MARK GOLDMAN

CITY ON THE EDGE

BUFFALO, NEW YORK

Prometheus Books

59 John Glenn Drive
Amherst, New York 14228-2197

Published 2007 by Prometheus Books

Inquiries should be addressed to
Prometheus Books
59 John Glenn Drive
Amherst, New York 14228–2197
VOICE: 716–691–0133, ext. 207
FAX: 716–564–2711
WWW.PROMETHEUSBOOKS.COM

17 16   8 7

Library of Congress Cataloging-in-Publication Data

Goldman, Mark, 1943–
    City on the edge : Buffalo, New York / by Mark Goldman.
        p. cm.
    Includes bibliographical references and index.
    ISBN 978–1–59102–457–6 (pbk. : alk. paper)
    1. Buffalo (N.Y.)—History. 2. Buffalo (N.Y.)—Social conditions. I. Title.

F129.B857G63 2007
974.7'97—dc22

                                                                    2006032866

Printed in the United States of America on acid-free paper

This book is dedicated to the many people, both professionals and volunteers, who through their hard work and commitment keep alive our communal memory. These people include archivists and teachers, storytellers and librarians, webmasters and webmistresses, preservationists and gardeners.

CONTENTS

INTRODUCTION

Born and raised in midtown Manhattan, I moved to Buffalo in September 1967 to enroll in the graduate history program at the University at Buffalo. Growing up, New York City had been the center of my universe. I knew it and loved it and thought that at UB I would do my graduate work on the history of the city of my childhood. What I have always loved most about New York is the democratic nature of its public places; the egalitarian vitality of its streets; the friendly, communal character of its parks; the stimulating pluralism of the subway; and the strong sense of place that defined its neighborhoods. I wanted to know more about how all of that happened—what it was about the historical development of New York that had led to the creation of a way of life I found so appealing. For these reasons, I fully expected to spend my years at UB focused on the study of my native city.

At that time, I lived close to Delaware Park. While watching a Little League baseball game there one day, a woman sitting next to me on the bleachers called out to her son who had just come to the plate: "C'mon, Mikey! Show 'em what a Black Rock kid can do!" What, I wondered, was all that about? Turning toward the woman, I asked, "A Black Rock kid? What's 'Black Rock?'" "Black Rock? You don't know Black Rock?" she answered. "That's a neighborhood. That's where we're from."

Curious to know more, I decided to investigate. It didn't take me long to discover that Black Rock was a small, proud, clearly defined, and unique historic neighborhood that reflected many of the same qualities and characteristics that so drew me to the neighborhoods of New York. I continued to study the neighborhood in earnest for two years, photographing its streets and buildings, uncovering its newspapers, photographs, and other records, and interviewing its current residents in an effort to understand the historical forces that had shaped this most interesting place.

My research and investigation into the history of Black Rock piqued my curiosity about the rest of the city and soon, accompanied by my infant son (who would sleep only in a moving car), I was regularly exploring the city's endless fascinating highways and byways, its nooks and its crannies. I considered myself an urban archeologist, using my eyes, my camera, and my instincts to look for any and all shreds of information that would reveal to me the story of the city that I was coming increasingly to know and to like.

Combining a scholar's interest with an entrepreneurial instinct, I created a "Rubberneck Tour of Buffalo" in 1974. In an interview with *Buffalo Evening News* reporter Karen Brady, I explained that for five dollars (which included lunch at the Broadway Market), I would take people on a two-and-a-half-hour guided tour of the city, during which they would hear the story the city's economic, social, and architectural history and development. In the days following the feature of my tour in Ms. Brady's "Karen's Corner" column, my phone rang off the hook. Hundreds of people were interested in the tour and for a dozen or more consecutive Saturdays, I shepherded groups of around forty people around the city that they loved but knew little of. I was making solid extra money and so, too, was Blue Bird, the old bus company I was using to transport tourgoers. Indeed, after about six weeks of tours, the president of the company called me up with an offer to take me out for lunch. Leaning over the table after the meal, he said, "Kid, I want to buy out your operation."

However, what I had was not an operation; it was an idea. And while my interest in the tour began slowly to dwindle, my interest in Buffalo's history continued to grow. Realizing that I had gathered a growing amount of material, I began in the late 1970s to write a book. Written during a difficult and trying time both in my own life and in the life of the city, the book, which I called *High Hopes: The Rise and Decline of Buffalo, New York* (SUNY Press, 1983), was pessimistic at best and cynical at worst.

In the years following the publication of *High Hopes*, my ideas about Buffalo began to change. Two of my kids were attending school at City Honors and as a result we all shared in the promise of Judge John T. Curtin's vision of a new, multiracial and pluralistic community. If the city could integrate its schools, I thought, there was nothing that we the people of Buffalo, following Curtin's visionary lead, could not accomplish. It was with this hope and promise in mind that I wrote my second book on Buffalo, called *City on the Lake: The Challenge of Change in Buffalo, New York*(Prometheus, 1992). Ending with a lyrical description of Stanley Swisher's magnificent rose garden at the Erie Basin Marina, the book implied that despite the challenges of a history of decline, recreating community, like creating a stunning garden on reclaimed industrial land, could, with lots of hard work and faith, be accomplished.

It was my faith in myself, my love of Buffalo, and my long-held belief in the transformative power of the performing arts that led me in 1990 to open The Calumet Arts Café. Located in a long-abandoned, yet still-magical building on Chippewa Street, referred to by many as "the street of broken dreams," the Calumet, as much as anything, represented to my mind a vision and an ideal. For here, on this lost corner of a decaying downtown, I would build a profitable business that would, by showcasing the best and most interesting artists in the world— Flamenco and Tango dancers, the world's greatest jazz musicians, poets, writers, and performers from Tibet, Africa, and Latin and South America—point the way to a new and different kind of future for the city of Buffalo.

My faith in the ability of individuals to improve the quality of community life grew during my ten years at the Calumet. I was inspired by the public's response to the work that we were doing there and I became increasingly aware of the impact that the work of others, as individuals or as members of a steadily growing number of grassroots organizations, was having in places all over the city. However, like so many other like-minded people, I was becoming increasingly frustrated and disappointed by public officials who, distracted by the lure of big-money, "silver-bullet" projects, failed to recognize the incredible power that local people working on small, local projects can have on the life of a community. But despite the shortsighted leadership of local politicians, we have lost neither our faith in ourselves nor our faith in our community. We remain committed to doing the work that we know will heal and renew this city that we love.

It is this combination of faith in the city's people and distrust of its leadership that imbues my latest effort to write the history of Buffalo. Some of the material revisits and revises my earlier work. Much of it is new. *City on the Edge* begins with the high hopes created at the turn of the century when Buffalo was chosen as the site for both the Pan-American Exposition and the Lackawanna Steel Company's enormous waterfront production facility. The book proceeds chronologically through the entire twentieth century, narrating and analyzing the critical events that occurred in the life of the city and how people in private and public life responded to them. This book, as did *City on the Lake*, ends with a garden. I hope you enjoy it.

Council Districts

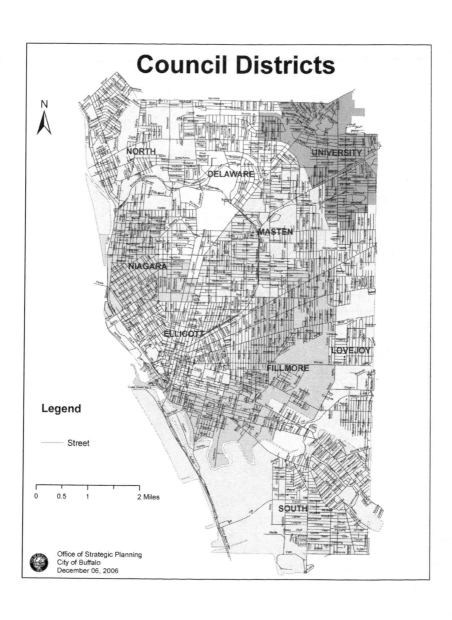

N

NORTH

UNIVERSITY

DELAWARE

MASTEN

NIAGARA

ELLICOTT

LOVEJOY

FILLMORE

Legend

—— Street

0   0.5   1   2 Miles

SOUTH

Office of Strategic Planning
City of Buffalo
December 06, 2006

chapter I

THE PAN–AMERICAN EXPOSITION AND THE LACKAWANNA STEEL COMPANY

High Hopes in Early Twentieth–century Buffalo

President William McKinley liked world fairs. They were, he said, "the timekeepers of progress. They record the world's advancement." He had been to the Columbian Exposition in Chicago in 1893 and the Cotton States Exposition in Atlanta two years later. He did not want to miss the Pan-American Exposition, scheduled to open in Buffalo in May of 1901.

McKinley had hoped to be in Buffalo for the opening of the Exposition but his wife, Ida, was ill. Because he never traveled without her, he postponed the trip, sending in his stead Theodore Roosevelt, the vice president. Upon returning to Washington, Roosevelt raved about the Pan-Am, telling the president that he was particularly impressed by the Electric Tower. Over the objections of both his wife, who suffered from epilepsy and hated to travel, and his personal secretary, George B. Cortelyou, who worried about the president's safety, McKinley resolved to go to Buffalo to see the Pan-American Exposition for himself. On September 4, 1901, the presidential party, with both Ida McKinley and Cortelyou in tow, pulled into Buffalo.[1]

As a result of America's stunning victory in the Spanish-American War and the territorial acquisitions that followed, McKinley, the leading spokesman of a newly discovered national strength and brazen self-confidence, was well liked. He held a vast appeal,

13

particularly in Buffalo, a city whose international exposition embodied and glorified the goals of the president's expansionist foreign policy. His popularity transcended class and party lines, making him the most admired president since Lincoln. The Pan-American had been planned during the heady days following the conclusion of the war against Spain and now, as hundreds of thousands of Americans descended on Buffalo to pay homage to Pan-Americanism, the city became the national symbol of the country's pride. Never had American power been more apparent. In March 1901, three months before the Exposition opened, Emilio Aguinaldo, the leader of the insurrection against American occupation of the Philippine Islands, was captured by US Marines. In May, the Supreme Court ruled that the Constitution Bill of Rights were not applicable in the territories recently captured from Spain. In June, one month after the Pan-Am opened, the Cuban Senate added the Platt Amendment to their constitution, which, written by an American senator, authorized the United States to intervene at any time in order to preserve law and order in that technically sovereign country. And in July, two months after the Pan-Am opened, William Howard Taft was sent to Manila to become the first American governor of the Philippine Islands. Like most Americans, the people of Buffalo were proud of these achievements. They were proud of themselves as well, for the Pan-American Exposition tapped the same source of inspiration in Buffalo that McKinley's foreign policy had inspired in the nation at large. McKinley's visit affirmed their achievement and they waited eagerly for the opportunity to welcome their president.

President McKinley's arrival in Buffalo at 5:00 p.m. on Tuesday, September 4, 1901, was clouded by what some would later call an ominous event. As the presidential train pulled into the Terrace Railroad Station overlooking Lake Erie, it was greeted by a twenty-one-gun salute. In his eagerness to honor this most popular president, the cannoneer, a Coast Guard officer and veteran of McKinley's Civil War regiment, had placed the cannon so close to the railroad tracks that the salvo shook the presidential car violently. Although there were no injuries and only minimal damage to the train, the presidential party was worried about Mrs. McKinley, who was greatly unhinged by the incident. As the train left the station and headed north to the exposition grounds, a dozen or more people, screaming "anarchist," pounced on a short, swarthy man who had been standing near the cannoneer.

Several minutes later, however, the train pulled safely into a special platform built at one of the entrances to the exposition grounds. Wearing a black frock coat and a high, black silk hat, President McKinley, his right arm tightly around his wife's waist, disembarked. Following a short and ceremonious greeting by John G. Milburn, president of the exposition's board of directors and the city's leading lawyer, President and Mrs. McKinley, watched by a crowd of more than sixty

thousand, st
and made a
veyed to Mi
sition. They
Milburr
Earlier that
had the Fre
weekend of
eons in the
Milbur
power brok
1874 at the
the firm of
by 1900, th
pelling and
sessed a br
the time w
ness, law, a
forever remake the city's economy.

the Buffalo General Electric Company; and
International Street Railroad Company, a
and friend of John Milburn. There w
senting the New York Central Rail
Erie County Savings Bank and t
resenting the Third National
The luncheon was sh
Shortly after the elabor
tact with Rogers, too
Buffalo's distinct
possessed all of
economy r
them, h
Mesa
La

Because Milburn's law firm was among the city's most powerful institutions, its partners could, with a phone call, dramatically alter the direction of the entire area's economic life. One of Milburn's partners was William A. Rogers, who, like so many power brokers, wore a variety of different hats. In addition to his work at Rogers, Locke and Millburn, Rogers was president of some of the largest iron manufacturing companies in Western New York, including one he owned called the Rogers Iron Mining Company. Rogers's base in the local economy was further strengthened by his position as board member of both the Marine National Bank and the Erie County Savings Bank.[3] Milburn and Rogers had, along with their clients (particularly Charles and Frank Goodyear and John J. Albright), acquired large amounts of stock in the Lackawanna Steel Company in Scranton, Pennsylvania. In the late 1890s, as a result of their contacts with Lackawanna Steel, they learned that Walter Scranton was looking for a new location for his company. In an effort to attract Scranton's attention, they invited him to a luncheon at Milburn's Delaware Avenue home during the weekend of July 4, 1898. The powerful barons of Buffalo's emerging industrial economy were there to greet Scranton: Jacob F. Schoellkopf Jr., of Niagara Falls Hydraulic; John J. Albright, of Ontario Power; Frank and Charles Goodyear, of the Goodyear empire of mining, lumbering, and shipping; Frank B. Baird, of the recently organized Tonawanda Iron and Steel Company; John N. Scratherd, president of the Lumber Exchange and the developer behind the Ellicott Square Building; George Urban Jr., president of

William C. Ely, president of the
director of the Exposition, and client
re lawyers, too: William B. Hoyt, repre-
oad; Carleton E. Sprague, representing the
e Grand Trunk Railroad; Loran L. Lewis, rep-
ank; and Milburn's partner, William A. Rogers.
uded in secrecy.[4] Only later did the details leak out.
te meal was served, Milburn, maintaining close eye con-
the floor and, in a florid yet businesslike manner, touted
dvantages as an industrial center. Buffalo, Milburn exhorted,
the necessary conditions and ingredients for the creation of a new
ted firmly in industry: natural resources, power, and labor. Each of
said, were cheap and inexhaustible: the iron recently discovered in
, Minnesota, which was shipping uninterrupted to Buffalo on the Great
es; the power of Niagara Falls; and, finally, the labor force, more than fifty
thousand immigrants from Eastern Europe who, because they were not unionized,
would work long, hard, and cheap.

While nothing was decided on that day in July 1898, Milburn and his colleagues remained in close contact with Scranton, speaking with him regularly by
telephone throughout the fall and winter. During this period, it seems, Scranton
made his decision and, on March 23, 1899, he came to Buffalo to finalize the deal.
The next day, he traveled to South Buffalo along with John Milburn, John
Albright, William Rogers, and a few other carefully selected players in the high
stakes world of industrial entrepreneurship. There, tramping along the muddy
lakefront, Scranton considered the area as a possible location for his steel company. Albright, who seemed to be the man with the most money and desire, immediately volunteered to buy the land. He fronted the money to John Milburn, who,
as president of the Pan-American, would be able to buy the land at much lower
prices under the pretext of using it for the Exposition.[5]

By the end of April, Milburn, using more than $1 million provided by John
Albright, had acquired more than a thousand acres of lakefront property. When it
became apparent that the Lackawanna Steel Company wanted still more land,
both the state and the City of Buffalo stepped in, the former donating three hundred acres, the latter twenty-five. When asked how he was able to so quickly and
easily effect such a transfer of public land for use by a private company (the city's
twenty-five acres had been intended for the construction of a waterfront park),
Milburn, the great dealmaker, replied, "It was merely a question of forms."

Added to the gift of public lands was a financing package that pleased
Scranton and his board of directors. Looking for local participation without local

control, Scranton insisted that local investors provide no less than 5 percent and not more than 10 percent of the $40 million needed to launch the venture. By early 1900, Albright and Milburn quickly raised $3 million from among their friends and colleagues. The last million came from the Vanderbilts. The investment was, according to William B. Hoyt, their local attorney, "Precautionary ... to conserve the interests of the New York Central Railroad."[6]

By the end of 1900, two enormous communities were growing in Buffalo: one, in South Buffalo, soon to become a separate and independent city known as Lackawanna and the other, rising quickly on the edges of Delaware Park in North Buffalo, at the fairgrounds of the Pan-American Exposition.

It is not surprising that both of these events, unfolding almost simultaneously, were orchestrated by virtually the same people. Milburn had a large circle of friends and business colleagues and was able to call on many of them to help him with his two most challenging projects. If Milburn was the majordomo, his friend and partner John J. Albright was right there with him, not only pacing off and then purchasing the land that became home to Lackawanna Steel but, as a director of the Pan-American, making many of the critical choices regarding what got built and who built it. It was Albright who made sure that his favorite architect, Edward B. Green, was commissioned to design two of the exposition's major buildings, the Electricity Building and, more significantly, the art gallery. Although the Albright Art Gallery opened in 1905, a few years later than he had hoped, Albright altered the landscape of this part of Buffalo as much as he had in Lackawanna.[7]

Other Milburn colleagues—a group of men with interconnected business and social relationships—were similarly involved, serving primarily behind the scenes with the Lackawanna deal and more publicly on the board of directors of the Pan-American Exposition. Baird, Albright, Urban, Goodyear, and Sprague, all in attendance at Milburn's pivotal July Fourth meeting, were, with Milburn himself as president, members of the board of directors of the Pan-American. Clearly, it helped to know the right people, and these men certainly did. One of the board's members who for unknown reasons was not at that fateful luncheon was George K. Birge, owner not only of Birge Wallpaper but, by 1900, of the Pierce Arrow Company as well. When his daughter married a young architect named George Cary, Birge did what he could to see that Cary was chosen to build the New York State Pavilion, the only building at the exposition meant to be permanent. Several years after the pavilion became the Buffalo Historical Society, Birge's grandson and Cary's nephew, Charles Cary Rumsey, was selected to execute the sculpture known as *The Centaur*, which was subsequently installed on the historical society's front lawn. In what seemed to be a Birge-Cary family affair, Cary's sister-in-law, Evelyn Rumsey Cary, was asked to design the exposition's poster, a moody art nouveau depiction of "The Spirit of Niagara."[8]

While no contemporary commentators seemed to notice the insularity of the group responsible for these two monumental events in the history of the city, people, particularly the press, could not help but notice the scope and scale of the building activities involved. As construction proceeded on both projects, the local press described them in intimate and rhapsodic detail.

The most generous prose was reserved for the Electric Tower, designed by John Galen Howard. It was both the tallest and, because of its spectacular lighting, most famous building at the fair. Kerry Grant, in a fascinating and richly illustrated book on the "light, color and architecture of the Pan-American Exposition," noted that the Electric Tower evoked, in a gigantic flood of gushing water flowing day and night, "all the power of Niagara Falls." At the top of the 410-foot tower was an 18-foot statue of the "Goddess of Light," which at night was lit with more than forty thousand lights. "Here," wrote one visitor, "is nocturnal architecture, nocturnal landscapes, nocturnal gardens and long vistas of nocturnal beauty. At a distance the Fair presents the appearance of a whole city in illumination." "The Tower," wrote another reporter,

> is a great center of brilliancy. There are perhaps not a half million electric bulbs, but there are hundreds and thousands of them and you are willing to believe that there may be millions. It shines like diamonds, a transparent, soft structure of sunlight. There it stands, glowing with the lights of many thousand bulbs flashing its image in the basin at its feet, showing its gleaming dome to the people in neighboring cities. Its beauty is transcendent.

At the base of the Electric Tower were two colonnades that formed a semi-circle around the "Court of Fountains," which was then in turn surrounded by six buildings dedicated to manufactures, liberal arts, machines, transportation, agriculture, and electricity. While most of the buildings were designed in what was called the "Spanish Renaissance Style," the fairgrounds appear today to have been an incongruous mix: the New York State Building was a copy of the Parthenon, while the midway contained a number of Islamic minarets and Italian loggias, and Luchow's Alt Nuremburg boasted more than two dozen medieval turrets.[9]

And everywhere there were flowers, thousands and thousands of them, all under the care of Frederick W. Taylor, the superintendent of horticulture. There were three hundred thousand roses, ten thousand cannas, hundreds of beds of delphiniums, pansies, verbenas, and geraniums, and, according to Taylor, "the largest display of water-lilies ever made." There were, in addition, tulips: "It's doubtful," Taylor said, "whether there was ever seen in America a finer and more beautiful tulip show than resulted from the carefully planned plantings made in the autumn of 1900."[10]

No part of the Pan-Am was more popular with the press and the public than the midway, which contained a wide and fantastical array of buildings and activities. There were countless restaurants, the "Trip to the Moon," a "scenograph" of the Johnstown flood, which recreated that whole disastrous event—the gathering storm, the bursting dam, the torrents of flooding waters, and the deaths of thousands. In addition, the midway contained "whole transplanted native villages with real natives in them." Among the most popular was one called "Darkest Africa" and another called the "Old Plantation." Here, as the *Buffalo Evening News* reported,

> Genuine Southern darkies, two hundred of them, ranging in years from wee, toddling pickininies to negroes, grey and bent with age, can be seen each day at the Exposition at their different occupations and pastimes. Lovers of negro melodies will have a feast. Many of the darkies have been selected because of their special talents as singers and banjo players and they will dance and sing to the seductive tinkling of instruments exactly as the Negroes of the south used to do in the long, long ago.

Lest anybody worry, the *News* reassured its readers that "the negroes were selected from the best class of southern darkies, for "Skip" Dandy, the concessionaire, has the reputation of not tolerating anything shiftless or degrading about him."[11]

Not everyone was pleased by Dandy's "Old Plantation." Indeed, one of Buffalo's most respected African American citizens, a woman named Mary Talbert, was sickened by it. Born in Ohio in 1866 and educated at Oberlin College, Talbert moved to Arkansas in the late 1880s to teach high school in Little Rock. Talbert came to Buffalo in 1891, following her marriage to a well-established realtor, an African American named William H. Talbert. The Talberts lived on Michigan Avenue, next to the Michigan Avenue Baptist Church, one of the city's oldest churches, and the location during the 1850s of an abolitionist meeting place and a "station" on the underground railroad. The Talberts were active in the life of their community. In 1899, Mrs. Talbert became one of the founding members of the Phyllis Wheatley Club of Colored Women, the city's first affiliate of the National Association of Colored Women's Clubs. With their motto "Lifting as We Climb" as inspiration, Talbert's Phyllis Wheatley Club created an ambitious program of services for local families. Given her intelligence and sophistication, she was appalled by the depiction of her people at the exposition.

As someone familiar with W. E. B. Du Bois's work at the Paris World's Fair in 1900, she knew that it didn't have to be that way. Du Bois, she knew, had created at Paris a full-scale exhibit documenting the achievement of African Americans in industry, literature, and journalism since the Emancipation Proclamation. The exhibition included photographic documentation of educational institutions such as Tuskegee, Fisk, and Howard, and Talbert wanted the same for Buffalo. In the late spring of 1901, Talbert petitioned the Pan-American's board of managers, insisting that Dandy's concession be dismantled and replaced. While her petition was denied, Talbert and her sisters in the Wheatley Club were energized by the frustration of their failed effort and began subsequently to organize for an even greater effort. Four years later, in July 1905, W. E. B. Du Bois, John Hope, Monroe Trotter, and other African American leaders responded to Talbert's invitation and met at her house to discuss the formation of a group that would lead their movement. From the Talbert's home on Michigan Avenue, the group crossed the Niagara River to the Canadian side of Niagara Falls. There, next to the "mighty current" of water from which they wished to launch their protest, these leaders formed the Niagara Movement, which by 1909 became the National Association for the Advancement of Colored People.[12]

While the press took little notice of Mrs. Talbert's efforts, they did pay a great deal of attention to the seemingly sudden, almost "magical" appearance of the enormous complex of buildings that the Lackawanna Steel Company was erecting on the shores of Lake Erie just south of Buffalo. It was, said one newspaper, "a veritable cradle of steel." To another it was the "Magic City." A reporter for the *Buffalo Times* wrote:

> On entering the gates the visitor is first impressed with the immensity of the plant before him. As far as his eye can reach he can see the signs of industry, see the furnaces belching out their molten contents, the cupolas spouting fire, smoke and cinders like the dragons of song and story. From the great brick structures housing the huge machines come the roaring and pounding of the big wheels driven by thousands of pounds of pressure. Across the yards come the shrieking donkey engines pulling their weighty loads to and from the mills and everywhere there is a nerve-wracking roar of sound and a bewildering rush of men and machines.[13]

Another reporter, writing for the *Commercial Advertiser* in early 1902 was equally hyperbolic:

> A new city is springing up; it is the new Buffalo of which so much has been heard.... Cities all over the country are striving for factories; they realize that they are the life blood of commercial eminence, but no city, however persistently it may have angled, has landed so enormous an enterprise as that which is spreading itself over the two and a half miles of water front property at Stony Point.... There have been many mythical beginnings for the new Buffalo, but the real, the genuine is finally here.[14]

Like the Pan-American Exposition in North Buffalo, in South Buffalo, this equally fantastical place was being created; over the coming decades, the steel mill would shape the hopes and tease the dreams of a whole generation of Buffalonians.

Given his interest in industry and his well-known support for its growth and development, it is notable that President McKinley expressed no known desire to visit the emerging steel plant. He was, his host John Milburn knew, eager and intent instead to visit the Pan-American Exposition.

In anticipation of McKinley's presence at the Pan-Am on the second day of his visit to Buffalo, the crowd at the exposition—more than 116,000 people—broke records. The great rush came after supper:

> Every street car was loaded and passengers clung to the steps. The whole city, it seemed, was traveling to the Exposition. At six pm about thirty thousand people were admitted through the various gates. The grounds had never looked so crowded. Buildings were visited by throngs. The shows were packed at every performance. The restaurants were overwhelmed. From every quarter a flood of humanity bore down upon the esplanade until it was difficult even to worm one's way through the crowd.[15]

The first entertainment to come was a concert by John Philip Sousa. Sousa, who had played at the Bicentennial Exposition at Philadelphia in 1876, the Chicago World's Fair in 1893, the mid-winter California Fair in 1894, the Atlanta Cotton States Exposition in 1895, and the Paris Exposition in 1900, had been brought in from the Boston Food Fair to play for the president. Then came Henry J. Pain, the "Fire Works King," whose name was synonymous with pyrotechnics. At the Paris Exposition, Pain had launched a three-figured display symbolizing the ideals of the French Revolution. At the St. Louis Fair he used fireworks to create an embodiment of the Louis and Clark Expedition. For Buffalo, he promised the "largest pyrotechnical display ever seen."[16]

At sunset, the exposition grounds were illuminated by fifty powerful fires in five different colors. A large number of lighted balloons came next, followed by the discharge of one hundred three-pound rockets fired simultaneously from different sections of the fairgrounds. Ten batteries of mines were then put in motion. Next came five hundred colored lights, discharging electric comets in a continuous stream, and a salvo of ten thirty-inch bombs with five colors each. A series of ten national streamers followed, and then ten huge shells, each of which detached one hundred parachutes and fifty silver umbrellas. Next came a display called "The American Empire." At one thousand feet, four large bombs exploded together. The first formed the outline of the United States, the second and third the outlines of Cuba and Puerto Rico, and the fourth splattered into a series of small shells representing the Philippine Islands. But the best was saved for last. For the finale, thousands of tiny fireballs exploded at once, creating a gigantic, sparkling likeness of William McKinley. The sky filled with shining letters: "Welcome President McKinley, Chief of our Nation and our Empire." McKinley, his aides noted happily, seemed to have enjoyed every minute of Pain's display, and after personally thanking the master of pyrotechnics, the president returned to the Milburn home.

On September 6, President McKinley awoke early, as was his custom. At 7:15 a.m., fully dressed for the day in his habitual black frock coat and black silk hat, he eluded the small secret service entourage that surrounded the Milburn house and took a solitary walk down Delaware Avenue before, it was later learned, Milburn himself, concerned for his safety, rushed him back inside. Later that morning, accompanied by a host of city and exposition officials, the McKinleys boarded a train for Niagara Falls. They visited the falls, walked along the gorge, and toured the Niagara Falls Power Project, which the president referred to as "the marvel of the Electrical Age." After lunch, the presidential party returned to Buffalo. Mrs. McKinley went to the Milburn house to rest, and the president went to the exposition, where he was scheduled to meet the thousands of people who, in spite of the oppressive heat, were waiting at the Temple of Music, a large, vaguely Byzantine structure on the north side of the fairgrounds.[17]

In the middle of the waiting crowd was Jim Parker, a six-foot-six-inch African American waiter from Atlanta who had been standing outside the temple since mid morning. Finally, at 4:00 p.m., the doors of the Temple of Music opened and hundreds of people made an orderly, single-file procession to the front of the auditorium, where the president, flanked by Milburn and Cortelyou, stood waiting. It was more than ninety degrees in the room, and everybody carried handkerchiefs, either wiping their brows or waving them at the president. In the crowd, too, was Leon Czolgosz, who used his handkerchief to conceal a tiny handgun. As the fast-moving line brought him directly in front of the president, Czolgosz shot twice into McKinley's abdomen. Parker (referred to in the press as "the Herculean Negro" or "Giant Jim"), who was standing directly behind the assailant, smashed him to the floor. Czolgosz was pounced on and beaten by the attending soldiers and guards. McKinley was carried out amid the screeching pandemonium in the room and, several minutes later, was rushed in an electrical ambulance to a hospital on the exposition grounds.[18]

Milburn took command immediately. When he learned that Dr. Roswell Park, the medical director of the exposition, was in Niagara Falls performing a lymphoma operation, he pointed to Dr. Matthew D. Mann, one of several physicians who had gathered at the hospital, and told him to take charge of the case. Mann, a professor of gynecology at the University of Buffalo Medical School, examined the president and determined that unless his wounds were immediately sutured they would prove fatal. Thus, at 5:30 p.m., the city's leading gynecologist (but a man with limited experience in abdominal surgery) began to operate on the president of the United States. Park, who had been brought back to Buffalo on a special train, entered the hospital after the operation had begun. He noticed immediately that Mann was working under the most difficult of conditions. Like all the buildings at the exposition, the hospital was a temporary structure, ill equipped to handle any but the most routine medical emergencies. There were, for example, no electric lights at all in the operating room, which forced one of the attending physicians to improvise by using a looking glass to reflect the rays of the setting sun.

The operation itself was fairly simple. There had been two bullets, and the first had merely grazed the president's skin. Although he could not find the second bullet, Dr. Mann was not concerned. It had caused no apparent damage to the intestine or to other abdominal organs and he therefore assumed that it was safely lodged in McKinley's lumbar muscles. He closed the wounds in the front and back walls of the president's stomach and, to everyone's great relief, completed the operation, after which McKinley was carefully transported by electric ambulance to Milburn's Delaware Avenue home.

As word spread throughout the fairgrounds that Czolgosz was being held in one of the rooms in the Temple of Music, a large and unruly crowd gathered around the building, threatening to break through the cordon of guards that surrounded it. Crowds also blocked the electric paddy wagon that transported Czolgosz from the Temple of Music to police headquarters downtown. At the Franklin Street police headquarters, two National Guard regiments held at bay the hundreds of people who had gathered to surround it. A different kind of crowd, however, quiet and respectful, stood outside Milburn's house. Dr. Park described the scene:

> The passage through the crowd and down Delaware Avenue was one of the most dramatic incidents I have ever witnessed. The fair grounds were crowded that day and it seemed as though the entire crowd had gathered to witness this event. Every man's hat was in his hand and there were handkerchiefs at many eyes. I never saw so large a crowd so quiet.[19]

The recently renovated Milburn house was converted into a virtual military camp. Outside, it was surrounded by armed guards. Inside, special telegraph machines were installed—the house became the center of an international communications network. Across the street, press tents were set up for the more than two hundred and fifty newsmen covering the story, the most, it was reported, that had ever covered a public event. All of them rejoiced when Dr. Mann issued the first of many medical bulletins. The doctors were "gratified," Mann reported, by the president's condition. "The results," he said, "cannot yet be foretold [but] hopes for recovery are justified."

As the president and the people of Buffalo settled in for what appeared to be a long period of recuperation (John Milburn engaged rooms for his family at a downtown hotel), the rest of the world reacted to the news. Europeans, recently shocked by the murder of King Umberto of Italy and the attempted assassination of Kaiser Wilhelm, were particularly concerned. Czar Nicholas II and the Russian royal family, cruising off the Danish coast, arranged to meet with Kaiser Wilhelm on his royal yacht, the *Hohenzollern*, in the North Sea. There they agreed to double their security measures and to avoid, at least for a while, all public appearances.

In New York City, people were more concerned about the whereabouts of J. P. Morgan than they were with the medical bulletins emanating from the Milburn house in Buffalo. The shooting of the president had triggered dire predictions of a stock market collapse and many people, by now accustomed to the fiscal heroics of Morgan, desperately wondered where he was. Some reports had him closeted with advisors on his private yacht, the *Corsair*. Others said he was in conference in his private room at Delmonico's. Still others said he was busy on the telephone in the library of his Murray Hill mansion. Morgan, meanwhile, had hired three private detectives to protect him.

In a basement room at Buffalo's police headquarters, Leon Czolgosz confessed: "Not until Tuesday did the resolution to shoot the President take hold of me. It was in my heart—there was no escape for me. I could not have conquered it had my life depended on it.... I am an Anarchist," he said, "a disciple of Emma Goldman. Her words set me on fire." Within hours, a national search for the notorious anarchist leader began. The next day, at the request of the Buffalo police department, Goldman was arrested in Chicago.

The Buffalo police began a relentless search of the East Side, where so many of the city's Polish immigrants lived, looking for suspects to question, people who might have encountered Czolgosz on his several trips in and out of the city, people like Charles Nowak, whose hotel he had stayed in; a man named Pasczek, in whose tavern he had drank; and Paul Redlinski, a barber who had cut Czolgosz's hair a week earlier. On a tip from two local priests, the police arrested Helen Petrowski, a twenty-five-year-old schoolteacher. According to the priests' report to police, she had been teaching anarchism and free love. They further claimed that Petrowski's late husband, also an anarchist, had died because of his "constant brooding on the subject of the ideal social fabric which fatally affected his brain." Along with Mrs. Petrowski, the police arrested "a dark curly-headed man with a decidedly Polish appearance" and a Russian Jewish physician and social activist who, in 1894, had led a march of the poor on Buffalo's City Hall.[20]

But the press and the police were far more intrigued with the possible link to Emma Goldman. Everything, it seemed, pointed in her direction. Not only had Czolgosz mentioned her as a source of inspiration but the police said that in jail, on several different nights, he had talked about her in his sleep. Czolgosz's ruminations were given further substance when a local psychiatrist told the police that certain details of the assassination attempt—particularly Czolgosz's use of a white handkerchief—suggested a feminine touch.

The district attorney in Buffalo immediately initiated extradition proceedings, but the Chicago police stalled. Under intensive questioning, Goldman, whose family lived in Rochester, admitted having visited Buffalo and the Pan-American Exposition twice during the summer, but denied ever having met with Czolgosz. She was, she said, opposed to the use of violence. She even volunteered to nurse the wounded president back to health (she had studied midwifery and nursing in Vienna). Although they were convinced of her innocence and refused to comply with the district attorney's extradition request, the Chicago police detained Goldman for fifteen days, considerably longer than Nowak, Pasczek, Mrs. Petrowski, and the others, who had been released for lack of evidence. When finally allowed to go, she was denied the right to lecture in Chicago, and her magazine, *Free Society*, was denied the use of the mails. Her family suffered, too. Her father was forced to leave his synagogue in Rochester, and his furniture store was boycotted for months.

Meanwhile, the optimistic medical bulletins about President McKinley continued. Gradually, the shock of the assassination attempt wore off and the city began to enjoy the attention it had garnered as the unofficial capital of the nation. The comings and goings of the nation's political celebrities, who had convened in Buffalo following the shooting, were discussed in minute detail: Theodore Roosevelt had dined at the home of Ansley I. Wilcox, about half a mile south of the Milburn house on Delaware Avenue; Philander Knox, the attorney general, and John Hay, the secretary of state, had stayed at the Buffalo Club; and Elihu Root, the secretary of war, had addressed the Buffalo branch of the Grand Army of the Republic on how the government was coping with the emergency.[21]

The doctors reported continued progress in the president's condition. On September 9, they told the press that "if the President continues to improve we may safely say that he is convalescent." Senator Mark Hanna, a close personal friend of the president, said that "any day now he will be smoking cigars again." On September 10, following a conference with the president's physicians, Roosevelt summarized the situation: "I am absolutely certain," he said, "that everything is coming out all right." Two days later, in spite of reports that McKinley had spent a restless night, Roosevelt announced that he was leaving for his home in Oyster Bay, Long Island. That same day, William I. Buchanan, the director of the Pan-American, announced plans for "President McKinley Day" at the Exposition, a special day to celebrate the recovery of the president. The celebration was necessary, Buchanan said, to dissipate any possible odium that might have been cast upon the Exposition and "to raise it from a landmark of doom to a symbol of happiness."

At 6:00 p.m. on September 12, the president's physicians reported that the president was "not so good." McKinley had just taken his first oral meal since the shooting (he had previously been fed intravenously) and was not able to digest his food. However, he was given calomel and oils and by midnight he had moved his bowels. The trouble was reported to have passed. However, by 2:00 a.m. on September 13, it became clear that the president was suffering something far more serious than indigestion. His pulse, which had been abnormally high ever since his operation, quickened still more, and his heart weakened considerably. Dr. Park arrived at the Milburn house at 3:00 a.m., and at 6:00 a.m. Senator Hanna, who had just returned home to Cleveland, once again set out for Buffalo on a special train. Stunned by the sudden activity at the Milburn house, crowds began to congregate along Delaware Avenue. Fearing the worst, chief of police William Bull activated three hundred police reserves to contain a threatening crowd of close to two thousand people, who marched down Main Street in the direction of police headquarters, where Czolgosz was held.

However, nothing that had happened—not the summoning of McKinley's friends, family, and cabinet members; not the desperate effort to contact the vice president, who was mountain climbing in the Adirondacks; not even the increasingly pessimistic reports of the medical team—could convince some people that the end was near. Congressman Alexander of Buffalo told a crowd of still trusting reporters that "[i]t is not true that the physicians are without hope or that those gathered in the house are despondent. Everybody about the house is hopeful. The two men who know him best, Cortelyou and Hanna, are cheerful and confident."

But Alexander could not wish away the truth, and McKinley weakened steadily throughout the day. At 4:00 p.m. on September 13, his pulsations increased again, and one hour later he suffered a heart attack. Aware himself of the futility of further efforts to save him, at 8:00 that night, McKinley asked to have a last word with his wife. At 9:00, he lost consciousness, and at 2:10 the following morning he died. That morning, the Pan-American Exposition was closed for the first time, and at a hasty swearing-in ceremony in Wilcox's house on Delaware Avenue, Theodore Roosevelt became the twenty-sixth president of the United States.

What was most upsetting about President McKinley's death was how unexpectedly it came. After days of nothing but optimistic reports about his health, the news of the president's death confused and angered the public more than it saddened them. It became apparent that from the beginning there had been little grounds for optimism and, while nobody was accusing the medical team of outright deceit, there was no question that the public had not been told the truth. In the hours following McKinley's death, some of the details began to emerge. Dr. Park said that once the bullet had penetrated the abdomen, the president was a doomed man. He was, he said, amazed that McKinley had lived as long as he had. Another said that there was no case record of a person the age of the president surviving a serious stomach wound. Citing the recent case of a Princeton quarterback who had been shot in the stomach by a spectator, another doctor said that regardless of age or physical condition, a stomach wound was fatal more often than not.

Most shocking of all was the fact that ever since Tuesday, September 12, the president's physicians had been aware that gangrene had set in. And while they believed that they had removed the poisoned areas, there was every reason to suspect that the disease would spread. Cortelyou had urged the doctors to again search for the bullet and even had Thomas Edison send his most sophisticated x-ray machine to Buffalo for that purpose. However, satisfied that the bullet could cause no harm, the doctors refused to reexamine the wound. The autopsy confirmed Cortelyou's suspicions, and what the doctors must certainly have guessed on Tuesday: the spread of gangrene along the path of the unretrieved bullet into the stomach, kidney, and pancreas had killed the president.

Two days after McKinley died, a grand jury, meeting for the first and only time, indicted Leon Czolgosz for murder. His trial proceeded expeditiously. It opened on September 23, and by the end of the first day, a jury had been selected. On the second day, both prosecution and defense attorneys completed their cases, the judge charged the jury, and in less than half an hour a guilty verdict was returned. The case was closed twenty-four hours after it opened.

Czolgosz's trial was a sham from the start. Most disturbing was the conduct of the defense. Czolgosz was defended by two court-appointed lawyers, Loran L. Lewis and Robert G. Titus, aging former judges who had not argued in court for years. On the opening day of the trial, Lewis asked the judge that the court be in session only four hours a day:

> Neither Judge Titus nor myself is a young man and neither of us is in perfect health. We have had little opportunity to consult with each other. We believe that the trial will not be injured by having short hours. We have concluded to ask Your Honor during this trial to sit from ten to noon in the morning and from 2 to 4 in the afternoon. I mention four P.M. because my home—my summer home—is in Lewiston and the train leaves at 4:40.[22]

Their apparent lack of zeal extended into their courtroom procedural practice, too. Titus and Lewis made only the most perfunctory challenges of the jury, and the result was a shocking miscarriage of justice. All of the jurors admitted that they were inclined to find Czolgosz guilty and that they would consider acquittal only if presented with reasonable evidence to the contrary. Czolgosz's lawyers made no effort to communicate with their client, called no defense witnesses, and constantly apologized to the court for their client's "dastardly act," while through it all tearfully referring to the greatness of "our martyred President." But their most serious shortcoming was their failure to raise the issue of the defendant's sanity. While they instructed the jury that Czolgosz must be considered sane before he could be found guilty, the lawyers made no attempt to offer any testimony or evidence dealing with their client's mental state at the time of the shooting.

There was nothing to prevent Titus and Lewis from raising the question of Czolgosz's sanity. Indeed, the presiding judge had already done it. In his charge to the jury, Judge Truman White said that if Czolgosz was "laboring under a defect of reasoning" at the time of the crime, he should be acquitted. The Erie County Bar Association, too, had been concerned about the sanity question; in order to be absolutely certain that they would be able to bring Czolgosz to trial, the bar had at least gone through the motions of deliberating the defendant's mental condition. On September 8, two days after the shooting, Czolgosz was examined by a team of local psychiatrists and an expert in forensics from Bellevue Hospital in New York. They determined that Czolgosz was indeed sane and thereby fit to stand trial. They enumerated their findings: He was, they said, not a victim of paranoia because "he has not systematized delusions reverting to self and because he is in exceptionally good condition and has an unbroken record of good health." Nor, they concluded, was he a "degenerate." The phrenologically oriented physicians stated that their examinations revealed none of the stigmata of degeneration: "His skull is symmetrical; his ears do not protrude, nor are they of abnormal size and his palate is not arched." Dr. MacDonald from Bellevue concurred in a separate report. "Czolgosz is," he said, "the product of anarchism. He is sane and responsible."[23]

Yet these hastily written reports could not still the many questions that began to surface in the months after Czolgosz's execution. A growing number of psychiatrists were becoming convinced that a closer scrutiny of Czolgosz's personal history—the death of his mother when he was twelve, his father's subsequent remarriage to a woman he detested, his constant brooding and dreamy behavior—combined with an attempt on the part of his attorneys to introduce testimony dealing with the question of his sanity, would have raised serious doubts in the minds of the jury about the defendant's sanity at the time of the crime. But these were questions that the legal fraternity in a city desperately bent on vengeance were unwilling to ask. Had McKinley lived, Czolgosz would have received a maximum of only ten years' imprisonment. But the president had died, and the law entitled the people to their revenge.

In the meantime, Milburn and Buchanan tried to rescue the Pan-American Exposition from the wreck of McKinley's assassination. Throughout the summer, every nation in the hemisphere and every state in the union had been honored with a special day at the Exposition. However, after the shooting of the president, the country lost its taste for the Exposition and, as the weather turned colder, the tourists stopped coming. Buchanan declared November 1 as "Buffalo Day" in a desperate effort to at least make the Exposition's closing day a success. It did not work. Mayor Diehl would not even consider proclaiming another civic holiday, and all but a few businessmen ignored the request of the exposition's board of directors to grant half-day holidays to their employees (even William C. Ely refused to lower streetcar fares for the day).

"Buffalo Day" began in failure—and ended in mayhem. That night, the exposition was completely wrecked. The newspapers were aghast:

> People went mad. They were seized with the desire to destroy. Depredation and destruction were carried on in the boldest manner all along the Midway. Electric light bulbs were jerked from their posts and thousands of them were smashed on the ground. Some of the Midway restaurants were crushed into fragments under the pressure of the mob as if they were so much pasteboard. Windows were shattered and doors were kicked down. Policemen were pushed aside as if they were stuffed ornaments. The National Glass Exhibit was completely destroyed. Pabst's Cafe was demolished and Cleopatra's needle was torn to the ground.[24]

Frank C. Bostock, "The Animal King," whose live animal show was one of the Exposition's most popular, reported trouble, too. Earlier in the summer, Regal, one of his largest African lions, had died of heat prostration. Now, on the last day of the Exposition, Jumbo the Elephant, his star attraction, who was billed as the world's largest animal, became unmanageable. Bostock had recently acquired Jumbo, who weighed nine tons, from the British Army, where he had been decorated by Queen Victoria for bravery in the Afghani Wars. Over the course of the summer, Jumbo had entertained the multitudes with his friendliness, giving rides to thousands of children eager to be walked around the large outdoor arena on the back of an animal reputed to be the world's largest. Suddenly, however, Jumbo took a frightening turn for the worse. In early September, he refused to eat. Then, on the morning of Buffalo Day, he attacked Bostock. That afternoon, he knocked his keeper unconscious. Bostock, sensing an opportunity, decided to destroy the beloved Jumbo and announced that he would hold a public execution at the stadium on the exposition grounds. Tickets, at fifty cents each, would be available at the gate. "It is likely," Bostock said, "that Jumbo will be hanged, or choked to death with chains, in which case other elephants will be used."[25]

While Milburn and Buchanan had no objection to the execution, they were appalled by Bostock's announced method, which, they said, was simply not in accord with the ideals of the Pan-American. If, however, Bostock chose to electrocute the elephant, they would withdraw their opposition. Milburn, as always, it seemed, got his way. On Saturday afternoon, November 3, more than seven thousand people filled the Pan-American stadium to witness the electrocution of Jumbo. The mammoth elephant was chained to two large wooden blocks in the center of the stadium. Long electric wires connected him to a transformer several hundred yards away. Bostock stood in front of him and made a short speech. He told the crowd about Jumbo's military career. He recalled the long voyage from the kingdoms of Africa to the Niagara Frontier and how hard it had been for Jumbo to adjust to life along the midway. These events, Bostock said, had completely altered Jumbo's sanity. He had become a killer, and death by electrocution was the only solution. With no further delay, Bostock gave a signal to Lewis Mills, the electrician, who pulled a lever that sent eleven thousand volts of electricity into the elephant.

Although it could power the streetcar lines, illuminate the Electric Tower, and drive the engines at Lackawanna Steel, the electricity that poured out of Niagara Falls could not penetrate Jumbo's thick hide. Jumbo stood, dazed and confused, and stared out at the people, many of whom laughed uncontrollably. Bostock, himself incredulous, promised over the din of laughter that there was nothing to worry about and that tickets would be refunded. Jumbo's execution was stayed and the giant elephant, who had survived his own execution, remained an attraction for years to come.

Leon Czolgosz was not so lucky. Since the moment he shot the president on September 9, Czolgosz had been hounded by crowds. First, there was the bloodthirsty mob at the Temple of Music. Then, there was the mass of people who had waited for days outside his jail cell inside Buffalo police headquarters, uncertain of what would transpire. And now, on September 26, as he arrived at Auburn Prison, more than three thousand people converged at the railroad station in an effort to get their hands on the man who had assassinated the president. Under heavy guard, Czolgosz walked amid the screaming, clawing crowd and made his way slowly into the prison. Once inside, he succumbed to the stress. He became hysterical and fell to the ground, shrieking and writhing on the floor. He was immediately strapped into a chair and injected with a sedative. Again, as at the trial, little time was wasted in dispatching the jury's verdict of execution by electricity. Afraid that Czolgosz, like Gaetano Bresci before him, would kill himself in his cell, the execution was scheduled one month after the jury verdict. On October 29, 1901, Leon Czolgosz died in the electric chair. Local newspapers reported the details:

> Warden Mead of Auburn raised his hands and at 7:12:30, electrician Davis turned the switch that threw twenty-seven hundred volts of electricity into the living

body. The rush of immense current threw the body so hard against the straps that they creaked perceptibly. The hands clinched up suddenly and the whole attitude was one of extreme tenseness. For forty-five seconds the full current was kept on and then slowly the electrician threw the switch back reducing the current volt by volt until it was cut off entirely. Then, just as it had reached that point, he threw the lever back again for a brief two or three seconds. The body, which had collapsed as the current reduced, stiffened up again against the straps. When it was turned off again, Dr. McCauley stepped up to the chair and put his hand over the heart. He said he felt no pulsation but suggested that the current be turned on for a few seconds again. At 7:18 the current was turned off for a third and final time. At 7:20 the warden announced: "Gentlemen, the prisoner is dead."[26]

One week later, John Milburn announced that the Pan-American Exposition had lost more than $6 million and that the company would have to default on more than $3.5 million in bonds. Milburn informed the board of directors that he was going to Washington where he would meet with New York's congressional delegation in an effort to convince Congress to pass a Pan-American relief bill. He hoped, also, to meet with President Roosevelt, who was reportedly sympathetic.

Despite this, Milburn's spirit was unbroken. He denied that the money lost on the Exposition was "a foolish expenditure," as some had charged. The Pan-American was, he said, a "masterpiece," and the city its "chosen showcase." Milburn asked the board to remain positive, to remember the millions of dollars that had poured into the city, and to believe that the Exposition had made Buffalo known all over the world, a city destined, he said, to rank with New York and Chicago.[27]

Yet somehow Milburn was not convincing. His words did not ring true. Nothing had turned out as Milburn had hoped. The Exposition for which he had worked so hard had ended in a nightmare of violence and destruction. Milburn, always looking ahead, did not like what he saw. Three years later, he left for New York, where he accepted a partnership in a law firm.[28]

In early December 1901, the Exposition buildings were sold to the Harris Wrecking Company of Chicago. A local committee was formed to buy and preserve the Electric Tower as a lasting monument to the Exposition, but it failed to raise the necessary funds. On January 20, 1902, the statue of the Goddess of Light was sold to the Humphrey Popcorn Company of Cleveland and the Electric Tower was finally torn down.[29]

While the one magical city was being dismantled, the gigantic complex of factories being built by the Lackawanna Steel Company was nearing completion. By 1904, the company had already built six open-hearth furnaces, mills for the production of light rails, steel plate, and steel slabs, and a "merchant mill" for a variety of smaller, diversified items. In addition, the company had built a new ship canal exclusively for iron ore from Mesabi (in 1905 close to 80 percent of all of Mesabi's iron ore was sent to the ports of the lower Great Lakes, much of it to Buffalo), and had constructed miles of railroad tracks, some linking the plant directly to the coal regions of western Pennsylvania and others connecting it directly to the large national railroad distribution system. The company was producing and selling millions of tons of steel, most of it to American railroads, but also a significant amount to international customers, particularly in Asia and the Pacific. In June 1906, Lieutenant Commander Shiegetoshi Takehuci of the Imperial Japanese Navy visited the plant and placed a multimillion-dollar order for armor plating. By the end of that year, Lackawanna was filling similar orders from Russia, Germany, and England.[30]

In 1906, the first year that the company was in full operation, Lackawanna Steel shipped more than one million tons of steel. Their net earnings reached $5 million. Within one year, however, the fortunes of the company faded, caught up in a cycle of decline that hit the whole industrial economy, which, led by the railroads, sunk into the economic depression of 1907. Production dropped by more than 40 percent and, by the end of the year, only two thousand of the company's six-thousand-man workforce remained employed. In early 1908, the salaries of office workers were cut by 10 percent and mill hands, who normally earned between twelve and seventeen cents per hour, now received a flat hourly rate of twelve cents. Despite losses of more than $1 million in 1908, the president of the company, Edward A. Clarke (the company's board had replaced Walter Scranton in 1904 with Clarke, a professional manager with a Harvard business degree, who, they felt, was better suited to lead the company into the new century at their new location) was optimistic and predicted an early return to full employment. The press, disappointed by the sudden reversal of the fortunes of a company that they had previously touted, was not so sure. "There is no warrant," the usually bullish *Commercial Advertiser* wrote, "for published statements intimating that the steel business is picking up again."[31]

Indeed, for the first time, the press began to pay close and gruesomely detailed attention to the accidents that occurred at the plant. In the spring of 1908, the *Buffalo Times* told the story of a man named Julius Kolas, who was hit by a falling piece of ore while working at the plant. "He was taken to the Emergency Hospital," the paper reported, "where it was found that both his hips were smashed, his right arm fractured and that he had internal injuries. He died on the operating table." Later in 1908, the *Times* reported that:

> August Pfohl, a young man employed at the rolling mills at the Lackawanna plant, was severely and perhaps fatally burned while taking away the red-hot iron from the rolls. Pfohl was standing in front of the rolls which, curling up like a snake, wound themselves around both of Pfohl's legs. He is resting at home as easily as can be expected and it is thought that he will be able to return to work. His legs however will be useless."[32]

More attention, too, was paid to the conditions in the company's employee housing complex. The newspapers reported on the unpaved streets, lack of sewers, poor sanitation, and the potential for fires. In the summer of 1908, the *Buffalo Express* intimated that waste discharged from the plant might well be contaminating Buffalo's drinking water. Hinting obliquely at what they felt to be true, the newspaper said that "the working class is not responsible for existing conditions and while it is not our intention to state who is, these are conditions that could easily be changed by the steel concern itself or by township authorities."[33]

Disappointed by the steel company that it had done so much to promote, the local press was disillusioned, and it questioned whether the community had not been "had." Unaware that the city's fate in the new industrial order was no longer in local hands, the press demanded accountability. Why, they wondered, had no dividends been paid on company stocks? Why had four thousand workers so abruptly lost their jobs? Why had local stockholders not been granted more power within the company? And why, finally, had the president of the company, Edward Clarke, still not moved his home and office to Buffalo? Battered and bruised by the seemingly false promises of both the Pan-American Exposition and the arrival of the Lackawanna Steel Company, people wondered how, when, and if the high hopes of this first decade of the new century would be realized.

NOTES

1. Among the many treasures in the scrapbooks at the Buffalo and Erie County Public Library's Grosvenor Collection are four volumes dedicated to President William McKinley. These fascinating books are filled with chronologically arranged clippings from the local press. They begin with McKinley's arrival in Buffalo on September 5, 1901, and end, four volumes later, with the death of McKinley's assassin, Leon Czolgosz, in the electric chair three months later. A good place to start is with the article headlined "McKinley Is Here," which appeared in the *Buffalo Express* on September 5, 1901, and can be found on page 11 of the first volume of these scrapbooks.

2. For biographical information on Milburn, see Bob Watson, *A Law Firm and a City: Hodgson, Russ, Andrews, Woods and Goodyear and Its Predecessor Firms, 1817–1981* (Buffalo, NY: Hodgson, Russ, Andrews, Woods & Goodyear, 1981), pp. 69ff.

3. For more information on William Rogers and the other businessmen active in the efforts to recruit Lackawanna Steel to Buffalo, see Chuck LaChiusa's brilliant Web site on Buffalo history and architecture, http://www.freenet.buffalo.edu/bah/h/lacksteel/index.html.

4. Information relating to the opening of the Lackawanna Steel Company's Buffalo facility is extensively covered in a one-volume scrapbook in the Grosvenor Collection at the Buffalo and Erie County Public Library, called "The Lackawanna Steel Company." It

contains clippings from the local press on all aspects of this momentous event, beginning in 1899 and ending in 1908. For information on Milburn's luncheon, see the May 1902 *Buffalo Times* article on p. 83 of the scrapbook.

5. "Albright Purchases South Buffalo Land…Deeds Filed," *Commercial Advertiser*, May 9, 1899, Lackawanna Steel Company Scrapbook, Grosvenor Collection, BECPL, p. 13. Other related articles are "Buying Land" (pp. 7–8) and "Mystery Ended" (p. 23).

6. "Vanderbilt Invests in New Steel Mill," *Buffalo Courier*, June 2, 1900, Lackawanna Steel Company Scrapbook, Grosvenor Collection, BECPL, p. 23.

7. For information regarding the relationship between J. J. Albright and E. B. Green, see Chuck LaChiusa, "Edward Brodhead Green—Biography," http://www.ah.bfn.org/a/archs/ebg/ebg.html.

8. Chuck LaChiusa, "The Pan Am Who's Who," http://www.ah.bfn.org/h/panam/links.

9. Kerry Grant, *The Rainbow City: Celebrating Light, Color and Architecture at the Pan American Exposition* (Buffalo, NY: Canisius College Press, 2001), p. 74ff.

10. Frederick W. Taylor, "The Horticultural Exhibits at Buffalo," *Everybody's Magazine*, October 1901, http://www.panam1901.bfn.org/documents/hortarticle.html.

11. For views and a description of "Darkest Africa," see "One Hundred Views of the Pan American Exposition," Film no. 264, vol. 4, BECPL. In addition, see Peggy Brooks-Bertran and Barbara Nevergold, "Africans, Darkies and Negroes: Black Faces at the Pan American Exposition," http://www.buffalonian.com/history/articles/1901-50/ucqueens/UncrownedQueens.html.

12. Chuck LaChiusa, "Mary Talbert—Chronology," http://www.freenet.buffalo.edu/bah/h/tal/index.html.

13. "A Magic City," *Commercial Advertiser*, September 15, 1900, Lackawanna Steel Company Scrapbook, Grosvenor Collection, BECPL, p. 342.

14. *Commercial Advertiser*, February 6, 1902, Lackawanna Steel Company Scrapbook, Grosvenor Collection, BECPL, p. 72.

15. "President's Day," *Commercial Advertiser*, September 5, 1901, McKinley Scrapbook, vol. 1, pp. 16–21, Grosvenor Collection, BECPL.

16. "Fireworks," McKinley Scrapbook, vol. 1, Grosvenor Collection, BECPL.

17. McKinley's activities on September 6, 1901, are minutely chronicled in a series of stories from various local papers that are clipped and arranged in the first volume of the McKinley Scrapbook at the BECPL. See, for example, "Biggest Day at the Fair," *Morning Express*, September 6, 1901, McKinley Scrapbook, vol. 1, p. 31, Grosvenor Collection, BECPL.

18. The events surrounding McKinley's visit to the exposition, his shooting, treatment, and death, as well as the arrest, trial, and execution of Leon Czolgosz are extensively covered in all four volumes of the McKinley Scrapbook at the BECPL. See also, "President William McKinley in Buffalo, NY" at http://www.freenet.buffalo.edu/bah/h/mckinley.html.

19. *Buffalo Morning Express*, September 8, 1901, McKinley Scrapbooks, vol. 2, pp. 34–41, Grosvenor Collection, BECPL.

20. "Helen Petrowski's Strange Story," *Buffalo Courier*, September 11, 1901, McKinley Scrapbook, vol. 1, Grosvenor Collection, BECPL.

21. "Recovery Is Now Assured," *Commercial Advertiser*, September 10, 1901, McKinley Scrapbook, vol. 2, Grosvenor Collection, BECPL.

22. The McKinley Scrapbook is filled with a vast amount of information regarding Leon Czolgosz: his family, his early life, his arrest, his detention, his trial, and his execution. See particularly "Czolgosz Plot Laid," *Commercial Advertiser*, September 16, 1901, McKinley Scrapbook, vol. 1, Grosvenor Collection, BECPL; "Sweet Justice for Czolgosz," *Commercial Advertiser*, September 17, 1901, McKinley Scrapbook, vol. 3, p. 129, Grosvenor Collection, BECPL; "Assassin's End," *Buffalo Express*, October 30, 1901, McKinley Scrapbook, vol. 4, Grosvenor Collection, BECPL. See also an excellent contemporary account in C. F. Donald, *The Trial, Execution, Autopsy and Mental Status of Leon Czolgosz* (Buffalo, NY, 1902).

23. See "Quotes About the Trial," McKinley Assassination Link: A Documentary History of William McKinley's Assassination," http://www.mckinleydeath.com/quotes/trial.htm.

24. "Buffalo Day at the Exposition" Pan-American Scrapbook, vol. 22, Grosvenor Collection, BECPL.

25. "Bostock's Farewell," *Buffalo Morning Express*, October 28, 1901, Pan-American Scrapbook, vol. 23, Grosvenor Collection, BECPL; "Elephant to Be Killed," *Buffalo Morning Express*, November 7, 1901, Pan-American Scrapbook, vol. 22, Grosvenor Collection, BECPL; "Jumbo Still Lives," *Buffalo Commercial Advertiser*, November 9, 1901, Pan-American Scrapbook, vol. 23, Grosvenor Collection, BECPL.

26. "Assassin's End," *Buffalo Morning Express*, October 30, 1901, McKinley Scrapbook, vol. 4, Grosvenor Collection, BECPL.

27. "Milburn Hopeful for Pan American Funds," *Commercial Advertiser*, November 5, 1901, Pan-American Scrapbook, vol. 18, Grosvenor Collection, BECPL.

28. "Milburn to Be a New Yorker," *New York Times*, December 16, 1903, p. 1.

29. "Goddess of Light Sold," *Commercial Advertiser*, December 12, 1901, Pan-American Scrapbook, vol. 22, Grosvenor Collection, BECPL.

30. "Great Progress at Steel Plant," *Buffalo Evening News*, September 29, 1901, Lackawanna Steel Company Scrapbook, Grosvenor Collection, BECPL, p. 56.

31. "Big Shake Up at New Steel Plant," *Commercial Advertiser*, September 15, 1903, Lackawanna Steel Company Scrapbook, Grosvenor Collection, BECPL, pp. 166–67. See also, "Resignation of Walter Scranton," *Buffalo Evening News*, January 3, 1904, Lackawanna Steel Company Scrapbook, Grosvenor Collection, BECPL, p. 176.

32. "Burned to a Cinder in Fluid Iron," *Buffalo Morning Express*, May 10, 1907, Lackawanna Steel Company Scrapbook, Grosvenor Collection, BECPL, p. 213.

33. "The Lackawanna Steel Company's New Villages," *Buffalo Morning Express*, August 8, 1908, Lackawanna Steel Company Scrapbook, Grosvenor Collection, BECPL, p. 221.

chapter 2

PATTERNS OF DAILY LIFE
IN THE INDUSTRIAL CITY

Despite concerns about the new steel company, it was clear by the early years of the twentieth century that the process of industrialization would dynamically reshape Buffalo's economy, introducing diversification in almost every field of endeavor. Industry boomed, particularly in iron and steel. In 1910, more than ten thousand people worked in more than one hundred fifty iron and steel factories throughout Buffalo, most of them, unlike Lackawanna Steel with its six thousand workers, in small plants scattered around the city's neighborhoods. Despite the size of the steel industry, however, it did not dominate the local economy. Other industries had come to play an increasingly important role: more than thirty-six hundred people worked in the auto industry, thirty-four hundred in the manufacture and repair of railroad cars, and eighteen hundred in the manufacture of copper, much of it used for beer barrels. Buffalo's commercial orientation, rooted in the city's traditional function as a clearinghouse for the raw products of the Midwest, remained strong. On one typical September day of that year, thirty-one ships arrived in the harbor, carrying lumber, livestock, pig iron, corn, flour, barley, rye, and more than one million tons of grain. The next day, thirty-three boats docked, despite warnings of high winds off of Detroit and the threat of a tugboat workers' strike in Green Bay and Chicago.[1]

In 1910, Buffalo remained the greatest grain port in the world and showed every sign of so remaining. The dozen or so gigantic steel elevators that lined the lakefront handled two million bushels of grain daily, with a storage capacity of more than twenty million bushels. Because of its superb shipping and storage facilities, Buffalo was second only to Minneapolis as a milling center. In 1894, George Pillsbury, the Minneapolis flour magnate, built a huge steel grain elevator in Buffalo. The following year, the H-O Cereal Company of New York moved its plant to Buffalo. H-O, the manufacturer of Korn Kinks, "the world's most nutritious breakfast food," employed nine hundred workers in 1905. But the largest milling company in early twentieth-century Buffalo was the Urban Company. The first in the United States to be powered by electricity, the Urban mills were capable of producing one thousand two hundred barrels of flour a day. George Urban Jr., the president of the company, was particularly proud of a manufacturing process that was capable of making uniform particles of flour. The advantage of this breakthrough, Urban maintained, was that the amount of water required to make dough would be constant and, thus, all of the flour particles would become dough at the same time.[2]

The grain trade led naturally to the development of a brewing industry and, by 1901, there were nineteen independently owned breweries in the city, producing more than seven hundred fifty thousand barrels a year (barrel making was a big business in Buffalo, too). The largest, the Gerhard Lang Company, produced three hundred thousand barrels a year. Like so many of the city's German-owned companies, the Lang brewery was a second-generation business owned by Jacob Gerhard Lang, a graduate of Doctor Wyatt's School of Technical Brewing in New York City. Lang's beer, like the other beers brewed locally by Philip Schaefer, William Simon, Magnus Beck, and others, was known throughout the Northeast and Midwest.[3]

While trade in grain led to the manufacture of flour, cereal, and beer, the passage of lumber through the port of Buffalo made the city one of the nation's great lumber centers. In the early days following the completion of the Erie Canal, Buffalo merchants handled the shipment of lumber and were involved in all aspects of the lumber trade. Some, like Frank and Charles Goodyear, who had purchased millions of acres of Pennsylvania timberland, had come to control the initial stages of lumber production. In 1905, the Goodyear brothers bought half a million more acres of timberlands on the Bogue Lusa Creek in Washington Parish, Louisiana. Their outfit, the Southern Lumber Company, built several saw mills and a railroad, and planned a town "complete with its own colored quarters." Chronicling the history of his family, a scion of the Goodyears wrote: "On May 13, 1907 Frank H. Goodyear died of Bright's disease, worn out with ceaseless activity and worry. Although only five feet eight inches in height, he weighed two hundred and twenty pounds and overeating was undoubtedly a cause of his early death."[4] His appetite had obviously been enormous, and although it killed him, it helped reshape the economy of the city of Buffalo.

The excellence of Buffalo's shipping facilities made the city second only to Chicago as the most important livestock center in the world. Arriving from Canada and the western United States on lake boats and railroads, millions of head of cattle, sheep, and hogs were processed yearly at the city's enormous East Side livestock yards. There was even a special bank that catered strictly to the needs of the countless livestock dealers, commission merchants, wholesale butchers, and meatpackers who comprised this extensive industry. Livestock contributed to the diversity of the city's manufacturing base. In 1909, Jacob Dold, president of the largest packinghouse in Buffalo, wrote:

> There is no part of the animal which is not used. Certain glands, membranes, tissues, and bone oils are sources of valuable medicinal preparations. Some of the bones of better quality are converted into knife handles, buttons, etc.; other bones, after yielding their content of fats, oils and glue stock are used for poultry foods, and fertilizers. The intestines are converted into sausage and other containers strings for musical instruments. Hoofs and horns are converted into combs and other novelties. Hair bristles are used in the manufacture of brushes and upholstery. The blood is used in certain meat food products.[5]

Soap was another byproduct of the livestock industry. In 1910, the Larkin Soap Company, which was founded in 1875, had become, as the result of an aggressive marketing campaign developed by John D. Larkin's brother-in-law, Elbert Hubbard, one of the largest in the world. What livestock was to soap, lumber was to furniture, and by the early years of the century, Buffalo boasted some of the finest furniture manufacturers in the country, most famously the Kittinger Company.

Buffalo had other industries, which had nothing to do with either interstate commerce or heavy industry. One of these was the production of chemicals. The first and one of the largest chemical companies in the area was founded in 1901 by Jacob and Alfred Schoellkopf, whose father Jacob had already made a fortune in electrical power. His sons made their fortunes when their company, National Aniline, sold chemicals to the Allies during World War I for the manufacture of explosives.[6]

Growing rapidly, too, and very quickly capturing the imagination of Buffalonians, was the automobile industry. In 1899, a man named Truman Martin, the manager of a company named the New York Electrical Vehicle Company (it was owned by the Whitneys of New York Central fame), opened a dealership for their electric automobiles in Buffalo. One year later, George N. Pierce, a bicycle manufacturer, whose bicycles were known around the world, began the production of a gasoline-powered automobile. In 1901, the Pierce "motorette," a two and three-quarters horsepower car with a maximum speed of 15 miles per hour, finished first in a Fourth of July race between Buffalo and New York. In 1903, Pierce had three automobiles in his line: a 5-horsepower runabout, the 6.5-horsepower "Stanhope," and the pride of the company, the 16.5-horsepower "Arrow." Pierce reported that in all three models "the noise of the exhaust has been entirely eliminated, owing to a new system adopted in construction." Prices for Pierce's automobiles ranged from $1,000 to $2,500.[7] In 1906, Pierce moved from his old plant on Hanover Street in South Buffalo to an enormous new factory that he built on Elmwood Avenue adjacent to the tracks of the Belt Line Railroad. With 250,000 square feet of floor space, the plant, with more than eight hundred workers, was one of the first in the country built specifically for the manufacture of automobiles.

In 1900, another company, the Conrad Motor Carriage Company, began production of a steam-powered vehicle. One year later, they, too, switched to gasoline and began manufacture of a light runabout and a 12-horsepower touring car. The founder of the company, F. P. Conrad, had gone to Paris to learn from the French, and he vowed upon returning to Buffalo that he would produce a car that "would not require an engineer to operate." In 1902, there were five hundred automobiles in Buffalo and a chapter of the Automobile Club of America actively lobbied on behalf of the city's growing number of motorists. By 1910, more than three thousand five hundred people were employed in the city's rapidly expanding automobile industry.[8]

More than anything, however, the railroads remade the local economy. Drawn to Buffalo because of its location at one of the nation's great transfer points—the city's location, wrote one newspaper in 1907, was "an alluring bait to the energetic railroad magnates"—railroads completely altered the way people worked and lived. By 1910, Buffalo was served by eleven different trunk lines and was second only to Chicago among the leading railroad termini in the United States. There were seven direct lines connecting Buffalo with six different East Coast cities; six direct lines to Chicago, Kansas City, Omaha, and St. Louis; and two direct lines between Buffalo and Pittsburgh. The New York Central was so big that it had its own police force (some officials of the Pennsylvania Railroad complained that they should also have one). The railroad companies had created a new industry in the city. They owned thirty-six hundred acres of city land and had laid six hundred sixty miles of track within the city limits. They directly employed twenty thousand men and indirectly gave work to thousands more in the car wheel shops, palace car shops, locomotive and freight car shops, and in the largest bridge company in the world, all of which were located in the city.[9]

The massive network of factories and railroads that comprised the infrastructure of industry had a dramatic influence on neighborhood patterns in Buffalo. By the early twentieth century, the East Side, where railroads, factories, and cheap housing converged, had become home to most of the city's immigrant groups, none larger than the Poles. By 1910, the Polish community on the East Side of Buffalo had grown to almost fifty thousand people. And finally, after more than twenty-five years of growth and development, the area began to attract the attention of outsiders.

In 1909, John T. Daniels, a social worker in charge of what was called the "Buffalo Social Survey," moved into the neighborhood in an effort, he said, to document "the history and the current conditions of the Poles in Buffalo." Amid increasing concern about the high rates of poverty in the Polish community and the high rates of crime that seemed to go with it, the Buffalo Social Survey studied the community over a six-month period in late 1909 and early 1910. There were, Daniels said, more than eighty thousand Poles living in Buffalo, proportionately more—20 percent of the total population—than in any other city in the nation. Daniels's study, which appeared in the *Buffalo Express* but was covered by the other papers as well, was divided into five topics: "History and Progress of the Poles"; "Wages and Livelihood"; "Housing and Living Conditions"; "Education of the Rising Generation"; and, to the great consternation of many in the Polish community, a topic that Daniels called "Lawlessness and Criminality." Daniels pored carefully over police records and clearly documented that a disproportionate amount of crime in the city was in fact committed by Poles. Defending himself against the attacks of Polish partisans who accused him of prejudice, Daniels insisted fruitlessly that this was a function of poverty, not of any weakness in the Polish character.[10] Daniels was impressed with the churches and the hold they seemed to have on the people of the Polish neighborhood. They were massive structures with gigantic congregations: St. Stanislaus boasted twenty thousand members; St. Adalbert's, eight thousand; Transfiguration, six thousand; Corpus Christie, six thousand; and Assumption, the smallest, had a mere eight hundred. Daniels studied the religious as well as the secular life of the community and was particularly interested in how people worked in their chosen occupations. Neighborhood patterns, Daniels seemed to conclude, were shaped as much by industry and the nature of work as they were by patterns of ethnicity. Industry's demand for labor was voracious and, by 1910, more than 50 percent of the city's labor force worked at industrial jobs, with many, if not most of them, Poles. Factory work in the neighborhood—in the railroad yards, car repair shops, machine shops, metal factories, breweries, barrel factories, and so on—was plentiful, and the men in the Polish community gravitated to it. Here, in large brick factories crammed between the small wood-frame houses that lined the streets, recently settled Poles found all kinds of work. Following his survey, Daniels concluded that "if all the Poles in Buffalo would be taken away over night many of the large factories in the city might as well go away also."[11] Work on Buffalo's Polish East Side, Daniels discovered, was not limited to gritty industrial work. Indeed, Daniels revealed the existence of a small but healthy entrepreneurial economy. Moving street by street in St. Stanislaus Parish—through Coit, Detroit, Sycamore, Emslie, and the others—Daniels found them filled with small stores and businesses, a total of 184 groceries, 176 saloons, 44 butcher shops, 32 "market men at the Broadway market," 34 cobblers, 14 drugstores, 2 architects, 3 moving picture theaters, four photographers, and one piano teacher. While pleased with the progress of this homegrown economy, Daniels was concerned about the lack of a Polish business presence on Main Street: "A few Polish names along Main Street as an entering wedge for more would do wonders in drawing the attention of the public to the business progress of the Poles." In addition, he said, "it would stimulate the Poles themselves to break away from their exclusively Polish moorings and steer their course into the vastly larger American field with its vastly greater opportunities."

How the patterns and processes of industry, transportation, and ethnicity came together to create separate communities within the city is perfectly demonstrated in the story of a neighborhood still known as Assumption Parish, near Black Rock. It started in 1883, when the New York Central Railroad Company built a new railroad called the belt line. In an effort to decentralize industrial development and to better link the factories of the city, the belt line, for both freight and passengers, opened up whole new areas of the city for development. Whole new neighborhoods were spawned, none bigger than Assumption Parish, which, by the early years of the twentieth century, had become a deeply rooted, industrialized, Polish-Catholic neighborhood. At first a simple stop on the belt line, the area soon became a major node that attracted both new factories and new residents, most all of them Poles who had left their old East Side neighborhood in search of opportunities on the new frontier of Assumption Parish. The pace of development quickened. Assumption Church was constructed on Amherst Street in 1888, and factories followed: Pratt and Letchworth Steel, Pratt and Lambert Paint, and the biggest one of all, Pierce Arrow, which built its mammoth new plant at the corner of Elmwood and Great Arrow in 1904. Still more came and, by 1910, the Assumption neighborhood was the most industrialized in the city.[12]

While railroads created new neighborhoods, they also divided existing ones. Railroad tracks like the belt line cut through the city at street level. Not only were these crossings extremely dangerous (the newspapers of turn-of-the-century Buffalo were filled with gruesome details of accidents to man and beast caused by the street-level railroads) but by crisscrossing entire sections of the city, they effectively divided the city into separate and virtually impassable sections. Black Rock and Assumption Parish, though adjacent to each other, were completely isolated from each other by a fortress-like conglomeration of street-level railroad crossings. The tangible notion of "the other side of the tracks" imbued a sense of separatism to these neighborhoods, which was further reinforced by the separatist and parochial patterns of the immigrant groups who lived in them.

Separate and parochial, too, were the Italians. At the turn of the century, the Italian population of Buffalo was growing fast, with approximately thirteen thousand in 1890, twenty thousand in 1900, and more than fifty thousand by 1920.[13] The Italian immigrants came from all over Italy, but particularly from the dozens of towns and villages that dotted the gorgeous mountains and valleys of southern Italy and Sicily. Thousands upon thousands of heartbreaking departures later, these people—from Abruzzi and Calabria, Campobasso and Campagna, Enna and Noto, Messina and Palermo, and each speaking the dialects of their region— found themselves on the streets of Buffalo: the Campobassini headed to Seneca and Swan streets on the East Side; the Calabrese to South Buffalo; the Abruzzese to Roma Avenue; and the Sicilians, the largest group, to the old waterfront area around Canal Street and to the tiny side streets near the waterfront on the Lower West Side. Sometimes, entire Italian towns were emptied by these migrations. By 1910, for example, eight thousand of a total population of twelve thousand people in the medieval mountain town of Valle D'Olmo ("Valley of the Elms") had moved to Buffalo, where they lived—brothers and sisters, uncles and aunts, cousins, grandparents, and paesani—cramped together on the waterfront streets of the Lower West Side. These migrations of whole families, clans, and even villages provided strength, security, and islands of refuge. Family, faith, home, and memory sustained these immigrants in an uncertain new world, creating both community in the new and continuity with the old.[14]

The boom years for Buffalo's Italian community were the early years of the century, a time of frenzied community-building activities that energized the newly arrived immigrants. In 1902, on a small plot of land on Court Street, just off Niagara Square, the city's first Italian parish church, St. Anthony of Padua, opened its doors. That same year, a new building for School 2, whose nine hundred students were nearly all Italian, opened on the Terrace. In 1905, as more Italians moved into the old Canal Street area known as "the Hooks," the church of the Madonna del Carmine, known as Mt. Carmel, opened on a street whose name, "Le Couteleux" (one of the village of Buffalo's earliest settlers), surely must have been difficult for the parishioners to pronounce. One year later, as the numbers of Italians on Swan Street grew, St. Lucy's opened to accommodate them.

There were other foreigners, too, in much smaller numbers. Nevertheless, there were enough of them to attract the attention of the press and those citizens who cared enough to notice. In 1904, Annie Danes, a social worker for the Charity Organization Society, a social agency whose mission was to help the poor, gave a speech at the Twentieth Century Club titled "Our Foreign Population." Referring to the smaller, less visible groups, she mentioned the Greeks, the Syrians, and the Jews. According to Danes, there were, at the time, approximately seventy-five Greeks living in Buffalo, most living on a long-abandoned alley called "Blossom," on the edge of the central business district, between Broadway and Sycamore. Many of them, she said, worked in the candy business, like the family of Peter Sperios Niarchos, the city's most successful Greek businessman, who owned the Buffalo Candy Company.

Living nearby were several hundred Lebanese, also known as "Syrians," who, as early as 1904, had founded their own church, St. John Maron, on Seneca Street. The apparent leaders of the congregation were George Joseph and Nahmi George, owners of a factory at 415 Seneca Street (not far from the church), which manufactured men's shirts and overalls. Danes, said the *Buffalo Express* reporter who covered her speech,

> gave a vivid description of Lebanese weddings which, according to her description, were street-weddings that lasted for several days. She was delighted by the excitement the event created in the public life of the community. "When one of the girls of the colony is married a grand feast follows the ceremony. Then comes a three day dance where the Oriental custom is followed as vigorously as in Syria (Lebanon)."[15]

In addition, Danes reported, there were a growing number of Jews, more than six thousand of them at the turn of the century, most of whom lived on the side streets just east of downtown, between Broadway and William Streets. Here, on and around William Street, a growing first-generation neighborhood of Russian and Polish Jews quickly took root, and it was here that a handful of synagogues, kosher butcher shops, bakeries, and food and clothing shops formed the bustling center of Jewish community life in Western New York.[16]

In the early years of the twentieth century, the city's neighborhoods were shaped not only by the patterns of ethnicity but by the movement through the city of electric streetcars, by then the dominant form of public transportation. Winding its way in and around the streets of the city's countless neighborhoods, the electric streetcar tied the city together in a way that had not been possible earlier. For the price of a nickel, Buffalonians, whose lives for so long had been limited to places they could reach only by foot, found a new freedom to move around the whole city. By 1900, electric streetcars traveled on streets throughout the city, including Bailey, Baynes, Best, Broadway, Cazenovia, Clinton, Connecticut, East Ferry, East Utica, Elk, Elmwood, Genessee, Herman, Hertel, Jefferson, Kensington, Main, Niagara, Seneca, School, Sycamore, and Utica. The lines were distinguished by different numbers and different colors, which enlivened the movement of these long, kaleidoscopic vehicles through the streets: the Albany and School streetcars in burgundy; the Allen and Ferry cars in green; the Bailey cars in yellow; the Baynes and Hoyt cars in green; the Clinton and Jefferson in red; and the Elmwood in dark red.[17] Streetcars were responsible for two historic changes in the city. First, they encouraged movement of people out of and away from their old neighborhoods in the center of the city. Thousands of people moved their families and, as a result, whole new residential neighborhoods—"street-car suburbs"—sprung up on the fringes of the central core. From the old neighborhoods, where small frame homes shared the streetscapes with hulking grain elevators, a new generation of Buffalonians hopped on the streetcar lines as their ancestors had hopped on ships. Suddenly, whole sections of the city's cramped old neighborhoods were drained as people in Black Rock, the East Side, and the Old First Ward took a streetcar line and moved to Riverside, to Kensington-Bailey, to South Buffalo, and beyond. Soon there were suburban lines that also moved people to and from the city, a phenomenon that occurred twenty years before the automobile accelerated a process that would, in the days after World War I, become known as "suburbanization." By 1910, these lines included the Buffalo, Depew, and Lancaster, the Buffalo and Gardenville, the Buffalo and Grand Island, the Buffalo and Hamburg, and separate lines to Lockport, Niagara Falls, Tonawanda, and Williamsville.

The electric streetcar not only created entirely new residential neighborhoods, it was also, as much as anything, responsible for the rise of the modern central business district. Now, for the first time, thousands of Buffalonians, whose social and cultural activities had been for so long confined to the limits of their ancestral neighborhoods, could leave and come downtown. Retail business in the area boomed as large new department stores opened to accommodate the flood. Hotels, theaters, restaurants, and music halls sought downtown locations, as the social and cultural center shifted from the neighborhoods to downtown. In 1910, the electric streetcar had become the chief mode of transit for people of all ages and classes: businessmen commuting to work; industrial workers on their way to factory jobs; housewives on family errands; and children traveling to and from school.

The electric streetcars fed an unprecedented downtown building boom. National corporations, local banks, department stores, and real estate developers sought downtown locations at the center of an emerging regional central business district. Change was apparent everywhere. Shelton Square at Main Street and Eagle, for example, had, since the 1820s, been watched over by the twin towers of the First Presbyterian Church on the northwest corner and St. Paul's Episcopal Church across the street on the southwest corner. For the better part of a century, these symbols of the city's pioneering days had stood tall and steady as the landscape around them gradually changed. By the late 1880s, pressure on them had grown too strong to resist and, in 1889, the trustees of one, the First Presbyterian, succumbed. Eager to move to "a neighborhood not so shut in by business," they sold the magnificent church to the Erie County Savings Bank and relocated to "the circle," on Fredrick Law Olmsted's recently completed Richmond Avenue. The old church was quickly demolished and replaced by a spectacular gothic revival structure that was to be the headquarters for the Erie County Savings Bank. As downtown became increasingly accessible and more and more people sought it out as an entertainment destination, the area churches, whose memberships were in decline as people moved away from their old neighborhoods, were eager to sell. Churches were easily adapted to theaters. For example, the Lafayette Presbyterian Church on Lafayette Square, became, in 1896, the Lyceum Theatre, the largest one in the city, with more than two thousand seats. Other churches gave way under similar temptations, with many of them transformed, often haphazardly, into large, garish theaters or vaudeville houses. In 1904, the North Presbyterian Church on Main and Huron was demolished and replaced by the Hippodrome Theatre. Soon, the Central Presbyterian Church on Pearl and Genesee followed, giving way to the Majestic Theatre. In 1906, the magnificent gothic revival St. John's Episcopal Church, built in 1846 on Washington Street, was torn down and replaced by the Statler Hotel, just across from the recently completed Ellicott Square Building. There were other new theaters in the booming downtown, places like the Star on the corner of Pearl and Mohawk, with one thousand five hundred seats, and the Court Street Theatre, just down Court from Lafayette Square near Franklin, with a capacity of eight hundred. The Star also had its own restaurant, called Yhen King, which claimed to be Buffalo's first Chinese restaurant. By 1910, there were almost ten thousand seats in downtown Buffalo ready to accommodate the unprecedented numbers of people who had discovered downtown as the entertainment center of the metropolitan area.[18]

    In scope and scale, nothing was bigger than the Ellicott Square Building. Containing eight hundred separate offices in a ten-story square building that covered an entire city block, it was, when it opened on May 1, 1898, the largest office building in the world. In 1910, the Ellicott Square Building boasted well over a thousand tenants. While the majority of them were lawyers, there were also corporate headquarters, brokers of all kinds, real estate agents, bankers, stationers, private detectives, two shoe stores, several restaurants, a handful of physicians and dentists, chiropodists, hairdressers, architects, and jewelers, as well as the local office of the Berlitz School of Foreign Languages. The building's restaurant, owned and operated by Ellsworth Statler, served more than five hundred lunches a day.[19] More than any other building, Ellicott Square contributed to the pressure cooker of activity that made downtown the bustling center of the metropolis.

Just up Main Street lay Lafayette Square, another emerging center of activity in the new downtown. By 1910, Lafayette Square was flanked by large new office buildings, the recently completed Lafayette Hotel, and the city's leading department stores, including Kleinhans, S. H. Knox, J. N. Adams, and Hengerer's, billed as "the largest department store between Chicago and New York." As much as anything, it was the Buffalo Public Library, built in the late 1880s, which contributed to the excitement and vitality of Lafayette Square. The building was large and beautiful, a dark, romantic, castle-like Romanesque structure that embraced the street, giving spectacular definition to the east side of the square. More so than the building, the activities within the library did much to alter the character and function of this part of downtown. First, the library's vast and growing collection of materials attracted, by 1905, a circulation of more than one million. Noting this, a weekly periodical titled the *Buffalo Chronicle*, wrote in 1905: "It is doubtful whether any city in the country can show so large a percentage of circulation in proportion to population."[20] Second, in addition to their own collection, the library hosted and incubated the leading cultural institutions of the city: the Buffalo Fine Arts Academy, the Buffalo Society of Natural Sciences, and the Buffalo Historical Society. Other organizations had their meeting rooms there, too, like the Bohemian Sketch Club, the only artists' organization, it claimed, "run by artists for artists." While each of these institutions would eventually have homes of their own, until they did, the central library served as a stimulating space for these groups, each of which, with creative and scholarly constituencies, added not only to the synergy within the library building but to the rest of downtown as well. The library had become "the brain" of an increasingly "smart" downtown.

Nearby, just down Court Street, on Niagara Square, other places of learning were built in the 1880s. Buffalo's Central High School was constructed on Court Street and on Niagara Square rose the Women's Educational and Industrial Union, a remarkable Romanesque complex of masonry offices that were linked by repeating rows of arches. Around the corner from Lafayette Square was the Washington Street Market, the largest retail market in Buffalo. It occupied one large square block and was owned and operated by the city. Situated in the middle of the block, between Washington, Chippewa, and Ellicott streets, the market included a large, medieval-style brick building, which served as its focal point. The cavernous interior of the market was reserved for butchers, all of whom operated their own stalls. Against the walls of the building were stalls reserved for poultry, butter, cheese, fruits, and vegetables, all, one reporter noted in 1887, "tastefully and effectively displayed." The market provided wonderful street theater, diverse and operatic in its form and function: "Wagons are allowed to stand on the sides of the streets which surround the marketplace and pedestrians walk along the sidewalks and buy from these wagons. Then there are stalls in front of the market where crockery, tins, knit goods and variety articles of all sorts may be bought." The principal market days were Tuesdays, Thursdays, and Saturdays. But it was, according to one account, "Saturday, of course that is the greatest market day and from early morning till midnight the narrow pavements between the stalls are so crowded that even market-men and farmers can scarcely find room to move about." On Saturdays, the market stayed open late and then the place came alive: "This is the vendors' festival night and whole families come and see the fun. The market is lit by gas and many of the outside stands use torch lights so that as one approaches the market at night the scene is a brilliant and active one."[21]

By the early years of the century, as traffic and congestion grew, Lafayette Square, which for years had been known as Lafayette Park, a lush urban public place with thickly planted trees, bushes, and many benches for its patrons, was destined for change. Downtown interest groups—the new retailers and theater, hotel, and restaurant owners—joined by a powerful new lobby, the Buffalo Auto Club, which had more than a thousand members, were eager to see the park better adapted to the area's rapidly changing needs. In 1912, the Buffalo Common Council, without much hesitation, approved a resolution to "devote to street purposes all that part of the Park except a small circle around the Soldiers and Sailors' Monument." Lafayette Park had become a traffic circle.[22]

In 1900, Johnson Park, which took its name from Ebenezer Johnson, the city's first mayor, was still an elegant residential neighborhood within walking distance of the central business district. Like the town squares of London on which it was modeled, it had become by the turn of the new century a venerable residential quarter. The tree-lined mall, home to many of the city's most prestigious families and the site of the Buffalo Female Academy, an exclusive private school for the daughters of the elite, was lined with large wood and brick homes. Adjacent to Johnson Park and extending from Delaware Avenue was the private estate of Bronson C. Rumsey. Rumsey's estate, known by 1900 as Rumsey Park, was a veritable forest of trees. The estate featured a large lake, which, fed by a natural spring, filled much of the property from Carolina Street to Delaware Avenue. The property was designed by the English architects Henry and Edward Rose, who were brought to Buffalo by Rumsey for the commission. The park, as described in a remarkable book of photographs titled *The Picture Book of Earlier Buffalo*, published in 1912 by the Buffalo Historical Society, was gorgeous:

The topography of the spot was carefully studied and the native forest trees were augmented by judicious planting. A boat house, a tiny Swiss chalet, was set at the water-side and a little Grecian temple, now destroyed, bespoke the taste of the owner. The gardens near the house were terraced, set with flowers and fountains. For half a century this beauty spot in the heart of the city was the joy of its owner and his friends. It was the ideal setting for many festivities and social gatherings and in the skating season no place was so popular for those privileged to use it as Rumsey Park."[23]

But a new century had arrived, a time when the rapidly expanding central business district was devouring the land that lay around it. For the central business district to thrive and to realize its potential as the economic focal point of the metropolis, all roads had to lead to it. Johnson Park and the Rumsey estate stood in the path of Elmwood Avenue, which, the boosters of downtown insisted, should be extended through them both and into the heart of downtown. By the early 1900s, a coalition of downtown interest groups was created, which included merchants, bankers, real estate agents, and hoteliers. Under the forceful leadership of J. N. Adam, owner of one of downtown's newest and largest department stores, and W. C. Ely, president of the International Railway Corporation, owner and operator of the city's streetcar lines, both of whom stood to benefit mightily from the extension of Elmwood, the coalition lobbied for an improvement they deemed vital to the realization of their visions for downtown. Over the weakened opposition of the residents of Johnson Park who, despite the presence of many individuals listed in Buffalo's Social Register, lacked the clout of the emergent downtown leaders, the Common Council unanimously approved the measure. In 1907, another chapter in the long, continuing saga of upheaval in the life of the city began. Homes were demolished and Rumsey's lake was filled in. The Rumseys, like many other residents of Johnson Park, left. So, too, did the Buffalo Female Academy, moving to Bidwell Parkway, in a newer residential part of town. In 1914, a public school, Hutchinson Central, was built near the site. The Rumsey estate was eviscerated and Johnson Park was bisected by Elmwood Avenue's new route downtown. When a few years later a new hotel, the Tourraine, opened at the corner of Johnson Park and Delaware Avenue, it was, an advertisement said, "located in the center most section of downtown Buffalo."[24] One reality was replaced by another, as Johnson Park, for so long the bucolic home of the city's "best" families, began its new life as a battered, tawdry, and increasingly marginal neighborhood on the fringes of downtown.[25]

Conditions changed quickly. By the turn of the century, automobiles, particularly electrical ones, were becoming increasingly popular in Buffalo. By 1910, with close to a thousand cars and trucks on the road, it was impossible to ignore the

importance of the automobile in the daily life of the city. While still seen primarily as pleasure vehicles, efforts were being made to commercialize them. No one
pursued this more aggressively than a physician named Truman J. Martin. In
1896, having recognized the value an automobile would offer a doctor, Martin
brought to Buffalo from Connecticut an electric version called the "Stanhope."
Since there were no charging stations in Buffalo, Martin, who lived at North
Street and Delaware Avenue, kept the car in his stable and charged it by tapping
into the electrical supply at the nearby Lenox Hotel. Three years later, Martin,
who now was reported to "represent the Whitney interests in Buffalo," bought the
old Brown Riding Academy on West Utica Street and converted it into a garage
for the storing and charging of electric automobiles. Later that year, Martin began
testing what he said was the "first public auto omnibus service in the country."
There were two of them—one for fourteen passengers, another for twenty—
which Martin demonstrated in several test runs from Main and Seneca Street,
over to Chippewa, and up Delaware Avenue to Chapin Parkway.[26] Toward the end
of 1899, another outfit—the Buffalo Automobile Company—was formed with the
intention of running

> a line of public omnibuses along some of the most popular streets in the city. It is
> planned to have a line of horseless conveyances running out Delaware Avenue and
> another out Richmond Avenue. The object will be to afford cheap public con-
> veyances to such people as reside at a distance from the present streetcar lines.[27]

Earlier that same year, another recently formed enterprise, called the
National Motor Transit Company, entered into a one-year contract with the Park
Board of Buffalo to operate an automobile transit service that traveled along what
would become, sixty years later, the route of the city's first intra-urban highway,
the Scajaquada Creek Expressway. Four cars, leaving every half hour, traveled
from Lincoln Parkway, along "the main road south of the Meadow," past the zoo,
to Humboldt Parkway and Main Street. One year later, Dr. Martin, who had left
his medical practice to work full time at the Buffalo Automobile Company, recognized the increasing popularity of the new form of transportation and organized the Buffalo Automobile Club.[28] Martin was bullish about the future of autos
in Buffalo. "It is," he said, "the city of bicyclists. It is bound to be the city of automobiles too." The city, he said, "is especially suited to the pleasures of the auto
on account of its many miles of smooth pavement and delightful parkways which
cross, re-cross and encircle the city." Noting that "the city is already full of automobiles," the time was ripe, he said, to form the auto club, an organization that
would, he promised, "advance the rights and privileges of the growing number of
people in this city who own and drive automobiles."[29] It was only a question of

time, some people began to realize, before these "rights and privileges" would forever change the way the people of Buffalo lived in and experienced their city.

In 1903, an enormous roughly circular building at the corner of Edward and Franklin streets, known as the "cyclorama," was converted into a seven-hundred-car garage, the city's first. It was the largest parking garage in the state of New York and the second largest in the country. According to a 1903 article in the *Express*, the cyclorama was more than just a garage; it was "built in the French fashion with a large turn-table in the center of the main floor." Owned and operated by the Auto Roundhouse Company, the facility had what were called "retiring rooms with shower baths." Every effort was made to accommodate the rapidly growing number of Buffalo motorists. It seems the city's battles in the long war with the automobile had begun.

While the electric streetcar was beginning to drain the city's older neighborhoods, both luring their inhabitants to newer streetcar suburbs and drawing them inward to the booming downtown, neighborhoods would remain the focal point of local life for years to come. In 1910, every main street in every neighborhood of the city supported businesses that created an energetic street life. All of the commercial strips—Allen, Grant, Connecticut, Fillmore, Jefferson, and the rest—were packed with the vitality of small businesses, all of which served the people who lived within steps of the stores. A 1910 street-by-street directory of the city's businesses reveals the tightly woven fabric of its streets: on one block alone—the two hundred block of Allen Street—the directory reports that there were two barbers, two salons, one cigar store, two doctors, a post office substation, two butchers, a milliner, a dressmaker, a druggist, a candy and ice cream shop, and one Chinese laundry.[30] And then there were the saloons—hundreds and hundreds of them on side streets and main streets in every corner of the city. Indeed, the 1910 city directory devotes more than nine pages to listing in alphabetical order the names of every bar in Buffalo. In the social and convivial environment of the neighborhood saloon, everyone had a place to go—a local neighborhood hangout, away from the house and the family, but still close to home. Even the parks, designed by Olmstead as a place of escape from the increasing pace of urbanization, were filled with people. A reporter, writing on a cold and sunny day in January 1906, described the scene at the lake in Delaware Park: "As one stands on the bridge and views them from a distance they appear very much like a swarm of black flies upon a ground of sugar. The crowd is often so dense that their movements are hardly perceptible."[31] Everywhere, it seemed, there was a complex and intense overlap of uses that supported a vibrant public culture, lived out daily on the streets and in the neighborhoods of the city.

Despite the increasingly ominous presence of the automobile, turn-of-the-century Buffalo possessed a highly developed sense of urbanism. In the neighborhoods and the central business district, in the parks and on the waterfront, people lived in an urban environment that encouraged and sustained a high degree of density, with an overlapping mixture of places and spaces. People, and lots of them, were everywhere: in the crowded tenements of the immigrant poor; on the miles of tree-lined streets in the city's working and middle-class neighborhoods; on the sidewalks of the city's voraciously expanding downtown; and even on the broad boulevards of Delaware Avenue and Chapin Parkway, where Buffalo's wealthy families lived.

NOTES

1. Information on Buffalo's economy in 1910 is taken from H. W. Hill, ed., *Municipality of Buffalo, A History, 1720–1923*, vol. 1 (New York: Lewis, 1932), pp. 727–845.

2. Ibid.

3. Ibid.

4. J. T. Horton, *History of Northwestern New York* (New York: Lewis, 1948), p. 220.

5. Hill, *Municipality of Buffalo*, vol. 1, p. 811

6. Ibid.

7. Industry in Buffalo Scrapbook, vol. 2, pp. 31–37, Grosvenor Collection, BECPL.

8. Hill, *Municipality of Buffalo*, vol. 1, p. 839.

9. Ibid., p. 824.

10. John Daniels, "Buffalo's Foreign Population," *Buffalo Express*, March 16, 1910.

11. Daniels's richly detailed articles appeared in the *Buffalo Times* throughout 1910 and can be found in the Buffalo's Foreign Population Scrapbook in the Grosvenor Collection at the BECPL.

12. For information regarding the impact of industry and railroads on the city's neighborhoods, including Black Rock, see "City of Buffalo Atlas, 1894," http://www.erie .gov/atlases/buff_94/city_atlas.html, which can be reached from the "maps" section of Cynthia Van Ness's Web site, http://www.buffaloresearch.com.

13. These numbers are drawn from articles included in the Buffalo's Foreign Population Scrapbook, vol. 1, Grosvenor Collection, BECPL.

14. For the patterns of Italian settlement, see Virginia Yans-McGlaughlin, *Family and Community: Italian Immigrants in Buffalo, 1880–1930* (Ithaca, NY: Cornell University Press, 1971), pp. 109–133

15. *Buffalo Express*, January 1, 1904, Buffalo's Foreign Population Scrapbook, vol. 2, p. 341, Grosvenor Collection, BECPL.

16. Selig Adler, *From Ararat to Suburbia: The History of the Jewish Community of Buffalo* (Philadelphia: Jewish Publication Society, 1960), pp. 160–214.

17. *Paul's Dictionary of Buffalo* (Buffalo, NY: Peter Paul Press, 1897), pp. 159ff.

18. For the process of change that occurred in downtown and on Main Street, see Frank Severance, ed., *Picture Book of Earlier Buffalo*, vol. 16 (Buffalo, NY: Buffalo Historical Society, 1912), pp. 105–51, 309–47.

19. There is a great deal of information on the Ellicott Square Building in the vertical files of the Buffalo and Erie County Historical Society. See also any of the many turn-of-the-century guidebooks and directories to business activity in Buffalo, which are housed in the Grosvenor Collection at the BECPL.

20. *Buffalo Chronicle*, 1905, p. 7. The *Chronicle* was a periodical, which was published for two years between 1904 and 1905. It is shelved in the Grosvenor Collection at the BECPL.

21. See *Paul's Dictionary*, p. 167, as well as the many articles on the city's markets in the Grosvenor Collection at the BECPL. For a good photograph of the market, see http://www.vintageviews.org/vv-ny/AE/cards/b032.html.

22. For a photo of Lafayette Park before the transition, see http://www.ah.bfn.org/a/lafsq/index.html. For a story from the newspapers on the transition, see the Local History Scrapbook, vol. 1, p. 245, Grosvenor Collection, BECPL. See also a great article on the "Lafayette Square Improvement" in the Chamber of Commerce publication *Live Wire*, January 1913, pp. 77–80.

23. Severance, *Picture Book*, p. 417.

24. *Buffalo Express*, October 18, 1909, p. 5.

25. The changes that occurred in Johnson Park can be followed by studying City of Buffalo atlases in 1894 and 1915 and by studying the land use changes referred to in Severance's *Picture Book*, pp. 411ff. For great photos of the transition that occurred there, see http://www.wnyheritagepress.org/photos_week_2005/rumsey_park/rumsey_park.htm.

26. "Rigs in the Park," *Buffalo Express*, February 9, 1899, Industry in Buffalo and the Niagara Frontier Scrapbook, vol. 6, p. 39, BECPL.

27. "Park Carriages," *Commercial Advertiser*, February 16, 1899, Industry in Buffalo and the Niagara Frontier Scrapbook, vol. 4, p. 39, Grosvenor Collection, BECPL.

28. The Kensington Bicycle Company, the first company to actually produce automobiles in Buffalo, manufactured its first electrical automobile earlier, in 1899.

29. "Automobiles in Buffalo," *Buffalo Courier*, May 25, 1902, Industry in Buffalo and the Niagara Frontier Scrapbook, vol. 4, pp. 51–61, Grosvenor Collection, BECPL.

30. *Mill's Business Directory of Buffalo, 1910* (Buffalo, 1910), Grosvenor Collection, BECPL.

31. *Buffalo Evening News*, January 19, 1906, Parks and Playgrounds Scrapbook, Grosvenor Collection, BECPL.

chapter 3

EARLY TWENTIETH–CENTURY BUFFALO THROUGH THE LENS OF CHANGE

I n 1913, the forty-six-year-old Buffalo Historical Society published a poignant volume called *The Picture Book of Earlier Buffalo*. Written by Frank H. Severance, the society's director, the book was filled with haunting photographs taken over a twenty-year period. The *Picture Book*, like a family album, was a wistful and nostalgic look back. Produced by a generation that was witness to the radical transformation of its city, this striking volume documented the heavy price the city paid in the loss of cherished buildings, the erosion of familiar places, and the endless daily upheavals at the turn of the twentieth century. Divided into chapters bearing nostalgic titles such as "Old Time Churches," "The Changing Times," "Vanished Main Street," and "Glimpses of Yesterday," the book's nearly five hundred pages were filled with dozens of photographs, many of them taken by the great photographer G. Hunter Bartlett. The photos were accompanied by descriptive text that illustrated as well as any other primary source just how radical the upheaval was. Severance and Bartlett worked on this project over the course of several years; in periodic presentations to concerned groups of citizens throughout the decade, they shared their somber findings. Bartlett's wife, Mary, was in attendance at the Buffalo Library in February 1906 when the two men showed, as she noted in her diary, "a set of 125 lantern slides of early Buffalo homes."

There was a newspaper article about their presentation that Mrs. Bartlett later clipped and pasted in her scrapbook. "The slides," the article says, "are mostly views of old buildings which have been torn down. It is one of the finest sets of views of early Buffalo ever exhibited and it is very valuable." Like Eugene Atget, his contemporary in Paris, Bartlett used his camera both to "stop time" and to raise the ire of his contemporaries—he captured and presented to a fascinated public the impact of modern life on the traditional landscape of the city.[1]

Severance and Bartlett were among a growing number of people, most of them well-established white Anglo-Saxon Protestants who, during the early years of the new century, were shaken by the rapid and dramatic changes that were occurring to the form, fabric, and function of Buffalo. Like members of their social class in cities throughout the country, these men and women were appalled at the intrusions of industry and the railroads into the fabric of their city, angered by the losses that had occurred at Johnson Park, distraught at how the waterfront was being turned into a dumping ground for industry, and saddened by the demolition of so many of the private home, and churches that had for so long characterized the landscape of the city. They worried not only about Buffalo's physical landscape but about its social structure as well, particularly the unknown but clearly destabilizing impact and influence of so many immigrants, most of them poor, and most of them Catholic. Worried about the future, they began to work together in an effort to influence, if not control, the forces that were so dramatically altering the nature and quality of daily life. Their efforts to bring order and beauty to the increasingly disturbing and chaotic state of the city led them eventually to take up the cause of city planning.

Inspired by the carefully planned fairgrounds at both the Columbian and the Pan-American Exposition, a new generation of Buffalonians, like civic leaders in other American cities, began, under the rubric of "The City Beautiful" movement, an effort to bring order and beauty to Buffalo. The year of the Pan-American Exposition witnessed an intense outburst of activity with the formation of four groups dedicated to conservation and beautification: the Niagara Frontier Landmarks Association, whose purpose was to "locate along the Niagara Frontier suitable monuments to commemorate historical events"; the American Institute of Architects Committee on Municipal Art; a local chapter of the National League of Improvement; and, at the end of the year, the Society for the Beautification of Buffalo. Known for sometimes angry, always passionate language, Dr. Matthew D. Mann, the physician who had operated on President McKinley, was the society's first president. At its founding, Mann declared "war on all things that tend to deface the beauty of Buffalo. . . . Doom begins for such eyesores as gaudy billboards, belching smokestacks, unkempt parks and factories in residential areas."[2]

Mann was deeply troubled by the railroads and the impact they had on the landscapes and streetscapes of the city. The railroads not only "penetrated" the city but they determined land use in neighborhoods and on the waterfront. By 1910, railroad companies owned 42 square miles of railroad yards and 660 miles of track on which moved more than fifteen thousand railroad cars. More than five thousand acres of land in the city were owned by the railroad companies.[3] The size and scale of the railroad companies' operations were overwhelming, particularly in the heavily industrialized East Side and on the waterfront. Writing in 1907, Mann angrily stated that "Buffalo has maintained the attitude of a suppliant" toward the railroads, turning over to them far too much of the places and spaces in the city that belonged by right, he felt, to the people who lived there:

> "We have allowed practically all of our waterfront to be taken by the steam railroads. Scott Street during almost its entire length is a railroad shambles. Prime Street is another dedicated by piracy to the uses of the Delaware, Lackawanna and Western."[4]

Mann and his colleagues were also concerned about the impact the industrial infrastructure had on the city's schools and, in an effort to increase the public's awareness of this critical problem, the society, in 1902, documented the problem and distributed a report titled "Sanitary Conditions in the City's Schools." Among schools cited were School 2, located on Terrace and Genesee, which, the report said, was "one block from the Erie Canal, half a block from the Central railroad tracks and a saloon. Foundries, machine shops and planning mills are on both sides and a four story tenement is seven feet from the playground." Another problem school was School 3, on Perry and Illinois in the Old First Ward, which, the report said, was "completely surrounded by industries and every room is deficient in air space." In addition, at School 10, on Delaware and Mohawk, a "malt house in the rear is a nuisance and causing trouble by dust as well as by smell." To this new generation of public citizens concerned about beauty and order, the devastation of the city's landscape was unacceptable. In the early years of the twentieth century, they dedicated themselves to an effort to control, if not stop, the industrial destruction of Buffalo.[5]

One of the society's first actions was to retain the services of Charles M. Robinson, a leader of the increasingly influential city planning movement known as "City Beautiful." Robinson, a resident of Rochester, made several visits to Buffalo throughout the year and late in 1902, he made a wide-ranging report to Dr. Mann's society. Robinson, who was much in demand as a consultant, provided essentially the same report wherever he went and, as elsewhere, he urged Buffalo to concentrate its efforts on the waterfront and the central business district. Robinson paid no attention to the spreading miasma of industrial uses; he concentrated instead on the more sculptural elements of city planning, limiting his recommendations to the construction of a union station on the waterfront, which would be linked by a Haussman-esque grand boulevard to a newly remodeled Niagara Square.[6]

While there seemed to be little that this new generation of gentlemen planners could do about the larger issues of intrusive land use by railroads and industry, they were able to achieve significant results in their efforts to improve the landscape through beautification. The society worked hard on the beautification of Gates Circle and, in 1902, they were instrumental in the selection of the architectural firm of Green and Wicks as the designers of the sunken fountain located at its center. They were also concerned about Niagara Square and, while their ambitious plans for the creation of a monumental civic center would have to wait, the society led the effort to bring the City Beautiful ideals of order and monumentality to the square. They turned for inspiration, as did almost everybody in turn-of-the-century urban America, to the Columbian Exposition, where they called on the Exposition's leading lights, Daniel H. Burnham and Carrere and Hastings, to design the square and a monument, which, in 1907, would be dedicated to the late William McKinley.[7] In 1907, the society invited Bryant R. Flemming, a professor of landscape architecture at Cornell, to address the group on "The Importance of City Planning." Drawing on a rich planning tradition that began with Ellicott and continued with Olmsted, Flemming told the group that it was time for "Buffalo to adopt a far reaching plan, a plan so broad in its scope as to cover her needs for all time."[8] While it would be years before Buffalo actually had its first "master plan," the society, believing deeply in the value of planning, persisted in what became a seemingly endless effort.

Mann and his colleagues, like reformers in other cities during the progressive era, were also concerned about vice. In 1905, he organized yet another group, this one called the Citizens Committee of One Hundred. Three years later, the group published what they called the "Expurgated Report on Vice Conditions in Buffalo," which identified three different types of houses of prostitution, dozens of which were located on streets just east of downtown. There were three on Elm and a half dozen on Ellicott, Seneca, Virginia, Michigan, and Oak streets. The first types of houses were termed the "Disreputable Houses," where, the group said, "[T]he girls are kept for hire.... The exterior of these places, in most instances plainly shows their character: heavy lattice doorways, brass rails up the steps, red lights and shades and in most cases each occupies a complete house or building." The second types of houses were the "Assignation Houses," which, according to the group, were also "easily known by their canopied and lattice doorways. These are places where rooms are rented for couples and drinks are served.... If the male comes without a companion, the proprietor has a list from which she telephones and secures a companion." The third category listed in the report was "saloons," each of which had "rooms [in] which street-walkers and women of the tenderloin assemble and solicit business of the men who come into the saloon." The report described one of these, located on Ellicott and Genesee, in detail:

> The woman proprietor has been running notorious places in Buffalo for the past fifteen years.... [T]he main room is on the second floor, fitted with a hand-operated electric piano. About twenty tables are arranged close to the wall and the center of the room is kept clear for dancing.

It was raucous and fun, a place where those so inclined could listen to provocative music: "Ragtime singing and dancing goes on constantly. At 3 am there were one hundred men and women in the room and everything was full blast." The report provided an interesting aside as to the growing popularity of automobiles. Most of the patrons, it seems from the report, were driving downtown. They were "young men who came in some of the many autos standing on the street outside."[9]

The reform efforts of the progressive era in Buffalo were, as in the rest of the nation, extensive. Its promise filled the air and people in all parts of the community dedicated themselves to the mantra of progress through change. Many of these activists were women. Some, like Maria Love, a society doyenne whose family had settled in Buffalo in the early part of the nineteenth century, when the city was still a village, worked aggressively in the hope of transforming the way Buffalo dealt with the problems of poverty. Love's father, Judge Thomas Love, had been a fervent abolitionist and it was from him, she claimed, that she derived her ardor for reform. In 1884, she opened the city's first free kindergarten, the Fitch Crèche, named for the philanthropist Benjamin Fitch, from whom Love raised the funds. Unafraid to dirty her hands in the business of politics, Love organized parents and pressured politicians so that, in 1899, the Crèche was finally incorporated into the structure of the public schools. In the early 1890s, she had traveled to London, where she made several visits to Toynbee Hall, the world's first and foremost settlement house. She also met with the leading London social workers of her generation. Love became convinced that poverty was rooted in and worsened by the conditions in which the poor lived. Only when neighborhoods were improved, she argued, would the problems of the poor be remedied. Upon her return to Buffalo she began to work with other concerned citizens in the community to develop what she called "The Church District Plan." Modeled after the parish system, the city would be divided into districts, each under the jurisdiction of a church, whose job it would be to centralize and coordinate the "poverty programs" in its district. By thus taking politics and politicians out of the business of poverty, these reform-minded advocates of the church district plan hoped to improve the delivery of services to the poor, thereby improving the conditions in which they lived.[10]

Love worked out of the Fitch Institute, on the southwest corner of Swan and Michigan, in a building named after its benefactor. The large brick building was a dynamic center for social service. The institute housed the headquarters of the Charity Organization Society, a private charity that provided support to the poor, an emergency hospital, the Fitch Crèche, the headquarters of the Fresh Air Mission, the Buffalo Civil Service Reform Association, an organization called the Trinity Cooperative Association, and the offices of the Cradle Beach Camp, an overnight camp operated by the Fresh Air Mission. The excitement of this progressive and creative work environment proved synergistic. In 1895, another agency for the poor opened around the corner on Seneca and Louisiana streets. Called Welcome Hall, it, too, was founded by a woman, Mary Remington, who, having taken the advice of Ms. Love, lived in the neighborhood where she worked, which she described in 1900 as "predominantly industrial, the men being engaged largely in what is generally referred to as unskilled labor, though a more correct term would be underpaid labor." Welcome Hall was a respite from the neighborhood, for inside the four-story brick building was a gym, a library, a kindergarten, and classes where the neighborhood residents, mostly Lebanese and Greek, studied English.

Both Love and Remington were members of the city's oldest church, the First Presbyterian and, like so many of the church-based reformers of their day, they were as concerned with the "moral elevation" of the poor as with their material conditions. However, while their preachments were filled with predictable homilies about righteousness and individual responsibility, there was no question that Love, Remington, and their colleagues were moving beyond these Victorian blandishments. Indeed, for these female founders of the city's most important social service agencies, there was a growing understanding of the importance of the neighborhood and the role that it had to play in the remediation of conditions created by poverty. In 1900, the authors of Welcome Hall's annual report said that the development of "neighborhood consciousness" was necessary. The goal of effective social work, they insisted in language that remains relevant today, was to "convince the neighborhood that it has within itself the power of its own renewal."[11] It was with this in mind that another citizen-based group, the People's Gardens Association, began to advocate for the creation of what they called "community food lots" in Buffalo. By 1909, the superintendent of the poor, a man named Fredrick C. Almy, recognized the need for and the validity of community-operated vegetable gardens. He created a new office called the superintendent of the people's gardens. By 1910, Almy reported that there were more than one hundred fifty acres of land in the city under cultivation, which provided food for four hundred families.[12] Maria Love functioned as comfortably on the streets of the immigrant East Side as she did in the world of Buffalo's Protestant gentry. In addition to her many charitable activities, she was a devoted member of her church community, a founding member of the Twentieth Century Club, the nation's first all-female club, and was a regular participant in the many balls, pageants, and galas that characterized so much of the social life of the city's elite. Not so with Mabel Ganson, a contemporary of Love's who, unlike Love, bitterly turned her back on her upbringing.

Born in 1870 into a wealthy Buffalo family of flour milling fortune, Ganson left the city early in the new century never to return. She moved to New York City where her home became a salon and hangout for radical artists and writers, people like John Reed who, in the years before he went to Russia to cover the revolution, lived with Ganson in her chic Greenwich Village apartment. Years later, after she'd left New York to continue her bohemian life in Taos, New Mexico, Ganson, formerly Mabel Dodge and, as a result of a subsequent marriage, Mabel Luhan, wrote a book titled *Intimate Memoirs*, which documented her early years in Buffalo. The book, published in 1932, projects a bleak vision of life among Buffalo's elite. The silence of winter, for so many a balm, was for her eerie and frightening. "In the winter time there was never any sound on our streets except of people's voices and these were muffled by snow ... the streets were dark. ... Everybody was at home."

Home for Luhan was a large mansion on Delaware Avenue (currently the site of an outsized Walgreen's drugstore), "a deathly place" where "the blinds were always drawn" and "there was never a sense of life." "Each house," she said, "held its own secret, helpless shame." Behind the thick walls people were alone, alienated from self and isolated from each other. "There was," she said in tones that anticipated Diane Arbus, "hardly any intimacy between friends and people had no confidence in each other." Life, Luhan suggested, was dull, predictable, and uneventful, "flowing on in an apparently commonplace way, until once in a while something happened." Continuing without pause, she wrote: "Donald White would be found hanging on the gas fixture in his bedroom, naked except for a pair of white gloves. Caroline Thompson would suddenly be seen no more among her friends and no one would mention her absence."

More distressing to this curious, intelligent, but bitter child of luxury was the "lovelessness" of her family and the cold, distant, and stilted behavior that colored their relationships. Her father was "the man in my house that I called Father and who brushed me in the hall with a look of dislike." Her mother, it seemed, was brusque and businesslike, a woman who spent her time "ordering her household" and controlling her servants, and who, above all, was "proud of the appearance of her windows from the street." She recalled little closeness with her parents and remembered that she ate separately from them, "for we were allowed to be with grown-ups for a while after dinner. They would return and sit in two big chairs in the subdued atmosphere of that loveless house. They did not laugh or joke with me nor with each other."

Despite her unhappy recollections of her childhood, Luhan did not fault her family and their circle for their behavior. Indeed, in the end, as if feeling sorry for them, she dedicated her volume of memories to her home town: "We are all," she wrote, "inevitably perhaps, loyal to our town. I like my Buffalo as I knew it, just as I like and admire now those grown-ups who surrounded me and who endured so gallantly and with such robust courage, the terrible emptiness of their lives."[13]

Other women, also daughters of the old, white Anglo-Saxon Protestant gentry, saw their life and times through the lens of photography. Perhaps sensing that people in a rapidly changing community would be eager to capture themselves in those quickly passing moments, photographers were very early drawn to Buffalo. In 1840, only one year after the photographic process was first made public, a physician opened the city's first daguerreian studio. Before the decade was out, the studio offered sales of the latest German and American cameras, plates, cases, and chemicals. The popularity of photography increased with the improvement of photographic technology and the introduction of flexible film and the handheld camera in the 1880s. In 1880, a group of serious and talented amateur photographers formed the Buffalo Camera Club. Dedicated to the advancement "among its members of the knowledge of photography in all of its branches," the camera club sponsored workshops, discussion groups, and exhibits of both its own members' work and that of photographers throughout the Northeast. In that year, it was reported that there were five hundred "known photographers" in Buffalo.[14] The founder of the camera club was G. Hunter Bartlett. Bartlett, who had been taking photographs in Buffalo since the 1880s when, according to Buffalo historian Paul Redding, he took photographs of people, streets, buildings, and social and outdoor events using the new dry-plate cameras. In order to more quickly develop and print his shots, Bartlett built a fully equipped dark room on the third floor of his home on Park Street, located in what would later become known as Allentown.[15]

Other photographers used their art at the turn of the century to express a wistful and somewhat haunting look at the changing urban landscape. Among the most active members of the camera club during that time were three women: Charlotte Spaulding, Rose Clark, and Clara Sipprell. Born in 1879, Spaulding, the daughter of a wealthy and socially prominent lawyer, returned to Buffalo after college determined to make photography her life's work. She was a beautiful woman, with dark, deeply set eyes. From the scant available evidence, she seemed to have lived an unconventional life. Spaulding concentrated her work on dark, shadowed images of women, always alone or with their children, and never with their husbands. Her ambition took her to New York City, where she studied with the emerging giant of twentieth century photography, Edward Steichen. Committed above all else to her career, Spaulding did not marry until 1909 when, at the age of thirty, she wed the son of John J. Albright, the steel magnate whose donation earlier in the decade had made possible the construction of the Albright Art Gallery. Her career as a photographer did not survive her marriage and in 1910 she stopped taking pictures.

Marriage and photography, it seemed, were incompatible. Two of the other most active and creative photographers of the early twentieth century were Clara Sipprell and Rose Clark, neither of whom ever married. Sipprell moved to Buffalo from Ontario, Canada, in 1895. After twenty years in Buffalo, she moved on to New York, where she soon rose to prominence, becoming one of the great female photographers of her time. Rose Clark, on the other hand, came to Buffalo from Indiana in the 1890s to teach art at St. Margaret's School and lived and worked in the city for all but a few years until her death in 1942. One of the most successful members of the Buffalo Camera Club, Clark was invited by Alfred Stieglitz in 1904 to exhibit in his New York gallery where her work was, one critic commented, "second only to Steichen's."

The work of these photographers, who now called themselves the Buffalo Photo Pictorialists, caught the attention of Cornelia Bentley Sage, the assistant to the director at the recently opened Albright Art Gallery. Sage was fascinated by the work of Alfred Stieglitz and, soon after the gallery opened in 1901, she urged the director, Charles M. Kurtz, to mount a show of Stieglitz's work. Sage was born in Buffalo in 1876 and studied art as a girl at the Art Students League of Buffalo. Sometime in the mid-1890s she went to Paris, where she studied at the Ecole du Louvre. Upon her return to Buffalo she became active in the Buffalo Fine Arts Academy and worked closely with John J. Albright and Edward B. Green as they planned and built the white marble Albright Art Gallery. Sage was a good friend of John Albright's daughter-in-law, the photographer formerly known as Charlotte Spaulding, and an eager devotee of photo-pictorialism. As a result of her efforts, the Albright mounted a show in 1907 titled "The Buffalo Pictorialists," which was devoted to Charlotte Albright and her colleagues. Under Sage and Kurtz's aegis, the Albright became one of the first museums in America to recognize photography as an art form. Together they had established contact with Stieglitz in New York and were in the process of arranging the first ever museum show of his Photo-Secession Group when, in 1909, Kurtz died unexpectedly. Appointed acting director of the gallery in 1910, Sage immediately mounted, in

November of that year "The International Exhibition of Pictorial Photography," the most ambitious photography exhibition ever held in the United States. Shortly thereafter, she was appointed the first female director of any major American museum.[16]

The work of the Buffalo Pictorialists was characterized by an almost anxious and withdrawn treatment of its subjects. It appeared at odds not only with modernism but also with the increasingly mechanized world. The few images that the pictorialists made of streets and factories were idealized and abstract, taken at a distance or from behind a screen of billowing clouds. Bearing such classic titles as "Commerce" and "Industry," the photographs represented uncomfortable attempts to come to terms with life in the modern city. Unlike the Buffalo Pictorialists, however, other photographers, particularly those working for the newspapers, plunged right into the grit of twentieth-century city life. The local press had discovered the city's newest residents and sent photographers into the immigrant neighborhoods to document their daily lives. Several went to the Canal Street area known as "the Hooks," which was Buffalo's "Little Italy." In contrast to the muckraking photographs of Jacob Riis and others in New York City, the work of Buffalo's photographers was celebratory. While there was an occasional shot of a muddied, run-down street lined with ramshackle tenements, most of the images were wholesome photographs, which included children playing in the street, families sitting happily on chairs set up on the sidewalk, individuals working in a macaroni factory, and even a dignified portrait of Mrs. Louis Roffo sitting in the parlor of her Prospect Avenue home. One of the photographers was George F. Hare, who, with his brother, would come to own Hare and Hare, Buffalo's most successful photographic studio for most of the twentieth century. Hare's portraits were quiet but beautiful: a cobbler at his bench; a laborer with his shovel; an organ grinder, smiling, standing next to his instrument; and countless young mothers with their babies cradled in their arms. Hare's portraits of the men, women, and children of Buffalo's Italian neighborhood, which appeared in the *Buffalo Times* in 1907, are, like the work of his contemporaries Steichen and Stieglitz, romantic and deeply evocative.[17]

Several other photographers and writers were drawn to the "Italian colony" in and around the Hooks during this time. What seemed to appeal most to them was the extent to which so much of daily life was lived on the neighborhood's streets. In stark contrast to the dark interior life of Victorian America, the Italians of Buffalo seemed to live much of their lives outside and in public. "It's a life full of sunshine," said one article in the *Express* in April 1907: "The houses are old, the people are crowded together, but out in the street the sun shines warm and the people really love it."[18] With some envy, this reporter compared what he found there to the pale and drab Anglo faces found in other sections of Buffalo: "How many people in our city really appreciate the joy of warm sunshine? Down here they really know what it is." And when every summer the streets in the vicinity of St. Anthony of Padua on Court were closed for the Festival of St. Anthony, the press celebrated the parade and the procession of the Virgin with not a trace of condescension.

> The Church is at the center of the Italian population and yesterday the streets of the neighborhood resembled a festival day in another land. All the colors of the rainbow were upon the women and the waistcoats of the men were not a whit less gorgeous....More than one thousand Sicilians of the various societies marched in procession headed by a band of their own all the way to the Bishop's mansion out on Delaware Avenue to escort him to the parish. Escorting the bishop, the parade moved back down Delaware Avenue to The Terrace to Canal to Evans to Fly and LeCouteleux.[19]

"The marshal of the parade," a mesmerized unnamed reporter wrote, "was James Napoli, mounted and resplendent in the officer's uniform of the Societa Castellucio. Behind him came the following groups of men and women from San Fele, San Rocco and others."[20]

The newspaper accounts of life in Buffalo's "Italian colony" were far from critical or condescending. They tended toward an understanding of just how difficult their adjustment process was and were supportive of their efforts to balance the demands of both old and new worlds. Eland J. Gjessing, for example, who both wrote and took photographs for a story that was published in the *Express* in 1908, was sympathetic to the impact the Americanization of the immigrants' children had had on traditional Italian family values. Referring to School 2, Gjessing wrote that "the school language is English...and no opportunity is given to the children to learn the Italian language in its purity (as opposed to the dialects)." This, Gjessing said, should be deplored: "The families of these children, while wishing to be loyal Americans, see with sorrow and regret that their children are losing all knowledge of their traditional language and culture."[21] (In the same article, Gjessing reported that for the school choir "only national airs such as 'America' and 'My Country 'Tis of Thee' are in order.")

The press raved about Charles F. Ryan, the principal of School 2 and, in articles written about him during a tenure that lasted from 1900 through 1927, lauded his role in the Lower West Side Italian community. Known as "il padre degli Italiani," Ryan, who spoke fluent Italian, was "the best known American-born man in Buffalo in the Italian community. He belongs to their societies, attends St. Anthony's and accepts many invitations to dine, attend weddings and other festivities in Buffalo's Little Italy."[22]

Newspapers also applauded the migration of a growing number of Italians to

the Hooks, pleased that their arrival was displacing the rough waterfront crowd—
"driving out the fellows of loose morals," said one reporter—who had for so long
tainted the area as one of the bawdiest in the nation. In 1907, the name of the
street—Canal—was officially changed to Dante Place, in recognition of the
neighborhood's renewal.[23]

Moreover, the press appreciated the colorful characteristics of the Italian
immigrants. A monthly magazine titled *Buffalo Saturday Night*, which was published for a few years in the early 1920s by Lee Heacock, had one correspondent
named B. J. Ruby, who wrote regularly about Buffalo's immigrant neighborhoods.
Ruby loved the Hooks and visited the area regularly:

> Go down some warm evening and stroll through the section and you will find
> yourself in a miniature Naples, a little city so strange and unfamiliar that you
> can scarcely believe you are in twentieth century America. You will find the
> streets crowded with a colorful and motley collection of swarthy skinned
> people. You will see perspiring madonnas in flaming calico dresses and brilliant
> head-cloths. Probably they will be sitting, upon the doorsteps of their queer
> homes. Most likely a glass-fronted home which looks like a store, or a saloon.
> Indeed, in the old days, it was a saloon; and standing where the Italian mother
> now stands, stood a flashily dressed, bejeweled wastrel, ogling the drunken
> sailors who passed by. But now you see the sturdy, competent mother gathering
> her black-haired, white-toothed bambinos about her with the desperate,
> yearning love which Italian mothers always display. You will see the husband
> and father not far away. He will be dressed in an eye-smiting, purple suit prob-
> ably, a lavender shirt perhaps, and a gorgeous, yellow-flowered necktie. He will
> be doing the family marketing very likely, puffing a thin, twisted Italian cigar as
> he goes from store to store.
>
> Outside the store you will see long strings of chestnuts, and inside Italian
> cheeses of all kinds. You will also see a profusion of red and green peppers of
> which the Italians are very fond; many different kinds of pastry, cakes and hot
> loaves of bread. And, of course, the never absent macaroni, sometimes in white
> sheets in a modern sanitary carton. And the inoffensive silver skilled garlic is
> everywhere....
>
> In this strange place in which the names of the street have an ethnic
> flavor—Dante, LeCouteleux, Maiden Lane and Peacock, for instance, not the
> least fascinating place is the Marionette Theatre on Dante Place near the Com-
> mercial Street bridge. Stop in for a moment and meet the "maestro" of the
> puppet show, fat-paunched, be-mustached fellow of sixty odd, wearing baggy
> trousers and an old sweater. His name is Salvatore Rizzo and he has conducted
> the Marionette Theatre here for twenty years. In the hot summer months he lays
> down the marionettes and tells the stories himself. The little theatre is always
> filled with the men, women and the children of the neighborhood.[24]

Another reporter named Beth Stewart, who wrote for the *Courier* in 1921, was also drawn to Rizzo's marionette theater. Rizzo had come to Buffalo from Palermo, one in a long line of Palermarinos who had made the ancient art of Sicilian puppetry and marionettes his own. Stewart was clearly drawn to the excitement of life in this dynamic Italian neighborhood and enticingly described it to her overwhelmingly American audience:

> To find the teatrino, you turn onto Dante Place. On the right, as you leave the Commercial Street bridge, you walk a little way along the street with its huddled domesticity and teeming shops and fruit stands, past crates of fowls and strings of onions, past doorways filled with children and men and women who carry on the Italian tradition of life in the open. Suddenly you are arrested by a vision of knighthood and deeds of valor. Quaintly painted curtains setting forth the adventures of Troilus and Renaldo fill the windows of what once was a little shop. It's the "teatrino" of Salvatore Rizzo.... The habitués of Rizzo's teatrino have imbibed a love for the marionettes in their Southern Italian homes when, bereft of schools they had had to rely on the oral rather than the printed story. Night after night they enjoy their pipes while following the fate of Orlando, Riccardo and Guido Santo whose deeds of valor form for them the way of escape to their ideal.[25]

While the new immigrant neighborhoods had unquestioned appeal to many Buffalonians, they created an equal amount of concern, particularly for the growing group of reformers eager to end the ward system of government. Throughout most of the nineteenth century, political power, like so much of daily life in the city, was decentralized and rooted in the city's thirteen wards. Some were enormous, like the Fifth Ward, which comprised more than fifty-five thousand people and covered the entire East Side. Others, like the Fourth Ward, on the near East Side, with fewer than five thousand people, were small. Each ward, regardless of its size, the value of its assessed property, or its importance in the life of the city, sent two representatives—aldermen—to the Common Council. The aldermen, unchallenged by weak, single-term mayors whose powers were primarily titular, controlled the political system and chose all of its commissioners—of public health, education, police, streets, schools, and fire. While this system worked well for the neighborhoods, particularly the well-organized ethnic ones, where a solid block of votes could control the ward's delegation, it was a disaster for the newly emergent, increasingly powerful central business district. Because the ward system was created prior to the rise of downtown as the focal point of the metropolis, the central business district had no ward of its own. Instead, its power was fragmented, or parsed out, to the wards surrounding it. Given the increasing importance of the central business district and the increasingly influential role that the lawyers, bankers, and businessmen who worked there played in the daily life of the city, it was only a question of time before these men challenged the hegemony of the wards and the neighborhoods they represented in the hope of creating a political system for the city that more accurately reflected their own power and influence.

Their quest, which took years to realize, began in 1880 when downtown business interests rallied around the mayoral candidacy of Grover Cleveland. Cleveland ran as a reformer and, following his election in 1881, he launched an effective effort to weaken the control the ward-based aldermen exercised over the city's political culture. Elected governor one year later, Cleveland carried the banner of reform to Albany and from there he inspired further efforts for political change at home. His actions and words led to the formation in 1889 of the Buffalo's Citizens' Association, which was led by the emerging young power broker, John Milburn. In what was to become a power struggle between downtown interests and the neighborhoods, Milburn's group launched a crusade to break the power of the ward-based aldermancy. Consisting of a handful of prominent bankers, lawyers, and other downtown business leaders, the Citizens' Association, after meeting regularly throughout 1889, in early 1890 proposed a new charter for the city of Buffalo that, had it been adopted, would have ended the ward-based system of choosing representatives. What Milburn and his colleagues instead proposed was a system whereby representatives would be chosen by voters in the city at-large. While bitter opposition from the ward-based political leaders, led by "Blue-Eyed Billy" Sheehan, a popular and powerful Irish American politico from South Buffalo, led to a compromise, it became clear by the 1890s that the days of aldermanic control of city politics were numbered. Criticism of the ward system grew more intense and more effective during the first fifteen years of the new century, following a series of crippling strikes and the controversy over the efforts to create a publicly supported university.[26]

Founded during the middle of the nineteenth century, the University of Buffalo had become a loosely knit collection of professional schools that consisted of a medical school (1845), a school of pharmacy (1886), a law school (1887), and a school of dentistry (1887). Only after Charles Norton, a local lawyer and one of the founders of the law school, was appointed acting chancellor of the university in 1905 did a concerted effort begin for the creation of a publicly supported liberal arts college, a place, Norton hoped, where those graduates of the city's high schools who were unable to afford private school could continue their education. Norton's choice for the location of the school was on some of the land left vacant from the Pan-American Exposition. There, in an emerging cultural center near both the recently opened Buffalo Historical Society and the Albright Art Gallery,

Norton saw the perfect site for his projected university. First, however, he would need money—$29,000 for the first year—which would, Norton said, pay for nineteen faculty members. (There was no money for a library, dormitory, or gymnasium which, Norton said, were "not necessary for a city college.") When Norton turned to the Common Council for help, he triggered one of the city's many on-again, off-again conflicts between Protestants and Catholics.

As part of his promise to provide three hundred full-tuition scholarships to deserving graduates of local high schools, Norton asked the Common Council for an annual bequest of $75,000. The Diocese of Western New York, concerned about Norton's close relationship with Dr. Roswell Park, whose text on the history of medicine gave more credence to Darwin than to Genesis, opposed. The Common Council, with much of its power rooted in the immigrant, Catholic neighborhoods, hesitated. One councilman objected to a statement from Park's text that said that "[o]nly when students of science emancipate themselves from the prejudices and superstitions of the theologians did medicine make more than perceptible progress." The book was, this councilman said, "sectarian, bigoted, libelous, scandalous and injurious to the people I represent and therefore I cannot vote for any contract with the University."[27] One of the city's leading Protestant theologians, the Rev. Dr. Raymond P. Sweeny of the august First Presbyterian Church, now jumped into the fray. "We regret," he said later in 1909, "that certain clerical members of the Roman Catholic church have injected a religious question into the discussion and have been active in inciting and organizing opposition to the foundation of the college. Our only desire," Sweeny continued, in what to the city's hundreds of thousands of Catholics must have seemed a patronizing tone, "has been to place this city where it belongs in the matter of education and to give to every man and woman, Catholic, Protestant, Jew or Gentile, an opportunity to obtain in Buffalo an education that will fit them for life." Resistance in the council stiffened and, in 1911, it agreed to support the scholarships only if the councilmen themselves were given control of the university's governing council.

After the collapse in 1911 of the recently completed Col. Ward Water Pumping Station, disappointment and anger with the Common Council grew. Demands for change intensified when, later that year, an investigation revealed that construction of the station was marred by illegal contracts, faulty construction, and inflated budgets. Questions and concerns about the effectiveness of local government increased two years later during a long, contentious, and sometimes violent strike by workers on the city's electric streetcar lines. When in April 1913 the International Railway Company fired seventy-four employees suspected of union activities, the streetcar workers' union, the Amalgamated Association of Street and Electric Railway Employees of America, went on strike. One month later, two thousand department store workers commenced a strike. Many were surprised by this, particularly at Hengerer's, where the company had taken what they thought were painstaking efforts to satisfy their employees: counter girls were given seats behind the counters and employees had their own water fountains, a lunch room, and a medical emergency room. Alone among businesses downtown, Hengerer's had its own health insurance program, paid for jointly by the company and its employees. The workers went on strike anyway, and by the end of May 1913, they were joined by still more strikers, this time the more than six thousand members of the Machinists' Trade Union.[28]

The calls for change gathered momentum. In 1912, Mann and yet another group called the Civic Improvement Committee proposed that a city planning commission, made up of private citizens appointed by the mayor, be placed in charge of any and all decisions regarding land use. In what seemed to be a replay of the confrontation over the city's role in the creation of the University of Buffalo's liberal arts college, the ward-based and Catholic aldermen objected and soundly rejected the committee's proposal. Frustrated by a political system that appeared backward and, at the same time, denied them power, in 1913 Mann and his committee, whose members included such lions of the local establishment as John Albright, John Larkin, Fredrick Schoellkopf, and A. Conger Goodyear, met at Goodyear's Bryant Street home to "discuss the advisability of organizing a non-partisan citizens committee for the purpose of putting a full and complete non-partisan political ticket of able competent men in the field next fall." Hoping for nothing less than a coup that would end the rule of the ward-based alderman, these gentlemen reformers announced the creation of a "Citizens Ticket" for the mayoral election in the fall of 1913.[29] The men were angry, frustrated, disappointed, and appalled that the beloved city their ancestors had built was being held hostage by what they saw as "gangs from both political parties." What they wanted, like their Progressive Era brethren in cities throughout the country, was a government that, in the words of their candidate for mayor, a young lawyer named John Lord O'Brian, was "non-partisan and unbossed. The Citizens Movement," O'Brian said, "is based on the idea that our own city affairs are business matters and should be kept free from politics." Governance for them was rooted in morality, good works, and idealistic notions of democracy, and they were shrill in their denunciation of what, according to O'Brian, was "the present city policy of tolerating flagrant immorality." Using words that clearly connoted a double meaning, they pledged themselves "to the creation of a clean city."

Although badly beaten in 1913, O'Brian's Citizens Party was strengthened from the battle and, along with an expanding group of reformers, it lobbied successfully for the passage of a bill in 1914 that created a new charter for the city, which would be implemented in January 1916, contingent upon approval in a 1915 citywide referendum. This new charter proposed a sweeping revision of local government that called for the complete elimination of the ward-based aldermanic system. Despite the overwhelming opposition of Buffalo's deeply entrenched, neighborhood-based political establishment, the new charter was passed, and on January 1, 1916, a commission form of government made its debut in Buffalo. The new charter abolished both the Board of Councilmen and the Board of Aldermen and concentrated all power, both legislative and executive, in the hands of five commissioners. The commissioners, elected not by wards but rather by voters at-large, each had their own bailiwicks, including public safety, finance and accounts, public works, parks and public buildings, and public affairs, which included the city's schools and "overseeing the poor." The charter retained the office of the mayor, who functioned strictly as titular head of the city. In one bold sweep, a political revolution had occurred, whose primary effect was the radical centralization of political power in Buffalo.[30] Emboldened by their successful struggle to bring order and stability to the political structure and encouraged by their efforts to make city planning and urban design a priority of public policy, a new generation of reformers, despite the looming threat of world war, looked hopefully and confidently to the future.

NOTES

1. See Mrs. Bartlett's fascinating multivolume scrapbook, which deals with a broad range of topics—obituaries, social events, and other local happenings—in the manuscript collection of the Buffalo and Erie County Historical Society. The society also has boxes filled with hundreds of Dr. Bartlett's photographs.

2. See Matthew Mann Scrapbooks, vol. 2, p. 88, manuscript collection, Buffalo and Erie County Historical Society. Dr. Mann left several volumes of scrapbooks, which contain an array of material, including letters, programs, travel receipts, and other compelling materials.

3. "Rail Companies Growing Land Ownership," *Buffalo Times*, April 3, 1910, The Railroads Entering Buffalo Scrapbook, p. 3, Grosvenor Collection, BECPL.

4. Mann Scrapbooks, vol. 2, p. 14.

5. Reference to the republishing of the report is in the Mann Scrapbooks, vol. 3, p. 11. See also the 1898 "Sanitary Report of the Buffalo School Association," Grosvenor Collection, BECPL. The children of the wealthy had less to worry about; by the early years of the twentieth century, the city's three most important private schools—Nichols, Park, and the Buffalo Seminary—were all located in new neighborhoods far removed from the gritty realities of life in the core of the industrial city.

6. Robinson did have a good idea for the lighting of Main Street. Like all good City

Beautiful advocates, he loathed billboards, particularly, he said, "the extraordinarily vulgar display of electric signs." He had a better idea: "If the lights now tortured with huge letters of script or print were untangled and spread along the facades into a beading at the height of the first stories, you would find your Main Street transformed into a veritable court of honor." Robinson's report can be found among the pages of the Mann Scrapbooks, vol. 11.

7. Reynar Banham, et al., *Buffalo Architecture: A Guide* (Cambridge, MA: MIT Press, 1982), p. 54.

8. *Commercial Advertiser*, May 16, 1907, Clubs and Associations Scrapbook, vol. 1, p. 296, Grosvenor Collection, BECPL.

9. This small report can be found among the pages of the Mann Scrapbooks, vol. 2, Manuscript Collection, Buffalo and Erie County Historical Society.

10. For more on Maria Love, see Karen B. Little, *Maria Love: The Life and Legacy of a Social Work Pioneer* (Buffalo, NY: Canisius College Press, 1994).

11. Annual Report of Welcome House (1900), p. 11, Grosvenor Collection, BECPL.

12. Little, *Maria Love*, p. 59.

13. Mabel Dodge Luhan, Dedication, *Intimate Memories* (New York: Harcourt Brace, 1933).

14. Anthony Bannon, *The Photopictorialists of Buffalo* (Buffalo, NY: Media Study, 1981).

15. Paul Redding, "G. F. Hunter Bartlett as Documentary Photographer," *Niagara Frontier* (Autumn 1967): 64ff.

16. For biographical information on Sage, see "Cornelia Bentley Sage Quinton (1876–1936)," Ask/Art: The American Artists Bluebook, http://www.askart.com/askart/artist.aspx?artist=80059. See also Benjamin Townsend, *100: The Buffalo Fine Arts Academy, 1862–1962* (Buffalo, NY: Albright-Knox Art Gallery, 1962), pp. 25–26.

17. Hare's marvelous undated photos are filed at the Lower Lakes Marine Historical Museum. Hare also took haunting photographs of the Polish East Side. See Buffalo's Foreign Population Scrapbook, vol. 1, p. 204 and the Charities in Buffalo Scrapbook, pp. 385–89, both of which are housed in the Grosvenor Collection at the BECPL.

18. Buffalo's Foreign Population Scrapbook, vol. I, pp. 93–94.

19. *Buffalo Express*, August 14, 1905, Buffalo Churches Scrapbook, vol. 5, p. 41, Grosvenor Collection, BECPL.

20. Ibid.

21. *Buffalo Express*, April 5, 1908, Buffalo Churches Scrapbook, vol. 5, p. 145, Grosvenor Collection, BECPL.

22. *Buffalo Times*, November 24, 1901, Buffalo's Foreign Population Scrapbook, vol. 2, p. 235, Grosvenor Collection, BECPL; *Buffalo Express*, January 17, 1926, Buffalo's Foreign Population Scrapbook, vol. 2, p. 253, Grosvenor Collection, BECPL.

23. For more on this topic, see Mike Vogel, Edward Patton, and Paul Redding, *America's Crossroads: Buffalo's Canal Street* (Buffalo, NY: WNY Heritage Press, 1993).

24. B. J. Ruby, "A Visit to Buffalo Little Naples," *Buffalo Saturday Night* 1:20, p. 4. Ruby wrote similar articles titled "A Visit to Buffalo's Black Belt," *Buffalo Saturday Night* 4:23, pp. 4–5 and "The William Street Jewish Quarter," *Buffalo Saturday Night* 1:22, p. 4. *Buffalo Saturday Night* can be found in the Grosvenor Collection at the BECPL.

25. *Courier Express*, June 26, 1921, Buffalo's Foreign Population Scrapbook, vol. 1, p. 145, Grosvenor Collection, BECPL.

26. J. T. Horton, *History of Northwestern New York* (New York: Lewis, 1948) pp. 347–350.

27. Ibid., pp. 359ff.

28. Richard Fleischman, "Violence in Buffalo: The 1913 Street-Car Strike," *Niagara Frontier* 30, no. 1 (1983): 3–20. This publication is available at the Buffalo and Erie County Historical Society.

29. Mann Scrapbooks, vol. 4, pp. 117ff, Manuscript Collection, Buffalo and Erie County Historical Society.

30. Horton, *History of Northwestern New York*, p. 359.

chapter 4

THE 1920S AND THE
RISE OF THE MODERN CITY

Except for the War of 1812 when, on New Year's Eve of 1813, the British burned the village of Buffalo to the ground, war had been good to Buffalo. The Civil War strengthened the city's dominance as a great inland port and gave birth to its industry. The Spanish-American War fostered the patriotic energy that created the Pan-American Exposition. Thus, it was not surprising that, by and large, Buffalonians greeted America's entry into World War I with fervor. Months before President Wilson's declaration of war on April 2, 1917, local business and political leaders, perhaps haunted by the ghosts of 1812, formed the Niagara Defense League, whose goal was to protect the Niagara Frontier.

From the time of America's entry in the war until the Armistice one year later, the people of Buffalo engaged in countless parades, demonstrations, and other public expressions of patriotism. The streets were filled regularly with crowds of celebrating people. While support for the war was widespread and genuine, the fervent public demonstrations were hardly spontaneous. Indeed, like the Liberty Loan bond drive, they were carefully orchestrated events.[1]

In Buffalo, as in every other city, the Liberty Loan drive developed a marketing machine for their bonds that was unique for its time. The director of the local drive was the influential and highly regarded lawyer, Walter P. Cooke, whose mission, he said, was "to help develop a war ideal in the people of this city by appealing to certain instincts and patriotic sentiments. We must concentrate," he said, on "democracy, loyalty, gratitude and sympathy." With a publicity committee and an educational bureau, the drive spent thousands of dollars simply marketing its product. It made no attempts to hide its intent: "The function of the Education Bureau was to reach as many houses in the city as possible with propaganda for the purpose of creating an informed public opinion in regard to the war and of developing and fostering patriotism." The educational bureau had four divisions. One was for "house visitations." According to their strategy, cooperating social agencies "agreed to carry on patriotic teaching in connection with family visitation." Another was "neighborhood activities," whereby the city was divided into seven settlement house districts wherein the settlement house would be used as a "center for patriotic instruction" by hosting "inspirational talks" and by sponsoring lectures. During the lectures, stereopticon slides pertaining to the war, produced by the citizen photographers of the Buffalo Camera Club, were exhibited.[2] There was also a women's division of the bond drive, whose members were urged to make themselves "propagandists among their own circle of friends." Great efforts were made to organize immigrant women, particularly Poles, who would act as leaders of the bond drive in their own communities. Polish women, regarded as solid, hardworking, and unquestioning, were viewed as "naturally loyal. Their ready response offers a splendid opportunity for driving home lessons in American ideals and in good citizenship."

The police, too, were brought into the campaign and, in what was referred to as "the final combing-out process," every one of the city's fifty-five thousand homes was visited in the fall of 1917 by a member of the police department. Under the careful eyes of the police officers, each household was to fill out not only a form requesting that it be visited by a representative of the Liberty Loan committee, but also a pledge card that indicated the size of the bond they would buy.

The hype surrounding the Liberty Loan drive helped stimulate the superpatriotism and paranoia that characterized so much of the political climate of the 1920s. Hardly had war been declared when Mayor Louis P. Fuhrmann, a secondgeneration German American, formed the "Committee on Americanization," which consisted of fifty "leading citizens from the immigrant and native communities." Insisting that "either a Buffalonian is an American and nothing else or he isn't an American at all," Mayor Fuhrman pledged to make Buffalo an "English speaking city." When coupled with his promise to "wake up Buffalo and stir the laggards to a deeper sense of duty to flag and land," Fuhrmann's message frightened the more than one hundred thousand first- and second-generation Germans who lived in the city. The pressure on the city's Germans was suddenly intense. This long-favored ethnic group, idealized since the middle of the nineteenth century as hardworking, thrifty, successful, and as an "American" kind of immigrant, was the object of suspicion, anger, resentment, and discrimination. While the older generation—the Schoellkopfs, who had made millions in electrical power; the Klincks and the Dolds, the extraordinarily successful meat packers; and the Scheus and the Langs, who had made their fortunes in the beer business—had little to worry about, the more recent arrivals, those thousands of Germans who had come to Buffalo since the beginning of the century, were constant objects of the vigilant.[3]

Many succumbed to the pressure. The German-language newspaper, *Der Welt burger*, published continuously since the mid-1840s, faced a rapidly declining readership. When a harsh federal law was enacted that required all newspaper articles that contained references to the United States to be translated and read by the government prior to publication, the publication shut down. Names of banks and insurance companies were changed, most famously the Germania Building, renamed as the "Liberty Building." Thousands of individuals dropped or Anglicized their German names, and long-standing cultural and community institutions, now suddenly besieged by the changing climate of patriotism and paranoia, went underground.

Many, however, were able to weather the storm. While the German language was eliminated from the curriculum in the public schools, most German cultural groups continued their activities. Despite what was clearly a state of fear in the city, German music and singing groups—the Buffalo Orpheus, the Saengerbund, the Froshsinn Singing Society, and the Teutonia Liederkranz—continued to meet, practice, and perform throughout the war. Other community groups and institutions—the Buffalo Turn Verein, the Humboldt Club, and the Emmaru Maenner Verein—remained active in their old East Side headquarters throughout the period. Many, indeed, seemed eager, despite the atmosphere of hostility, to express their "Germanness." In late 1917, in the midst of the passionate, intensely patriotic second Liberty Loan drive, the German Deaconess Hospital announced a campaign of its own to raise $200,000.[4] In politics, too, Buffalo's Germans asserted themselves. In 1917, the city's Germans rejected the mayoral candidates of both Republican and Democratic parties, both of whom were German Americans and both of whom scrambled to outdo each other's patriotic rhetoric, voting instead for the Socialist party candidate, a man named Franklin Brill. Despite its local newspaper having been banned, its candidates for mayor and other local offices having received no coverage in the press, and its demands for an end to the draft and a negotiated peace settlement, which were repeatedly characterized as disloyal, the Socialist party received more than fourteen thousand votes, just missing a victory over the Republican candidate to qualify for the runoff in the general election. Like Socialist candidates in New York City,

Chicago, and Milwaukee in 1917, Brill was a peace candidate in an atmosphere of militarism and xenophobia, and he found an enormous amount of support in Buffalo's increasingly isolated and alienated German community. Although not particularly Socialist in outlook and ideology, members of the German community used their votes as a way of expressing their doubts about the war. If, in the process, they risked alienating themselves from the rest of the nation, it was a gamble it seemed they were willing to take.[5]

If the war years were tough on Buffalo's German community, all of the city's immigrants were affected by Prohibition. Alcohol had always been associated with immigrants, and Prohibition, the culmination of close to one hundred years of temperance activities, was a powerful assault on the economic and social structure of immigrant community life. Economically, it destroyed the beer business and, in the process, undercut the power of the city's German Americans. Socially, it undermined the tavern, which was the focal point of the immigrant community. It is no wonder that from the beginning, Buffalo's immigrants, like most everybody in the city, were staunchly opposed to Prohibition. Indeed, in 1922, Francis X. Schwab, a former beer salesman and president of the Buffalo Brewing Company, was elected mayor on a repeal platform.[6]

Despite the magnitude of its threat, the city in general and the immigrants in particular quickly learned to live with Prohibition—by persistently and defiantly violating it. While some local breweries went out of business, a few managed to remain open by selling both legal (two percent) beer and "needle beer," in which alcohol was illegally injected. Similarly, almost unlimited amounts of bootleg liquor were available.

Almost as if it were planned with Prohibition in mind, the Peace Bridge between Buffalo and Canada opened with royal fanfare in 1927 and quickly became the primary pipeline for bootleg liquor trucked into Buffalo from Canada. Using either this or liquor they made in their own stills, most neighborhood tavern owners were, despite the obstacles, able to keep their institutions alive and well during these hard times. While there were periodic raids on the local saloons and speakeasies—Diamond Lil McVan's, Galdyz's, Richie Roth's, Jew Minnie's, and Ann Montgomery's were the most popular—law enforcement was sporadic and relaxed. By 1927, the Anti-Saloon League launched a campaign to "dry-up Buffalo," while the Ku Klux Klan, in Buffalo at least, was as concerned with violations of the Prohibition law as they were with the growing presence in the city of Catholics, Negroes, and Jews.[7] Although at times laughable and easily circumvented, Prohibition did not amuse the immigrant community.

No laughing matter, either, was the attempt to restrict immigration with the passage of the National Origins Act of 1924. World War I had had a devastating impact on immigration, suspending for more than five years the free and relatively inexpensive access that had for so long existed between southeastern Europe and the United States. Trips between Buffalo and Warsaw, Budapest, and Palermo had been everyday occurrences. Indeed, several Italian and Polish travel agents made small fortunes in this business. More significant than the contact that had existed between the Old World and the New was the commonly held assumption that this freedom would continue, and that it was just a question of time before a man would be joined by his family, by his neighbors, and eventually by many of his villagers. However, the complex and international chain of events that had created the world of immigrant Buffalo came to a sudden end when the war commenced in August 1914.

While there was a renewed flood of immigration after the war's end, that, too, came to an end following the passage in the early 1920s of quotas that severely limited the number of newcomers, particularly the Jews and Catholics of southeastern Europe. Many Buffalonians favored some restrictions on the numbers and kinds of immigrants allowed into the country, particularly in 1919, after a long and controversial strike at Lackawanna Steel sparked wild notions about Bolshevik and foreign radical conspiracies. The National Origins Act of 1924, however, with harsh and restrictive quotas for immigrants from Catholic and Jewish communities in Eastern Europe, went well beyond the moderate restrictions favored by most Buffalonians. Yet, despite the impact of the bill on the city's immigrant communities, there was, with the exception of activists within the Jewish community, little effort to oppose it.

It was not easy to be Jewish in Buffalo in the early twentieth century. Unlike New York, Philadelphia, or Chicago, where Jews, through force of numbers, began to play an important role in the cities' civic life, Jews in Buffalo (about thirteen thousand in 1920, or about 4 percent of the population) were vastly outnumbered by the majority populations and were therefore far less secure. The Jewish community, particularly the poorer, recently arrived Russian and Polish Jews who lived on the East Side, was cohesive and organized from the very beginning, with a full range of social, religious, and cultural activities and institutions. There were numerous synagogues, several newspapers, literary circles, and Zionist and labor organizations, and a theater known as the Little Theatre, which specialized in pacifist and socially conscious agit-prop. During the mid-1920s, when the community was undergoing considerable turmoil as large numbers of blacks began to move in, the Little Theatre produced a play called "In Abraham's Bosom," a story about a black youth's struggle against racial prejudice.[8] While these activities took place within the confines of the Jewish community itself, separate and apart from the community at large, opposition to the National Origins Act of 1924 meant that for the first time, Jews would have to go public as Jews. This was, as a man named Joseph Braun knew, a risky business. [9] Braun, who was thirty years old in 1924, was president of a small but successful insurance business, most of whose clients were gentiles. Born in Buffalo into a first-generation German-Jewish family, Braun, who had grown up in the prosperous, Protestant social environment of Buffalo's West Side, had many friends in the non-Jewish community. He belonged to an organization of downtown businessmen and a downtown luncheon club, and was an active member in the Buffalo Rotary. Although raised in a traditional Jewish household, Braun had for years belonged to Temple Beth Zion, a reform and largely German-Jewish congregation. Other than his annual attendance at High Holy Day services, Braun was casual about his religious affiliation. Being Jewish, he felt, played an insignificant part in his life; many of his gentile friends didn't even know he was Jewish.

Life changed for Braun after World War I, as the Jewish community, now bigger and more prosperous, became more self-consciously organized. The year 1918 saw the first issue of the *Buffalo Jewish Review*, a newspaper still published today. One year later, the newly organized Federation of Jewish Social Services opened its headquarters in a downtown hotel. A Jewish old people's home, the Rosa Coplon, was built in the heart of a prosperous neighborhood next to the First Presbyterian Church at Symphony Circle. Meanwhile, throughout the decade, Zionism, a subject long frowned upon by the city's assimilationist-minded German-Jewish establishment, became more acceptable. People like Henrietta Szold, Vladimir Jabotinsky, and Chaim Weitzman came to Buffalo, raising interest, eyebrows, and money, by speaking before ever-larger community groups. The Jewish community, it seemed, was coming out—and never more visibly than in 1924, when, more so than any of the city's other immigrant groups, Jews from both the established German-Jewish community on the West Side and the recent Jewish immigrants on the East Side, vocally protested the National Origins Act. Unlike the restrained rhetoric of the immigrant press—the *Catholic Union and Times, Everybody's Polish Daily*, and the *Italian Corriere*—the *Buffalo Jewish Review* was frank in its attack. It openly denounced "these Nordic theories of racial supremacy" and called the bill "anti-Semitic, anti-Catholic and anti-American." [10] In response to these public protests, Braun, who had recently led a fund drive for the Jewish Federation, began to organize the entire immigrant community of Buffalo against the bill. Working with two Polish priests and one Italian priest (the bishop of Buffalo refused to participate), Braun organized a citywide protest. With the support of the mayor and the Common Council, which passed a unanimous resolution against the bill, Braun and the others attracted an audience of more than two thousand Jews, Poles, and Italians to Buffalo's auditorium. The

Jewish Review noted that "the Broadway Auditorium last Sunday presented a scene that was unique and inspiring. Three groups that hitherto have been separate have united in a common protest against the Johnson Immigration Bill."[11] Their protest, however, failed. The bill became law, and, like other American cities that were to be denied the positive effects of immigration, Buffalo suffered terribly.

In ever-growing numbers, however, African Americans migrated to the city, most settling in the East Side. While there had been a small number of African Americans on Buffalo's East Side since the 1820s (the Bethel AME Church, currently located on East Ferry Street, was founded on Michigan Avenue in 1832; the Michigan Street Baptist Church, which followed in 1845, still stands at its original Michigan Avenue location), their numbers increased during the First World War when demand for labor grew. By 1920, there were four thousand five hundred African Americans in Buffalo. Ten years later, as a result of "the Great Migration," there were close to fourteen thousand. Almost all of them moved into the Jewish East Side, in the area in and around William, Michigan, and Broadway.[12]

One of the earliest known descriptions of the emerging African American community on the city's East Side appeared in 1921, in a fascinating, sporadically published weekly called *Buffalo Saturday Night*. The story, titled "Local Color: A Visit to Buffalo's Black Belt," noted the tremendous influx of blacks into the city during the First World War. According to the writer, B. J. Ruby, "Munitions plants, chemical plants and construction work drew them to Buffalo by the hundreds and thousands and one has only to walk through the colored quarter to realize that there are many thousands of colored people here now." In terms that today's readers would find offensive, the writer urged his audience to visit the area:

> If you have eyes in your head you cannot but find it interesting. You may find much that is bestial there. You will perhaps get a glimpse of rough, savage beauty, you may hear jangling, drunken, rag-time, you may hear the soft chant of Negro hymns. I do not know what you will see or hear if you visit the Negro colony, but you will always find life there—primitive, uncivilized, passionate life and that is always interesting. Begin your exploration on the corner of Clinton and Washington Street. Stand for a moment in the blaze of light under the Hotel canopy and look down Clinton Street. If the sky is not moonlit, the darkness of the street pierced only by an occasional lance of light from a corner arc-light, will seem like the yawning mouth of a cavern. I suggest this procedure, because it will give you a feeling of reckless intrepidity as you stride boldly into it. If you are frightened too much, stop at Flore's for one of his celebrated wieners and drink over his mahogany bar a cup of hot boullion. Thus fortified go on. When you reach Oak Street, turn north and when you reach Vine Alley turn east again. No resident of Buffalo but has heard wild and true tales of the doings in Vine Alley. But they are

true no longer; Vine Alley is now merely a shabby row of negro dwellings. You may roost here from sunrise to sunset and to dawn again but you will see nothing more exciting than the people going to church on Sunday morning. For there is a negro church on Vine Alley—the First African M. E. Church. And incidentally, to watch the colored people as they go to church is an interesting sight these days. They come to church in automobiles nowadays—the curbs are lined with autos; and they are mostly big cars too. And such splendor of raiment! Such gay ribboned hats! Such wondrous cravats! Such shiny, stiff shirt-bosoms! No rags and tatters for your modern negro. The most gorgeous costume is none too good—especially for Sunday meetin'. When you get to the other end of Vine Alley you will be at the juncture of Michigan, William, Clinton and Vine, and here in the very heart of the black belt I can safely leave you to your own resources, for no matter in which direction you go, you will still be in the negro quarter. Near this point where I leave you, you will find the sidewalks thronged. with cola-red ge'men. You may ask yourself why, but if you watch closely you will have your answer. You will see one of them approach the door of a stairway leading to rooms over a restaurant. He presses the bell a certain number of times. If he has given the signal correctly, the latch, electrically controlled as in many apartment houses, will click open, and he will enter, closing the door carefully behind him. What is the lure upstairs? Ah!, You have guessed it—African golf, galloping bones, the great indoor sport of the negro craps!"[13]

The African American community grew throughout the 1920s. In response to the needs of the expanding population, black-owned enterprises proliferated, including hotels, nightclubs, funeral parlors, cleaners, drug stores, restaurants, candy stores, saloons, and even a Negro baseball team. Sherman Walker's Funeral Home, the Ruth-Patrick Drug Company, the My Cab Company, and the McAvoy Theater were substantial and successful operations. But success did not come easy. In the middle of the 1920s, local banks bowed to pressure from white-owned cab companies and refused to extend a loan to My Cab. The effort to run My Cab out of business failed, however, when the business secured a loan from a New York City bank.

Self-help groups within the black community flourished. One of the earliest was the Colored Musicians' Union of Buffalo, founded in 1917 by individuals who had been denied membership in the white musicians' local. Others included a grocery cooperative; several Negro lodges; the Negro Businessmen's League; the American Colored Workmen's League; a chapter of Marcus Garvey's United Negro Improvement Association; the Big Brothers' Association (founded by older, established East Side blacks to help ease the settlement problems of the new southern migrants); and the Michigan Avenue YMCA, built in 1926 by a local black architect named John R. Brent.[14]

While there was no black-owned bank, the community boasted several news-papers: the *Buffalo Enterprise*, the *Buffalo American*, the *Buffalo Criterion*, and the *Voice*. In addition, according to a study completed in 1927 by Niles Carpenter, chairman of the University of Buffalo's recently founded School of Social Work, there were fifteen Negro churches with Negro pastors; four Negro physicians, three dentists, one lawyer, and one architect; two Negro newspapers; two Negro undertakers; one Negro real estate company; and several Negro-owned restaurants, hotels, and cabarets, all on the black East Side. Despite the growing structure of a black-owned economy, "few Negroes," Carpenter concluded, "have achieved a measure of success in direct competition with whites."[15]

The East Side remained integrated for years, and Jews and blacks, finding so much in common, created an alliance and an allegiance that lasted well into the civil rights era so many years later. Jews and blacks mixed at the public market-place; in the neighborhood's many jazz clubs; at School 32 on Clinton Street; and at the intersection of William and Jefferson, where the Jewish Community Center shared the corner with the headquarters of the Brotherhood of Sleeping Car Porters. However, despite the coexistence of Jews and African Americans on the East Side of Buffalo, Jews left in growing numbers, as they moved to newer and more desirable neighborhoods on Humboldt Parkway and in North Buffalo. As they left, the African Americans quickly filled the vacuum.

Buffalo's economy, meanwhile, was in the midst of a different kind of upheaval. As Europe crumbled, devastated by the horrific events of the Great War, the rap-idly developing industrial infrastructure of the nation as a whole, including Buf-falo, benefited. Indeed, even before America's spring 1917 entry into the war, it was clear that the demands of the fighting armies were helping to feed develop-ment in the city's neighborhood economies, particularly ones like Black Rock, where industry had come to play such an important role. In 1915, anticipating that the war in Europe would revolutionize their nascent industry, the Curtiss Aeroplane Company built its first plant on Churchill Street in Black Rock. In August 1916, Pratt and Letchworth Steel, located near the railroad tracks in Black Rock, where now sits one of the area's most popular supermarkets, sold ten thousand tons of castings of high explosive steel to J. P. Morgan, the British gov-ernment's purchasing agent in the United States. Later in 1916, still a year before American entry into the war, Pierce Arrow won a generous contract to produce trucks for the allied cause. In 1914, there were 50,596 people in Buffalo employed in manufacturing. By 1921, there were more than 112,000.[16] In Buffalo, as in the rest of the nation, the years that followed the war were a time of opti-mism and confidence, rooted in Buffalo's case in the existence of four "key indus-tries"—steel, grain, lumber, and rubber. These key industries were defined by the local Chamber of Commerce as industries around which others would grow because of mutual dependence on the product. Buffalo's key industries, it stated, assured the city "indefinite prosperity." Facts tend to bear out this optimism. It is true that, throughout the 1920s, Buffalo's economy was dynamic, diversified, and strong. The older industries—grain, steel, and lumber—employed more people and produced a larger finished product than ever before. Meanwhile, three new major industries—airplanes, chemicals and automobiles—began to exert an increasingly dominant role. Wartime defense contracts had turned Buffalo's two largest airplane companies, Curtiss and Wright, into industry leaders, producing more than half of all wartime American planes. By the mid-1920s, they employed more than six thousand people and produced a combined total of more than one hundred and fifty planes per year. When the two companies merged in 1929, they formed the largest plane manufacturing company in the world. Buffalo, with its municipally owned and operated airport built in 1927, ten years before New York City's La Guardia Airport, had quickly become the center of the nation's airplane industry.[17]

The 1920s also saw the rise of the chemical industry in both Buffalo and nearby Niagara Falls. Within a period of a few years, this entirely new industry spawned companies whose impersonal names made no reference to either place or person—Carborundum, Niacet, Canadium, Vanadium, and the Alox Chemical Corporation (Hooker, named after the company's founder, was an exception). The petrochemical industry, located primarily in Niagara Falls, employed more than fifteen hundred people by the end of the decade. Niagara Falls was its choice of location due to the presence of its electrical power. Initially developed by Jacob Schoellkopf, the German immigrant who had made his first fortune in the tanning business, the business of producing and selling electrical power at Niagara Falls had become a gigantic enterprise by the 1920s. Nothing, indeed, was more responsible for the accelerated development of the Buffalo region as an industrial center than the availability of cheap and plentiful electrical power.

Added to planes and chemicals was the growth of the automobile industry. Buffalo was particularly proud of the Pierce Arrow Company. Unlike most other automobiles, the Pierce Arrow was produced by teams of workers, not assembly line automatons—Pierce Arrow workers handcrafted each automobile in a manner reminiscent of the Roycrofters. As a result, Pierce Arrow automobiles were well made. The company had retired the Glidden Cup, a trophy earned for having won the roundtrip automobile race between New York City and Bretton Woods, New Hampshire, three years in a row. In addition, its Touring Landau of 1910, which featured a built-in lavatory with running water, was one of the most coveted automobiles in the prewar years. When, during the war, the government needed fast, reliable, and well-built vehicles, it turned to Pierce Arrow, which began to produce trucks in the same careful, handcrafted tradition. In 1916, George Birge, the president of the company, sold it to a group of investors from New York City. The new owners replaced the traditional Pierce Arrow method of team production with an assembly line. Auto production increased in Buffalo during the 1920s; by the end of the decade, close to thirteen thousand people worked in the industry, including several thousand at General Motors, which had built a factory in the city in 1923.[18]

The strength of the Buffalo economy was rooted in its diversity. Area spokesmen never failed to tout it, particularly the Chamber of Commerce, whose monthly publication, *Buffalo Business*, gives a fascinating glimpse into how local business leaders saw and understood the economy of the city. One 1925 article noted that there were fifteen thousand people working in twelve automobile factories, thirteen thousand in machine and foundry shops, two thousand in furniture, three thousand in packing and slaughtering, and three thousand in soap factories. The city's streetcars and railroads, meanwhile, employed two thousand switchmen. Buffalo, the chamber pointed out, also maintained a vital small-scale and largely locally owned economy that employed large numbers of skilled and semiskilled workers. There were a dozen shoe factories that employed 228 men and 28 women; half a dozen clothing factories with 368 male and 1,386 female workers; several large machine and tool factories with more than 3,000 employees; thousands of painters, glaziers, varnishers, and enamellers in the local construction trade; 2,378 electricians; 1,865 plumbers; 5,077 carpenters; and 1,180 bakers. While manufacturing, with close to one hundred thousand workers, clearly dominated, Buffalo's economy had increasingly become service oriented; by the end of the 1920s, more than thirty-five thousand men and women worked in trade, primarily in the retail sector. Other than retail, women worked as teachers (more than six thousand out of a total of 8,567 teachers in the city were women), nurses, and in a job category referred to as "personal and domestic service." (There were very few female lawyers and physicians. Of the close to one thousand lawyers and nine hundred physicians, there were only thirty-seven and fifty-seven women, respectively.) However, despite the predominance of industry and the rapid growth of the service sector, the old waterfront jobs remained vital. In 1930, there were still more than five hundred sailors and deck hands and almost three hundred longshoremen and stevedores working on the city's waterfront.[19] As a center of assembly, manufacturing, and distribution, there was no city, its boosters insisted, more strategically located than Buffalo. Indeed, it was the city's location that reinforced the general sense of confidence that most people had in the local economy. The theme was perennial and unchanging. Year in and year out, professional boosters touted Buffalo's location and its excellent position athwart the world's greatest stream of commerce: the great American heartland in the west (the wheat fields of Kansas, the hills of Minnesota packed with iron ore) and the giant industrial centers to the east. Nothing was more important to the success of the economy than Buffalo's location on this important trade route. Recognizing that, the city's business and political leadership fought to protect it. When, during the 1920s, rumors grew that the governments of the United States and Canada might build a "St. Lawrence Seaway," a direct water route between the Great Lakes and the Atlantic Ocean, the Chamber of Commerce and other Buffalo leaders angrily insisted that that could never and would never happen. Protected by location and cushioned by diversity, Buffalo's economy would remain, they felt, stable and immune to the vagaries of the business cycle.

Most contemporaries also felt that the city's economy was further protected by the arrival of large national corporations who, during the 1920s, began to acquire some of Buffalo's smaller companies, both those locally owned or (like Lackawanna Steel) outsider-owned. The purchase in October 1922 of Lackawanna Steel by Bethlehem Steel, the second-largest steel company in the United States, was, at that time anyway, good for the area. During the nearly two decades since it opened, the company had made few improvements; the massive factory complex had become increasingly antiquated. Immediately following its acquisition (for what was considered the bargain price of $60 million), Bethlehem Steel initiated modernizing improvements that cost in excess of $40 million. There were other acquisitions in the steel industry, too, as Republic Steel, based in Cleveland, bought the Donner Steel and Iron Company. Meanwhile, Rogers-Brown Steel was acquired by the National Steel Company.[20] Buffalo's grain business was another prime target for large, national corporations eager to strengthen their control over the industry. Standard Milling of New York built a gigantic elevator and flour mill on the Buffalo waterfront. Commander-Larabee and International Milling, both of Minneapolis, bought out several local operations, while building new facilities of their own. Elevators, mills, and even bakeries were brought into the national network of the grain industry. In 1927, Greenan's Bakery, "the largest and best equipped cake bakery in this section of the country," was bought by the Purity Bakery Company of New York City.

For good or bad, local ownership eroded in other economic sectors as well. Consolidations, mergers, and acquisitions doomed the *Commercial Advertiser*, a newspaper published in Buffalo since 1828. The *Enquirer* followed in 1926. In 1929, the *Buffalo Times*, locally owned for fifty years, was bought by Scripps Howard. In that same year, the gigantic Fox Movie Company bought up five local movie theaters.

Some of the acquisitions and consolidations were local. In 1918, the Schoellkopf family of Buffalo consolidated two separate small power companies into the Niagara Falls Power Company, which immediately became one of the largest in the country. In 1925, the Schoellkopfs merged the Niagara Falls Company, the Niagara, Lockport and Ontario Power Company, the Tonawanda Power Company, and the Buffalo General Electric Company into a gigantic holding company called the Buffalo, Niagara and Eastern Power Company. Four years later this, along with the New England Power Company and the Mohawk and Hudson Power Company, was merged into yet another holding company called the Niagara Hudson Power Company. Based in Buffalo, the company dominated electrical utilities from the Hudson to the Niagara River.

Mergers and consolidations also strengthened the power of several local banks. In the early 1920s, there remained a few small private banks, many of them neighborhood-based and immigrant-owned. Immigrants were moving out of their neighborhoods, however, and the big downtown banks expanded. The smaller banks, caught up in these changes, were either merged or went out of business. Thus, for example, the Commercial Trust Company bought out Michael Lunghino's Bank and the Ortolani Brothers Bank. Far larger and more significant bank mergers also occurred. In 1919, there were thirteen commercial banks in Buffalo, but by 1927 there were only six. The largest was the Marine Midland Bank, which had begun the decade as a major commercial bank. It ended it as the centerpiece of a gigantic financial holding company, the Marine Midland Corporation. By 1929, Marine Midland owned 97 percent of the capital stock of seventeen banks throughout New York State.[21]

Because they were intertwined with the rest of the economy, banks and bankers were particularly close to the power industry. As a result of their dominance and control in both finance and electricity, the banks' presidents and directors played a critical role in the life of the economy. George F. Rand, president and chairman of the Marine Trust, was also a director of the Niagara Hudson Power Corporation. Jacob Schoellkopf Jr. was vice president and general manager of the same power company, and served on boards in an overlapping network of corporate power and control: Manufacturers' and Traders' Bank (M&T Bank), and several power companies, including Niagara Falls Power, Tonawanda Power, and New England Power. His brother, Paul, was an officer of both the power company and Rand's Marine Trust. Walter P. Cooke, partner in Kenefick and Cook and a leading corporate attorney, was director of Rand's Marine Trust, Goodyear's Southern Lumber Company, and the Niagara Hudson. His partner, Daniel Kenefick, was on the board of M&T Bank, Buffalo General Electric, and Niagara Electric. Lewis G. Harriman, president and chairman of M&T Bank, also served as a director of the Niagara Hudson. These men had other business interests as well. George Rand was a director of the Remington-Rand Company, the Cleveland Transit Company, the General Baking Company of Minneapolis, and the Metropolitan Casualty Company of New York City. Schoellkopf, too, was a director of the Metropolitan, where Harriman was active in a variety of investment companies throughout New York State.[22]

In addition to their business interests, these men took an active role in the ongoing efforts to bring order to the chaotic downtown business district through city planning. Concerned about the rapid and seemingly random growth of their city, yet confident about the city's growth, the men were convinced that Buffalo's future could not be positively realized without a careful and "scientific" approach to its planning. Thus, in 1920, a group of citizen activists, consisting primarily of bankers, lawyers, and downtown business owners, formed the City Planning Association (CPA).[23] Under the leadership of Chauncey J. Hamlin, an attorney whose personal wealth enabled him to devote most of his activities to public improvement, the CPA, continuing the movement that had begun twenty years earlier with the Society for the Beautification of Buffalo, lobbied the Common Council to pass a resolution that would give city government unprecedented power over the planning and use of land. It was a sweeping proposal that established the city's first official planning body, the City Planning Committee, and at the same time granted city government the power to acquire land through eminent domain for the location of public buildings. The council, however, required a referendum on the matter. Thus, Hamlin and the CPA, working out of offices in the Buffalo Public Library on Lafayette Square, issued bulletins and press releases, made phone calls (their number was Seneca 3455), arranged for speeches and press conferences, and seized every possibility and created every opportunity to convince the public of the importance of approving the resolution in the November referendum. The public did just that, and, in January 1921, the City Planning Committee was created, with Chauncey Hamlin as its first chairman.

Hamlin was eager to make the most of the opportunity that people like him had been waiting for for years. He turned his eyes to Chicago, which, since the Columbian Exposition in 1893, had dominated the field of architecture and city planning. While Hamlin was too young to have visited the Columbian Exposition, an earlier generation of Buffalonians, people like John Milburn and John Albright (Albright had taken his architect E. B. Green with him) had seen it. By the early years of the twentieth century, Chicago's leading architects—Daniel Burnham, Louis Sullivan, and Frank Lloyd Wright—had done some of their finest work in Buffalo. Nothing, however, was more influential than the Chicago Plan. Designed by Daniel Burnham in 1909, the Chicago Plan, with its vast monumental boulevards, its ceremonial civic center, its grandiose public buildings, and its sense of cleanliness and order, appealed to people around the country who, by the end of the century's first decade, were overwhelmed by the rapid, haphazard, and (in the words of the City Beautiful movement) "chaotic" growth of the modern city. By calling for the construction of a complete system of wide radial thoroughfares leading from the downtown core as well as a series of highways that circled the central business district, Burnham's plan for Chicago was the first major attempt by a planner to account for and to accommodate the automobile. Burnham's Chicago Plan became, for better or for worse, the blueprint for cities across the country, including Buffalo. In 1920, Burnham's successor, Edward C. Bennett, who had taken over Burnham's practice following his death, was brought to Buffalo by Hamlin and the gentlemen planners of the CPA to provide advice and consultation to the City Planning Committee.[24] Bennett's Buffalo Plan of 1920 was an ambitious and visionary effort to create a planning strategy not only for the city but for the entire region; it was a plan, Hamlin and its other advocates were convinced, that would solve what they believed were the two most pressing problems of the day: the threat to downtown posed by growing vehicular congestion and the threat to the entire region posed by the dangerous and disorderly sprawl of the metropolitan area.

Nothing more dramatically altered the relationship that existed between people and the landscape of the city than automobiles, which, by the early 1920s, had come to dominate the way people understood the problems of their city. For years, there had been an active automobile lobby in Buffalo. The automobile industry, with close to four thousand employees and the Buffalo Automobile Club, with close to three thousand members, were forceful proponents of the automobile. The auto club's monthly magazine, the *Motorist*, published the latest news of the automobile world and fought all the battles dear to the heart of every motorist, particularly limits on speed, which, although regularly liberalized, were invariably considered far too restrictive.[25] More significant than the particular issues that the automobile lobby fought for was the increasing acceptability of the vision of the city as an automobile-centered community, a place where the private automobile, far more than public transportation, was destined to become the dominant form of transportation. Private autos required public highways, however, and by the early 1920s, an increasingly irrepressible movement grew in Buffalo, as in cities across the nation, for their construction.

The CPA agreed: "The rapid development of the automobile industry has created conditions which must be taken care of. Bear in mind," the CPA reported in 1921, in their periodic publication called the *Live Wire*, "that there is one car to every eleven people in Erie County and the number is growing." Writing in 1926 in the *Live Wire*, George H. Norton, the city engineer and a member of the CPA, wrote that "this problem of street traffic is today the most pressing of all of our planning problems."[26] There were, he said, more than eighty-three thousand cars per day entering the central business district from the newer neighborhoods in north and south Buffalo. Concerned that the increased congestion would choke off access to downtown and that commuters, rather than deal with the growing traffic nightmares, might just choose to stay where they were, the CPA argued for the creation and implementation of an integrated approach to the problem of vehicular congestion. "This is," Hamlin wrote,

> the era of highway transportation. The day of the automotive movement of passengers and freight is at hand. The growth of cities is becoming more and more dependent upon the development of thru highways. What the Buffalo of tomorrow will be depends on very great measure upon the highway plans made by the Buffalonians of today.[27]

In order to relieve the growing congestion caused by increased use of cars and trucks, Bennett's plan insisted that a new road be built around the periphery of the central business district. This road, a four-lane, grade-level arterial called the "Cross-town Traffic Way," would begin at Elmwood and North Street and end at Swan and Washington, thus encircling the central business district and thereby facilitating the movement of traffic around the downtown area. The new highway, its advocates said, would "save" downtown, for not only would it ease the movement of vehicles, it would create a brand-new boulevard, which, they argued, would "afford splendid sites for stores, apartment houses, semi-public and public buildings." In addition, if that were not enough, the CPA argued that the new road "will make for a more unified city." Convinced of the correctness of their views and undaunted by the scope and scale of the project (something that, had it been built, would have radically uprooted long-established patterns of life throughout the entire city), the CPA believed that their plan, the largest and most ambitious for the area since the construction of the Erie Canal, would "create no real obstacles."

While the "Cross-town Traffic Way" would enable motorists to move around the city without moving through it, wider streets and avenues, the gentlemen planners of the CPA believed, would make it easier to enter the traffic way from outlying areas. "The general use of the automobile and truck," the CPA wrote in one of its publicly distributed publications, "has placed a great burden of traffic on city streets and they must be improved to meet these conditions." Better highways and widened streets, they thought, were essential if the central business district were to slow the growing trend toward the suburbs. In 1923, M&T Bank published a widely distributed, free brochure called "Planning the City."[28] One article, written by Fenton Parke, a founding member of the CPA, articulated an increasingly popular vision for Buffalo. He argued that since downtown's growth and vitality depended on the automobile, the construction of highways was essential. Highways, Parke insisted, would not only provide insurance against what was then referred to as "decentralization," they would also lead to still greater growth.

With this in mind, in 1924, the CPA called for the widening and extension of "all of the twenty-four radial streets entering the city." George Norton, the city engineer and the official in charge of the city's streets, went still further, insisting that every street in the entire city should be widened on each side by three to four feet. Without widened streets, Norton believed, "the city will choke and die."

The *Buffalo Motorist*, the influential publication of the Buffalo Automobile Club, agreed:

> Every major artery in the city should be widened to its maximum width...plenty of wide, well-paved streets are not only an asset of immeasurable value, but under the stress of modern traffic these thoroughfares are an absolute necessity.[29]

Much of the widening efforts were focused on Delaware Avenue, the tree-lined, mansion-filled locale of Buffalo's affluent. Delaware Avenue was Buffalo's equivalent of Woodward Avenue in Detroit and Euclid Avenue in Cleveland. It was quickly becoming the city's major artery, the avenue that connected the booming neighborhoods in north Buffalo to the booming business section downtown. The avenue, particularly following the completion of the Statler Hotel in 1923, had become increasingly commercial, and, by the middle of the decade, office buildings and stores lined Delaware Avenue from Chippewa to Tupper. The pressure to widen it even more increased, and when, in the mid-1920s, the city engineer announced a plan for its widening, most people supported it. Some, however, were opposed, unwilling to pay the steep price to be exacted for the improvement: the loss of hundreds of elm trees that, towering high over the avenue, defined the street for so many. Charles Burchfield, a painter who had moved to Buffalo in 1921, was appalled. He protested the plan in a painting called *Civic Improvement*. Somebody else wrote a poem called "Our Martyred Beauties: A Sacrifice to Greed and Power: Pace, Haste, Destroy and Lay Waste."[30]

Trees, for years, had been an important part of Buffalo's streetscape. When they were lost, by man's hands or by nature, the results were devastating. Frank E. Karpick, who served as the city forester from 1929 until his retirement in 1968, was a loving guardian of the city's rich arboreal heritage. He treated the trees when they were sick and repaired them when, as in the vicious ice storm of 1929, they were damaged. In an article written in that year for a national magazine called *American City*, he chronicled the storm's ferocity: "The arching elms for which Buffalo has long been famous suffered a terrible experience on December 17th and 18th, 1929 from which it will take a long time to recover." Karpick spent days riding up and down the streets of the city to document the damage: "On these days a sleet storm, the worst in local history, visited the city. While all the trees bore the brunt of the storm," it was, he wrote, his favorites, "the elms which suffered most."[31]

Some suggested alternative and less destructive solutions to the problems of traffic congestion on Delaware Avenue. One proposed a ban on parking. Another argued that if buses ran on Delaware then "many people would use this method to get downtown instead of their own cars." Widening, however, was the easier, tested way, however, and in 1924, Burchfield's haunting image of hundreds of trees chopped cruelly to the ground became a reality. Anything, it seemed, that impeded the free flow of traffic, was expendable. In 1927, a man named Miller McClintock, director of the Erskine Bureau for Street Traffic Research at Harvard, delivered a talk in Buffalo on "How the City Traffic Problem Will Be Solved." Among the many ideas and suggestions that Erskine offered was the dictum that "the streets need to be cleared of all private encroachments such as newsstands, merchandise displays, peddlers carts and advertising wagons." McClintock, like so many of his generation, paved the way for the end of street life that the people of Buffalo had for so long known.[32]

Hamlin and the other planners of the 1920s were as concerned with regional planning as they were with plans for the city itself. "Few people realize," Hamlin's CPA said in 1920, "that now over 700,000 people inhabit the metropolitan area.... Growing at a rate of 22 % a decade, the area will contain over 1,000,000 people in twenty years and over 1,500,000 by 1960." "The Buffalo of tomorrow" will become a region "so thickly populated that there will be practically one continuous city of several millions from Lackawanna to Niagara Falls." The rapid growth of the region, the CPA insisted, required the creation and implementation of a master plan for the entire region. In speeches and in press releases issued throughout the summer of 1920, Hamlin and his colleagues spread the gospel of regional planning. "Proper city planning," Hamlin said, "will not only aid Buffalo to attain her place among the great industrial centers of the world, but will permit her to grow sanely and economically with the great efficiency, preventing mistakes that would cost our citizens millions to correct later." In one of many press releases, the CPA pronounced that a "city that makes its opportunity by grasping an efficient and economical plan for the entire region will be building its foundation on a rock of success and prosperity." Armed with these convictions, Hamlin became one of New York State's most articulate advocates of regional planning.

Regional planning had already become a hot topic by the early 1920s and Buffalo, under Hamlin's aegis, was a center of its activity. In 1923, the New York State Legislature created the New York State Commission on Housing and Regional Planning. In November 1924, following a statewide conference held in Buffalo on regional and city planning, the Niagara Frontier Regional Planning

Board (NFRPB) was created, with Hamlin as chairman. One year later, he arranged for the National Conference on City Planning to hold its national conference in Buffalo. Hamlin was hopeful that the event, which, he said, "will bring together four hundred of the leading planning professionals in the US and Canada," would provide further encouragement and inspiration to the city's planning movement.

Regional planning was given yet another boost with the completion in 1927 of the Peace Bridge between the United States and Canada. The bridge, with one end in Buffalo and the other across the Niagara River in Fort Erie, made possible the creation of what Erie County engineer George C. Diehl called the "International City," with more than one million people living in a large swath of land that included all of southern Ontario as well as Buffalo and its surrounding suburbs. In 1927, Diehl's office published a large fold-out map that indicated in bright orange the two-hundred-square-mile area he called the "Greater Niagara Region." In lectures throughout the community, Diehl proposed that a free trade zone be created that would revolutionize the economic and political life of the area.[33]

Diehl, as much as anyone, recognized the impact the automobile was exerting on the metropolitan area. Writing in 1921, he stated that "motor traffic has become so tremendous in volume that city lines today are little more than political divisions... Business and social movements pay little or no attention to them." He was concerned, he said, that there simply were not enough streets within the city limits to "meet the requirements of modern traffic" unless the streets of the city were connected to new highways outside the city limits. What was needed, he said, was a comprehensive plan for highway improvement throughout Erie County. Indeed, throughout the 1920s, it seemed that nearly every day new highways—often called "major traffic ways"—were proposed: bridges and a new highway across Grand Island; extensions of existing roads and highways; and the construction of a bevy of new ones that would better connect all of the disparate communities that dotted the emerging metropolitan area.

Some, like Frank C. Perkins, president of the Buffalo Common Council, went further. Perkins, like so many people who cared about downtown, knew that even though the population of the city was still growing (from 506,775 in 1920 to 573,076 in 1930), its rate of growth—13 percent—was the smallest in the city's history. More significantly, the city's growth was dwarfed by the astounding growth (from 250,000 in 1920 to 340,000 in 1930, an increase of 26 percent) of the surrounding suburban areas. In 1927, *Buffalo Business*, the Chamber of Commerce's monthly publication, reported that "for the first time in Buffalo's history, there is more building activity in the suburbs immediately surrounding Buffalo than in the city itself. In the Village of Kenmore," the journal reported, "in the townships of Tonawanda, Amherst and West Seneca, the value of building construction was 27% greater than the value of new building within the city of Buffalo."[34] Something had to be done, and later that year, Perkins, with the hearty support of many in the downtown business community, proposed the incorporation of the towns of Kenmore, Lackawanna, Tonawanda, Amherst, and the city of Niagara Falls into one regional city of Buffalo. Modeled on greater New York, Perkins envisioned this new conglomeration as one that would function as a federation of separate boroughs, a two-tiered system that would somehow balance home rule with regionalism. Confident that "the outside communities need Buffalo more than we need them" and that it was but a question of time before "they will rush forward to be enveloped in our arms," Perkins was willing to wait.[35] Matthew D. Young, a supervisor in the Town of Tonawanda, felt otherwise. "I don't know how Mr. Perkins judged the sentiment," he said, "but I have talked to quite a few people and they are all opposed to it." Fenton Parke, the president of the City Planning Association in the late 1920s, didn't care. He insisted that "we must turn our attention to the annexation of the suburbs."[36] Hamlin and the CPA recognized the seeds of downtown's decline even earlier and, as part of Bennett's master plan, they insisted that he include proposals to counter the downward trends. Bennett's plan, similar to the one that he and Burnham had proposed for Chicago, proposed the construction in downtown of an architecturally impressive neoclassical civic center. It would be centered on a drastically restructured Niagara Square, with its focal point a new city hall on the square's west side. The city hall building, which in Bennett's drawing far exceeded the size of the structure that was eventually built, towered over the existing streetscape, a gigantic, St. Peter's-like structure with a soaring dome of impressive height. It would, Bennett hoped, "stand as the symbol of civic order and unity" for the people of Buffalo.[37] Flanked at great distances by two overpowering and formal Neoclassical public buildings, a "Hall of Records" and a state office building, the goal of Bennett's plan, known both as "the City Hall Group" and "the Court of Honor," was to re-create Niagara Square as the symbolic center of the entire metropolitan area. For Hamlin and the others who believed so deeply in the power of the monumental to alter the fortunes of a city, the city hall group was "Buffalo's opportunity." In 1928, Hamlin wrote sincerely that "such improvements as are indicated are going to make every one of the hundreds of thousands of visitors who come to Buffalo go away with a feeling of regret that they have not made their homes in our beautiful city."[38]

The CPA's master plan for downtown was the first of many that were advanced during the twentieth century for Buffalo's downtown renewal. Although not all of their specific plans were realized, their concepts about Buffalo's downtown remained influential in subsequent years. While the "Cross-town Traffic Way" was never built, for example, the concept of a street-level highway through the heart of the city surfaced, and, in the forms of the Kensington Expressway, the Sca-jaquada Creek Expressway, and the Elm-Oak Arterial, were realized. (Another, the Lower West Side Arterial, was planned but never built.) Bennett's CPA-commissioned civic center was also realized, albeit in much-altered form. By the early 1930s, Niagara Square, with the exception of the recently built Statler Hotel, was given over completely to governmental uses. The replacement of heterogeneous land use with a homogenous zone for government functions, a cardinal principal of City Beautiful planning ideals, has made contemporary efforts to revitalize downtown as a diverse and dynamic center of activity even more difficult.

There was no greater embodiment of the ideals of City Beautiful architecture and city planning than the Albright Art Gallery building. Located on a hill overlooking Delaware Park Lake and built in the purest Greek Revival style, the gallery in its form and purpose embodied the essence of the City Beautiful. It is, therefore, somewhat ironic that by the mid-1920s, the Albright, this most classic of neoclassical buildings, began to pave a daring path of modernism that would sustain it through the rest of the century. The groundwork that had been laid by Charles Kurtz and Cornelia Sage earlier in the century continued with William M. Hekking, who succeeded Sage as gallery director in 1924.[39] Hekking came under the wing of A. Conger Goodyear, a director of the gallery's board, and together they aggressively pushed the Albright in the direction of modernism. In 1926, Goodyear organized an endowment program called the "Fellows for Life," which raised funds to buy the works of such significant modern and contemporary artists as Morisot, Matisse, Rodin, Brancusi, Gauguin, and Cezanne. Goodyear, as the chairman of the Art Acquisitions Committee, next added his own considerable funds to those raised from the Members for Life campaign, and made a series of startling and increasingly controversial acquisitions, including works by Morisot, Gauguin, Augustus John, Epstein, Brancusi, Noguchi, Degas, Cezanne, and Matisse. It was Goodyear's prodding that led the Albright to bring the annual show of the Societé Anonyme to Buffalo in 1927 (the only city outside of New York to host it). Founded by Katherine Dreier and Marcel Duchamp in 1920, the Societé Anonyme was one of the world's most persuasive advocates of modernism. In an article written for the *Buffalo Arts Journal* in 1927, Dreier congratulated the Albright for its boldness in exhibiting the work of Brancusi, Archipenko, Zorach, Kandinsky, Stella, Duchamp, Moholy Nagy, and others from among the world's leading contemporary artists.[40] Following this exhibition, Goodyear bought and donated to the gallery a painting by Picasso called "La Toilette." It was the gallery's first Picasso, and made it one of only six museums in the country to own a work by this daring artist. This acquisition, combined with Goodyear's unequivocal embrace of modernism, turned the more conservative gallery board against him. Over the strenuous objection of Goodyear's young protégé, Seymour H. Knox Jr., who recognized the Picasso as a great work of contemporary art, Goodyear was removed from the board. In a fit of pique that would last for years, Goodyear left Buffalo and moved to New York, where he shortly thereafter became a founder and the first president of the Museum of Modern Art. He never lost his love for Buffalo, however, and during the 1930s he continued to play an important role in the cultural life of the city as it confronted the challenges of the Great Depression.

NOTES

1. For details about the home front during World War I, see H. W. Hill, ed., *Municipality of Buffalo, A History, 1720–1923*, vol. 2 (New York: Lewis, 1932), pp. 856–71; J. T. Horton, *History of Northwestern New York* (New York: Lewis, 1948), p. 377ff.

2. Obituary of Walter P. Cooke, *Buffalo Evening News*, August 5, 1931, p. E2.

3. For information on Fuhrman and the Americanization committee, see Horton, *History of Northwestern New York*, pp. 405ff.

4. Ibid.

5. For information on the mayoral election of 1917, see Michael Rizzo, *Through the Mayor's Eyes: The Only Complete History of the Mayors of Buffalo, New York* (Buffalo, NY: Old House History, 2005) p. 224.

6. Ibid., pp. 235–47.

7. For information on the Ku Klux Klan in Buffalo, see Shaun Lay, *Hooded Knights Along the Niagara: The KKK in Buffalo, New York* (New York: New York University Press, 1995).

8. A. Parnell, "The Little Theatre on William Street," *Buffalo Arts Journal* (November–December 1927): 543–44. For information on the Jewish community, see the *Buffalo Jewish Review*, which can be found in the archives at Buffalo State College. See also Selig Adler and Tom Connolly, *From Ararat to Suburbia: The History of the Jewish Community of Buffalo* (Philadelphia: Jewish Publication Society of America, 1960).

9. "Joseph Braun" (an alias), interview with the author, March 1981.

10. "Mean-Spirited Immigration Bill," *Buffalo Jewish Review* (April 12, 1924): 12.

11. "Large Crowds Protest Bill," *Buffalo Jewish Review* (June 13, 1924): 1.

12. Lillian Williams, *Strangers in the Land of Paradise: The Creation of an African-American Community in Buffalo, 1900–1940* (Bloomington: Indiana University Press, 1999), pp. 123ff.

13. B. J. Ruby, "Local Color: A Visit to Buffalo's Black Belt," *Buffalo Saturday Night* 4, no. 23: 4–5.

14. Williams, *Strangers in the Land of Paradise*, p. 123ff.

15. Niles Carpenter, "Nationality, Color and Economic Opportunity in the City of Buffalo, *University of Buffalo Studies* 5, no. 4: 95–145.

16. D. J. Sweeney, ed., *History of Buffalo and Erie County, 1914–1919* (Buffalo, NY, 1921).

17. *Chamber Contacts*, April 13, 1926, p. 1. *Chamber Contacts* can be found in the Grosvenor Collection at the BECPL.

18. There is a great deal of information on the Pierce Arrow Company at Chuck LaChuisa, "History of Buffalo, Pierce-Arrow Autos—Links," http://www.ah.phpweb hosting.com/h/pierce/tc.html.

19. *Buffalo Business*, February 1925, pp. 17–39.

20. This and the following information on Buffalo's economy in the late 1920s is taken from Horton, *History of Northwestern New York*, pp. 412–14.

21. Ibid.

22. See *Poor's Register of Directors of the United States, 1929* (New York: Standard and Poor, 1929), p. 389.

23. The City Planning Association dominated any and all talk regarding city and regional planning during the 1920 and 1930s. A great deal of material pertaining to the City Planning Association is kept in the "city planning" vertical files in the Grosvenor Collection at the BECPL.

24. For information on Burnham and the City Beautiful movement, see William Wilson, *The City Beautiful Movement* (Baltimore: Johns Hopkins University Press, 1989).

25. *Buffalo Motorist* can be found in the stacks in the Grosvenor Collection at the BECPL.

26. *Live Wire*, November 1926, p. 11. *Live Wire* can be found in the "city planning" vertical files in the Grosvenor Collection at the BECPL.

27. *Live Wire*, November 1926, p. 7.

28. "City planning" vertical files, Grosvenor Collection, BECPL.

29. *Buffalo Motorist*, June 1929, p. 41.

30. *Civic Improvement* was featured in an exhibit at the Burchfield-Penny Art Center called "City Critique: Burchfield's Commentary on the Early Twentieth-Century Metropolis," which ran from October–November 2005. See the catalog of that exhibition. The poem "Martyred Beauties" appeared in the *Courier Express*, March 20, 1930, Trees Scrapbook, vol. 1, p. 18, Grosvenor Collection, BECPL.

31. *Town Tidings*, July 1930, Trees Scrapbook, vol. 1, p. 53, Grosvenor Collection, BECPL.

32. *Buffalo Motorist*, July 1927, p. 13.

33. George Diehl, "Buffalo, An International City," "city planning" vertical files, Grosvenor Collection, BECPL.

34. *Chamber Contacts*, February 2, 1927, p. 1.

35. "Perkins Proposes Regional City," *Courier Express*, March 11, 1928, p. 12.

36. "More Annexation Talk," *Buffalo Evening News*, May 15, 1928.

37. Quoted in Wilson, *The City Beautiful Movement*, p. 282.

38. *Live Wire*, April 1928, p. 109.

39. Thompson, *100 Years*, p. 141.

40. *Buffalo Arts Journal*, March 1927, p. 167.

chapter 5

ART AND LIFE IN THE DEPRESSION DECADE

Despite its vaunted economic diversity, Buffalo was devastated by the Great Depression. Unemployment had been increasing slowly in 1928 and 1929. By the end of 1930, more than 20 percent of all construction workers, cabinetmakers, carpenters, machinists, toolmakers, painters, varnishers, glaziers, railroad and streetcar workers, and factory workers were out of work. The city did not know what to do, but tried desperately to deal with what was generally referred to, in the newspapers at least, as "the present emergency." The mayor, grasping at straws, formed numerous committees: the Committee for the Stabilization of Employment; the Mayor's Clothing Campaign Committee; and the Committee on Economic Recovery.[1] None of these efforts worked, not the mayor's committees, not the Sunday school children's drive to collect old shoes, not the Boy Scouts' call to collect food, and not the Man-a-Block campaign, which pooled the funds of families on each street in order to hire unemployed men to do landscape and maintenance chores. Not even the heroic efforts by private charities to do what they had always done in times of economic crisis seemed to work, as it was beyond their organizational ability and financial resources to have any significant impact. At the end of 1930, the Charity Organization Society, the largest private charity in the city, announced that because of their deficit of $25,000, they would have to curtail relief work.[2] Meanwhile, economic indicators continued to plunge. By 1932, building permits were down by 50 percent, the number of wage earners by 30 percent, and average weekly earnings by 17 percent. Steel production was off by 38 percent and flour milling by 22 percent.[3]

Relief rolls mounted. In 1932, the City of Buffalo paid out $6 million in welfare benefits to 21,706 families—more than one hundred thousand people. The county added close to $1 million, while the state government reimbursed the city for 40 percent of its welfare budget. Costs were enormous, and the benefits were small and closely monitored. Money from the city's welfare fund could be used solely for the purchase of food. Only in clearly demonstrated emergencies would welfare funds be allocated to pay for shelter and fuel. Similarly, public funds could not be used to purchase clothing, and in July 1932, the mayor, Charles E. Roesch, reporting that "the clothing situation is growing increasingly acute," announced the formation of an old clothes collection campaign. Under the city's welfare provisions, a single person could receive no more than two dollars per week in food vouchers. Regardless of size, no family could receive more than the maximum weekly allotment of $10. In order to most efficiently budget their money, housewives were advised that one-quarter of their food allotments should be used for milk or evaporated milk, whichever was cheaper; one-fifth for vegetables such as canned tomatoes, cabbage, potatoes, and greens; one-fifth for cereals such as oatmeal, wheat cereal, cornmeal, flour, rice, macaroni, and bread, plus dried beans and pears; and one-fifth for such fat as lard, salt pork, butter, or margarine, and sugars such as molasses, sugar, or corn syrup. The balance could be used to buy meat, fish, cheese, coffee, and tea. Food allowances were cut as prices fell, and a family of five, granted six dollars a week for food, faced further reductions. In July 1932, the mayor announced that "experts are being consulted to advise welfare workers on an absolute minimum that will not endanger health."[4] People were losing faith. In the fall of 1930, Charles Burchfield painted *Rainy Night*, a depiction of the intersection of Broadway and Ellicott. The city looked bleak, grim, and hopeless.[5]

The Chamber of Commerce, however, continued to believe in the resiliency of the city's diversified economy and, in early 1932, predicted that "no doubt Buffalo will feel the present economic crisis less than will most American cities." A local editorialist felt that it was all up to the people themselves: "If those with jobs buckle down to them; if those with properties start using them; if those with money get it to work, there will be prosperity for all."[6] And, if all else failed, the city's past could always be remembered. Thus, Buffalo, in the midst of the Depression, celebrated the centennial of its incorporation as a city. Using the Pan-American Exposition as a model, the organizers of the 1932 centennial erected another plywood village on a downtown park overlooking the waterfront. Here—in Centennial Park—they built a stadium, a midway, aeroplane exhibits, and several large exposition buildings.

Like the Pan-American, the centennial had several columned proscenium entrances. There was also a tower—a large erector set-like structure hung with sparkling lights of different colors—called the "Tower of Jewels." A fireworks spectacle illustrated scenes from the life of George Washington. The whole community, it seemed, joined in this look backward. Several newspapers featured articles that highlighted "distinctive events in the life of our city," while a radio station sponsored an eight-night serial during the first two weeks of July. It was trumpeted as "a musical drama, taking eight nights to present, which will tell the story of Buffalo's progress from pioneer days to the present."[7]

There was a sadness to the centennial. Not only did it seem to trivialize the past and deny the present; it seemed specious that it would redeem the future. "Our Centennial," one editor nonetheless wrote, "will act as an incentive for each to play his part in achieving the glorious future that lies just ahead in the second century of the history of Buffalo."[8] Another had convinced himself that "the Centennial will give expression to the faith that Buffalo people have in the future of their city." The rhetoric of community uplift and optimism that characterized the centennial celebration went quickly out of style, however. Shortly after the inauguration of Franklin D. Roosevelt, a massive flow of federal and state funds to the city created a genuine spark of hope and enthusiasm, which made the boosterish hype of the centennial seem out of place.

New Deal benefits came slowly but when they did finally arrive, the sums were enormous. Throughout most of 1935 and 1936 there were almost daily announcements of federally funded public works: $4.5 million for public housing; $1.2 million for airport modernization; $2 million for a downtown auditorium; $750,000 for a concert hall (and thousands of dollars for the creation of the Buffalo Philharmonic Orchestra); $1 million for the modernization of the zoo; $2 million for a federal office building; $1.3 million for a stadium; $500,000 for a new police headquarters; and hundreds of thousands of dollars for schools, street widenings, playgrounds, tennis courts, and swimming pools. The largest single grant of all—$15 million—was for the construction of a new sewer. Between 1935 and 1937, more than $45 million was spent on permanent projects in the city of Buffalo, which employed more than seventy-five thousand men and women. Although less than the initial promise of one job for every family on relief, the New Deal was an unprecedented effort to provide work and relief for those who needed it.[9]

People were concerned, however, that despite the apparent return to some semblance of normalcy—economic indicators, including wages, employment, and steel production, were all up by the mid-1930s—the number of families supported by public funds continued to increase. In March and April 1936, for example, the federal government reported that for every family that went off relief because of work, two families went on. During the summer of that year, 142,960 people—25 percent of the city's population—still lived on relief or make work. The WPA in Buffalo was spending money at the rate of $60,000 per day, yet it could employ only half of the able-bodied workers on the city's relief roles.[10]

As prosperity slowly returned, skilled workers left their public relief jobs and returned to the private economy. In addition, as relief work became increasingly dominated by the unskilled, criticism mounted. There were so many people cleaning up at the airport, it was charged, that no planes could land. Articles, letters to the editor, and editorials in all of the papers began to warn about the dangers of increased public welfare, of the "opiate of relief and relief employment," of "relief and the impairment of human values," and of "welfare chiselers." Soon, politicians, newspaper writers, and community leaders, Democrats as well as Republicans, began to talk seriously about "going back to private charity" in the hope of spurring thousands of workers into jobs in private industry. People argued that only a return to private charity, an older, more demeaning system of outdoor relief, would force people back to work.

Some thought that the problems were political as much as they were structural. Indeed, following months of newspaper reports in 1937 that mayor George J. Zimmerman and several members of his administration had used WPA funds to finance their payrolls, a special grand jury was created to investigate the allegations. In early 1938, a councilman was convicted of receiving fraudulent payments from the city, the streets commissioner was convicted of payroll padding, and the mayor himself was charged with the taking of unlawful fees in connection with the $15 million federal sewer project. By the end of 1938, nine councilmen and former councilmen had been indicted. Although several priests charged that the indictments were part of an "anti-Catholic plot," the charges stuck. Several of the politicians went to jail. Mayor Zimmerman died while out on bail.[11]

Oddly enough, 1937, which saw the collapse of the venerable Pierce Arrow company and the investigation of the mayor, had begun as a good year for Buffalo. Not only were federal public works grants at their highest level but the local economy appeared to be following the rest of the nation back to some semblance of economic prosperity. Steel, for example, had been coming back slowly since 1934 when, following a loss of over $8 million in 1933, Bethlehem Steel reported a profit of $5.5 million. While people were pleased with this progress, the president of Bethlehem, Eugene Grace, was criticized bitterly in the local press when it became public that he had received an annual salary of $180,000 since 1932.[12] Still, at only 34 percent of capacity, business was slow. Part of the problem at Bethlehem was that its primary product was heavy steel sheetings used in the manufacture of railroad cars. Desperately eager to be independent of that crippled industry, in 1935, Grace invested $20 million in the construction of a new plant at Lackawanna that would manufacture the lighter steel sheets used in the manufacture of automobiles.[13] It was a dangerous gamble. It soon looked, however, as though the move had paid off. In March 1937, rumors that had been circulating for several months were now confirmed: for close to a year the General Motors Company had been quietly purchasing more than 160 acres of waterfront land overlooking the Niagara River, just north of the Buffalo city line. GM, it was announced, was going to build a $12.5 million Chevrolet plant that would employ from three thousand to four thousand workers in the manufacture of automobile axles and the assembly of automobile engines.[14]

People were ecstatic. There would be a new steel mill and a gigantic new automobile plant. The economy was changing; new directions were emerging and nothing, certainly not the quickly shelved park that Erie County had planned for the GM site, would stand in the way. Work proceeded quickly and, with no strikes or other interruptions, the plant began production in March 1938, less than one year after construction had begun. GM had been looking at Buffalo as one of several places to build new plants. Ever since the sitdown strikes in Detroit and Flint in 1937, the company had wanted to move away from the solid union towns in Michigan. Buffalo, a steel town with a nonunionized workforce in its heavy industries, seemed to fit the bill. Other companies thought so, too. In the spring of 1937, the *Buffalo Evening News* reported that the Chrysler Company was considering a move to Buffalo to join GM. "Labor trouble in Michigan has given added impetus," the paper noted, "to the decentralization movement."[15] However, labor organizers followed GM's, move and, in late 1936 and early 1937, the Congress of Industrial Organizations (CIO), targeting automobile and steelworkers, began actively organizing the industrial workers of Buffalo.[16]

It was not going to be an easy job. The economy had just begun to recover. Following Bethlehem's modernization, steel production in Buffalo, at 90 percent of total capacity, was at a record high. Factory wages, averaging $28.85 per week in early 1937, were finally back to their 1927 level. Factory employment, meanwhile, was higher than during any year since 1927. Workers were understandably reluctant to jeopardize their recently acquired status by joining a union. The Depression, while over in the minds of many, was still vivid. Besides, ever since the steel strike of 1919, the steel industry had taken harsh measures to discourage unionism. Yellow-dog contracts, effective company unions, and a notorious company police force had deterred organization activities at both Bethlehem and Republic. No inroads had ever been made at local automobile plants.[17] Workers, thus, were afraid of unions, afraid for their jobs, and thankful for what they had.

Indeed, as had been true in Detroit and Flint, it was difficult for the CIO organizers to find grievances. Wages, between $12 and $15 per day in steel and auto plants, were far better than in other industries. There had also been vast improvement in hours worked. Both Bethlehem and Republic had instituted the eight-hour day and five-day workweek in the late 1920s. While automobile workers tended to work longer hours, most of them welcomed this as a cushion against the layoffs that occurred annually as companies shut down their plants to prepare production for the coming year. Thus, local steel workers and autoworkers were in no rush to join the Steel Workers Organizing Committee (SWOC) and the United Auto Workers (UAW). With no help from local organized labor—the American Federation of Labor (AFL) in Buffalo refused to cooperate with the CIO—and with fear of company reprisals keeping most of the workers away, the CIO organizing drive bogged down. When a premature and badly organized strike of steelworkers was called in April 1937, it was easily and effectively squashed by a combination of worker apathy and company policemen.[18]

The real problem with the steel strike of 1937, and indeed the larger problem of the CIO in Buffalo, was that its radical leadership simply did not reflect the characteristics and the ideology of the local workforce. Following the strike of 1937, Marxist leadership, particularly strong among the SWOC, was now seen as an obstacle to organizing the rank and file. Once it realized that organized labor needed different friends if it was to survive in Buffalo, the CIO began to purge Communists from local leadership positions. The CIO suddenly abandoned its support of the Marxist Labor Institute, which had dominated labor education in Buffalo since the early 1930s, and, in a complete about-face, joined the bishop of Buffalo in sponsoring the Catholic Labor College. The CIO's campaign for respectability took yet another turn when in 1940 it stopped efforts to organize a separate labor party and instead forged an alliance with local Democrats, which has lasted to this day.[19]

With the Catholic Church and the Democrats in their camp, the CIO found success. By early 1941, organizers for the SWOC had penetrated Bethlehem and completely undermined the company union. In February, they called a strike. With the support of the bishop, who extolled them from the pulpit, the mayor, who refused to grant police protection to strikebreakers, and the president of the United States, who threatened to cancel Bethlehem's defense contracts unless the company dealt with the union, the SWOC prevailed. Later that year, Republic Steel also recognized the SWOC, and GM bestowed recognition on the UAW. While the CIO certainly deserved much of the credit for the triumph of industrial unionism in Buffalo, it was clear to everyone that without the support of the church and the federal government, the victory would never have been theirs. Besides, industry could afford to be in a giving mood, for by late 1939 and early 1940, war in Europe had led to a dramatic improvement in the economy in Buffalo, as in the rest of the nation. Business in Buffalo turned a handspring in 1939.

It was perhaps the sudden buoyancy in the local economy that fed a growing optimism in the world of culture and the arts. In the late 1920s, the torch of modernism in Buffalo had been passed to Seymour Knox Jr., who, from 1926, when he first joined its board, to his death in 1990, was the most influential figure in Buffalo's progressive and uniquely modern cultural life. Knox, whose father had made his first fortune by parlaying his five and dime store into the F. W. Woolworth chain (he made his second as president of Marine Trust Bank), was a committed advocate of all that was modern in all of the arts. Knox aggressively built on the modernist tradition established by his predecessors at the gallery, taking a leadership position there and assertively pushing it to the forefront of American modernism. From the time of his first acquisition in 1927, when he purchased the gallery's first Matissse, *A Late Afternoon Glimpse of Notre Dame*, to his last in 1989, Knox was one of the century's most creative benefactors of the modern arts.[20] It was Knox's lifelong enthusiasm and support for modern art in all its forms that, more than anything, enabled Buffalo to become, by the mid-1960s, one of the world's great centers of modern art. Under Knox and the new curator, Gordon B. Washburn, who became director at the age of twenty-seven in 1931, the Albright became a committed bastion of modernism. In addition, despite Goodyear's stormy departure from Buffalo, he and Knox stayed in close contact throughout the 1930s, forging a long-lasting relationship between the MoMA and the Albright.

Under Knox, the relationship between Buffalo's Albright and New York's Museum of Modern Art became closer. A growing number of shows and expositions at the Albright were curated by the MoMA—a Matisse drawing show in 1933; an "Art of Today" show in 1936; and a retrospective photography show in 1937. The MoMA sent speakers, too, and soon the leading lights of global modernism were making their way to Buffalo and the Albright. The following is a list of those who came and the topics they discussed:

Frank Lloyd Wright, "Modern Architecture" (November 1932)
Maurice Sachs, "Modern Art in Europe" (March 1933)
Lewis Mumford, "The Machine and its Influence" (November 1934)
William Lescaze, "Functional Architecture" (November 1935)
Iris Barry, "On Liking the Wrong Movie" (March 1937)
Henry A. Lappin, "The Greatest of the Arts: Poetry" (March 1938)
Walter Behrendt, "Modern Architecture" (October 1938)
Walter Gropius, "The True Sources of Modern Architecture" (January 1941)[21]

Knox and Washburn were concerned not to push their modernist agenda too hard. Knox, particularly, was sensitive to the ostracism that had followed Goodyear's effort (which had been perceived by many as forced feeding) to wean a conservative community away from tastes that had been so long in the making. Intent on their mission, yet fearful of failure, they created a structure for the development of modern art at the Albright that would insulate them from the more conservative tastes of their peers. They would, they announced in January 1939, create a room of contemporary art "dedicated to the continuous display of contemporary art," which would personally be controlled by Knox. Funded with $100,000 from the Knox Family, the Contemporary Room would be administered by a special committee responsible not to the board but, rather, to the president of the Fine Arts Academy, an office filled by Knox himself from 1939 until 1975. Knox and Washburn advised both the board and the public that the Contemporary Room would, by definition, be "contemporary and experimental." Their project created a visionary path for the Albright, which has guided it into the next century.[22]

The first show in the Contemporary Room comprised works that were lent by the premier galleries of New York and Europe. It featured dozens of the world's leading modern artists, including Matisse, Picasso, Derain, Klee, Braque, Modigliani, Kollwitz, Hopper, Prendergast, Marin, and others. The show attracted thousands of people over the course of a month and brought A. Conger Goodyear back to the gallery for the first time since he left ten years earlier. He was thrilled at how far the Albright had come and, in an introduction to the show's catalog that Seymour Knox had invited him to write, Goodyear who, like Knox, identified personally with the goals and objectives of modernism, stated: "Modern art is a free art, an expression of the genius of men and women who refuse to be bound to a meticulous and slavish imitation of their ancestors."[23]

Modernism, however, was not limited to the Contemporary Room. In the spring of 1939, the Albright featured an exhibition of twentieth-century "Banned German Art," with works from the greatest German Expressionists, including Beckmann, Ernst, Feininger, Grosz, Klee, and Lehmbruck. In 1940, Washburn's last year at the Albright, the gallery showed "Sixty American Paintings from the Whitney," including Bellow, Burchfield, and such leading modernists as Kunyioshi, Gorky, Marsh, Soyer, and Prendergast. Together, Washburn and Knox pushed the Albright to embrace architecture as well. Not only did the leading lights of modern architecture lecture at the gallery but significant architectural shows were also held during Washburn's tenure. One, curated by the MoMA in 1939, dealt with "Three Centuries of American Architecture." The subject of the other, which was Washburn's last show at the gallery and which was curated by the great architectural historian Henry Russell Hitchcock, focused on "Buffalo Architecture, 1816–1940."[24]

As a result of Knox's eye for the new and different, the Albright became one of the first museums in the country to acquire the works of two unknown African American painters: Horace Pippin, whose haunting self-portrait was purchased by Knox in 1941, and Jacob Lawrence, whose shadowy watercolor of blacks riding the New York subway (titled *Going to Work*) was bought by Knox in 1944. But it was Washburn's and Knox's acquisitions of contemporary art—seventy-five major purchases, including works by Soutine, Roualt, Modigliani, Roualt, Derain, Redon, Chagall, Miro, Leger, and others—that had, by the time of Washburn's departure in 1940, created growing national attention toward the Albright as a center of modern art.

By the end of the 1930s, Buffalo had become one of the country's most innovative cities for music. The local music world was the beneficiary of Cameron Baird, one of the city's wealthiest and most successful businessmen. Like so many families in Buffalo, the Baird family's wealth was rooted in iron and steel. Baird descended from a long line of iron manufacturers who could trace their origins in the business to the 1820s. Cameron's great-grandfather built the first blast furnace west of the Alleghenies at Bush Creek, Ohio, in 1829. His grandfather, Samuel Baird, built the first blast furnace in Hocking Valley, Ohio. His father, Frank B. Baird, was born in Marietta, Ohio, in 1852 and followed his father and his grandfather into the pig iron business. Working at first for his father and then for Hanna Furnace in Cleveland, in 1888, Baird, like so many ambitious men of his day, moved to Buffalo, which was a rapidly growing center of economic opportunity. One of the first to use coke for the making of iron, Baird's business expanded rapidly and, by the early 1890s, he owned three iron foundries along the Niagara River in Tonawanda. In 1900, he combined them to create the largest foundry in the city, the Buffalo Union Furnace Company. Baird, like the great industrial titans of the day, had grand visions for himself and for his community. He recognized early on the importance of the Pan-American Exposition and was one of its most active directors, working aggressively to use the exposition as a way to better the opportunities for his adopted city. Baird was closely involved in the planning of the bridge across the Niagara River that would eventually link Canada and the United States at Buffalo. By 1927, Baird's dream was realized when, as president of the Peace Bridge Company, he joined members of the British royal family at the opening ceremony of the Peace Bridge. His son, Cameron, meanwhile, had just moved back to Buffalo after graduating from Williams College and, in 1927, he and his brother William founded the Buffalo Pipe and Foundry Corporation, a company that specialized in the manufacture of sewer pipe.[25]

Cameron Baird was passionate not about steel but about music. As a high school student at the Nichols School, he had formed the school's orchestra. In the late 1920s, he was one of the founders of the Buffalo Chamber Music Society and, in 1930, he began to conduct the Buffalo Oratorio. In the early 1930s, he traveled to Europe regularly, studying conducting in Salzburg with Bruno Walter and composition in Paris with Nadie Boulanger and in Berlin with Paul Hindemith. He was particularly close to Hindemith, and when that giant of twentieth-century music was forced out of Hitler's Germany, Baird arranged for his immigration to and settlement in Buffalo, where he stayed for more than a year, lecturing on music at the University of Buffalo, before going on to Yale.

Hindemith was a friend of another famous German refugee then living in Buffalo, the architect Walter C. Behrendt. On March 13, 1938, Hindemith, under the sponsorship of Cameron Baird's Chamber Music Society, performed several of his works at a recital at the Nichols School, with Behrendt's wife as accompanist. It was in Europe, too, that Baird first heard the Budapest String Quartet, one of the great young string quartets in Europe. Baird arranged for them to visit Buffalo where, on January 12, 1931, they gave a recital for the Buffalo Chamber Music Society. The Budapest immediately became a mainstay of the Buffalo music scene—they performed in Buffalo at least once a year here through the mid-1960s.[26] And in 1962, they became the resident string ensemble at UB.

With his regular returns from Europe to Buffalo throughout the 1930s, Baird remained closely involved with the city's varied and exciting music scene, particularly the Chamber Music Society, which Baird had helped found. Baird, however, was particularly concerned about the status of the symphony orchestra, which, by the middle 1930s, had fallen into flux. In 1934, Baird patched together the outlines of what would soon become the Buffalo Philharmonic Orchestra. Working closely with Fredrick Slee, Baird's lawyer and an accomplished violinist, and Samuel P. Capen, the chancellor of UB, Baird brought Lajos Shuk, a cello virtuoso and director of the New York Civic Symphony to Buffalo and formed an orchestra of seventy local musicians, all paid for by the WPA. Shortly thereafter, the Buffalo Philharmonic Orchestra Society was founded and a series of light concerts was presented during the 1935–36 season. With the outlines of the fledgling orchestra in place, Baird was eager to ensure a dedicated source of funds. He thus formed the Buffalo Philharmonic Society, the purpose of which was to raise supplementary funds for the Philharmonic. When in 1939 Baird was informed that federal funding for the symphony was to cease immediately, he personally provided the $10,000 necessary to pay the musicians. With his funds in addition to those raised by the society, a conductor named Franco Autori from the Dallas Symphony was brought to Buffalo to conduct what was now known as the Buffalo Philharmonic Orchestra.[27] Soon, they would have a new music hall.

What Seymour Knox and Cameron Baird were doing for the arts in the 1930s, Thomas B. Lockwood, a leading member of Buffalo's bar, was doing for the world of letters. Fascinated by the world of books, Lockwood had, by the early 1930s, assembled a collection of more than three thousand volumes, one of the best-known collections of rare books and first editions in the country. Like so many collectors of his generation, Lockwood followed the Grolier's Club list of "One Hundred Books Famous in the English Language," collecting in the process some of the great works of English literature in their most prized editions: the 1590 and 1595 editions of Spenser's *Faerie Queene*, the four seventeenth-century folios of Shakespeare; the two volumes of the collected works of Ben Jonson (1616, 1640); as well as first editions of *Paradise Lost* (1667), Johnson's *Dictionary of the English Language* (1755), Shelley's *Prometheus Unbound* (1820), and the novels of Sir Walter Scott. Lockwood's first editions of American authors were some of the most prized: Melville's *Moby Dick*, Whitman's *Leaves of Grass*, and Hawthorne's *Scarlet Letter*. In 1935, he donated all of these books, as well as $700,000, to UB for the construction of the Lockwood Memorial Library. His choice to direct the new library was Charles D. Abbott, an English professor who had taught at UB in the late 1920s and had gone from there to the University of Colorado.[28]

Charles Abbott wanted to collect but knew that the kind of collection Lockwood had created was no longer possible. Nonetheless, Abbott, an adventuresome and radical risk taker, was eager to make a name for his new library as a center of something that was daring, exciting, and modern. He began to concentrate on his first love: poetry, particularly contemporary poetry. His plan for what he called simply "the poetry project" was clear and narrowly focused: to build a library devoted exclusively to the first editions of twentieth-century English-language poetry. This was a bold and creative decision made at a time when contemporary poetry was anathema in the academic world, where, it was said that the only good poet is a dead poet. Few studied contemporary poetry, few wrote about it, and even fewer collected it. The world of contemporary poetry was controversial and virgin territory, and by collecting it, Abbott planned to create a unique role for the new library at UB. Abbott was a persuasive man and was able to convince Lockwood, whose collecting habits had been traditional, of the value of the poetry project. Thus, in 1937, with great enthusiasm and commitment, Thomas Lockwood and Charles Abbott announced the establishment of the poetry collection at the University of Buffalo library.[29]

Abbott's vision had a tremendous impact on both the university and the community, transforming the former into one of the country's great centers of contemporary poetry and raising for the latter a higher profile, which placed Buffalo at the epicenter of modern art and ideas. Nothing better describes the passion and excitement of Abbott's poetry project than Abbott's own colorful account of its origins:

> It was October 1935. Modern poetry it was to be. The first order went out for books: T. S. Eliot, Robert Frost, Edith Sitwell, Elinor Wylie, W. B. Yeats, whatever appeared in the booksellers' list at considerate prices. The financial limitation was severe.... Small funds could be raised, however, through an organization of the library's friends. They were enough for a modest beginning. We would endeavor

to build, piece by piece, a collection of books which would include every text by a twentieth-century poet writing in English.... In this one field we would construct a bibliographer's paradise and, what is more important, provide the textual and interpretive scholar of later generations with what his counterpart of today can seldom consult in one library: the whole sequential body of a poet's printed work. Whoever the Wordsworth or the Coleridge of our age may turn out to be, his de Selincout or Lowes may hope to find on our shelves the sources for his study.[30]

As an English professor, Abbott had been as interested in the creative process as he was in the finished product. He was fascinated by poetry and the creative contortions that poets experienced in the process of writing their works. "Suppose," he wondered, "the world really possessed the beginnings of poems, the rough drafts, records of all changes of mind?" As an educator as well as a collector, he wanted the poetry collection to serve as a resource for generations of future students eager to learn about poetry's creative process. "This was," he continued, with his typical energy and passion, "a thought that has never left me and this library, thanks to Tom Lockwood's understandings, is the development of that thought." What Abbott wanted was to preserve the material development of a poem from its first fragments to its final published form—"the whole sequential body of a poet's printed work." He needed, therefore, the working elements, the shards, scraps, and detritus that comprised the fitful starts, the changes of mind, the gradual flow of work that eventually became the finished poem. "Manuscripts!" he wrote:

> We needed manuscripts if we were to help the scholar in his struggle to penetrate towards the core of the puzzle; if our projects were to assist in the pushing back of the barriers that obstruct knowledge; if the beam of light were to be turned full upon 'l'action qui fait'... manuscripts—not "fair copies," not the neat and pretty simulacra of a poem in the best behaved handwriting... [but] all the tangible sheets a poet uses in making a poem. Something like that might give the theorist real bricks and mortar.[31]

To get these source materials, he wrote hundreds of letters to poets, booksellers, and publishers, asking them to send him anything and everything they had. He asked them to "empty the contents of their waste baskets" and send him the scraps. In one letter, Abbott, ever the salesman for his poetry project, described his mission and purpose with typical exuberance: "Our collection," he said, "achieves its full authority from the manuscripts which are being contributed by the poets themselves. These, in their best form, consist of rough drafts, trial versions, transitional stages, etc.... Since such materials constitute a kind of case history of the poets' mind in action, they are likely to be of considerable value to future scholars."

Ever proud, Abbott concluded what became his standard letter with praise for the project: "The Lockwood Collection," he said, "has become one of the most important extant collections of English and American manuscript stuff since 1900 and we are more anxious than I can tell you to persuade you to send in materials."

According to Abbott, the responses began pouring in: "[P]oets, with some exceptions, are a gracious, indulgent, amenable breed of men. They did read their letters." Some sent mocking responses, especially to Abbott's persistent request for worksheets. Why, one English poet wrote, would Abbott want "worksheets which had probably been used to jam the bathroom door and prevent it from becoming open in a high wind?" Sometimes, veritable treasures appeared: "Most thrilling of all," Abbott said, was "a collection of material from Genevieve Taggard so complete, so detailed, so exhaustive, that almost no footprint of the mind was lost in the record; materials that conveyed, like nothing I had ever seen before, the sense of excitement, of agonizing growth, that accompanies invention." By 1938, Abbott had received letters, notebooks, printed books, and worksheets from such contemporary poets as T. S. Eliot, John Crow Ransom, Marianne Moore, W. B. Yeats, Stephen Spender, W. H. Auden, Gertrude Stein, Edith Sitwell, and Wallace Stevens, who responded to Abbott's solicitation by sending him the working manuscript of his signature poem "The Man with the Blue Guitar."

With the support of Capen, who arranged for a $1,500 grant from the Carnegie Corporation (Capen was a master at securing grants, even during the driest years of the Great Depression), Abbott and his wife, Theresa, took a three-month tour of Europe, with stops in Scotland, Ireland, and Paris, to meet with poets and acquire their manuscripts. Abbott wrote about his journey with great energy and good humor, describing how his landlady was somewhat disapproving of the gaggle of raggedy poets who made their way to her house to visit the Abbotts. Soon, Abbott reported, she caught on and "would even go so far as to suggest special foods that visiting poets might appreciate."[32]

"The flux of poets at Ebury Street was steady," Abbott wrote, and no visit was more interesting or more productive than that of Stephen Spender, who came for lunch. "I've got just what you want," Spender informed Abbott before presenting a work-a-day, functional volume that "contained nearly all the poems of his 1933 collection." According to Abbott, it was

one of the significant poetic achievements of the decade. Each poem was there in a completeness that staggered the eye: version after version, false starts and blind alleys, phrase groping for content, metrical filings, images jostling each other in the rush to finality. It was an experience just to examine it, an irresistible absorption into the process of the imaginative creation. It was the real right thing, without any qualification—perhaps the nearest possible approach to the fury and the pain of "making."[33]

Abbott's return to Buffalo at the end of April 1938 was noteworthy enough to be covered by the *Buffalo Evening News*, which trumpeted his arrival: "Just returned from England, Charles D. Abbott, librarian of the Lockwood Memorial Library at the University of Buffalo, disclosed today that he has collected manuscripts, notes and books from one hundred and twenty English poets making the Lockwood Library the only depository in the world for this collection of material of modern poetry." The *News* continued in detail, unusual for a news item concerning poetry: "In three months in England Mr. Abbott, accompanied by his wife, obtained manuscripts, notes and other original drafts of some of the most famous English work." The securing of Robert Bridges' "Testament of Beauty" particularly impressed the *News*. Lockwood, the *News* boasted, "is the only library in the world with any of the late poet laureate's manuscripts." By the time of Abbott's 1938 return, an overwhelming number of manuscripts had been delivered to his office at Lockwood. After yet another purchasing trip—"on this trip through the Middle West, Californian and several southern states, I expect to contact 150 to 200 poets, including twenty to twenty-five in California"—Abbott desperately sought an assistant, someone with great instincts about poetry. At the recommendation of his brother, John, he soon found the person he was looking for.

Abbott and his wife, Theresa, lived at his wife's family home—Gratwick Estate—a large, somewhat dilapidated home situated on several hundred wilderness acres in the Genesee River valley, about fifty miles from Buffalo. It was, one regular visitor reported, "another of those big estates with several houses inhabited by different members of the (Gratwick) family but in this case all of the money was gone."[34] The Abbotts were casual and expansive hosts and, according to those who remember, there were always large numbers of houseguests, people who, like William Carlos Williams, would come for the weekend and stay for weeks. Among those who regularly visited Charles and Theresa Abbott were his brother John and his wife, Iris Barry, who lived in New York City.[35]

The Abbotts were intrigued by Barry, who was widely known and respected in the late 1920s as a film critic. She was one of a handful of people in the world who believed that film was an important art form. Alfred Barr, the founding director of the Museum of Modern Art, knew of her work and encouraged both Iris and her husband John to join him at the MoMA, with John as director and Iris as curator of the first film department in museum history. A. Conger Goodyear, MoMA's first president, agreed, but "because it is highly unusual to consider films as art or as a medium worth preserving," he urged Barr not to publicize his intentions until after the film department was up and running. The Rockefellers supported Barry's vision and, in 1935, with a grant of $120,000 from their foundation, Iris Barry and John Abbott accepted the offer.[36]

Like her brother-in-law, Charles, who, alone among his colleagues in Buffalo, recognized the value of collecting and preserving the work of contemporary poets and writers, Iris Barry recognized that film would soon be regarded as the great artistic medium of the age. Like Abbott's first editions, films needed to be collected, preserved, cataloged, and inventoried. In 1936, John Abbott and Iris Barry, in a trip that anticipated by two years the one taken by Charles and Theresa, went to Europe to purchase as many silent and avant-garde films as they could find. Driven by their mission, in the fall of 1937, they co-taught a pioneering course called The Film as Art at the Columbia University Extension.

The contribution that John Abbott and Iris Barry made to film is significant but little known. Prior to the founding of the film library at the Museum of Modern Art in 1935, there were no film archives, no film exhibitions, no "art" theaters, and no film societies. The Abbotts's notion that original films, like the musings and throwaway drafts of contemporary poets, could possibly be considered the building blocks of art and therefore worthy of preservation was truly visionary. It is no wonder that Barry's efforts appealed to Charles, the newly appointed director of the Lockwood Memorial Library. Thus, in 1935, the year that MoMA opened its film department, Abbott organized the Buffalo Film Society. Using a press release that his brother had given him from the MoMA, Abbott crossed out the words "Museum of Modern Art" and replaced them with "The Buffalo Film Society" and announced the formation of "an organization which will sponsor showings of those moving pictures from the past, both foreign and American, which are important historically or aesthetically. Its aim," Abbott continued, "is primarily educational and its hope is that it may foster a new and intelligent interest in the film as a medium of artistic expression."[37]

Cosponsored by the Albright Art Gallery, where Gordon Washburn and Seymour H. Knox were eager to push the gallery to the forefront of modernism, the Film Society's first event was a lecture by Iris Barry on March 10, 1936, titled "Why We Like the Wrong Movies." The first series, offered in the fall of 1936 and shown at the Elmwood Theatre, featured the most daring European films. The series opened with the 1919 German film titled *The Cabinet of Dr. Caligari*, which was being "shown for the first time in its entirety in America." Others shown that first year were *The Love of Jeanne Ney*, a 1927 film by German director G. W. Pabst; Emil Jannings's 1924 film called *The Last Mile*; René Clair's first film, *Paris qui Dort*, made in 1923; and *Etoile de Mer*, described by Abbott as "an advance guard film directed in France in 1928 by the distinguished American photographer Man Ray."

Abbott, who seemed to spend his days writing solicitous letters to poets and writers all over England and the United States, now began to write to university presidents and academic colleagues, imploring them to support the film project. To J. D. Bennett, president of Sweet Briar College, he wrote: "Are you at all, either historically or aesthetically, interested in movies? If so, I want to bring to your attention a scheme which I think has many possibilities." To the president of Swarthmore College he wrote: "I am pestering you with this letter because it is my brother who is attempting for the Museum of Modern Art to organize the whole scheme (the film project) and because I feel very strongly that there ought to be in every college community some means for the preservation of historically important old pictures and new foreign pictures which communal interests never find it worth their while to preserve."[38]

John and Iris Abbott visited Charles and Theresa regularly at Gratwick Estates. It was during one of those visits in the summer of 1939 that Charles, who had been increasingly overwhelmed by the steady flow of manuscripts, asked his brother and sister-in-law if they knew anyone who would be willing to become his assistant in charge of the ever growing and disorganized poetry project. As fortune would have it, they'd met a woman earlier that year, a friend, they said, of Ezra Pound, who had brought her to see them at the MoMA in the hope that she might find a job there. Her name, they said, was Mary Bernard and, according to Pound, she was a poet. Bernard, who lived in New York City and was friendly with Pound, Marianne Moore, William Carlos Williams, and other local poets was, according to the Abbott's, eager for work. Charles Abbott was curious and, in the summer of 1939, he invited Bernard to come to Buffalo to begin work as the first curator of what had by then come to be called the poetry collection. She was thrilled, and recounted later that "within one or two sentences casually spoken, Pound had made the connection between me and the one job in the country that I was suited for."[39] Bernard was inspired by Abbott's vision and his passionate mission to collect materials that would enable students to study the creative process of contemporary writers and poets. She recognized the radicalism of his work and knew that "no self-respecting scholar would waste his time on living writers." "Most American professors," she wrote, "including those at the University of Buffalo," thought such work "strange, not to say scandalous." Abbott himself recognized the loneliness of the task, she said; he believed that the poetry collection would come to be recognized for its significance "perhaps in a hundred years."

Bernard's tenure as curator of the poetry collection, which lasted until 1943, was fruitful. Her presence freed Abbott to spread his missionary zeal, and enabled him, with Bernard's assistance, to teach a course at UB in the fall of 1939 called "A New and Experimental Course in British and American Poetry," for which he used the manuscripts, notebooks, and workbooks that he had collected. He was proud of his groundbreaking work and proclaimed it in his course description: "Since the materials are not fair and final copies, but genuine trial notes, rough drafts, corrected copies and run down scrawls bearing on poems, the student will get closer to the creative mechanism of the artists than the reader of the final printed copy ever could."[40]

Abbott was proud also of the readings that were held in the wood-paneled surroundings of his office in Lockwood, where a small and carefully chosen assembly of the wealthy wives of Buffalo, upon whom Abbott came increasingly to count for support, were invited to attend readings by Robinson Jeffers, May Sarton, Alfred Noyes, William Carlos Williams, Leonara Speyer, and Louis Untermeyer. On his early 1942 visit, Untermeryer brought as a gift to the collection letters from Amy Lowell, Vachel Lindsay, and Sara Teasdale. When William Carlos Williams came to Buffalo later in the year, recalled Bernard, he brought, "to my surprise, a big carton full of letters.... I think we now have most all of the Williams letters."[41]

In 1939, Wyndham Lewis, the great but highly erratic English painter and writer whom Abbott had befriended in London, also came to Buffalo in the hope of finding work as a portrait painter of Buffalo's "smart set." Bernard was assigned the task of squiring the petulant, opinionated artist. Although commissioned by Samuel Capen to paint his portrait, Lewis did little other work in Buffalo. He did, however, write a novel called *America, I Presume*, about an English author traveling through the country. The book, housed in the poetry collection, describes Buffalo in scathing terms, using the name "Nineveh" and describing the "Ninevites" in the intense, critical way that could be expected from a debauched and barely sober English writer. (While Lewis's descriptions of "Ninevah" are sophomoric and not particularly interesting, his book contains a lyrical description of the effect created by the elms along Delaware Avenue. The view, he wrote,

> is unexpectedly attractive. "A city in a wood," it is called.... As I looked down on it from a tall hotel, in the autumn, I saw nothing but a copper ocean of foliage, in which the broken peaks of houses were submerged. It was as if one were looking down upon the Bois de Boulogne, in which a piece of Paris, or of some Dutch city, had been planted. And down below, beneath the trees, it is likewise a place of great urbanity.[42]

Bernard, too, wrote about Buffalo in unflattering terms:

> Beside the snow, the wind and the cold, there was the ice underfoot all winter long.... Crutches, slings and plaster casts abounded on the campus. During the frequent blizzards pedestrians clung to ropes stretched on downtown streets. The combination of ice and wind made it almost impossible to stand up, let alone proceed without the assistance of ropes.[13]

But more than the weather, it was the people she met, and in particular the well-to-do social set with whom Abbott surrounded himself, that she did not like. She was put off by what she felt was a disconcerting formality and superficiality. She described a cocktail party that she'd been invited to on December 7, 1941. Stunned by the Japanese attack on Pearl Harbor, she was flabbergasted that the event was mentioned by not one of the guests. She wrote that she herself brought it up but was dismayed by what she sensed was their lack of interest. "I was made to feel that I had introduced an unsuitable subject into the conversation," she wrote. Puzzled beyond comprehension, she left the party convinced that she would "never, never understand Buffalo." She did feel, however, "that it might make a good setting for a murder mystery."[44]

Bernard loved her work, however, and was very good at it. During her stay at the poetry collection, she had gone a long way toward realizing Abbott's lofty expectations. By 1945, the poetry collection boasted more than ten thousand printed books, including first editions by every living English and American poet, three thousand sets of poets' worksheets, twenty-five hundred letters, and three hundred fifty literary magazines, including the *Little Review*, the *Hound and the Horn*, the *Savoy*, the *Chap Book*, and more. The prodigious letter writing and peregrinations of Abbott and Bernard had also brought to the collection such gems as Pound's *El Lume Spento*, Yeats's *The Wandering Oisin*, Dylan Thomas's *18 Poems*, Wallace Stevens's *Harmonium*, T. S. Eliot's *The Wasteland*, and the collected poems of Marianne Moore. Together, the two had created one of the world's great depositories of modern poetry. In 1943, Bernard left the poetry collection, intensely proud of the work she had done.[45]

The 1930s were, as we have seen, important years in the development of modern art in Buffalo, a period when patterns and traditions in music, art, and architecture were shattered, and when new directions were created, which placed Buffalo at the center of the world of contemporary art and culture. In 1937, Cameron Baird returned from Europe, poised to introduce to Buffalo audiences the sounds of modern music. In January of 1938, Charles Abbott began his path-breaking journey to Europe in quest of modern manuscripts for his fast-budding poetry project. One year later, the Albright Art Gallery announced the opening of Seymour Knox's Room of Contemporary Art. And in the middle of it all, Eliel Saarinen, one of a new generation of European modern architects, was hired to design the new Kleinhans Music Hall.

Like the arrival in Buffalo of Charles Abbott, the choice of Saarinen to design the new music hall was a momentous event in the cultural and intellectual life of the community. While Buffalonians became, like most Americans, increasingly aware of the powerful modern movement that was sweeping Europe, no building designed in the modern style had been built in the city since the completion of Frank Lloyd Wright's Martin House in 1905. While there were plenty of modern ideas—indeed, during the 1930s the great exponents of a modernist ethic in architecture, including Frank Lloyd Wright, Lewis Mumford, Walter Behrendt, Mies van der Rohe, and Walter Gropius, had each delivered lectures at the Albright—there were no modern buildings. Thus, when in 1934 the last will and testament of Edward L. and Mary Seaton Kleinhans left close to a million dollars for the construction of a new music hall in the city of Buffalo, most people assumed that the job would go to the city's favorite architect, Edward B. Green. Green was the architect's architect, and since the end of the nineteenth century his firm had designed countless homes, churches, schools, and public facilities in whatever was the fashionable style of the day. Designs for Romanesque churches, Sullivanesque office buildings, Richardson-like private homes, and neoclassical post offices and halls were churned out of the office in what, during a sixty-year career that began in 1890, must surely have been one of the longest and, in terms of its impact on one city, most influential architectural practices in the country. Indeed, shortly after the Kleinhans' bequest was made known, Green submitted a design in 1935 for the construction of a music hall, a large neoclassical structure that he would have attached to the Museum of Science in Humboldt Park. Green's design, which combined elements of Symphony Hall in Boston and Severance Hall in Cleveland, was heavy-handed and predictable.

Within a year, however, the location for the new hall had been resolved. While there had been proposals for a site in Humboldt Park and at the Rose Garden in Delaware Park, there was little inclination by either city officials or the Buffalo Foundation, the Kleinhans' executors, to use park land for the new concert hall. The problem was resolved when, in late 1935, the Buffalo Foundation received as a gift from the family of Truman Avery the site of his Newport-like mansion on the circle at Richmond and Porter avenues. While Avery's magnificent home was being demolished, the foundation continued its search for an architect. George F. Rand, the chairman of the Buffalo Foundation, liked the work of Kidd and Kidd, a local architectural firm headed by two brothers F. J. and William Kidd. The Kidds were Rand family architects, having designed several homes for the family as well as the Rand Building (1929), a large office tower located on Lafayette Square in downtown Buffalo, which served as the headquarters of the Marine Trust. In May of 1938, the Kidds were hired as the architects of the new music hall. The applecart was quickly upset, however, when about one month later, Edward P. Letchworth, the lawyer for the Buffalo Foundation, casually showed Kidd's drawings to another of his clients, a woman named Esther Link. When asked what she thought, Link winced in horror and said, "You really want to know? I think it is a disaster."[46]

The plan for the hall showed a forbidding fortress-like structure, which, with six pilasters marching down the large limestone face, each topped with portraits of great composers, resembled a Depression-era city hall or post office. Esther Link was appalled. While Link had no formal knowledge of architecture, she was well educated and self-confident. She'd traveled widely (her resume mentions trips to many European capitals) and she was proud of her experience as both a high school music teacher and as vice president at Pitt Petri, a high-end retailer of expensive house wares and accessories, where she handled all construction and remodeling issues. On her resume, she wrote that she had had "[e]xperience in working with architects, artists, artisans, in connection with the decorating of the various shops here and in New York. Also in developing items for the shop with the manufacturers and artists."[47] She had learned much, her resume suggested, from her father, "a foreman of interior carpenters for builders and various other mills who worked on the interior of churches, banks and pretentious homes." In addition, she had attended talks by architects at the Albright and had traveled widely in Europe, coming quickly to the realization that there was a whole new world of modern European architecture of which Americans knew little. She was a particularly ardent admirer of the work of Eliel Saarinen, whose design of a central railroad terminal in Helsinki had made a strong impression on her. It was this lofty, bold, and strikingly modern structure that she thought of when she so imperiously dismissed the Kidd design that Letchworth had shown her. Letchworth listened and asked if she would not mind putting her thoughts in writing.

Link enthusiastically complied with Letchworth's request and, in a letter written in July of 1938, she expressed passionately her ideas about architecture. While she recognized the unlikely possibility of their selecting an architect from out of town, Link, in her long and rambling letter, said that if the choice was hers, she would go to Frank Lloyd Wright and "to the Swiss, Lescares [*sic*] (however he spells himself) anyway the Swiss architect who put up that famous modern building in Philadelphia." (Link was referring to William Lescaze and the modern Philadelphia Savings Fund Society building he had designed in 1932.) You may have heard him," she wrote Letchworth, "at the Art Gallery...excellent." Link wrote about architectural principles, making it clear that she favored a design that was "indisputably original and creative." It must not be, she said, referring to the designs of Green, Kidd, and the other Buffalo architects who had submitted drawings, "a cross between Greek classical and someone's vague impressions of 'modernistic.'" Once the best and not necessarily most expensive architect is chosen, "I should let the architect brood over it all until he hatched out a plan that would," she urged in the language of a convinced modernist, "provide for everything so that the building will result in great unity, a kind of inevitability and great beauty." Anticipating the kind of public reaction that this type of design would provoke, she urged Letchworth to stand fast: "Then I would devote myself to helping the architect achieve those results, warding off all chisellers, all faint hearted, would be modifiers, etc., etc....A hard and ungrateful task." Even then, she wrote, the worst was still to come. "Then I would steel myself against the critics and all conservatives who wondered how Mr. Letchworth could so far have forgotten his usual good taste to sponsor such a monstrosity."[48] Link's letter made a strong impression on Letchworth, who now asked her to make a detailed presentation to Rand and Philip Wickser, another foundation board member. Link was well prepared, and brought to the meeting photographs of Saarinen's work in Helsinki, particularly her beloved railroad station, as well as pictures of the campus that Saarinen had just completed for the Cranbook School in Bloomfield Hills, Michigan. The men, impressed as much by Link's passion as by Saarinen's design, began to hedge on their commitment to Kidd. Shortly after the July 1938 meeting with Link, the board of the Buffalo Foundation supported Letchworth's motion to "endeavor to secure Eliel Saarinen as consultant on architectural plans." Saarinen, however, declined the position as consultant, saying that it would quickly lead him to become the "insultant." In the meantime, Letchworth, who was moving in his own mind toward Saarinen, was concerned about undermining Rand's favorite architect. In September 1938, he diplomatically invited Kidd to join him on a trip to visit Eliel and his son Eero Saarinen at their home in Cranbrook, Michigan. Letchworth loved the visit and was moved and impressed by the strikingly modernist but warm campus of the Cranbrook School. Upon his return, he met with Rand and Wickser in an effort to find a way to hire Saarinen without offending Kidd. It was decided that the Kidd firm, with money provided by the foundation, would employ Saarinen as the "designing architect" while the Kidds would be charged with supervising construction.[49]

Meanwhile, Saarinen worked quickly and, one month later, he submitted his design. It was simple and organic and followed Sullivan's iconic adage of modernism that form must follow function. "As a concert auditorium is," Saarinen said, "to its innermost nature a musical instrument . . . its formation must derive accordingly. . . . Metaphorically speaking," he continued, "the concert hall, by means of its form, must be part of that music played within its walls."[50] In attempting to capture in his building the spiritual essence of music, Saarinen had set a lofty goal for himself—this was, he said, "the spiritual program of the design work."

Saarinen's thoughts on this subject are important in that they help us understand the continued beauty and appeal of his magnificent hall. For Saarinen "the shape and character of the main auditorium were conceived as a 'musical instrument' where the solution to the problem had to come from within in accordance with the demands, both spiritual and practical, of such an instrument. In this process it was the aim of the designers to create an architectural atmosphere in the auditorium so as to tune the performers and the public alike into a proper mood of performance and receptivity, respectively. This was," he said, "the spiritual issue."

Link was ecstatic. In a letter to Letchworth written shortly after she'd seen Saarinen's plans, she wrote that to my mind, he has never done anything better. To me, the plan sings. The very building with all its lines and contours and mass dispositions follows a pattern as inevitable as classic music. You have the fluidity of melody, the element of similarity and contrast, the pulsation of rhythm—the whole expressing such beauty and poetry and grace and still retaining the shape, the simplicity and naturalness of a raindrop.... The amazing thing is that despite all these rigid limitations and exacting demands, such a brilliant solution should be evolved.[51]

Despite Link's enthusiasm and the support of a majority of the directors of the Buffalo Foundation, the Saarinen plan was jeopardized by the fact that the balance of power on the board of directors of the Kleinhans Company had shifted to the City of Buffalo, which, because of strings attached to a federal grant of $800,000 allocated to the project, had a majority on the Kleinhans board. The idea that a major commission, in the midst of a depression, should go to an out-of-town architect, particularly one whose design was so blatantly modern, was a hard one to sell, and the six city officials on the board balked. When it looked bad for Saarinen (one of the members referred repeatedly to him as "Mr. Sarazan," confusing the Finnish architect with the popular American golfer Gene Sarazan), Philip Wickser intervened with a ploy meant to delay the proceedings. A panel should be convened, he said, to help with the decision. Handpicked by Wickser, the panel consisted of three of the best known practitioners of modern architecture of the day, including Ralph Walker, J. Andre Fouilhoux, and Harrie T. Lindeberg. Wickser's strategy worked and, following the panel's unanimous recommendation, the board of directors of the Kleinhans Music Hall selected the Saarinen plan by a five to four vote, with one abstention. With relentless passion and the support of willing members of the community, Link's crusade on behalf of a bold and contemporary plan for Buffalo's new music hall had prevailed. Prevailing, too, was her insistence that the two large Chinese ginkgo trees on the Kleinhans site be saved. They were moved to where they still stand on the circle near the hall.[52] When Saarinen's visionary hall opened to the public in October 1940, it was universally recognized as one of the greatest concert halls ever built in the United States. For years to come, Saarinen's Kleinhans Music Hall was to play a vital role in the flourishing cultural life of the Buffalo community.

Another modernist working in Buffalo during the 1930s was Walter C. Behrendt. One of the founders of the Bauhaus, Behrendt, like the rest of his colleagues in that hotbed of modernism, left his homeland following Adolf Hitler's rise to power. By the mid-1930s he was working in Buffalo, hired by the ever-active City Planning Association (CPA) to help them wrestle with the challenges of the automobile and the threat that it posed to the city's central business district.

The 1930 census confirmed the fears of Chauncey Hamlin and his CPA colleagues. Although the city's population, pulled by the vitality of the city's booming economy, was still growing, the 13 percent growth during the decade examined was the smallest increase in the city's history. Many, particularly the downtown interest groups that had fought so hard during the 1920s to keep downtown competitive, were disappointed. Fenton Parke, owner of an active downtown real estate firm and occasional president of the CPA, was dismayed. "There had been hope and expectation," he said, "that the official figures (for Buffalo's population) would exceed 600,000." (The US census in 1930 reported that Buffalo's actual population was 575,000.)[53] The surrounding suburbs, meanwhile, grew rapidly, from just under 250,000 in 1920 to 340,000 ten years later, an increase of almost 40 percent. In 1927, *Buffalo Business*, the Chamber of Commerce's monthly publication, reported that "for the first time in Buffalo's history, there is more building activity in the suburbs immediately surrounding Buffalo than in the city itself. In the village of Kenmore, the city of Lackawanna and the townships of Tonawanda, Amherst and West Seneca, the value of building construction was 27% greater than the value of new building within the city of Buffalo."[54]

The growth of the suburbs, combined with the rise of newer outlying neighborhoods in the northern and southern parts of Buffalo was driven by the automobile, and as vehicular use grew, so, too, did congestion. By the early 1930s, the numbers of people entering downtown on daily trips began to decline in cities throughout the country, and Buffalo was no exception. The number of cars, however, continued to increase, and traffic congestion worsened. Growing problems of parking and congestion downtown may have been misleading. Increasingly, the people of Buffalo, like those in cities throughout the Northeast, found downtown less desirable as a destination for work and for entertainment.[55]

Growing vacancies during the Depression were compounded by the fact that assessments for real estate tax purposes did not keep up with the decline in revenues. This was yet another factor that led landlords to abandon their downtown buildings and move out to newer areas that were not only more convenient but offered far lower rates of assessments. What was true of commercial users was true even more so of manufacturers who, throughout the 1930s, moved a growing number of their operations to outlying areas.

Nothing, it seemed, posed a greater threat to the dominance of downtown than traffic congestion. Downtown interest groups knew that unless steps were taken to ease the movement of traffic to and within the central business district more and more people and businesses, unwilling to do daily battle with it, would leave. Afraid that the difficult problem of driving into and out of the city was already undermining downtown's dominant role in the life of the metropolis, downtown interest groups throughout the 1930s proposed a series of sweeping renewal projects that would, they hoped, remedy the problem.

Parking was then, as now, central to their thinking. While some off-street parking lots and spaces had been created during the 1920s (most famous was the three-story Statler garage, demolished in the early 1990s for the new federal building), most people sought parking spaces on the streets. But this only worsened congestion during the late 1920s. As a result, planners during the early 1930s began to give much more serious thought to off-street parking.

Ironically, the Depression brought some relief. As the economy declined and a growing number of businesses closed, building owners, facing ever-higher vacancy rates, realized that their properties would have greater value if used as surface parking lots. There was, according to one story in the *Courier Express*, "an increasing growth of off-street parking caused by the obsolescence of many downtown buildings. Many office buildings," the paper said, "have been or are now being torn down due to lowered income from the property." At least now landlords would be able to pay their taxes. On side streets all over downtown, half-empty office buildings were demolished and a bumper crop of off-street parking lots, known as "taxpayers," filled the increasingly pockmarked streetscape of downtown Buffalo.[56] The Depression also accelerated the street-widening efforts of the 1920s. Unemployed men, paid by the job-creation programs of the New Deal, were put to work on streets all over the city, narrowing sidewalks, cutting down trees, doing all the things that we now know are detrimental to the city. The two volumes on "Streets" in the Buffalo and Erie County Public Library's scrapbook collection are filled with poignant stories about the widening of the streets; they include pictures, maps, photographs, and comments. Invariably, the neighbors, worried about the changing character of their communities—the loss of their trees and the damage to the scale, form, and function of their neighborhoods—objected. Invariably, however, the politicians, the local councilmen, and the mayor, blinded by federal largesse and limited in their thinking, insisted on going forward with their plans and, as a result, most of the main streets in the city—Elmwood, Franklin, Washington, Elm, North, Virginia, Allen, Mohawk, and Huron—were widened. As they were, the delicate balance of homes, business, and stores, and the diverse mixture of uses that characterized so many streets of the city, was altered as place after place succumbed to the pressure of the automobile. As this happened, more residents left and local stores and businesses, faced with a dwindling customer base, closed their doors for good. Meanwhile, traffic worsened and the problems of downtown escalated.[57]

Despite a great deal of concern with the automobile, there were some who thought that the problems of the city, downtown in particular, might be improved with better public transportation. While the *Buffalo Motorist*, the publication of the local chapter of the Automobile Association of America, argued that in the interest of vehicular flow all trolley lines in the city should be eliminated, the *Buf-*

falo Evening News felt otherwise and insisted that mass transit could, if improved, deal effectively with the problems of traffic congestion in downtown, but only if the International Railway Company (IRC), a private company that had had a monopoly on the city's buses and trolley cars for years, was replaced. The *News*, like many others throughout the community, had become angry and disappointed at the level of services that the IRC provided. "The transportation situation in Buffalo is altogether unsatisfactory," the *News* commented in a 1931 editorial. "Year by year it grows worse. Steadily the IRC is curtailing service. There is never an extension of tracks. As a result thickly populated sections of the city lack proper transportation facilities." Perhaps recognizing that it was this, maybe even more than the proliferation of autos on narrow streets, that exacerbated the problem of traffic congestion, the *News* angrily criticized the IRC and said that "their system is admittedly the poorest to be found in any city of the first class in the country." The *News*, like many others at the time, was willing to consider the creation of a municipally owned transit system, which would, it felt, "give the city a powerful club to force adequate service."[58]

As the problems of downtown worsened throughout the 1930s, calls for the creation of a master plan for the city became louder and more insistent and led a growing number of groups and individuals to endorse what was called "the gospel of city planning." Chauncey Hamlin, for one, was frustrated and, in 1935, fifteen years after he had founded the CPA, he lamented: "We still have no accepted master plan for the development of the city or the region and we continue to suffer all of the handicaps which the lack of that imply." A year later he bemoaned the "almost impossible well of despondency in which city planning now finds itself."[59] Concerned that the advocacy work of his volunteer organization was getting nowhere and that the problems of "decentralization and suburbanitis" were growing greater, Hamlin urged that the city charter be amended in order to provide for the creation of what he called a "high grade, experienced planning board appointed on the basis of training and ability, not political party ties." Without such changes, he argued, neighborhoods would become blighted, downtown would stagnate, and the city would continue to lose its population to the suburbs. Skeptical of the city's commitment, Hamlin and the CPA went a step farther. More eager than ever to create and implement a master plan for their city, they brought to Buffalo Walter Curt Behrendt, one of Europe's best-known city planners and a recent refugee from Hitler's Germany.

Behrendt, a colleague of Gropius, Mies, and other Modernist founders of the Bauhaus, had served as chief city planner for Berlin prior to his emigration from Germany in 1937. Having been hired to teach at Dartmouth, Behrendt met there a young architectural student from Buffalo named George Metzger. The son of a prominent local architect and a member of the CPA, Metzger was fascinated with the handsome, inspiring, if overbearing and dogmatic, Behrendt. Thrilled by his sweeping vision of the well-planned and well-ordered city, Metzger, eager to bring the exciting German to Buffalo, discussed the idea with UB's chancellor.[60] Since his installation as president of UB in 1924, Capen worked diligently to involve the university in the life of the city. Aware of Behrendt's European reputation, and sensing the impact he might have on Buffalo, Capen seized the opportunity to hire him. Working closely with Metzger and his colleagues at the CPA, Capen created an ambitious proposal for the German planner. Behrendt would divide his time between the university, where he would develop a city planning curriculum, and the community where, working with his UB students at what Capen called the "Planning and Experiment Station," Behrendt would develop a master plan for the city. The idea, Capen said, "bridges the gap between academic study and professional practice in the same manner that a hospital with its staff of interns completes the training of a physician."[61] Although a fully functioning school of architecture and environmental design was not created at UB until 1972, the seeds of that program were planted by Capen and Metzger in their 1937 plan for Behrendt.

The lack of funds did not bother Capen and, with aid from the Rockefeller Foundation, his hopes for his bold venture in city planning were realized. In September 1937, Behrendt moved to Buffalo to become professor of city planning and housing at the School of Social Work, and director of the CPA's newly established Planning and Experiment Station, which was, according to Chancellor Capen, "the first of its kind in the country."[62]

Behrendt was greeted with enthusiasm by downtown interest groups and the university community. His picture—he had a long angular face, piercing eyes, and was always seen holding a pipe purposefully in hand—appeared regularly in the newspapers where he was touted as the man who would, through the power of his ideas, fix the problems of an increasingly troubled downtown.

By May 1939, Behrendt was ready. He presented the master plan that he and his students at the Planning Station had been working on for more than a year. To a rapt audience of the city's "kings and captains," held at the prestigious and private Saturn Club, Behrendt outlined his proposal for what, in deference to the world's fair then being held in New York, he called "The Buffalo of Tomorrow." Like so many in his profession, Behrendt saw the city in largely abstract and symbolic terms. First and foremost, he said, was the creation of "a master plan for Buffalo." Such a plan, overseen by "an authority with sweeping powers to enforce its provisions must be created and implemented lest," Behrendt predicted, "the city will become permanently spoiled by unplanned building."[63]

Behrendt, like so many people charged with planning in Buffalo, was drawn to the waterfront. While the waterfront at or near the terminus of the Erie Canal, an area tightly packed with towering cement grain elevators, remained economically viable, the area north of it, between the canal and Porter Avenue had, by the early 1930s, begun to lose many of the small factories, machine shops, and other light industrial activities that had been there for so long. As this part of the waterfront began to lose its economic function, planners and others who thought about these kinds of issues began to cast about for a new and different way to think about this prime piece of city real estate. Buffalo's waterfront, with its broad, curving shoreline, its clear and unbroken view of Lake Erie, and the dramatic confluence of the lake and the river, was a site that was far too tempting to ignore. Some saw it as the most desirable location for a new railroad station. Another, Mrs. Lewis Rogers, president of the Buffalo Federation of Women's Clubs and a member of the City Planning Association, in 1923, outlined her "dream of the Niagara River front as a New Riviera: a terraced line of beautiful homes and mansions built along the Niagara River.... When this River front is built up," she said, "the same reference will be made to it as the manors along the Hudson, Grosse Point and other river banks where people have picked out beauty spots for their homes."[64] Mrs. Rogers' vision gained momentum during the 1930s, after the centennial buildings had been removed, and it inspired Behrendt.

Behrendt, a high-minded Modernist who scorned the ordinariness of everyday life in Buffalo, saw the waterfront as one continuous park filled with Le Corbusier-like highrises and townhouses, a high-income "new town" in the heart of the city.[65] Behrendt's ideas for the waterfront were visionary. He was appalled that Buffalo's access to the waterfront was littered and marred almost beyond recognition by the proliferation of countless commercial and industrial uses. "At present," he said, "the whole district along the harbor, between Georgia and Lower Main Street, is a rather disreputable sight. The docks show signs of neglect; some of them show decayed walls, others are fully deteriorated. The smaller slips are partly filled with sunken barges." Referring to the vast potential that the waterfront offered the community (as have several generations of planners who followed), Behrendt observed that apparently the water "has never been alive in the consciousness of its inhabitants because it has never been given a proper and decent development demonstrating the important part it plays in the life of the city."[66] With this in mind, Behrendt proposed a sweeping reclamation of the waterfront for recreational purposes. All railroad tracks should be removed, he said, and all land between downtown and the northern boundary of the city should be cleared. In its place, he said, "a green zone" should be created, which would, upon its completion, "link finally and forever the people of the city to their waterfront."

Like so many progressive thinkers of the day, Behrendt had a regional vision for the development of the Buffalo metropolitan area. The primary challenge, he argued, was to control "unchecked decentralization"—what we would today call "sprawl." Like so many planners of his day, his strategy, modeled on the English New Town movement, called for "organized decentralization" in the form of self-contained clusters of mixed-use communities. These "settlements" of people, dispersed carefully around the metropolitan area and separated by open space, would function as "satellites" of the downtown business district to which they would be linked by a series of connecting highways.

Behrendt had no interest in the city at the street level. Like so many of his generation, he was unable to understand the workings of a pluralistic, multi-faceted American city. While he liked and appreciated Buffalo's planning tradition, which began with Joseph Ellicott and continued with Olmsted, he was, in fact, repelled by everyday elements of life in Buffalo—the crowded, cluttered, littered, and random aspects of living in the city. Downtown Buffalo, he said, confirming the concerns of the CPA and other downtown interest groups, was "in a state of rapid and steep decline." Part of the problem, claimed Behrendt, was the "panorama of visual clutter and disorder" that he found there. What was necessary instead was "uniformity in city planning." "People in our time," he said,

> seem to be afraid of using uniformity as a means of architectural design. They obviously hold that uniformity proves lack of originality. They are mistaken.... Uniformity certainly secured a much better effect than is achieved in present times in the streets of our modern cities when everybody thinks he must differ from his neighbor to prove his personal taste.

Based upon the ceremonious and formal approach taken in the design of the recently completed city hall, he expected to find those patterns repeated elsewhere in the central business district and its surrounding neighborhoods. Instead, in walking around downtown, he was surprised to find a lively, if dense and overcrowded, Italian neighborhood. Court Street behind city hall, he said, "continued on in a rather dilapidated form, bordered on both sides with poor residential structures contrasting most strikingly to the architectural dignity of Niagara Square." He was dismayed to see a large billboard posted on a building high above the square. Walking farther down Court Street through the large and bustling Italian neighborhood of St. Anthony's Parish, Behrendt, handsomely decked out in tweeds and wearing a Mac with his pipe in hand, was shocked by what he found. "There I saw, believe it or not, a goat nibbling at some weeds along the curb." Having looked, he said, "for beauty not ugliness, splendor not squalor," Behrendt, as if to threaten his provincial readers, remarked that "[i]n a German city there would have been issued an order forbidding any encroachments of these kinds."[67]

St. Anthony's Parish, the teeming Italian neighborhood that so offended

Behrendt, meandered down to and around the waterfront, filling the streets and alleys with the confusing, serendipitous mix of uses that we so long for today. Behrendt, like planning professionals throughout the world, had higher hopes for the city's waterfront. All of it, he said, all of the land from city hall to Carolina Street, with its acres of ancient streets, houses, schools, and stores should come down, replaced, he insisted, with a Le Corbusier-like "Ville Radieuse" of immaculate new high-rises, all located in a garden, a "fashionable residential district with handsome homes and apartments overlooking a waterfront restored to its natural beauty."[68] Another downtown neighborhood that Behrendt visited was a turn-of-the-century Italian community located in the hook of land that poked out into the Buffalo Creek between Lower Main Street and Court Street. Some knew it as "Canal Street," others as "Mt. Carmel Parish," but most knew it as "the Hooks." By 1936, the neighborhood, already on its last legs, was rocked by a gas explosion in a house on LeCouteleux Street that killed five people on New Year's Day. News of the fire filled the local papers, and demands for the demolition of the neighborhood, bandied around casually for years, became louder and more insistent. "This is a heavily congested area," the county supervisor said in a telegram to the housing director of the public works administration, "containing many old tenement buildings that would be a worth while project for the Federal government to allocate funds for slum clearance."[69] Father Pasquale Tronolone, pastor of the parish church, Our Lady of Mt. Carmel, reflected the thinking of many of the residents of the Hooks. "All of these homes," he said, "should have been torn down years ago." Charles Borzilleri, the first Italian-born graduate of the University of Buffalo Medical School and the founder of Columbus Hospital, which served the people of the neighborhood, agreed. "The whole Dante Place section is a disgrace to the city of Buffalo." The city agreed, too, and by 1938, using powers enumerated in a 1936 state law, which gave the city the right to condemn and remove "unsafe and unsanitary buildings" with consent decrees, had demolished and cleared almost all of the neighborhood's homes, businesses, factories, and other buildings. In what was a harbinger of things to come, in the summer of 1937 alone, five hundred families were moved out, many to the city's first public housing project, Lakeview, in preparation for the demolition of their former homes. A reporter for the *Courier Express* described the scene: "Gaping areas have taken the place of old brick buildings destroyed according to law. Dante Place, Commercial Street and many interesting alleys that used to be a veritable din and clatter in days gone by are like a graveyard for quiet..."[70] While most greeted the clearance of the Hooks, there were some people, notably a group of painters, who were angry and upset. "Painters Fear Day When City's Picturesque Spots Will Fall in Clean-up Drive," announced a headline in the *Courier Express* in 1939.[71] The Hooks, with its exotic mix of people, places, and old buildings, had been a favorite haunt of area artists and painters, like William Swanekamp, the president of the Buffalo Society of Artists—Victor R. Millonzi and Tony Sisti had also worked there. Sisti wondered what the fascinating combination of factories, elevators, and small buildings might turn into if preserved. Perhaps, he mused, the area could become like Greenwich Village or the Vieux Carre, populated by artists, and a magnet for tourism. "We believe," Sisti said, "that Buffalo and Buffalonians ought to take stock of what the city had in the way of beauty and color and preserve it."

Walter Behrendt, however, felt otherwise. It was places like the Hooks that his plans, unveiled in January 1940 at the Albright Art Gallery, would eliminate. Called "Buffalo, City of Tomorrow," the show, with its installation created by a graphic designer from Eliel Saarinen's studio at Cranbrook, was viewed by more than twenty thousand people. Behrendt himself, however, was not there. He had left Buffalo for good six months before, leaving behind the problems of the city as he had found them—in the hands of the local politicians and downtown businessmen who would, for better or worse, make the plans and the decisions that the rest of the people who stayed would have to live with.

Perhaps Behrendt sensed that the time was ripe, that the days of the city's great growth were behind it, and that it was time for him to move on to new commissions. Behrendt was well aware that the increase in Buffalo's population, barely 13 percent during the 1920s, as against 40 percent for the suburbs, showed virtually no growth during the 1930s. The growth of the suburbs, meanwhile, even during the Depression, continued rapidly and relentlessly, increasing by more than 20 percent. Perhaps he sensed that no matter how well he was treated and no matter how much he was wined and dined by the city's downtown business community, Buffalo would never submit to the rigor and discipline of any master plan, let alone his. Certainly, some of his sponsors at the CPA felt this way. One of them, the executive vice president of the Chamber of Commerce, Samuel Botsford, walked out of Behrendt's Saturn Club presentation in frustration, saying, "This is perhaps the 150th meeting I have attended where similar programs have been discussed."[72] Daniel W. Streeter, the president of the Chamber of Commerce, felt much the same. "One of our biggest errors," he said several years later, "has been to draw plans on tablecloths around cups of pink sherbet at civic gatherings. Too many of these plans are disposed of as soon as the table covering hits the laundry."[73] Increasingly, it seemed, the people who cared about downtown were frustrated and disappointed in their tireless efforts to understand and control the forces that were so drastically reshaping their community. Blaming the changes sometimes on vehicular congestion, sometimes on "neighborhood deterioration and blight," and sometimes on the failure to adopt a master plan for the region, the CPA and the others who cared about downtown floundered. When their plans and ideas did finally become the basis of public policy more than ten years later, the results, as we will see, were disastrous.

NOTES

1. The efforts to deal with the challenges of the Depression are best captured in the Welfare Work Projects Scrapbook in the Grosvenor Collection at the BECPL. This scrapbook contains dozens of articles on this topic from all the local newspapers. I have referred specifically to the following: "$83 Million Plan for City Works Prepared by ERB," *Buffalo Evening News*, April 23, 1935, Welfare Work Projects Scrapbook, pp. 26–27, Grosvenor Collection, BECPL; "New Millions Promised City," *Buffalo Evening News*, May 11, 1935, Welfare Work Projects Scrapbook, p. 28. For an excellent discussion of the increased role of the federal government in dealing with the problems of the Depression, see J. T. Horton, *History of Northwestern New York* (New York: Lewis, 1948), pp. 430–31.

2. "COS in Dire Straits," *Courier Express*, October 12, 1930, p. 1, Welfare Work Projects Scrapbook, p. 11, Grosvenor Collection, BECPL.

3. *Chamber Contacts*, November 1933, p. 1.

4. "Food Reductions Pose Health Threat," *Courier Express*, August 14, 1932, p. 11, Welfare Work Projects Scrapbook, p. 66, Grosvenor Collection, BECPL.

5. For a photo of the painting, see the catalog of the exhibition: *Charles Burchfield: A Retrospective Exhibition at the Albright Art Gallery, April 14–May 15, 1944* (Buffalo, NY: Buffalo Fine Arts Academy, 1944), plate 27. This catalog can be found in the Grosvenor Collection at the BECPL.

6. "Permanent Relief Problem Is City's Depression Heritage," *Buffalo Evening News*, May 4, 1936, Welfare Work Projects Scrapbook, p. 76, Grosvenor Collection, BECPL.

7. There are two scrapbooks in the Grosvenor Collection at the BECPL that are dedicated to the centennial celebration of 1932. Unfortunately, pages are not marked in these scrapbooks. The information here comes from the following articles: "Enthusiastic Crowd Cheers Progress of Centennial," *Buffalo Evening News*, June 27, 1932, and "Buffalo, One Hundred Years Old, Opens Its Celebration," *Courier Express*, July 2, 1932.

8. Kate Burr, "The Why of the Centennial," *Buffalo Times*, June 14, 1932.

9. "US Providing Buffalo with Many Improvements," *Courier Express*, August 25, 1935, Welfare Work Projects Scrapbook, p. 32, Grosvenor Collection, BECPL.

10. Ibid.

11. Michael Rizzo, *Through the Mayor's Eyes: The Only Complete History of the Mayors of Buffalo, New York* (Buffalo, NY: Old House History, 2005), pp. 260–62.

12. "Bethlehem Chief Salary Increase," *Courier Express*, March 22, 1932.

13. "Bethlehem OKs $20 Million for Lackawanna," *Buffalo Evening News*, February 1, 1935, Industry in Buffalo and the Niagara Frontier Scrapbook, vol. 4, p. 139, Grosvenor Collection, BECPL.

14. The arrival of General Motors in the late 1930s was well covered by the local press. Numerous clippings can be found in volume four of the Industry in Buffalo and the

Niagara Frontier Scrapbook, pp. 72–107. See also, "Huge New Plant for Frontier," *Buffalo Business*, March 26, 1937, p. 1.

15. James R. McDonnell, "The Rise of the CIO in Buffalo, 1936–1942," PhD diss., University of Wisconsin, 1970, p. 28.

16. Ibid., pp. 72–74.

17. Ibid., pp. 88–94.

18. Ibid., pp. 101–109.

19. Ibid., p. 113.

20. Acquisition dates are posted next to each painting displayed at the Albright-Knox Art Gallery.

21. See the Albright Art Gallery's *Gallery Notes* for each of the years listed. The annual *Gallery Notes* contains listings of all the talks, exhibitions, and other activities held at the gallery.

22. Fascinating articles on the opening of the Contemporary Room can be found in the Buffalo Fine Arts Academy Scrapbook, which is stored in the Grosvenor Collection at the BECPL. See particularly, "New Art Room Open," *Courier Express*, January 15, 1939, and "Contemporary Art Gets Gallery Room," *Buffalo Evening News*, January 5, 1939. There is a wonderful photograph of S. H. Knox Jr. and A. Conger Goodyear, two of the founders of the Contemporary Room, which is pasted on p. 64 of the Buffalo Fine Arts Academy Scrapbook.

23. *The Room of Contemporary Art* (Buffalo, NY: Albright Art Gallery, 1939).

24. "Buffalo Architecture," *Albright Art Gallery Exhibitions, 1940* (Buffalo, NY: Albright Art Gallery, 1940).

25. For background on Cameron Baird, see Andrew Stiller, *Golden Anniversary Commemoration of the Buffalo Philharmonic Orchestra* (Buffalo, NY: Buffalo Philharmonic Orchestra, 1985), p. 45, which is housed in the "music" vertical file in the Grovesnor Collection at the BECPL.

26. Ed Yadzinski, *Cameron Baird, 1905–1960: A Legacy* (Buffalo, NY: Buffalo Philharmonic Orchestra, 2005). This publication can be found in the Music vertical file at the Grosvenor Collection, BECPL.

27. Stiller, *Golden Anniversary Commemoration*, p. 47.

28. The University Archives at the University at Buffalo has seventeen boxes of material related to Charles D. Abbott. This list of books donated to UB by Thomas Lockwood comes from a typed sheet in a loose-leaf binder, which introduces and outlines the collection. For help locating these materials, see archivists John Edsen and Bill Offhaus.

29. The best background on the establishment and the early days of the poetry collection can be found in Charles D. Abbott's introduction to *Poets at Work: Essays Based on the Modern Poetry Collection at the Lockwood Memorial Library, University of Buffalo* (New York: Harcourt Brace, 1948) pp. 1–37.

30. Ibid., p. 7.

31. Ibid., p. 11.

32. Ibid., pp. 17ff.

33. Ibid., p. 22.

34. Annette Cravens, a regular at the estate, in discussion with the author, November 2004.

35. Ibid.

36. Information on the creation of the Film Society of Buffalo can be found in Charles Abbott's correspondence, announcements, catalogs, etc., which are located in the Abbott Papers (box 11), University Archives, State University of New York at Buffalo.

37. Ibid.

38. This particularly passionate letter was written on March 5, 1935.

39. Both the meeting with the Abbotts and the Pound connection are described in Mary Bernard, *Assault on Mount Helion: A Literary Memoir* (Berkeley: University of California Press, 1984), p. 167ff.

40. Robert Bertholf, comp., *HERE: Fifty Years of Poetry in Buffalo*, CD-ROM, University at Buffalo Poetry/Rare Books Collection *Fifty Years of Poetry in Buffalo*, 1996.

41. Bernard, *Assault on Mount Helion*, p. 171.

42. Wyndham Lewis, *America, I Presume* (London, 1940), p. 106. In July 2006, Michael Basinski, curator of the UB Poetry Collection, acquired a copy of *America, I Presume*, which had belonged to Charles Abbott. Entered in the margins of Abbott's copy, in his own writing, are the actual names and places of the people described in the book.

43. Bernard, *Assault on Mount Helion*, p. 172.

44. Ibid., pp. 191–92.

45. For an overview of the material in the Poetry Collection, see *Special Collections of the University Libraries* (Buffalo, NY: University Libraries, SUNYAB, 1984).

46. This account draws on Matthew Ginal's fascinating study titled "The Architectural History of Kleinhans Music Hall," an unpublished graduate student paper dated spring 1988, which is housed in the archives of the State University of New York at Buffalo.

47. Ibid.

48. Esther Link to Edward Letchworth, July 11, 1938, quoted in Ginal, "The Architectural History of Kleinhans Music Hall," appendix A.

49. Ginal, "The Architectural History of Kleinhans Music Hall," p. 32.

50. Ibid., p. 34.

51. Ibid., p. 36.

52. "Trees Saved," *Buffalo Evening News*, April 15, 1939, in "Trees" Scrapbook, p. 43.

53. Census data was kept by the City Planning Association and it, along with Parke's comments, can be found in the "city planning" vertical file in the Grosvenor Collection at the BECPL.

54. *Chamber Contacts*, February 12, 1927, p. l.

55. Robert Fogelson, *Downtown: Its Rise and Fall, 1880–1950* (New Haven, CT: Yale University Press, 2001), p. 230.

56. For a graphic view of empty storefronts and offices in downtown during the late 1920s, see the incredible photographs taken by George Hare in the Hare and Hare Collection, which is housed at the Lower Great Lakes Maritime Museum in downtown Buffalo. For a fascinating discussion of "taxpayers," see Fogelson, *Downtown: Its Rise and Fall*, pp. 229–30. For examples of "taxpayers" in downtown Buffalo, see "Parking Lot Claims Another Landmark," *Buffalo Evening News*, December 3, 1940, Buildings Scrapbook, p. 247, Grosvenor Collection, BECPL and "Seven Story Downtown Building, 48 Years Old to Be

Razed to Become Parking Lot," *Buffalo Evening News*, August 28, 1937, Buildings Scrapbook, p. 235, Grosvenor Collection, BECPL.

57. For a good understanding of this conflict, see the many articles about the widening of Elmwood Avenue between Virginia and Allen Streets in the Streets Scrapbook, vol. 2, pp. 56ff. In addition, see "Public Hearing to Decide Fate of Shade Trees," *Courier Express*, October 1, 1936, p. 32; "Council to Act on New Elmwood Widening Proposal," *Courier Express*, February 7, 1939, p. 26; "Mayor to Veto Elmwood Widening Plan," *Courier Express*, February 10, 1939, p. 24.

58. "Foot-Dragging by IRC," *Buffalo Evening News*, April 11, 1930.

59. "Board to Work on Master Plan," *Buffalo Evening News*, August 1, 1936, p. 13.

60. "City's Major Planning Problems to Be Discussed at Civic Luncheon," *Courier Express*, November 28, 1937, City Planning Scrapbook, vol. 2, p. 81; Josephine Hardwicke, "First Planning Station Formed Here," *Buffalo Evening News*, December 4, 1937, City Planning Scrapbook, vol. 2, p. 82. Metzger's efforts to bring Behrendt to Buffalo are covered in other material contained in the "city planning" vertical files in the Grosvenor Collection at the BECPL.

61. Hardwicke, "First Planning Station Formed Here."

62. "Capen Lauds City Planning Station," *Courier Express*, December 6, 1937, p. 22. Volume two of the City Planning Scrapbook (Grosvenor Collection, BECPL) includes several articles on Behrendt and his stay in Buffalo. See "Buffalo Leaders Hear Plan for 'City of Tomorrow,'" *Buffalo Times*, May 5, 1939, City Planning Scrapbook, vol. 2, pp. 95–98. See also a three-part series on Behrendt written by Julius Goodman, which appeared in the *Buffalo Times* between June 1, 1939, and June 4, 1939, City Planning Scrapbook, vol. 2, pp. 103–13.

63. See Julius Goodman's June 1939 articles on Behrendt in the *Buffalo Times*.

64. This small item was taken from the *New House News* (August 15, 1923, p. 5), a fascinating magazine that appeared only once or twice during the 1920s.

65. See Julius Goodman's June 1939 articles on Behrendt in the *Buffalo Times*.

66. City Planning Association, "A City Planner Looks at the City," printed by the City Planning Association, 1939 and glued into the City Planning Scrapbook, vol. 2, p. 80, Grosvenor Collection, BECPL.

67. "Goats Grazing Behind City Hall," *Buffalo Times*, May 5, 1939, City Planning Scrapbook, vol. 2, p. 99, Grosvenor Collection, BECPL.

68. Julius Goodman, "Behrendt in Buffalo," *Buffalo Times*, June 4, 1939, City Planning Scrapbook, vol. 2, pp. 112–13, Grosvenor Collection, BECPL.

69. Mike Vogel, et al., *America's Crossroads: Buffalo's Canal Street* (Buffalo: Western New York Heritage Press, 1993), p. 312.

70. Vogel, et al., *America's Crossroads*, p. 327.

71. "Imagination Not Destruction Could Remedy Housing Ills, Say Artists," *Courier Express*, August 13, 1939, Buildings Scrapbook, pp. 345–46, Grosvenor Collection, BECPL.

72. "95th Annual Banquet of BCC," *Courier Express*, January 7, 1939, p. 13.

73. M. H. Baker, "New President, Urges Five Year Plan to Better Buffalo," *Courier Express*, June 15, 1939, p. 22.

chapter 6

THE HOME FRONT

ong before the events at Pearl Harbor, millions of dollars in federal contracts began to pour into what was increasingly being referred to as the "Buffalo-Niagara Falls industrial area." This pattern was not unprecedented—in 1936, the Senate Munitions Committee revealed that in 1915, two years before America entered World War I, J. P. Morgan's banking firm had delivered a $28 million contract to Bethlehem Steel and a $30 million contract to Buffalo Copper and Brass. With tensions again escalating in Europe and the Pacific, preparations for war would bail out Buffalo's economy. In September 1939, two months before Congress repealed the Arms Embargo Act, the United States government signed a million-dollar spare parts contract with Curtiss Wright. Things got better still once the embargo was actually lifted. By the end of 1939, Bethlehem Steel, making close to ten thousand tons of steel per day, was breaking all production records. There were more than fifteen thousand people employed in Buffalo's steel industry, twelve thousand of them at Bethlehem. The *Buffalo Evening News*, in an end-of-the-year wrap-up, was ecstatic.

> The steel companies here hastily gathered men and materials together, took idle production facilities and made them useful again.... Chemical and dyestuff makers put out calls for men,

raised wages... the railroads added men to put the transportation plant in better running order. Aircraft companies here had fifty to sixty million dollars of foreign aircraft orders fall into their laps.... Heavy industry has begun to shake off its lethargy. Lake commerce finished up the year with such a rush that the harbor was literally choked with boats.[1]

The spree continued. In January 1940, with new contracts in hand, Bell Aircraft, with twelve hundred employees in its Buffalo factory, moved into a brand-new plant that the federal government had built for it in Niagara Falls. By the end of the year, Bell employed more than thirty-two thousand people. The expansion at Curtiss Wright, with fifty-three hundred employees in 1940 and forty-three thousand three years later, was equally dramatic. In 1943, eighty-seven thousand people were working at three area General Motors plants, producing motors for engines and airplanes. By 1943, Buffalo, with more than $5 billion in war supply contracts, did more war business with the federal government than all but four cities in the country. Local officials were proud that their city, "with only seven-tenths of one percent of the nation's population was producing 2.5% of all America's war goods." Bell, which produced more than one-half of all the American aircraft sent to Russia during the war, manufactured more than nine thousand Airacobras, the only single-engine pursuit plane armed with a cannon. Curtiss Wright made another pursuit plane—the P-40—and shipped more than a thousand of them to England. The British Air Force was particularly pleased with the Curtiss Tomahawk, which, "in one encounter attacked thirty Messerschmidts over the North African desert, destroying four and damaging many more without a loss." Bethlehem Steel produced twelve thousand tons of steel daily for tanks and railroad cars, while Republic Steel was used for cannon shells, gun barrels, tanks, and trucks. Gould Coupler made armor coatings for locomotives and tanks; Central Machine Works manufactured trucks "especially designed to be driven on the rugged terrain of China"; Spreichtool was the largest manufacturer in the world of bomb racks; and American Car Foundry was the nation's largest producer of howitzer shells. Some of the other materials for war produced in Buffalo included steel armor for ships, machine guns and ammunition, bombshells, chemical warfare equipment, diesel-powered invasion barges, tugs, parachutes, medical and hospital equipment, weather recording equipment, rubber rafts, uniforms, marine engines, firefighting equipment, amphibious cars, army cots, pontoons, and TNT.[2] The war was good for Buffalo, and everybody tried to get into the act. Hosts of new companies were spawned in the scramble to win war contracts. Officers for two banks formed Ships, Inc., in October 1941 and began to build ships under contract to the navy. Lake Erie Shipbuilding formed Buffalo Shipbuilding, which, with millions more in navy contracts, began to produce small craft.

Houdaille Industry, makers of precision auto parts, formed a subsidiary called Buffalo Arms and, employing more than five thousand workers, manufactured ordnance for the British Army.

Government orders for weapons came as a pleasant and welcome surprise after the Depression. It was easy and profitable to do business with the United States government. The government was interested in output and was willing to pay for it. No longer would contracts be given to the lowest bidder. War was not the time to reward efficiency; government contracts paid the costs of production plus a profit. The United States government had become the ultimate customer; not only did it buy the material and equipment its suppliers produced but, in the cases of Bell and Curtiss Wright, it built their plants as well.

For most people, the war was a windfall. With more than 458,000 people in the labor force (225,000 of them in war-related industries) earning a combined total of more than $10 million in weekly wages, prosperity was unprecedented. With only eight thousand unemployed, crime was down, relief rates had sunk to their lowest levels since 1929, and department stores reported that the Christmas season for 1943 was the best in history. In fact, according to a spokesman for the Chamber of Commerce, it was "Christmas every week in Buffalo."[3]

If the prosperity generated by the war was unprecedented, so, too, were the problems. The conversion of the economy to production for war and the mobilization of a workforce sufficiently large and skilled was a massive and extraordinarily difficult task. Again, as during the Depression, local government was forced to defer to Washington.

This was bound to happen, and it always does during wartime. The loss of power might not have happened so quickly, however, had local government been less concerned with political spoils. In the fall of 1941, the mayor, Joseph J. Kelly, ignored the local branch of the Office of Civil Defense and created a civilian defense organization of his own. When a local political reporter, widely known as a friend and supporter of the mayor, was placed in charge of the new organization, the director of civil defense resigned. According to one student of the American home front, Buffalo had become

one of the chief eyesores in the civilian defense program. The town had no auxiliary police, no air raid warden, no flashlights or helmets. One practice blackout was held in December 1941. The fire engines were brought out and the sirens turned on. The sirens promptly burned out.[4]

With political patronage and mismanagement rife, the state stepped in and, in May 1942, passed legislation that required that cities throughout the state set up local war councils, which should consist of a diverse board of businessmen, bankers, and city officials. Buffalo's war council was chaired by a leading Republican judge and lawyer; it was administered by a stockbroker named Dudley Irwin (when Irwin resigned to become an officer of the Manufacturers and Traders Bank, he was replaced by James B. Wilson, "a well-known Buffalo football coach, sportsman and attorney"). The Buffalo War Council was given vast and sweeping powers over virtually every aspect of daily life in the city: "The purpose of the Council is to coordinate and make efficient utilization of every facility and every resource of the community in support of the war effort." Yet despite the breadth of its responsibility—victory gardens and child care, salvage and public transportation, subversive rumor control and recruitment of farm labor—and the size of its membership (seventeen hundred block leaders plus more than a thousand volunteers)—the council had very little power of its own. Most of the time it was simply enacting rules and regulations that had been developed in Washington. Now more than ever, more than during World War I, more even than during the Depression, the federal government had become supreme in everyday affairs of the city.[5] The most challenging problem was to mobilize the workforce for employment in the defense industry. By 1940, signs of a labor shortage had begun to appear. Afraid that a critical labor shortage would lead the government to take its defense contracts elsewhere, business and political leaders willingly accepted and even called for federal manpower controls. In early 1942, the Chamber of Commerce demanded a government-sponsored labor draft as the only means of effectively allocating available manpower. Newspapers followed. One, reporting that local defense plants were "stymied in further stepping-up production by the scarcity of labor," joined in the call for a labor draft and cheered when, in February 1942, President Roosevelt ordered that all plants with government contracts lengthen their workweek to forty-eight hours and pay time and a half after forty hours.

Washington imposed other measures as well. Many teachers, ministers, college students, and public employees, unable to work full-time, joined "victory shifts" and worked part-time in Buffalo's defense plants. There was a "Farm Cadet Plan," whereby Boy Scouts, Girl Scouts, and students under fifteen were bused to surrounding farms to help with the harvest. Vagrants and drunks, too, were enlisted by what was referred to locally as "sunrise courts." Here, early in the morning, men arrested for loitering, vagrancy, and drunkenness could choose between jail or work in a defense plant. Even the influx of migrants (four thousand in 1941 and thirty thousand in 1943), whose need for shelter was as pressing as the city's need for workers, hardly made a dent in Buffalo's increasingly critical labor shortage.[6] Women undoubtedly helped. There had always been women in the workforce—more than sixty thousand, in fact, a year before Pearl Harbor. Still more were needed, however, and, beginning in early 1941, the federal Work Manpower Commission (WMC), in conjunction with the Buffalo War Council, took elaborate measures to lure more women, particularly married women with children, into the workforce. By June 1943, there were close to two hundred thousand women working in the city's defense industries. Women had finally joined the industrial workforce in large and impressive numbers.[7]

Women worked under a different and more intense set of pressures than men. While many had made the shift to industrial work from lesser-paying, prewar jobs, others, particularly mothers, were not only working for the first time but were doing so under conditions of a rapid speedup in production. (Many mothers chose to work the "owl" shift. Beginning at midnight, they could be home in time to help get their children to school.) Thus, the absentee rate among female workers was higher than among males. In an effort to combat it, local industries, with state and federal grants, opened daycare centers on their premises. (For some reason, however, daycare centers were never popular with working mothers of Buffalo. "Most working mothers," according to the chief administrator of the Buffalo War Council, "preferred to make informal arrangements with neighbors or relatives for the care of their children.")[8] Despite the host of "incentives" offered to female workers, noticeably lacking among them was equal pay for equal work. Indeed, despite national policy to the contrary, women in every branch of local industry, with the exception of iron and steel, still earned about 30 percent less than their male coworkers.

Despite all of these measures, however, Buffalo, over the strenuous protests of many of its community leaders, was declared a "labor shortage area" in October 1942. Citing the need for eighty-three thousand new workers in the forthcoming year, Buffalo's manpower mobilization program was placed under the direct control of Anna A. Rosenberg, the regional director of the WMC. Functioning as a kind of industrial czar for the area, Rosenberg's many visits to the city were greeted with a combination of anxiety and uncertainty lest her findings result in still stiffer regulations of local industry. Under her authority, WMC representatives regularly inspected all defense-related plants and reported on a range of issues that make minute by comparison the most stringent regulations of contemporary regulatory agencies. Through detailed and extensive inspections and questionnaires, Rosenberg's investigators gathered information on wages and hours, on utilization of labor, on training programs, and on racial and sexual discrimination. Rosenberg was diligent in her work and refused to tolerate the prejudicial hiring policies that had for so long been a part of local industry. In countless speeches to community leaders, she insisted that they overcome the city's labor shortage by making "maximum use of women and other minorities." She went well beyond the problem of the labor shortage, exhorting her audiences that the "people of Buffalo must realize that minority groups just don't exist any more. There must be no closing of doors to people because they are members of minority groups."[9] Her constant prodding, combined with the critical labor shortage, created unprecedented opportunities for the city's minority groups. Not only women but blacks, too, worked in places long denied to them. Buffalo's booming economy during World War II brought growth and opportunity to Buffalo's African American community. In a report prepared in 1943, the State Committee on Discrimination reported that 14,506 blacks, 7 percent of the workforce, were employed in Buffalo's 104 war-related industries. Lured by the promise of steady, good-paying work, thousands of blacks migrated north. The number of blacks in Buffalo grew from 17,694 in 1940 to more than 25,000 in 1945. Prospects for blacks remained good even after the war. The State Commission Against Discrimination reported in 1947 that "Buffalo Negroes today enjoy occupational opportunities and more civil rights than in almost any other metropolitan area in the country." The Urban League concurred, stating that due largely to a stringent antidiscrimination law in effect in New York State since 1945, blacks were holding their own. Of the fourteen thousand blacks who had found industrial jobs during the war, the league said that 90 percent had either retained them or found better ones. Nonetheless, the Urban League reported that much of Buffalo's economy, particularly its nonindustrial sectors, remained off-limits to members of Buffalo's African American community.[10] Since it opened in the mid-1920s, the Buffalo chapter of the Urban League had made small but relentless efforts to find jobs for blacks in the local economy. Its progress was slow and painstaking, its rewards small and provisional. The 1947 report of the league's industrial department indicated that "the situation is very encouraging...a Negro salesgirl has been placed at Hengerer's. J. N. Adam is next on the list. At Hengerer's there is a Negro forelady supervising ten persons. There are girls doing semi-clerical work as a result of long range planning and ground work." In addition, "Nurse training has been secured in Meyer Memorial Hospital, after many years of struggle and petition and all hospitals, except the Buffalo General, accept Negro patients." Meanwhile, the Buffalo Bills, then in the All-American Conference, signed Edward L. Conwell, their first black player, a sprinter and member of the 1948 US Olympic Team. These positive results were mitigated by the balance of the report. While pleased that there were two blacks on the faculty of the University of Buffalo, there were, the league said, no black professors at State Teacher's College, and no black teachers in any Buffalo high school. In addition, "There has never been a Negro intern in any local hospital and no medical school graduates in the last twenty years."[11]

Despite enormous growth of the labor supply, the labor shortage continued. The newspapers were filled with want ads. On just one day in June 1943, Curtiss Wright advertised for bench hands, auto mechanics, sheet metal workers, radio electricians, accountants, box makers, estimators, tool designers, template makers, and general laborers; National Biscuit advertised for packers, checkers, wrappers, porters, truck greasers, and salesmen; and American Optical offered to train workers to become lens grinders. Something had to be done.[12] In June 1943, Rosenberg implemented what was called the Controlled Referral Plan, the most sweeping federally regulated manpower mobilization plan ever used in an American city. By placing the hiring process completely in the hands of the WMC, the Controlled Referral Plan took the hiring process out of the private sector. No longer would a company be able to do its own hiring. No longer could a worker seek work or switch jobs on his or her own. Instead, everything would be arranged by and cleared through the United States Employment Service (USES).

Not everyone liked the plan. Organized labor, in particular, was most resistant. The head of the United States Steel Workers, about to enter the service, said that "putting the plan into effect is contrary to what we're fighting for on foreign battlefields." Others questioned Rosenberg's authority: "We feel she is putting the plan into effect over our heads." Many were bothered that "[i]t's not a Buffalo made plan." But Rosenberg was adamant; she insisted that the plan "will become operative regardless of how the community views it."

Buffalo was being bypassed. By determining who needed how many workers and when, the USES controlled almost the entire workforce in the city of Buffalo. According to the plan, a company had to make its case for more workers before the WMC. The commission would then decide the merits of the appeal. Sometimes, as in the case of the commission's deliberations over General Drop Forge's request for more workers, they consented:

> They are using quite a few women. During week prior to visit, employed 20 additional women, and are willing to employ women wherever possible. This week they are putting on 20 more women who are being employed as drill press operators, core inspection grinders, sand blasters and snag press operators, as well as working in the machine shop. They have 65 women on production. They have lost 32 the first month. They expect to lose a total of 22 men for the next 6 months.... Absenteeism, during week of 10–24, was 10%. It started declining and is about 6% a week. Their backlog is increasing because of lack of manpower. They have a total of 631 males employed. Need 2 tool makers. They are exploring the possibility of subletting some of the die work. They need 2 machinists to work as setup men; in processing shop they want 2 grinders to fill up empty machines; need 15 machinists... 3 lift truck operators; 3 finish molders; 2 forge inspectors; 2 die storagemen; 1 planer; 2 shipping clerks.... They have three million dollars of Army and 2 million dollars worth of Navy unfinished business. Both have # 1 Urgency Rating.... They are one hundred thousand castings behind for Cleveland Diesel Engine Company. Backlog of one hundred fifty thousand forgings for gears; two hundred thousand on engine

parts. Other part of their production goes into engines which probably will go into landing craft. They were given 25 workers just recently. In view of the critical situation, I would recommend that they be given about 50 workers. I have a suspicion the shipping clerks will assist in loading heavy castings.[13]

Other times, the commission did not approve labor requests. In late 1943, the Chase Bag Company asked for more workers:

They require eleven workers. Their male workers are utilized primarily on heavy operations. They have twenty-one males and fifty-six females. As far as the urgency, they are low on the List. That can be made someplace else. As far as I am concerned, I think we should reserve the workers for more essential work. We have the mills for storage, and facilities to accomplish the shipment, they need the containers. Has this Company plants located in other towns than Buffalo? If so, I suggest this be made some place else. Do not add to list. Advise Company to make bags in some of their other plants where there is no labor shortage.[14]

While the WMC, through the Controlled Referral System, controlled the local workforce, the Office of Price Administration (OPA), in countless regulations aimed at containing wartime inflation, monitored the price of almost every item that people ate, wore, or used. With only nine enforcement offices (the OPA never revealed how small their staff actually was), there was only so much they could do. Charged with patrolling the whole county, the Buffalo division of the OPA decided to only go after the big offenders; during the war years, meat packers, hotels, restaurants, gas stations, dairies, and other providers of food, gasoline, and tires were charged with and oftentimes sued for price gouging. Even more difficult to enforce was the statewide ban on pleasure driving. Forced to choose between giving up trips to the beach or a ballgame, playing golf, visiting friends, or other favorite pastimes or using public transportation to get there, many people chose the latter. Almost as many, rather than surrender their cars, violated the law, and in most cases received lenient treatment. Following his retirement in early 1944, the chief enforcement officer of the OPA, torn between civic pride and the knowledge he had gained, reluctantly admitted that during the course of the war one in every five business establishments in Buffalo and Erie County had received some kind of warning from his office.[15] There were other problems that the normal workings of the private economy and the local government simply could not handle. One of them was transportation. Because the federal government's War Production Board had ended the manufacture of private automobiles, because new tires were no longer available due to the reassignment of rubber supplies, and because deliveries of crude oil were drastically rationed, the burden of transporting the more than three hundred thousand workers to and from their places of work fell on public transportation. Under orders from the Office of Defense Transportation (yet another wartime federal agency) the Buffalo War Council implemented a system of staggered work hours similar to that used in other industrial cities. According to this schedule, heavy industry would operate from 7:30 to 3:30, downtown business and government offices from 8:00 to 4:00, and public and parochial schools from 9:30 to 3:30. By the end of 1943, Buffalo's streetcar and bus system was handling close to four hundred thousand commuters a day.[16]

Production for war had become the primary measure of achievement, and by these standards Buffalo had done remarkably well. People were proud of the part the city had played in making the United States the "Arsenal of Democracy." They applauded the success of its defense-related industries as they do today its sports team and boasted about its achievements as their own. One of the city's newspapers, in a loss of its journalistic distance, extolled Curtiss Wright's P-40:

> The P-40 lunged at Tojo's squadrons and broke them up. They plastered Jap ships. They escorted our bombers and when the bombers were gone heroic young Americans, British and Aussies loaded bombs into the P-40's and dropped the eggs on the Japs' advancing line.

Congratulations were also extended to the Buffalo Arms Company for its success in manufacturing .30- and .40-caliber firearms, and to Bell, Chevrolet, and Westinghouse, all of whom, along with Curtiss Wright, had won the coveted Army and Navy "E" award for excellence. The city was proud of itself, too, and never tired of extolling its citizenry, diversified and yet seemingly unified, which, according to the historian of the Buffalo War Council, "had buried their vast differences and submerged all political, religious and class distinctions and had met the challenge of total war."[17] There was a great deal of truth to these claims. In the workplace, at least, more progress than ever had been made in eliminating the racial and ethnic barriers that had for so long fragmented the people of Buffalo. (Still, in 1943, when the federal government planned to build public housing for black defense workers in South Buffalo, the outburst from that predominantly Irish community was so vociferous that the plan was dropped. It was decided to expand existing public housing on the increasingly black East Side instead.)[18] In addition, perhaps because the vast majority of the German American community were staunch supporters of the war effort, there was none of the anti-German bitterness and rancor that had existed during World War I. However, in the streets of the city's German neighborhoods, the German American League, or "Bund," was active, and enjoyed the support of many. Imitating in structure the procedures of the Nazis in Germany, the Buffalo Bund offered a "frauenshaft" for women, a "madchenshaft" for girls, and a "Jegenshaft" for boys. Selected members of these groups were sent to Germany throughout the 1930s to learn, as John T. Horton writes, "the Nazi gospel first hand.... Thence they returned well indoctrinated to help propagate the gospel in foreign parts." From their headquarters at the "Café Vaterland," at Genesee and Bailey, and on buildings at Bund-operated camps in Olcott Beach and in East Aurora, the Bund displayed, hanging alongside the American flag, the German imperial flag and the swastika of the Third Reich.[19]

Indeed, despite the war, the blackouts, the rationing, the long hours, and the unprecedented disruption in the daily life of virtually everyone, a sense of public calm, security, and confidence seemed to prevail. Even crime rates—robberies and rapes, murder and arson, fraud, counterfeiting, and juvenile delinquency— declined significantly. Brought on perhaps by prosperity, perhaps by a common sense of purpose, Buffalo seemed to be united as never before.

To see this, however, as a spontaneous, somewhat mystical response of a suddenly cohesive, highly motivated community would be to miss the point. Without the strong and controlling hand of the federal government it would have been impossible for Buffalo, like any other city in the country, to have risen to the occasion of war. Then, as during the Depression, it was Washington that virtually commandeered local government, leading it when possible and forcing it when necessary to develop and implement the programs that it deemed essential to the challenge. For better or for worse, the Depression and then the war forever changed the relationship that had historically existed between Buffalo and Washington. In the years ahead, Buffalo would become ever more dependent (sometimes as the beneficiary, sometimes as the victim) on programs and policies developed by the federal government.

Buffalo's population, recorded in 1940 at 575,000, swelled to over 600,000 by the end of the war, a result of the thousands of people who had trekked to the city to work in its booming wartime economy. Many left when the war ended and moved back home. Others, in ever growing numbers, moved to the city's suburbs, which continued their rapid growth. Throughout the 1930s, those difficult years of national depression, when jobs were scarce and money tight, a growing number of people still found a way to leave the city and move to the suburbs. In Buffalo, as in cities throughout the nation, the population of the city was stagnant at around 575,000 people while, meantime, the surrounding suburban population grew by 92,000 to a total of 338,000, an increase of more than 40 percent by 1940. "People leave the city and Buffalo loses population to the suburbs," a 1942 City Planning Association brochure proclaimed.[20]

In the meanwhile, downtown's problems continued to worsen in the years after the war. By 1940, the central business district could claim only 25 percent of metropolitan area sales versus their 52 percent share ten years earlier.[21] Not only were sales dropping and office vacancy rates rising, of even greater concern was the massive drain on the city's treasury that the move to the suburbs had caused. In 1948, the *Buffalo Evening News* reported that

> the shift of city dwellers to the suburbs is at the fastest pace in years, resulting in the construction of more than five times as many homes in the outlying section as in the city itself.... New homes appear to be popping up overnight in areas that a few years ago were favorite hunting spots of local nimrods. Former farm lands and barren fields have been transformed into thriving communities, self-contained with new schools, churches and large shopping centers."[22]

In 1940, Buffalo still raised more than two-thirds of its own revenue from property taxes, more than half of which came from the central business district. By the end of the decade, property values in downtown, adjusted for inflation, were lower than they had been in 1929. Something had to be done—something soon, and something big.

The automobile, which dominated thinking about city planning during the 1920s and '30s, exerted still more influence in the post–World War II years. Buffalonians, like people all over the country, could not wait to throw off the wartime controls that had so specifically regulated their use of cars. They had had enough of gas rations, of limits on when they could and could not drive, and of jam-packed rapid transit. They began to plan well before the war was over for what everybody fully expected would be the new golden age of the automobile. By the war's end, the mechanism for bringing it about—a sweeping plan for the construction of a whole new system of city and region-wide highways and arteries—was in place. In 1943, New York State had passed a thruway bill and, in 1946, the state, in conjunction with planning officials in Buffalo, made public their "Urban Area Report on the New York State Thruway and Arterial Routes in the Buffalo Area."[23]

The report, which became the bible for transportation planning in Buffalo for the next thirty years, was rooted in the belief that the city's survival required that it take immediate steps to accommodate the projected enormous increase in private vehicle ownership. The vision of the city articulated in this document was that of a large, downtown business district surrounded by ever growing numbers of suburban residential communities (few people realized then the extent to which the suburbs would become virtually self-sustaining and independent). Since, the planners argued, more and more people would be leaving the city for the suburbs, the city would have to develop strategies for handling the private automobile. "Suburban traffic," the report said, "must be given high consideration in the logical treatment of any conditions within the city."[24] Given this notion, local streets could no longer serve their traditional function of being local paths of movement and transportation; no longer could they remain relatively small routes, linking neighborhoods to each other and to downtown. Instead, they would have to be transformed into large arterials on which fast-moving vehicular traffic would be able to travel quickly between suburban residential areas and the downtown business district.

The plan was ambitious and expensive. According to its dictates, a system of highways, like that envisioned by Walter Behrendt, would be built around the city—"a cordon virtually encircling the city"—which would be linked to the downtown area by a series of connecting arteries. Since the main concern of the plan was to distribute and disperse downtown-bound suburban traffic, streets would have to be widened considerably so that they could, in the words of the planners, "intercept traffic on all the main arteries leading into the city and to carry that traffic freely to the downtown area." Congestion and bottlenecks as cars approached downtown would have to be avoided at all costs. Traffic, the report emphasized, must be free-flowing, uninterrupted, and unburdened: "Unless provision is made for the uninterrupted flow of vehicles from the Thruway [the major highway intended to link the city to the suburbs] onto the streets, and they in turn have the capacity to receive this concentrated flow, there will be blocked intersections and heavy congestion at every point."[25] Downtown interests—the City Planning Association, the Buffalo Chamber of Commerce, the Buffalo Real Estate Board, the Main Street Association, and others—desperately wanted the new thruway to enter directly into the heart of the central business district, terminating there much like the canal had more than a hundred years before. In an elaborately designed, carefully illustrated brochure in support of what they called the "mid-City thruway," the CPA outlined their proposal. Welles Moot, chairman of the City Planning Committee, supported the midcity route, saying that the planned location of the new highway on the banks of the Niagara River "would serve only tourists." What was more, Moot argued, it would "bypass downtown by skirting around it along the River." The thruway, Moot and the others felt, was "a great opportunity, perhaps the last, to strengthen and preserve downtown. A thruway that brought motorists directly into the heart of the central business district was the surest and most effective means to connect commuters to their offices and shoppers to their stores."[26] According to a proposal advanced by the ever-active CPA, the three-hundred-foot-wide highway would enter the heart of the city from the north, cross at grade from the Niagara River at North Tonawanda, follow Delaware Avenue south past Delaware Park and Forest Lawn Cemetery, proceed downtown, across Main and Michigan streets, and down Washington to Seneca Street, where it would link up with the thruway at the southeastern end of the city. Lest residents in affected areas wonder about the impact of the highway on their neighborhoods and their homes, the report assured them that the highway would be separated from the neighborhoods it passed through by a one-hundred-foot-wide green space, which would, they said, be developed as public space for "many small parks, playgrounds, tennis courts and wading pools." Indeed, its advocates claimed, the midcity highway route would improve the city's neighborhoods. Traffic congestion within the neighborhoods would be relieved, "blighted areas would eliminated," and downtown would become more accessible.[27] This proposal, like Bennett's 1920 plan for the Circuit Traffic Way, would have had a shattering and unprecedented impact on the life and structure of the city. The homes of thirty-four hundred families, the report acknowledged, would be demolished, and countless businesses would have been irretrievably lost. However, since the highway would be through areas that were "substandard" anyway, "the problem of relocating them," the report said, without suggesting a strategy, "will be simple."

Governor Thomas E. Dewey felt otherwise and rejected outright a proposal that in scope and scale would have dwarfed any renewal project proposed before or since. At a speech at the 1945 annual meeting of the CPA, the governor recognized the controversy about the location of the new highway. "Some people," he noted, "would like it on the West Side where it would be a more beautiful scenic drive. Others," referring to many in the audience, "would like it further to the east (of downtown) where," the governor admitted, "it would greatly relieve your congestion." The facts, however, were that no one had a choice. Unapologetically, with seemingly little response from the audience, Dewey, in a comment that revealed a great deal about how planning decisions were made in New York State, said that "it will all be decided by Charlie Sells," New York's supervisor of public works. "I know," Dewey assured his listeners, "that when Charlie gets through with his surveys and announces his decision, you will accept it as the best job an engineering expert can do."[28] Sells, for better or for worse, chose the banks of the Niagara River, and following its completion in 1949, thoughts turned to completing the remainder of the proposed new highway system. While the Niagara section of the thruway linked Buffalo with Niagara Falls, Tonawanda, Grand Island, and other suburbs in the north and west, it did nothing to connect Buffalo to the east, where the greatest suburban growth was occurring. What was needed, it was felt, was a system of highways that ran from east to west. Not only would this provide a direct link between the city and the new suburbs, it would also bring the airport within direct and easy reach of downtown. Thus, using the 1946 study as their rationale, state and city planners in 1953 outlined their proposal for the construction of five new highways that would cut across the city along five different east-west axes. Superimposed upon the existing pattern of the city's streets, parks, and neighborhoods would be a massive grid of five superhighways, whose purpose would be to join the rapidly growing surrounding suburbs with a rapidly declining central city.

The price that would be paid for this plan, as we will see in a subsequent chapter, was enormous, and the damage has so far been irreparable.

And then there was the parking issue. Welles Moot, the chairman of the City Planning Commission since 1948, was, like so many of his generation, convinced that the survival of downtown depended on solving "the parking problem." Parking had been a major concern of the mayor's Post-War Planning Committee, which, under the supervision of Henry Osborne, the traffic advisor for a municipal department called the Division of Safety, issued a postwar planning report in 1943. Osborne was concerned about the city's ability to handle the growing volume of automobiles; there were, he said, one hundred forty thousand registered vehicles in Erie County in 1943:

> Are we going to be prepared to handle traffic movement on our street system in the post-War era? Our motorists have been restricted in the amount of their driving during the war period, speed has been reduced by Federal mandate, so when this war is over, will we be able to handle the pent up emotions to go places and do things? We must plan now and start to make these improvements so that they will be available the moment the motorist has the gasoline.[29]

Street widenings, for years the method of choice for dealing with the increase in cars, had never worked and should, Osborne said, be discontinued. The primary function of streets, he insisted, was the movement of traffic: "[T]hey are too valuable to be used as parking lots." Parked cars should, he advised, be removed from the streets altogether and located instead in "planned and consolidated parking facilities."

While planners and city officials worried about the car, many people, it seemed, continued to rely on public transportation. Indeed, at the end of the war, the character and personality of the city was still, to a great extent, colored by rapid transit. In 1945, for example, a weekly entertainment magazine called *Buffalo Trends* told its readers how to use public transportation to get to places of interest. To get to the Albright, it wrote, "take the Elmwood bus." For the Museum of Science, "take a Delaware or Elmwood bus or any Main Street car going north and transfer to a Porter-Best bus."[30] Even as late as 1955, Buffalonians continued to rely on buses, which still carried two and a half times as many shoppers downtown as did automobiles. Indeed, in that year, Buffalo added eleven new buses. However, the days were numbered for rapid transit; the number of people who cared about and fought for public transportation began to dwindle and by the late 1940s and early 1950s, public transportation, outside of all but the biggest cities, was doomed. Indeed, public transportation was rarely part of the equation and in 1955, a year when the newly organized transit company Niagara Frontier Transit boasted that Buffalo was "one of the few major American cities with all modern bus service," three city-owned parking ramps with a combined capacity of two thousand automobiles opened in downtown Buffalo. Four years earlier, in 1951, the Marine Trust opened the first drive-in bank in the city. Located at Main and Seneca, the low, ranch-style building had the look of a drive-in restaurant where smiling waitresses on roller skates took orders.[31] The people who cared about downtown wanted it both ways—they wanted their cars and their public transportation—and for a while, at least, it seemed that they could have both.

But Moot, like most of his colleagues in the planning profession, was far more concerned with cars, particularly how and where to park them. In a report issued in 1949, he minced no words. "The downtown parking problem, he said, "is our most serious and most urgent problem.... Unless something is done promptly we can expect a continued migration of Buffalo's downtown business to the suburban areas." Given what Moot said was "the required ratio" of one space for every two cars, the city, with only eleven thousand spaces and forty thousand cars per day entering the city, was already nine thousand spaces short. With projections indicating fifty thousand cars by 1960, Moot projected a need for fourteen thousand new spaces. Of these, sixteen hundred should be in three parking ramps, built and operated by the city, and the rest—23,400—would be on surface parking lots. Mayor Joseph Mruk agreed. Not only, he said, would the city build three ramps, it would also encourage the private development of parking facilities downtown "by assisting in the condemnation and assembly of necessary sites."[32] The campaign to build parking spaces for twenty-five thousand automobiles began in 1950. The process, which fifty years later is still ongoing, destroyed streets and buildings and left many people to wonder if there might soon be nothing left in downtown but an ever-growing sea of parking lots. The people of Buffalo watched as the fabric of their city came tumbling down. Falling with it was their history and their heritage and, unbeknownst to them, their future as well.

NOTES

1. *Buffalo Evening News Almanac, 1940* (Buffalo, NY: Buffalo Evening News, 1941), p. 179.

2. For wartime industries, see J. T. Horton, *History of Northwestern New York* (New York: Lewis, 1948), pp. 440–41. The best way to track the impact of the war on the local economy is to use the Industry in Buffalo and the Niagara Frontier Scrapbook, which is housed in the Grosvenor Collection at the BECPL.

3. "Best Christmas Shopping Season Ever," *Buffalo Evening News,* January 19, 1944, p. B1.

4. R. R. Lingeman, *Don't You Know There's a War on? The American Home Front, 1941–1945* (New York: Houghton-Mifflin, 1970), p. 171.

5. Dudley Irwin, *The Buffalo War Council: How One City Met the Challenge of Total War* (Buffalo: Saxen and Pfeiffer, 1945), pp. 10ff.

6. The story of wartime manpower questions is covered in detail in Leonard P.

Adams, *Wartime Manpower Mobilization: A Study of the World War Two Experience in the Buffalo-Niagara Falls Area* (Ithaca, NY: Cornell University Press, 1951).

7. Irwin, *Buffalo War Council*, p. 27. For images of women in Buffalo's war-time workforce, see the photos of Marjory Collins in the collection of the Library of Congress, http://www.memory.loc.gov/cgi-bin/query/b?ammem/fsaall:LC-USW3-028182-D:collection=fsa.

8. Ibid., p. 41.

9. "Regional Man Power Chief in Buffalo. Labor Shortage, Piracy Under Study," *Buffalo Evening News*, October 1, 1941, Industry in Buffalo and the Niagara Frontier Scrapbook, vol. 6, pp. 44–45, Grosvenor Collection, BECPL.

10. Victor Einach, "Channels of Defense," an unpublished report written in 1943 for the Council of Social Services, Buffalo, New York, pp. 32–43 (Grosvenor Collection, BECPL).

11. Buffalo Urban League, *Annual Report, 1948*, pp. 5–6, Grosvenor Collection, BECPL.

12. "Immediate Study Ordered of War Plant Labor Needs, *Buffalo Evening News*, October 2, 1942, Industry in Buffalo and the Niagara Frontier Scrapbook, vol. 6, p. 46, Grosvenor Collection, BECPL.

13. Adams, *Wartime Manpower Mobilization*, pp. 110–12.

14. Ibid., p. 113.

15. Milton Friedman, director, OPA, Buffalo Branch, personal communication with the author, April 1982.

16. Ibid.

17. Irwin, *Buffalo War Council*, p. 33.

18. Leland Jones, former Ellicott District councilman, personal communication with the author, October 1988.

19. Horton, *History of Northwestern New York*, p. 435.

20. See "city planning" vertical files, Grosvenor Collection, BECPL.

21. *Buffalo Business*, April 1941, p. 11.

22. "Spreading Out," *Buffalo Evening News*, September 2, 1948, City Planning vertical files, Grosvenor Collection, BECPL.

23. "Report on the New York State Thruway and Arterial Routes," New York State Department of Public Works, 1944. This report can be found in the files of the New York State Department of Transportation Offices, 100 Seneca Street in Buffalo, NY.

24. Ibid., p. 4.

25. *Buffalo Business*, April 1946, p. 42.

26. "The Mid City Thruway," City Planning Association, "city planning" vertical file, Grosvenor Collection, BECPL.

27. Thomas E. Dewey, "The Thruway and Buffalo's Future," lecture, Annual Meeting of the City Planning Association, Buffalo, NY, December 1945.

28. Ibid.

29. Henry Osborne, Post-War Planning Committee Report, 1943, "city planning" vertical files, Grosvenor Collection, BECPL.

30. *Buffalo Trends*, August 11, 1945, p. 49.

31. There are two great photos of the drive-in bank in the Banks Scrapbook, vol. 2, pp. 184–86, Grosvenor Collection, BECPL.

32. "City Owned Ramp to Cover Entire Block," *Courier Express*, August 14, 1951.

chapter 7

BUFFALO AT MID-CENTURY

Deep blues and purples, rich pastels, a bright sun shimmering on the lake, dark furnaces and factories in the background—these were the colors and images that appeared on the cover of *Fortune* magazine in July 1951 for the story titled "Made in Buffalo," which included twelve pages of stunning photographs "portraying the industrial diversity of a great city." The text was detailed and read like copy from the Buffalo Chamber of Commerce. As recorded in *Fortune*, Buffalo was the eleventh-largest industrial center in the country that year, the third-largest producer of steel, the largest inland water port, the second-largest railroad center, and the "first city in the world" in flour milling—Buffalo produced enough flour to supply every family in the country with half a loaf of bread every day. The city had twelve railroad freight terminals that served forty-five thousand trains a year, and five passenger terminals serving fifty thousand trains a year. And with more than half a million people living in the city itself and a million and a half in the metropolitan area, Buffalo was the fifteenth largest city in the country[1] Even though Curtiss-Wright, the giant airplane manufacturer, had moved out of the area in 1946, Buffalo remained an industrial giant. The city's five iron and steel plants employed close to thirty thousand workers, one-eighth of the city's total labor force, according to *Fortune*. Buffalo's American Brass Company was the "number-one fabricator of copper and brass sheet, strip, and tubing," and Chevrolet's Tonawanda plant produced a third of all Chevy engines. The city hosted heavy industries like Lake Erie Engineering, Eastman Machine, Buffalo Forge, and Worthington Pump, manufacturers of cloth-cutting machines, presses, and machine tools. There were electrical equipment manufacturers: Sylvania, Westinghouse, and Western Electric; electrochemical companies: Carborundum, Hooker, and Vanadium; brewers: Magnus Beck, Iroquois, Phoenix, and William Simon; a number of renowned specialty companies, including Kittinger Furniture, "known the world over" for the furniture it made for the re-created colonial village in Williamsburg, Virginia; and Birge Wallpaper, famous for its "unusual twelve-color presses." While to the casual visitor, *Fortune* wrote, "the city may seem as conventional, unassuming and unexciting as a businessman in a blue-serge suit...behind its unexceptional facade [Buffalo] reveals a fascinating industrial kaleidoscope." More impressive still were the photographs by Victor Jorgensen. They depicted the city as a powerful, even overwhelming, industrial behemoth that was also sleek, modern, and successful. The city had, it seemed, despite worries to the contrary, survived the transition to peacetime.

They were right, so it seemed, for Buffalo continued to boom throughout the 1950s, and growth occurred in all sectors of the economy. In 1955, *Buffalo Today*, the monthly magazine of the Chamber of Commerce, reported that there were four hundred fifty thousand people working in the Buffalo area, twenty thousand more than the year before. Their combined earnings, the chamber proudly claimed, were more than $2 billion. With 215,000 of the people (a record number) working in industry and manufacturing, Buffalo's blue-collar population was the tenth-largest in the country.[2] Buffalo, the chamber boasted, was "a workingman's town." Forty-two percent of the labor force worked in manufacturing (as compared with 25 percent for New York State and 26 percent for the nation) while 75 percent of total earned income came from wages and salaries. With so many people working in industry, Buffalo's per capita income of $2,500 in 1955 exceeded the national average by 25 percent. This, coupled with low taxes and, according to the chamber, "unchanged living costs," created a genuine sense of optimism and the feeling that things could only get better.

Generous defense contracts (more than $325 million in 1955) continued to play a significant role in the area's economy. Bell Aircraft, which since the war had switched from combat planes to the development and production of jet engines and guided missiles, still employed one hundred forty thousand people. Bell, whose workers earned more than $1 million a week, contributed significantly to the area's economic wellbeing—the company spent over $400,000 weekly in the local economy buying materials and supplies. In 1955, demonstrating that it was

on the cutting edge of emerging technologies, Bell announced that it had purchased "an electronic brain" from IBM for use in "scientific calculations."[3]

Expansion was apparent throughout the entire range of the metropolis's
highly diversified economy. In 1955 alone, Chevrolet added ninety-five hundred
employees, Buffalo Tool and Dye saw an 80 percent increase in the production of
dyes, and Barcalo, the maker of the Barcalounger, opened its third plant in the
city. Not only did *Fortune* smile on Buffalo but in 1955, *Holiday* covered the city,
too. The writer of the piece, interested mostly in the social life of the rich, was
impressed by the city's economic vitality. "Metropolitan Buffalo," the author
wrote, "is a tremendous manufacturing center with possibly the most diversified
industry of any American city. It leads the nation in flour milling. It manufactures
railroad car wheels, dredges, hair-pins, internal combustion engines, nylon stock-
ings, pipe organs, airplanes, steam radiators and practically anything else you can
think of including merry-go-round horses."[4] These conditions, however, could
not last forever, and times were changing. Buffalo's industrial infrastructure—its
factories and railroads—was aging, and its workforce, as the result of a series of
crippling yet successful strikes, was deeply entrenched. Its population, too, was in
decline. In addition, beginning in 1952, a small yet significant number of Buffalo's
industries began to leave. Spencer-Kellogg, the largest maker of linseed oil products in the United States, announced in January 1952 that it was closing its Buffalo plant. It was, the owner said, fifty years old and out of date. Others followed.
Dupont decided that it would build a $10 million plant in Ohio to manufacture a
product—mylar—that it had developed in Buffalo. National Anilene, now owned
by Allied Chemical, had also, it seemed, lost its loyalty to the local community,
announcing that it would begin processing coal tar products at a plant in Virginia,
while Hooker Chemical chose Mississippi over Niagara Falls as the site of a new
chlorine plant. The reason, the company said, was "a combination of circumstances including cost of land, the labor situation and the cost of doing business
in New York State." Most people, unable to face the reality of the dramatic
upheavals that were occurring within the community, failed to grasp the significance of these events. Commentators remained boosterish in the face of
unsettling facts. The *Courier Express*, responding to the rash of corporate departures in 1952, remained optimistic: "Buffalo's economic position, with its low cost
of power, its skilled labor and its shipping advantages, is far too secure to bring
about any wholesale economic dislodgement."[5]

Commerce was even more vulnerable than industry. The movement of goods
and material by water had made Buffalo what it was, and despite more than fifty
years of dominance by industry and railroads, Buffalo's self-image remained
rooted in trade. The city's symbol—a lake boat floating on the rippling waters of
Lake Erie, a canal boat moving slowly down the still waters of the Canal, and the

lighthouse of the Buffalo harbor—continued to serve as the seal of the city. In 1950, as in 1850, Buffalo was still, so many said, the "Queen City of the Lakes." But the facts were beginning to say otherwise. The city had long ago lost its historic function as a port of transshipment, and by midcentury, most of the processing industries that had at one time provided a diversified and stable economic base—lumber, tanning, and the manufacture of soap, for example—had all but disappeared. Even the beer industry was in trouble.

While the number of breweries had been reduced during Prohibition (there had been seventeen in 1919, but only five in 1933), and the number of brewery workers was down from two thousand to twelve hundred, production remained steady. After the war, however, sales and production declined precipitously. While Buffalonians were drinking more beer than ever (per capita consumption was estimated at twenty-two gallons per year in 1955), the beer they drank was increasingly made elsewhere. National companies—Schlitz, Budweiser, and Miller—in a concerted effort to destroy home-based breweries in cities throughout the country, invaded local markets and successfully undercut local breweries (Anheuser-Busch, for example, opened a local distributorship in Buffalo in 1953).[6] The local industry staggered under this intense pressure from the large national companies. It simply could not compete. Not only did Buffalo breweries lack the cash to mount more than regional sales campaigns, their plant facilities were also old and obsolete, and it seemed they were unwilling to modernize. While breweries in other cities had introduced automated processes in virtually all aspects of the industry, local family-owned breweries continued to operate largely by hand. Workers still poured all of the ingredients, washed the gigantic kettles, and uncorked, cleaned, rinsed, and stacked the returned kegs by hand. In 1964, Arthur Newman, a business representative for Brewery Workers Local No. 4, went on a national tour of modern breweries. When he returned to speak to the few local brewers still remaining in Buffalo about the new automated processes he had seen, he received little response. Newman told the papers: "People didn't care. They never believed it would happen."[7] By the end of the 1960s, Iroquois was Buffalo's last remaining brewery. It closed in 1972.

While reinvestment may well have turned the tide in the beer business, there was nothing, it seemed, that local business leaders could have done about the St. Lawrence Seaway. Not that they didn't try. Ever since it was first proposed in the early 1920s, Buffalonians were deeply concerned about the impact that this kind of project would have. By extending the navigable portion of the St. Lawrence River from Montreal into Lake Ontario, the seaway would provide a direct inland water route between the Great Lakes and the Atlantic Ocean. It would, as a result, completely bypass Buffalo. The impact, as anybody aware of the city's history should have known, would be disastrous. Since the 1820s and 1830s, Buffalo's raison d'etre had been its location at the mouth of the Great Lakes and its direct connection, first via the Erie Canal and then the railroads, with the Atlantic Ocean. By the middle of the nineteenth century, Buffalo had become one of the world's great inland ports and the flour-milling center of the world. By the early 1950s, all of this was threatened by the planned construction of the St. Lawrence Seaway. The opposition rallied. Delegations of local businessmen descended on Washington and, in 1953, the Common Council, in a resolution that claimed the seaway should not be built because it would be vulnerable to Soviet air attacks, approved funds for still more lobbying. Other Buffalonians either were or pretended to be more optimistic. Frank A. Sedita, who was elected mayor in 1958, said the seaway would make Buffalo "the most accessible city on the North American continent," while an editorial in the *Evening News* crowed, "Seaway Bolsters City's Stature as Great Center of Commerce." One business executive said, "The Seaway means push and purpose for this community." Another claimed, "Smart men will see the potential here and ten years from now Buffalo will enter a period of great growth. I don't know anything that can stop it."[8] The impact of the St. Lawrence Seaway, notwithstanding the strangely deluded hopes of those within the community who supported it, was devastating. From the day it opened in the summer of 1959, the lake-bound freighters that had for so long sailed from the west toward Buffalo as their final destination, came no more. Lured by a water route that took them directly from the Great Lakes to the Atlantic Ocean, those great lake steamers, their holds filled with the products that for so long had formed the basis of Buffalo's diverse manufacturing economy, were lost forever, never to return. Buffalo's long-dreaded nightmare had finally come to pass; the city, which for so long had dominated the stream of commerce on the Great Lakes, was now bypassed as a dead-end route. As a result, an entire range of waterfront industries—boat companies, ship chandlers, ship repairers, and shipbuilders—closed. In 1962, the American Shipbuilding Company closed down, the last vestige of an industry that had been in Buffalo since 1812. The grain industry, consisting primarily of grain storage and the manufacture of flour, suffered the most. Since the middle of the nineteenth century, Buffalo had been the grain storage capital of the world, harboring millions of tons of Midwestern grain in its internationally renowned grain elevators. Now, as increasing amounts of grain were shipped to Montreal via the seaway, Buffalo's significance as a port of storage quickly eroded.

The construction of the St. Lawrence Seaway was not the only event that doomed grain storage and flour milling in Buffalo. Other developments were equally harmful, including freight rates. For years, the Interstate Commerce Commission (ICC) had maintained artificially low rates for the shipment of grain by lake boats. By the early 1960s, however, the ICC revised its rate structure and it became far cheaper to ship grain on railroads directly from the Midwest to ocean ports on the East Coast.[9] Squeezed between a new rate structure on the one hand and the St. Lawrence Seaway on the other, Buffalo's grain industry, once the foundation of the city's prosperity and the source of its pride, struggled desperately to survive.

Some argued that Buffalo should have won the battle over rates, that the mills, if only they had cared, could have convinced the ICC to maintain their favorable rates. However, by the late 1950s the grain and flour businesses were no longer locally owned. The national corporations that owned the local mills—Cargill, International Milling, Standard Mills and Pillsbury—had little commitment to the local economy. With these corporations standing aloof from the issue, the struggle over rail rates fell to organized labor, the Chamber of Commerce, and the local political establishment. Without support from the mills, the *Courier Express* commented in 1959, there was little chance that Buffalo could win the rate restructuring case. Angered and frustrated by an economy increasingly dominated by outside interests, the newspaper concluded that the grain companies didn't really care, that "big companies with nationwide or worldwide operations have told their executives to steer clear of the problems of an individual city."[10] They did, and Buffalo suffered.

The impact of the decline of the city's grain-based economy was masked by the continued rise of the industrial economy, which rebounded to the benefit of many, particularly Buffalo's growing African American community. By 1956, the director of industrial relations for the Buffalo Urban League was pleased to report that "the Niagara Frontier is leading the country in integrating the Negro in industry and commerce."[11] While Buffalo's African American population had doubled between 1940 and 1950, by the latter year, the thirty-six thousand blacks living in Buffalo, most all of them in the Ellicott District, still represented a mere 6 percent of the city's total population of 575,901. While their numbers were small, to the white ethnics who had been living there for generations—the Germans in the Fruit Belt and Cold Springs, the Jews on Jefferson and William, and the Italians on Swan Street—they were large enough to motivate them to leave. Some went to outlying neighborhoods: Italians to South Buffalo; Jews to Humboldt Park and North Buffalo; and most, like the Germans, to the suburbs. Between the end of the war and 1950, whites were leaving the city at the rate of twenty-two per day, a more rapid rate, according to the Urban League, than any other city in the country (though followed closely by two other aging industrial cities, Cleveland and Pittsburgh).[12] As the African American population grew throughout the 1950s, race increasingly dominated the public agenda, particularly at the Buffalo Board of Education. For now, at least, as long as Buffalo's black population was small and black children were a minority in a handful of East Side schools, nobody, let alone the Board of Education, cared. There were other issues during the 1940s and 1950s that seemed more pressing.

Buffalo's Board of Education, appointed by the mayor, consisted of five members, which were carefully selected so as not to offend any of the city's ethnic groups. There was always one Irish American, one Italian, one Pole, one Protestant, and at least one Jew. (Although they made up only 2 percent of Buffalo's population in 1950, Jews were thought to be especially concerned about education. Blacks, with 6 percent of the population, were not represented on the board.) The board was a mixed group of business people, professionals, and would-be politicians, who served for no pay—people like Lester Gross, who owned a hat-manufacturing company; Mary Kazmierczak, a neighborhood doctor who lived over her office on the Polish East Side; Pasquale P. Rubino, an occasional candidate for political office and the proprietor of a well-known West Side funeral parlor; Sam Markel, a dentist; and Peter Gust Economu, maitre d' at the Park Lane Hotel, a favorite haunt of the city's business and political power brokers. The superintendent of schools was Robert T. Bapst, born on the German East Side in 1888, a graduate of local parochial schools, a respected Latin scholar, and a deeply religious Catholic—"the most prominent Catholic layman in Buffalo," the *Buffalo Evening News* wrote at the time of his appointment in 1935.[13] Bapst was proud of his management skills and boasted that Buffalo spent less per pupil on public education than any of the "big six" cities in New York.[14] (His critics argued that had he cared less about the parochial schools he would have been a more effective advocate for the public schools.)

Because of Bapst's Catholicism, the Board of Education was particularly sensitive about keeping religion out of the public schools. When in January 1949 the Kiwanis Club sought the permission of the board to advertise and sell tickets for a traveling performance of the world-famous Passion Play from Oberammergau, West Germany, the board refused. Board members were even more adamant when the club asked to have students released from school to see the play. Over Bapst's objection, the board denied the request and told the Kiwanis Club to schedule the performance on a Saturday.

Sometimes the separation of religion and public education was a ruse to hide other fears. In March 1950, a Jewish philanthropist offered to place a copy of the Jewish Encyclopedia in each of the schools' libraries. Samuel Markel, the Jewish member on the board, advised against it, saying that the book was "religious in character." Most of the board members, however, wanted to accept the books. Chairman Michael B. Montessano thought Markel's position was excessive. He said the board was "leaning over backwards for fear that someone may construe it as an action bordering on the religious." When it began to appear that Montessano would prevail, Markel revealed his real motive. He was opposed to the gift, he said, because it was an open invitation to anti-Semitic vandalism. Revealing the rawness of this particular wound, Markel said, "Somebody may go in there and take those books and deface them, and may use it as a means of poking fun at a group." The board reversed itself and, acceding to an understood ethnic prerogative, rejected the offer of the encyclopedias. Ethnic prerogative was again recognized in 1950, when Mary Kazmierczak received permission from her fellow board members to collect funds and clothing in the schools for the Polish Relief Fund.[15]

The board was particularly proud of its vocational schools. The mural on the entrance walls at Burgard High School, painted in the heroic, romantic style of all the murals created in the 1930s by the federal Works Progress Administration, reflected this pride. The picture, on two huge walls, is of the city's skyline. The sky is bright blue, with gleaming, colorful buildings in the background; the city's factories and the airport are prominently displayed (for years Burgard has offered courses in automobile and aviation mechanics). In the foreground are handsome, Nordic-looking young men, white work coats covering their suits and ties, diligently repairing cars, trucks, and planes.

The growth of wartime industries had increased the demand for vocational education and by 1950, more than half of the boys of high school age in Buffalo were enrolled in the city's six vocational schools (there was only one vocational school for girls).[16] Each of the schools specialized in the skills needed by one of Buffalo's dominant industries. McKinley offered courses in pattern-making and molding; Burgard in car and airplane tool and die making; and Buffalo Technical, a highly competitive technical rather than a vocational school, in engineering. The State Education Department (SED), while pleased with the condition of vocational education in Buffalo, was concerned that there was an overemphasis on industrial training. Compared with students in Rochester, Pittsburgh, Boston, and Chicago, the SED said in a 1956 report that not enough of Buffalo's youngsters were being prepared for careers in the business world. The report implied that Buffalo was failing to provide its children with the skills necessary for the modern age. The SED's analysts thought that "the relative stability of the economic life of the area is assured," but they wanted to take no chances and, in a prescient reminder, urged the Board of Education to think about the future by adapting vocational schools to the needs of the changing economy: "Specialized education in the vocational fields must be broad enough to condition trainees in other areas as jobs shift as a result of labor-saving equipment and the like."[17] The SED was also concerned about "inter-group relations" in Buffalo's public schools. Noting that "it appears that the relative concentration of certain ethnic groups in particular sections of the city will persist for several generations," the department urged school officials to "concentrate...on interschool activities as a way of teaching better inter-group relations." The SED was also worried about a group of high school students who were neither college-bound nor in vocational programs. These youngsters, 60 percent of all the students in Buffalo's high schools, were destined, the SED said, to work at manual labor jobs, called "operational," which required few skills. These students needed "pre-employment preparation, including some business and management skills and certain social skills involved in dealing with the public." Buffalo had a high dropout rate (20 percent in the academic high schools and an incredible 50 percent for students in vocational programs), and the SED proposed a program to allow dropouts to reenter school on a part-time or full-time basis, "as their experience after leaving school reveals the need for further education."

While Buffalo's dropout rate was high, the number of students going on to college—15 percent—was low, the SED noted. In an industrial economy that had revealed few weaknesses, this was acceptable. Welles Moot, as active in education as he was in city planning, and author of a 1949 board of regents report on vocational education, saw no cause for concern. "I don't believe in pushing them," Moot told the *Buffalo Evening News* in 1949. "If they don't want to go to college they shouldn't be forced to. If they want to go to work after they finish high school, let them go to work."[18] The Board of Education seemed to agree, for when Superintendent Bapst resigned in 1950, he was replaced by Benjamin D. Willis, a nationally known expert on vocational education.

By now, however, the Board of Education had begun to devote more attention to the growing numbers of black children in the city's public schools and, in 1954, in a sweeping change of high school districts, the board did what it could to reinforce Main Street as a racial barrier between the African American East Side and the white West Side. One of the schools that moved in the process was Buffalo Technical, which had for years been the flagship of Buffalo's vocational schools. A degree from "Tech" was a ticket to success in the engineering field, and admission to the school, located on Cedar Street on the city's East Side, was prized by the first- and second-generation immigrant families who lived near it. While the school remained almost exclusively white, by the mid-1950s the neighborhood around the school was increasingly African American. In addition, under growing pressure from parents as well as from the skilled trades unions that drew new members from the school, the board, as part of the sweeping school boundary changes made in 1954, moved the school into Hutchinson Central, which was located on Elmwood Avenue, on the West Side. At the same time, lines at East High, located on Northland Avenue, were redrawn so that, by the mid 1950s, East became widely recognized as "Buffalo's Negro high school." As a result of the redistricting decisions of 1954, the city's schools, like its neighborhoods, were fast becoming racially isolated. The situation worsened after the May 1956 riots on the popular Crystal Beach boat, the *Canadiana*.

Crystal Beach was a large, old-fashioned amusement park located on the Canadian shore across Lake Erie from Buffalo. Though dismantled in 1989, it was beloved by many. Scruffy and shabby, with the look of another era, it would have been perfect for a film set in the 1930s or 1940s. There was a large dance hall, an outdoor beer garden, and buildings where the gentle pastel colors of neon lights radiated softly from within glass bricks. Cheap and close to Buffalo, Crystal Beach, like Coney Island in New York City, had been the most popular outdoor summer recreation spot in the area for almost a century. There was hardly anybody in Buffalo who hadn't had a ride on the Comet roller coaster; or nursed "Crystal Beach suckers," multicolored lollipops that were hand-dipped at the park; or eaten french fries with white vinegar, washed down with loganberry juice, the rich, dark, syrupy concoction that has dripped down the chins of generations of Buffalonians.

Most people got to Crystal Beach by car, a twenty-minute ride across the Niagara River via the Peace Bridge. Until 1956, many others took the Crystal Beach boat, the *Canadiana*, a large, old, three-decked wooden steamer that had been making the hour-long trip up the river and out onto Lake Erie since the amusement park opened at the turn of the century. Hardly fancy or elaborate, the boat was nonetheless pleasant and the trip relaxing. People sat on the decks to picnic and sun themselves, and in the evening, a band played dance music in the rear of the ship. The 1956 season started, like all summer seasons, on Memorial Day. "That was like the beginning of summer," recalls Bill Robinson, a black man now in his mid-seventies:

> We all looked forward to it, the boat and all. Back then, if you were in any club or gang or what have you, the thing was to go to the beach on Memorial Day. And you'd go in your gang's clothes. The El Dorados wore matador pants and purple jackets. The El Tones had turquoise jackets with black trim. The Conservative Lovers... they were a girl's gang... wore dark blue. The Sweethearts had purple jackets with a dragon stitched on the back.[19]

On Wednesday night, May 30, 1956, the last boat back to Buffalo was packed. There were nearly a thousand passengers, most of them teenagers, many of them black. Fighting had broken out at the amusement park earlier in the day, and the Ontario Provincial Police had arrested nine of the troublemakers, four of them white, five black. When the *Canadiana* pulled away from the pier at Crystal Beach at five past nine that night, all seemed well. It was a rainy night and many passengers were below decks, huddling to keep warm. Then, suddenly, midway through the dark Lake Erie passage, fighting broke out between groups of black and white teenagers. Gangs—the morning paper called them "rampaging gangs"—rushed back and forth over the decks of the ship. The paper further reported that "switch-blade knives were brandished. Youngsters were shoved to the deck. Above deck roving groups of Negroes attacked the outnumbered whites. Girls were beaten mercilessly and youths who attempted to defend themselves were slugged and kicked without feeling." The evening paper reported that black teenage girls started the riot by attacking white girls. "'All of us white children were sitting together,' [said] the sobbing white girls, being escorted home by their parents and the police. 'They kept laughing at our shorts and began hitting us. They threw some of us to the floor. They were running up and down the decks. The Negro boys joined in.... The parents were afraid to break it up....'" Buffalo police officer Jeremiah R. Cronin said, "I'd never seen anything like it in all my years in the department."

The next day, the local press carried the news in large headlines. "Nightmare Boat Trip from Crystal Beach. Public's Wrath Runs High," said the *Courier Express.* "Violence Erupts at Crystal Beach... Tensions Brewing," said the *Evening News.* The story was repeated in papers throughout the country. The *New York Daily News* reported in a caption under a wire photo that "Youths Riot at Crystal Beach." The *Washington Post* said, "Teens Battle at Amusement Park." Meanwhile, Governor Averill Harriman expressed "grave concern" and urged authorities in Buffalo to investigate. United States Attorney John Henderson, worried about "subversive connections with the incidents aboard the *S.S. Canadiana,*" asked the FBI to do the same.

By the middle of June, the FBI had identified witnesses. The story they told was one of fear, confusion, and panic. One witness said that she had seen a "small white boy, about seven years old, being attacked by a colored girl about thirteen or fourteen years old." There were other reports of "Negro girls accosting white girls, pulling their hair, scratching them and causing them to become hysterical." Others thought the fight had been precipitated by "rival Negro gangs in from the Ellicott and Cold Springs neighborhoods." Others were not quite sure what they had seen. One witness claimed to have seen Negro girls attack white girls, but was able to identify neither attackers nor victims. Another said she wasn't sure "whether the victim was Negro or white." One who had sought shelter from the rain below deck said she was not even aware there had been a disturbance aboard the steamer. The captain of the *Canadiana,* Edward M. Solomonson, was equally nonplussed. He'd never felt the situation was bad enough to call the coast guard. "Similar events happened before," he said, "This was just a little bit more than ordinary."[20]

Southern newspapers saw it differently and seemed to relish the news. Under a photograph of policemen struggling with unruly blacks, the *Washington Daily News* wrote that "Holiday Outing Is Day-Long Race Riot." The *Daily News* in Jackson, Mississippi, accused the northern press, particularly the *New York Times* and the *New York Herald Tribune,* of virtually ignoring what they saw clearly as a "race riot." These same papers, the *Daily News* wrote, who "lather themselves with indignation and accusing headlines when discord rears its ugly head in the South, just can't see, hear or speak of comparable evil when such breaks out at home or just down the road at Buffalo."

Most in Buffalo disagreed. While there were several meetings of politicians, concerned ministers, and lay leaders to discuss the "implications of the riots for race relations," the public stance of community leaders was that the riot aboard the *Canadiana* was caused by juvenile delinquents and was not a "race riot." There were, the *Buffalo Evening News* said, "too many undisciplined punks—male and female—traveling in gangs looking for trouble." The absence of any adult partic- ipation, the paper continued, "clearly refutes any too-easy assumptions that the underlying problem was a breakdown in community race relations." The mayor, Chester Kowal, saw the incident as "part and parcel of Juvenile hooliganism." King Peterson, the black councilman from the Ellicott District, felt the same way. It was not a race riot, he said; rather, it was "a fight caused by unruly and dan- gerous teenagers." L. L. Scruggs, a highly respected African American physician, held the same opinion. "It is unanimously agreed by the Negroes in Buffalo that this was not a race riot," he said. The Board of Community Relations, while not discounting "racial tensions" as a cause, agreed with the mayor that the primary problem was indeed "juvenile hooliganism." Joseph DeCillis, the police commis- sioner, and Frank E. Evans, the president of the Urban League, reassured the community in a joint statement that there was "no racial problem in Buffalo and there is no cause for alarm on that score." Some dissented from the consensus. Victor Einach, Buffalo field representative of the State Commission Against Dis- crimination, said that blacks had "a strong chip on their shoulders." Whites, on the other hand, "refuse to face up to the fact that racial problems exist." The head of the youth board agreed. "Anyone who denies that there are tensions in certain areas of this city is blind," he said. Rev. Kenneth A. Bowen, president of the Buf- falo branch of the NAACP, was much less sanguine than other spokesmen in the black community. He expressed his sorrow that the summer had opened with this kind of conflagration, "especially since it seems to be between racial groups."[21]

What actually happened on the *Canadiana* that rainy night, two and a half miles out on Lake Erie, made little difference to the white people of Buffalo. No matter how hard the press and the politicians tried to convince them otherwise, the great majority of white Buffalonians saw the riots as an outburst of violence by blacks against whites. The white people of Buffalo were frightened, and many of them, particularly the immigrants who had been living in the neighborhoods of the East Side for generations, decided to leave. The exodus gathered momentum during the 1950s, and by the end of that decade, the US census reported that more than eighty thousand white people, 15 percent of Buffalo's white population, had left the city for the suburbs.[22]

For a while, anyway, according to social historian William Graebner in his wonderful book on teenage culture in Buffalo during the 1950s, there existed "the possibility of an interracial community based on a shared black youth subculture."[23] Much of this had to do with George Lorenz, a disc jockey known as the "Hound Dog," who became by the mid-1950s one of the nation's premier rhythm and blues and rock and roll disc jockeys. Lorenz, who had been programming rhythm and blues on a small radio station in Niagara Falls, moved to Buffalo in the early 1950s and was soon broadcasting live from a nightclub on William Street called the Zanzibar. The Zanzibar was owned by two brothers named Burt and Ralph Glaser, whose father, a Jewish immigrant, owned a nearby tire store. Like Leonard and Phil Chess in Chicago, the Glasers had a strong affinity for the culture of their Harlem-like neighborhood, and in their racially mixed club they programmed the era's leading rhythm and blues stars, including Fats Domino, Little Richard, LaVerne Baker, and others. Throughout 1956 and, in fact, on that unhappy weekend in May, the Hound Dog broadcast his primarily black music on WKBW radio while he promoted live rhythm and blues shows at the Memorial Auditorium. Lorenz was phenomenally popular, particularly with white audiences, a fact that Graebner attributed to questions of race. "Lorenz," he wrote, "was at the center of a complex set of relationships between white and black cultures. Though white, Lorenz was responsible for transmitting the energy and sexuality of black culture to white teenagers.... His Zanzibar broadcasts attracted interracial audiences... and his auditorium promotions were usually interracial events, attended by blacks and whites who sat side by side to watch a racially mixed card."[24] Sadly, the passions created in the wake of what many saw as "the riots" on the *Canadiana* made these kinds of activities and interactions increasingly difficult.

Meanwhile, Buffalo's rapidly growing African American population, most all of whom lived on the East Side, created a desperate shortage of housing and schools in that part of town. In 1958, after years of politicking by Cora P. Maloney, the African American woman who represented the Masten District on the Common Council, the Board of Education agreed to build a new school in the heart of the East Side at the corner of Masten and Ferry. While some African Americans were concerned that the new school's location east of Main Street would make it segregated, Joseph Manch, the new superintendent of schools, assured them that "any thought of segregation is one thing I won't stand for." The racial question, he said, would be dealt with later, when district boundaries for the new school were drawn. When Cora Maloney reminded Manch that just four years earlier the Supreme Court had found that segregated education was inferior education, Manch proffered reassurances that "the court was concerned with schools in the South, Mrs. Maloney, they were not concerned with schools in Buffalo.... We just don't operate that way."[25]

The NAACP didn't agree with Manch. In 1962, the local chapter of the NAACP reported that there were twenty-eight schools with black majorities and seventeen, all on the East Side, that were 100 percent black. Stating that Buffalo "has taken a back seat among cities in the fight for integration," chapter president Raphael A. DuBard demanded that the Board of Education, using a variety of strategies including site selection and redistricting, "fulfill its educational and legal responsibilities by entirely desegregating the school system." In June 1963, New York State Commissioner of Education James F. Allen corroborated DuBard's data. Reporting "clear and overwhelming evidence of racial imbalance" in the Buffalo public schools, Allen ordered the board to produce a remedy to be implemented in January 1964.[26] It might have appeared that time had begun to run out for the board, but Allen seemed less than committed. The board seemed to sense this and responded halfheartedly to the order. At the suggestion of Superintendent Manch, the board considered a voluntary transfer plan that would permit any child in any school in the city to transfer to any other school if space permitted. Space, not race, Manch said, would be the determining factor.

In a world seemingly removed from the rough and tumble of Buffalo's increasingly racially polarized world of politics and public policy, the arts, under the leadership of a group of enlightened men and women, flourished during the decade of the 1950s as never before. By the late 1940s, Cameron Baird had left the iron business, selling his interest in Buffalo Pipe to his brother William. Free from business concerns, he instead devoted himself full-time to his position as violist with the Buffalo Philharmonic Orchestra. When the war ended, he resumed his travels to the musical capitals of Europe. During this period, he helped found the great Casals Festival, which was held annually first in France and then in Puerto Rico. Back in Buffalo, motivated equally by his love of music and his eagerness to see it flourish in his home town, Baird began discussions with Samuel Capen, the chancellor of the University of Buffalo, who had worked closely with Baird to form the BPO in the mid-1930s, about the possibility of creating a department of music at UB. Baird was interested in the university's musical life as well as the musical life of the wider Buffalo community; it had been his hope, as chairman of the City Planning Association's subcommittee on the new music hall, to locate a new facility on the university's Main Street campus. Now, more than a decade later, he had the opportunity to influence the musical world of the campus as founding chairman of a new music department. Discussions with Capen proceeded quickly and in 1951 the first department of music in the history of the university was created under the chairmanship of Cameron Baird. A new and exciting era in the musical life of the city was about to begin.

Working out of a small converted house on Winspear Avenue, just off campus, Baird and a staff of one built a department that by the time of his death in 1960 had become a center of musical excellence that was recognized throughout the world. A great opportunity occurred in 1954 with a bequest from Fredrick Slee. Like Baird, Slee was torn between music and business. As a student at Harvard Law School at the turn of the century, Slee studied as much music as he did law. He also studied in Europe as one of the first American students of the already acclaimed Nadie Boulanger. By the 1920s, however, he was practicing law in Buffalo, having become by then one of the city's most respected corporate lawyers. As a specialist in the iron and steel business, he represented, among others, Bethlehem Steel, Frank Baird's Union Iron, and, when it opened in 1927, Cameron and William Baird's Buffalo Sewer Pipe.[27] While Slee's office was the epicenter of Buffalo's powerful world of iron and steel culture, his Buffalo home on Saybrook Place had become one of the great music salons west of the Hudson River, where, in a specially built performance space, such chamber music greats as Jascha Heifitz, Zino Franscati, Janos Starker, Fritz Kreisler, and others performed during their visits to Buffalo. By the late 1940s and early '50s, Slee had become particularly close to Cameron Baird, working with him at both the BPO and the chamber music society. Slee was also excited about Baird's new music department and shared with Baird a vision of a great musical mecca, like Boulanger's Sorbonne—a place where young people would come to learn, study, and perform with the best and most creative musicians in the world. When Slee died in 1954, his widow Alice revealed that he had left the full value of his estate—close to $800,000—as an endowment to Baird's music department. The purpose of the Slee bequest was specific—the money was to be used to bring to UB, every year "in perpetuity," a distinguished American composer, "a master teacher of harmony, counterpoint and fugue equal to a professor at the Paris Conservatory." In addition, Slee, who above all adored the Beethoven quartets, insisted that his bequest be used to fund an annual cycle of the complete Beethoven String Quartets. The quartets would be performed at UB by a string quartet of "international repute" and in a specific sequence prescribed in detail in his will.[28]

Baird was thrilled with the gift and wasted no time in implementing the terms and conditions of the Slee bequest. He immediately recruited one of the world's best chamber groups, the Budapest String Quartet, which had for years visited, rehearsed, and performed informal recitals at the Baird's home in Eden and at the Slee's home in Buffalo. Since the Budapest String Quartet was no stranger to Buffalo, Capen Hall at UB was packed when they performed the first Slee Beethoven Cycle in November 1955. The *Buffalo Evening News*, recognizing the opportunity the Slee cycle offered to the people of Buffalo, was thrilled: "Just to contemplate what these cycles can mean to the cultural future of the community puts any sincere music lover in a glow. In very few cities can a music student hear within the space of two weeks all the string quartets of Beethoven or ponder the fearless and gushing genius of the man and be inspired by the spiritual truths revealed in his music."[29] The Budapest String Quartet, as resident artists at the university, performed the Slee Beethoven Cycle every year between 1955 and 1966.

Baird was ambitious for his department and eager to make the appointment of the first Slee professorship a significant one, one that would bring the attention of the whole music world to Buffalo; he wanted to recruit the best and most famous. In September 1957, Aaron Copland accepted Cameron Baird's invitation to come to Buffalo as the first Slee Professor of Music.

Despite the acclaim that Copland and the Budapest brought to it, UB's music department grew slowly under Baird. By 1958, there were one hundred twenty-five students enrolled in music courses, more than fifty music majors working with a small faculty of five full-time professors, and more than twenty members of the Buffalo Philharmonic Orchestra teaching part-time. The Slee bequest, however, was doing its work well and, increasingly, Buffalo and the new department of music at UB began to acquire the respect and legitimacy that Slee had sought and Baird had worked so hard for. Slee's Beethoven cycles came to be recognized throughout the music world as a unique contribution to chamber music, and the Slee professorships continued to attract some of the most interesting and sometimes controversial composers, including Mexican composer Carlos Chavez; Leon Kirchner, whose 1953 piano concerto had won a Naumberg Award; and Ned Rorem, the Pulitzer Prize–winning composer, whose piece "Eleven Studies for Eleven Players" was dedicated to Cameron Baird. Under Baird, UB's music department became one of the most daring academic programs in the country, attracting the attention and curiosity of the world of the avant-garde.

Baird, who donated half of the $1.5 million cost, commissioned Paul Schweiker, one of the country's best-known architects of the modern style and the chairman of the Yale School of Architecture, to design a building to house the new department. Baird had envisioned an integrated fine arts center with three distinct parts, one each for drama, music, and art. His great dream was to house a performance space for opera. "What a wonderful thing it would be," he mused in 1958, "for the Metropolitan Opera to come to Buffalo as it does to Toronto and Cleveland."[30] Funding and bureaucratic problems ensued, and Baird was forced to settle for a more modest hall dedicated strictly to music. As was often the case with signature buildings designed by marquee architects, the building, though fraught with horrific structural problems that often caused the basement to flood, won *Progressive Architecture*'s award for "Best Building for Advanced Education" in 1957. Following Baird's premature death from cancer in 1960, the building was named Baird Hall in his memory. By the time of his death, Baird had created a music department that was on the cusp of world recognition. In the years that followed, the seeds that Baird had planted would bear fruit; the music department at UB achieved the goals for which he had so long labored.

Baird's pathbreaking and adventuresome work at the music department was mirrored by the work of his colleague at the university, Oscar A. Silverman. As chairman of the English department, Silverman, a Yale-educated scholar, was, like Niles Carpenter, Charles Abbott, Cameron Baird, and others on Capen's campus, a public educator who was as committed to his community as to his students. Capen encouraged his faculty to integrate their scholarly lives with the life of the community, and few were more adept at this than Silverman. Handsome, debonair, extremely affable, and very well liked, Silverman, much like Charles Abbott, was a wonderful ambassador for the arts in general as well as for the university in particular. Silverman was also a dynamic and popular classroom teacher who loved his craft. Accessible and eager to share his knowledge and his personality, Silverman taught regularly in the university's noncredit night school and for years was the host of a popular weekly radio program on the arts. Like Abbott, Silverman was socially smart, with a keen but sensitive sense of where the money in Buffalo was and how best to get it. And, like Cameron Baird, his friend and colleague at the music department, Silverman was a brilliant cultural entrepreneur, able to chart new directions that brought distinction not only to UB but to the city as well.

In the fall of 1949, on a sabbatical with his family in Paris, Silverman, "with hundreds of other people, went a number of times to see the exhibition of books, manuscripts, memorabilia, etc of the late James Joyce, who had died in 1941." Silverman was struck by the exhibition, impressed particularly by its structure and arrangement, which, he said, was "like a clever labyrinth" by which "the visitor himself progressed through Joyce's life, personal and literary." He was impressed by the "many examples in small notes...of the first or second or third drafts of the various episodes of *Ulysses*." "In addition," Silverman recounted with the excitement of great discovery, "there were many notebooks illustrating the working habits of the author in preparing *Finnegans Wake*." The materials of the Joyce exhibition, Silverman recognized instantly, fit perfectly with the mission of Charles Abbott's poetry project. "The whole comprised one of the most striking exhibitions of the creative talent—in this case the talent of a genius—at work that anyone could be privileged to see." The exhibit, Silverman knew, had been organized in the hope of selling selected items to raise funds for Joyce's family. Following several hurried telephone calls to Charles Abbott, the director of the Lockwood Memorial Library at UB, the two men, recognizing instantly the value that this "magnificent" (in Silverman's words) collection of Joyce material would have for the university, resolved to purchase them for Lockwood Library.[31] Chancellor Capen was happy to underwrite the project, but, he told Abbott and Silverman, as he had told George Metzger years before, the money for the project would have to come from private funds of local patrons of the arts whom Silverman, as the university's favorite emissary to the community's rich and famous, had come to know. Appealing to his friends in the community, Silverman raised the money, and in the fall of 1950 the bounty arrived: boxes filled with manuscripts representing all stages of the development of most of Joyce's works. In addition, there were "many letters, two decades of reviews, press clippings and journal articles on his works from the world over, family portraits, as well as his personal library and effects."[32] With his brilliant, stealth-like acquisition, Silverman, like Abbott before him, was adding to what was fast becoming one of the world's great manuscript collections.

Silverman's influence at the university transcended his chairmanship of the English department. Indeed, it was Silverman who had persuaded Capen to hire Baird in 1950, and it was Silverman who a year later persuaded Seymour Knox to sponsor what Silverman called the university's "Niagara Frontier Convocation," an ambitious two-day symposium held on December 7 and 8, 1951, to discuss nothing less than "The Outlook for Mankind in the Next Half Century." Silverman, with significant financial support from Knox, had invited scholars, scientists, artists, and writers from all over the world to discuss topics of concern from world peace to the arts and sciences. None was more interesting or better attended than a program titled "Will the creative arts thrive or degenerate during the next fifty years?" Chaired by Knox himself, the panelists consisted of a host of artists and intellectuals who had done so much to place Buffalo at the forefront of the world of modern art: Oscar Silverman; Edgar C. Schenck, director of the Albright Art Gallery; A. Conger Goodyear, representing the MoMA; Andrew C. Ritchie, former director of the Albright and then-current director of painting and sculpture at the MoMA; Alexander B. Schneider, from the Budapest String Quartet; the great contemporary painter Ben Shahn, whose stained glass windows would soon grace one of the city's principal synagogues; and the poet William Carlos Williams.[33]

During his visit to Paris, the gregarious Silverman had befriended Sylvia Beach, the original publisher in 1922 of *Ulysses* and the owner of Paris's world-famous Left Bank bookstore, "Shakespeare and Co." By the late 1950s it became apparent to Silverman that Beach was willing to sell her entire collection of Joyce materials. Eager and excited, Silverman shared this information with his friends in the community, and two of them, Dr. and Mrs. Walter Stafford, were curious to see for themselves the extent of the collection. Silverman recounted: "A hasty trip was arranged; and the Saturday after Thanksgiving [1959], the first week of jet service to Europe, the three of us descended on Paris." Months passed and finally the persistence of Silverman and "the charm of the young woman, Mrs. Stafford" paid off. Beach, after great heart-wrenching difficulty, agreed to sell her vast Joyce materials to the University of Buffalo. "Finally," Silverman wrote, "details were arranged, and in the next summer, at Miss Beach's insistence, we returned to Paris to sort and to plan and to transport the treasures to Buffalo." By September 1959, the Sylvia Beach Collection had been added to the Wickser Collection in the Lockwood Memorial Library. It was a treasure trove of Joyceiana, including, most significantly, twelve more workbooks of episodes from *Ulysses*. This was not all, however, as, according to Luca A. Crispi, a Joyce scholar at UB, "Sylvia Beach also sent over twelve hundred pages of typescript and eight hundred pages of galley proofs, all with additions and corrections by Joyce."[34] Silverman's initial coup was augmented still further when, following the sudden death of Beach in 1962, UB was offered the opportunity to buy the rest of her collection of Joyce material. Again, it was the Staffords who made the purchase possible. The Beach purchase was a mother lode. Crispi, who cataloged it, reported that it contained "two hundred and twelve letters from Joyce to Beach, further first editions signed by the author and dedicated to her, translations, more photographs, as well as other significant manuscripts and letters." Beyond that, Crispi reported, "there were many letters, two decades of reviews, press clippings…family portraits as well as his personal library and effects."[35] "Now," Silverman concluded triumphantly upon the arrival of the Beach material, "the University of Buffalo Library has one of the great Joyce collections in the world."

Seymour Knox, meanwhile, was in the midst of passionate and inspired collecting of his own, which lasted with little interruption until his death in 1990. Between 1945 and 1955, Knox had acquired 158 paintings, 78 prints, 31 drawings, and 12 pieces of sculpture. Among them were works of the greatest artists in the world; including Henry Moore, Picasso, Matisse, Braque, Kokoschka, Rousseau, Rouault, Modigliani, and Mondrian; American painters Charles Sheeler, Arthur Davis, Stuart Davis, Marsden Hartley, Georgia O'Keeffe; and Gaugan's "Yellow Christ."

Knox's buying became more aggressive following the appointment in 1955 of Gordon M. Smith as director of the Albright Gallery. Between the time of Smith's arrival and 1957, Knox bought forty-five paintings and sculptures for the gallery, all but one of which was completed in the 1950s. No sooner had the paint on many of them dried than Knox and Smith snapped them up. A Franz Kline completed in 1953 was purchased by them in 1956. A De Kooning completed in 1955, a Rothko, completed in 1956, and a Lichtenstein, completed in 1962, were all bought the year they were painted. A Sam Francis, painted in 1952, was hanging on the walls of the gallery in 1956. A painting by Philip Guston, completed in 1956, was bought in 1957. A Jaspar Johns, completed in 1959, was bought the same year, and Rauschenberg's "Ace," completed in 1962, was exhibited to excited crowds in early 1963. Smith and Knox—"Mr. Albright and Mr. Knox," as they were known in the astounded art circles of New York and Paris—knew what they wanted and became bold and visionary tastemakers of the contemporary. They pushed the Albright and, with it, their hometown to the forefront of the world's contemporary art scene. In Smith's first year alone, Knox and Smith worked through galleries in Paris, London, and New York, as well as with the artists directly, to buy works by Gorky, Pollock, de Kooning, Gottlieb, Hans Hofmann, Franz Kline, Mark Rothko, and Sam Francis. By the end of the decade, the Albright possessed the leading collection of Abstract Expressionist art in the world. At the end of 1957, an exhausting and exhilarating year, Smith reported that "the Albright has always been in the vanguard in its acquisitions. It has not waited for artists to receive national acceptance but has frequently bought their work before they received it."[36]

The rest of the world also recognized the role and standing of the Albright. Writing in the *Baltimore Sun* in 1958, Kenneth Sawyer, the paper's widely regarded art critic, said that "the Albright is considered in museum circles as the hottest institution in America. It used to be the Museum of Modern Art but now the Albright is the touchstone and Buffalo is the envy of every other city in America as its modern collection is far and away the best today. It is courageous and magnificent."[37]

Downtown Buffalo, meanwhile, continued to struggle. Throughout the 1950s, politicians and planners in the city, as in the rest of the nation, became increasingly desperate, seeking salvation in ever-larger, ever-more expensive, and ever-more disastrous policies of urban renewal. For those who cared and thought they knew, the renewal of the city, its downtown and its neighborhoods, could be found only in big projects and large-scale developments. Only these types of ventures, they argued, had the potential to renew large areas and to make the kind of impact, both real and symbolic, that they felt was necessary to improve the struggling city. Since the 1940s, most professionals, including planners like Ladislas Segoe, a consultant retained by the City Planning Association in 1944 to help them generate postwar plans for downtown, espoused this point of view. Segoe, who served as a consultant to Detroit, Toledo, and other cities that would become part of the arc of cities referred to as the "Rust Belt," told a large Buffalo audience in 1944 that nothing less than "a complete remodeling of the central city was required to adapt it to modern conditions."[38] These ideas gathered force as downtown's problems mounted in the postwar years. At a 1955 roundtable sponsored by *Architectural Forum*, the leading journal of the design profession, and attended by architects and planners from all over the country, there was much discussion about creating "a clean slate" in downtown, of "using the same kind of genius that is being used in the development of new towns and shopping centers" for the renewal of central business districts. One presenter suggested that success required "ripping out no less than one hundred acres of old buildings for a completely re-planned rebuilding of the city." The general sense of the conference was that "downtown cannot reestablish itself by half measures; it cannot make-do but rather must make itself as beautiful and desirable and as accessible as the new outlying districts are." Lewis Mumford, the great guru of urbanism, seemed to have agreed. Writing in the *New Yorker* in 1955 (how, it is interesting to ponder, did his readers in New York City respond to the advice he proffered?) Mumford insisted that the only way for the city to compete with the "lure of the suburb" is by "rebuilding the interior of the city with gardens and parks and open vistas so that it too will be desirable and habitable."[39] "Rebuilding" required demolition, and throughout the 1950s, whole blocks in downtown were cleared. The goal of such demolition was often nothing more than increasing parking capacity.

In 1951, Common Council president Peter J. Crotty, who earlier in the year had proposed the widening of Delaware Avenue from Niagara Square north to the city line, suggested the demolition of two square blocks of lower Main Street for the creation of a thousand-car parking ramp. Not only would this help the businessmen there, Crotty said, the surface lot would be "an enhancement." He argued that "the area needs beautification" and should "be rid of the semi-slums there."[40]

Most downtown business interests—bankers, real estate developers, the Chamber of Commerce, and the press—agreed that municipally owned and operated parking ramps were critical to the future of downtown. In 1951, Alfred G. Bourne, an officer at Gurney, Overturf, and Becker, which, like the other big downtown realtors, was afraid of the suburbs and was therefore ever eager to grasp at straws, said that even when the move to the suburbs "was just starting, there [were] a good many vacancies in downtown office buildings and more vacant stores than ever."[41] Citing "deplorable parking conditions," the answer, he felt, like so many others, was plenty of cheap, city-owned parking. In October 1951, the Common Council approved the creation of a municipal parking agency and authorized a $3 million bond issue for the construction of three of five proposed parking ramps. Mayor Mruk was thrilled, believing that these ramps were somehow a cure-all that would, he said, lead to "the preservation and expansion of existing trade; the stabilization of existing business trends and the prevention of decentralization of business and shopping."[42]

The ramps were just the beginning. Some, like the planning consultants Nathaniel D. Keith and Carl Feis, retained by the city in 1957, would go further still. The mixture of uses that characterized downtown, they said, exacerbated the parking problem. The city, therefore, should be rezoned and completely replanned so that each sector of the city's economy—office, retail, financial, and service—would have its own separate, preferably clustered location within downtown. Only this way, they argued, would the "parking problem" be eliminated.

The conversion of building sites to parking lots occurred at the hands of private owners, too, who, like those who came before and after them, realized a higher rate of return on their properties. The most infamous case occurred in 1950, when despite editorials in newspapers throughout the country and a few faint-hearted efforts locally to save it, Frank Lloyd Wright's world-renowned Larkin Administration Building was torn down so the owners could build a parking lot. The building had been deteriorating for years, abandoned by its owners and neglected by the authorities. An article in the *Buffalo Evening News*, which featured a photograph of the crumbling building with all of its windows broken and shattered, bore the headline: "City's 'White Elephant' Falling to Ruin ... No use for Larkin Building in sight." The article told the full story:

> The five story brick structure, once the most modern office building in the country, gradually is approaching a state in which it will be entirely useless. Every double-paned window is shattered. The tall iron gate which graced the entrance has toppled from rusted hinges. The iron fence topping a low brick wall around the structure went into a wartime scrap collection. The Larkin Building, a headache to the city since it was acquired in tax foreclosure proceedings in 1945, cost $4,000,000 to build and was designed by Frank Lloyd Wright, a nationally famous architect. Offers to purchase it for around $25,000, far less than its assessed valuation of $239,000, including land, have been turned down. A national advertising campaign that cost $6,000 brought inquiries but no offers. The state rejected a suggestion that the building be converted for emergency housing and the county took no action on a proposal to make it headquarters of the Welfare Department. [43]

It was not, it seems, that the owners did not know its value or its worth; it was just that they did not care enough to do anything about it. For years, fabulous buildings, so many of which had lost their value in a city hit by economic depression and then stunned by suburbanization, buildings whose absence we mourn today, had been coming down, usually for parking lots. This devastating process, which deprived future generations of the great treasures of the past, accelerated in the 1950s.

The price was high; the losses irreparable. Acquisition of the ramp sites and demolition of the buildings proceeded quickly. Reporting in the spring of 1954, the *Evening News* said: "A sizeable chunk of Buffalo's history will be powdered into dust when wreckers' hammers begin thudding against the buildings at Main and Seneca streets, clearing the way for municipal erection of off-street parking facilities." With some sense of regret and loss, the paper described the building at 215 Main Street, which was being demolished: "The granite structure with its second floor façade of Greek columns and heavily cross-barred windows, was built in 1894, obviously as an ornate financial center." [44] Also demolished for a ramp that was built at Washington and Eagle was the breathtakingly beautiful Hotel Buffalo, which through the 1920s was the city's proudest and most elegant hotel. Down, too, came the Germania Insurance Building on the corner of Main and Lafayette Square. A six-story cast iron building built in 1875, it would have, had it been allowed to stand, rivaled any building in New York's SoHo, the country's great district of cast-iron architecture. Bought by the Tishman family of New York realtors in 1956, who planned to build on the site a contemporary, Miesian box of a building, the Germania did not come down without a fight. "The wreckers," the *Buffalo Evening News* reported in August 1957, "who still will have to tear it apart with acetylene torches, will learn that in the 1870s good buildings were not put up to be torn down."[45] Allan C. Tishman could not wait. "We're excited about it," he said. "We're anxious to get the first brick off the old building to remove any doubts there may be about a new building going up." Tishman had big plans for the site: it was to showcase a twenty-story glass, curtain-walled building, which was designed by the internationally known New York modernist, Emery Roth. It was to be the first skyscraper built in Buffalo in twenty-five years.[46]

The Germania Building was not, at least according to the *Buffalo Evening News*, going to be missed: "[T]here are few left to shed any tears as it comes tumbling down." The same also seemed to be true when, in early 1959, M&T Bank bought back from the Federal Reserve a building that the bank had built in the 1880s. The bank needed, it said, "more customer parking." It was a heartbreakingly beautiful building, built in an imposing Greek Revival style and surrounded on three sides by monumental marble columns. Insley Smith, in charge of the Buffalo branch of the Federal Reserve, was pleased. "We're glad," he said, "that the M&T bought it because it is in a position to utilize the property to the best advantage of that area of Buffalo."[47] In September of the same year, the Spencer-Kellogg Building, a stately four-story Federal-style brick building at the corner of Niagara Square and Delaware Avenue, which dated to the early 1830s, was also torn down for parking. The adjacent Erlanger Theatre at 120 Delaware was also being torn down. The owner, Darwin Martin Jr., said that a new parking lot was needed. Martin, whose father had commissioned Frank Lloyd Wright to build his home, known today as the Martin House, "regretted," he said, "that no economically feasible plan had been found to preserve it."[48]

Some, like Irving Saperston of Saperston Real Estate, would go further still. Saperston, like the other big downtown real estate companies, rarely saw a renewal project he did not like, particularly when new construction was involved. In a speech delivered to the Chamber of Commerce in 1958, Saperston advanced yet another plan that had the backing and support of many of the downtown real estate interests. The goal, as always, was more parking and easier traffic flow. The target, as it had been almost fifty years before, was Lafayette Square, which, along with the elaborate Soldier's and Sailor's Monument, Saperston planned to demolish. In its place, Saperston would build an underground parking garage with space for more than a thousand cars. Gone, too, if Saperston had had his way, would have been downtown's last farmer's market, the Washington Market, which would have been replaced by a four-square-block surface parking lot. According to the Saperston plan, traffic flow would be enhanced by the conversion of most downtown streets to one-way traffic. But Saperston's plan was not all slash and burn. For downtown to thrive, he said, children must be brought downtown. "Bring them back," he proposed, "with clowns, prizes, suckers and free movies."[49]

Parking lots, like weeds, grew up along the streets of downtown Buffalo; by the end of the 1950s, a growing number of formerly teeming downtown corners were lost to the vast, empty expanses of asphalt parking lots. Some residents, like long-time Buffalo attorney Edward Jaeckle, wondered if it was worth the price. In an interview in 1957, following the demolition of yet another downtown business block, Jaeckle spoke about how he was saddened by the changes, the loss of small businesses, stores, and especially good places for lunch, "places such as Tony Kaiser's at Washington and Mohawk, Frank Offerman's at Main and Mohawk, Tony Schasri's on Court Street, Billy Rose's, La Porta's and Leffler's. They were good, cheap and a lot of fun."

Others argued that these kinds of losses, and the steady and relentless erosion of historic patterns of living in the city, were small compared to the gain to be had. When the first parking ramps opened at Washington and Mohawk and down the street at Washington and Eagle in 1955, they were greeted with enthusiasm by Steven Pankow, one in a long list of mayors who saw the salvation of downtown in parking lots. Pankow promised (and perhaps even believed) that downtown Buffalo would, as a result of the ramps, "become once again the business, shopping and financial center of Western New York for a considerable radius."[50] He said that parking lots "show that Buffalo has arrived at a new and wonderful age." The Chamber of Commerce seemed to agree. With ten thousand parking spaces available (as compared to Moot's recommended twenty-five thousand), the chamber felt that Buffalo had "solved the problem of parking." Now, it said, "there really is no other vital problem or threat to Buffalo's downtown business district." As if the chamber was not quite convinced itself, it also adjured: "Don't anyone, anyone, sell downtown Buffalo short."[51]

The neighborhoods, meanwhile, were experiencing troubles of their own. For awhile, following the passage of the National Housing Act of 1949 and the creation of a new urban public policy known as "urban renewal," there was hope: in addition to the sweeping powers of eminent domain that they already possessed, city governments were now given incalculable amounts of federal dollars to "renew" themselves. In Buffalo, the work started in the Ellicott District, for more than a hundred years home to Buffalo's East Side African American community. The problems of the Ellicott District become serious during the 1940s when a huge influx of African Americans—more than eight thousand, according to the Urban League—came to Buffalo to work in the city's massive war-time economy. Buffalo's African American population, 17,694 in 1940, continued to grow after the war, reaching more than 36,645, or 7 percent of the city's total population, by 1950. Almost all of these migrants had moved into the Ellicott district where conditions were worsening.

In an article titled "The Negro Community in 1948: A Story of Bad Housing," the *Buffalo Evening News* cited the findings of the 1948 annual report of the Urban League: "The facts it recites," the *News* reported, "are a shock to civic complacency."[52] Citing the huge influx of new black settlers during the war, the Urban League's report said that the Ellicott District had "become a breeding place for crime." Noting the "definite correlation between poor housing, morality, delinquency and crime," it warned that Buffalo "may experience race riots like those in Detroit and Chicago if measures are not taken to relieve the desperate Negro housing needs." The *News* concurred, and citing the Housing Act of 1949, it warned that "Buffalo had better lose no time equipping itself to take advantage of the program: the clearing of our slums is too urgent to risk 'missing the boat' for want of a local initiative."

Conditions—overcrowding, high rents, and neighborhood blight—worsened, and in its 1951 annual report, the Urban League reported that the "trend toward ghetto living in the Ellicott District is the major social problem in the Negro community."[53] Even the white community could no longer ignore the dramatic changes that had taken place. One downtown banker, eager to expedite the project, concurred. "It is," he told the *Evening News*, " a colored slum of the worst kind." Like so many of his colleagues among the downtown community, he was concerned, he said, because Ellicott was "just a stone's throw from our best downtown district." In July 1952, the *Buffalo Evening News* commented that "the good people of Buffalo who think they live in a sleek, clean, tree-lined city would be shocked beyond description if they see the conditions in the Ellicott District."[54] Overwhelmed by the flood of southern blacks into their community, many of the older, more established African American families who had lived in the Ellicott District for years moved out. Excluded from the suburbs by the notoriously discriminatory housing policies of the federal government and the equally discriminatory housing covenants that had been passed throughout suburban America by townships in conjunction with the real estate industry, these blacks moved into the neighborhoods vacated by the white ethnics. Despite its distinctly racist overtone, there was something perversely beneficial about the movement of whites to the suburbs. Had whites not left in such large numbers; there would have been no place for blacks to move. Racial conflict would have been exacerbated by conflicts over turf, and race relations would have deteriorated even more than they did.

Blacks, in fact, were not overconcerned by the departure of whites. Indeed, Rev. Kenneth Bowen, president of the local chapter of the NAACP, was pleased with the progress of the transition. Commenting on the phenomenon in 1956, he said, "The movement of second-generation middle-class Negroes from the Elli-cott District to the Cold Springs and the Humboldt Park section has been steady, smooth and successful, devoid of friction." Thus, for those blacks able to afford to buy homes in these suddenly abandoned neighborhoods of the East Side, the white exodus was a blessing, which allowed them to escape the deterioration of the old Ellicott District where worsening conditions created growing concern.

In June 1955, the Common Council announced that it would authorize the demolition of twenty-nine city blocks and one hundred sixty acres—a massive square block in the Ellicott District that spanned from Michigan Street in the west to Jefferson in the east and from William in the north to Swan in the south. The area was to be cleared and replaced with a development, which the council prom-ised would include a "new town in town" consisting of clusters of private, single-family garden homes, apartments, two high-rise low income housing projects, and a state-of-the-art community center.

While many in the black community, including Leland D. Jones, the district's councilman, and King Peterson, his successor, favored renewal of the area, they, like many of their constituents, were opposed to the sweeping demolition and clearance project outlined by city and federal authorities. Some of them, particularly the homeowners, favored what was called the "Baltimore Plan," whereby federal funds would be used for renovation and restoration of existing homes. The Baltimore Plan, pioneered in that city by the federal Home Owners' Loan Corporation (HOLC), called for neighborhood conservation in Baltimore's Waverly neighbor-hood. Waverly was an old inner-city neighborhood of thirty-nine blocks and seven thousand residents. Four out of every five Waverly families owned their own homes. The HOLC program included three elements that, had they been applied in Buf-falo, might well have prevented the havoc eventually wrought by urban renewal here. The first called for the physical restoration of deteriorated housing; the second for the drafting of a long-term neighborhood plan; and the third for the cre-ation of the Waverly Neighborhood Conservation League, a community organiza-tion dedicated to monitoring and protecting the renewal of the neighborhood. Pro-moters of this approach eschewed the radicalism of urban renewal, speaking instead of a more organic approach to neighborhood renewal. "Just as the application of curative remedies will preserve the vigor and delay the eventual death of the human body, so can definite preventive measures be taken in the case of the urban community."[55] In Baltimore, the HOLC went further still and proposed the creation in every large city of a "Department of Conservation whose sole function would be, by precept, example and inspirational activity, to promote community stabilization projects in potentially and partially depreciated sections." While aware of the Baltimore Plan, Jones, concerned that the two public housing projects planned for the renewal area would only increase the isolation of blacks in the Ellicott District, urged a program of small-scale, scatter-site public housing. The *Wall Street Journal*, in a front-page article on urban renewal in Buffalo written in April 1958, agreed.[56] The problems in the Ellicott District, the *Journal* reported, were serious. Most of the area, it said, "is a slum: a dingy thicket of clapboard houses, one room churches and scabrous saloons." Despite this, the *Journal* said that many of the residents were in fact homeowners who supported the Baltimore Plan as a means to renew their neighborhood. These suggestions, however, were ignored. In January 1958, six years after the Ellicott District Urban Renewal Program was first announced, demolition and clearance of the neighborhood began. Within weeks, sixteen hundred African American families and more than two hundred businesses, over eighty owned by blacks, were lost. The residents scattered. The better-off homeowners moved to the Humboldt Parkway neighborhood. Some, the poorer tenants, were placed in the recently completed Dante Place projects, while others waited in the hope of finding apartments in the promised Ellicott projects. Most, however, more than a thousand families, moved up Jefferson Avenue into the Fruit Belt, where they were joined by the crush of blacks moving into Buffalo from the South at a rate of ten per day throughout the 1950s. The sudden in-migration of large numbers of new residents frightened the long-established residents of the German neighborhood. They, too, fled in turn, leaving the Fruit Belt—with streets named Cherry, Peach, Grape, and Lemon—to its new African American residents.

Obliterated, too, were the residences of more than a thousand Italian American families and more than a hundred of their businesses, all located in the ancestral Italian parish of St. Lucy's on Swan Street. Most of the people in St. Lucy's had been there since the late nineteenth century, having settled in along the many tangled side streets of the iconic Italian neighborhood. The church itself, on the corner of Swan and Chicago, was a stunning Victorian structure flanked with a peaked-roof rectory and an attached three-story brick school building. Nearby were stores and businesses rich in meaning and heritage to a new generation of Italian Americans: Bocce Pizza, Santora's, Christiano's Bakery, Chef's, and DiTondo's restaurants.[57] The people left (most of them moving to South Buffalo), the businesses closed, and the neighborhood died. In December 1960, the Reverend Monsignor Carl J. Fenice held the last mass at St. Lucy's. Urban renewal had destroyed in one year what it had taken fifty-six years of community building to create. Fenice was incredulous: "We were bewildered by the whole operation," he said. "It all happened so fast. There was such good, solid brick housing in the parish. That money could have done a lot of rehabilitation. What galls me is that that plot of land where our church stood is still vacant."

Meanwhile, flush with federal funds and the apparently thrilling sight of a century-old neighborhood crashing to the ground, Mayor Frank Sedita, in the summer of 1959, announced a new plan for the renewal of another ancestral African American neighborhood, Cold Springs, in the vicinity of Ferry and Jefferson. The plan, which called for the razing of most of the homes and buildings on close to eight hundred acres and replacing them with high-rise rental units, inspired the instant and vociferous opposition of Dr. Gerald N. Murphy, an African American dentist with an office on East Ferry Street. "This proposal," Dr. Murphy said, "is the most radical and impractical ever suggested for our neighborhood. It would be of irreparable harm to our community residents.... A trip through Cold Spring," he said, "gives evidence that less than 2 percent of the structures are beyond rehabilitation." Murphy suggested, instead, that for this neighborhood "made up of homeowners and over nineteen block clubs, a far more practical approach would show that rehabilitation is the best answer to the threat of blight and impoverishment."[58]

A similarly radical approach to urban renewal was taken toward the city's waterfront. In the late 1950s, Mayor Sedita, in a tradition that went back at least to the 1920s, advanced a scheme for the development of the area. Though much of the waterfront was taken up by the Niagara section of the New York State Thruway, there was a large chunk of land nestled between Niagara Street and the river and Porter Avenue and city hall that Sedita, like Walter Behrendt before him, cast his covetous eyes upon. The area, so close to downtown, so dense and overcrowded, was filled with thousands of first- and second-generation Italian Americans. In the words of Mayor Sedita, it was "ripe and ready, for relocation and renewal." In 1958, Sedita announced that the waterfront area, known as the "Lower West Side," was designated as "an urban renewal area." Two hundred and ninety-two acres west of Niagara Street would be cleared and replaced, he promised vaguely, with "high and middle income apartments and town houses, commercial development and a marina."[59]

When several years later the full impact of these several plans to renew the city's neighborhoods and its downtown were realized, nothing—not the neighborhoods, not downtown, not the streets, homes, or businesses, and not the long-cherished buildings that had for so long distinguished the character and fabric of the city—was immune from its devastating hand. Urban renewal was, as will be seen, a sweeping, unprecedented process, a virtual blank check, which enabled a small group of politicians and, in the case of the central business district, downtown businessmen to remake as they chose the form and the function of the entire city.

During the same period, Buffalo suddenly appeared on the radar screen of Joseph P. McCarthy, the Red-baiting senator from Wisconsin. Staff members of his

Senate Investigations Subcommittee had been in and out of Buffalo in late 1953 and early 1954 investigating Communist infiltration into local defense plants. Westinghouse, where the radical United Electrical Workers (the UEW had been expelled from the CIO in 1949 for alleged Communist domination) had a strong following, was singled out for particularly close scrutiny. Believing McCarthy's estimates that there were a hundred thirty members of the Communist party in Buffalo (he later revised his figures to thirty-nine), the House Un-American Activities Committee (HUAC) decided to add Buffalo to its list of cities to visit. Its informers had provided them with additional information, and, finally, in October 1957, the HUAC came to Buffalo.[60]

The first to testify were the professional informers, federal officials paid to infiltrate the ranks of the suspected Reds, who were intent on naming names. They gave the names of individuals who, they said, had organized Communist cells in industries and in neighborhoods throughout the city. There was, they said, a "Riverside club," an "Ellicott club," a "Polish club," and an "Italian club." In addition, they said, there were communist "cells" at Bethlehem Steel, Republic Steel, Westinghouse, Bell Aircraft, American Radiator, Chevrolet, and Ford. Organized by "colonizers," mostly individuals who came to Buffalo from New York City after the war, these clubs, the witnesses told the committee, made Buffalo "a serious Communist operation." One of them, paid to say exactly what the committee wanted to hear, said that "the penetration is quite extensive in this community. We have uncovered various colonizers in fifteen to eighteen different legitimate organizations in this area." Another witness swore that there were between five hundred and six hundred of these "colonizers" in the city. The committee, however, had learned from McCarthy's histrionics the danger of bandying around false figures and they immediately covered themselves. The actual number of party members in the city was irrelevant, Edwin O. Willis, a Democrat from Louisiana, said. In fact, he said, "there is a fallacy in undertaking to appraise the threat of the operation on the basis of numbers," for the Communists, who are "very deliberate in seeking out nerve centers and key positions within unions and various industries themselves, have a power far greater than their numbers would ever indicate."

The "colonizers" themselves were next to testify; over a two-day period, as their testimony became public, certain patterns emerged. The informers had done their jobs well and had caught the witnesses in embarrassing lies. Many of them, it became clear, had in fact come to Buffalo after the war, primarily from the New York City area, and had sought positions in the city's many industries. In applying for their jobs, many of them, anticipating the hostility of their prospective employers, lied about their backgrounds. Although none denied coming from "the City" (in those days before the advent of the state university and the inundation of the Buffalo area by New Yorkers, their accents glaringly stood out), they did lie about their education histories. Several of them, graduates of Queens, Brooklyn, and City colleges, had indicated at the time of their hiring that they had had no college education.

When confronted with this (the committee produced the college transcripts of the witnesses concerned), and with other questions about who they were and what their motives for coming to Buffalo were, most sought the protection against self-incrimination offered by the Fifth Amendment. Others took the more risky option and pleaded the First Amendment, thereby making themselves liable for a contempt indictment. Stanley P. Ingerman, a steelworker, was one of the witnesses who when asked to name the names of Communists cited the First Amendment and refused. (The committee didn't really need these names, as they already had them. Their interest was not in information but in intimidation.) He would, he said, talk about himself but nobody else. Gilbert Cohen took the same position. Cohen aggressively challenged the committee, denouncing it for attacking, not defending, American traditions. Cohen refused to talk, he said,

> first, because it affects my freedom of speech and association under the First Amendment. Second, the resolution creating this Committee is too vague. Third, this inquiry is outside the Committee's jurisdiction. Fourth, the Congress did not delegate to this Committee the authority which it claims. Fifth, my rights under the due process clause are violated. Sixth, this investigation involves exposure for the sake of exposure. Seventh, I believe that this investigation is injurious to American democracy and I believe it is my duty to do what I can to resist.

Other witnesses resisted too. One woman, Helen Mintz, a Jew and a practicing lawyer in Buffalo since 1934, was a particularly sought-after victim. She had been active in radical politics for years. An early member of Buffalo's small pro-loyalist Spanish Committee during the late 1930s, a member of the Committee Against War and Fascism, a supporter of Henry Wallace's campaign for president in 1948 (she had helped to organize Paul Robeson's benefit concert for Wallace at Kleinhan's Music Hall in that year), and an ardent Zionist, this woman was a prime suspect. She, too, however, refused the protection of the Fifth Amendment and used her testimony instead as an opportunity to denounce her informer as a liar and the committee as lawless and despotic.[61] Other women were paraded before the committee during those two days in October 1957. Several, whose husbands had been called to testify about their activities in area industries, were accused of joining local service organizations including the YWCA, the Jewish Community Center, and the Red Cross. Their intention, the committee said, was to spread Communist propaganda "by meeting young housewives in their homes and communities."

After two full days of testimony, the committee concluded its hearings. While they had hoped for more pliant witnesses, they were pleased with the "evidence" that they had acquired. "There has been confirmed," Willis said, "a pattern of Communist techniques of penetration of heavy industrial establishments of which this Buffalo area had many that are vital to our defense and economic well-being." Willis made no attempt to provide the confirming evidence, admitting that the witnesses had not helped him. But that, he said, was sufficient confirmation. "Many of the witnesses have been completely uncooperative with the Committee. But they have, in a negative way, helped to complete the factual picture which we have been trying to develop here as elsewhere throughout the nation." Their conclusions, in other words, had been foregone.

What the committee had revealed, however, was something about the nature of the Communist activities that had in fact taken place in Buffalo. The facts of the matter were that there had been a policy of "colonization." Many of the people who were indicted had in fact come to Buffalo with the expressed intention of trying to organize among the people in general and the workers in particular within the community. Operating as individuals—most of the people subpoenaed by the HUAC had neither seen nor met one another until then—and never part of a centrally organized and controlled party, the activities of these people were small in scale, humble in scope, and generous in aspirations. The witnesses had become active in their unions and in their communities to fight for such progressive causes as improved work conditions, health and safety, and equal opportunity for black workers.

But the committee was threatened by these people—these Jews and blacks and women and New Yorkers—and frightened by what they stood for. Their fear was contagious, and the witnesses were treated as pariahs by the rest of the community. For two days the newspapers printed their names and their pictures and ran stories with inflammatory headlines (such as the one in the *Courier Express*, October 3, 1957) that read "Housewife Denies She's a Red Now But Is Silent on Past") as if they had been convicted at a criminal trial. While the United Auto Workers protected their members who had been subpoenaed, the steel workers union did not, and refused to support those who had testified unless they signed a non-Communist pledge. The Jewish community, despite the heavy-handed anti-Semitism of the probe (the lawyer for the committee, in questioning a witness who worked at the Jewish Center of Buffalo, asked: "This establishment at which you are presently employed is under the auspices of the Hebrew Church, is it not?"), was equally silent, while the Bar Association of Erie County refused to condone the action of those lawyers who chose to represent their subpoenaed clients. Even the Niagara Frontier branch of the American Civil Liberties Union refused to get involved, and issued a statement that "neither the attorneys representing witnesses nor the ACLU should in any way be identified with the views of any of the witnesses."

Not only did the committee intimidate the community, it pandered to it, too. In his concluding statement at the end of the hearings, Gordon H. Scherer, a Republican from Ohio, assuaged the people of Buffalo. "If it is any consolation to the people of Buffalo," he said, "it is apparent from the testimony that by far the great majority of Communists in this area are not natives of the city of Buffalo. ...Practically all of them come from the City of New York, particularly those who came to colonize the industries of Buffalo." Worse yet, Scherer concluded, "those are the individuals who have college educations." Thus, by feeding the city's fear and distrust not only of outsiders in general but of educated outsiders in particular, the HUAC hearings set the stage for the traumatic controversy that emerged between the city and the University of Buffalo during the mid-1960s.

A far more serious and immediate threat to the people of Buffalo was Dutch Elm Disease, which by the mid-1950s had begun to ravage the city's arboreal paradise that had been lovingly cared for since the late 1920s by the city forester, Frank Karpick. As we saw with the widening of Delaware Avenue, Buffalo's trees had been in jeopardy for years. Karpick followed their gradual loss closely and mourned when the widening of Elmwood Avenue between Niagara Square and Allen Street in 1939 led to the loss of dozens more. Karpick commented that Elmwood, stripped of its trees, had taken on the appearance of "a naked street in a western mining town—bleak and bare."[62] Karpick's knowledge of the city's vast inventory of trees was detailed and intimate and from the lyrical tones of his writing, it seems as if he found within them the seeds of the city's salvation. In "Before Our Eyes," an article for a short-lived local weekly called *Town Tidings* written in July 1940, Karpick described in loving detail the trees of Buffalo. It is worth reading his writing in its entirety.

> As we stroll along Richmond Avenue on a hot, July day, we can readily appreciate the shade of the tall, stately elms, growing on both sides of this thoroughfare. We gaze aloft, as if to utter a silent prayer of thanks and our eye immediately is attracted to the beautiful Gothic arch, formed directly over the center of the Avenue, where the tips of the branches meet.
>
> Before our eyes, we have the most beautiful specimen of shade trees planting in the City of Buffalo—aye, in the world, we can almost say without fear of contradiction.... In spite of their beauty, even elm trees would be rather monotonous if they were used to the exclusion of all others. The planners of this city, knowing this, gave us a diversified planting so as to hold our interest.... Along North Street, Linwood and the other nearby streets we find quite a few hard or sugar maples. These trees are quite desirable as shade trees....

Northampton Street presents an older Norway maple planting, while Woodette, off Elmwood and Paul Place, of Seneca, have the same maples although considerably younger.

Hughes Avenue has Scotch elms about twenty-five years old and the same variety of elm was planted a good many years ago along Hertel Avenue near Main Street. French Street, from Kehr to Moselle, is planted with European linden and they surely present a beautiful sight with their symmetrical cone shape.... On Timon Street we have a planting which is quite colorful, especially in the winter. Here we find the London or Oriental Plane. The fruit or "button balls" which it carries most of the winter, gives it an appearance of a decorated Christmas tree.[63]

Spread by a fungus carried by insects, the dreaded Dutch Elm Disease, whose impact on elms was invariably fatal, had first entered the country in 1933 on elm-burl logs imported from France. Trees infected with the disease were first discovered in New York in Westchester County and on Staten Island and, by the spring of 1934, more than twelve hundred diseased elms had been discovered in the New York City area. Karpick, who knew that more than 60 percent of Buffalo's three hundred thousand trees were elms, was deeply concerned. "Now," he told the *Buffalo Evening News* in October 1946, "Rochester and Binghamton are on the suspect list too."[64] However, by the early 1950s it was too late, and in April 1952, Karpick reported that a tree, located in the Old First Ward, had been diagnosed with Dutch Elm Disease. "The actual disease," Karpick said, describing the process of the plague in simple yet ominous prose,

> is a fungus that gives off sticky spores. The fungus grows under the bark where the beetle lives. The beetle lays eggs below the bark and the wood. Then, the eggs hatch and larvae develops. The sticky spores adhere to the larva. The beetles proceed immediately to the top branches whither they feed on the twigs, opening up the bark. This allows the fungus to impregnate the bark. Once infected the tree will die within one year.[65]

All the public could do, Karpick said, was to watch for the disease's three symptoms. When the symptoms were spotted, he recommended that people immediately report them to him. First, he said, the leaves would turn yellow, and then brown. This would be followed by "a noticeable wilting in the upper branches." Third, the last and most telling symptom, he said, would be the death of the tree's small twigs and branches.

The concern was immediate and widespread. One newspaper urged that "[d]rastic action is needed to save the city's elm trees." Another suggested that the state and the federal government be brought in to "help us save our cherished

trees."[66] Indeed, in 1953 the New York State Department of Conservation established a special laboratory at the South Park Conservatory to fight the increasingly threatening disease. By the end of the year, Karpick, sickened by what he
knew was happening, reported that one hundred forty trees had already died. The
numbers grew, slowly at first, and then with increasing rapidity throughout the
decade: 151 in 1953 and 481 in 1954. In July 1954, John A. Ulinski, the city park
commissioner, at the instigation of Karpick, declared a "state of emergency" in
connection with the city's war against Dutch Elm Disease. Karpick, who until then
had been hopeful, had lost all optimism: "In spite of the fact that we did our best
to remove and dispose of all the infected and infested trees, as soon as we possibly
could after they were located, the number of cases increased."[67] By March 1958,
the Erie County Board of Supervisors, deciding that the problem was "too big"
for the county, said that there was little they could do and "passed the problem
back into the laps of the municipalities." As the disease spread, the city, helpless
to prevent it, could do little more than diagnose and eliminate. Each year the
number of stricken trees grew, so that by 1960, as the old decade ended and the
new one began, more than two thousand trees on streets and sidewalks in neighborhoods all over Buffalo had been cut down and removed.[68]

NOTES

1. "Made in Buffalo," *Fortune*, July 1951, pp. 91–102.

2. *Buffalo Business*, July 1955, pp. 17–22.

3. Daniel Norton, *Larry: A Biography of Lawrence D. Bell* (Chicago: Nelson-Hall,
1981), p. 221.

4. *Holiday*, August 1955, pp. 94–103.

5. "Solid Foundation for Buffalo Economy," *Courier Express*, March 15, 1952, p. 31.

6. The best history of brewing in Buffalo can be found in Stephen R. Powell, *Rushing
the Growler: A History of Brewing in Buffalo* (Buffalo, NY: Apogee, 1996). See also, "Beer and Buffalo," *Buffalo* 39, no. 1 (1964): 32–34, which was written during the last days of the industry.

7. "Sad Days for Local Breweries," *Courier Express*, February 15, 1964, p. 34.

8. There is a great deal of material on the seaway, which had been discussed since the
1920s, at both the Buffalo and Erie County Public Library and the Buffalo and Erie County
Historical Society. This material is drawn from E. A. Momberge, "St. Lawrence Seaway
Issue Rises Again," *Buffalo Business*, November 1945, pp. 22–27; "St. Lawrence Seaway at
Last," *America*, May 22, 1954, pp. 212–19; and P. D. Fahnestock, "Buffalo and the St.
Lawrence Seaway," an article published in the *Buffalo Evening News* in 1954. In addition to
the extensive materials listed in the local history card catalog, there is a large, article-filled
scrapbook on the "St. Lawrence Ship Canal" in the Grosvenor Collection at the BECPL.

9. "Struggle over Rail Rates Continues," *Courier Express*, July 15, 1959, p. 1.

10. Ibid.

11. Buffalo Urban League, *Annual Report, 1956* (Buffalo, NY: Buffalo Urban League, 1956), p. 14.

12. Buffalo Urban League, *Annual Report, 1950* (Buffalo, NY: Buffalo Urban League, 1956) p. 4.

13. "Bapst Appointed Superintendent," *Buffalo Evening News,* July 24, 1935, p. 1.

14. "Educational Expense in Buffalo," *Courier Express,* October 5, 1949, p. 12.

15. Buffalo Board of Education, *Minutes of the Buffalo Board of Education, 1950* (Buffalo, NY: Buffalo Board of Education, 1950), p. 854. This volume is stored in the offices of the Board of Education on the eighth floor of Buffalo City Hall. The *Minutes* from 1966 to the present are housed in the Grosvenor Collection at the BECPL.

16. Ibid., p. 1113.

17. Quoted in Buffalo Board of Education, *Minutes of the Buffalo Board of Education, 1956* (Buffalo, NY: Buffalo Board of Education, 1956) p. 770.

18. "Regents Wanted Changes in Vocational Ed," *Buffalo Evening News,* November 20, 1949.

19. This and the following information on the riots aboard the *Canadiana* is contained in FBI file number 45-9258, which was provided to the author by Dr. Bill Graebner, a history professor at the State University of New York, Fredonia.

20. William Graebner, *Coming of Age in Buffalo: Youth and Culture in the Post War Era* (Philadelphia: Temple University Press, 1990), pp. 120–29.

21. "*Canadiana* Incident Stirs Discussion on Race," *Courier Express,* June 2, 1956, p. 12.

22. "Census to Show Steep Population Loss," *Buffalo Evening News,* July 19, 1960.

23. Graebner, *Coming of Age in Buffalo,* p. 34.

24. Ibid.

25. Buffalo Board of Education, *Minutes of the Board of Education, 1958* (Buffalo, NY: Buffalo Board of Education, 1958), p. 101.

26. "Allen Pushes Board on Integration," *Courier Express,* June 23, 1963, p. 32.

27. For good background information on Cameron Baird, see Penelope Prentice, "Cameron Baird: Undersung Hero of Good Music in Buffalo," *Buffalo Spree* (fall 1986): 125 and "Cameron Baird, Music Leader and Industrialist, Dies at 54," *Buffalo Evening News,* May 5, 1960. Both articles can be found in the "music" files in the Grosvenor Collection at the BECPL. See also, Ed Yadzinksi, "Cameron Baird—A Legacy," http://www.music.buffalo.edu/bpo/CB-narr.htm.

28. Biographical information on Slee is from his obituary in the *Buffalo Evening News,* May 19, 1954. See also the Local Biography Scrapbook, vol. 22, p. 178, Grosvenor Collection, BECPL. Further information can be found in the Slee Family Collection, at the BECPL and at the University at Buffalo Music Department.

29. "Quartet in Slee Debut," *Buffalo Evening News,* November 1, 1955.

30. John Dwyer, "Cameron Baird Builds up UB Team to Be Proud of," *Buffalo Evening News,* April 5, 1958.

31. Oscar Silverman, "Why James Joyce?" *Grosvenor Society Occasional Papers,* February 1964, pp. 1–5.

32. Luca Crispi, "ReCollecting Joyce at Buffalo: Revising and Completing the Catalog," ed. Sam Slote and Wim Van Mierlo, *Genitricksling Joyce: European Joyces Studies 9* (Atlanta: Rodopi, 1999), pp. 13–26.

33. "The Future of the Creative Arts: A Symposium, as Part of the Niagara Frontier Convocation," *University of Buffalo Studies* 19, no. 4 (1952).

34. Crispi, "ReCollecting Joyce."

35. Ibid.

36. J. Benjamin Townshend, *100: The Buffalo Fine Arts Academy,* 1862-1962 (Buffalo, NY: Buffalo Fine Arts Academy, 1962), p. 34.

37. Jean Reeves, "Growing Kudos for Albright," *Buffalo Evening News*, December 8, 1958.

38. Ladislas Segoe, *The Modern City* (Buffalo, NY: Buffalo City Planning Association, 1944). This volume can be found in the "city planning" vertical files in the Grosvenor Collection at the BECPL.

39. Lewis Mumford, *From the Ground Up* (New York: Random House, 1960), p. 121.

40. "Council Directs Crane to Get Plans Ready for Main St. Project," *Buffalo Evening News,* June 13, 1951, City Planning Scrapbook, vol. 2, p. 210, Grosvenor Collection, BECPL.

41. "Shift of Business Offices to Fringe of Downtown Viewed as Growth Sign," *Buffalo Evening News*, April 22, 1953, City Planning Scrapbook, vol. 2, p. 226, Grosvenor Collection, BECPL.

42. "Mruk Cheers Ramps," *Courier Express*, October 15, 1951, p. 12.

43. "City's White Elephant Falling to Ruins," *Buffalo Evening News*, October 15, 1947, Buildings Scrapbook, p. 182, Grosvenor Collection, BECPL.

44. "Larkin Building Called Monument," *Buffalo Evening News*, November 16, 1949, Buildings Scrapbook, p. 183, Grosvenor Collection, BECPL.

45. Dean Richmond, "Former Federal Reserve Bank to Be Auctioned," *Buffalo Evening News*, December 17, 1958, Buildings Scrapbook, p. 120, Grosvenor Collection, BECPL.

46. There are good newspaper stories on the demolition of the Germania Building and the construction of the Tishman Building in the BECPL Grosvenor Collection's Buildings Scrapbook, pp. 309–17. See particularly Bob Watson, "Tishman Building Opens, Is Called Test of Buffalo's Downtown Redevelopment," *Buffalo Evening News*, November 19, 1959, and Bob Watson, "Tishman Building Opens…," *Buffalo Evening News*, November 19, 1959.

47. "Old Reserve Building to Be Razed, Replaced by Parking Lot at Main and Seneca," *Buffalo Evening News*, February 9, 1959, Buildings Scrapbook, p. 121, Grosvenor Collection, BECPL.

48. Dean Richmond, "Historic Kellogg Bldg. to Be Wrecked for Parking," *Buffalo Evening News*, September 25, 1959, Buildings Scrapbook, p. 167, Grosvenor Collection, BECPL.

49. Bob Watson, "Revolutionary Plan Offered to Improve Downtown Area," *Buffalo Evening News*, April 22, 1958, City Planning Scrapbook, vol. 2, p. 240, Grosvenor Collection, BECPL. See also J. Edmund de Castro, "Old Insurance Building Had Fine View of a Growing City," *Buffalo Evening News*, October 8, 1957, Buildings Scrapbook, pp. 43–44, Grosvenor Collection, BECPL.

50. "Ramps Key to Future of Downtown, Pankow Claims," *Buffalo Evening News*, April 13, 1955.

51. "Chamber Urges Completion of Downtown Ramps," *Courier Express*, May 2, 1955.

52. "Shortage Here Hits All Classes but Poor Suffer Most," *Buffalo Evening News*, April 23, 1949, p. 41.

53. Buffalo Urban League, *Annual Report, 1951* (Buffalo, NY: Buffalo Urban League, 1951), p. 2.

54. "Conditions in Ellicott District Worsen," *Buffalo Evening News*, July 18, 1952, quoted in John Teaford, *The Rough Road to Renaissance: Urban Revitalization in America, 1940–1985* (Baltimore: Johns Hopkins, 1989), p. 32.

55. For a good general discussion of the Ellicott Urban Renewal program, see Neil Kraus, *Race, Neighborhoods and Community Power: Buffalo Politics, 1934–1937* (Albany: State University of New York Press, 2000), pp. 85–119.

56. Quoted in the *Courier Express*, April 6, 1958, p. 1.

57. "Last Mass Scheduled May 1 at St. Lucy's," *Courier Express*, April 15, 1960, Churches in Buffalo and Western New York Scrapbook, vol. 9, p. 285, Grosvenor Collection, BECPL. See also, "Old Days at St. Lucy's Recalled," *Courier Express*, August 30, 1964, p. 7A.

58. Fred Turner, "Plan to Raze Two Areas Criticized," *Buffalo Evening News*, August 5, 1959, City Planning Scrapbook, vol. 2, p. 248, Grosvenor Collection, BECPL.

59. "Mayor's New Waterfront Plan," *Buffalo Evening News*, November 18, 1960, p. A1.

60. This and the following are taken from "Investigation of Communist Activities in the Buffalo, New York area," Hearings before the Committee on Un-American Activities, House of Representatives, October 2 and 3, 1957.

61. Helen Mintz, personal communication with the author, September 1979.

62. "Public Hearing to Decide Fate of Shade Trees," *Courier Express*, October 1, 1936, p. 32; "City Trees Menaced by Dutch Elm Disease," *Buffalo Evening News*, April 3, 1952; Trees in and Around Buffalo Scrapbook, p. 75, Grosvenor Collection, BECPL. See also, "Buffalo Faces Battle to Save Its Elm Trees from Dutch Disease," *Buffalo Evening News*, May 15, 1952, Trees Scrapbook, p. 76, Grosvenor Collection, BECPL.

63. Frank E. Karpick, "Before Our Eyes," *Town Tidings*, July 1940, Trees Scrapbook, p. 53, Grosvenor Collection, BECPL.

64. "Forester Says City Trees Neglected," *Courier Express*, May 29, 1946, p. 12.

65. "Dutch Elm Disease Threatens Elms," *Courier Express*, May 18, 1952.

66. Ibid.

67. Ibid.

68. Ibid.

Little Money's Grocery, Niagara Street

Symphony Circle and the First Presbyterian Church

The Michigan Street Baptist Church

Cazenovia Park

Bidwell Parkway

Sunset, from the foot of Porter Avenue

Fourth of July 2006 on Niagara Street

The trees of Timon Street in the Fruit Belt

The Colored Musicians Club at Broadway and Michigan

Wedding at the old Central Terminal

Richmond Avenue

Stanley Swisher In his rose garden at the Erie Basin Marina

Young gardeners at the Massachusetts Avenue Project

New citizens, July 4, 2006

The "oldest tree in Buffalo," Delaware Park

Rosa Gibson on Wohlers Street

The Days Park fountain

Angolan couple in their Niagara Street store

DOWNTOWN AND THE
NEIGHBORHOODS DURING THE 1960S

Little love seemed to be lost for the city's elm trees. As always, leadership in Buffalo, dazzled by increasing amounts of federal money, was far more focused on rebuilding the declining central business district and the decaying neighborhoods.

By the late forties and early fifties, this drastic approach to what was considered neighborhood blight had broadened. Under the aegis of urban renewal, more tracts of land, comprising neighborhoods where thousands of people lived, were scheduled to be cleared in an effort to save the city. By the mid-1950s, those who cared about downtown had come to accept the notion that only large-scale reconstruction of downtown would work.

Robert T. Coles, a young architect from Buffalo, did not agree. Indeed, in a particularly prescient article written in 1963, Coles argued that these highly touted public policies for the renewal of downtown might well have the opposite effect. At MIT Coles had studied with Charles Abrams, the little-remembered but highly influential and iconoclastic teacher about city life. Abrams, along with Jane Jacobs, revolutionized the way cities are thought about today. Abrams and Jacobs both lived in Greenwich Village—Abrams on Tenth Street, between Fifth and Sixth Avenues, and Jacobs around the corner on Hudson. It was in these neighborhoods, these intimate places, on the streets where people walked and on the stoops where people sat, that Abrams and Jacobs learned about cities. Unlike their colleagues, the two had been lecturing and writing throughout the 1950s about the importance of the street and the pedestrian in the life of a downtown. In a series of articles published by *Fortune* in 1958 under the title "The Exploding Metropolis," Jacobs and another urbanist, William H. Whyte, articulated new and different ideas about how best to renew American cities. In an essay titled "Downtown Is for People," Jacobs argued a point that went unheeded until it finally resonated more than twenty-five years later. "Designing a dream city," Jacobs wrote, "is easy; rebuilding a living one," she said, "takes imagination." Deeply worried about the neat, spanking new, and cleanly swept plans that appeared in threatened cities all over the country, Jacobs wrote: "We are becoming too solemn about downtown. The architects, planners and businessmen are seized with dreams of order and they have become fascinated with scale models and bird's-eye views." Arguing for a vision of the city that she came to know and love on the streets of New York, Jacobs urged her readers to learn from the street. To know what makes a city great, she said, "You've got to get out of your car and walk. Walk," she insisted, " and you will see that many of the assumptions on which (today's) projects depend are ... wrong."[1]

While most people, including those in the design profession, were heedless of Jacobs's warning, Coles heard her visionary cry and understood. Charles Abrams also concurred; in "Downtown Decay and Renewal," an article published in 1961, the same year Jacobs's monumental work *The Death and Life of Great American Cities* went to press, Abrams wrote that for downtown to meet the challenge of the suburbs, it must be made more urban and "above all more walkable." Claiming that "a pedestrian revolt is long overdue," Abrams proposed that cities appoint a "Commissioner of Pedestrians in order to catechize the Commissioner of Traffic." Abrams, like Jacobs, was passionate about the importance of healthy and vital streets. "The surrender of streets to the automobile," he wrote, "has reached scandalous proportions in some cities as sidewalks have ruthlessly been cut down to slivers. Benches have been removed. Great gaping spaces for parking have replaced small shops so that downtowns now look like an old man's mouth with his dentures out." Abrams offered advice that has still not been taken by those charged with making plans for Buffalo. "The problem," he advised in 1961, "is how to make a city vibrate and continue vibrating.... This should challenge a profession that has paid all too much attention to the stock devices of slum demolition and projects and too little to the hidden secrets of what gives a city its impulse and makes people move toward life."[2]

Between his classes with Abrams and a trip to Europe, Coles had learned his lessons well; when he returned to Buffalo in 1961, his views about cities and how their problems should be dealt with were strikingly different from his colleagues.

He wasted little time in launching a broad and stinging critique of the efforts of his contemporaries to revitalize downtown Buffalo. He was sickened and appalled by the demolition of so much of the traditional fabric of the city, the streets and the buildings that had for so long defined its scale. He argued instead that preservation and rehabilitation would likely prove to be more effective tools of urban renewal than the planners' habitual method of drafting grand plans that encouraged sweeping demolition. In 1963, writing for *Buffalo*, the monthly magazine of the Chamber of Commerce, Coles said that "in wandering through the downtown neighborhoods, one sees so much that could be saved; one wonders whether it might be better for Buffalo to rehabilitate what it already has to attract its former residents back into the city rather than to build at tremendous cost new towers in the horizon in the midst of blight and deterioration." Coles "missed the unusual shapes and forms of the old," and using terms like "human scale," he wrote that "pedestrians are overlooked in downtown renewal plans." Pedestrians, he suggested, and not cars, should be given preference. "Why not," he asked, unknowingly anticipating the incredible popularity forty years later of a weekly summer event called Thursdays in the Square, "give Lafayette Square back to the pedestrian?" He decried the demolition of the Larkin Building and "the destruction in the name of development, the making way for something new, slick and often bad." He also criticized the new office buildings on Delaware Avenue where, he said, "We see the wholesale waste of land in the blocks between Allen and North Streets, the anti-urbanness in a section so close to downtown." Here, like elsewhere, he said, "We are mistaking newness for goodness, even to the point of possibly destroying the Wilcox Residence...the finest example of Greek Revival architecture still standing in Buffalo." And in a cry that has still to be fully heard let alone understood by city leaders, Coles passionately preached that "[W]e must recognize, as urban renewal advances in Buffalo, that the city is urban; that every great city is characterized by denseness, compactness, cohesiveness; that there can never be suburbia in the city—regardless of the reasons put forth."[3]

But these were not, it seemed, the qualities that the decision makers were looking for in a planner. For example, when in 1956 Eugene W. Fitzgerald was appointed to the post of director of planning, he was cited for his "wide experience in municipal engineering" and for his experience "in charge of coordination of arterial plans and design, advising the public works commission on public construction and planning, right of way lay-outs, drainage and other construction specifications."[4] Unlike planners of Fitzgerald's ilk, Coles saw the problems of his city from a different perspective and, in a stinging rebuke to the auto-friendly plans that dominated the day, he harshly criticized the recent spate of highway construction. Referring to the work of Fredrick Law Olmsted, Coles argued that "parks and parkways are useless to a people who are immersed in the automobile age. Delaware Park has already been bisected by an expressway and the trees along Humboldt Parkway have been toppled by bulldozers preparing the new Kensington Expressway." For the sake of the city, Coles pleaded, this had to stop. "Only an indifferent society could permit this destruction to go on." Learn from the past, he urged, and realize "that the decline of any city has been related directly to the rise of the automobile.... Will we ever realize that the city and the automobile are incompatible and that the solution we see in more urban expressways and downtown parking is no solution at all?" Indeed, he concluded, "Rather than waste more millions, destroy more neighborhoods and drive more people from the city, we should study closely the new rapid transit systems being developed in Toronto, San Francisco and Stockholm and see how they can be applied to Buffalo."

The following month, Milton Milstein, president of the Western New York chapter of the American Institute of Architects and the downtown establishment's favorite architect, repudiated Coles's point of view and in another article in *Buffalo* "disclaimed any identification with (the Coles) article." Indeed, he insisted, they should continue to do just the opposite of what Coles had proposed. Milstein warned that "we must not discourage our potential driver market. Let us instead pamper it with the most direct and convenient access it can have to its destination and (then when it is there) provide for it a system of economical or even free parking, if possible." Milstein had no reluctance to alter dramatically the city's historic street pattern if it meant aiding the movement of automobiles in and around the city. In 1962, he proposed that the city eliminate the radial street system at Niagara Square, which Joseph Ellicott had laid out in 1805, and replace it with a grid. As Milstein said, "It is a well known fact among our planners that Niagara Square's radial plan does not fit modern-day traffic circulation."[5]

That the thinking of Milstein, not Coles, had prevailed became apparent to everyone following the release in 1960 of the Little Report, which called for and ultimately led to the radical remaking of downtown Buffalo in the early 1960s. Reflecting an intellectual climate that believed deeply in the ameliorative effects of sweeping, large-scale, downtown renewal plans—plans that called for change, in Mumford's words, "from the ground up"—the Little Report would not have been possible without the legal mechanism and the financial capability provided by the Housing Act of 1949. Originally designed to clear slums and build new housing, by the early 1950s the Housing Act of 1949 had become the cover under which was carried out drastic and radical programs designed to renew the central business districts of America's increasingly ailing cities. Although one of the basic provisions of the law was that urban renewal funds were to be used only for "a slum or a blighted, deteriorated or deteriorating area ... which the federal administrator approves as appropriate," by the mid-1950s urban renewal officials in Washington, under heavy pressure from downtown interest groups in cities

throughout the country, became increasingly willing to apply the criteria originally designed for distressed residential neighborhoods to downtown business
districts.[6] But first they needed a plan. Thus, in 1959, the Buffalo Redevelopment
Foundation (BRF), an alliance of downtown businessmen—bankers, department
store owners, real estate owners, and their associated law firms—modeled after
Pittsburgh's highly touted Allegheny Conference, retained Arthur D. Little Company, "the oldest consulting firm in the world," to devise the plan for the renewal
of downtown Buffalo. The price was high—Little's fee was $125,000, $85,000 of
which was paid for by the foundation, the rest by the city—but the stakes, as well
as the foundation's hopes for the project, were higher still.

Francis N. Smith, the president of the Marine Trust and head of the BRF,
welcomed the Little team to Buffalo in July 1959. "Buffalo's central business district," Smith said, "is in transition. Business and cultural activities, traditionally
located in downtown, have been shifting to the periphery. As a result, the core of
the city has suffered and the prevailing investment climate reflects an uncertainty
on the part of the business community as to the future of downtown Buffalo as a
commercial center."[7]

The Little team insisted that the problems of downtown transcended the particular problems of high office vacancies (12 percent in 1958 versus a 5 percent
rate for other cities of its size) and a dwindling share of regional retail sales. To a
certain extent, the report argued, the problems had more to do with image than
reality. "Downtown's major problem," the consultants said, "is to overcome the
existing image it has in the public mind. It is not," they said, "considered dynamic,
pleasant or exciting.... As it is," they continued, "downtown Buffalo does not have
the busy, bustling atmosphere that contributes so much to a shopping trip. It carries only limited appeal as a place to live, work, shop and play. A visit downtown
is not an experience. It's a chore."[8]

For downtown "to retain its function as a regional shopping destination," the
Little Report insisted, "it must take on another look.... It is clear that a plan must
be developed which will meet the requirements and tasks of today's and
tomorrow's shopper." Since large-scale developments are "the secret" of suburban
shopping centers, the city should abide by the mantra of the day, "land must be
assembled by parcels, not a half a block or a block, but several blocks in size and
scale."

The Little people, like Walter Behrendt before them, were concerned about
the proximity of what they called "blighted areas" to the central business district—the old, primarily poor, Italian Lower West Side and the rapidly growing
African American community on the East Side. They were encouraged, they said,
by the "steps being taken in the Ellicott District to upgrade blighted areas there"
and the "efforts to develop higher income housing on the Waterfront." Banking on

the gentrification of these surrounding areas as a way to "enhance the competitive position of the old central city," they urged that rents in the new high-rise apartments planned for the area, "be keyed as high up the income scale as the demand permits."[9]

The ongoing renewal of the Ellicott District and the waterfront did not ease their concerns about "the presence of large ethnic groups [clearly a reference to African Americans, who were at the time the only "large ethnic group" in the vicinity of the central business district] that had not yet been absorbed by the rest of the community" and the impact that they would have on plans to revive downtown. In a reference to the increasing number of wig shops and other specialty shops that catered to the expanding African American customer base in downtown (the movement to the suburbs of a growing number of whites was changing the racial mix of the central business district, creating concern and discomfort among downtown interest groups), Little said that the influx of these "marginal retail establishments" created "an unsightly appearance" and contributed to a sharp decline in pedestrian traffic.

While the Little group noted the continued presence of several large retail stores, it was concerned about the 1960 closure of J. N. Adams' Main Street store and worried about the continued health of AM&A's, Hengerer's, and other remaining department stores. According to the group, the situation, "caused by the rise of the suburbs whose impact on the social and economic life of the central city has been disastrous," was dire. Though comprised of neither architects nor planners, neither builders nor businessmen, the Little firm insisted that "the most direct and effective way to attack [the] problem" was "to change the area's physical appearance by the construction of new facilities. Physical change is essential if Buffalo's central business district is to enhance its competitive position."

The Little Report's vision for downtown was radical; it required a drastic overhaul of the entire central business district. In recognition of the inevitability of continued population decline, the Little Report envisioned a city comprised of freestanding and self-contained sectors, separate satellites, really, with a central business district surrounded by residential districts that would be separated by "greenbelts" and linked by highways. Given the city's shrinking population, the Little Report said that the central business district needed to be "physically tightened up and the retail core contracted." The "new center" of the city would be a two-block area bounded by Court Street on the north, Pearl Street along the west, Church Street on the south, and Main Street on the eastern margin. Whole blocks of downtown Buffalo, the Little Report recommended, should be torn down and replaced with an integrated, unified, self-contained "complex," which would contain an enclosed retail mall, underground parking, and a new office tower. Also planned was a development that the Little Report said was "similar to Rockefeller

Center, with high-rise office buildings, enclosing a small public park." With an attitude that would increasingly characterize thinking about the revitalization of downtown, later referred to as "build it (as long as you use public money), and they will come," the Little group was cavalier about the already high office vacancies. This was not a concern, the report said, because "new office and retailing facilities will create their own markets." The new complex, connected by grade-level arterials to the city's new "circumferential highway system," and with plenty of cheap parking available, would "allow downtown Buffalo the opportunity to redesign itself as a plaza."

Parking, as cheap as possible, was critical. "So long as the average plaza shopper is able to park her automobile close to the store at no cost, downtown shoppers will suffer a competitive disadvantage. Therefore," the Little Report recommended, "every effort should be made to reduce the cost of parking in downtown Buffalo."[10] Thus, the report seemed to say, that only by copying the tactics and strategies of the suburbs, by building what they had come to fear most—a mall—could downtown hope to compete.

The Little Report claimed that the Main Street project, combined with new and renewed satellite residential areas in the Ellicott District and the Lower West Side, would enable downtown Buffalo to become "a sanctuary of shopping by offering it the competitive leverage and the opportunity to redesign downtown Buffalo." The rhetoric notwithstanding, the Little group was clearly uncertain about these vague predictions. Indeed, after all the promised demolition and destruction, after all the streets that would soon be lost and all the buildings that would soon come down, they could still provide "no assurances that a development of this nature will alter current downtrends. There is, at best," the report concluded, "a considerable measure of speculation involved in such a project."[11]

But downtown leadership—Mayor Sedita, the Buffalo Redevelopment Agency, and the politicians, planners, architects, lawyers, real estate brokers, and construction companies who stood to benefit from such a massive project—wanted badly to believe. Afraid, threatened, and increasingly desperate, the city's leadership, unable to develop renewal strategies that reflected the history, heritage, and character of its own community, swallowed whole the formulaic, "cookie cutter" ideas promoted by the Little team. With Mayor Sedita and the coalition of downtown business interests now reconstituted as the Greater Buffalo Development Foundation (GBDF) fervently behind it, the Little Report became the blueprint that would guide, for better or for worse, the city's plans to revitalize its downtown. Sedita, simultaneously presiding over the urban renewal plan that obliterated his childhood neighborhood on the Italian West Side, was ecstatic: "This planned face-lifting of downtown with green space, a realignment of traffic with wide perimeter roads and the removal of ugly ancient buildings will rejuvenate the entire core."[12]

Sedita, in fact, wanted to go still further; he proposed that a major overhaul of traffic patterns be added to the Little plan. With not even a nod to public transportation, Mayor Sedita proposed the construction of that perennial favorite, "an inner traffic ring around the central core." In addition, he called for doubling the width of Chippewa Street along its length from the west side of the city to the east by demolishing all properties, including the vaunted art nouveau masterpiece, the Calumet Building, on the south side of the street.

City leaders knew that the Little project would be expensive, but they were not concerned. After all, that was what federal urban renewal funds were for. If the project, Sedita said, "is packaged and attacked as an urban renewal project the costs are not prohibitive." Sedita had, he said, "been briefing urban renewal officials in Washington about the proposals and they have showed enthusiasm for the plan." All that remained for Sedita to do to qualify for federal urban renewal funds, he said, "is provide the proof that the area is blighted." In February 1961, after a public hearing, the city planning board declared a five-block, fourteen-acre site "substandard, unsanitary and therefore blighted." Federal housing officials, under intense pressure from downtown coalitions like the GBDF all over the country, quickly rubberstamped Sedita's request, just as they did similar requests from mayors all over the country. The power they conferred upon him was enormous. Armed with the designation of large chunks of the city's core as "blighted," Sedita was given vast leeway to alter the form and function of much of downtown Buffalo including, but not limited to:

> A) the acquisition and clearance of all substandard structures and of existing uses incompatible with the land use objectives of this plan; B) the vacation of streets and subsequent redevelopment in accordance with the overall design objectives; and C) the development of new commercial complexes, public open areas and necessary community facilities.[13]

Gradually, the pieces came together. The Little Report provided the rationale, Sedita provided the cover of "blight," the federal government provided the power and the money, and the project was underway. Everybody was on board—the banks who lent the money, the politicians who made the deals, the real estate companies who brokered them, the lawyers who negotiated them, the demolition companies that tore things down, the construction companies that built replacement structures, the architects who drew up the plans, and the newspapers that wrote the stories. It was an enormous team effort, launched and executed by a fraternity, a mutual admiration society that, convinced of the righteousness of its cause, would destroy the city in order, it believed, to save it. They celebrated their work and they celebrated themselves. Singing each other's praises in a powerful chorus of consent, they could not do enough to help each other. The language as much as the content of a resolution passed unanimously by the Common Council in 1963 reveals the spirit and the thinking of the time. The resolution was introduced by Thomas Santa Lucia, the councilman from the Niagara District who would vote several years later to have his own neighborhood declared an urban renewal district. "Now, therefore," it read, "let it be resolved that the Common Council of the City of Buffalo does hereby express and declare its intent to such private developers, engaged in the revitalization of the central business district of Buffalo, to cooperate with and support the said program to the fullest extent possible and to proceed diligently to accomplish all things required ... to make possible and assist the said redevelopment Program."[14]

Everybody was on the same page. Headed by Charles Millard, M&T Bank, which with $12 million invested was the largest private lender, would not only help fund the Little recommendations but would soon use urban renewal power and money to build a new headquarters of its own. Pleased with the team effort and cooperation of the city, Millard voiced his approval: "The cooperative attitude of Mayor Kowal [Kowal had replaced Sedita as mayor in 1961; Sedita returned in 1965] and the Common Council ... encourages me to believe that we may expect similar cooperation from other official bodies whose help is necessary to the successful redevelopment of downtown Buffalo."[15] The banks thanked the politicians and the newspaper thanked the banks. In a news article (not an editorial) written several years later, *Courier Express* reporter Ray Dearlove concluded an article titled "Buffalo's Banks Lead the Way in Rejuvenating Downtown" with the following: "Downtown Buffalo's redevelopment progress continues on the move. And the city's banking institutions are moving right along with it and behind it."[16] Finally, after years of waiting, a plan was in place that the downtown establishment and the local media believed would save downtown Buffalo.

The Little Report, issued in November 1960, became the final blueprint for the most massive development project in the city's history. Given that the various concerned parties fawned over each other on behalf of the Little Report, there is no wonder that the many pieces of the project fell quickly in place. The GBDF retained a group of five local architectural firms to develop a plan that would integrate the new buildings, the retail mall, and a planned parking structure, all of which were included in the five-block shopping and business center that Little proposed. "Feeling the urgency of a bold and significant step towards large scale renewal," the new planning team, headed by the omnipresent Milstein and known as the Architect's Redevelopment Collaborative (ARC), immediately suggested that the scope of the project be broadened by adding six more blocks. Eagle and Niagara Streets would be eliminated and buildings of many sizes, shapes, styles, and functions would be torn down. In their place would rise a fourteen-acre superblock; anchored by the Liberty Building on the north and a brand-new headquarters for the Erie County Savings Bank on the south, it would be bigger by far than any suburban mall built to date.

The goal was nothing less, Milstein's report said, than to "save the city." The vast reconstruction project would be managed and controlled by the mayor, the ARC, and the bankers and businessmen who comprised the GBDF. Decisions about concept, function, and design of buildings, for so long in the hands of a varied and fragmented collection of landlords and tenants, would now be centralized so that "a proper degree of control" could be exercised throughout the long and complicated redevelopment process. Overall design decisions were in the hands of a "design review board" whose function was "to assure the proper degree of design control over full project development." It is perhaps understandable that the architects charged with the reconstruction and re-creation of downtown paid so much attention to and cared so much more about the form of their project than about its function. Indeed, they had little interest in or understanding of how cities, their neighborhoods, and their downtowns actually worked. What mattered most, the ARC believed, was appearance. If it was new, if it was expensive, if it was grandiose, and if a well-known, preferably European architect designed it, it had to be good. Form and design were absolutely essential to the success of the project. "There is no time or latitude for failure to observe the recommended design spirit which will represent a bold step towards reshaping the very heart of our city."[17]

Milstein's design was predictable. It comprised a series of modernistic slabs and towers—a massive structure built on one large, rectangular superblock; it looked like all the other plans to revitalize all the other dying downtowns in all the other cities that by the early 1960s had become so desperate for change. The design was enormous and sleek, but it was also removed and separated from the streets and the city around it. The heart of the plan was the Main Place Mall, designed by the Viennese architect Victor Gruen, who, as the designer of the country's first downtown shopping mall in Detroit, was known increasingly as "the father of the enclosed mall." Gruen's mall, which within ten years of its completion in 1966 was riddled with the same kinds of social and economic problems that affected all of his other "offspring," had, at least according to him, a higher purpose. Not only would it restore the commercial health of the central business district, he said, it would also "fill an existing void by affording opportunities for social life and recreation in a protected pedestrian environment by incorporating within it civic and educational facilities."

During the time that Milstein's architect's collaborative, in conjunction with Gruen, performed the reconstruction design work, the GBDF brokered the deal. It formed its own realty corporation called "Backers Realty," which proceeded, using funds provided by the members of the GBDF, to buy options on all of the property in the renewal area. Samuel R. Fusco, a Connecticut real estate developer who had been working for years on similar projects in Bridgeport, New Haven, and Hartford, was chosen by the GBDF as the "designated developer" of the project. Buffalo, it seemed, was eager to join those other desperate cities apparently willing to destroy their downtowns in order to save them. Partnering with Hammerson, a British development company, and Amatruda, a company from New York, Fusco created a new company called HFA, which, now armed with a $12 million loan from M&T Bank, proceeded to acquire all the property that lay within the proposed superblock. Fusco, whose renewal work in New Haven was the centerpiece of what would, by the middle 1960s, become a textbook case of failed urban renewal projects, was "willing to bet on Buffalo." He appreciated particularly the role of the local banks: "Bankers generally are conservative in nature. But in Buffalo they are out to do things; taking risks not normally expected."[18] Soon Fusco, whose $30 million portfolio of real estate in downtown Buffalo came to comprise the entire redevelopment project (the mall as well as the two office buildings), had become the single largest landlord in the city.[19]

By the fall of 1965, "Main Place," as it was called—a project that involved the demolition and clearance of fourteen acres of land in the historic heart of the city—was well underway. The banks, in the language of the GBDF, "were the showstoppers."[20] First came the headquarters for M&T Bank, which had acquired and was now demolishing an entire block of buildings across Main Street from the mall. Western Savings Bank followed, demolishing their headquarters at Main and Court, a magnificent Greek Revival building, which, built in 1848, was the oldest building in New York State used continuously as a bank. The Erie County Savings Bank followed M&T and, in June 1963, the bank, located at the corner of Main and Church Street for more than seventy years, announced that it was adding its building and land to the site being assembled for the buildout of the plans put forward in the Little Report.

The press was ecstatic. "An entire city block in the heart of downtown Buffalo," reporter Bob Watson wrote in the *Buffalo Evening News* in June 1963, "is being purchased and plans are to clear it to make way for a multi-million dollar bank building for the Erie County Savings Bank." The area, known as the "Kremlin Block," was a random group of small mid-nineteenth-century office buildings that somehow managed to fit into the tiny triangle of land between Main, Niagara, Eagle, and Shelton Square. The Kremlin Block, named for its fortress-like sense of strength and stability, housed scores of offices and businesses that ranged from restaurants, drugstores, bars, and liquor stores, to shoe stores, haberdasheries (like Brownie's Clothing and Blisky's Men's Shop), loan companies, jewelers, a bakery, and a Deco restaurant. The largest and oldest building in the Kremlin Block was Kremlin Hall, built by Benjamin Rathbun in 1832.[21] A lavish building with stores on the first floor, a hall with a seating capacity of a thousand on the second floor, and offices on the third and fourth floors, the Kremlin, which the *Courier Express* said "evidences its past grandeur in plaster frescoes, curving wood stairs, balustrades and faded ceiling designs," was still fully occupied at the time of its demolition in the summer of 1963.[22] Occupied, too, was a wooden shed in the lobby of the Kremlin, which housed a shoeshine stand. Owned and operated by the Ricigliano family since 1905, it was destined, at least it seemed to Mike Ricigliano, for demolition. "It used to be," he said, "that people would walk five or six blocks for a good shine. Now they won't walk across the street.[23] Down, too, came the elegant sandstone building with its repeating Italianate arches that had, since the 1860s, housed the original AM&A's department store. Two years later, in 1965, the Erie County Savings Bank was demolished, which, with more than six hundred thousand square feet of space was the largest building ever demolished in downtown Buffalo. As striking and as memorable as any building ever built in the city, the Erie County Savings Bank, a whimsical "Gothic fortress," replete with turrets, flying buttresses, and a large, central banking room, was one of the great "public rooms" in a city that had once been filled with them. Edward P. Gabriel, president of Niagara Wrecking, foresaw no difficulty in razing what the *Courier Express* called "the rusticated granite baroness." "We have the original working plans," he said. "It's just a matter of working in reverse."[24]

Bob Watson, a *Buffalo Evening News* reporter whose beat was the downtown business scene, was no more or less enthusiastic than his colleagues among the local media. Watson, however, did seem to take a particularly perverse pleasure in the destruction of so much of the fabric of the city. In a January 1964 article titled "New Buildings Changing Downtown Look of City," Watson was rhapsodic: "The wonderful sounds peculiarly identified with old buildings coming down and new buildings going up finally filled the air in downtown Buffalo in 1963. There will be more of this in 1964, still more in 1965 and 1966 when the rebuilding of downtown, particularly along Main Street reaches a probable peak." Watson also provided a timetable for the redevelopment:

> In April [1964], the Merchants Mutual starts construction of its new building. At the same time the new Court-Franklin parking ramp will open. In May the Western Savings Bank moves into the new building it has been putting up on Main St. north of Court Street. A few days after, the wreckers will go to work tearing down the old Western Savings Bank on the corner of Main and Court.... This new bank building, plus the new library that will be finished in 1964 and the Tishman office building at 10 Lafayette Square, will give all of Lafayette Square a completely new look. Farther down Main Street, south of Swan, the Marine Trust expects to begin an enormous building project in late 1964. Marine had bought or offered to buy all the property in the entire block on the east side of Main all the way down to Swan Street."[25]

And so on it went until, Watson concluded, "all the pieces will fall into place." As more and more buildings came down, the rhetoric of glee intensified, at times seeming orgiastic. Again, in September 1964, Watson boasted that "one of the largest downtown building demolition projects in the country started today in Buffalo. The razing of more than six acres of old buildings to make way for the construction of new ones will go on for more than a year." Alfred Bourne, from the real estate firm known today as Gurney, Becker and Bourne, one of the prime movers of the GBDF, was, like the rest of its members, joyful at the prospect, apparently believing that the more that came down, the more would go up. "This is undoubtedly one of the largest concentrated building demolitions going on in any central downtown area in the country."[26]

Demolitions, as Watson had promised, continued throughout the mid-1960s. The *Courier Express* trumpeted the changes in June 1965:

> Here's a diagrammed aerial view of the heart of old downtown Buffalo which clearly shows some of the many changes in progress these days. Along Niagara Street the Morgan Building is coming down and the old Niagara Hotel is already gone. On Main Street the same fate has befallen the old AM&A's store. On the other side of Main Street a whole block has been leveled to make way for the new twenty-one story M&T Building. New parking lots also dot the area.[27]

Lost in this radical process of change was the diurnal—the everyday patterns and activities of people who lived in and on the fringes of downtown. Up to and through the 1950s and early '60s, downtown was bounded on both the east and west by thousands of people who lived in the surrounding neighborhoods. These places—the Ellicott District; up and down Elm and Oak streets; the Lower West Side—were within easy walking distance of downtown; it was the activities of the people who lived in these neighborhoods that gave downtown the kind of round-the-clock vitality that Buffalonians long for today. By the early sixties, these neighborhoods had been ravaged by urban renewal. As their residents were forced to move, they lost the easy access to the vast and varied emporium that Main Street had been. Now, deprived of their customers, downtown retail establishments could no longer survive. Increasingly they gave way to "higher and better uses" of their property. In 1962, the city sold the mammoth Washington Street Market to the Buffalo Savings Bank. This giant, a maze-like outdoor bazaar had served the neighborhoods on the near east side of the city for almost a hundred years; however, now deprived of its customers in the recently gutted Ellicott District, it had clearly outlived its purpose. Besides, the bank needed the space for parking. Two years later, the bank also bought the nearby A&P supermarket at the corner of Chippewa and Washington. In operation since 1895, it had been the oldest operating store in that historic chain.[28]

Few doubted the wisdom or questioned the efficacy of the policies and procedures that so radically altered the form and the function of the central business district. The process was reported on diligently by the local press, which, like the
public at large, expressed neither anger nor remorse. In 1965, a reporter for the
Courier Express referred to the demolition of so much of Main Street as "a normal,
natural development reflecting the inherent stability of the community's growth,
heartening to say the least."[29] That same year, the *Buffalo Evening News* printed a map
of "the emerging downtown with its bright new look," which showed that "the
refreshing effect of the razing of neglected structures and building new ones is
spreading in downtown Buffalo." Indeed, it seemed that the press drew a perverse
pleasure from such destruction and demolition. It seemed to enjoy the carefully calculated yet clearly self-destructive attack on its own history, and its response fueled
the optimism of those who supported the project. Both dailies—the *Courier Express*
and the *Buffalo Evening News*—were cheerleaders for the project, and from the time
the Little Report was released in the summer of 1960 to the time the first demolition company appeared on the scene, both papers covered the unfolding process in
lively and optimistic detail. Maps, drawings of models, and photographs appeared
regularly, all supported by positive commentary.

The reconstruction process continued throughout the 1960s. In the summer of
1968, it was still ongoing. In an article in the Chamber of Commerce monthly magazine *Buffalo*, Dick Baldwin reported that "bulldozers and cranes are cutting wide
swaths through Buffalo while wreckers' balls and torches are toppling hundreds of
old homes, business places and industrial buildings in an ambitious face-lifting program for the Queen City." With no certainty as to what would replace them all, or
when it would happen, Baldwin could only say that "the demolition is making room
for officially designated urban renewal projects, for highway construction projects
and for a privately financed downtown redevelopment effort." Given the number of
buildings being demolished, Baldwin acknowledged that it was "difficult to compile
statistics about them." All he could say was that "hundreds of buildings are
involved." He listed some of the "better-known buildings to feel the sting of the
wreckers' hammers: the thirteen-story Hotel Buffalo, the eighty-two-year-old
Hotel Worth, the ornate Erie County Savings Bank, the old Buffalo Times Building
on Main street, the old Palace Theatre nearby, and the St. Paul's and St. Mark's
United Church of Christ on Ellicott Street between Tupper and Goodell." While
he expressed concern that "their destruction is removing millions of dollars of
assessed value from the city tax roles," he was hopeful, if vague, that these might "be
offset by some of the new construction planned for downtown and other areas."[30]

By the end of the 1960s, the damage had been done. Entire neighborhoods
and a vast swath of the city's historic heart of downtown had been demolished and
cleared. Hundreds of millions of dollars had been spent, thousands upon thou-

sands of people had been uprooted, countless homes, stores, and businesses had been ruined, and some of the country's most stately architecture had been destroyed. Downtown, deprived of the thousands of people who for so many years had lived on its fringes, continued its decline, abandoned by stores, offices, and businesses that followed the customers to the rapidly growing suburbs.

Urban renewal was doing no better in the neighborhoods. In the Ellicott District on Buffalo's East Side, urban renewal, as a result of failed policies and politicians, had by 1960 become a dirty word. More than $13 million of federal money had been spent with nothing to show for it other than two public housing towers and a litter-filled field. It was, according to an article in the *Courier Express* in 1963, "a 72 acre wasteland in the heart of the city." People were appalled that here, so close to downtown and in plain sight of so many, "vacant lots littered with junked cars, piles of garbage and rats' nests were the most visible result of thirteen years of work in the ambitious Ellicott Project.... After a decade, Buffalo urban renewal programs," investigative reporter Dick Hirsch wrote, "can be summed up this way: all talk and no action. Despite the plans and headlines, not one new cellar has been dug, not one new brick has been set in place and not one dollar of valuation has been added to the shrinking tax base."[31]

Continued delays led to an investigation of the Ellicott District urban renewal project by the federal government's General Accounting Office (GAO) in late 1966. Deeply critical of the process, the GAO report referred to the "chaotic state of the city's planning and redevelopment machinery." The *Buffalo Evening News* was concerned, wondering if the report should not "serve as a further warning to Buffalo that grandiose hopes for redevelopment of substandard areas may turn out to be unattainable."[32] The whole project had become hostage to an arcane political process, stuck in the mire of local politics, subject to incessant wrangling between mayor and council and the conflicting aims and claims of suspect developers. The damage, meanwhile, was enormous. The Italians of St. Lucy's and the African Americans of the Ellicott District had lost their historic neighborhoods. The people of the Fruit Belt, overwhelmed by the migration of African Americans, some from the Ellicott District, still more from the American South, panicked and ran. Homes and businesses were lost, race relations were poisoned, and the patterns of daily life in the city were traumatized by events that people still talk about today.

The failures of urban renewal in the Ellicott District, however, did not deter political leaders in Washington and Buffalo; by the mid 1960s, they were ready to try again, this time with the city's waterfront. This time, they promised, it would be different—this time it would work. A new group of consultants, City Planning Associates, East, pledged: "The Waterfront project will serve as a pilot project to demonstrate the feasibility of the comprehensive relocation and renewal pro-gram."[33] For years, the waterfront in Buffalo, as in other cities, had been the city's greatest workshop, a massive hodgepodge, an economic engine where, in the crowded and littered warrens of the area, ships, wharves, grain elevators, factories, shops, barns, and yards comprised the ramshackle landscape of the busy, com-merce-driven district. And, of course, people lived there too, mostly immigrants and their children and, by the early twentieth century, mostly Italians.

Initially, there was "the Hooks." However, following the demolition of that neighborhood in the thirties and forties, the Italians and Sicilians left the area and St. Carmel's Parish and moved a few blocks north to join their countrymen in St. Anthony's Parish, the tightly packed neighborhood between city hall in the south, the Niagara River in the west, Porter Avenue in the north, and Niagara Street in the east. Now that neighborhood, too, was threatened. In 1963, the Common Council approved a sweeping urban renewal plan for the area. Only one of the fourteen councilmen, William G. Buyers, who represented the North district, only a mile or two away from the targeted area, opposed: "I am not for progress at the expense and complete decay of the rights of the individual. The people living there," he said, referring to the mostly Italian American population on the Lower West Side, "either like living there or can't afford to live anywhere else. What's going to happen to them?" The others (even the councilman from the African American Masten Dis-trict, a neighborhood that had been overwhelmed following the demolition of the Ellicott District), though unsure about what to do with the people who would be displaced as a result of implementing it, found the Lower West Side urban renewal plan difficult to resist. All of the council members, people with names like Petrella and Makowski, Lewandowski and Santa Maria, people who themselves had grown up in neighborhoods like the one they were now voting to destroy—people who should have known better—supported the project to demolish and rebuild the Lower West Side of Buffalo, but for what they were not sure.

Within a year, however, even the city seemed to have given up on the project. In a half-page ad targeted toward developers in the *Buffalo Evening News* in January 1964, the city put the entire Lower West Side out to bid. When not one response was received, Sedita, who had been reelected as mayor in 1963, and who had become increasingly desperate, became convinced that only a cleared, "shovel-ready" site would attract developers. The mayor promised that he would use $27 million in federal funds to acquire the properties, relocate the tenants, clear the whole area, and then turn it over to a willing developer. Sedita's announcement was blandly, but brutally, spelled out in an article written in the *Courier Express* in March 1965: "The City is in the process of acquiring from the present owners all of the property in the redevelopment area. Buildings will be demolished, resi-dents will be relocated and existing streets will be removed at public expense.

After the property is cleared," the article continued, "the land will be sold to a developer who will construct new buildings in accordance with a re-use plan adopted by the city and approved by the federal government. New streets... and new parks and recreation areas will be built."[34]

Many of the residents of the neighborhood wondered why. They had been living there for years. They, their parents, and their children had all gone or were then going to St. Anthony's on Court Street, to School 1 on Busti, and to Hutchinson Central High on Elmwood. It was a good neighborhood, one of those warm and friendly places where, it was said, the sound of tarantellas could be heard through wide-open windows. It was the kind of place for which a new generation of Americans are so nostalgic, that people still think about, and writers, like Joe Giambra, who grew up there, write about:

> Chico Vacanto, his sister, Franny. Godspeed. Piano man, Jimmy Gelia, singing heartfelt blues inspired by a brother with everything to lose. Mister Catanzaro: fresh Boston fish, mussels and clams. A little place; merluzzi, scungili, calamari. The depression, the Lindberg case. Downtown, the YMCA, Johnny Re, Horace Collichio, smart, bold. Toomy, Freddie Mogavaro: a station: tires they fixed, gas they sold.
>
> Andrews Hall. A hot, summer night—may it never end. A wedding at Bronzini's. Sam Scamacca, Jebber Calabrese, a four-piece band, an abundance of rhythm; the widows dressed in black. Draft beer in glasses, pop: Queeno, Oscar's, Nehi. Ham sandwiches in wax paper wrapped, cold pizza, homemade cookies... who could ask for anything more. Agnes Alessandra, their sons and Louisa lived upstairs. In front of the store children wait religiously to board Mule's carousel: miniature horses, colorful moments of happy, galloping abandonment, innocent faces, thrilled, turning, always turning, counterclockwise.
>
> With a swim in the moss of Lake Erie, the summer nights began. At the foot of Georgia, from Efner Heights we ran full force toward the water. Sykie Sicurella, Louis Petrotta always around. Benny Baia, his father Joe, enjoying ice cream.
>
> Back on Busti and Carolina, Mister Alphonso the elder, a good and honest man, without a vice, sold fish packed in ice. He pushed a cart while his youngest son Charlie thrilled us with song. The Virginia Street Pastry Shop, the Why Not Café, Nick's Lounge and Izzy Termini's Italian Marching Band. The Turf Club and Scotty's Clam Bar, Angelo the Barber. 326 Busti here Mr. LaCort cigars he made. Ravioli, the best in the world, made right here at Herman Abbarno's Subway Grill. The Marlowe Theatre, Baffo's La Cantina. Marranca's, your car he fixed.[35]

The people liked their neighborhood and, like the fruit trees and the vineyards that they had planted in their backyards, they had planted their roots deep in the Lower

West Side. Now that it was being torn up and destroyed, no one seemed to notice, let alone care—not the politicians who enthusiastically supported the program and not the newspapers, which barely touched on this horrific story of public policy gone wrong. Joe Ritz, a reporter for the *Courier Express*, was an exception. He had heard about the plans for the renewal of Niagara Street and wrote an article about it in the fall of 1966. For the better part of an afternoon, Ritz walked around the neighborhood, talked to the residents, and took notes. He wrote:

> Many waterfront residents are still mystified over the use of federal, state and city taxpayer money to buy homes and commercial structures, clear them and sell the land to developers on the theory that the buildings to be removed from the Waterfront Project area are slums or "substandard" structures. A decade ago 7th Street was peopled almost entirely by Italian American families, many of them closely related. Since plans for developing the area were announced in 1960, several families have moved out.

Ritz reported that "the street is still predominantly Italian-American. Gardens and fruit trees flourish in back yard plots. The interiors of the homes are well-kept and comfortably furnished." As far as Ritz could tell, the neighborhood was in good shape. The people in the neighborhood

> resent the scattering of neighbors and relatives and their relocation from familiar stores, churches and gathering places. Perhaps to understand the residents' feeling one has to be a gardener. One has to have nursed a cherry tree from a sapling, protected it from diseases, watered it, fed it, worked it so that it is capable of bearing one hundred quarts of fruit and then face the certain knowledge that it will be destroyed one afternoon by a clanking bulldozer.[36]

For two years or more the demolition went on. Writing in *Buffalo* in July of 1968, Dick Baldwin, who had become somewhat expert about the events on the Lower West Side, described the impact on the residents of the neighborhood:

> Many of the most moving emotions, however, were evident during the demolition of row upon row of modest homes along such streets as Carolina, Georgia, Fourth, Efner, Trenton, Seventh and Busti Avenue. Tears were shed, too, when the corner stores, the neighborhood taverns and the other small businesses fell under the wreckers' ball. These were the places where memories lingered. For many families, these modest neighborhoods were the only homes they had known in Buffalo.[37]

Baldwin was worried about when, if ever, the promised renewal of the cleared neighborhood would take place. "It is," he said, "anyone's guess how long it will take for construction to begin on the promised apartments, commercial and public buildings, roads, parks and other improvements. If the history of the Ellicott Redevelopment Project and the Thruway Industrial Park Pilot Project are any indication of what is to come, it may be a long wait."[38]

Among the oldest and sturdiest in the city, the lost housing stock of the Lower West Side had been amazing: tall, narrow, wood frame and brick Italianate structures that sported latter-day Eastlake porches and carpenter's gingerbread, built in the 1850s and 1860s, and ornamented into the 1890s. The area designated for clearance was an attractive, lively, and interesting neighborhood. Charles Burchfield, Buffalo's great watercolorist, came to know the place while working as a designer in the Birge wallpaper factory around the corner at Niagara and Maryland streets (the current site of a McDonald's franchise). His *Little Italy in Spring*, painted in 1927–28, depicts the Seventh Street neighborhood below Maryland that was demolished in the 1960s. One sees two- and three-story Victorian homes with gardens and porches in front; a woman hanging laundry in an empty lot; others talking on a corner in a cluster; a man selling fish from a hand-drawn cart; children watching a hurdy-gurdy man play his tunes; tall, bent trees in the foreground; and Lake Erie in the background, receding as far as the eye can see. Yet Mayor Sedita, who had grown up in the neighborhood—"Little Frankie from Efner Street"—had told them that it was time to go.

Despite all the acquisition and demolition, all the efforts to create a "shovel-ready" site, and all the efforts to market the area (a second full-page ad in the *Buffalo News* in early 1965, intended to lure developers, promoted the site to the highest bidder: "The Waterfront Project will reclaim for the future prosperity of Buffalo the vast potential of Buffalo's lakefront...complementing the lake front development a commercial and technical support service network will rejuvenate the downtown commercial fringe").[39] There were no takers until finally, in March 1965, with great fanfare from the *Buffalo Evening News*, a developer from New York City announced that he would build three thousand luxury apartments on the site, constructed in four twenty-story buildings on the waterfront, west of Niagara and south of Virginia. However, when the plan failed to materialize, the city, unable to develop, let alone implement, any plan for the area that in 1958 had been so ceremoniously designated for urban renewal, in 1967 turned all those acres of empty land on the waterfront over to state and its newly created "super agency," the Urban Development Corporation (UDC).

Under the leadership of Edward J. Logue, a master planner in the tradition of Robert Moses, who had presided over highly praised and publicized clearance and renewal projects in New Haven and Boston, the UDC took up where the city left off. Logue promised that the company would build an entire community between Niagara Street and the Niagara River, a mixed-use development for ten thousand people with a school, recreation facilities, and high- and low-rise apartments for moderate- and low-income subsidized housing. Under the procedure, the city acquired properties from each owner, then issued a contract to a demolition company to tear the structures down. Once the buildings were down, the city sold (gave away, really) the property to as yet unnamed developers who were to build as yet unknown projects. Almost all of the money the city spent on the venture was provided by the federal government.

The project and its process was described in a thoughtless, tasteless—even obscene—way, as if nothing had ever existed on the site, let alone a vibrant community that had struggled to stay alive. The UDC said it would "create a New Town in Town," a place "arranged in a village like atmosphere" where "suburban-style housing joins the urban Renaissance."[40] Designed by Paul M. Rudolph, Logue's handpicked architect, the project was "keyed" to parking plazas, "because the car is the focus of arrival and departure no matter where you live." Rudolph was greeted with the same deference and unquestioning adoration as Walter Behrendt had been before him. In a 1971 article in the *Courier Express*, Modesto Argenio reported credulously: "As Rudolph sees it, the area (west of Niagara and south of Virginia streets) is on the verge of sprouting anew, like Brasilia, from a jungle of slime and blight." But Rudolph, according to Argenio, had a much larger agenda—a vision of Buffalo modeled on his mentor Le Corbusier. "If Rudolph has it his way," he wrote, "all the slums of Buffalo will be bulldozed, giving way to clusters of high rise homes towering sixty stories in the sky." For now, however, work focused on what Rudolph and the UDC called "The Waterfront Village": a planned community that would house nine thousand people in twenty-four hundred housing units built around shops, playgrounds, and a new school.[41] Today, we know, the project as built bears hardly the slightest resemblance to Rudolph's grandiose vision. Named "The Shoreline," the complex consists of clustered, sand-colored concrete buildings that several hundred low-income tenants and a school. It is surrounded by large, empty grass fields and littered common areas. It is a barren, concrete development in the heart of the city where once there had been a thriving neighborhood.

This, however, is not meant to romanticize an urban landscape that by 1960 was showing serious and considerable "patterns of blight." Indeed, considering that most of the housing units in the city were made of wood and that more than 85 percent of them in 1960 were more than thirty years old, a great deal of the city's housing stock, much of it in the older, poorer neighborhoods close to downtown, was in need of repair. Unfortunately, the public policies implemented to deal with the problems of aging residences were extreme and counterproductive. Rather than the radical "carpet-bomb" approach that was taken, what the city desperately needed was a more thoughtful approach to the problems of neighborhood decline, one that was built on respect for the past as well as the complex and carefully constructed patterns of the present.

No neighborhood was safe from the scourge of federal eminent domain powers. While Buffalo used federal money to tear apart entire communities in the city, the federal government and the Army Corps of Engineers tore out the heart and soul of the traditional home of the Seneca Indians at the Allegany Indian Reservation. In a July 2003 article titled "Roots of Seneca Anger" written by *Buffalo News* reporter Michael Beebe, a new generation of Western New Yorkers learned about the horrors of the Kinzua Dam project. "'Kinzua,'" Beebe wrote, "is a Seneca word roughly translated as 'fish on a spear.' To the Senecas who live here, Kinzua has a different meaning—betrayal." The Kinzua dam, seventy-five miles south of Buffalo, just south of the Seneca reservation in Allegany County, was built in the early 1960s to control the periodic flooding of the Allegheny River that occurred in Pittsburgh. Built by the Army Corps of Engineers, the dam created the Allegheny Reservoir, a popular twenty-five-mile-long lake that draws thousands of boaters every year. The dam and the subsequent reservoir took ten thousand acres of the Senecas' finest land, one-third of their two-hundred-year-old Allegany Reservation. "Most of it," Beebe reminded his readers, "is flooded; the rest is treeless muckland. Another third of Allegheny, ten thousand acres of mountain slopes above the lake, will never again be accessible."

Acting much as they did in downtown Buffalo, the Ellicott District, and then again on the waterfront, government officials responsible for the dam project, Beebe reported, "never asked the Senecas for their land. They took it." Using the power of eminent domain, they ignored the terms of the Treaty of Canandaigua, a treaty that George Washington himself had signed in 1794. Beebe described the destruction that occurred when the federal government took over their land:

> Marshals from the federal government came first, handing out legal notices to the Senecas, telling them their land was condemned, telling them that it was time to move. Next came the government moving vans, the fires set to their homes, the giant scissors-like machines that ripped full-grown trees out of the earth, denuding the ancient hunting grounds. As the trucks packed up their belongings and the Senecas began the move to modern, ranch-style houses the government built in Jimerstown and Steamburg, near Salamanca, many watched as their homes were set on fire, the ashes bulldozed into the earth... On September 16, 1966, the government dedicated the new dam near Warren, and the meandering Allegany River backed up to flood Seneca land, including the home of Handsome Lake, half brother of the great chief, Cornplanter and founder of the Longhouse religion. Besides the Allegany Reservation, Kinzua also flooded the 15,000 acre Cornplanter Grant, land that Pennsylvania gave the Seneca chief for keeping the Senecas neutral during the Indian Wars in Ohio.[42]

The wounds of Kinzua were deep and have yet to heal, and today's generation of Senecas vow never to forget. In Salamanca, in Buffalo's old Italian Lower West Side, and in the Ellicott District, the damage caused by the sweeping powers of eminent domain is irreparable. For years, the government willingly and thoughtlessly made use of a public policy that knew little and cared less how people lived and what was important in their lives. The tears and even the blood of generations—of Italians on the West Side, of African Americans on the East Side, of Senecas at Kinzua—is in much of the ground of Western New York.

Few traumas are more deeply etched in the memory of many than the tragedy of Humboldt Parkway, which was destroyed in the late 1950s and early '60s in a blatant act of urban destruction. No one who remembers the serene beauty of Fredrick Law Olmsted's parkway can understand how public officials charged with protecting the public trust could have conceived and then executed a plan so devastating in scale. Today, more than fifty years after it was destroyed, Humboldt Parkway has become part of Buffalo's communal memory, shared even by a new generation of Buffalonians for whom a name is all that remains of this vestige of another time.

By the early 1950s, rumors began to circulate in the Humboldt Parkway neighborhood that the state was planning to build a highway over the preexisting road. The Scajaquada Expressway would bisect Delaware Park and connect to the Kensington Expressway, which would replace the Humboldt Parkway. Both areas, it seemed, were expendable, and people whispered that the parkway was doomed. Bulldozers arrived in the late winter of 1958. *Buffalo*, the chamber's publication, reported that "demolition crews are busily at work razing residential and business properties." "In the first stage alone," the magazine claimed, "590 structures will be dismantled."[43] Ten years later, the project was nearly completed. Herbert F. Darling, Inc., the engineering contractor for the project, in a full-page advertisement in an unidentified publication, boasted about its work on the project. In the ad are two photographs: the first is an idyllic, tree-filled photograph of Humboldt Parkway, dated June 1968; the second is a photograph of a mud-filled construction site. The trees are gone, replaced by a giant steel crane. The caption reads: "The Hour Glass, November 1958." The conversion of Fredrick Law Olmsted's Humboldt Parkway into a massive traffic feeder called "The Hour Glass" was an enormous undertaking that required, Darling said, excavation of a roadway that was 120 feet wide and three-quarters of a mile long; 280,000 square feet of sheet piling; 35,000 square yards of concrete for paving, retaining walls and sidewalks; 35,000 lineal feet of stone curbing; 42,000 lineal feet (nearly eight miles) of conduit; 7,000 lineal feet of steel railing; the construction of two overhead bridges and the rebuilding of a mile and a half of service roads, curbing, and sidewalks. "What's going on in Buffalo's hour glass? Other than 35,000 cars a day..." Darling asked the publication's readers.

The advertisement proudly provided the answer: "What was known as Humboldt Parkway in July 1968 is now a complex of construction that will provide five lanes of traffic in each direction [which] must be completed in December 1970." By that time, many had left. Those who stayed watched in disbelief as trees— twenty the first week, and hundreds over the months that followed—were removed from the rich soil that was soon to be covered with concrete.[44]

From their home on Humboldt Parkway, Dr. Lydia Wright and her husband, Dr. Frank Evans, watched the same sight. Fredrick Law Olmsted had laid out the parkway as a woodsy link to join Humboldt Park to Delaware Park. The parkway, the African American couple from Baltimore knew, held the neighborhood together. It was the place where the children played together and the grownups walked and talked. Like everybody else in the neighborhood, Wright and Evans came to the parkway to sit, to walk, and to socialize with friends and neighbors. The couple had tried to stop the project by organizing their neighbors and lobbying officials in Buffalo and Albany about the plan to build a highway through the heart of their neighborhood; they received no response.[45]

There was little that the couple and their band of neighborhood activists could do. Like many road-building schemes, this one had broad support within the power structure of the community. The Chamber of Commerce liked it and had supported it from the beginning. Buffalo was "on the threshold of a great and unlimited future," it declared. "This is not the time to make little plans. To reject the expressway would be little short of treason." The mayor, Steven Pankow, liked the plan, too. Pointing out that most of the funds for the highway network would come from Albany, he said, "Never has Buffalo been offered so much for so little."[46]

Some felt otherwise. In 1961, the architect Robert T. Coles bought an empty lot near the junction of the Humboldt Parkway and the Kensington Expressway. Unlike his neighbors, Coles knew how to read surveyors' maps. These told him far more than the smooth assurances of state and city officials, who maintained that the highway planned for the area would be "consistent with the contours of Humboldt Parkway." When Coles designed and built his home at 321 Humboldt Parkway later that year, he placed the back of the house to the parkway so that it, and not the front, would face the six-lane highway that Humboldt Parkway had become.

Some changes in the neighborhood were less traumatic but were just as meaningful, affecting not the physical character of the neighborhoods themselves but in some way the people in them. For years, since the fairly widespread use of the telephone at the end of the nineteenth century, phone numbers in Buffalo, as in cities throughout the country, consisted of four numbers preceded by a place name that indicated the neighborhood where the household was located. With such monikers as "Summer," "Grant," "Delaware," "University," "Madison," "Riverside," "Mohawk," "Humboldt," "Cleveland," "Windsor," "Parkside," "Elmwood" and others, a person's phone number—"SU 2456," "GR 8896," "DE 1134," and so on—functioned much like their address, adding a layer of identification and a sense of belonging to a particular place. This, too, was lost when, in the mid-1960s, these colorful place-related phone numbers where replaced by seven-digit numbers with no connection to any place in particular.[47]

More was lost than place-related telephone exchanges. Indeed, an entire way of life, one deeply rooted in the daily and intimate contacts that occurred on and in the streets of the city's neighborhoods, was eroded. Consider, for example, the impact on the quality of neighborhood life brought on by the decline in street-oriented, neighborhood-based retail businesses. In 1940, the streets of the city were filled with thousands of these types of businesses. There were, according to the city directory, 218 retail bakeries, more than 600 barber shops and 500 beauty shops, 56 pool and billiard halls, 32 bowling alleys, 175 tobacco shops, 198 cleaners, 201 clubs, 268 confectionary and ice cream stores, more than 400 delis, 150 retail drug stores, dozens of retail florists, 45 jewelry stores, 200 butchers, 65 movie theaters, 160 tailors, 150 shoemakers, 1,200 restaurants and lunch rooms, and more than 1,000 retail grocery stores. By 1970, the changes were pronounced: 60 bakeries, 300 barbers, 250 beauty shops, 24 billiard halls, 55 tobacco stores, 75 cleaners, 150 clubs, 90 confectioners, 150 delis, 18 jewelry stores, 15 movie theaters, no more than a dozen shoemakers, and fewer than 500 retail groceries were left. What was lost was not only a strong, locally rooted and owned economy but with it a strong, sustaining, and supportive structure that gave neighborhood life power and meaning. With that loss came sadness, anger, malaise, and, as people were about to find out, a dramatic increase in crime and insecurity.[48]

In an effort to protect the uniqueness of place, the residents of one neighborhood—Allentown—began in the late 1950s and early 1960s to resist the drastic changes they saw around them. Allentown, with roots in the early nineteenth century, was an intriguing neighborhood, consisting of a tight network of small, tree-lined streets located between North Street, North Pearl Street in the east, Elmwood Avenue in the west, and Virginia in the south. Lined with a wide array of brick and wood houses in a broad range of architectural styles, the area went through a steep decline in the 1950s. By then, however, the neighborhood had begun to attract a small but vibrant group of artists and the area was beginning to take on a distinctly Bohemian aura. Dotted with small mom-and-pop stores and a few galleries and tiny restaurants, the area had a scruffy casualness to it that appealed to local artists. By the late 1960s, the artists Wes Olmsted and Ben Pirrone had rented studios there. Hanging out in local restaurants and cafes— "Kisses" at Allen and Wadsworth, Jerry Baker's Blacksmith Shop around the corner on Delaware, the Café Limelight, and Laughlin's bar across Main on

Franklin near Allen—a hip scene of artists, poets, performers, and musicians emerged, giving color and flavor to Allentown. Dave Sharpe, an Allentown poet and infamous regular at Loughlin's, everybody's favorite hangout, described the scene: "Those were exciting times in Allentown. Jazz people, beats, all got along down there. There was a looseness in Allentown in those times."[49] In April 1958, a few of the denizens of the neighborhood, meeting at Jerry Baker's Blacksmith Shop Restaurant at Delaware near Allen formed the Allentown Village Society, which in September of that year sponsored the first of what would become many Allentown art shows. "Allentown, the *Buffalo Evening News* reported in April 1958, "is a new name in Buffalo but it could become as familiar as Greenwich Village."[50]

The emergence of artists and the arts as vital forces of community renewal did not protect Allentown from the threat of demolition and urban renewal. It, too, was threatened by modernization, particularly the changes on Delaware Avenue, where late-nineteenth-century private homes were being bought up, demolished, and replaced by office buildings. By the late 1950s, the Benderson Company, which was fast becoming one of the area's largest and most aggressive developers, bought key corners on Delaware Avenue, all of them the sites of large, single-family Victorian homes. In 1958, Benderson demolished three of them at the corner of Delaware and Allen, including the hundred-year-old Sidway mansion on the northwest corner. The publication of the Chamber of Commerce blandly reported the development: "The Benderson Company plans to demolish the buildings to make room for a modern hotel and office building."[51] Two years later, the Buffalo Club, located in a sumptuous Victorian town house on Delaware near Edward, worried like everybody else about parking, acquired and demolished St. Mary's Infant Asylum and Maternity Hospital, a Byzantine warren of connected brick structures built in 1878. The *Buffalo Evening News* reported that "[i]t took just twelve hours on Saturday for the three Schwab boys [the Schwabs were one of the area's biggest demolition contractors] to bring down the brick and wood buildings."[52] Deeply concerned about these developments and the impact they could have on their neighborhood, a group of Allentown neighbors began to meet regularly in late 1959 at a residence on Irving Place.

Irving Place is a one-block street that runs north and south between North and Allen, just one block west of Delaware. First developed, like the other streets of Allentown, in the 1850s and '60s, by the turn of the century, Irving Place had become a street of stylish, single-family homes. Originally named "Bowery," as a place where trees bowered overhead, the new residents of the street, uncomfortable with the association with Manhattan's Bowery section, changed it to "Irving" in honor of the author Washington Irving. (Another author, F. Scott Fitzgerald, lived at 29 Irving with his family for a few years early in the twentieth century). The street was lined with rich, fanciful, and beautifully decorated Victorian houses, none more attractive and interesting than 54 Irving, the home, since her birth in 1890, of Allentown activist Olive Williams. "Passionately dedicated," one chronicler of Allentown wrote, "to preserving the old and comprehending the new,"[53] Williams, who was angered and appalled by the impact of the Benderson demolitions and sensed that the future of her neighborhood was intertwined with the integrity of its historic fabric, organized the North Street Association in 1960. Three years later, with an expanded mission, they changed the name of the organization to the Allentown Association.

By the mid-1960s their work began to bear fruit. The association had crafted its own plan for the conservation and preservation of Allentown, and more and more people, attracted to the increasingly artsy community filled with block after block of wonderful though rundown Victorian buildings, found their way to the side streets of the neighborhood. Writing about the area in 1970, the *Courier Express* noted that "the suburban exodus has drawn people away from many neighborhoods in the city during the last thirty years. But in Allentown," it said, "the population trend is in reverse." In what was one of the rare public recognitions of the value of historic preservation, the article said that it was "the historic, preserved aura of Allentown's buildings that give its residents a sense of deeper roots." By that year there were, according to Max Clarkson, the president of the Allentown Association, "more than three thousand people here, representing the most complete mix and cross-section of people of any neighborhood in Buffalo. Three things stand out for us," Clarkson said: "The diversity of the fascinating people, the historic and unique architecture and the life style."[54]

By that time historic preservation had begun to acquire some credibility and achieve some significant successes. In 1966, the Niagara Frontier Landmarks Society was founded by a group of men and women concerned about the loss of historic structures in Allentown. Nobody was more active than one of the society's founders, the architect Olaf Shelgren Jr. In 1965, Shelgren had hosted a representative of the National Trust for Historic Preservation, which was preparing a "Special Report on Historic Preservation for the United States Conference of Mayors." Noting that Buffalo was "a target for developers and politicians looking for the quick fix," the trust's representative, Audrey Bullock, said that "Buffalo's nineteenth century landmarks are not so obsolescent that they must be torn down and replaced by glass boxes."[55] However, it would be several more years before the work of Olive Williams and Olaf Shelgren would produce results.

Meanwhile, concerns about race continued to dominate the public's agenda, particularly in the spring of 1964, as the Board of Education debated the district lines for its new school, Woodlawn Junior High, located at the corner of Michigan and East Ferry on the city's East Side. For civil rights groups and those in Buffalo who cared about race relations, "Woodlawn," as it was called, was critical to the issue.

The civil rights movement in Buffalo was weak; it was less a movement than a group of scattered individuals, primarily African American and Jewish. In other cities, an alliance of black and Jewish groups had created and maintained the civil rights struggle ever since World War II. But in Buffalo, where blacks, like other ethnic groups, tended to be quiet and conservative, and Jews, in the absence of a large Jewish working class and a Jewish labor movement, were equally so, the civil rights movement lacked the drive and leadership that it had elsewhere. There were, however, a handful of dynamic, committed, and energetic individual activists, the most charismatic of them being Norman Goldfarb.[56]

Goldfarb was born and raised on Madison Street on Buffalo's East Side. The son of Jewish immigrants, Goldfarb's father was a rag peddler, and the boy spoke only Yiddish until he was five years old. When Goldfarb was in his early teens, the family moved to Humboldt Parkway, where they lived in a two-family home on Brunswick Boulevard, a street filled with Jewish families. Goldfarb went to School 78 and graduated from Fosdick-Masten, the local high school located on a hill overlooking the old Fruit Belt. He continued his education at the University of Buffalo on a football scholarship, where he played alongside Leland Jones, one of the great quarterbacks in that school's history. Goldfarb was drafted into the army during World War II, where he first became aware of discrimination against both Negroes and Jews. Goldfarb returned to UB after the war and became involved in the university's small but vocal "Jim Crow Must Go" movement.

Growing up on the East Side, Goldfarb had mixed easily with blacks. "Blacks were in my house and I was in theirs," he remembered shortly before he died in 1982. Goldfarb thought blacks and Jews were fighting the same struggle; during the 1950s and early 1960s, he almost singlehandedly fought against racial and religious discrimination in Buffalo's town clubs and golf clubs. As director of personnel for a local department store during the 1950s, Goldfarb argued relentlessly for the hiring and promotion of blacks. Given his attitudes and ideas, it was no wonder that Goldfarb became a leader of the struggle to make Woodlawn an integrated school. For Goldfarb, the Woodlawn redistricting case was a critical test for Buffalo, a barometer of the character of the community.[57] In speeches to community groups during the tension-filled winter days of 1964, Goldfarb said that Buffalo was at a "moral crossroads." It was time, he said, for the people of Buffalo to accept their "responsibility as citizens of the city of 'Good Neighbors' by supporting the creation of an integrated district for the new school." Goldfarb, along with two African American community activists—Raphael Dubard and Frank Mesiah, both of whom had gone to the August 1963 march on Washington—organized a citywide campaign to generate support for an integrated school. At community meetings and in newspaper ads, letters to the editor, and television talk shows throughout January and February 1964, they carried the fight to neighborhoods and community groups all over the city, engaging the people of Buffalo in a dramatic and intense debate. But their efforts, hampered by a tiny budget and hostile public opinion, could not match those of the opposition.

Two members of the Board of Education, Carmelo P. Parlato, from the Italian West Side, and Alfreda Slominski, from the Polish East Side, had other ideas for Woodlawn. Banking their political future on the easily aroused fears of Buffalo's ethnic voters, they aggressively argued for a plan that would have drawn students exclusively from an African American neighborhood east of Main Street. Superintendent Manch, meanwhile, continued to insist that Woodlawn would be integrated, saying that "the zone will cut across both sides of Main Street if I have anything to say about it." However, Parlato and Slominski's efforts garnered support throughout the city, and white pressure on Manch began to mount. By the end of January 1964, he said, he had received more than ten thousand signatures from parents west of Main Street as well as thousands from people in other neighborhoods not affected by the plan, all opposed to the creation of an integrated district for Woodlawn. Manch called the feeling among these parents "akin to panic."

While Manch claimed that he wanted to integrate Woodlawn, he was unwilling to exert the leadership necessary to leverage support in the community to counter the powerful and virulent anti-integration forces roused so effectively by Parlato and Slominski. When Parlato introduced his resolution in March 1964, all but one board member, Dr. Lydia Wright, voted for it. Another board member, Anthony Nitkowski, a leader of the International Association of Machinists and widely considered to be a liberal, joined the majority in favor of Parlato's exclusively East Side boundaries. "I came here to vote against this motion," he said. However, he added, "in the interests of unity I vote 'yes.'" Manch was the last to capitulate. "It is not now feasible," he said, "to draw the district lines for Woodlawn in such a way as to achieve a racial balance that would be meaningful or stable."

Manch and the members of the Board of Education had other problems as well. By the mid-1960s, Buffalo's public schools had experienced a steady decline in academic achievement. In 1965, 38 percent of the city's public school students failed to pass the state's regents exam. Statewide, only the Schenectady schools did worse. Among the state's big six cities—New York, Buffalo, Yonkers, Rochester, Syracuse, and Albany—none paid its teachers less, none had fewer teachers with baccalaureates, and none spent less per student per year than did Buffalo ($496, compared to a state average of $740). According to the National Educational Association (NEA), the problems of the Buffalo public schools were far more than academic or budgetary. The primary problem was citizen apathy. "One of Buffalo's most distinctive features," the NEA reported, "is its lack of interested, vocal, effective individuals with a commitment to public education." Change of any kind, the report suggested, would be long in coming.[58]

But race dominated the agenda and, in June 1967, James Allen, New York commissioner of education, increasingly impatient with what he regarded as Buffalo's half-hearted efforts to integrate its schools, gave Manch and the Board of Education a deadline. They had, Allen said, until November 1967 to submit a timetable for the development and implementation of what he called "a total integration plan." The timing of Allen's new order could not have been worse; at the end of June 1967, riots erupted on the East Side of Buffalo.[59] The trouble started late in the afternoon on Tuesday, June 27. Small groups of black teenage boys (some of the newspaper accounts referred to them as "gangs") cruised the streets around William Street and Jefferson Avenue, smashing car and store windows. By nightfall, more than one hundred fifty riot-equipped policemen had been dispatched to the area. Following a melee during which three policemen (all of whom, it turned out, lived in the suburbs) and one fireman were injured, crowds were quickly dispersed by a wedge of forty police officers who marched down the middle of Sycamore Street firing tear gas. The ghetto still smoldered the next morning, and fires still burned at William and Jefferson, Maple and Carlton, and Peckham and Monroe. Plate glass windows all along Broadway and Sycamore had been smashed and whole streets were littered with broken glass.

As the day wore on, the situation worsened. Beginning at about 4:30 in the afternoon, buses passing through the neighborhood were stoned. As night fell, the numbers of young black men who'd been taunting police and firemen from street corners all day grew larger and more menacing. Still more windows were broken, more fires were started, more cars were overturned, and more stores were looted. Taking no chances, Police Commissioner Frank Felicetta, an Italian American from the old West Side, dispatched more than four hundred policemen to the neighborhood. By early Thursday morning most of the crowds had dispersed. Fourteen African American teenage boys had been arrested, and forty people had been treated for injuries, fourteen of them for gunshot wounds. Manch, who had checked for damage at School 41 on Jefferson Avenue, was escorted out of the area under guard by a dozen policemen.

Leslie Fiedler, in his 1969 memoir *Being Busted*, wrote that he saw "young blacks in jeans and knotted bandanas, running like crazy cowboys down ghetto streets to smash store windows and steal TV sets."[60] Alistair Cooke, the English commentator, writing in the *Manchester Guardian*, saw it another way:

> Buffalo's Negroes seethe in an interior desert of slums rising like war ruins from empty lots stacked with litter and garbage. The hundreds of rampaging Negroes gave a grim twist to the saucy old folk song "Buffalo Boys Won't You Come Out Tonight." They came out in furious droves for three nights in a row to protest against their useless life in Buffalo's Negro ghetto and the civic indifference that perpetuated it.[61]

For some, particularly the city's old White Anglo-Saxon Protestant families, life continued relatively undisturbed. Indeed, in a neighborhood of their own on the lovely side streets—Cleveland, Highland, and Lexington—that gracefully ran between Elmwood and Delaware avenues, the rhythms of daily life that had characterized these streets for an entire century continued unchanged. In patterns similar to those exhibited by their immigrant neighbors, the remnants of the city's Protestant elite lived, happily it seemed, in a small, insular world of their own, in large, stately Victorian homes in the city, and in summer homes along the Canadian shore and in rural Eden and Clarksburg. Despite the seismic upheavals that were occurring in the city, this small group remained clustered in the neighborhood of streets off Delaware Avenue. Here, numerous families listed on the social register lived next to or directly across the street from one another. Their children played together and ice skated in each others' frozen backyards. They congregated at Westminster Presbyterian and Trinity Episcopal Church and met at the handful of private clubs that dotted the area. Buffalo's "first families" managed, against the raging storms of change in their city, to retain a private and privileged community of their own.[62]

NOTES

1. William Whyte, ed., *The Exploding Metropolis* (Garden City, NY: Fortune, 1958), pp. 157–84. This book, with essays by Whyte, Jane Jacobs, and others, is a must read for anybody interested in the planning profession's inability or unwillingness to understand what would soon become common knowledge.

2. Charles Abrams, "Downtown Decay and Revitalization," *Journal of the American Institute of Planners* 38, no. 1 (1961): 3–11.

3. Robert T. Coles, "An Architect Looks at Buffalo, *Buffalo* 38, no. 10 (1963): 32ff.

4. "E. W. Fitzgerald Named Buffalo's Planning Director," *Buffalo Evening News*, August, 23, 1956. City Planning Scrapbook, vol. 2, p. 237, Grosvenor Collection, BECPL.

5. Milton Milstein, "Another Look at Buffalo's Architecture," *Buffalo* 38, no. 11 (1963): 30ff.

6. For a good summary of the law and its applications, see Bernard J. Freiden and Lynne B. Sagalyn, *Downtown, Inc: How America Rebuilds Cities* (Cambridge, MA: MIT Press, 1989), pp. 195ff.

7. "Little Report Asks Major Rebuilding in Downtown Buffalo," *Buffalo Evening News*, December 8, 1960, p. 1, City Planning Scrapbook, vol. 2, p. 57, Grosvenor Collection, BECPL.

8. Arthur D. Little, *Downtown Buffalo Study: A Report to the City of Buffalo and the Greater Buffalo Development Foundation* (Cambridge, MA: Arthur D. Little, Inc., 1960), p. 112.

9. Ibid.

10. Ibid.

11. Ibid.

12. Called "*New Ideas for a New Downtown*," Sedita's 1960 report, which appears to be an in-house document, is a mimeograph, which is housed in the Grosvenor Collection at the BECPL.

13. Ibid.

14. Buffalo Common Council, *Proceedings of the Buffalo Common Council, 1963*, Part 2 (Buffalo, NY: Buffalo Common Council, 1963), p. 1436.

15. "Little Report Asks," p. 1.

16. "Buffalo Banks Lead the Way," *Courier Express*, 1969, Banking and Savings Institutions Scrapbook, vol. 2, p. 5, Grosvenor Collection, BECPL.

17. Architect's Redevelopment Collaborative, *Downtown Buffalo Shopping and Business Center* (Buffalo, NY: Architect's Redevelopment Collaborative, p. 19), "city planning" vertical file, Grosvenor Collection, BECPL.

18. For more on Fusco and his purchase of the Liberty Bank building, see "NYC Firm to Buy Bank Building," *Courier Express*, December 24, 1967, p. 1, Banks and Savings Institutions Scrapbook, vol. 2, p. 109, Grosvenor Collection, BECPL. See also Bob Watson, "Huge Downtown Rebuilding," *Buffalo Evening News*, July 30, 1964, p. 1, Buildings Scrapbook, p. 421, Grosvenor Collection, BECPL.

19. *30th Annual Report of the Greater Buffalo Development Foundation*, "city planning" vertical files, Grosvenor Collection, BECPL

20. "Ceremonies Mark Construction Start of M&T Building," *Buffalo Evening News*, June 16, 1965, p. 53, Banks and Savings Institutions Scrapbook, vol. 2, pp. 150–51, Grosvenor Collection, BECPL.

21. Bob Watson, "Demolition of Kremlin Block to Begin," *Buffalo Evening News*, June 10, 1965, p. 1. Buildings Scrapbook, p. 171, Grosvenor Collection, BECPL. See also "Ghosts of Kremlin Alley Give Way to City's Progress," *Buffalo Evening News*, November 23, 1965, p. 21, Buildings Scrapbook, p. 175, Grosvenor Collection, BECPL.

22. "Erie County Savings Bank Plans New Building on Kremlin Block," *Courier Express*, June 30, 1963, Banks and Savings Institutions Scrapbook, vol. 2, p. 49, Grosvenor Collection, BECPL.

23. "A Little Business Gives Way to City's Progress," *Buffalo Evening News*, November 11, 1965, Buildings Scrapbook, pp. 173–74, Grosvenor Collection, BECPL.

24. "Landmark's Adieu Stirs Nostalgia," *Courier Express*, January 22, 1967, Banks and Savings Institutions Scrapbook, vol. 2, p. 41, Grosvenor Collection, BECPL. See also, "Demolition of Bank Building Starts," *Courier Express*, July 11, 1967, p. 11, Banks and Savings Institutions Scrapbook, vol. 2, p. 66, Grosvenor Collection, BECPL.

25. Bob Watson, "New Buildings Changing Downtown Look of City," *Buffalo Evening News*, January 4, 1964, p. 1, Buildings Scrapbook, p. 412, Grosvenor Collection, BECPL.

26. Bob Watson, "Razing Six Acres of Buildings—Downtown Project Begins," *Buffalo Evening News*, September 30, 1964, Buildings Scrapbook, p. 430, Grosvenor Collection, BECPL.

27. Clare Allen, "Changing Face of Downtown Buffalo," *Courier Express Magazine*, September 26, 1965, p. 4.

28. "City Completes Sale of Washington Market to Buffalo Savings Bank," *Buffalo Evening News*, June 1, 1965, p. 27.

29. Allen, "Changing Face of Downtown," p. 4.

30. This quote accompanied a detailed map of new projects downtown that appeared in the *Buffalo Evening News* on September 28, 1963, under the heading "This map shows that the refreshing effect of razing neglected structures and building new ones is spreading in downtown Buffalo." See Buildings Scrapbook, p. 408, Grosvenor Collection, BECPL.

31. Dick Hirsch, "City Fails to Get Approval of Project," *Courier Express*, June 25, 1963, p. 7.

32. "Politicians Fiddle, Citizens Burn," *Buffalo Evening News*, June 8, 1963.

33. City Planning Associates, East, *City Planning East: A Community Renewal Project for the Waterfront* (Buffalo, NY, 1962). This mimeographed report can be found in the "city planning" vertical files in the Grosvenor Collection at the BECPL.

34. "Council Approves Waterfront Development Plan," *Courier Express*, October 23, 1963. p. 37.

35. From *Bread and Onions*, an unpublished play written by Joseph G. Giambra, private collection of the author.

36. Joe Ritz, "Mixed Thoughts on Waterfront Renewal," *Courier Express*, December 2, 1966, p. 18.

37. Dick Baldwin, "What Goes Up...Comes Down," *Buffalo* 43, no. 7 (1968): 15–18.

38. Ibid.

39. *Buffalo Evening News*, March 12, 1965, p. B2.

40. Peter Wolf, *Another Chance for Cities: The Current Program of the NYS Urban Development Corporation* (New York: Whitney Museum, 1970). This publication can be found in the Grosvenor Collection at the BECPL.

41. Modesto Argenio, "Architect Paul Rudolph Restyles Buffalo's Waterfront," *Courier Express Sunday Pictorial*, October 3, 1971, p. 4.

42. Michael Beebe, "Roots of Seneca Anger," *Buffalo News*, July 6, 2003, p. A1.

43. *Buffalo Business*, February 1958, p. 21.

44. This advertisement is part of the author's private collection.

45. Dr. Lydia Wright and Dr. Frank Evans, personal communication with the author, April 1989.

46. "Kensington Expressway Project Bargain Deal for Buffalonians," *Buffalo Business*, June 1954, pp. 28–29.

47. Buffalo telephone directories are housed in the Grosvenor Collection at the BECPL.

48. The Grosvenor Collection at the BECPL has a complete set of Buffalo's city directories beginning in 1829. Two wonderful discussions of the impact of urban decline of the character and quality of daily life in the modern city are Douglas Rae, *City: Urbanism and Its End* (New Haven, CT: Yale University Press, 2003) and Ray Suarez, *The Old Neighborhood* (New York: Free Press, 1999). See particularly the first chapter of *The Old Neighborhood*, appropriately titled "What We Lost," pp. 1–26.

49. *Art as Revelation: The Sculptures and Altars of Wes Olmsted* (Buffalo, NY: Burchfield-Penny Art Center, 2004).

50. "Allentown to Sponsor Art Festival," *Buffalo Evening News*, April 11, 1958.

51. "$500,000 Office Building Planned on Delaware Ave," *Courier Express*, March 7, 1957, p. 12, Buildings Scrapbook, p. 361, Grosvenor Collection, BECPL.

52. "St. Mary's Demolished for Parking Lot," *Buffalo Evening News*, August 1, 1960.

53. Louise G. McMillan, *Field Guide to the History and Architecture of Allentown* (Buffalo, NY: Allentown Association, 1985).

54. "Repairs Turn Allentown into Suburbia's Answer, *Courier Express*, November 30, 1970, p. 19.

55. "Buffalo's Historic Buildings Called Worthy of Saving," *Buffalo Evening News*, October 28, 1965, Buildings Scrapbook, p. 440, Grosvenor Collection, BECPL.

56. Sadly, there is little information on Norman Goldfarb, who for thirty odd years prior to his death in 1982 was one of the most active and interesting advocates for civil and human rights in the area. While his name appears in many of the newspaper articles dealing with these subjects, he did not leave papers or other records. The information contained herein on Goldfarb comes from anecdotes from people who knew him and worked with him. Particularly helpful were two of his colleagues, Richard Griffin and Marilyn Hochfield, both of Buffalo.

57. The Woodlawn redistricting case filled the pages of both the *Courier Express* and the *Buffalo Evening News* during the late winter and spring of 1964. The Buffalo Board of Education kept a scrapbook of relevant articles dealing with public education in Buffalo during the 1960s and 1970s, and all of the information presented in the following discussion comes from these papers. For years these scrapbooks were housed at the Board of Education's offices in City Hall. The scrapbooks are no longer there and their location is unknown.

58. "NEA Raps Buffalo Schools," *Courier Express*, February 15, 1965, p. 17.

59. From June 27, 1967, through the first week of July, the pages of both papers are filled with news stories on the riots of 1967. See also Frank P. Besag, *Anatomy of a Riot: Buffalo '67* (Buffalo, NY: University Press, 1967).

60. Leslie Fiedler, *Being Busted* (New York: Stein and Day, 1969), pp. 93ff.

61. Quoted in the *Spectrum*, University of Buffalo student newspaper, July 24, 1967.

62. *The Social Register of Buffalo, 1967* (New York: Social Register Association, 1968).

chapter 9

LIGHTNING STRIKES

Art and life during the 1960s

The upheavals that tattered and ripped the fabric of the city throughout the 1960s seemed to have had little impact on the arts, particularly after 1962, the year that lightning struck Buffalo, energizing a thrilling and spectacular outburst of artistic expressions. It was in that year that this great, gray, muscular giant of a city, a city known for its blue-collar stolidity, its working-class neighborhoods—a shot and a beer town if ever there was one—after years of gestation, burst to the forefront of the world's cultural scene. It began in January, when the Albright Gallery, with the addition of a new wing, became the Albright-Knox. It continued in September, when Buffalo's small commuter college, the University of Buffalo, merged with the State University of New York. And it ended in December, when Lukas Foss was hired as music director of the Buffalo Philharmonic Orchestra. These events created a new and exciting light in the city, a light that for those who chose to notice and to follow served as a beacon to a new and different kind of community—one filled with exciting challenges and possibilities, which, had they been fully realized, would have been truly revolutionary.

Much of the excitement revolved around Seymour H. Knox Jr., who had been the dominant force in the cultural life of the community since the departure from Buffalo of A. Conger

Goodyear in 1927. Combining his passion for the arts with an enormous private fortune rooted in retail (the Knoxes owned over two hundred fifty thousand shares of Woolworth and Company stock throughout this period) and banking (Knox was the chairman of the board of Marine Midland Bank from 1943 to 1970), Knox continued to be the preeminent cultural force in the city. In addition to serving as the president of the Albright from 1938 to 1977, he was chairman of the governing council of the University of Buffalo from 1949 to 1969 and served as Governor Rockefeller's hand-picked chairman of the New York State Council on the Arts throughout the pivotal decade of the 1960s. There was little that happened in the exciting world of the arts in Buffalo without "Shorty" Knox's knowledge, approval, and financial support.[1]

Closest to his heart was the Albright Art Gallery, and as its 1962 centennial approached, Knox began to conceive of building a new wing for the gallery, a contemporary building that would reflect the cutting-edge modernity of the collection he and Gordon Smith had assembled. There was something already modern about the Albright's gleaming, white Greek Revival architecture. Knox wanted the new building to contrast without contradicting, and to help him with the project, he contacted one of the great architects of the day, Gordon Bunshaft, a contemporary who, like him, was born and raised in Buffalo. A senior partner at Skidmore, Owings, and Merrill, Bunshaft had already designed some of the great modern buildings of the day, including that icon of modernism, the Lever Building in New York City. For Knox's Albright, Bunshaft proposed a structure that was equally pure and strikingly beautiful, a glass cube that, because of its simplicity, juxtaposed and blended perfectly with its Greek Revival neighbor: "The white goddess and her new consort"; "the white pearl and the black diamond." The setting, Bunshaft said, made his work easier. "We were blessed," he said in an interview in 1962, "by the beautiful setting—Delaware Park. Those beautiful trees which form our backdrop are something which money can't buy."[2]

Bunshaft's building was gorgeous, an instant landmark in the world of contemporary architecture, and its opening in January 1962 was a major event in the art scene of the United States. *Time* magazine covered it in elaborate detail. The magazine was particularly taken by the role of the gallery and its prime benefactor in the life of the City of Buffalo. "The 533,000 citizens of Buffalo, though not celebrated for their love of art, have in their midst a museum envied throughout the US." Noting the strength of its modern collection, *Time* reported that "contemporary artists hold few places in higher esteem than the Albright Art Gallery." Their final tribute was reserved for Knox, who alone had built the collection, making it the finest contemporary art gallery in the country, and whose gift of more than a million dollars had built the new wing: "There are few men for whom the dealers of Manhattan, Paris and London have more respect than the

Gallery's Medici, its principal patron, Seymour H. Knox."[3] It was Knox, *Time* said, who had arranged for the opening show to be a Van Gogh retrospective, the largest ever held in the country. Among the works featured at that exhibition were some of the artist's best known: *The Potato Eaters*, *Vincent's House at Arles*, and *Vincent's Bedroom*.

People came from all over the world for the opening of what was now called the Albright-Knox Art Gallery; over 725,000 during the first year. They marveled at Bunshaft's Knox Wing, particularly the simple, all-glass cube that housed the auditorium. Glass was at the heart of Bunshaft's vision for the new wing. He wanted "the gray glass to act as a mirror to reflect the trees. It will," he said, "resemble a series of four murals of tree-sky reflections. At night it will flow with the lights inside."[4] Mostly, people commented about the glass of the auditorium, which tinted slightly gray, appeared black from the outside because of a double curtain wall. From the inside there is a clear view of the surrounding elm trees, which from the outside are mirrored in the windows. Gently backlit from the inside, the walls of the auditorium were, as Bunshaft had hoped, particularly striking at night. It was this gem of an auditorium, as elegant and pure a building as exists anywhere, which would, over the next ten years, house some of the most innovative cultural offerings of its time.

Even more than the building, the gallery's reputation was built on the quality of the collection that Seymour Knox had assembled, a collection that consisted of works of art that were consistently bold, daring, adventurous, and far in advance of public and even critical taste and attention.

Later in the year, an article that appeared in the *Toronto Telegram* and was reprinted in the *Buffalo Evening News* reaffirmed Knox's critical role in Buffalo's emerging contemporary art scene. "As a result of his efforts," the *Telegram* reported, "Buffalo's Albright-Knox Art Gallery is possibly the most exciting and dynamic public gallery in North America." The paper cited Knox's aggressive and inspired acquisitions: "Between 1954 and 1957 Knox gave 48 works. In the next year and a half he gave fifty more. Then between 1959 and 1961 he gave a further sixty-five works of art. The total for the seven year period was an incredible 165 pieces of painting and sculpture." Over the same period of time, this reporter noted enviously, the Royal Ontario Museum acquired five works of equivalent value.[5]

Artists, too, valued Knox's taste and appreciated the commitment he had made over the years to the best in contemporary art. In recognition of Knox, Clifford Still, perhaps the greatest living abstract expressionist, donated thirty-one of his paintings to the Albright-Knox in May of 1964. Still had kind words for Knox, saying that he had "complete confidence in Gordon Smith and Academy President Seymour Knox. They have," he told the *Buffalo Evening News*, "an understanding of my work and are willing to stand by it. Because of them conditions at the Albright-Knox are so different from the usual museum."[6] By thrusting art to the center of community life, Knox had single-handedly created an institution that the whole world admired and respected. In the process, he had redefined Buffalo to the world.

The aggressive effort by Knox and Smith to create a dynamic culture of modernism in Buffalo was joined by Alan Sapp, a friend of Oscar Silverman, who was recruited to succeed Cameron Baird as chairman of the university's music department following Baird's death in 1960. Sapp, a composer of contemporary music, a professor of composition a Harvard, a colleague of both Leonard Bernstein and Lukas Foss at Tanglewood, and a man deeply connected to the international network that comprised the cutting edge of music, was a bold and forceful advocate of the avant-garde. Sapp was puzzled at first: "Would I be interested in Buffalo? I hardly knew where Buffalo was: somewhere out west, I knew. I was the most provincial easterner you had ever heard of." He tread cautiously, coming to Buffalo first as Slee Professor of Composition, then finally accepting Silverman's offer in 1961.

Sapp was ambitious, creative, and entrepreneurial; immediately upon his arrival in Buffalo, he worked feverishly to create a high-profile music department whose primary purpose was to offer students "a fertilizing experience in the music of our time."[7] Sapp strengthened the contemporary foundations of his own department in 1962 when he hired the great American composer and pianist Leo Smit as Slee Professor. In the same year, at the urging of Oscar Silverman, he used money provided by the Slee bequest to sign the Budapest String Quartet as the university's resident string quartet. The next year, after Smit joined the faculty permanently, Sapp brought Virgil Thompson to the department as Slee Professor. Sapp's ambition extended beyond the campus to the whole community. An aggressive and persuasive apostle of all that was modern in the arts, Sapp endeavored to make Buffalo a mecca of contemporary art. Soon after his arrival, he eagerly sought out and befriended Seymour Knox and Gordon Smith and, by the fall of his first year in Buffalo, he had created a new position for himself as the gallery's music advisor. Next he set his sights on the Buffalo Philharmonic Orchestra and, in the fall of 1961, he was appointed a board member and, more specifically, chairman of the philharmonic's music advisory committee. His first job as chairman was to find a replacement for the great and august Josef Krips, who, since 1952, had been the musical director of the orchestra. From his new position, Sapp sensed that he had the opportunity to create a new and still more dynamic cultural community in his new hometown of Buffalo, New York.[8] But he needed the right man at the philharmonic: someone young and deeply committed to modernism. Some members of the board, particularly a lawyer named Robert Millonzi and a businessman named Irving Levick, were ardent and persuasive proponents of contemporary music; during the mid-1950s, they had gently prodded the German-born, stately, and old-world Krips to move in a more modernist direction. Krips had relented reluctantly; in January 1958 the BPO had sponsored the World Frontier Convocation Concert of American Music, at which Aaron Copland conducted the orchestra in Charles Ives's starkly modern piece *The Unanswered Question.* Later that year, Krips had given in still more; with funds donated by Robert Millonzi, the philharmonic had commissioned its first composition, a piece by American composer Norman Lockland called *Light out of Darkness.* Krips, it seemed, was becoming more willing to program contemporary music. Indeed, in 1961 and 1962 he conducted works by Webern, Honegger, Stravinsky, and Max Reger. And in February 1962, at the urging of Sapp, Krips led the BPO in a daring contemporary work by Sapp's good friend, the American composer David Diamond, titled *Elegy in Memory of Ravel.* Sapp was thrilled and in a note to Krips wrote: "As you know, I am personally delighted with this kind of program with its formal endorsement of contemporary music." Krips drew the line, however, at the avant-garde. Despite Sapp's persistent requests, he was unwilling to commit in advance to perform the work of the Slee composers in residence at Sapp's music department. Krips's decision to accept the music directorship of the San Francisco Orchestra beginning in the fall of 1963 provided Sapp with the opportunity he'd been waiting for. Now, suddenly, the stage was set for lightning to strike.[9]

Sapp wanted desperately to bring to Buffalo a more daring and contemporary music director, a person who shared his ambitions to make Buffalo a center of modernism in music. So, too, did Millonzi and Levick who, with Sapp, had become the guiding forces on the orchestra's board. They wanted somebody young and charismatic, someone like Leonard Bernstein, the very modern model of an orchestra's music director. Sapp, Millonzi, and Levick sought out Lukas Foss. Born in Berlin in 1922, Foss, who had been victimized by the Nazis like Steinberg and Krips before him, escaped first to Paris in 1933 and then to America in 1937. He attended the Curtis Institute of Music, where he was a classmate of Bernstein's, studied composition with Randall Thompson and Paul Hindemith, and conducted with Fritz Reiner and Serge Koussivitsky. He'd been the pianist with the Boston Symphony from 1944 to 1950 before proceeding to UCLA, the center of the universe of contemporary music, where he had succeeded Arnold Schonberg as professor of composition. Although he had never had a full-time conducting position, it was his reputation as one of the world's best-known composers of the avant-garde and his Bernstein-like good looks and charisma that most excited Millonzi. Millonzi, as chairman of the BPO board, and Sapp, as chairman of the music advisory board, would use their overwhelming influence to bring Lukas Foss to Buffalo.[10]

Others were concerned, afraid that the audiences that Krips had so carefully and successfully cultivated would not welcome what one of the board members said was sure to be a "preponderance of contemporary works on the programs." Skeptical of this new musical direction, they were proud of the reputation that the orchestra had achieved under the leadership of Krips and his still-more-traditional predecessor, William Steinberg. Ultimately, they were concerned that a more pronounced drift to modernism might well jeopardize the BPO's standing as "the sixth greatest orchestra in the country." Sapp reassured them. Foss, he said, "was aware of the policy in Buffalo of working with the Music Advisory Committee for final program determination" and would, he promised, "build on the traditions established by his predecessors."[11] Realizing that the decision to hire Foss would create continued controversy within the Buffalo music community, Sapp proceeded cautiously. He sensed early on that if he were to realize his goal of making Buffalo a mecca of modern music, he would have to continue to provide cover for his controversial friend. In a letter to Foss written in November 1962, Sapp revealed his carefully planned and interestingly conspiratorial efforts to bring Foss and his brand of modernism to Buffalo.

> Everything is moving along much according to your plans, I trust. I am so extremely excited by all your ideas, your catholic point of view and your rigorous insistence on a new orientation in the musical scene here. This is, of course, precisely what I'd hoped for in all our earlier efforts in bringing you here. You may be assured that my position as musical advisor is essentially to insulate you as well as to provide long term continuity with the trustees; so in a real sense I can construe my role as being that of educating and persuading and explaining.[12]

Finally, Millonzi and Sapp prevailed. It was announced in December 1962 that beginning in the fall of 1963, Lukas Foss would become the next musical director of the Buffalo Philharmonic Orchestra.

Foss's impact not only on Buffalo but on the entire music world was immediate. Ecstatically received at his opening concert on October 26, 1963, Foss wasted little time, programming the Buffalo premier of Stravinksy's revolutionary ballet *Le Sacre du Printemps*. In the program notes, he said that Stravinsky's ballet was "second to none in its influence on contemporary composers and contemporary music in general." Then, in March, following a triumphant all-Bernstein program, which rocked the house when "Lenny" himself made a surprise appearance as a last-minute replacement for an ailing Andre Previn, Foss programmed the American premier of a piece written by the world's most controversial contemporary composer, Stockhausen's *Momente*. The *Buffalo Evening News* reprinted the review written by Eric Saltzman, eminent music critic for the New York *Herald*

Tribune, who had come to Buffalo for the concert and then stayed longer. "Buffalo," Saltzman wrote,

> is turning out to be quite a place for contemporary arts. The marvelous Albright-Knox is one of the best of its kind in the country. Now the Buffalo Philharmonic Orchestra under Lukas Foss, has become a pacesetter too. The reputation of this city for musical firsts is spreading rapidly with considerable effect.[13]

Under Foss's direction, the BPO had overnight gone from being a conservative, staid orchestra under the baton of a highly talented but deeply conservative Viennese, to the most radical and innovative large orchestra in the world.

Foss was, according to longtime *Buffalo Evening* News music critic Herman Trotter, turning Buffalo "into a real turmoil of experimentation." The city had become a place of pilgrimage for young musicians everywhere who wanted to be a part of this most exciting development in the world of music. One of these was Andrew Stiller, who in his *Jubilee History of the Buffalo Philharmonic* tells of the thrill and the joy he experienced in coming to Buffalo: "I loaded all of my worldly goods into a rental van and headed for Buffalo to begin graduate studies in composition at SUNY/Buffalo. To save gas and mileage charges, the AAA had mapped me a route that was practically a straight line between Washington D. C. and Buffalo—and as far as I was concerned every winding, two lane mile of it was paved with yellow bricks. Imagine," he continued "a town where the orchestra played the most demanding contemporary scores as a matter of routine! In such a utopia anything might happen. As the Emerald City on Lake Erie drew inexorably nearer, I actually bounced in my seat like a child and shouted 'Buffalo!' every once in a while. Never before or since have I looked forward to something with such anticipation."[14]

None of these earthshaking events would have been possible without the University of Buffalo, which since September 1962 had officially become a part of the State University of New York. Founded in 1856, the University of Buffalo, despite the visionary leadership of Samuel Capen and the exciting and truly significant work of many of his faculty, remained primarily a local institution, known as a "street-car college," a commuter school (the first dorm was not built until 1957) that primarily served the children of Buffalo's lower middle class. "It was not," as Leslie Fiedler, the American literary scholar who came to UB in 1965, wrote, "a great university...but it performed its intended functions in a way that kept the community around it happy." What "reassured the surrounding community," Fiedler wrote, "was the prevailing sense of a school which knew and accepted its predetermined place and whose students only sought to move up to the predetermined slot next above the one into which they were born."[15]

If the school knew its place, so, too, did its students. They were composed, Fiedler said, not of the white Anglo-Saxon Protestant elite, who sent their children away to exclusive private colleges and universities, and not of African Americans, "who were sorted out early into technical high schools." Rather, the University of Buffalo's student body was made up of the upwardly mobile children of Polish and Italian immigrants and large numbers of Jews. These students, Fiedler said, were "on their way to becoming dentists, pharmacists, accountants, teachers, technicians, insurance agents and real estate lawyers." They were young people, he wrote in his scintillating yet self-serving essay "Just Off Main: 1967," who were "acting out the All-American charade called 'Bound-to-Win,' 'Onward and Upward,' 'Getting Ahead' with the promise of a degree."

UB did its job very well, however, educating and creating virtually all of Buffalo's professional class. In 1955, all of the judges in both the city court of Buffalo and the Erie County Court were alumni of the UB Law School, as were the majority of the district's New York State Supreme Court judges. Similarly, 85 percent of all trained pharmacists, 61 percent of all physicians, 61 percent of all lawyers, and 82 percent of all dentists had earned their degrees at UB.[16] UB had become a place that could be trusted to educate the children of the city's upwardly mobile middle class without shaking them up too much; it was a school that could be counted on to reinforce the values and the expectations of the parents who sent their children there. For years, UB had lived up to these expectations, performing its function ably and willingly. As a former history professor defined it, UB was a "training center for the defense of American integrity and the betterment of American life."[17]

The university was growing rapidly during the 1950s, and Governor Nelson Rockefeller was concerned that UB, like other colleges across the state, was not equipped or prepared to handle the still-greater growth projected for the future. In early 1960, Rockefeller created a committee to explore the matter. Named for Henry T. Heald, the academic who chaired the committee, the Heald Report, which appeared in November 1960, documented what it called "the crisis in higher education." While there were 401,000 enrollments in 1959, the numbers, they said, would increase dramatically: 646,000 in 1965, 804,000 in 1970, and 1,270,000 in 1985. Given "the post-war birth rate, an increasing desire to go to college as well as the increased capacity of young people to go as a result of the higher income of their parents," the committee recommended an immediate expansion of the state university system (limited at the time to eleven campuses, consisting of teachers' colleges and two agricultural schools, which served fewer than twenty thousand students total) to accommodate the projected tide of new students. The report called for the establishment of a public university, which would offer "low tuition, high quality education to students on the basis of ability, not personal wealth."[18]

The committee's boldest and most ambitious recommendation was for the creation of two new universities—one at Stony Brook on Long Island and the other "upstate, either through the conversion of an existing private institution or through the development of one of the present campuses of the State University." Within hours of the release of the Heald Report, UB, under the leadership of its chancellor, Clifford Furnas, who, along with UB council president Seymour Knox recognized the unprecedented opportunity for his campus, initiated discussions with the state. While there were a great many concerns—faculty worried about the impact on their retirement plans, administrators were concerned about the loss of autonomy and the increased state bureaucracy, and everybody had misgivings about the lost sense of community that was sure to come—most everybody seemed to agree that the rewards were worth the risks. Undergraduate tuition, Furnas predicted accurately, would drop immediately from $1,000 to $500. Medical and dental school tuition would drop too, from $1,200 to $700. Meanwhile, faculty salaries, he promised, would increase immediately by over 10 percent while the operating budget in the first year alone would rise from four to fourteen million dollars. The greatest opportunity, Furnas said, would be in the budget for capital improvements, which would go, he promised, from $7 million in 1962 to $18 million the year after. By the spring of 1961, the deal was done; in the fall of 1962, the old, private University of Buffalo, merged with the state and became the State University of New York at Buffalo.

It was a staggering and unprecedented historical moment, not only for UB but also for the City of Buffalo. Rockefeller's vision for the new university was grandiose. Chosen to become one of the four "graduate centers" of the state university system, UB was overnight transformed from a small commuter college into a great and complex university, "the Berkeley of the East," in the boosterish, heady idiom of the day. Local leadership in Buffalo was stunned and overwhelmed by the development; they recognized it instantly as a great and long-term opportunity for the continued development and progress of their community. "The 'new' University of Buffalo," the *Courier Express* predicted in an editorial in March 1962, "will sooner or later touch the personal lives of most everyone who lives in this city."[19]

Alan Sapp was one of the most enthusiastic supporters of the merger. In his estimation, the creation of the state university in Buffalo offered a rare and unique opportunity for the city. It was, he said, "urban renewal at is most spectacular." He saw the "long-range advantages that the expanded university will bring to the Niagara Frontier." The impact on culture and the arts would be particularly dramatic and would lead, he predicted, "to new directions in the cultural affairs of the community." He believed that the university would lead the way in creating an urban public policy with the arts as a focal point. He wanted, he said, to decentralize the cultural activities of the community and bring the arts, music, dance, and lectures from the university into the neighborhoods where the people lived. Sapp envisioned UB playing a central role in re-creating "the public artist—the town musician, the town actor, the town dance—a tradition from the Renaissance which we will need to revive."[20]

Sapp recognized that the new university offered the city of Buffalo a rare and historic opportunity to play a new and dynamic role as a center of the arts in America, and he longed to seize it. Working with Lukas Foss shortly after his arrival in Buffalo in late 1963, these two apostles of contemporary art and music applied for and received two million dollars from the Rockefeller Foundation (the Rockefeller Foundation, ever eager to bring modernism to new, outlying outposts, had funded Behrendt's position at UB more than thirty years earlier) to create what Sapp and Foss called "The Center of Creative and Performing Arts." Sapp and Foss were great educators, deeply interested in how and what young musicians, both composers and performers, learned. Like Charles Abbott, who understood the value of deconstructing the creative process of poetry so that its lessons could be applied in the creation of further poems, Sapp and Foss recognized the relationship between process and product across artistic disciplines and particularly in music. As a professor of composition at UCLA, Foss had initiated the process of freeing performers of classical music from what he said was "the tyranny of the note" by encouraging them to improvise in their performance, "to invent something like jazz improvisation but in the classical field." Foss recognized the value of this process for composers, too, who would be forced to hear their music in new and changing ways. The impact of improvisation had had a powerful affect on Foss, helping him to shed neo-classical composing traditions to become instead, in his own words, a "wildly adventurous experimental composer." Sapp and Foss wanted to embed this interrelationship between composer and performer deeper into the creative process and hoped that the Center of Creative and Performing Arts and its offshoot, the Creative Associates, an ensemble of talented musicians, which coalesced around Foss, would accomplish that.

Sapp and Foss were as committed to the new musician as they were to the new music; they were eager to alter the process by which so many young and talented musicians went directly from the conservatory to a position in an orchestra. Wanting to create opportunities for young musicians to grow at the beginning of their careers, Foss and Sapp saw the center as a dynamic and stimulating locus of musical growth. Their purpose, the two men wrote, was to create at SUNY Buffalo, "an atmosphere dedicated to study, creation and performance of new music and to bring together the best and the brightest young musicians, scholars, performers and composers." The Center of Creative and Performing Arts awarded year-long fellowships, which provided the "creative associates," as they were known, the opportunity to study, compose, and perform without "the stultifying effects of the commercial music world."

The Creative Associates had an instant and long-lasting impact on the university, thrusting it, exactly as Sapp had wanted, into the forefront of the international avant-garde. With its promise of well-funded, no-strings-attached fellowships, word of the Creative Associates spread quickly to music centers all over the world. Suddenly, the most promising young people in the world of avant-garde music were flocking to Buffalo. David Rosenbaum, a violinist-composer, was one of them. "I was at the University of Illinois," Rosenbaum remembered, "and I already knew that there were all kinds of interesting things going on in Buffalo; that it was high profile."[21] Pianist/composer George Crumb came from Europe. "The existence of the Center in Buffalo was known in Europe as a good example of a place that didn't exist there: a center that existed for the purpose of doing only new music and having a mix between composers and performers who were also composers. That idea was completely new."

The grant for the Creative Associates was a feather in the cap of the university and a wonderful opportunity for the city. Indeed, it was the city itself and the strong supportive network that existed among Buffalo's cultural organizations that had encouraged the Rockefeller Foundation to support the associates. The foundation, according to Professor Sapp, was impressed with "a University with almost limitless expansion of services and resource, a leadership committed to the arts and strong relationships to the Albright-Knox Art Gallery and the Buffalo Philharmonic." What they noticed particularly, Sapp said, was "a pervasive spirit of adventure and change that all combined to underlay the formation of the Center within the University of Buffalo." Sapp, who with his other colleagues in modernism had done so much to create and implement the unique and exciting changes in the cultural life of Buffalo, was thrilled with the success of the Center of Creative and Performing Arts and the Creative Associates who worked there. In an interview a year and a half after the center opened in September 1964, Sapp said that he was pleased that the center had become "one of the really outstanding things going on in the whole university. It has set a national pattern and is known all over the world. It has brought the university a distinguished complement of creative people from all over the world and in the process it has changed completely the whole character of this university." For Sapp, the center was "a model and a mechanism for experimentation, innovation in curriculum, international education and in a whole realm of developments within the arts. The Center is a community of artists working in series and in parallel. It is unique in American university and metropolitan life." The location of the center in Buffalo, Sapp insisted, was no mere accident of location. Indeed, it was Sapp's belief that there was something about the quality and character of the city itself that encouraged these kinds of artistic developments: "Buffalo," he said, "was an ideal city in which to try an experimental program."[22]

John Dwyer, the highly respected music critic of the *Buffalo Evening News*, understood what Sapp was trying to achieve, and he recognized the opportunity that Sapp's center offered the city. "There will be young professional musicians—performers, scholars, educators and composers. They will design and present concerts, hold forums and panels on new trends, seek to bring the community at large into the music picture and form special cultural 'cadres,' or lecture/performance teams, for visits to area schools." Dwyer saw the creation of the Creative Associates in Buffalo as momentous, and he encouraged the whole community to support them. "The development has national significance and it is most heartening to the University and to the BPO that a deciding factor in awarding this rich grant for Buffalo was the growing artistic climate of Western New York."[23]

The Creative Associates, Lukas Foss said, "was my child" and, like any proud parent, he was eager to show off. There was no better venue anywhere than the new and magnificently modern auditorium that Gordon Bunshaft had designed for the new wing at the Albright-Knox Art Gallery. And it was here, beginning in November 1964, that Foss offered the first of what would be many "Evenings for New Music." The lure of Buffalo to creators and aficionados of new music became irresistible, and following the first "Evening" in November 1964, Buffalo's place on the international music map became secure. One month later, Foss took the Creative Associates to New York, where they performed "An Evening for New Music" at the Carnegie Recital Hall. In attendance were Leonard Bernstein, Morton Feldman, Gunther Schuller, Elliot Carter, and other giants of contemporary music. These luminaries would continue to spread the word about Buffalo. Sapp's stimulating impact on the music department was mirrored throughout the university community; with enormous infusions of state funds to attract the best and brightest young scholars in the country, UB was in fact fast becoming "the Berkeley of the East."

No segment of the UB community grew more glamorously than the English department. Bruce Jackson, one of its members, wrote about it many years later in a February 1999 piece in *Buffalo Beat*, a local weekly:

> For at least a decade, beginning in the early 'sixties, the University of Buffalo English Department was the most interesting English department in the country. Other universities had the best English departments for history or criticism or philology or whatever. But UB was the only place where it all went on at once: hot-center and cutting-edge scholarship and creative writing, literary and film criticism, poem and play and novel writing, deep history and magazine journalism. There was a constant flow of fabulous visitors, some here for a day or week, some for a semester or a year. The department was like a small college: 75 full time faculty teaching literature and philosophy and film and art and folklore, working

about stuff and making stuff. Looking back on it from the end of the century, knowing what I now know about other English departments in the country.

The names are just part of it. There were other writers and critics here, and more who came soon after, some to stay and some to visit: the critic Dwight Mac-Donald, the story-writer Donald Barthelme, the scholar Angus Fletcher, the poets Charles Olsen, Robert Creeley, John Logan, Irving Feldman and Robert Haas, the novelists John Barth and John Coetzee, the critics David Bazelon. and Leon Edell. And there were writers and artists and thinkers in other departments who were part of our community of words and ideas: Raymond Federman, Rene Girard, Michel Foucault, Olga Bernal, Eugenio Donato, Lukas Foss, Helene Cixous, Warren Bennis, John Sullivan.[24]

In 2004, Jackson, whose work flourished in the rich atmosphere of this department, again reminisced:

> If you spend much time around Buffalo you're almost certain to hear tell of the legendary English department that existed at the University at Buffalo in the late nineteen-sixties and early nineteen-seventies. Like a lot of legends, there's some truth to those stories and a good deal of imaginative reconstruction. It's true that Al Cook, who chaired the English department in those years, assembled in a very short time a spectacular faculty. But it's also true that many of the people who were part of the scene that is imagined so fondly weren't in the English department at all, and some weren't even faculty members of UB but were rather friends or working associates of people who were. Furthermore, the UB English Department of legend took place over time, not all at once. People came and went; some were here briefly, some were here early and some were here late. The UB English Department of legend is more of an idea than a fact.

> What happened here in the late nineteen-sixties and early nineteen-seventies wasn't a department, but a dynamic cultural scene and an extended process, and there is only one place it really does exist: in the work of Harvey Breverman. In Breverman's pictures you find dozens of the people who populated that scene and process: Michel Serres, Olga Bernal, René Girard and Raymond Federman in French (Federman would later move into the English department); John Sullivan and Jack Peradotto in Classics; Larry Chisholm in American Studies; Al Cook, Homer Brown, Robert Creeley, John Barth, Diane Christian, J. M. Coetzee, and Dwight Macdonald in English. And the visitors and friends and colleagues: Robert Duncan, Alain Robbe-Grillet, Michel Foucault, Ruthven Todd, Allen Ginsberg, John Ashbery, Jim Dine and so many others.[25]

The vibrancy of these departments was dynamic and synergistic. Said Jackson:

"We had the advantage of having the entire University of Buffalo as a resource. Leslie Fielder, Jack Barth, Leon Edell and the others were there. It was very intellectual and very much fun. You had a chance to meet all kinds of people. I've never had an opportunity like that since.... I had a great time in Buffalo." Carol Plantamura, a great American soprano, fondly remembered her years as a Creative Associate: "The Budapest String Quartet was in residence there. I went to all of their performances. I found the Slee Beethoven cycles thrilling. Listening to the Budapest, looking at Paul Zukovsky, the violinist, playing the Ives Violin Sonata and breaking a string and keeping on going...just taking in all those performance and practice ideas.... All in Buffalo, New York."[26]

John Barth was a member of the English department during those heady years (Barth taught at UB between 1965 and 1974). In his 1984 novel, *The Friday Book*, he recalled that "it was altogether a stimulating place to work during those troubled years: Pop Art popping at the Albright-Knox Gallery; strange new music from Lukas Foss, Lejaren Hiller and his electronic colleagues; dope as ubiquitous as martinis at faculty parties and, across the Peace Bridge, endless Canada, to which hosts of our young men fled as their counterparts had done in other of our national convulsions.... I confess to missing that lively make-it-new spirit of the Buffalo Sixties."[27]

Nils Vigeland, a teenager growing up in Buffalo in the mid-1960s and himself destined to become a leading composer of contemporary music, felt the impact on the streets of the city. He recalled some years after that he "didn't realize until later that the childhood [he] had in Buffalo was unusual." He wrote: "I thought it was normal that six times a year these wild concerts would happen with all these amazing people. I thought it was normal that you would run into Lukas Foss on Elmwood Avenue. It wasn't until later that I realized that it was one of those special places in a special time, like Vienna in 1900. It really seemed like that to me."[28] Christyne Lawson, a member of the dance faculty, agreed: "The whole place was just like we were in the middle of the center of the Earth. And it really was Buffalo. I mean that's the kind of feeling that you got."

One of the high points of the arts scene occurred in February and March 1965, when Buffalo's entrepreneurial advocates of the avant-garde—Sapp, Smith, and Foss—joined forces with Seymour Knox to create and present in Buffalo an unprecedented festival of contemporary culture called the "Buffalo Festival of the Arts Today." It was the kind of partnership—the festival was cosponsored by the UB music department, the Albright-Knox, the BPO, and the New York State Council on the Arts—which Sapp had long dreamed about. With almost all funding for the two-week-long event coming directly from Knox (even though he was chairman of the New York State Council on the Arts, Knox, more concerned with the artistic purity of the program, discouraged Sapp from applying to the council for funds), the festival was, according to *Life* magazine, "the most all-encompassing hip, with it, avant-garde presentation held in the US to date."[29]

The festival, a mix of visual arts, music, dance, film, and theater, drew over three hundred thousand people. While most events were held at the Albright-Knox, there were several concerts at Kleinhans and four plays by Eugene Ionesco premiered at Upton Hall on the Buffalo State College campus. While much of it was self-consciously and aggressively modern—people did not know quite what to make of John Cage's "Metronome," in which one hundred metronomes were set off simultaneously—a great deal of it was a serious effort to create a modernistic agenda for the arts while at the same time creating a place for Buffalo at the center of the art world. In both these regards, the Buffalo Festival of the Arts Today was highly successful.

Lukas Foss and Allan Sapp were at the center of much of the action. On Sunday afternoon, February 28, with his Buffalo Philharmonic Orchestra performing at Kleinhans Music Hall, Foss offered a program featuring the music of Morton Feldman, Pierre Boulez, Penderecki, and a world premier by Lucciano Berrio called *Traces*. The concert was followed by a symposium titled "Tomorrow?" which was held at the Albright-Knox auditorium and was introduced by Sapp and led by Foss. On the panel were the leading lights of the American avant-garde: poet Gregory Corso, composer Morton Feldman, painter Larry Rivers, and critic Harold Rosenberg.

The next day, Sapp introduced John Cage, who delivered a lecture to a packed room at the Albright-Knox auditorium on "Contemporary Music." In the evening, over one thousand people went to Upton Hall on the Bufffalo State College campus just across Elmwood Avenue for a recital of original works performed by Merce Cunningham's Dance Company.

And so it continued into the next week. There were poetry readings by Robert Creeley and Randall Jarrell, recitals of new music by the Creative Associates, the screening of new films by Andy Warhol and Jonas Mekas, much-heralded concert presentations of the work of Xenakis, and Cage and Foss's own "Baroque Variations," which, according to music critic John Dwyer, received "five curtain calls and a standing ovation."[30]

Meanwhile, Seymour Knox's gallery was filled with the latest in European and American kinetic art. One piece, an eight-foot-tall sculpture called *Cysp I*, was, the catalog said, "programmed through a cylinder-like electronic brain." Active in darkness and still during the day, *Cysp I*, which emitted periodic percussive sounds, was the hit of the show. Another piece of kinetic sculpture, *Chronos V*, was programmed to project colors and abstract images on the walls and ceilings of the gallery.

By the time the festival ended in early March 1965, *Time* magazine reported that over 313,000 people had attended festival events: one hundred fifty thousand had seen the art exhibit, three thousand had attended the Ionesco plays, and sixty-five hundred had gone to the various concerts. The national press covered the festival, too, and there were stories about the festival in the *New York Times*, the *New Yorker*, and *Time* and *Life* magazines. *Life*, in a story headlined "Can This Be Buffalo?" reported the large numbers of people who came to the concerts, lectures, recitals, and exhibitions. Reporting that "musicians played iconoclastic works to runaway houses," *Life*, under a photograph of an enormous crush of people trying to enter the gallery, reported that police had been called to direct traffic and keep order. Howard Taubman, the dean of American music critics, was deeply impressed. "Do you think that New York is hep? That Paris is with it? Shuffle off to Buffalo if you want to see and hear a concentrated concatenation of the arts as their far-out practitioners are pulling, pushing, distorting and rearranging them these days." Taubman was surprised at the local response to the festival. "It has been embraced as chic. Every event, including the talks, has played to overflowing houses. Everyone, even the people who have only read or heard about the goings on, are talking about it."[31]

The *Buffalo Evening News* was proud of the festival, viewing it as a significant event in the life of the community—one that could, if built upon, point Buffalo in new and exciting directions. An editorial written during the festival said,

> Those who regard Buffalo as a staid and conservative community, not given to new ideas, presumably are unaware of the city's growing importance as a cultural center in which contemporary innovations have a place alongside traditional art forms. We don't pretend that the public or large segments of it will like or understand everything it sees or hears during the festival. We rather suspect, however, that even those who may shake their heads in confusion will take genuine pride in the vitality of the community's cultural and educational resources and in its readiness to expose itself to the ideas and works of contemporary artists.[32]

It had been a magical moment for Buffalo. Robert Creeley, who would soon join the faculty of the UB English department, remembered sitting in an audience in the auditorium of the Albright-Knox for a solo performance by Merce Cunningham: "And there was John Cage, Jasper Johns, who'd done one of the sets, and Marcel Duchamp.... I remember Ginsberg reading.... It was just this incredible star-studded yet intimate, terrific group of people. It was just this fantastically active confluence of people in a very classic Buffalo setting and it was just delicious."[33] Rene Levine, the coordinator of Foss's Creative Associates, recalled walking up to the gallery for an evening's performance. "From the street," she said, "the jewel-like glow of the brilliantly lit glass cube seemed distinct and sharply etched in the night. Inside, you could see people in clusters, some descending to the seating well. It was special, magical. You hoped there'd be enough room for you too."[34]

Within days of the festival's conclusion in March 1965, Allan Sapp wrote a letter to the Rockefeller Foundation, informing them of the success of the Buffalo Festival of the Arts Today. It was, he wrote, "the first." The next, he promised, would be bigger and, most certainly, he assured them, "even better."[35]

The Second Buffalo Festival of the Arts Today opened on March 2, 1968, and continued through March 17. It was a broad survey of the latest trends in art, music, drama, dance, films, literature, and architecture. With Sapp as the ringmaster, Buffalo's leading cultural and educational organizations—the Buffalo Fine Arts Academy, the Buffalo Philharmonic Orchestra, the State University of New York at Buffalo, Buffalo State College, the New York State Council on the Arts, and the Studio Arena Theatre—worked closely together, creating and mounting forty-six programs and events within the two-week period. The focal point—the event around which the others revolved and related—was an art exhibition, "Plus by Minus: Today's Half-Century," which was organized by Douglas MacAgy, an internationally known critic and author. The show consisted of more than three hundred pieces, which occupied all fourteen of the Albright-Knox's interior spaces before spilling out onto and all over the gallery's grounds. The exhibition featured over one hundred works by the constructivist Nahum Gabo; it provided a comprehensive representation of revolutionary Russian art; and it also displayed work by other contemporary artists. According to an art critic for the *London Times* who came to Buffalo for the festival, the show was "one of the most important exhibitions of 20th century art in the United Sates in the past twenty five years.... The Buffalo Arts Festival," he wrote, "is the outstanding event of its kind in the United States."[36]

Karen Brady, a reporter for the *Buffalo Evening News*, wrote that with the festival on there was "a different feeling in the air"; the festival "had brought thousands of curious visitors to the Albright-Knox Art Gallery.... It [had] brought license plates from all over America to fill the parking lots of the Gallery, of Kleinhans Music Hall, of Buffalo State University and the State University of Buffalo. And it [had] brought a vast array of critics, cameramen, musicians, dancers, artists and writers from all over the world."[37] Another correspondent, writing for *Dance Magazine*, agreed: "This week in Buffalo they didn't light a match but set off a bomb. The resulting cultural explosion, officially known as the 'Second Buffalo Festival of the Arts,' may well be the loudest and most brilliant in the country." The reporter, describing the excitement in the city, was ecstatic.

On the day of the opening, the air of Buffalo ... recalled Venice during its biennial international exhibition and Spoleto at the time of Menotti's summer festivals. Artists, musicians, poets, dancers, composers, museum men, collectors from all over the world were under each other's feet. Last minute rehearsals were going on in every available auditorium in the city. The hitch is that someone with two free weeks, sitting down to figure out all the permutations and combinations of events in the wonderfully hectic schedule, still could not get to it all.[38]

The programming for the festival was varied and impressive, the obvious result of a meticulously planned, carefully orchestrated, and well-funded effort by local cultural entrepreneurs and organizations to bring to Buffalo the best and most exciting work in the fields of music, art, theater, dance, and film then being produced. Among the vast and varied programs that took place during those two weeks in March 1968 were readings by John Barth, Charles Olsen, Louis Zukofsky, and Allen Ginsberg; three programs of dance by the Merce Cunningham Company; concerts by the Buffalo Philharmonic Orchestra and the Creative Associates, as well as recitals by John Cage, Yannis Xanakis, and Lukas Foss; lectures by architects and city planners R. Buckminster Fuller and Constantin Doxiadis; a panel on playwriting with Edward Albee, Richard Barr, and Alan Schneider; a new film by Jonas Mekas called *New York Diaries*; and the world premiers at the Studio Arena Theatre of Edward Albee's *Box* and *Quotations for Chairman Mao*.

"Can this be Buffalo?" *Life* magazine asked rhetorically again as it had three years earlier. "Yes, it can be Buffalo—and is. It is no surprise," *Life* continued, "that any big American city offers plenty of art and culture. But Buffalo last month exploded in a two-week avant-garde festival that was bigger and hipper than anything ever held in New York or Paris. In fact, one Sunday the cops had to be called to handle a traffic jam at the Albright-Knox Art Gallery which finally had to be shut because 66,500 art lovers were trying to get in."[39] People, like Congressmen Thaddeus Dulski, were proud of their city; on March 13, 1968, Dulski introduced into the *Congressional Record* an article that had appeared in the most recent issue of *Time* magazine.

Most people think of Buffalo, when they think of it at all, as a sooty industrial port on a blustery bluff overlooking on Lake Erie. They ought to try shuffling off to Buffalo some time. Ask any contemporary art lover and he will tell you that Buffalo is the home of the Albright-Knox Art Gallery, one of the nation's finest and most up-to-date art collections. Ask any experimental music lover and he will tell you that since 1963 Lukas Foss, one of the nation's most venturesome young composers, has been leading the Buffalo Philharmonic through the a-melodic intricacies of Krzysztof Penderecki, Luigi Nono and other twentieth century composers.... Buffalo, in the six years since the Albright-Knox added its glass-walled new wing, has taken giant strides toward becoming a vociferously militant acropolis of the avant-garde arts. Though the later term is out of vogue in Manhattan, it is used with force and conviction in Buffalo where the cab drivers lecture their fares on the horrors of modern art and where Foss reminds his listeners that the word avant garde is military in origin. The artist, in his view, is meant to act as a sort of spiritual shock-trooper for society, forcing it to become aware of new conflicts and realities whether it wants to or not.[40]

By the middle of the 1960s, the cultural life of Buffalo had reached a level as high and as sophisticated as any city in the country. In this blue-collar industrial community, known far more for its brawn than its brains, a handful of individuals who cared deeply about their city and were passionate about the arts, attempting to use the latter to remake the former, worked together to create a vital and dynamic cultural force that, had it been sustained, would have redefined the role and function of Buffalo in the life of the nation. For what Allan Sapp, Seymour Knox, and Lukas Foss wanted, like A. Conger Goodyear and Cameron Baird before them, was to build and sustain a community where cultural expression was defined by artistic daring and adventure; a place that would, because it was stimulating, exciting, and forever "kinetic," function as a magnet, attracting the best and most inventive artists of the time; a place that, through the force and power of its artistic expression might, like Florence before it, have transformed itself. Their efforts, which began in the mid-1930s and continued without interruption through the mid-1960s, bore rich and delicious fruit, producing a burst of artistic energy that by the end of the 1960s was recognized and admired around the world.

In the midst of the great burst of artistic energy and enthusiasm at the end of the 1960s, the State University of New York at Buffalo, with a tenfold increase in the projected number of students by the mid-1970s, knew that it had to expand. New buildings had been regularly added to the 1920s core of original buildings, and there appeared to be ample room for still more construction. However, a second option had far more appeal to the master-building Governor Rockefeller. In 1963, he instructed Vincent Moore, of the New York State Office of Planning Coordination, to explore the various possibilities for construction of a new, second campus for UB.

Even before Moore began his deliberations, the choice for the new campus had been narrowed down to either a large plot of vacant land on Buffalo's downtown waterfront or a much larger space in the far reaches of suburban Amherst. Although Moore purported to make an objective presentation, it was clear from his conclusions that he favored the Buffalo waterfront. While the suburban Amherst site did offer larger amounts of unencumbered land (some of the waterfront was tied up in complicated urban renewal projects), Moore seemed convinced that the advantages of the waterfront outweighed those of Amherst. Besides, Moore said, the waterfront site offered a unique challenge to the university and a special promise to the city: "The situating of a university within the heart of Buffalo might provide stimulation for the solution of many bewildering problems of the urban setting by minds of latent imagination and intellectual curiosity." The trustees of the State University of New York (SUNY), however, felt differently. Even though they had commissioned Moore, they rejected his recommendation. In June 1964, they voted unanimously in favor of the Amherst site.[41]

The question of the new site for the university had not yet become the critical issue that it would be later. UB was growing rapidly and was otherwise occupied. By early 1966, students and faculty, increasingly concerned about the war in Vietnam, were becoming militant. In the spring of that year, furious and frightened students entered and occupied President Clifford Furnas's Hayes Hall offices, protesting his insistence that selective service exams be held on campus. In an atmosphere of growing dissent, it was simply a question of time before members of the university community demanded that the issues of the new campus be reopened.

In the spring of 1966, a coalition of university and community groups called CURB (Committee for an Urban Campus) was formed to fight for the waterfront site.[42] By now, the site controversy had become an important local issue. CURB, chaired by Robert T. Coles (the African American architect who'd made a daring critique of urban renewal years before), had the support not only of all the local black political and social organizations but also of virtually every downtown business and political group, including the newspapers and the banks. In an age of increasing concern with the problems of the city in general and of the inner city in particular, the controversy over the site of the new campus had become a prime indicator of one's "urban" credentials. An urban campus would, it was said, "add a dimension of relevance and pertinency to the University's role and function." BUILD (Build Unity, Independence, Labor, and Dignity), a Saul Alinsky-organized civil rights group, maintained that far more was at stake in the decision than the mere location of a campus. Rather, the group insisted, "the issues before the State University Trustees is whether to turn away from the critical challenges of the future or to face them squarely and deal with them creatively." In addition to the array of downtowners and African American community groups, a growing number of faculty members at UB began to speak out against the Amherst site where, one group felt, "the suburban location will reinforce any tendencies of the University to insulate its student body from the rest of the society."[43]

Even Governor Rockefeller himself began to offer hints that perhaps he, too, had begun to reconsider. The 1968 Republican convention was less than two years away and Rockefeller, still in those days before Attica considered a liberal, was counting on the support of those blacks and liberals who overwhelmingly supported an urban campus. The tilt toward the waterfront appeared to be gaining still more support when it was announced that as of September 1967, Martin Meyerson would become the new president of UB. An internationally known city planner and former dean of the prestigious College of Environmental Design at the University of California's Berkeley campus, Meyerson would, everybody assumed, naturally favor an urban location for the campus. Indeed, shortly after the start of Meyerson's tenure, Governor Rockefeller insisted on yet another report on the question. To help him and the SUNY trustees make what Rockefeller promised would be his final decision, Rockefeller, thinking that an outsider would be more objective, appointed the president of Rutgers University, a man named Mason Gross, to help him choose the location of the new UB campus.

Gross made every effort to be objective. Under his auspices, meetings were held on campus and students, faculty, and alumni were carefully polled and consulted. Most of the university's constituents strongly favored the suburban site in Amherst. The staff, those hundreds of people, most of them women—the secretaries and nonteaching professionals who worked eight-hour days and really kept the university going—already lived in the suburbs and therefore favored the Amherst location. The majority of the faculty, too, leaned toward Amherst. Many of them, young and hired fresh out of graduate school in the flush, early days of the university's initial growth period, had themselves grown up in the suburbs. Coming to Buffalo from all parts of the country, they had little feeling for or commitment to this particular city. In addition, many of them viewed themselves as academic stars on the make, whose stays in Buffalo would be brief—long enough merely to build resumes that would earn them better jobs at still better universities elsewhere. For these young faculty members, the rapidly growing, highly mobile suburb of Amherst was the perfect location for the new university. When the results of the faculty poll were counted, it was determined that "a majority of the faculty have indicated a desire to live outside of the core city."[44]

The alumni of UB felt even stronger than the faculty. For they, Fiedler's upwardly mobile "dentists, pharmacists, accountants, teachers, technicians, insurance agents and real estate lawyers," had already made it to the suburbs, and they wanted their children to live there, too. In a strong statement following a poll of the group, the president of the alumni association reported, "We do not feel it is incumbent upon the university to solve the urban renewal problems of Buffalo at the expense of future generations of students." They'd moved away from the city and now they wanted their children to do the same.

All of these efforts to involve the university community in the decision ultimately meant nothing. Indeed, all of the hearings, meetings, polls, and surveys were little more than a charade. The SUNY trustees had already made their decision, and regardless of who believed what—be it Meyerson, CURB, the faculty, students, or alumni—the Amherst site was a foregone conclusion. When Gross issued his report in February 1967, many people were disappointed but few were surprised. Gross's rationale—that Amherst offered three times the building space and twice the parking space (all of which, presumably, was required if the university was to effectively serve the forty thousand-odd students, faculty, and staff who were supposed to be there by 1975)—may well have been sound, but somehow the argument was not convincing. Gross believed that the size of the Amherst parcel was what made the difference, that if located on the waterfront, the "university would be so limited by that site that it could not achieve its true potential." Others felt differently. The university, they believed, by moving to Amherst, had rejected the city. While UB may have acquired a new campus, many wondered if they had not in the process lost a soul. Yet the decision was made. But Rockefeller and the SUNY trustees were not convinced, and beginning in the late 1960s, construction of the new campus began in the farthest reaches of suburban Amherst.

The decision to build the campus in Amherst has assumed somewhat mythical proportions in the life of the contemporary city. In the conversations Buffalonians love to have about "what's wrong with Buffalo," virtually everyone agrees that a downtown location for UB would have done more to revitalize the city than any other project that has ever been on any planner's drawing board. And yet, somehow, for mysterious reasons that remain the source of endless speculation, term paper topics, newspaper articles, and cocktail party conversations more than thirty years later, the new campus was built not downtown, not on the waterfront, but in Amherst. Conspiracy theories abound. University trustees, say some, wanted it in Amherst because they owned tracts of undeveloped land there. Downtown businessmen, say others, didn't want it downtown; they didn't really want all those disheveled, radical students hanging around. Others argue more rationally (though their critics disagree) that there simply was not enough space on the downtown waterfront for the kind of massive, wide-open campus that the trustees of the state university wanted to build. While a lot of people doubted the wisdom of the decision, the riots that tore apart Buffalo's black ghetto on the East Side in July 1967 convinced many of them that perhaps the governor and the SUNY trustees had been right after all.

Meanwhile, there was turmoil of a different kind on UB's Main Street campus. Enrollment had grown rapidly and steadily since 1962, not only increasing the size but dramatically changing the character of the student population. During that period of rapid growth, an increasing number of students, many of them from working-class families in New York City—the children of cab drivers, high school teachers, and civil servants who could for the first time afford to go to college—poured into Buffalo, bringing with them the excitement, color, and creative dynamism of their native city. By 1967, UB had become the most stimulating and avant-garde cultural showplace in all of Western New York. Fiedler describes the atmosphere that he found when he arrived from Montana in 1964:

We are visited not only by poets but by successful Jewish novelists and lost Gentile ones, absurdist playwrights, underground filmmakers, stand-up comedians, folk singers, mime troops, rock guitarists, electronic musicians, designers of geodesic domes, structural linguists, pop artists, puppeteers, defenders of mass culture or polymorphous perverse love, Zen Buddhists, Russians on good will tours, jazz flutists, nude dancers, Black Power organizers, pianists who play with their feet as well as their hands, and pianists who sit motionless over the keyboard, daring the audience to laugh. And before each event, there is a reception, after each a party; sometimes when visitors overlap, two or three parties combined into one: all in all a nonstop festival, a continuous ball—as the All-American Cultural Road show rolls into Buffalo for a one-night stand between Albany and Ann Arbor, New Paltz and Chicago.[45]

Among the artists who appeared on campus in the spring of 1967 were three East Village iconoclastic poets and musicians who called themselves the Fugs. Announcing that they were delivering "Tomorrow's Orgasms Today," the Fugs performed at an "Angry Arts Festival" at UB in March 1967. The *Spectrum*, the student newspaper, which under the editorship of yet another New Yorker had become increasingly outrageous—at this point more culturally shocking than politically radical—reviewed the concert, printing the names of the Fugs's songs: "Jack-Off Blues," "Wet Dream Over You, Baby," "I Couldn't Get High," and a song dealing with American foreign policy called "River of Shit."

The review provoked an immediate reaction within the community, with politicians in both Amherst and Buffalo complaining bitterly and loudly. A strong antistudent stand was becoming increasingly popular in Buffalo as in the rest of the country. One local politician in Amherst vowed that when the university completed its move to his town, he would do everything possible "to prevent such groups from appearing" there. The *Spectrum* continued to aggravate the raw nerves of respectable Buffalo opinion. Throughout the fall semester of 1966 and into the spring of 1967, the *Spectrum* became increasingly outspoken and critical of the selective service tests administered on campus (anyone who scored a seventy or better was exempt; the rest were eligible for the draft) and the dress code in a student-subsidized restaurant frequented primarily by administrators. At the same time, the *Spectrum* vocally supported such campus groups as the SDS (Students for a Democratic Society) and LEMAR, a student group that advocated the legalization of marijuana. The paper's positions combined with its eagerness to print scatological material earned it the scorn of many of the still-to-be-radicalized student body and the bitter opposition of a growing number of influential off-campus figures (a group calling itself the Christian Family Movement had sent letters to all businesses advertising in the *Spectrum*, urging that they stop in the name of decency).[46]

Relations between the university and the community were still further strained less than one month later when Leslie Fiedler, one of the university's best-known professors, was arrested on a drug charge: not for selling drugs and not even for using them, but rather for "maintaining a premise where narcotics are used." Fiedler's house, Erie County Sheriff Michael Amico admitted, had been under surveillance for days; his phones had been tapped; and a paid undercover agent, masquerading as a hippie-like friend of Fiedler's daughter, had planted a listening device in Fiedler's home. Fiedler, who had earlier incurred the rage of the community by serving as faculty advisor to LEMAR, knew throughout his three-year-long trial that the verdict would go against him. He didn't stand a chance in this venue. Subject to relentless harassment by gawking neighbors; by his bank, which declined to renegotiate his mortgage as he sought to raise cash for the trial; and by his insurance company, which cancelled his homeowner's policy, he knew that he would lose, "since what was being judged was not my specific guilt but [our] general role in the community as outsiders and dissenters."[47]

As turmoil on the old campus accelerated, so, too, did the planning of the new one. Nelson Rockefeller's appetite for architectural overkill is well known. The mall at Albany, begun during the early years of his governorship and barely completed before his death in 1979, is a windswept monstrosity, its superhuman scale awesome and overwhelming. His plans for the new UB campus in Amherst were equally grandiose. One of Rockefeller's favorite architects was Buffalo-born Gordon Bunshaft. Since his truly magnificent addition to Buffalo's Albright-Knox Art Gallery in 1962, Bunshaft, the most influential partner in Skidmore, Owings, and Merrill, the world's most influential architectural firm, had been designing increasingly larger and more monumental buildings. As far as Rockefeller was concerned, the bigger the better. In the spring of 1967, Rockefeller had the State University Construction Fund (SUCF) hire Bunshaft to prepare a preliminary master plan for the new UB campus.[48]

In November 1967, Bunshaft's plan appeared on the front pages of Buffalo's newspapers. It defied description. What was pictured was a single "building" (the local press, not knowing quite what to call it, put the word in quotations) nearly one mile long and one thousand feet wide. It was, a spokesman for the SUCF said, "to be the largest single architectural undertaking in the country and possibly the world." It would, the SUCF continued, "dwarf the Pentagon." Within this enormous structure (later buildings like this would be called "mega-structures") would be housed all of the academic departments of the university, all classrooms, all libraries, all research facilities, all offices and laboratories, and all recreational facilities. It would even contain a hospital. Surrounding this mind-boggling mega-thing were to be thirty colleges—"centers of identification," Meyerson called them— where thousands of students and faculty would live and learn together. Bunshaft's new campus would serve a university community of forty thousand people and would be built at a cost of between $600 million and $650 million.[49]

The plan was too much for most people to swallow. Even the sophisticated Meyerson thought that it was inappropriate, and soon the plan was withdrawn amidst a chorus of criticism (the university downplayed the significance of this and said that Bunshaft's plan was but one of many being considered). Meanwhile, a group of engineering students, fearing for their campus lest the likes of Bunshaft and the others have their way, proposed a plan of their own. While based on the requirements for the new university, their model had a completely different form than what had emerged from Bunshaft's office. Using a variation of the quadrangle, the design that had typified American and European colleges for several hundred years, the engineering students suggested that the buildings of the university should be small in scale and located around the perimeter of a large circle. The effect of this design, unlike Bunshaft's mile-long horizontal shaft, would be to contain the activities of the university in a linked enclosure traditionally characteristic of campus designs.

The final plan revealed by the SUCF in June 1968 was much closer to Bunshaft's original plan than to the students' alternative. While the mile-long mall had been trimmed considerably, the plan still centralized and concentrated virtually all of the university in a single structure referred to as the "Spine." In order to scale down the size of the original mega-structure, the "Health Sciences," as they were called, were removed and placed instead in twenty-four separate towers. Lest anyone suspect that these revised and seemingly more humble plans represented a concession by the university, Robert Ketter, the officer in charge of campus construction (his official title was vice president for facilities planning) and the man who two years later became president of the university, explained the support system that this new campus would require. It would need, Ketter said, a new highway system capable of carrying thirteen thousand cars per hour (four times the existing capability), a rapid transit system joining the campus to the city, a seventy-five-acre park for research activities, seventy-five acres of commercial property, thirty-five to forty thousand units of new housing, and parking for over five thousand cars.[50]

Meanwhile, back on the Main Street campus, upwards of twenty-five thousand students, faculty, and staff continued to live in cramped, overlapping, yet somehow satisfactory and pleasing quarters. The university was expanding rapidly, every year hiring dozens of new faculty members at a time (in the spring of 1967, over 120 faculty were hired for the coming fall semester). Thus, with more students, more faculty, more radicals, and more reason to be angry than ever before, UB, like campuses throughout the United States, became ever more involved in anti–Vietnam War activities. For several years, there had been a small yet continuous stream of antiwar protests, but by the fall of 1967 these were galvanized by the march on the Pentagon in October. Now, with frequency and ferocity, significant numbers of students and faculty became involved in protests at the UB campus.

Antiwar activities continued throughout the winter and spring of 1967–68. Recruiters for Dow Chemical and other companies involved in war production were harassed, campus research projects funded by the Department of Defense were constantly trashed, and draft cards were regularly burned. As long as these activities were confined to the campus itself, there was little trouble from the community. While the Common Council of the City of Buffalo had voted overwhelmingly in favor of a motion objecting to the use of state facilities for antiwar activities, there was little politicians could do about what happened on the campus. But it was a different matter when the protests spilled over into the rest of the community.

In the summer of 1968, antiwar activities were taken directly into Buffalo's residential West Side, where several students, already found guilty of draft evasion, sought asylum in a Unitarian church on Elmwood Avenue. Finally, after several tense days of efforts by the minister to mediate between the students and the federal agents outside the church, the Feds stormed in and forcibly arrested the students, who at that point became known as the "Buffalo Nine."[51]

The trial of the Buffalo Nine, who were charged with assault and resisting arrest, occupied the attention of UB's antiwar movement throughout the fall. When in February 1969 one of the Buffalo Nine, a student named Bruce Beyer, was convicted on two of three counts, the university exploded. Unlike the other irritants, there was something about the trial of the Buffalo Nine, the seriousness and commitment of the defendants, and the violent assault on the church by the federal officials, which captured the imagination and ignited the energy of a large proportion of the student population. Meeting at the gym the night after the verdict to express their solidarity with Beyer, twenty-five hundred students demanded an end to American involvement in the war and an end to UB's participation in defense-related research. Meyerson, whose flexibility with students (considered "patronizing" by them and "permissive" by the community) had helped to earn him the job as president of the university, agreed on this latter point and expressed his hope that no such projects would be permitted in the future. He agreed also to cancel classes temporarily so that teach-ins on the war could be held.[52]

His attempt to mollify the growing student anger failed. When on March 19, 1969, Beyer was sentenced to two concurrent three-year terms, real violence broke out as several hundred students (local papers referred to them as "rampagers") set fire to several buildings that were part of a navy research project. From there they jubilantly entered administration offices at Hayes Hall, where several climbed to the bell tower of that hundred-year-old building and began to clang uproariously the bells of the university. Meyerson's reputation in the community as a capitulator to the students grew still more when he, choosing to avoid confrontation, allowed them to leave Hayes at their leisure. He further outraged the community (there had already been formed in Buffalo an organization called Mothers Against Meyerson) when, the very next day, he expressed his support for a cause that had become increasingly important to many in the university community. Now, only six months after ground for the new campus had been officially and ceremoniously broken, Meyerson publicly urged that Governor Rockefeller stop all work there until the labor force was equitably integrated. (Rockefeller subsequently complied, imposing a moratorium on all campus construction. A year passed before the integrated construction crews were in place and work resumed.) On the next day, March 21, 1969, a handful of Buffalo councilmen demanded that Meyerson be fired for his "weak" action as president of the university.[53] Meyerson's troubles with the community were exacerbated by his educational philosophy. For Meyerson did not want to duplicate in Buffalo the worst aspects of the California system, a large and lonely "multiversity" that had somehow managed to lose sight of the personal as well as the educational needs of the individual student. Thus, he supported enthusiastically the creation of separate colleges—those "centers of identification"—where faculty and students would live and learn together according to their particular interests. By late 1969 and early 1970, however, several of these colleges had taken on lives and identities of their own well beyond the range of possibilities that anyone had ever imagined. Several of them, committed to a nontraditional education in which students and people within the community-at-large would somehow learn with and from each other, had leased office space in storefronts off campus, on Main Street. College A, as it was called, had become a particularly nettlesome problem. Dedicated to social change and student activism as much as it was to nontraditional education, College A, with its bevy of disheveled, bearded students and faculty walking around and hanging out in their Main Street storefront, made a lot of the local people very angry. Offering courses—and for credits, too—for subjects that few people had ever heard of, let alone understood (subjects like "Conflict and Change in the Local Community" and "Social Change in America"), College A was an outrageous affront to what most people in Buffalo regarded as sound education.[54] As had happened once before, earlier in the century, the content of the university's education again became the legitimate subject of political discussion, with Buffalo councilmen hearing witnesses and debating questions that had most always remained beyond the pale of city politics. One member of the Buffalo Common Council, reflecting the views of more than a few of his colleagues, said that "we are concerned over this—the kind of program at College A—and I feel that the University needs a definition of education which excludes this sort of aimlessness. Education should have more concrete goals."

It was bad enough that public funds were being spent on such notions of education; it was much worse when those notions began to ooze out into the rest of the community. (One college, an offshoot of College A, called Rosa Luxemburg after the notorious German Communist, was concerned primarily with taking radicalism directly into the community. Their brochure said: "It does little good to know abstract theories of racism and imperialism if one cannot impart this knowledge to a high school student, or a young housewife, in your neighborhood.") This, more than the content of the courses offered at College A, was what most concerned the people in the surrounding neighborhood. In response, they formed the Concerned Parents Group to deal with the question. Located directly across the street from a parochial school, the college, the Concerned Parents argued, was luring neighborhood children there and encouraging them to "dropout of school and church." It was, many charged, harboring runaways and initiating them into a world of sex, drugs, and radicalism. When a local politician revealed that ten of the instructors of the Social Change in America courses were facing prosecution on criminal charges ranging from assault to vandalism and antiwar activities, it heightened still further the anger and anxiety of this particular neighborhood as well as the anger and anxiety of the community at large. The events of February 1970 made the situation worse still.

It was easy to create a crisis at UB in the early spring of 1970 and, like the events that have triggered cataclysms throughout history, the spark that ignited the confrontation between police and students on the night of February 27, 1970, was quickly forgotten. It all started at a demonstration against the allegedly racist practices of UB's basketball coach. At the end of a freshman basketball game between UB and Canisius, students took to the floor chanting "Power to the People," "Ho-Ho-Ho Chi Minh," and "Serfustini [UB's basketball coach] is a racist."[55] While campus security, which had been alerted that a demonstration might occur, was able to peacefully disperse the crowd, the game, already much delayed, was postponed. Meanwhile, the demonstrators, increasingly aroused, joined other students coming out of yet another rally in another building and, together, this group of approximately one hundred people made its way to Hayes Hall, where at 9:30 at night, the university's acting president, Peter Regan (Meyerson had taken a year-long leave of absence in September 1969), was working in his office. After entering the building and then the lobby in front of Regan's office, the students saw approximately twenty university security police, unarmed (though fully outfitted in riot gear), approaching the building. Upon seeing them coming their way, the students quickly dispersed, breaking several windows in Regan's office as they left. Sensing that this time they would be pursued, the students ran to Norton Union, several hundred yards away. They entered and hastily gathered tables and chairs to barricade the doors so as to block the campus police who were indeed on their heels. Reinforced by officers from the Buffalo police department (to this day, despite extensive testimony and depositions, nobody seems to know for sure who called the Buffalo police) law enforcement officials smashed through the doors and began to violently chase the students through the halls of the union. Within less than an hour, the policemen had gone, leaving behind them the wreckage of several badly beaten students, a badly damaged student union, and a bitterly hurt and angry student body.[56]

While there was tension, anxiety, and a great deal of uncertainty following the police raid, the union was relatively quiet and activities were soon almost back to normal. Regan, however, now holed up in security headquarters at the other end of the campus, thought differently; even though he had apparently received information to the contrary, he acted on the assumption that the violence in Norton had continued. Once again, Buffalo police were dispatched to the student union. While quiet returned to Norton some time after midnight, student anger could not be contained. The next day—Thursday, February 26—several thousand students marched vigorously to Hayes Hall shouting, "We Want Regan." From there they continued on to the campus security building where, linking hands across the street, they sang endless choruses of the National Anthem and "America the Beautiful." With over four thousand students "on strike," there were no classes held anywhere on the campus. The State University of New York at Buffalo was under siege. By Sunday, sensing that another outbreak of student anger was imminent, Regan again summoned the Buffalo police. By midday, as three hundred fully armed police officers outfitted with highly polished, knee-high leather boots and riot helmets patrolled the grounds of their campus, hundreds of faculty members and students marched in silence around its perimeter mourning the death of their university. This time the police stayed. Indeed, they remained on the premises despite an overwhelming faculty vote demanding that Regan have them removed. When Regan refused to comply, forty-five members of the faculty, on March 15, 1970, peaceably entered the lobby in front of his office, sat down on the floor, and vowed not to move until the police left the campus. They were arrested several hours later.

The events of the spring 1970 semester at UB were traumatic for everyone involved. Indeed, none of the participants—students, faculty, police, and administrators—will ever be able to forget what happened. While students risked their lives (although none were killed, at least twenty-one were hospitalized) and faculty their careers, the police and the members of the administration were better protected, the former by their strength and equipment, the latter by an agile instinct for survival. President Meyerson, away from the campus on a year's leave of absence, had already announced that he would not be returning to UB. He had, he said, accepted a new job as president of the University of Pennsylvania. Acting president Regan, meanwhile, overwhelmed by the events of the spring of 1970, also announced his resignation later that year. He was, he said, resuming his position at the University of Buffalo medical school in the department of psychiatry. Most of the lessons learned from that breakdown of the university in the spring of 1970 were abstract and difficult to identify, having to do with the nature and function of institutions of higher learning. In some cases, however, the lessons were clear-cut and easy to surmise. Such was the case for the people charged with planning the new campus in Amherst.

Actually, it was far more than a new campus that Rockefeller, the SUNY trustees, and the planners and architects wanted to build. Rather, it was, in the phrase increasingly popular among those expectant master builders, "Brasilia in America," a whole new environment filled with monumental and dramatic structures that would capture the imagination of the world. The planners were thrilled by the magnitude of the challenge. In 1970, the director of the SUCF wrote that

> the scale, complexity and coordination of this project require that the State University Construction Fund create an organizational framework and develop new techniques to augment the traditional planning process. More than twenty planning firms are working in a coordinated effort to ensure that the resultant facilities not only satisfy the University's program, but also realize the potential of the site and the atmosphere of activity envisioned there to bring new life to the land. Never has the development of a single university been more potent with possibility.[57]

Only the best, the brightest, and the most expensive architects would be permitted to work on the major buildings of the new campus: from New York came I. M. Pei, Ullrich Franzen, and the firm of Davis-Brody; from Chicago came Harry Weese; and from Cambridge came Sasaki, Dawson, and DeMay. Although Bunshaft's mile-long mega-structure had been rejected, his concept of a spine or, as the architects liked to call it, a "central activity corridor," remained the dominant feature of the plan for the new campus. (Angered by the rejection of his comprehensive plan for the university, Bunshaft had withdrawn from the project. He got revenge on his hometown, however, when he was hired by the Marine Midland Bank to build their Buffalo headquarters—he used the opportunity to erect a vertical version of his mile-lone monstrosity at the foot of Main Street.) The primary difference between Bunshaft's mega-structure and the revised plans was that in the revised plans, Bunshaft's single structure was broken into two smaller spines, each of which contained three linked buildings. The first spine included all of the administration offices, three specialized libraries, fifty-two classrooms, several "food service areas," and a conference theater. Included in the second spine was the law school, a gigantic building with office space and classrooms for over twenty-five hundred students, and the library, an enormous structure, which, with its one-million-volume capacity and over thirty miles of shelves, would be three times larger than the library on the Main Street campus. Although not a part of this second spine, a ten-story office building housing the English and modern language departments was directly linked to it by a pedestrian overpass. A half-mile away from these two spines was yet another mega-structure, a place called the Ellicott Complex. It was, in the words of the SUCF, "an environment which, though massive in scope, consists of a series of smaller, intimate spaces designed to combat the vastness and impersonality frequently associated with large universities." This detail of the design was Meyerson's antidote to the "multiversity."[58]

Other than its enormity, what most distinguished the design of the new campus from the old UB campus was its sudden and dramatic departure from the idea of centrality and enclosure, which had not only dictated the form of the Main Street campus but, indeed, had been the dominant concept in the design of universities throughout the world since the Middle Ages. On the new UB campus, there were no quadrangles, no fountain areas, no plazas, no enclosed courtyards—no places and no spaces, in other words, where the individuals who composed the college community could come together. How, in the absence of these kinds of places, people wondered, could a sense of community ever develop?

NOTES

1. Despite his very public role, Knox was a very private person. He seemed to have given very few if any interviews and very little was written about him. For a good account of his life, see his obituary, T. Buckham, "Seymour H. Knox, Jr., Banker, Patron of the Arts, Philanthropist, Dies at 92," *Buffalo News*, September, 27, 1990, p. A1.

2. "Albright-Knox Addition Lets Art Dominate, Designer Says," *Buffalo Evening News*, January 19, 1962, Buffalo Fine Arts Academy Scrapbook, p. 316, Grosvenor Collection, BECPL.

3. "'Shorty's' Triumph," *Time*, January 12, 1962, pp. 54–57.

4. The opening of the Knox wing was a major event in the life of the city, and the press covered it extensively. Many of the articles were clipped and pasted in the Buffalo Fine Arts Academy scrapbook in the Grosvenor Collection at the BECPL. See, for example, "Art Gallery's Magnificence Is Hailed in Dedication Eve," *Courier Express*, January 19, 1962, and Margaret Fess, "$2 Million Gallery Dedicated Today," *Courier Express*, January 19, 1962.

5. Ray Jerome, "Buffalo's Stellar Albright-Knox." This article first appeared in the *Globe and Mail* (Toronto) and was reprinted in the *Buffalo Evening News*, August 26, 1964, p. B18.

6. "In the Right Hands: C. Still's Gift to Gallery," *Buffalo Evening News*, May 2, 1964.

7. Minutes of the Board of Directors of the Buffalo Philharmonic Orchestra, October 18, 1962, box 1, folder 4, Allan Sapp Collection, University Archives, State University of New York at Buffalo. The minutes of these meetings offer fascinating insights into the conflicts within the board over the direction of the BPO.

8. Ibid., December 28, 1962.

9. Ibid.

10. Allan Sapp to David Laub, President of the Buffalo Philharmonic Orchestra, December 11, 1962, box 2, folder 3, Allan Sapp Collection, University Archives, State University of New York at Buffalo.

11. Ibid.

12. Allan Sapp to Lukas Foss, February 11, 1963, box 1, folder 5, Allan Sapp Collection, University Archives, State University of New York at Buffalo.

13. Saltzman's review was reprinted in the *Buffalo Evening News*, March 4, 1964, p. B16.

14. Andrew Stiller, *Jubilee History of the Buffalo Philharmonic Orchestra* (Buffalo, NY, 1985), p. 15. This publication can be found in the "music" vertical files in the Grosvenor Collection at the BECPL.

15. See Leslie Fiedler, *Being Busted* (New York: Stein and Day, 1969), pp. 91–177.

16. *Spectrum* 5, no. 18 (1955).

17. Milton Plesur, personal communication with the author, April 2, 1986.

18. Henry T. Heald, "Meeting the Increasing Demand for Higher Education in New York State," November 1960, University Archives, State University of New York at Buffalo.

19. "The 'New' University of Buffalo," *Courier Express*, March 13, 1962, p. 22. In addition, the University Archives at UB has two folders, which contain primary sources on the merger process.

20. Allan Sapp, "New Direction in Cultural Affairs," lecture, Model City Conference, Buffalo, NY, January 19–20, 1967.

21. Renee Levine-Packer, "In the Center: The Center of the Creative and Performing Arts in the State University of New York at Buffalo," master's thesis, State University of New York at Buffalo, April 6, 2000, p. 11.

22. Allan Sapp to Gerard Freund, Associate Director of the Rockefeller Foundation, February 18, 1964, Allan Sapp Collection, box 4, folder 12, University Archives, State University of New York at Buffalo.

23. John Dwyer, "Creative Associates' Ambitious Dreams," *Buffalo Evening News*, March 11, 1964, p. B12.

24. Bruce Jackson's e-magazine, *Buffalo Report*, http://www.acsu.buffalo.edu/%7ebjackson/englishdept.htm.

25. Ibid.

26. Levine-Packer, "In the Center," p. 24.

27. John Barth, *The Friday Book* (Baltimore: Johns Hopkins University Press, 1984), p. 44.

28. Levine-Packer, "In the Center," p. 37.

29. "Can This Be Buffalo?" *Life*, April 23, 1965, pp. 63–64. This and other clippings

are stored in the vertical file labeled "Buffalo Festival of the Arts Today, February 27–March 13, 1965," which is stored at the Albright-Knox Art Gallery library in Buffalo, NY.

30. John Dwyer, "Futuristic Music Brings Drama, Creative Brilliance to Festival," *Buffalo Evening News*, March 6, 1965, "Buffalo Festival of the Arts Today" vertical file, Albright-Knox Art Gallery.

31. Howard Taubman, "Festival: Buffalo Offers Arts of Today; Program Includes 4 Plays by Ionesco, *New York Times*, March 8, 1965, p. 34.

32. "'Art Today' Show Attracts 14,383 in Day," *Buffalo Evening News*, March 1, 1965, p. 19.

33. Levine-Packer, "In the Center," p. 46.

34. Ibid., p. 38.

35. Allan Sapp to Gerard Freund, Associate Director of the Rockefeller Foundation, March 18, 1965, "Rockefeller Foundation Support of Creative Associates, 1964–1965," box 4, Allan Sapp Collection, University Archives, State University of New York at Buffalo.

36. G. Needham, "Buffalo Traces Mainlines of 20th Century Art," *London Times*, April 10, 1968. This clipping is stored in a vertical file at the Albright-Knox Art Gallery library titled "Second Buffalo Festival of the Arts, March 2–March 17, 1968."

37. Karen Brady, "That Special Feeling—It's the Festival Air Making Buffalo Buzz," *Buffalo Evening News*, March 15, 1968, "Second Buffalo Festival of the Arts" vertical file, Albright-Knox Art Gallery.

38. S. J. Cohen, "Merce, Mao and More in Buffalo," *Dance* 42, no. 45 (1968): 8.

39. "Can This Be Buffalo?" pp. 61–64.

40. Dulski's remarks were clipped and filed in the "Second Buffalo Festival of the Arts" vertical file, Albright-Knox Art Gallery.

41. Vincent Moore's report is part of the author's private collection.

42. For a good discussion of the controversy over site selection, see Linda Levine, "A Waterfront Campus?" *Western New York Heritage* (Winter 2002): 55ff.

43. "'BUILD' Urges City Campus," *Courier Express*, January 28, 1967, p. 12.

44. "Faculty Statement Wants Amherst Site," *Buffalo Evening News*, January 21, 1967, p. A1.

45. Fiedler, *Being Busted*, p. 105.

46. See the ads and announcements for activities on the campus in *Spectrum* 17, no. 49 (1967): 49.

47. Fiedler, *Being Busted*, pp. 129ff.

48. "Buffalo Architect Hired to Create Master Plan for New UB Campus," *Courier Express*, April 11, 1967, p. 12. See also, "Architects Chosen for UB Amherst Campus," *Buffalo Evening News*, November 7, 1967, p. 17.

49. "UB Project a Mammoth One—$600 Million, 12,000 Acres Campus," *Courier Express*, November 12, 1968, p. 9.

50. "New UB Campus Plan Almost Complete," *Buffalo Evening News*, June 21, 1968, p. B1.

51. The *Spectrum*, the University at Buffalo's student newspaper, covered Bruce Beyer and the "Buffalo Nine" in detail from the time of their arrest in August 1968 through to their February 1969 trial. An excellent summarizing piece on the case from the perspec-

tive of students at UB is Linda Hanley, "Buffalo Nine On Trial Today," *Spectrum* 9, no. 34 (1969). The *Spectrum* is housed in the University Archives at the State University of New York at Buffalo.

52. Ibid.

53. "Demands Grow for Meyerson's Resignation," *Courier Express*, March 22, 1969, p. 16.

54. "Experimental College Projects Stir Controversy," *Courier Express*, February 22, 1970, p. 1; "Picketing of College A Resumed by Mothers," *Courier Express*, April 23, 1970, p. 17.

55. *Spectrum* 20, no. 70 (March 16, 1970); *Spectrum* 20, no. 71 (March 23, 1970).

56. *Spectrum* 20, no. 70. See also "45 of Faculty Arrested at Sit-in at Hayes Hall," *Courier Express*, March 16, 1970, p. 1.

57. State University Construction Fund, "SUNYAB Amherst Campus Plan" (Albany: State University Construction Fund, 1970), p. 2. This report is housed in the University Archives at the State University of New York at Buffalo.

58. Ibid.

chapter 10

THE 1970S

A Decade of Loss

What happened to Buffalo during the 1960s and '70s was a tragedy. The years measured hard times, even for the big and glamorous cities, places like New York and Boston. Times were harder still for the dark and dirty rust belt cities of the industrial heartland—Cleveland and Pittsburgh, Youngstown and Buffalo. With their industries eroded by foreign competition and undermined by disinvestments and mismanagement, these once great cities stared at a gloomy and uncertain future. Their tax bases shrank, their expenses soared, and their public services were diminished or dismantled. People left by the thousands. While Buffalo's population had been dropping since the end of World War II, the loss during the 1970s was staggering and unprecedented. The population went from 462,768 in 1970 to 357,000 in 1980, as 23 percent of the population left the city. While some of this loss was caused by lower birth rates, most of it was because people were leaving in droves, some to the "sunbelt," most to the suburbs. It was a massive exodus that in just a few years decimated neighborhoods in all parts of the city.

The worst of it occurred in the old, white ethnic neighborhoods, places like Fillmore-Leroy and Broadway-Fillmore, places that were now increasingly populated by African Americans. Fillmore-Leroy, on the northeast side of Buffalo, developed as a streetcar suburb early in the twentieth century. Like the adjacent Genesee-Moselle and Walden-Bailey neighborhoods, it was originally settled by first- and second-generation German and Polish families that had moved away from the old East Side. During the 1970s, these families again picked up and left, moving to newer and nicer neighborhoods in the adjacent suburb of Cheektowaga. Magnificent, old Catholic churches, places like Blessed Trinity on Leroy, St. Bartholomew's on Grider, and St. Matthew's on Wyoming, were emptied of congregants. The loss was heaviest at Blessed Trinity, one of the most beautiful churches in all of Buffalo. Built in the early 1920s by a local architect named Charles Oakley, the church, according to *Buffalo Architecture: A Guide*, is an "extraordinary re-creation of North Italian church architecture." It is, according to a 1944 article written for the Buffalo Historical Society, "true Lombardic in style resembling the beautiful church of San Teodora in Pavia, Italy. The bricks," the author says, "were shipped from Exeter, New Hampshire, where they were made by a colony of French workmen, who used the same tools and methods that were used centuries ago by French artisans. They are reddish brown, antique in appearance, irregular in shape and when the edifice is first approached, the thought occurs that the bricks appear as though they had been set in place by the parishioners, one by one as they filed by."[1] Blessed Trinity held onto to most of its sixteen hundred families throughout the 1950s but by the mid-1960s, large numbers of African Americans had moved into the area; the mostly white families that had resided in the parish for decades began a mass exodus. By 1980, the residents of Fillmore-Leroy were almost all black; Blessed Trinity, with fewer than four hundred families, could barely hold its own.[2]

Polish Americans, who had lived in the Broadway-Fillmore area for over a century, were also leaving. Through the mid-1950s, the still-majestic intersection of these East Side arteries remained, after Main Street, the busiest commercial corridor in Buffalo. On the ground floors of the buildings that lined Broadway were clothing emporiums and cigar stores, jewelers and bakeries, soda fountains and beauty shops, branch banks and delis. Above them, on the second floors, were the offices of doctors, lawyers, accountants, and businessmen. There were large department stores, too: Neisner's, Zolte's, and, the largest of them all, Sattler's, which was known as a mecca of shopping and excitement for several generations. Across the street from Sattler's was the Broadway Market, a cavernous, publicly owned structure where butchers and bakers, produce merchants and candy makers, all with long, hard-to-pronounce Polish names, marketed their wares to the people of the neighborhood. By the mid-1970s, this area—main streets like Broadway and Fillmore as well as the side streets—was fast becoming a slum. The main streets were filled with empty storefronts and the pot-holed side streets, strewn with garbage, were lined with wood-frame homes, some burned out, many in a state of terminal decay. The threat, if not the reality, of racial change haunted all of the city's neighborhoods, even those that were far removed from the East Side.

There is no better-located neighborhood in Buffalo than Riverside. Hugging the shores of the Niagara River, the view from many of the neighborhood's streets is staggering; second-story porches disclose magnificent views of the swift river, the lightly wooded Canadian shore, and on summer afternoons, the slow, orange sunsets over the water. Old-timers in Riverside, people who have been around since the 1950s, talk nostalgically of the fishing clubs that used to line the river's banks, of boating and swimming off the shore, of walking along the banks of the old Erie Canal towpath. It is all talk and memories now; in 1958, Riverside's access to the waterfront was obliterated by the construction of the Niagara section of the New York State Thruway. Riverside residents fought hard against it, and when it became clear that their efforts had come up short, they held a mock funeral to mourn their lost waterfront. In the mid-1970s, a pedestrian bridge spanning the thruway was installed; people today can walk over the highway to the river's bank, but it's not the same, not even close. There is a long, concrete ledge that hugs the river's edge, and pedestrians can stroll along its length, but it's as close to the thruway as it is to the river; it's noisy, dirty, and not a bit like the old Riverside waterfront. Like parks in neighborhoods throughout Buffalo, however, Riverside Park, designed by Frederick Law Olmsted, is lovely; its long views of the Niagara River continue to attract the area's people throughout the year.

There had been isolated pockets of settlement in Riverside since the late nineteenth century, but it was not until the 1920s that the neighborhood really grew, filling up with Germans and Poles from Black Rock and large numbers of Canadians attracted by the prospect of viewing their native land from the American side of the Niagara. There were jobs there, too, good-paying factory jobs. By the 1940s and 1950s, Riverside had become, like South Buffalo, a solidly Catholic, largely blue-collar neighborhood, prosperous and, thanks particularly to the magnificent Niagara River, a very pleasant place to live.

By the late 1970s, however, Riverside had lost not only its access to the Niagara River but its industrial base as well; gone were its largest factories: Pratt and Letchworth and J. H. Williams, two large steel mills, and Wood and Brooks, an internationally known manufacturer of piano keys. On summer evenings and on weekends, men decked out in ill-fitting polyester uniforms bearing the names of sponsoring taverns play softball on a field named for the J. H. Williams Steel Company. As the sun sets, the Williams field—"J. H." as it's called in the neighborhood—is draped with the long, slender shadows that stretch from the hulk of the abandoned steel plant. Across the park, on Vulcan Street, the border between Buffalo and the Town of Tonawanda, another empty factory, the large, poured-concrete structure that once housed the Wood and Brooks piano key factory, stands as a silent memory of better times.

But Riverside was tough, what some might call a redneck bastion. Except for a handful in the Jaspar Parish housing projects, few African Americans lived in Riverside. In 1972, as part of one of the early half-hearted attempts to desegregate the city schools, a few dozen blacks were bused to Riverside High. They came as close to being lynched as anyone ever has in what Buffalonians call the "city of good neighbors."

Still more fuel was poured on the smoldering racial fires burning in Buffalo when on Thursday morning, September 9, 1971, more than twelve hundred black and Hispanic inmates took control of all five cell blocks at the maximum-security state prison in Attica, a small, rural town thirty miles southeast of Buffalo. The inmates seized forty-three white guards as hostages. Within hours the media descended on the town, focusing the eyes of the nation on the frightening confrontation. All three Buffalo television stations had reporters on the scene around the clock, examining every minute detail of the unfolding drama: the comings and goings of the corrections commissioner, Russell Oswald; the status of William Quinn, a guard from Buffalo who had been hurled from a second-story cellblock window; the arrival of black militant Bobby Seale and radical attorney William Kuntsler, whose presence at the scene had been requested by the prisoners; and the efforts of Herman Schwartz, the UB law professor chosen by the prisoners to negotiate their case with state authorities.[3]

For a while it seemed that Schwartz, tireless in his efforts, might be able to negotiate an end to the uprising. On Thursday night, September 10, one day after the takeover, he flew off in a state plane at midnight to Manchester, New Hampshire, where Federal District Judge John T. Curtin, away at a conference, signed a federal injunction barring administrative reprisals against the prisoners. But it soon became apparent that neither the state nor the prisoners were in any mood to negotiate, particularly after the prisoners, rejecting an ultimatum from Commissioner Oswald, paraded eight blindfolded hostages around the prison's D Yard, holding knives at their throats. Meanwhile, Governor Rockefeller had already decided to retake the prison by force. At 9:50 on Monday morning, September 13, 1971, four hundred state troopers entered the prison. An official report issued a year later by the New York State Special Commission on Attica recounted the ensuing events: "Forty-three citizens of New York State died at Attica Correctional Facility between September 9 and 13, 1971. Thirty-nine of that number were killed and more than 80 others wounded by gunfire during the fifteen minutes it took the State Police to retake the prison on September 13." The commission concluded somberly, "With the exception of the Indian massacres in the late 19th century, the State Police assault which ended the four-day prison uprising was the bloodiest one-day encounter between Americans since the Civil War." The commission was sympathetic to the inmates, who, they said, were "demanding recognition as humans," and for whom confrontation was the only language that could "call attention to the system." Thus, the report concluded, "the possibility that the Attica townspeople will again hear the dread sound of the powerhouse whistle is very real."[4]

Like the riots on the Crystal Beach boat twenty-one years earlier, the uprising at nearby Attica shocked and terrified the people of Buffalo. Whites in particular were repelled by the images that flashed relentlessly across their television screens—black prisoners in hoods and bandanas, strutting arrogantly and angrily, bare-chested and sweating in the heat of the prison yard. Never had the images of black power been more graphically displayed; for the whites of Buffalo, "Attica" became a buzzword for terror. Meanwhile, for the younger, more militant members of the black community and the activists on the university campus, Attica quickly became a symbol of the violence and perversion of racism. For those fighting for school integration, "Attica" made that struggle seem less attainable than ever.

But the story of the Buffalo neighborhood known as Parkside suggested that racial integration was, despite the challenges of the time, still possible; by the end of the 1970s, the efforts of a handful of that neighborhood's citizens were proving successful. Adjacent to Fredrick Law Olmsted's magnificent Delaware Park, Parkside, with its gently curving streets and its spectacular view of Olmsted's meadow, has, since its initial growth and development in the late nineteenth century, been one of the most desirable neighborhoods in the city. Because of the proximity to Main Street, near both Canisius College and the old campus of the University of Buffalo, Parkside's reasonably priced Victorian homes have long attracted the local academics. Parkside also attracted upwardly mobile, second- and third-generation ethnics, particularly Irish Americans. When block-busting realtors, hoping to prey on the fears of the white residents of Parkside, began hovering around the neighborhood in the late 1960s, a handful of concerned neighborhood activists, eager to defend their community against the tactics that had destroyed so many others, organized the Parkside Community Association (PCA). By the early 1970s, the efforts of the PCA were beginning to pay off. Though blacks were moving into the neighborhood in increasing numbers, the whites of Parkside, encouraged by the work of their community association, stayed. By the end of the decade, a time when so many other neighborhoods succumbed to the frightening cycle of events that caused blight and decline, Parkside not only survived but thrived as a racially mixed, inspiringly beautiful middle-class neighborhood in the heart of the city.[5]

Parkside was not the only neighborhood where residents began to take an increasingly active role. Indeed, in neighborhoods throughout the city, people began to recognize and exercise the power they had in numbers. In an effort to reclaim their communities from decades of failed public policy and horrific historical events, the people of Buffalo had begun to fight back.

In Allentown, residents had begun the long and painstaking process of historic preservation. In Parkside, residents had demonstrated that racial integration could proceed smoothly. On the African American East Side, a grassroots organization called "BUILD" (Build Unity, Independence, Liberty, and Dignity), trained by Saul Alinsky's Industrial Areas Foundation in Chicago, had begun, as a result of successful initiatives in housing and community development, to restore power and pride to its shattered neighborhoods. In Fillmore-Leroy, a grassroots organization known as FLARE (Fillmore-Leroy Community Development Corporation), led by Father Walter Kerns of Blessed Trinity, struggled to delay and derail panic-spreading, block-busting real estate agents. Citizen activists were sprouting up everywhere. In an effort to protect Olmstead's Delaware Park from city plans to increase automobile access, a group of citizen activists, led by Delaware District Councilman William B. Hoyt, formed the Delaware Park Steering Committee. By the end of the decade, the steering committee had successfully lobbied for the implementation of many traffic-calming measures and had begun work on a master plan that would lay the groundwork for the creation in the 1990s of the Olmstead Conservancy. Flexing their muscles and using their brains, by the end of the decade, neighborhood groups all over the city were proving the power and the creativity of people working together. Few activists were more successful than Francisco "Frankie" Perez, the founder of the Puerto Rican-Chicano Coordinating Committee, who, in an effort to bring strength and stability to the growing Puerto Rican community, led his neighbors in a battle to defeat plans for the Lower West Side Arterial.

There had been a small Puerto Rican community in Buffalo since the mid-1940s, when many Puerto Ricans migrated from the island and from New York City to work in Buffalo's defense industries. Others came later, drifting into the city from surrounding agricultural areas, where many worked as seasonal farm laborers. At first, Buffalo's Puerto Ricans settled on the East Side, but with the expansion of the black population there in the 1960s, they gradually began to move to Niagara Street and the Lower West Side. In that neighborhood, amid the rubble of an area destroyed by decades of failed urban renewal policies, some recognized the promise of creating a new community of their own.

First, however, they would have to deal with the highway planners who, since the publication of the 1946 *Urban Area Report*, had done their best to realize the vast and lofty goal of bisecting the settled area of the city with an intricate system of street-level highways. By the early 1970s, four of these highways—the Niagara Extension of the Thruway, the Skyway, and the Scajaquada Creek and Kensington Expressways—had already been completed. All that remained to be built were the Elm-Oak Arterial on the East Side and the Lower West Side Arterial. Many residents of the West Side feared that completion of the planned project would reduce their neighborhood to what Douglas Rae, in his powerful book about urban renewal in New Haven, called "a wasteland of automotive infrastructure"[6]

The purpose of the Lower West Side Arterial was to connect the Niagara section of the thruway along the Niagara River to the Kensington Expressway, which terminated just east of the central business district. As planned, the expressway would cut a wide swath through both downtown and the mostly residential Lower West Side along the approximate route of Virginia Street. For years it had remained unclear what form the new highway would take. Some argued for street-level construction while others advocated for an elevated highway that would cast shadows on street-level activities as commuters sped across town. By the late 1960s, a consensus began to develop for a street-level route—despite what officials conceded was "a closely built-up area with many churches and other costly buildings." Plans, they promised, would "adapt to the requirements of this densely settled area." Though some of the area's most significant buildings were scheduled for demolition—great late-nineteenth-century structures like the Buffalo Club, the Montefiore Club, and the Grosvenor Library—state planning officials assured locals that the buildings would be "replaced with grass and trees."

Meanwhile, as the planners planned, Lower West Side residents who could afford to leave made plans to get out. "Planners' blight" began to set in; some residents sold their homes, others moved out but held on to their old homes, converting them for the short term into income-producing multiple dwellings, while holding out in the longer term for a potentially lucrative state buyout when construction of the arterial began. Soon, absentee ownership, high turnover, and abandonment began to plague the area. Efforts by residents to halt the cycle of decay were frustrated by cutbacks in city services and by banks and insurance companies unwilling to invest in a neighborhood destined for condemnation. In late 1971, the federal Department of Housing and Urban Development (HUD) denied a $2.5 million grant requested by a local community development organization called the Niagara Frontier Housing Development Corporation for the rehabilitation of homes in the neighborhood on the grounds that "the project is in the probable roadway corridor of the proposed West Side Arterial."[7] Meanwhile, people continued to leave, particularly the Italian Americans who'd been in the neighborhood for years. In 1960, there were nineteen hundred families, mostly Italian American, at the Church of the Immaculate Conception on Elmwood and Edward Streets. By 1973, there were under five hundred, all but a handful of which were Puerto Rican.[8] (The Church of the Immaculate Conception closed completely in 2004.)

Since the mid-1960s, when planning for the arterial began in earnest, state and city officials had been reluctant to involve the public in their decisions. In a memo to Edward Ummiker, the city's planning engineer, New York State district engineer Norman Krapf wrote that he had been "advised to proceed swiftly with the development of the plan.... Let's assume," he said, "that we have [the public's] blessing before going ahead with the public hearing." By the early 1970s, however, times had changed, and in compliance with new and strict guidelines for community involvement, the New York State Department of Transportation initiated a well-orchestrated and broad-based effort to elicit the opinions of community residents affected by the planned arterial. Operating out of an office on Maryland Street in the heart of the neighborhood, the DOT, in the spring of 1973 distributed brochures in English, Italian, and Spanish that explained the project and encouraged participation: "In keeping with the spirit of community involvement in transportation development studies the Department of Transportation is willing to consider any alternatives offered by local citizens." Throughout the spring and summer, eight community meetings were held in eight different locations throughout the Lower West Side. Finally, in May 1974, the DOT offered up nine different choices, which ranged from building nothing at all to constructing, at a cost of $30 million, a partially depressed and partially elevated highway that would cut through the city along the originally planned route from the river to the Kensington Expressway. From the language of the presentation, it seemed that the state was looking for a way out. "If at any point in this process," a DOT official said in May 1974, "local officials and citizens show a definite, overwhelming opposition to a project of this kind, it would be deemed infeasible and removed from the program."[9]

Opposition to the project was, in fact, increasing, particularly among the growing number of Puerto Ricans settling on the Lower West Side. Puerto Ricans—over two thousand of whom would have to be relocated if plans went forward—had the most to lose and the least to gain by the construction of the arterial. Now, a group of young community activists known as the Puerto Rican-Chicano Coordinating Committee, which Francisco Perez and Jose Pizzaro had founded, stepped to the forefront in opposing the state's road-building plans.

Pizarro was from New York City, one of the many New Yorkers who had come to Buffalo in the late 1960s to study at the new state university. Having cut his teeth as a student activist, organizing cultural and political events for the several hundred Hispanics attracted to the university by its low tuition and generous incentive programs, Pizarro liked Buffalo and, after graduation, decided to stay. Housing was cheap, and though the city lacked the dynamism and vibrancy of New York's Puerto Rican community, life in Buffalo was easier and friendlier. Besides, for an educated Puerto Rican like Pizarro, there was a future in Buffalo—the new federal block grant program had created many opportunities in politics and community organizing at the grassroots level.

Perez was born in the small Puerto Rican town of Moca. He had come to Buffalo in 1953 when his father, a fruit picker already in the United States, sent for him, his mother, and his brothers and sisters. His father, by that time, had found work at Bethlehem Steel and a permanent residence on Niagara Street, on the Lower West Side. Perez grew up in Buffalo, graduating from Grover Cleveland High School, which was still mainly Italian. After two years at the University of Puerto Rico, Perez returned to the Lower West Side where, in 1971, he, Pizarro, and a few others formed the Puerto Rican-Chicano Coordinating Committee. Having seen how urban renewal on the waterfront had wrecked the Italian community, Perez and Pizarro began to use their organization to fight the West Side Arterial. By the early 1970s, "far too much Puerto Rican concrete had been poured on Virginia Street," one veteran of the struggle remembered, "for anyone, including New York State, to jackhammer it out without a fight."[10]

Indeed, by the early 1970s a whole new community, a veritable "Little San Juan," had been created on Virginia Street. Everything came together there, group after grassroots group, with politics heavily on their minds—the Puerto Rican-Chicano Coordinating Committee, Allianza, the Spanish Speaking Political Caucus, the Buffalo Hispanic Association—together and separately, they wrestled with the problems of community building. Father Antonio Rodriguez, the pastor at Immaculate Conception Church, joined the upsurge of community involvement. He was a small, suave Spaniard with a Madrileno lisp. "Father Rod" had worked first at St. Anthony's, the Italian church on Court Street, where he came to see the American immigrant experience with his own eyes. He couldn't understand the American emphasis on the melting pot and remembered how shocked he'd been when his superior at St. Anthony's told him angrily never to address a parishioner in his native Spanish. Rodriquez was convinced that the real purpose of urban renewal was to purposefully break up the city's ethnic enclaves.

Nearby, Father David Gallivan had pressured his superiors at Holy Cross, the old "Italian church" on Niagara and Maryland, to hold Spanish services. "Father Dave" had been a missionary in Peru; his perfect Spanish, combined with his South Buffalo Irishman's political instinct, made him an excellent mediator between his Italian and Spanish parishioners. Alternatingly hosting Italian and Spanish saint's days, Holy Cross, like Immaculate Conception, anchored the Puerto Rican community on the Lower West Side. By the early 1970s, meanwhile, the Virginia Street Festival, with its parade, its ragtag tumble of booths, its homegrown salsa and son bands, its profusion of Mexican and Puerto Rican delicacies, and its "Dancin' in the Streets" spirit, had become an institution. The neighborhood bodegas, shabby as they looked to outsiders, were important ingredients in creating community strength and self-confidence, for only there could the Puerto Ricans in the neighborhood find the plantains and mangos, the aquacate and Cafe Bustelo, and the bright green, potent-smelling olive oil they had left behind.

Despite their increasing visibility, Puerto Ricans had very little political power. Lost amid the large number of blacks who made up the Ellicott District, where they'd originally settled, Puerto Ricans had never been part of the political mainstream in Buffalo. Isolated and neglected in their neighborhood, Puerto Ricans eventually developed their own grassroots community leadership. Few grassroots leaders were more effective than Frankie Perez. Articulate and widely read, gregarious and comfortable with people, energetic and passionate about the process of community organization and the importance of cohesiveness in the life of an ethnic community, Perez was educated, be told a reporter in 1976, at "the University of Virginia Street." "Without a sense of community in a city like Buffalo, you can't make it," he said. Perez understood community; he'd seen its ebb and flow while growing up on the West Side. He remembered watching *West Side Story* at the Allendale Theater in the adjacent Allentown neighborhood and dancing all the way home, feeling proud to be Puerto Rican. He remembered attending classes on Seventh Street, at old School 73, which had been torn down as part of the Shoreline renewal project. He remembered the principal who slapped him when she overheard him speaking Spanish to his little sister in the hallway. He remembered the guidance counselor who steered him to McKinley Vocational School so he could learn carpentry instead of encouraging him to go to Grover Cleveland, the academic high school from which he eventually graduated. His studies in archaeology and the pre-Colombian culture of the indigenous Arawak and Taino Indians at the University of Puerto Rico awoke in him a sense of racial and ethnic pride hard to find on the streets of the Lower West Side. This pride, along with his acute and seemingly innate political skills, made Perez a powerful and extremely effective leader in his community.

By the mid-1970s, Perez had become chairman of the four most important grassroots organizations on the Lower West Side: the Lower West Side Resource and Development Corporation, the Virginia Street Development Corporation, the Virginia Street Festival, and the Puerto Rican-Chicano Coordinating Committee. Having become the leading power broker in the Puerto Rican community, it was easy to forgive his bombast when, referring to the populist former mayor of New York City, he called himself "the LaGuardia of the Lower West Side." Perez hadn't traveled much, but he had been to Chinatown and Little Italy in Manhattan and Bedford-Stuyvesant in Brooklyn, where he visited the comprehensive community renewal project started there by Robert Kennedy during his short tenure as a US senator. Perez was particularly taken by Chinatown and Little Italy though; he was impressed with the dynamic communities that ethnic minorities had created, and he was eager to replicate the pattern on Buffalo's Lower West Side. However, before he could do that he would first have to kill the proposed West Side Arterial.

By 1974, the Puerto Rican community had strong allies in its fight against the arterial. Both of the city council members from the affected areas had joined the fight, as had the powerful Allentown Association, which sensed that its efforts to preserve and revitalize the Allentown community were severely threatened by the arterial. The new mayor, Stanley Makowski, who had succeeded Frank Sedita that year and was far more in touch with community sentiment than his predecessor, was also opposed to the arterial. In a letter to the state DOT he wrote, "We should come down to earth, recognize reality, and end the agony which has been caused in the community."[11]

By this time, both newspapers had reversed their position. Several editorials throughout the spring and summer of 1974 urged the Common Council to go on record against the arterial. Having reviewed the DOT's environmental impact statement for the arterial, the Environmental Protection Agency also strongly condemned the project. The agency said that the arterial would create more rather than less congestion and would encourage urban sprawl and lead to wasteful and inefficient use of energy and land. Urging the city to forget the arterial and turn instead to public transportation, the EPA concluded, "We believe that the only proposal which would make possible the survival of the city...is one which emphasizes alternatives to the automobile."[12] On October 1, 1975, the Common Council acted, requesting that the state withdraw its plans for the West Side Arterial. On January 12, 1976, the state assembly unanimously approved a measure introduced by Assemblyman Hoyt that removed the Lower West Side Arterial from state highway law.[13] That night, Frankie Perez threw a party at PRCC headquarters on Virginia Street. Now, finally, he was free to pursue his plans for the revitalization of the area.

In downtown, too, grassroots groups were stirring, increasingly concerned about the 1972 plan to build a convention center at public expense. Mayor Sedita, ever eager to latch onto any publicly funded urban renewal project that bore even the faintest glimmer of hope for downtown revitalization, had by the early seventies become an ardent proponent of a new convention center for downtown Buffalo. In 1972, he included an $11 million item in his budget for its construction. Convinced that the convention center was a key piece in the revival of downtown, both the Courier Express and the Buffalo Evening News enthusiastically endorsed it.[14]

Many people disagreed. In late 1972, another Alinksy trained citizens group called the Alliance of Consumers and Taxpayers (ACT) announced its opposition to the use of public funds for the construction of the convention center. Much to the shock and anger of Sedita and the rest of the urban renewal establishment, ACT launched a citywide campaign that secured enough signatures to force a referendum on the question, which was scheduled for November 1973. When the proposal was overwhelmingly defeated, the powers that so desperately wanted the project built prevailed on Erie County, where a referendum was not required, to step in.[15] Seemingly convinced that a new downtown convention center was just what this rapidly declining, increasingly shabby end-of-an-era industrial city needed, Erie County adopted the convention center as its own silver-bullet project, commissioned the local architectural firm of DeDonado and Renaldo, and built, to everybody's lasting regret, the city's convention center. The rest, as those who continued to live in Buffalo quickly came to realize, is history.

Given the continued decline of downtown during the early 1970s there was little, it seemed, that anything, let alone a convention center, could do to save it. Indeed, it is quite likely that the new convention center, whose construction required the demolition of several buildings containing offices, business, and stores, hurt more than it helped. More businesses left, more stores closed, and even the number of those most promised convention center residuals—hotel rooms—declined following the convention center's opening. William Hassett, a well-connected developer/politico and the owner of the Statler Hilton Hotel, was among the most enthusiastic supporters of the convention center. Within two years of its construction, when new business for his hotel failed to materialize, Hassett sold the hotel at bargain basement prices to new owners who immediately converted it to an office building. In fact, if anything, the new convention center accelerated downtown's relentless slide. A city's urban fabric—its ecosystem, if you will—is extremely sensitive to change. A long-loved building demolished here, a surface parking lot there, one or two ugly buildings somewhere else—resonate throughout the body that is the city. And when the change is as monstrous and outrageous as the convention center—a several-hundred-thousand-square-foot whale of a building that blocked long-standing views of the lake, tore the heart of the city's historic street pattern, and destroyed at least one whole street (Pearl) by erecting a wall that Stalin probably admired from afar—local residents and business are bound to suffer equally monstrous and outrageous consequences.[16]

By the middle of the 1970s it was no longer possible to ignore the activist energy, talent, and creativity that was gushing out of the streets and neighborhoods of the city. In 1974, Buffalo, in its implementation of the Community Development Act, created guidelines and procedures for citizen participation that were unprecedented in the nation. This watershed event came as a result of an important change at the highest level of city government.

When Frank Sedita, the mayor who had surrounded himself with old-line ethnic politicians who operated the entrenched departments in city hall, retired because of illness in 1974, he was succeeded by Stanley Makowski. For years a councilman from the Polish Broadway-Fillmore District, then a councilman-at-large, Makowski was well liked and respected as a "nice man," a person with more confidence in his character than in his intellect. He often extolled his own humbleness. "I am," he once said, "a simple guy. I never went to college. I'm just a grain scooper at heart." (You didn't have to be Irish to scoop grain in Buffalo.) Unlike Sedita, however, people said that Makowski was weak, afraid of power, and reluctant to use it. He was not afraid of change, however. In 1974, he turned to one of his youngest aides, Joseph E. Ryan, for help in creating a new and different way for the city to distribute the $11 million annual block grant that the Community Development Act of 1974 had promised.[17]

Ryan, from St. Mark's in Parkside, had graduated from Cornell. After serving in a naval underwater reconnaissance unit in Vietnam, he returned to Buffalo eager to enter politics and government. Deeply committed to citizen participation and having been very active in Sedita's 1969 reelection campaign, Ryan convinced the mayor to create what he called the "Citizen's Advisory Committee." In 1971, Ryan became its director. Aggressive, intelligent, and ambitious, Ryan quickly became impatient with city hall's department heads, many of whom were political hacks, old hands at the tribal back-scratching that characterized so much of Buffalo's ethnic politics. They loved elections, Ryan knew, and were great at winning them, but they seemed to know little and care less about actual governance. In an effort to circumvent their power to create a system that would allow block grant funds to pass as directly as possible into the communities involved, Ryan, working with William Price, the recently elected council member from the University District, created a new and dynamically different structure. Like Ryan, Price was a Vietnam veteran. Price was passionate about Buffalo and, after law school and an internship with Mayor Lindsay in New York City, Price returned home. Elected councilman in 1974, Price recognized the opportunity for change offered by the Community Development Act. As a newly elected councilman he "jumped," he said, "at the chance to try out our notions about how a city is rebuilt and preserved."[18] Price, like Ryan, wanted to open the process so that departmental heads couldn't "get together in a back room and divide the money up for their pet projects." Ryan and Price hoped that by building a power base of their own, rooted as much as possible in the neighborhoods, they could bypass the existing leadership. In order to convince the mayor of the strength of their proposal, they asked one of Ryan's aides, a woman named Louise Granelli, to put it in her words.

Granelli's ideas were rooted in her childhood on Buffalo's West Side, where she was raised at 16th and York Streets, in Our Lady of Loretto Parish, a tight-knit community like those found in nineteenth-century Italy. Granelli went to School 38 on Vermont Street and to Grover Cleveland, her neighborhood high school. By then she'd become a self-described "West Side beatnik": there weren't too many Italian girls on Buffalo's West Side, she said, who wore black tights, a black skirt, and turtleneck. In college—first at Rosary Hill, a local Catholic college, and then at UB—Granelli became increasingly active in the civil rights movement and later against the Vietnam War. She left UB after the school administration called police onto campus during the 1970 protests and devoted the next several years to the movement. "It wasn't a scene," she remembered proudly. "For our little set of rock-hard American beliefs we were threatened, harassed, busted, jailed, terrorized, beaten, and in a few cases extinguished." Through it all Granelli never left the West Side. Recognizing her intelligence and her commitment to citizen participation, Joe Ryan hired her at the Citizen's Advisory Committee (CAC).

The proposal that Granelli created for Ryan and Price breathed her upbringing on the Italian West Side. A city was "a process," she argued, an interconnected "continuum of relationships from family members to family members, from house to house, from house to block, from block to neighborhood, from neighborhood to community, and from community to city." Policies for the improvement and development of the community could work only if they reflected the "sense of community" and the way people lived in the city. Therefore, she wrote, community development block grant money should be given directly to the communities involved. The mechanism she advocated was the division of the city into twelve planning districts based not on the existing council districts but rather on lines that were generally understood to reflect traditional neighborhood boundaries. Each district would elect people to run a neighborhood development corporation that, working with a community coordinator appointed by the CAC, would plan and develop housing and neighborhood development projects. If approved by the Common Council, the projects would be funded with block grant funds and implemented by the neighborhood corporation.

Makowski, who prided himself on his responsiveness to emerging political ideas and groups, liked the proposal. Prodded by Ryan and Price, he implemented the program that was soon recognized nationally for the extent of its citizen involvement (in May 1975, the *Wall Street Journal* dispatched a reporter to Buffalo to cover the story). Makowski's effort to decentralize the administration of the grant program encountered stubborn opposition from established groups, including old-guard politicos; black community leaders, who were afraid that the better-organized white ethnic neighborhoods would take advantage of the program; and the leaders of the Democratic political machine, who were afraid that too many jobs would be handed out without their say. Makowski, however, prevailed. In late 1974 and early 1975, a series of public meetings were held in the twelve newly created "planning districts." Organized by Ryan and Granelli, the meetings were forums where residents, community leaders, priests, and politicians came together to engage in heated, confusing, and seemingly endless struggles over how to allocate block grant money. For the first time ever, grassroots community organizations from all over the city were becoming intimately involved in the development of plans and programs regarding the future of their neighborhoods. "Give us the lumber, the hammer, and the nails," said Norm Bakos, a neighborhood leader from East Lovejoy, "and we'll rebuild our own barns." Granelli, in an interview with the *Wall Street Journal* in May 1975, said that at every meeting she'd heard one clear and consistent message: "Every single neighborhood said 'Don't give us new communities, give us our own communities back!'"[19] While not everyone liked the program, and many criticized its results, it was clear that in Buffalo, more than any city in the United States, citizens had been given unprecedented power to decide how to spend federal funds for their city's renewal. Now, said Bill Price, "It's up to us to us to make it work."

Grassroots organizations produced upheaval and change not only in local politics but in the arts scene as well, where the avant-garde activity that had characterized the 1960s remained very much alive. In 1974, a handful of visual artists, working out of studios in a converted icehouse on Essex Street on the city's West Side, formed an organization they called "Hallwalls." Poetry and the written word were flourishing in Buffalo during the 1970s too. Stimulated by the presence at the university of such world-renowned writers and poets as John Logan, John Barth, Leslie Fiedler, Robert Creeley, Carl Dennis, Irving Feldman, and Ray Federman, Buffalo's reputation as a center of contemporary writing arts, particularly poetry, spread. The poetic ferment occurring in Buffalo came not only from academe but from the streets of the city as well. Stimulated particularly by the energy of Robert Creeley, who was deeply committed to integrating poetry into the life of the community, poetry seeped into the life blood of Buffalo. Jonathon Welch, a young English graduate student who had come to study with Creeley, opened a cooperative bookstore in 1971 called "Talking Leaves," which quickly became a mainstay in Buffalo's literary community. In 1973, Dennis Moloney, a poet and landscape architect, founded the White Pine Press. In 1975, Debra Ott, another student who had come to Buffalo to study with Creeley, founded the Just Buffalo Literary Center. Motivated by its mission "to create and strengthen communities through the literary arts," Just Buffalo, located in a basement office in the Allentown Community Center, began a Writers in Education program. Soon, a group of poets known as the Niagara Erie Writers began meeting there and, in 1977, in recognition of the importance of poetry in the life and texture of the community, the *Buffalo Evening News* began a monthly poetry page, which almost thirty years later continues to provide a stimulating outlet for Buffalo's poetic voices.[20]

Hallwalls was at the center of much of the artistic activity occurring in the city during the 1970s. The visual artist Kevin Noble, one of Hallwalls' founding fathers, remembered the early days:

> Although Hallwalls got its name from the fact that it was originally the hallway between a series of artists' studios, I always thought of it as more of a living room

than a hallway. From the beginning it was a place where a community of artists, writers, musicians and filmmakers came to meet and hang out. Some of the artists lived in their studios within the complex and this added to the sense of it being like a living room in a very large house. Usually at sometime between 10 and 11a.m., the artists and others who made up the community would start drifting into 30 Essex Street, the coffee pot was filled up and refilled as the day's activities began.

Writing about Buffalo's hip arts scene during the early 1970s, Anthony Bannon, then arts writer for the *Buffalo Evening News*, wrote:

Similar hot houses of artistic growth had just been established and Hallwalls promised connections with these organizations as well. The Center for the Creative and Performing Arts...the Creative Associates...the American Contemporary Theater, led by Joseph Dunn, originated vigorously experimental performance events in the old Pierce-Arrow factory. Media Study/Buffalo, whose faculty included James Blue, Tony Conrad, Hollis Frampton, Paul Sharits and Woody and Steina Vasulka, offered a city site for access to equipment and programming for film, video and electronic sound. The Center for Exploratory and Perceptual Arts (CEPA) focused on photography. A new, independent book store called Talking Leaves created an atmosphere of comfort and ferment. And Artpark, a New York State park for the arts in nearby Lewiston, offered residencies and work opportunities for the creation of temporary, site-specific outdoor sculpture and installations in all media...Meanwhile, key staff members at many venerable institutions, including the Buffalo Philharmonic Orchestra and the Albright-Knox Art Gallery, welcomed experimentation and collaboration. The English Department of the University of Buffalo assembled an impressive roster of professors, including John Barth, Robert Creeley and Leslie Fiedler. Artists from around the world visited Buffalo to test ideas, create work and teach in formal and informal settings, all in a climate of shared resources and institutional decentralization. One might legitimately argue that the roots of postmodernism lie largely in Buffalo.[21]

While there were daring and stimulating ideas at work in the world of neighborhood politics and the arts, the heavy hand of the past continued to dominate and stifle all thinking about the renewal of downtown. The worse things got downtown; the more people, businesses, and stores left; the more grandiose, ambitious, outrageous, and removed from reality became the plans advanced for its renewal. No plan for downtown renewal had been more unrealistic than the one proposed in 1971 by the well-known Philadelphia design firm of Wallace, McHarg, Roberts and Todd. Called the the "Regional Center: A Comprehensive Plan for Downtown Buffalo," the Wallace-McHarg plan, with its vision for "the total transformation of downtown Buffalo into a regional economic and transportation center," surpassed in breadth, scope, and ambition anything that had yet been proposed for the renewal of downtown Buffalo. Defying all trends and ignoring every economic and demographic indicator of steep and relentless decline, the Wallace-McHarg plan was based on the assumption that Buffalo would somehow not only stop shrinking but in fact would by 1990 grow to become a city populated by more than six hundred thousand people and the center of a metropolitan area with a population in excess of two million. According to the Wallace-McHarg plan, downtown would, could, and should be the dramatic center of it all. "The problem," the planners said, "is not whether Downtown will grow, but how the Downtown can be designed to produce an environment which will maximize its growth."[22] Drawn up over the course of a year, and in consultation with a long list of downtown bankers, lawyers, and businessmen, this was to be the uber-urban renewal plan, a transcendent, transformative approach to downtown renewal that would exceed in scope, cost, and impact anything yet tried in New Haven, that highly vaunted laboratory of social engineering and urban renewal. A complete and massive reconstruction program, they said, was required. The aim of the Wallace-McHarg plan was nothing less than to save the city; its authors were clear when they urged that "the City must do everything humanly possible to maintain the concentration of downtown and to provide an environment which will attract new development and new business downtown." Only this way, they warned, "can the fiscal solvency of the city be maintained."[23]

Conceptually, this plan, like all of the others meant to revive downtown, made sense. Downtown, unlike all other areas of the city, was still something of a profit center, a cash cow for an increasingly strapped community. In 1970, despite the losses of the past twenty years, downtown, which comprised less than 3 percent of the city's land area, still accounted for 25 percent of its revenues from property tax and retail sales taxes. In addition, downtown still supplied jobs to sixty-one thousand people, about 15 percent of the total jobs in the region. When compared to the rest of the city, where values and property taxes had been declining for years, downtown was a bargain that required far less overhead while generating far more revenues. While the investment required to save it was massive, many thought it might just be worth it.

There were four major, interrelated elements of the plan. First was the creation of a "smoothly operating movement system integrating pedestrian, rapid transit and vehicular traffic for the purpose of increasing the total number of daily trips to downtown." Second was the construction of an enclosed mall over Main Street from the Main Place complex to Chippewa Street. Third was increased parking for auto traffic. And fourth was the development of large amounts of new office space.

A brand new rapid transit system—"the major purpose of rapid transit is to preserve downtown," the authors said—was at the heart of the plan. Although they recognized and admitted that "transit ridership in the Buffalo metropolitan area is relatively low among large cities," they nevertheless proposed the creation of a hugely ambitious, metropolitan-wide rapid transit system. With lines going northeast to the new university in Amherst, southeast to the airport, south to Hamburg, and north to Tonawanda, this area-wide, integrated system, whose lines would all cross underground at Lafayette Square, would, when completed by 1990, create the "critical mass" necessary to support and sustain the above-ground renewal they anticipated for downtown.

The planners wanted, they said, "to create a balance between mass transit and the automobile." Hoping to have it both ways, to have their pie and to eat it too, they endorsed a highway-building program, which they surely must have known would have undermined their vision for public transportation. The plan endorsed the completion of the long-contemplated Lower West Side Arterial as well as the construction of a new highway on the eastern margin of the central business district. Called the "Elm-Oak Arterial," the planners proposed the construction of a depressed six-lane highway that would link up and connect the other highways that terminated downtown, the Niagara section of the thruway and the Kensington Expressway. In an effort to move traffic quickly in, around, and through the central business district, the plan argued for the elimination of downtown Buffalo's distinctive radial streets, which were originally laid out by Joseph Ellicott in 1805.[24] Downtown's streets would be made more "effective," they said, by eliminating more than six thousand on-street parking spaces. The plan indicated that to replace these on-street parking spaces, twenty thousand new off-street spaces would have to be built by 1990, "the end of the planning period."

Anchoring the new downtown would be the "Main Street Mall," which was not to be confused with the Main Place Mall that had opened in 1966, part of an earlier silver-bullet renewal plan. The new mall, conceived as an enclosed, sky-lit, air-conditioned, and heated structure, would completely cover Main Street from the old Main Place Mall north to Chippewa Street. The planners claimed that the enclosed Main Street would create "an entirely new environment," which, when integrated into the new mass transit, would offer downtown "the competitive advantage necessary to rival if not surpass suburban plazas."

There was more: thirteen million square feet of new commercial and office space in the central business district; a community college at the foot of Main Street; and a convention center that would, "acting as a catalyst," lead to the creation of three thousand new hotel rooms in the central business district by 1990. "These hotels," the plan said, "together with other convention oriented facilities will amount to $80 million in new construction in Buffalo's CBD by 1990."

Unrealistic, too, were the highways. The Wallace-McHarg plan itself revealed doubts about the necessity of the Elm-Oak Arterial, which it nonetheless made a key component of its recommendation. Part of a typewritten early draft of the plan was the following: "The Elm-Oak Arterial, while not necessary to handle the anticipated volumes of through traffic, represents a prior commitment by the New York State Department of Transportation to a full scale expressway in that corridor." Somebody, however, wanted it built, and built it would be, for in the margin next to those two lines is scribbled in authoritative red pencil, the instruction: "Rewrite!"[25]

This plan, like Little's plan less than ten years earlier, was surreal in its failure to understand the current reality of the city. The artist's renderings in the report showed tulips planted everywhere, elegant couples, all of them white, promenading up and down a covered pedestrian mall on Main Street, and still others sitting at outdoor cafes as if they were on the boulevards of Paris. Where, some wondered, was the gritty reality that was downtown Buffalo in the mid-1970s? Where were the bag ladies, the bums in their wool stocking caps, the clusters of African American teenagers, the wig shops, and the stores that sold knock-off designer sweat suits and outsized costume jewelry? Nothing could have been more alien to the current reality of the city than the plan proposed by these cynical planners from Philadelphia and their clueless clients in Buffalo. Everything about it was wrong and misguided. Where had they been for the past twenty years as Buffalo, like the other great cities of the Northeast, in decline for years, stood at the brink of desolation and despair? Did they themselves really believe that their projections of population growth and their visions of downtown as a magnificent regional mecca would possibly been taken seriously? Or didn't they really care? And what about Buffalo's leadership—the mayor and the Greater Buffalo Development Foundation—what were they thinking? What, in the lingo of the day, were these people smoking?

In addition to everything else, the new redevelopment plan called for the demolition of most of the increasingly decrepit buildings on Main Street that had once been home to Buffalo's profusion of theater houses; it went so far as to recommend the demolition of 70 percent of the existing structures on Main Street south of Chippewa, including the Market Arcade Building and Shea's Buffalo Theatre. In their place, the plan called for a new sports stadium. Fortunately, the city's new mayor, James D. Griffin, was willing to consider alternatives. He was drawn to a plan advanced by Harold L. Cohen, the new dean of UB's School of Architecture and Environmental Design, which proposed the creation on Main Street of a revived "Theater District."

Under Cohen's leadership, the School of Architecture and Environmental Design at UB, "The School," as it was called, had become one of the more exciting idea incubators in Buffalo. It had achieved some cachet for having been one of the few departments at UB that did not abandon the city. Instead, it occupied one of Buffalo's great industrial buildings, a sleek, turn of-the-century steel and glass factory on Main Street known as Bethune Hall. With Cohen at the helm, the school became an energetic laboratory of city-oriented design projects. Cohen was a strong and dynamic leader who had been able to attract to the school people like Reyner Banham, Edward Logue, Buckminster Fuller, and other internationally known designers, planners, philosophers, and tinkerers. It was Cohen's inspiration that led to a plan for creating on Main Street an "Entertainment District," which, when anchored by a mixture of office, commercial, and residential uses, was expected to become "one of the biggest and most innovative and exciting urban development efforts in the United States."

In the old days, of course, there had always been a theater district. It was so obvious, nobody bothered to call it that. As recently as 1960, the area was still bustling and lined with movie theaters. In October of that year, Shea's Buffalo had featured *It Started with a Kiss* with Glenn Ford and Debbie Reynolds. Up the street at the Teck, Frank Sinatra and Edward G. Robinson starred in *A Hole in the Head*. The May Britt and Curt Jurgens remake of *Blue Angel* was at the Palace; Richard Burton and Claire Bloom were appearing at the Center in *Look Back in Anger*; Sophia Loren and Tab Hunter were at the Paramount in *That Kind of Woman*; and Vincent Price played in *The Bat* at the Lafayette. But by the time Harold Cohen arrived in Buffalo, there was nothing left. The city had taken ownership of Shea's Buffalo for back taxes. The buildings adjoining it and across Main Street were either boarded up or housing down-in-the-mouth retail tenants trying to hang on. Cohen was committed to bringing them back.

For Cohen, the focal point of the Theater District was the group of historic late-nineteenth- and early-twentieth-century buildings that lined both sides of Main Street between Tupper and Chippewa. Shea's Buffalo was on this block. A magnificent, spacious, incredibly ornate 1920s movie palace with cantilevered balconies and a "Mighty Wurlitzer" that knocked the socks off generations of Buffalonians, Shea's had just been saved from demolition by the tenacious efforts of a group of preservationists called the Friends of Shea's. Across Main Street from Shea's was the circa 1892 Market Arcade Building. Intimate in scale, this indoor street was modeled on London's Burlington Arcade. Boarded up and vacant for years, Cohen's plan imagined the arcade, Shea's, and the turn-of-the-century commercial buildings adjacent to them as the thumping heart of the new Theater District. The concept was daring. Abandoned by developers, torn up by the seemingly endless chaos caused by the construction of the aboveground rapid transit line, Main Street was a shambles, a sea of mud filled with islands of debris. Cohen's vision seemed preposterous.

Cohen's plan, unlike the Wallace-McHarg counterpart, was rooted in the area's history. Cohen knew that for much of the twentieth century, Buffalo had been one of the dozen largest cities in the nation. And he knew that it had supported an entertainment district to match its size and diversity. Buffalo had hosted theaters, restaurants, dance halls, pinball parlors, billiard halls, and nightclubs that attracted countless residents as well as thousands of out-of-towners to downtown. The presence of so much nightlife had for years acted as a major economic generator for the entire city. Attracted by the presence of so many people in the arts, music, and the theater, many restaurants, music stores, dance academies, and theater supply outlets located in storefronts on the 600 block of Main Street and along adjacent side streets. It was some of this atmosphere and economic impact that Harold Cohen sought to recapture in his 1978 plan for Buffalo's Entertainment District.

Cohen was also drawn to the distinctive architectural character of many of the buildings in the area. These structures, most of them built between 1890 and 1930, offered many very fine examples of classical revival architecture typical of the period following the Columbian and Pan-American Expositions. Cohen also recognized that while not all of the buildings were architectural landmarks in and of themselves worthy of preservation, they were all part of a larger fabric, producing what he said were "façade combinations," "a whole ensemble" that created a rich architectural backdrop, a stage set that would most effectively house the various elements of his proposed "entertainment district." In an era when this kind of language was just beginning to be heard among people in the business of urban renewal, Cohen said that these buildings had "high architectural character and repairable structural condition which offer a unique potential for revitalization."[26] Using the area's "distinctive architectural heritage" as a foundation, Cohen recommended that the district's historic fabric be combined with the three legitimate theaters that remained to form the basis of a regional historic and cultural center. There were three key elements to Cohen's vision. The first was the creation of attractive spaces, inside and out, to promote arts, entertainment, and cultural activities. The second was a concerted public effort to shift the center of the region's cultural life to downtown Buffalo. And the third was to create housing opportunities within the new district. Such a plan, rooted in a deeply held faith in the transformative power of art and culture, would, Cohen believed, do more than anything to revitalize Main Street in downtown Buffalo. While various elements of Harold Cohen's vision for the creation of a broad and varied entertainment district in downtown Buffalo were realized—the restoration of Shea's Buffalo and the creation of mixed-use arts space in what was called "Theatre Place" were direct byproducts of Cohen's work—the plan, like all master plans, required disciplined commitment over time to a specific set of goals. In a civic atmosphere poisoned by desperation to get something, sometimes anything, done, this proved difficult to achieve.

NOTES

1. *Buffalo Architecture: A Guide* (Cambridge, MA: MIT Press, 1981), p. 222.

2. Walter Kerns, personal communication with the author, April 1989.

3. The pages of the *Buffalo Evening News* and the *Courier Express* were filled with stories from Attica throughout the fall of 1971.

4. New York State Special Commission on Attica, *Attica: The Official Report of the NYS Special Commission on Attica* (New York: Bantam, 1972), p. 226.

5. Ruth Lampe, personal communication with the author, March 1989. See also the Web site of the Parkside Community Association, http://www.parksidebuffalo.org/history.html.

6. Douglas Rae, *City: Urbanism and Its End* (New Haven, CT: Yale University Press, 2003), p. 334.

7. See the Niagara Frontier Housing Development Corporation papers in the "city planning" vertical files in the Grosvenor Collection at the BECPL.

8. Antonio Rodriguez, personal communication with the author, November 1988.

9. Norman Krapf, memo to Edward Umiker, "RE: West Side Arterial," October 15, 1969, "arterial" vertical files, New York State Department of Transportation, 100 Seneca Street, Buffalo, NY.

10. This and the following information comes from years of personal conversations between Mr. Perez and the author.

11. Stanley Makowski, letter to Norman, May 6, 1974, "arterial" vertical files, New York State Department of Transportation, Buffalo, NY.

12. "Environmental Agency Opposes Arterial," *Buffalo Evening News*, July 24, 1974, p. 1.

13. "Proposed West Side Arterial Seems Headed for Scrapheap," *Buffalo Evening News*, September 25, 1975, p. 35. See also, "Bill for New Buffalo Expressway Killed by WNY Assemblyman," *Buffalo Evening News*, April 20, 1970, p. 7.

14. The "Buffalo Business File" at the BECPL is a card catalog filled with drawers of cards that reference thousands of news articles that deal directly or tangentially with news pertaining to business. There are dozens of entries here under "Convention Center," which enables the student to following this controversy from its beginnings in the late 1960s.

15. "Citizens Group Organizes Against Convention Center," *Courier Express*, August 15, 1973, p. 11. The referendum, the events leading up to it, and the discussions in the wake of it are covered in detail in both the *Courier Express* and the *Buffalo Evening News* in the fall of 1973.

16. For the impact of the convention center on existing downtown retail, see the photograph at http://www.wnyheritagepress.org/photosofweek/convention_site.htm.

17. Much of the information on the Community Development Act comes from the author's familiarity with the program as well as from many conversations over the years about it with Bill Price, Joe Ryan, and Louise Granelli-McMillan.

18. Bill Price, personal communication with the author, November 1988.

19. "Citizen Participation the By-Word in Buffalo," *Wall Street Journal*, May 12, 1975.

20. Jimmie Gilliam, personal communication with the author, May 2006; Dennis

Moloney in discussion with the author, May 2006. See also R. D. Pohl's article on Creeley's eightieth birthday celebration, *Buffalo News*, May 19, 2006.

21. For this and more information on Hallwalls, see Ronald Ehmke and Elizabeth Licata, ed., *Consider the Alternative: 20 Years of Contemporary Art at Hallwalls* (Buffalo, NY: Hallwalls Contemporary Arts Center, 1996).

22. Wallace, McHarg, Roberts, & Todd, *The Regional Center: A Comprehensive Plan for Downtown Buffalo* (Buffalo, NY, 1971), p. 7, "city planning" vertical file, Grosvenor Collection, BECPL.

23. Ibid., p. 29.

24. Ibid., p. 35.

25. See the draft of the Wallace-McHarg master plan, "The Regional Center…A Rough Draft," which is stored in the "city planning" vertical files in the Grosvenor Collection at the BECPL. This fascinating document reveals the evolution of the plan from its conception to its final form.

26. *Entertainment District Report* (Buffalo, NY, 1979), p. 13. This privately published report was lent to the author by Harold Cohen.

chapter 11

JUDGE CURTIN STRIVES TO CREATE
A NEW KIND OF COMMUNITY

t five feet eight inches tall, John Curtin was handsome, with a ruddy complexion, gray hair, and strong, bright, Paul Newman-like blue eyes. Curtin, a United States District judge, has always been unabashed in his love for Buffalo, a city he knows inside and out. His knowledge of the history of Buffalo, the nooks and crannies of its neighborhoods, the locations of its churches and schools, the complexities of its various ethnic groups, is detailed and intimate. This, as much as his relaxed, unpretentious manner, helped earn him credibility as he presided over the city's school desegregation case—a case whose successful disposition was vitally dependent on the trust of the community. Caring deeply about the city and keenly aware of the power he had over the lives of the people who lived in it, Curtin sought from the beginning of the case to dispel the notion that he would act as a judicial ogre like Judge Garrity had in Boston. He did not want to appear insensitive to the impact of his rulings on the people in the neighborhoods. Curtin identified strongly with the city and shared in experiences common to many Buffalonians. He had lived in the city all his life, first in South Buffalo, in the house his father had built on Pawnee Parkway and, since the late 1940s, on a modest street of single-family homes in North Buffalo. A graduate of St. Theresa's, Canisius High School, and Canisius College, he joined the Marines following his graduation in 1941, serving for three years as a dive-bomber pilot of a single-engine Grumman torpedo plane. He was involved in "rear island action in the Guadalcanal area." For awhile, Curtin considered becoming an engineer, as his father and grandfather had before him, but he decided instead to go to law school at UB. He graduated in 1949 and entered general practice in downtown Buffalo.[1] On October 1, 1974, by then a federal judge, Curtin heard opening arguments in the Buffalo school desegregation case *Arthur v. Nyquist*, which time has proven a defining event both in Curtin's career and in the life of the city he loved.

By the fall of 1974, racial fears and tensions throughout the country had reached a peak. People around the nation had watched the "agony in the cradle of liberty," the desegregation confrontation in the streets of Boston. Just three months earlier, in June 1974, US District Judge Arthur Garrity had ruled that Boston's School Committee had deliberately created and maintained a segregated public school system.[2] Garrity ordered a two-phase remedy. The first phase, to take place that September, implemented a state-created desegregation plan. The second phase, to be fashioned by the School Committee, would become operative in September 1975. As lawyers in Judge Curtin's courtroom argued the merits of their positions, the Buffalo press closely covered the gruesome events that unfolded concurrently in Boston: five thousand white demonstrators marched through the streets of South Boston protesting Judge Garrity's order; black students were stoned as they made their way to South Boston High School; a black bystander was stabbed with an upended flagpole bearing the American flag; Sen. Edward Kennedy was harassed, jeered, and pelted with rocks and tomatoes as he addressed an antibusing rally in front of Boston's city hall.[3] Though a temporary calm returned to the streets of Boston, the seriousness of the passion and violence aroused by Judge Garrity's decision was not lost on the participants in the Buffalo case. The shadow of Boston would haunt the people of Buffalo for the next several years as they attempted to deal with segregation in their own city.

The plaintiffs were confident—particularly Norman Goldfarb and Frank Mesiah, the team who founded the Citizen's Council on Human Rights in 1963, and Raphael DuBard, the president of the Buffalo chapter of the NAACP, a man who had been active in the local civil rights movement since the early 1950s. They were no strangers in federal court. In 1969, when the New York State Legislature passed a law that prohibited appointed school boards (Buffalo was the only large city in the state that still had one) from "assigning or compelling" a student to attend any school on account of race, Goldfarb, Mesiah, DuBard, and a group of parents challenged Buffalo's school board. They had won that case and were confident that they could win this one, too.[4]

Goldfarb's commitment to social justice was deep and long-standing. Without him, say those who were involved in the struggle, the school desegregation case would not have happened. A passionate and persuasive crusader for racial justice, Goldfarb, who earned his living as an arbitrator for the Buffalo branch of the National Labor Relations Board, devoted all of his spare time to civil rights. From the mid-1950s until his death in 1982, "Norm," often working alone, politicked, advocated, argued, convinced, and wrote passionate and angry letters to state and local officials protesting segregation in the schools; to officers of private clubs that discriminated against blacks, Jews, and women (Goldfarb resigned from the Erie Downs Country Club in 1968 when it denied membership to a black family); and to individuals in cities throughout the nation who, like him, were, in his words, "fighting to foster better inter-group relations."

Goldfarb lived in the city and believed deeply in the promise of pluralism in Buffalo. While hundreds of his Jewish neighbors from the East Side and Humboldt Parkway were moving to the suburbs, Goldfarb stayed on, sensing that it was there, on the streets and pavements of the city, that one of the great dramas of this century's history was being played out. In 1970, he took the struggle into hostile suburban territory, addressing a meeting of the Board of Education in the gilded, nouveau-riche village of Williamsville, about three miles east of North Buffalo. Goldfarb urged his incredulous audience to join him in a metropolitan-wide solution to the problems of segregation in Buffalo's public schools. When the suit against the Board of Education and the city was filed two years later, in June 1972, Goldfarb was forced to monitor the case from his hospital bed, where he was recovering from open-heart surgery. Even with tubes protruding all over his body, Goldfarb was organizing, trying to convince the nurses that, like their aides, they should unionize. Following his release from the hospital, he immediately rejoined the team working on the case. When attorneys for the plaintiffs were taking pretrial testimony from a key witness, Goldfarb sat taking notes not about the testimony, he told his colleagues later, but for ideas in the suit he was planning to file against the Buffalo Yacht Club, which would charge them, he said, with racial discrimination.

As the date of the Nyquist trial approached, Goldfarb was confident, particularly following the US Supreme Court verdict in a 1973 case known as *Keyes v. School District Number One* in Denver, Colorado. What the 1954 decision in *Brown v. The Board of Education of Topeka* did for schools in the South, *Keyes* did for the cities of the North. For the first time, the Supreme Court ruled that segregation, whether caused by law or by demographic trends or neighborhood changes, violated the Fourteenth Amendment's guarantee of "equal protection." Writing one of the majority opinions, Justice William O. Douglas said, "It is time to state that there is no constitutional difference between *dejure* and *de facto* segregation, for each is the product of state actions and policies." Justice Lewis F. Powell of Virginia, known for his conservative views on the question of school integration, agreed. In a barbed separate opinion, he stripped away the facade that had allowed school systems in the North to avoid the burdens of school integration, which had been borne exclusively by schools in the South for close to twenty years. The distinction between de jure and de facto, he wrote, "has been nurtured by the courts and accepted complacently by many of the same voices which discovered the evils of segregated schools in the South." Quoting Sen. Abraham Ribicoff of Connecticut, Powell wrote, "Somehow residential segregation in the North was accidental or de facto and that made it better than the legally supported de jure segregation of the South. It was a hard distinction for black children in totally segregated schools in the North to accept." Because of that false distinction, Powell said, "No comparable progress has been made in many non-Southern cities with large majority populations." But their time had finally come. "In my view," he concluded, "we should abandon a distinction which long since has outlived its time, and formulate constitutional principles of national rather than merely regional application."[5]

Nearly a year and a half after the trial, on April 30, 1976, Curtin delivered his opinion. Over a photograph of a relaxed Curtin, large headlines in the *Evening News* announced the judge's decision. Most people thought he would find against the Board of Education, but few were prepared for the sweep of his judgment. The ruling was unequivocal. "It is the finding of this court that the defendants have violated the plaintiffs' Fourteenth Amendment rights to equal protection under the law by intentionally causing and maintaining a segregated school system." In a 156-page opinion reprinted by the *Evening News* in its entirety, Curtin said, "A thorough study of the board's action since the 1950s convinces the court that the already proven allegations of segregative actions and omissions are unfortunately not isolated incidents. The board's course of action for the last two decades, and more specifically since 1965, has been consistently dilatory, evasive, and at times obstructionist." Such board actions as the districting of Woodlawn Junior High and the use of language transfers to encourage whites to leave the segregated East High School district, Curtin found, had a "racial impact" that was "clearly forseeable." Curtin was strong and pointed in his criticism. "Like a clever photographer who uses an airbrush to eliminate what he does not want in a picture, the defendants try to haze over what the evidence clearly shows. But we are not dealing with art here and the Constitution does not permit this court to avoid the evidence, however unsightly."[6]

Curtin found equally reprehensible the actions of the Common Council. "Whenever the Board of Education was forced to implement integration plans, even if quite modest, the Council quickly shut off the money supply or enacted an ordinance that would effectively negate the board's actions. And, like the board, when it *was* forced to act, it would always find the route of least possible integrative consequences. Curtin's opinion concluded from the testimony of witnesses that the Common Council, by its opposition to portable classrooms, its refusal to fund the middle schools, and its antibusing regulations, had "willfully blocked whatever efforts the board did make to reduce school segregation." Other witnesses swore that the New York State Board of Regents and the state commissioner of education had "wrongly and unconstitutionally failed to reduce school segregation in Buffalo." Curtin further concluded that "unjustified inaction has aggravated the situation." New York State, Curtin continued, was also at fault. "However much the Board of Education or the Common Council procrastinated or wavered," he said, "an equal share of the blame for the segregation in the Buffalo public school system must be attributed to the state defendants." The Board of Regents and the commissioner of education "have the central responsibility for education in New York State," he said. It was a responsibility they "shirked," and in so doing, they "encouraged the city defendants to continue their own segregative actions. They … must be held accountable."

Eager to add his voice to the chorus of federal judges throughout the country who had found the distinction between de jure and de facto segregation untenable, Curtin was particularly clear about the relationship between segregated housing and segregated schools. In some cases, Curtin noted, the courts did not rely on testimony dealing with segregation in neighborhood housing. But the Buffalo case was different, he said, because the defendants relied so heavily on housing and neighborhood patterns as a defense. "The city defendants," he wrote, "cannot use residential segregation as a defense because as the evidence demonstrates they helped to create it." Curtin noted particularly the Ellicott Urban Renewal Project. The evidence showed that residential segregation in Buffalo was caused in substantial part by the policies and practices of the federal government, the Buffalo Municipal Housing Authority, the private real estate industry, and the Common Council. "The citizens of Buffalo, both black and white," the judge concluded, "have been affected by the legacies of these actions stretching back over many generations."

The *Buffalo Evening News* profiled Curtin as "The Man in the News." The writer of the story noted Curtin's educational background and his record as a US Marine fighter pilot in both World War II and the Korean War, but was particularly impressed by Curtin's relaxed demeanor. "He strolls casually from the bench as if walking through a park, unfazed by the heavy burden of court business. In chambers he sheds his robe unceremoniously, bursting into a few bars of 'When Irish Eyes Are Smiling'; coffee mug in hand, glasses pushed above his forehead, he walks to the outer office to check the day's agenda with his law clerk. In mid-conversation he bends over to touch his scuffed brown shoes, not quite succeeding. Later, after the hearings, he walks the block from the federal court building to the YMCA and chugs two and a half miles around the indoor track."[7]

"The opinions of the community" were critical to Curtin. In his ruling, he spoke extensively about the importance of involving the people of the city in the development of a desegregation plan. He said that any plan had to have as much community input as possible if it was to have any chance of being successful. Curtin's call for citizen involvement went beyond the concerns of the school desegregation case and reflected his deeper understanding of what constitutes a strong and healthy community. In his concluding comments, he wrote that:

> We should keep in mind that our nation is a nation of laws and we must follow the law, but it is also, and this, I believe, is most important in a problem such as this, a democracy where the best decisions are those in which individual members of the community have the ability to be heard and have their views listened to and considered and considered seriously. We have the duty as far as possible to integrate the schools in this district, I believe the board and the commissioner and the court have a responsibility to listen to the common-sense, practical views of the parents and the teachers and other people who are involved in this very complicated process. It is one thing to make decisions and it is another to be a parent of a small youngster or a teenager going off to school. They have insights which we cannot know until we listen to the views of all individuals in the community.[8]

In a rambling tone that suggests he was speaking spontaneously or at best from notes, Curtin continued:

> Too often, I think we all have had this experience or something happens, there are many complaints in the bars and beauty parlors and other places of commerce and activity but no one takes the time to meet with the people who are making decisions and this, I believe, is imperative.

Curtin had confidence in the willingness of the people of his community to deal with integration. While he believed that the surrounding suburbs had a responsibility to share the burden and appealed to them to do so, Curtin sensed that even if they didn't, the people of Buffalo could do it on their own. "Medieval Florence, a miserable hovel of a city compared to modern Buffalo, gave the world the Renaissance but it did it only because its leaders and its people believed that it could be done and willed that it should be done." In closing, Judge Curtin exhorted the citizens of the city to rise to the occasion, quoting Tennyson's *Ulysses*. "Come my friends, 'tis not too late to seek a newer world."

The *Evening News* applauded Curtin's "stern wisdom, moderation, and balance." By "holding the defendants' feet to the fire," it wrote, he had "caused them to move with more alacrity." The *Courier Express* added that "the instructions that have emanated from the court of Judge Curtin have had a dramatic effect on the school system. Everything seems to have moved along in a smooth and efficient fashion."[9]

In the summer of 1976, an ad hoc Coalition of Community Leaders and a religious group active in social justice issues called the Buffalo-Area Metropolitan Ministries both pledged to support Curtin's decision. Most significantly, Curtin's decision was supported by the newly appointed bishop of Buffalo, Edward Head, an Irish American from Brooklyn. At a December 1975 conference on "Positive Approaches to School Integration" sponsored by a group called the Buffalo Committee for Quality Integrated Education, Head had committed the diocese to the principle of "basic quality education and equal educational opportunity for every child in public as well as nonpublic schools." Hoping to involve Head in the desegregation process from the beginning, Judge Curtin wrote him a letter in August 1976 in which he explained his recent ruling and urged Head's participation in the development of the remedy.[10] The bishop's response was immediate. In a letter to his "Brothers and Sisters in Christ" in parishes throughout Buffalo, Head outlined "diocesan policy and guidelines to support quality integrated education in the Buffalo public schools." The bishop made himself perfectly clear. "Catholic schools," he said, "will not become havens for those seeking to avoid public school integration." Students seeking admission into a Catholic school would be admitted only if "the receiving officer is morally certain that the request for admission is consistent with the above stated diocesan policy."[11]

Somehow, it all seemed to be working. A justice department official who was in Buffalo to monitor the opening of the schools in September 1976, a man who had had similar assignments in Louisville, Boston, and Chicago, said, "This is the best school opening that I have ever seen.... Never in my entire experience have I been more gratified than I have been in Buffalo." Judge Curtin seemed not at all surprised. He expected, he said, "nothing less."[12]

Within a year, however, the challenges seemed far greater. By the fall of 1977, Curtin worried about the threats to efforts to desegregate Buffalo's schools posed by the racially charged mayoral election of that year as well as the seemingly endless decline in the city's economy.

With the exception of four short Republican years in the early 1960s, the Erie County Democratic Party, under the leadership of Peter Crotty and then Joseph F. Crangle, two classic Irish American political "bosses," had for years dominated local politics and controlled city government. Crotty lived his whole life in that great Irish American nesting ground in South Buffalo. Crangle, though born in South Buffalo, came of age in St. Mark's parish in the Parkside neighborhood adjacent to Delaware Park. Like so many of his peers, he had followed a route to success through Canisius College and then UB Law School. By the mid-1960s, he had become a dominant figure in the national as well as the local Democratic Party. Allied to the Kennedys, Hubert Humphrey, Pat Moynihan, and other politicians whose pictures lined his office at Democratic headquarters in the old

Genesee Building, Crangle, despite his comparative youth, was in style and substance very much a politician of the old school. A framed copy of "Loyalty," a homily by Buffalo's own Elbert Hubbard, hung on the wall outside his office door: "If you work for a man, in Heaven's name work for him; speak well of him and stand by the institutions he represents." By the 1970s, however, complacency within the Democratic Party and demographics—a shrinking white population that produced proportionately more black voters—had led to the decline of the party's influence. Finally, in 1977, the party brass lost control of city hall.

Crangle's man in that election was Leslie G. Foschio, a highly intelligent lawyer who, as Buffalo's corporation counsel, had argued the city's case in the school desegregation trial. A lackluster candidate, Foschio was trounced in the primary by two Democrats who ran in opposition to the party. One was Arthur Eve, the city's preeminent black politician who, as deputy majority leader in the state assembly, had played a key role in virtually every aspect of Buffalo's relations with the state. The other was James D. Griffin, a state senator the *Buffalo Evening News* described as "the dukes-up Irish Democratic independent from South Buffalo."[13]

Acting as a spoiler, Foschio drained enough white votes away from Griffin to hand the primary to Eve, who garnered virtually unanimous support from the African American community. The primary was a disaster for Crangle, who knew that a victory by either Eve or Griffin in the general election would deny him access to the patronage his political machine needed to survive. He sat out the general election. "Imagining an election without Crangle dominating the scene," wrote one local commentator, "is a little like watching the Bills without O. J., the Stanley Cup without the Canadiens, or the World Series without the Yankees." For Crangle, the election of 1977 was the beginning of the end.

Griffin, meanwhile, fell back on his Conservative Party ballot slot and in a three-way election between him, Eve, and John Phelan, a liberal Republican, Griffin won handily. Depicted as something of a redneck during the campaign by both Eve and Phelan, Griffin seemed to wear the tag proudly, boasting of his lack of education, his rise from private to lieutenant in the army, and his rough-and-tumble childhood in the Old First Ward, where he worked in the grain elevators and on the railroads before being elected councilman from the Ellicott District in 1963. To the city's white ethnics, Griffin was a hero—he triumphed in the 1977 mayoral election with more than a 40 percent plurality. Buffalo had entered the Griffin Era. Following his election, the city's attention turned to South Buffalo.

The best and fastest way to get to South Buffalo from downtown is on the Skyway, a high, arching "City of Tomorrow"-like elevated highway, right out of the 1939 World's Fair. Built by New York State in the late 1950s to connect Buffalo with the rapidly growing suburban "Southtowns," the Skyway is one of the most exciting and dramatic routes in Buffalo, a thrilling roller-coaster ride with breathtaking views. On one side is Lake Erie, sparkling and bright on sunny days, with the Canadian shore sharp and clear in the distance. The changing winter skies are best seen from here. Sometimes they are a ponderous, heavy, battleship kind of gray. More often they are fluid, with great marble cloud swirls and shadows pierced occasionally by radiant shafts of sunlight. On the other side of the Skyway is a fascinating and unique bird's-eye view of the grain elevators that for years were the lifeblood of Buffalo's economy. Massive, yet elegant, some were abandoned. Others were still regularly fed by the long conveyor belts that extended into the bowels of hulking Great Lakes grain boats. Sprinkled throughout this landscape were truck depots and rail yards filled with freight cars and locomotives.

But the Skyway was not the only way to get to South Buffalo. Some would say it wasn't even the most interesting way to get there. Another route goes through the streets of the city, by way of what people in the area call the "Old First Ward," or even just the "Ward," Buffalo's iconic Irish neighborhood.

The Ward was one of the oldest neighborhoods in Buffalo. Settled by Irish immigrants in the 1840s and 1850s, it still contained in the 1970s all of the visible landmarks of its early history as a nineteenth-century, working-class Irish neighborhood. The Irish settled the area because it was close to the terminus of the Erie Canal and to the grain elevators that still towered over the one- and two-family wood-frame homes that filled the neighborhood's tiny, quiet, tree-lined streets. Their names—Vandalia, Indiana, Illinois, Ohio—referred to the great American grain belt in the Midwest, reflecting its importance to the history of this community. Only one street—O'Connell—suggested anything Irish. To visit the ward was to make a wonderful journey into the city's nineteenth-century commercial roots, past the great grain elevators that the author Reyner Banham, in his book *The Concrete Atlantis*, called "the triumph of what is American in American building art." These grain elevators were landmarks in the development of modern architecture, significant influences on such great twentieth-century European architects as Le Corbusier, Walter Gropius, and Eric Mendelsohn. Writing to his wife in Berlin following a 1924 visit to the Ohio Street grain elevators, Mendelsohn said,

> Mountainous silos, incredibly space-conscious, but creating space. A random confusion amidst the chaos of loading and unloading of corn ships, of railways and bridges, crane monster with live gestures, hordes of silo cells in concrete, stone, and glazed brick. Then suddenly a silo with administrative buildings, closed horizontal fronts against the stupendous verticals of fifty to one hundred cylinders, and all this in the sharp evening light. I took photographs like mad. Everything else, so far now, seemed to have been shaped interim to my silo dreams. Everything else was merely a beginning.[14]

In the mid-1970s, the men who worked the elevators could still be found all over the neighborhood, in nicer weather sitting on their front porches, taking walks around the century-old brownstone parish church, Our Lady of Perpetual Help on O'Connell Street—"Pet's" to the locals. Others could be seen hanging out in the grain scoopers' tiny union hall, a hundred-year-old wood-frame building on Louisiana Street, or at Gene McCarthy's tavern, as Irish an Irish pub as ever there was. A county map of Ireland hung on the wall in the back room at McCarthy's, and the view from the window—railroad tracks, mammoth grain elevators, and the sunspangled waters of the Buffalo River—was a glance into the past. The bar was a meeting place for generations of Irish Americans, a place where politicians and lawyers, businessmen and scoopers met in goodwill to eat, talk, and reminisce. South Buffalo native, Joseph F. McMahon, a retired Buffalo Fire Department battalion chief and one among the last generation of Great Lakes grain shovellers, reported that McCarthy showed his goodwill by picking up the tab for all the regulars on the winter day in 2006 when he transferred the pub's keys, after more than forty years, to a new owner.[15]

The Ward, within a stone's throw of the Erie Canal's outlet to the lake, had been a place of plentiful work—in the factories, on the docks, and in the grain elevators that lined the waterfront. In 1853, five years after John Timon was appointed the first bishop of the Diocese of Western New York, St. Brigid's church was founded on Fulton Street in the Ward. Soon after, the Ward became a center of Irish Catholicism and a hotbed of Irish nationalism. Hatred of England ran deep in the Ward, as it did in Irish communities throughout the country. By the mid-1860s, the Ward had become a center of the Fenian Movement. With its outlandish goal of conquering Canada and then trading it for Irish independence, the Fenian Movement had great appeal among Buffalo's fervently patriotic Irish immigrants. That, in addition to the city's ideal location for the planned invasion, led to the Old First Ward being the center of the movement, the place to which arms were shipped and citizen soldiers dispatched and quartered. Although the invasion, launched on June 2, 1866, quickly fizzled, Irish nationalism lived on in Buffalo's Irish neighborhood.[16]

The Ward remained a strong and thriving Irish neighborhood through the early years of the twentieth century. In the early 1950s, Roger Dooley, born and raised in the neighborhood, used the First Ward as the setting for several novels. One, *The House of Shanahan*, traces three generations of a prototypical Irish American family. For Rose Shanahan, the novel's heroine, "the First Ward was not a political division or even a neighborhood, but a way of life, a state of mind."[17] By the time Dooley wrote his second volume, called *Days Beyond Recall*, which was set in the 1920s, the the Shanahans had moved to South Park, the street-car suburb just a mile away from the old neighborhood. Like many strivers from the Ward, the upwardly mobile Shanahans lived on McKinley Parkway, "The Delaware Avenue of South Buffalo," a broad, richly landscaped boulevard lined with large, comfortable, one- and two-family homes. Dooley writes:

> Even now Rose could hardly believe that this very parkway, where elms and maples had just begun to foreshadow an arch over the central strip, would soon be her home.... After Fulton Street the ample lawns, dotted with bridal wreath or snowball bushes, gave the street all the charm that Rose could have wished.[18]

McKinley was a beautiful street, the showplace of South Buffalo. There were many stately and magnificent monuments in South Buffalo, beautiful buildings like the fabulous Our Lady of Victory Basilica on Ridge Road, the border between South Buffalo and Lackawanna, and the 1898 glass-and-steel art nouveau South Park Conservatory. There were neighborhood landmarks too, schools and hospitals that have been area institutions for years: Mercy Hospital, Mt. St. Mercy School, and Trocaire College, run by the Sisters of Mercy. All over were lovely, quiet residential streets, like Pawnee Parkway, where Judge Curtin was born and raised. Many of South Buffalo's streets were named for Indian tribes—Tuscarora, Pawnee, Peconic, Niantic, Minnetonka, Seneca, Indian Orchard, and Indian Church—for south of the Buffalo Creek was where the remnants of the great Seneca Nation lived in the last years of the eighteenth century. By the mid-1800s, however, Seneca land had been sold and cleared for development. All that remains is a bronze plaque affixed to a large boulder in the middle of a small, shady park. Its fading letters tell the sad and haunting story:

> In this vicinity from 1780–1842 dwelt the larger portion of the Seneca nation of the Iroquois League. In this enclosure were buried Red Jacket, Mary Jemison, and many of the noted chiefs and leaders of the nation.[19]

For years, South Buffalo's economic foundation was the steel industry. Steel brought the Curtin family, like so many others, to South Buffalo. John A. Curtin, Judge Curtin's father, moved to Pawnee Place shortly before World War I, when he went to work at Bethlehem as an engineer. By the late 1930s he had become superintendent of mills at Bethlehem, in charge, Judge Curtin recalled, of the steel rolling mills, the rail mills, the structural steel mills, but not of the strip mills. Having lived with a "steel man" and worked at Bethlehem himself during summer vacations, Curtin knew the industry and spoke knowledgeably and fondly of it— how steel is made, the layout of the mills, the nature of the work, and the economic problems of the industry in general. Like a lot of people in Buffalo, Curtin was saddened by the fate of the industry. He wondered how a country that produces so little steel can long remain great.

Most of the men in the neighborhood worked either in the plants or on the South Buffalo Railroad that served them. The ones who didn't were likely to take jobs in the uniformed services, particularly the fire department, which had for decades been a virtual South Buffalo fraternity. It was not unusual for whole families to join the fire department. James Keane, a former councilman from South Buffalo and later the commissioner of emergency services for Erie County, had fifteen siblings. He and his brothers Dick and Mike were firefighters. His brother Neal was a battalion chief. Another brother, Bill "Puff" Keane, was killed in the line of duty. Jim's wife, Margaret, was a firefighter, too; she worked out of Station 3, on the Lower West Side. Her whole family, encompassing both the Whalens and the Healys, was filled with firefighters: Uncle "Whipper" Whalen; brother R. J. Whalen, like "Puff," killed in action; and cousins Ray and Dennis Sullivan and Danny and Jack Corcoran.[20]

Though the pay was low, the job was steady, the hours were flexible, and most of the firefighters and police officers in the city could easily hold second jobs. What's more, the fire department in general and the firehouses in particular were warm and friendly, like fraternity houses. In the yawning hours between fires and in the dangerous ventures into burning buildings, the ties formed in parish and neighborhood were bound still tighter. In the firehouses, as in the neighborhood, social life was safe, secure, and predictable. And, like work in the steel plants, it was always there.

Until the 1970s, that is, when economic tremors began to shake the old neighborhood. Like kids in neighborhoods throughout urban America, hundreds of South Buffalo boys had been drafted to fight in Vietnam. Many had been killed or wounded. They'd gone into the service after high school, after graduating from Bishop Timon, from Baker–Victory (a merged Catholic high school on the Lackawanna side of Ridge Road), or from South Park High School. Some had worked in the plants before they'd gone to war, killing time until they were called to duty. They served honorably, risked their lives in defense of their country, and when they came home they found that South Buffalo's safety and security were no longer certain. Their jobs went first. Employment at the grain elevators had been shrinking for years, and then, in 1970, Bethlehem Steel started laying people off, too. Everything began to crumble. The South Buffalo Railroad went next, and soon the Buffalo Iron Workers began to hurt. By the end of the 1970s, the ironworkers were getting a third of the work they'd had just a few years before. Many, like their brothers and fathers before them, gravitated in even greater numbers to the police and fire departments. But soon that line of work was increasingly hard to come by as well. In 1977, while presiding over the school desegregation case, South Buffalo's own Judge Curtin, of Pawnee Parkway, St. Theresa's parish, ruled against the police and fire departments. Both departments, he said, were guilty of long-term discrimination against African Americans, Hispanics, and women. In a ruling that rocked these bastions of privilege, Judge Curtin ordered the remedy: for every white male hired, a black, a Hispanic, or a female would have to be hired too. For South Buffalo, the rules were suddenly changing.[21]

The hardship of the plant closings and the pain of Judge Curtin's ruling were mitigated somewhat by the political rise of James D. Griffin. Solidly Democratic, Irish South Buffalo had always had strong political connections (Irish politicians had dominated the Erie County Democratic Party since the early 1950s), but Griffin was the first from South Buffalo to be elected mayor. With Griffin's election, they would for the first time dominate city hall as well.

Griffin, like so many people from South Buffalo, was born and raised in the Old First Ward. The family lived on Hamburg, Fulton, Louisiana, and Katherine Streets, he remembers. "We moved around a lot.... I guess we couldn't pay the rent." Griffin graduated from St. Brigid's, then married his wife, Margaret, a "Pet's" girl, before moving to Dorrance Street in South Buffalo, where the Griffins have lived ever since.

Griffin's election could not have come at a better time for South Buffalo. As jobs in local industry began to dry up and the police and fire departments came under court order, Mayor Griffin opened up city hall to his constituents, filling as many jobs as possible with people—mostly men—from South Buffalo. In a style that has characterized urban political machines since the late-nineteenth century, Griffin traded jobs for loyalty and in the process strengthened himself and his neighborhood.

South Buffalo needed all the help it could get. As the economy sagged and the population dropped, the community's cherished neighborhood Catholic schools suffered, too. This was happening throughout urban Catholic America, and Buffalo was no exception. The first consolidation of Catholic schools in Buffalo came in 1968 when St. Francis Xavier and St. John the Baptist, two schools in Black Rock, one of Buffalo's oldest Catholic neighborhoods, merged to become Our Lady of Black Rock. In 1970, five inner-city Catholic schools and three high schools, with a combined total of more than fourteen hundred students, were shut down completely.[22] The trends—a declining birth rate, the relentless migration to the suburbs, the growth of paid lay faculty that forced increases in tuition, and, since the early 1980s, a public school system that offered quality education for free—were too strong for even South Buffalo, where the tradition of Catholic education had been so solid. In the twenty years between 1966 and 1986, the eight Catholic schools in South Buffalo lost 70 percent of their enrollment. In 1987, St. John the Evangelist, one of the biggest, was permanently closed. Increasingly desperate, the diocese hired a local advertising agency in 1988 to promote Catholic schools. Ads appeared in print, on radio, on billboards, and on metro buses and trolleys. The ads proclaimed: "Our track record is right up there," "Personal attention works miracles," "Where God and discipline are still welcome." "We have a good product," the president of the Board of Catholic Education said, "It's time to sell it." The diocese, like people in neighborhoods throughout the city, was praying for a miracle. Judge John Curtin was no exception; throughout the proceedings of the school case he had worried about the city's economy, and he wanted a miracle, too. Wondering just how much more the people of the city could take, Curtin, in a September 1977 memo to his clerk, wrote, "I think it is appropriate in this kind of case to include the fact—in a footnote if not in the actual text—of the further decline of the Buffalo economy, the dropping of another thirty-five hundred jobs at Bethlehem."[23]

The steel and automobile industries had been booming throughout the years of the Vietnam War, employing over sixty thousand workers between them. The peak years were the late 1960s, when the economy expanded, defense spending increased, purchasing power grew, and people were optimistic about the local economy. Unemployment rates of only 4 percent in 1968 marked a record low. The steel industry was, in the late 1960s, enjoying a period of incredible profit and productivity; they were "in step," as one spokesman of the industry put it, "with the quickened pace of progress in Buffalo." The industry retained its compelling allure, with the local press using ever more mythic and heroic prose to describe it. In a two-page supplement on the industry written in late 1968, the *Courier Express*, in an article that included several imposing color photographs of the steel-making process, wrote: "Men who make steel are dwarfed by the titanic machines they control." Another picture illustrated "men releasing great torrents of fluid iron from volcano-like furnaces…this night shot of a black furnace resembles a volcano."[24]

By 1964, both Bethlehem Steel and Republic Steel, the two largest companies in Buffalo, had installed state-of-the-art basic oxygen furnaces able to produce as much steel in one hour as the old open-hearth furnaces had produced in six. Bethlehem's nearly twenty thousand employees in 1965 produced over six million tons of steel (Republic produced just over one million), making it the largest steel company in the nation. Never had Buffalo's steel industry been more prosperous; never did the future seem brighter.

The local automobile industry, too, was at its peak. With more than twenty-two thousand people working in the seven GM plants and the one Ford plant in the area, production and payrolls broke all previous records in 1964. Each year another payroll record was set. As a regional officer of the United Auto Workers said in 1964: "As far as the economy is concerned the greatest effect of all this boom and expansion is the fat paycheck that auto plant workers are pocketing."[25] The manufacturers of auto parts also did well: Buffalo Tool and Dye, American Radiator, American Brass, Dunlop Tire, and Trico, the windshield-wiper company, all had record years during the 1960s.

The tide turned quickly, however, and within a year or two, industry in Buffalo, particularly in steel and automobiles, entered a period of deepening crisis from which it has never recovered. Steel felt the downturn first. In 1971, in a sudden and shocking move, half of the workforce at Bethlehem was permanently laid off. People began to wonder if plans were in the works to permanently close the entire plant at Lackawanna. So extensive were the rumors to this effect that in January 1972, Bethlehem Steel felt compelled to explain itself in a half-page advertisement in the *Courier Express*. Lewis J. Foy, Bethlehem's president, first dealt with the issue of plant closings. He did not want to close any plants, he said, but certain features tend to make certain plants "sick." By way of diagnosing the "illness" at Bethlehem's Lackawanna facility, he cited "oppressive taxes," "unrealistic environmental control laws," and, most damaging of all, "an uncooperative labor force." Placing the onus on the workers and not on management, Foy concluded, "It is quite obvious that we're in deep trouble unless all of our employees improve their productivity."[26]

Conditions worsened during the 1970s. Unemployment rates, fueled by continued layoffs at Bethlehem, reached close to 9 percent in 1974 and hit a postwar peak of 12 percent a year later. With close to seventy thousand area workers unemployed, the press began to pay more attention to the problem. Noting that manufacturing jobs in Buffalo had fallen from 180,000 in 1954 to 154,000 in 1967, the *Courier Express*, in a front-page article in the summer of 1975, asked, "Has high unemployment become a way of life for the Buffalo area economy?" Descriptive rather than prescriptive, the story went on to explain the emerging crisis—why corporations were leaving; why Rochester, with a more diversified economy, was more successful; and how high wages and high taxes were contributing to industrial decline.[27]

Even the *New York Times* covered the story of unemployment in Buffalo. On February 9, 1975, on the cover of the most widely read Sunday magazine in the world, the *Times* printed a photo montage of the faces of Buffalo's unemployed men and women under the dramatic title "Down and Out in America: In Anger and Sadness People in Buffalo Tell the Story of Unemployment." A quotation on the front of the magazine from one of the people interviewed for the story read: "I didn't realize it was this bad." Inside were a series of interviews with men and women, factory workers and academics, clerical workers and professionals. Accompanied by sad-faced and somber pictures of the subjects, resembling the social documentaries of the Depression era, the article painted a picture of devastation and hopelessness.[28]

But the problems only worsened; 1977 was a particularly bad year. The American steel industry as a whole and the older factories in the industrial Northeast in particular faced financial collapse. Despite a $417 million tax credit from the federal government, Bethlehem Steel reported a fourth-quarter loss of $477 million, the largest quarterly loss in its history. Thirty-five hundred more workers were laid off at the Lackawanna plant. With only eighty-five hundred men left (there had been close to twenty thousand in 1965), half the plant was "mothballed," resulting in a 40 percent reduction in capacity.

Then, on Monday, December 27, 1982, the *News* reported that the Bethlehem Steel Company was going to shut down almost all of its steel-making operations permanently over the next six months. Thirty-nine hundred workers would be let go. Another thirty-four hundred workers who had already been put on temporary layoff would not be recalled. The company promised that thirteen hundred would remain employed in steel finishing operations, the bar mill, and on the galvanizing line. The *News* and the three local television stations treated the story as a tragedy, dispatching writers and reporters to the bars and union halls of Lackawanna, the small company town on Buffalo's southern border. The reporters interviewed workers and their families, telling the sentimental "human side" of the drama, while asking community leaders to speculate on what might happen now that the town was about to lose 70 percent of its tax base. The rhetoric of community leaders was predictable. Mayor James Griffin was "in a state of shock." Sen. Daniel Patrick Moynihan was angry. "You cannot simply close down a plant and say 'sorry,'" he said. Gov. Mario Cuomo announced the formation of a task force to deal with the problem.[29]

As if all this was not enough, the year 1977 was ushered in by the worst snowstorm in the city's history, the Blizzard of '77. Everyone in Buffalo remembers where they were on the Friday morning in January 1977 when the vicious, swirling torrent of snow and wind struck the metropolitan area. Locals cherish their memories of the blizzard; they share them often with those who are new to Buffalo and with those who are too young to remember—they even commemorate the event with an annual "Blizzard Ball."

"Brutal" is the word that most aptly describes the weather of January 1977. It was bad all over the East: snow in Florida, temperatures in the teens throughout Georgia, Virginia, and the Carolinas. It was particularly bad in the Midwest, where since Christmas the entire area had been wrestling with the meanest, coldest winter in memory. Buffalo had had a foot of snow in October. November's low temperatures broke a ninety-seven-year-old record, with another two feet of snow falling on the twenty-eighth and twenty-ninth of the month. There were storms throughout December, though Christmas Day was mild and pleasant. The day after Christmas was even nicer; by noon, the temperature had climbed into the mid-30s. Then, suddenly, the weather changed. It happens that way all the time in Buffalo: The wind roars off Lake Erie, with powerful gusts that force their way through the canyon of buildings on Court Street to whip around Niagara Square into the heart of the city. Traffic lights twirl and dance above windswept intersections and pedestrians struggling to stay on their feet clutch desperately at street lamps. Then the sky starts to darken and the temperature starts to drop. It was thirty-six degrees at noon on December 26, 1976. By early evening, it had dropped to ten degrees. The cold and snow continued into January: two inches on the first of the month, three on the second, four and a half on the seventh, and thirteen on the tenth. Four inches more followed on the fifteenth, and seven on the seventeenth. Meanwhile, with temperatures averaging fourteen degrees, the snow would not melt. Despite a much-heralded "snow blitz" and endless pleas to motorists to get their cars off the streets, snow removal proved difficult and ineffective. On January 18, the temperature was six degrees below zero. On the nineteenth, the temperature rose to the low teens but dropped down into single digits overnight. It hovered there—lows near zero, highs near twenty—through the weekend of the twenty-second and twenty-third. Meanwhile, the snow was mounting: thirty-four inches had already accumulated. Snowplowing proceeded at a snail's pace, hampered by scores of abandoned cars strewn throughout the streets and an exhausted crew that was, in the words of James Lindner, the city's streets commissioner, "shell-shocked." The weather had become front-page news, the daily headlines telling of a frustrated people wrestling with the relentless wind, cold, and snow of this bitterest of winters.

The forecast on Wednesday, January 26, was a bit more encouraging. There had been a letup in the snow, and the snowplow crews had finally made some progress. Within a week, Lindner said, "we'll have it back to normal." The National Weather Service predicted temperatures in the mid-30s. It warned, however, that should the warming trend continue, flooding was likely. But the next day, winds accompanied by heavy snow squalls returned, and the temperatures dropped once again to near zero. Fuel supplies dwindled, and Buffalo's schools and many businesses and factories closed for the balance of the week. Everyone lowered thermostats when Gov. Hugh Carey declared a "fuel emergency." The weather deteriorated overnight, and by early Friday morning, officials at the National Weather Service office at the Buffalo airport were very concerned about reports out of Ohio. The weather had worsened throughout the Midwest, and a storm was moving quickly across the expanse of Lake Erie. By seven o'clock in the morning, a vicious storm had struck Cleveland. Toledo and then Erie were next to feel the storm's fury. Officials at the National Weather Service considered issuing a "blizzard warning." The service described "blizzard-like" storms and "near blizzard conditions in Buffalo." Though it had never in its history predicted an actual blizzard, this was different. The Blizzard of '77 had arrived, and the people of Western New York had to be warned.

Weather reports were portentous:

Blizzard warning later this afternoon and tonight. Winds becoming westerly, increasing to twenty to forty miles per hour with higher gusts during the afternoon and tonight producing blizzard conditions and blowing and drifting snow. Occasional snow this afternoon accumulating up to three inches by evening. Bitter cold, with temperatures five degrees above zero or colder by evening. Occasional snow likely tonight. Lows five to fifteen below zero, colder in some valleys.

On Friday the twenty-eighth, between eleven o'clock in the morning and one o'clock in the afternoon, the savage storm finally arrived. It dwarfed anything that had come before, and it devastated all of Western New York. The *Evening News* reported that the area "lay prostrate, flattened by the most destructive and disruptive storm in memory." With winds up to sixty miles per hour, thick and heavy snowfall throughout the region, and temperatures close to zero, the storm was classified as a "severe blizzard." Thirteen thousand people were stranded downtown. At AM&A's department store, where three hundred were stuck, blankets and mattresses were distributed and the cafeteria stayed open throughout the night. It was the same story in department stores and offices everywhere. Six hundred people spent the night at city hall, many of them gathered around the one color television set in the building, watching *Roots*, the miniseries about one black family's history, which had gripped the nation that last week of January 1977.

On Saturday, January 29, President Jimmy Carter, who had been sworn into office less than a week earlier, declared a state of emergency in the area. A week after that he declared Western New York a "national disaster area." Two hundred and fifty National Guardsmen—by the end of the week there were more than five hundred—were mobilized and placed under the control of Thomas Casey, the Northeast regional administrator for the Federal Disaster Assistance Administration. Working out of a "Buffalo Command Zone" established at the State Office Building downtown, Casey mapped out his strategy. All vehicular traffic was immediately banned and streets leading to area hospitals were cleared. A convoy of milk trucks was arranged with the Upstate Dairy Cooperative and eight half-block-long tankers crawled along the New York State Thruway from Batavia to Buffalo. Meanwhile, the Red Cross organized a convoy to transport food from a supermarket warehouse in South Buffalo to Red Cross headquarters on Delaware Avenue. There, the food was packed up by tireless Red Cross workers and distributed to community centers throughout the city by dozens of volunteers: owners of snowmobiles and four-wheel drive vehicles, CB radio operators and volunteer firemen, workers at the public service agencies, the Salvation Army, and the Red Cross, and the staffs of hospitals and community centers. They worked without relief, as if at war.

The storm continued over the weekend. The sky cleared for a few hours on

Sunday afternoon, but by three o'clock, whirling black clouds again covered the city. On Monday and Tuesday the snow and wind increased again, and on Thursday still more snow fell. On Friday, one week after the blizzard first struck, squalls and heavy drifting combined with near-zero visibility produced conditions similar to those of the previous Friday. At dusk on Saturday, however, the sun slid down behind Lake Erie and the sky cleared. The night was bitter cold, but the wind died down, the clouds finally disappeared, and the rich, deep blue winter sky was filled with stars. The next day, everyone knew, would be beautiful.

Some people tried to explore the snow-covered city on foot. They awoke that morning to glistening, powder-white streets. The snow was piled high everywhere, and the sidewalks and driveways were buried under thick blankets of white. People dressed in layers of their warmest clothing. Then, pushing against masses of snow, they forced their doors open and ventured outside. Striking as the shimmering beauty of the snow-filled streets was the perfect quiet. All but emergency vehicles had been banned from the streets; the whole city was plunged deep into an eerie, awesome silence.

For some it was a time of fantasy. "It makes me think of poetry," one person remembered. "The quiet, the white city, the city in the clouds. It was so bright that there was little difference between day and night... streets and sidewalks went away. A city without streets, a city without going to work, a city on vacation, and all the kids were home. They piled the snow in the park... there were snow mountains everywhere. Next time I think we should pour food-coloring on the mountains and make them even more wonderful."

People couldn't travel very far that first day. But over the next several sunny days, the long-snowbound citizens began to be able to get around to different parts of the city. With schools and offices closed and automobiles banned, the streets were filled with people, some digging out, others pulling sleds stacked with filled grocery bags, and still others just wandering, gazing in wonderment at how the snow had transformed their city. People were friendly and concerned. They seemed to care about one another.

Gradually, over the next several weeks, Buffalo returned to normal, and people went back to their routines. The snow was cleared from streets and sidewalks (some of it was removed by a half dozen machines, Rube Goldberg-like contraptions borrowed from Toronto—these thirty-foot-long vehicles managed somehow to scoop, store, and then melt tons of snow while lumbering noisily up and down the side streets of the city's neighborhoods). Much of the snow was dumped in Delaware and La Salle parks, creating huge, packed, filthy mountains that did not fully melt until June.

Spring was unusually beautiful that year, and the summer of 1977 turned out to be one of the most pleasant in memory. People stopped talking about the blizzard.

No one, though, would ever forget it. These were hard times for Buffalo, years when the economic foundations of America's industrial cities were visibly weakened by changes in the world economy. But, like the blizzard, the battering of Buffalo's industry was a phenomenon over which the people of the city had little control. There was somehow a poignant connection between these two disasters, one natural, the other economic, and as the people of Buffalo struggled through them, the ties that bound them to their community were strengthened. To some it seemed that Buffalo was in its finest hour.[30]

NOTES

1. John T. Curtin, personal communication with the author, April 1989.

2. For *Keyes* decision, see http://faculty.washington.edu/qtaylor/documents/boston_bussing_case.htm.

3. For a great book on the impact of the Boston school desegregation case, see J. Anthony Lukas, *Common Ground: A Turbulent Decade in the Life of Three Families* (New York: Alfred Knopf, 1985).

4. Goldfarb himself left no apparent papers. However, there are people who remember him, and at various times over the years I have interviewed several of them, including Frank Mesiah and Marilyn Hochfield, two of his former colleagues in the civil rights movement.

5. "Judge Curtin Demands End to School Segregation," *Buffalo Evening News*, April 30, 1976, p. 1. This edition of the *Buffalo Evening News* also contained several other fascinating articles on the case.

6. See full text of decision, *Buffalo Evening News*, April 30, 1976, p. 9; "As Federal Judge Curtin Agrees He's Not Tough," *Buffalo Evening News*, March 14, 1976, p. 1.

7. "As Federal Judge Curtin Agrees," p. 1.

8. "Curtin's Order Shows Restraint, *Courier Express*, May 2, 1976, p. 22.

9. Ibid.

10. "Bishop Head Supports Deseg Ruling," *Courier Express*, December 12, 1975, p. 1.

11. Bishop Edward Head, letter to Judge John Curtin, May 5, 1976, *Arthur v. Nyquist* files, folder 4, chambers of Federal District Judge John Curtin.

12. "Uneventful First Day of School," *Courier Express*, September 8, 1976, p. 1. The growing number of people living in Buffalo's suburbs felt otherwise. They were concerned particularly about Curtin's plea that they join the city in bringing an end to school segregation (given that the Supreme Court had insulated suburban municipalities from court-ordered regional desegregation strategies, there was little else he could have done). School boards in all of the surrounding suburban communities quickly and flatly refused to heed Curtin's plea. The superintendent of schools in Williamsville, the wealthiest of Buffalo's suburbs, was fired for simply agreeing to discuss the matter with Buffalo Superintendent Eugene Reville. See "Williamsville School Head Dismissed over School Desegregation," *Buffalo Evening News*, August 26, 1976, p. 1.

13. The pages of both the *Courier Express* and the *Buffalo Evening News* from the summer and fall of 1977 are filled with stories about the election. See particularly, "Democratic Mayoral Hopefuls," *Courier Express,* June 12, 1977, p. 1; "As Focal Point of Bitter Campaign Crangle Points to Record of Success," *Buffalo Evening News,* September 22, 1977, p. 3; "Eve for Mayor," *Courier Express,* August 21, 1977, p. A1; "James Griffin Triumphs in Record Victory," *Buffalo Evening News,* November 9, 1977, p. 1.

14. Quoted in Reyner Banham, *A Concrete Atlantis: US Industrial Building and European Modern Architecture* (Cambridge, MA: MIT Press, 1986), p. 6.

15. Joseph McMahon and Edward McMahon, personal communication with the author, December 5, 2006.

16. See Mark Goldman, *High Hopes: The Rise and Decline of Buffalo, NY* (Albany, NY: SUNY Press, 1983), pp. 94–96.

17. Roger Dooley, *The House of Shanahan* (Philadelphia: Bruce, 1948), p. 21.

18. Roger Dooley, *Days Beyond Recall* (Philadelphia: Bruce, 1950), p. 37.

19. This plaque is located at the foot of Indian Church Road in South Buffalo.

20. Jim Keane, personal communication with the author, July 1988.

21. *US v. City of Buffalo,* 457 F. Supp 612 (W.D. NY 1978), p. 21.

22. "More Diocesan School Closings," *Courier Express,* September 15, 1970, p. 1.

23. John T. Curtin, memo to Michael Brady, September 2, 1977, *Arthur v. Nyquist* files, folder 5, chambers of Federal District Judge John Curtin.

24. "The Story of Steel," *Courier Express* Sunday Magazine, November 12, 1968, pp. 4ff.

25. *Buffalo Magazine,* July 1964, pp. 7–15.

26. "Foy Stirs Worries about Steel Plant," *Courier Express,* January 17, 1972, p. 1.

27. "Unemployment Continues to Climb," *Courier Express,* July 13, 1975, p. 1.

28. "Down and Out in America," *New York Times Sunday Magazine,* February 9, 1975, pp. 9ff.

29. "Cuomo Vows Help for Bethlehem," *Buffalo Evening News,* December 27, 1982, p. 1.

30. Erno Rossi, *White Death: The Blizzard of '77* (Port Colborne, Seventy Seven, 1999). The local history files in the Grosvenor Collection at the BECPL are filled with a broad and extensive range of compelling stories covering the blizzard story.

chapter 12

THE 1980S

where are we going?

By the early 1980s, after nearly twenty years of anxiety about busing, white parents in neighborhoods throughout the city were finally sending their children to schools on Buffalo's African American East Side. In September 1980, three thousand white children attended inner-city magnet schools in sections of the city whites hadn't regularly visited for years. More than eight hundred children attended six early childhood centers. Even suburban participation, that elusive symbol of success in urban public education, was on the increase. Indeed, there was not enough room for the hundred seventy suburban children who applied for admission to the magnet schools in September 1980.[1] But Judge John Curtin insisted on more effort, and in early 1981, Superintendent Eugene Reville, in response to still more pressure from Curtin, issued his most controversial plan to date, called "Phase IIIx."

Until then, white participation in the school desegregation effort had been strictly voluntary. Although schools in white neighborhoods like South Buffalo, Black Rock, and Riverside were paired with inner-city schools like Schools 31 and 61, parents in those neighborhoods could continue to send their children to their old neighborhood schools if they preferred. Reville's new program added an ultimatum: if enough whites did not volunteer, there would be "forced student assignments." A system of mandatory cross busing would be implemented that paired early childhood centers on the African American East Side with schools in white neighborhoods for children in grades three through eight.[2]

The reaction to the plan was loud and vocal. In letters written to Judge Curtin, citizens expressed their fears, anger, and concerns. Some contained threats. "Think it over, John Curtin," said one of them. "I hope you know the moral code. The good Lord reminded us that whoever hangs a millstone around the necks of little children shall be punished." Some were nasty, one suggesting that "the Goldfarbs and the Schwartzs" had paid him off. Some were poignant efforts to apply the lessons of the past to a very different present. One implored, "You must recall that for many years the Poles lived on the East Side, the Italians on the West Side, and the Irish on the South Side. We lived in segregation and managed okay. We enjoyed our neighborhood schools. But you are determined to destroy them." Some were thoughtful efforts to come to terms with the problem of race relations in the city. One man, a "grandfather concerned about his grand-children," who hoped they would grow up free of racial prejudice, claimed that "tolerance is best learned in the privacy of one's own home and not in a polarized bus or classroom." The man was afraid that the "spontaneous friendships" his grandchildren had with black children would be "terminated by court interfer-ence." Many letters contained specific requests not to close a particular school: "I know you are a busy man," wrote Dolores Landsman of Riverside, eager to keep her neighborhood School 79 open, "but we just cannot get anybody to listen.... Please, I'm begging you to really take a look into these things. We need your help." Some asked him to intervene in areas totally unrelated to the case, to "do some-thing" about the bands of teenagers roaming around Black Rock, the potholes on the streets of the West Side, high city taxes, and even the growing rate of infla-tion. To many people in Buffalo, Judge Curtin had become an omnipotent authority figure, a man with the power to bless or befoul the community at his choosing. Despite the wide range of responses, in practice, the great drama of school desegregation for the time being seemed to be going well.[3]

While people throughout the community had serious reservations about a forced integration program, it was the timing as much as anything that disturbed several members of the Board of Education and the Common Council. David Kelly, the board president, voted against the plan, fearing that the introduction of force could jeopardize the generally good feelings that had characterized white response to all of the other desegregation programs. "We've had a viable, produc-tive, and peaceful integration plan because it was implemented in reasonable time, not jammed down the throats of the people," he said. "We could be jeopard-izing all the good things we've done to date."[4]

In February 1981, Mayor Griffin lent his voice to the growing chorus of people now virtually begging Curtin to delay implementation of Phase IIIx. (The Common Council had already passed a resolution formally requesting that Curtin delay Phase IIIx.) At a public appearance at School 65 in Riverside, where emotions in this heavily white and Catholic neighborhood were raw on the question of busing, Mayor Griffin fanned the flames of resistance that had lain dormant for years. Speaking to parents in a school scheduled to be paired with an inner city elementary school, the mayor, whose own children attended parochial school in South Buffalo, railed, "It is that judge over there that is making the decisions. If he says 'bus' there's not a thing you or I can do about it, unfortunately." The plan, he said, "hurts the city badly." When asked if the fixed assignments called for in Phase IIIx would lead to white flight, he said, "Yes, it will, and I wouldn't blame anybody for leaving."[5] Soon after, Griffin softened his tone, and said it was not the busing he objected to so much as the end of voluntary measures. Mozella Richardson, an African American member of the Board of Education, saw it another way: "All my life I've been forced. Now I want to see someone else forced a little bit."[6]

Without the participation of white parents, Phase IIIx was doomed. In an intense effort to assuage fears, Reville, his invaluable colleague Joseph Murray, and several board members once again "worked" the city's white neighborhoods throughout the spring of 1981. Unlike public officials in Boston and Cleveland, and unlike their predecessors in Buffalo, Reville and Murray spoke directly, honestly, and frequently to community groups. There was no effort to mislead or deceive. To one group of Irish American parents in South Buffalo, whose two-, three-, and four-year-old children faced the prospect of being forced to attend early childhood centers in the black inner city, Murray said, "I'm going to look you in the eye and tell you what the facts are. You might not like them but I'm going to tell you: the schools have to be desegregated to the greatest extent possible and it may come down to forced assignments this September." He then asked rhetorically, "How bad is that? Call it forced busing, busing babies, whatever inflammatory rhetoric you might want to use. But our board acted in a responsible way and came up with a good program. The early childhood centers give you a good program at the end of the ride." Reville was equally forthright in a talk before Riverside parents at School 65. In a veiled reference to the obstructionist rhetoric of Mayor Griffin, Reville warned parents to be wary, and suggested that if they listened "to people who for political expediency tell you what you want to hear," the pain would be much greater. Referring to the racially charged demagoguery of the late 1960s and early 1970s, Reville reminded his audience that obstructionism had been tried and had failed. "That's why we're before the courts today," he said. When asked by a parent in Riverside just how much power Curtin had, Reville responded only partly in jest, "Enough to call out the 101st Airborne." To encourage white parents to cooperate, the board sponsored a series of well-publicized tours of several inner-city early childhood centers. Reville promoted the trips to his audiences—what they saw, he told them, would be what they got. "We have no choice," he said. "Judge Curtin is under pressure from the Second Circuit Court of Appeals to accelerate the process. There's no alternative."[7]

Despite the anxieties, the first day of school in September 1981 was a proud one for Buffalo. With more than half the city's forty-four thousand public school students riding buses to schools beyond the confines of their neighborhoods, the streets in every neighborhood of the city were calm and peaceful. The newspapers boasted of the achievements of the day. It was "a lesson in tranquility," said the *News*. The *Courier* reported in a banner headline, "Everyone Cooperates as Busing Commences." The integration specialist from the State Education Department reported that the implementation of Phase IIIx was exemplary. "We saw not one picket, not one so-called protective parent hanging around," he said. "I was impressed. I just finished visiting other cities undergoing desegregation—Indianapolis, Louisville, Saint Louis, Chicago, and Milwaukee—and this is not the way it usually goes." The Buffalo police commissioner concurred. "We had no incidents relating to busing, thank God."[8]

There were other things to be thankful for on that first day of school in 1981. While Buffalo's school population continued to decline, the loss of barely a thousand students (2 percent) was substantially less than in previous years. More significantly, the rate of decline in Buffalo was considerably lower than in school districts in the surrounding suburbs. White flight was limited to barely more than a handful of disgruntled parents who'd been able to finesse their way past the scrupulous Diocese of Buffalo admissions officers under the order of Bishop Head to deny admission to refugees from integration. Indeed, contrary to the expectation of Mayor Griffin, who had predicted a flight to the parochial system, the Diocese of Buffalo reported a 4.5 percent decline in enrollment in September 1981, as four hundred children had left diocesan schools that year to attend Buffalo's magnet schools.[9]

But the problem of racial isolation in Buffalo's schools was not yet completely solved. Enrollment figures for September 1981 showed that blacks made up 54 percent of the children in the schools; there were still close to three thousand black students in nine schools that failed to meet Judge Curtin's requirement that no less than 35 percent and no more than 65 percent of every school's population consist of minorities. According to the plaintiffs, this meant that 20 percent of all black elementary school children remained in segregated schools. The plaintiffs refused to accept this, and began a push for what they said would be "a final order." What they wanted, they said in the spring of 1982, was the pairing of four inner-city elementary schools with seven schools in white neighborhoods. The board objected, saying that such a plan would result in the busing of more than two thousand more whites while upsetting the racial balance in existing schools.[10]

Despite its continued legal struggle and a Reagan administration cut of federal integration funds from $6 million to $600,000, the Board of Education enjoyed a great deal of success and attention. Indeed, desegregation efforts in Buffalo were becoming a model for the nation. In an interview in the *News* in January 1982, James Barnes, the director of the National Educational Strategy Center in Hartford, Connecticut, said, "Over the past few years we've sent about five hundred people to Buffalo from other areas to look at the system. It's got to be the best there is." Several months later, the court-appointed desegregation monitor for Cleveland said, "I keep telling people here they should take a trip to Buffalo—they could learn a lot."[11] The apparent success of Buffalo's desegregation program occurred at a time of increasingly reactionary tendencies in Washington. Indeed, just as Buffalo was in the process of achieving its greatest success in desegregating its schools, the United States Senate passed its strongest antibusing bill ever. "Busing," said Senator Jesse Helms of North Carolina, "just doesn't work." The view from other cities suggested that perhaps he was correct. Boston's public schools were in terrible shape. They had lost more than thirty thousand pupils since court-ordered integration began in 1974, with the portion of the student body accounted for by white students falling from 70 percent to 30 percent. In Boston, there were more whites in private and parochial schools than there were in the city's public schools. In Cleveland, too, opposition to court-ordered desegregation had been intense—"as broad and as deep as you can imagine," the court-appointed monitor reported in January 1983. White flight in Cleveland, Detroit, and other cities throughout the North and Midwest had led to the virtual resegregation of their public schools.[12]

Judge Curtin was pleased with the progress being made, and for the first time since the case began, he put the burden on the plaintiffs to demonstrate that further racial balance was both desirable and even possible. Curtin seemed to agree with the board's argument that given the number of whites in the school system, further desegregation could not be achieved without destroying racial balance in existing schools. He hinted that, like judges in other cities, he might rule that despite the existence of two remaining all-minority schools, the system should be considered constitutionally desegregated. Curtin's ruling in August 1982 was a double-barreled victory for Reville's school board. Because it was "financially burdensome" and "disruptive," Curtin rejected the plaintiffs' proposal for the additional pairing of black and white neighborhood schools.

Meanwhile, desegregation continued to proceed smoothly. The one percent decline in school enrollment in September 1982 was the smallest in twenty-five years, much smaller than in all the other large cities of the Northeast. Furthermore, Buffalo's 52 percent minority student population was far lower than almost every large city in the country, 2 percentage points lower that the year before. In a ruling in May 1983, Curtin expressed satisfaction that the Board of Education had done all it could. Racial imbalance at the three remaining all-black elementary schools could not possibly be the result of segregative actions, he said. "The imposition of any new measures to desegregate the schools under the circumstances could only be viewed as counterproductive." While there were still some unanswered questions, Curtin said, the issue of desegregation had been satisfactorily resolved. "The board has met its burden of demonstrating that further desegregation of these schools is not practical at this time."[13]

Buffalo reaped the rewards of a difficult job well done. In May 1985, the *New York Times* lauded the city's efforts. The headline—"School integration in Buffalo hailed as a model for the U.S."—trumpeted the success: "Four years after a Federal judge ordered forced busing, the Buffalo public schools have come to be considered a national model of integration. Moreover, educators say, the schools here are the better for integration." The reporter, Michael Winerip, quoted Superintendent of Schools Eugene Reville: "The best thing that's happened to Buffalo is court-ordered desegregation. We've restored confidence in Buffalo public schools."[14] James Barnes of the National Education Strategy Center, Winerip wrote, reported that of the 531 school desegregation programs he had studied, "Buffalo is right at the top, right at the very top." Integration worked in Buffalo, the article said, because parents and teachers received a major role in designing the city's twenty-two magnet schools; because millions of dollars in extra federal funds were available to make the magnet schools special; and because of the extraordinary role played by Judge Curtin, who, with a delicate combination of firmness and sensitivity, brandished a court order that kept things moving.

Much of the success, Winerip wrote, was due to the creativity of school officials, who, by producing imaginative magnet programs, "sold integration to the people of Buffalo...by promising a better school waiting for children at the end of the bus ride." Winerip referred to the method employed by Buffalo administrators as the "velvet steamroller," which proved so appealing that "of the 30,000 students who were bused four years ago, only 15 percent had to be ordered onto buses by the Federal judge. Nearly one of every three Buffalo schools is a magnet school." Winerip touted Buffalo's achievement:

> Several months ago two dozen Japanese educators flew to Buffalo to see how such magnet schools work, and they were followed last month by a dozen superintendents from southern school districts. A few weeks ago, when a United States Justice Department lawyer involved in the prolonged school desegregation suit in Yonkers was looking for programs that might work there, he visited Buffalo.

Each year for the last five years, 300 to 400 white children have left private and parochial schools here to attend integrated public schools.

Buffalo's public schools improved as they integrated. In 1985, Buffalo students earned 165 New York State Regents scholarships, twice the number won in 1977. Fourteen students at City Honors High School won the generous and prestigious Regents Empire awards. A far higher percentage of Buffalo's third- and sixth-grade students passed pupil evaluation tests in reading and math than in any city in the state. Eight of the city's schools had received citations for excellence from the president of the United States, more schools than in any other city in the nation. Judge Curtin told Winerip: "I'm distressed by people who make statements nationally that integration doesn't work. It does work. It's plain wrong to say it won't. It's worked in Buffalo."

For the time being, at least, Curtin was right; the people of Buffalo had overcome the odds. An unprecedented degree of racial mixing had occurred in Buffalo's neighborhood schools, which had for years been bastions of racial isolation. Every day, thousands of children—white, African American, Hispanic, Asian, and Native American—ventured beyond the confines of their neighborhoods on school buses and metro buses, headed for magnet schools, vocational schools, early childhood centers, academic high schools, and neighborhood schools tucked away in all corners of the city. In the Fruit Belt and the Ellicott District, in Black Rock and Riverside, in South Buffalo and North Buffalo, on the West Side and on the East Side, the people of Buffalo made real the long-elusive goal of racial integration in the city's public schools.

Curtin rightfully deserved much of the credit. In 1986, the *Buffalo Evening News* selected him as one of its "Citizens of the Year," noting his "quiet power on the bench." Curtin's former clerk, Mike Brady, who had played a significant role during the early phases of the case, recalled Curtin's "judicial temperament." Curtin's wife, Jane, talked about his "patience," both in court and at home. Deeply aware of the difficult and complex changes he had required the people of the city to make, the judge had been patient. Patrick Martin, another clerk, said Curtin understood that "the carrot does better than the stick if you're willing to wait a bit longer for the results." Sometimes the judge had threatened to impose a solution or to appoint a "master"—but always he delayed, hoping to rely as long as possible on voluntary measures.[15]

Curtin had given the people of Buffalo power as well as time, insisting on extensive and meaningful citizen participation at every step of the desegregation process. "Curtin 'inserviced' everybody," said a principal, referring to the training sessions the judge required of all school personnel—building superintendents, crossing guards, and bus aides, not to mention parents and teachers. Because of the careful development insisted upon by Curtin, Pat Martin said, people "felt ownership in the process." Letting all the people affected by desegregation play a role in how it was carried out worked in Buffalo; it may well have worked in Boston, too. The president of the Boston School Committee told the *News* that he wished his city had done things differently. "If we had it to do over again," he said, "we would make sure, like Judge Curtin did in Buffalo, that the people of this city had some ownership of the plan." Citing the court-ordered pairing of all-white South Boston High with its all-black equivalent in Roxbury, he said, "In Boston it was just thrust on us."[16]

While Buffalo continued to have serious educational problems, the problems were more the result of larger, historical questions of culture, race, and class than of educational policy. And while much still needed to be done in the area of public education, much had already been accomplished. Judge Curtin's faith in the people of his community led him to empower people throughout the city to become involved in the critical issue of school desegregation. In the process, he reinforced a sense of commitment to community, which continued to motivate the people of Buffalo in following years. Like Eugene Reville and Joe Murray, Judge Curtin had appealed to the best instincts of the community; he had challenged the people of Buffalo to reach beyond the boundaries of their parochial experiences to achieve something that was unique in the annals of contemporary urban life.

Judge Curtin's lofty challenge to change, however, given the continued decline of the area's economy, had become increasingly more difficult to realize. By 1981, Bethlehem Steel's Lackawanna plant had virtually become history. Although five thousand workers still produced two and a half million tons of steel a year, the company had made it perfectly clear that it had no future in Lackawanna. In May 1981, the company's president, Walter Williams, said that while the plant was not "a shut-down target," he could not justify capital expenditures to modernize it. Bethlehem's problems at Lackawanna, he indicated, although aggravated by high local taxes, were structural, caused by the plant's "unfavorable location" and a product mix too heavily dependent on the automobile industry. The company had already spent more than $500 million at the Lackawanna plant since 1970, he said, and now there was little that either the company or the community could do. Williams said Bethlehem was committed to its new plants in Burns Harbor, Indiana, and at Sparrows Point, outside of Baltimore, Maryland, where it was investing $750 million.[17]

One year later, in June 1982, the *News* announced, "Strength of Buffalo Steel Industry Melting Away." The paper asked rhetorically, "Will fresh hot steel soon join Wildroot Cream Oil and the Pierce Arrow automobile on the list of things they don't make around here anymore?" Citing Bethlehem plant closings earlier in the year—a steel plant in Los Angeles and shipyards in Seattle—the *News* warned, "Don't bet against it."[18]

Six months later, on Monday, December 27, 1982, the *News* reported that Bethlehem Steel would permanently shut down almost all of its steel-making operations over the coming six months. Thirty-nine hundred workers would be let go. Thirty-four hundred, already on temporary layoff, would not be recalled. The company promised that thirteen hundred would remain employed in steel finishing operations at the bar mill and the galvanizing line.[19]

It should have been no surprise when Bethlehem Steel announced its closure in Lackawanna. For years, the people of Buffalo had been aware of the critical problems in the local steel industry. Community leaders, businesspeople, politicians, educators, and union representatives should have known and should have been working on plans and programs to save the plant. The story of Republic Steel, however, is somewhat different. Republic's mill in South Buffalo was much smaller than Bethlehem's, one of a series of small, integrated mills that the company had in Chicago, Birmingham, Troy, and Cleveland, which housed Republic's headquarters. It had been "a good little plant," remembered Frank Palumbero, president of Steelworkers Local 1743; it was compact, highly integrated, and capable of producing high-quality, low-priced steel. The South Buffalo plant could make *and* ship ingots to Republic's plant in Gadsden, Alabama, more cheaply than the Gadsden plant could make them. "It was like making soup," Palumbero said. "The smaller the kettle the better the soup." With only twenty-five hundred workers at its peak in the mid-1970s, Republic provided a good working environment; it was a plant where almost everyone knew one another. People liked it there, and the plant employed a number of families—fathers and sons, uncles, nephews, and cousins. As at Bethlehem, the workforce was integrated, and it was there, in the steel plants, that many of the workers in white South Buffalo first encountered African Americans.[20] Republic specialized in bar products for the automobile industry such as crankshaft steel and spring and coil steel, and as cars went, so did Republic. Business was good during the Vietnam era (the swan song years of American industry) and, in 1970, the company spent $40 million at the South Buffalo plant, replacing the open hearth with the basic oxygen furnace, raising the plant's capacity, and increasing its workforce. Bethlehem, of course, was moving in the opposite direction. The major cutback at Bethlehem's Lackawanna plant, followed by the opening of the gigantic Burns Harbor plant (where a much smaller workforce could produce far more steel), indicated that it would be increasingly difficult for the company's older plants to survive. Soon, Republic began to experience the same kinds of pressures. In 1970, the company closed its two oldest and smallest plants, in Birmingham, Alabama, and in Troy, New York. Nevertheless, Republic's Buffalo plant continued to do well throughout the 1970s. Profits were good and wages and benefits increased while capacity and employment levels remained steady. The combination of a decline in the domestic automobile industry in late 1980 and early 1981 and a cutback in bar business gave the company some breathing room, a chance to shut down temporarily and modernize. On August 15, 1981, the plant closed for six months so that the company could embark on a massive modernization and improvement program, spending $46 million on a state-of-the-art blast furnace, a new basic oxygen furnace, and a new blooming mill. The shutdown was temporary, employees were told, and the plant would reopen in December. By late November, the work was done, and Alan Marquardt, the superintendent of the blast furnace, was ready to go "pedal to the metal."[21] He heard nothing from headquarters in Cleveland, however, and began to worry that moisture would settle in the new blast furnace as the temperature dropped. Marquardt arranged to have enormous heaters installed in the furnace. Winter came and went and still the South Buffalo plant remained closed. While some continued to hope that it was just a question of time before the plant reopened, Marquardt, for one, was not surprised when, on June 1, 1982, he was told that the plant was going to stay closed for good. Despite its difficulties, the company behaved well, purposefully delaying the final shutdown to allow workers close to retirement to qualify for pensions. When the plant finally shut down in January 1984, well over half of the workforce received full pensions.

These events had a traumatic effect on the community and left nothing untouched. Most affected, naturally, were the industrial workers, the men who had grown up fully expecting that if all else failed, there would always be a job at Bethlehem or at Chevy. Indeed, these were not last resort jobs. Because they paid well and were highly unionized, they were considered secure and estimable forms of employment. A brochure written by the United Steel Workers in 1964 said:

> Once a steel worker always a steel worker. Perhaps the roar and clangor and blistering heat hammer such a respect in a man that he never can become bored with his job. Perhaps that is why a steel-maker never can be content except in the arduous toil and sweat that goes with the fabrication of hard metal. For here everything tells him that he is part of something stupendous, that he is doing something worthy of a man.[22]

That attitude had changed by the early 1980s. It was hard for these people, raised in the ethic of manly work, to accept the realities of Buffalo's economy. (By 1980 the newspapers had become almost morbidly obsessed with the traumas of unemployment. Revealing a Depression-era mentality, there were countless articles on handling stress, alcoholism, child abuse, and other behavioral problems that the newspapers generally attributed to unemployment.) A laid-off worker at Harrison Radiator told a reporter in 1982 that

I loved my job. I loved the pay, with two days off a week what more could anyone ask for. I was helping to build a good product (radiators for trucks and cars) and I went in there with the attitude that I was going to give those people the best damn eight hours I could. It made me feel like a man. Sitting around the house knocks your masculinity right down the drain.... Day after day, it's the same old thing. Nothing but stress.... I'm thirty five years old and I've never felt so insecure in my life."[23]

For Buffalo, 1982 ended gloomily. It was the year, *News* reporter Ray Hill wrote, that "Western New York took it on the chin...the year the bottom fell out ...the year we found a new subculture, the chronically unemployed."[24] The shutdowns at Bethlehem and Republic, and deep cuts at GM and Ford, badly weakened the rest of the economy. The entire city faltered as the list of closings lengthened. Retail chains, wholesale department stores, restaurants, shops, and service organizations went out of business. Even the *Courier Express*, the venerable daily newspaper that dated back to 1842, shut down that year. In the meantime, venerable institutions like the Buffalo Philharmonic Orchestra, the Albright-Knox Art Gallery, the Buffalo Museum of Science, and the Buffalo Historical Society teetered on the brink of bankruptcy.

At times it seemed hopeless. So it appeared on November 8, 1985, when Trico Corporation, the world's largest manufacturer of windshield wipers, announced that it was moving the bulk of its operations from Buffalo to the border of Texas and Mexico. The windshield wiper was invented in Buffalo by John Oshei who, after driving home on a rainy afternoon in March 1917, decided a gadget was necessary to mechanically wipe the rain from his windshield. Enterprising as well as creative, Oshei formed Trico, and from the 1920s on, it led its field. Housed in three aging but grand and imposing turn-of-the century plants scattered around the city, Trico was one of Buffalo's last remaining large family-controlled and locally owned companies. In the mid-1980s, the Osheis still owned close to 30 percent of Trico's outstanding stock.

Trico had been a good corporate citizen, and the Oshei Foundation was a magnanimous contributor to a broad range of community charities. However, notwithstanding this local commitment, the company, like a growing number of American manufacturers, decided to open a maquila ("contract work") plant in Mexico. Maquila operations have their origins in the mid-1960s, when changes in the tax laws encouraged American companies to take advantage of cheaper foreign, particularly Asian, labor. The new laws allowed an American company to ship manufacturing machinery and unfinished products into a foreign country, assemble the products there, and then bring them back into the US market, paying duty only on the value added during the assembly process. During the 1970s, this system led to the creation of assembly plants in Taiwan and other Pacific Rim countries.[25]

As the peso lost value during the early 1980s, Mexican businesspersons and government officials became interested in the program. In addition, the US Department of Commerce became interested in Mexico as a way to stem the loss of jobs to the Pacific Rim. Beginning in 1984, the Commerce Department sponsored conferences designed to introduce American companies to the cost-cutting advantages of the program. The labor movement throughout the country as well as the political leadership in Buffalo and other industrial cities was appalled at what they saw as a government-encouraged program of deindustrialization. Others saw it differently, arguing that the jobs that were headed for Mexico were being lost anyway; better that they went to Mexico than the Orient, since at least part of the product would be made in the United States. Toy manufacturer Fisher-Price, one of the most successful companies in the Buffalo area, set up twin plants on the Texas-Mexico border in 1984. If it hadn't done so, the president of the company said, "we'd be buying completed toys from the Orient."

For Trico, the maquila program sounded too good to be true. For years the company had comfortably dominated the windshield wiper industry. Unchallenged, Trico made little effort to modernize, and instead coasted on profits earned not from wipers but from its gigantic stock portfolio. In 1985, Trico owned nearly $62 million in common stock in General Motors, Exxon, and Ford. Under increasing pressure from foreign producers and American automakers, who demanded that Trico cut its price lest they begin buying from Japan, the company woke up. In 1985, company president Richard Wolf announced the decision to build an assembly plant in Matamoros, Mexico, and a distribution center across the border in Brownsville, Texas. Trico would equip the factory in Matamoros and stock it with windshield wiper components, all duty free. The components would then be assembled into finished products and shipped back across the border to the company's warehouse. Trico would pay duty only on the value added in Mexico. The cost savings, Wolf said, were too hard to resist. In Mexico, workers earned $1.20 an hour in wages and benefits. In Buffalo, Wolf told a stunned meeting of Trico workers, they received $14 an hour.

Buffalonians were horrified that their community and their workforce was being held hostage by what they saw as the slave labor of an underdeveloped country. Others viewed it differently. By 1988, more than two hundred fifty thousand Mexicans worked in maquila plants. The plants pumped more than $1.1 billion into the Mexican economy, behind oil but ahead of tourism in economic impact. The program, some said, would help Mexico deal with its terrible economic problems, give work to many who would otherwise slip across the border, and help the country pay its foreign debt. Small comfort, said others, to the industrial workforce of Buffalo.

Losing out to cheaper, foreign labor was nothing new to the proud unionized workers of Buffalo. But the maquila program was different, and it was particularly hard to swallow. In the months following the Trico announcement, Norman Harper, president of Local 2100 of the United Auto Workers of America, which represented the Trico workers, made several trips to the Brownsville–Matamoros area. He brought a tape recorder and camera with him, and the words and images he captured were shocking. Harper found teeming shantytowns that had sprung up on the dirt roads near plants owned by GM, Delco, and Fisher-Price. These ramshackle villages, with only minimal plumbing and sanitation, housed thousands of people, many of them young women, who had come from all over Mexico looking for work in the maquila factories. Some of them had found it but most had not. The unemployment rate on the border was higher than anywhere else in Mexico. Conditions in Matamoros, Harper's slides indicated, were desperate. There were few schools and medical facilities and hardly any municipal facilities of any kind. Harper said that the women and children of Matamoros lined up every day to cross the border to schools and hospitals in Brownsville. Rapid, unplanned expansion had turned the town upside down as companies and developers, using generous municipal handouts, constructed a host of jerrybuilt warehouses, homes, and shopping plazas. Something was terribly wrong, Harper fumed, when corporations were permitted to play vulnerable, low-paid workers of one country against high-paid but vulnerable workers of another. It was worse when governments encouraged it, he said. But this was exactly what happened in this cynical partnership, a compact between a desperate underdeveloped country and American corporations eager to improve their balance sheets by drastically cutting their labor costs. The only beneficiaries of the program were the corporations. Clearly, workers in places like Trico's Buffalo plants did not benefit. Nor, Harper said, did the Mexicans who moved in droves to the border to work in the maquila plants. Despite their government's alleged desire to make Mexico economically independent of the United States, the maquila program put Mexico's workers more at the mercy of the Americans than ever. Was Trico more committed, Harper wondered, to Matamoros than it was to Buffalo? Would it not move again when it found another place in some other corner of the world where wages were lower still? And what about the Mexicans who worked in the maquila plants, the young women who, earning so little, with so few benefits, had no job security?[26]

It was also too late for the eight hundred employees working at Westinghouse Electric near the airport in suburban Depew. Westinghouse, which manufactured electric engines, had bought its plant in 1947 from Curtiss-Wright, the great Buffalo-based airplane manufacturing company that had moved to California after World War II. Westinghouse grew continuously and, in 1970, when John Perry came to Buffalo to work for the company as strategic projects manager of motor operations, there were seventy-two hundred workers in the plant. But the engine plant had reached capacity, and the company, like General Electric and the US Electrical Motor Company, rather than expanding in the area, began to move its production out. Westinghouse moved its welding operations to Maryland and its copper wire production to Virginia. The number of Buffalo employees dropped steadily throughout the 1970s and early 1980s. For a while, the *Union Messenger*, the newsletter of the International Union of Electrical Workers, denied the obvious. "There are many topics of discussion circulating around the plant," the paper reported in early April 1986. "The main issue seems to be when and if it will all come to an end."[27] Perhaps in denial, the workers passed along alternative rumors that "due to an influx of orders the life of the Motor Division will be extended." But soon they could no longer deny it. In early 1987, with just under eight hundred employees left, Westinghouse announced that it would close.

By then, John Perry had a new job as coordinator of the Westinghouse Placement Center. In an interview in the *Messenger*, Perry promised the workers "the most humane plant close-down to ever take place." He began by organizing a series of workshops for Westinghouse workers on training for new jobs, personal finance (how to apply for unemployment insurance and deal with creditors), and food and health (how to apply for food stamps, Medicaid, and home energy assistance). "The top priority now," the union paper wrote, "is to pick up the pieces and resume industrial life again, as painful as it may be. We must begin to plan for our respective futures.... It is said that adversity is the glue that binds together the working people.... Let's make sure that rings true by sharing and caring for each of our brothers and sisters."

And then, in the end, there was steel. In May 1983, on Bethlehem Steel's last day of operation, the 79-inch bar mill produced a record 275 slabs of steel. "We wanted to go out in a blaze of glory," one of the workers said. In the middle of the night of August 16, 1983, a group of workers at Bethlehem's Lackawanna plant hoisted the international distress signal—an American flag flying upside down—on top of blast furnace C. The gigantic flag, over five hundred square feet and illuminated by two glaring thousand-watt mercury vapor lamps, could be seen for miles, from the shores of Lake Erie to as far north as Niagara Falls.[28]

In the spring of 1988, Joe Ritz, who years before had written so movingly about the impact of urban renewal on the Lower West Side, wrote an equally passionate piece in the *Buffalo News* about the demolition of the Bethlehem Steel plant. Titled "Once Mighty Bethlehem Steel Slowly Being Reduced to Rubble," Ritz's article dripped with nostalgia and sadness:

> Seen from the Father Baker Bridge, the once mighty Bethlehem Steel Corporation's Lackawanna plant—where motorists once looked for the rosy glow in the sky as the open hearths poured steel—is being reduced to rubble. Demo-

lition of the sprawling plant has been going on since late 1984, but the first phases consisted of tearing down long unused coke batteries and blast furnaces hidden from the eyes of the public by the deserted but untouched black metal buildings of the steel plant. Now, work by four demolition companies is rapidly proceeding on the 218-, 48-, and 54-inch bar mills.... Less visible is the No.3 open hearth, now rapidly becoming a tortured, twisted jungle of metal halfway to destruction.... Ironically, the scrap from the plant mostly will go to operating steel plants, including those owned by Bethlehem, to be melted down into new steel.

Demolition of the plant is half completed, according to Eliot Gordon, Bethlehem's supervisor of reclamation. "This is the largest demolition project in the country," he said. It will take at least another two years, Gordon said, before the demolition is completed. The ripping down of the largest single building, the massive basic oxygen furnace, which towers over the closed plant like a sooty metal castle, is expected to begin late this year or early in 1989.... When the project is completed, approximately thirteen hundred acres of waterfront property will become an empty field.... Even much of the railroad tracks on the property are being ripped up, although some will remain for use by a buyer of the land. In a year or so, Gordon said, motorists on the Father Baker Bridge will be able to see Lake Erie when they pass the former steel mill.[29]

No reader could avoid the conclusion that there was something irreversible about the decline of industry in Buffalo. The destruction of such a mighty edifice as the sprawling Bethlehem complex led people to wonder what could possibly be done to halt the decay. Staggered by the rapid devolution of its economy, Buffalo was, by the end of the 1980s, a city in search of an economic function. Its location, at the junction of what for so long had been the nation's most significant trade route, had been made irrelevant by the St. Lawrence Seaway. And now, its industrial economy, too, was becoming increasingly obsolete. The economy of the area had gone through a major shakedown. The shift of jobs out of manufacturing since the late 1970s was more pronounced in Buffalo than in any area in the country. By 1983, jobs in trade and services exceeded those in factories for the first time in the city's history. Between 1977 and 1987, more than 45,000 jobs—31 percent of Buffalo's manufacturing jobs—were lost (versus 25 percent nationally). In 1977, the manufacturing sector employed 28 percent of Buffalo's workers. By 1987, it employed only 18 percent. In addition, while the average pay of the local workforce had been among the highest rates in the nation, by the end of the 1980s, following years of layoffs, pay cuts, and concessions by a battered workforce, Buffalo had become a low-wage town. What had happened? What had gone wrong? People obsessively asked those questions, desperate to find answers. In the meantime, the decline continued, and the despair increased, striking at the core of the community, undermining family stability, weakening neighborhoods, and permanently altering the values and beliefs many people had long lived by.

During this time, those who cared about Buffalo's downtown continued to engage in a seemingly futile effort to save it. In 1977, a new federal plan for the revitalization of decaying downtowns was initiated. Called "Urban Development Action Grants" (UDAGs), policymakers rewrote the rules that had for years defined the relationship between public and private sectors in the development of the nation's downtowns. Patricia Harris, the Secretary of Housing and Urban Development, described the rationale for the program, stating that local government must "like a business be able to move quickly to take advantage of opportunities for coordinated economic and community development."[30] Hoping to overcome the unwillingness of private developers, local governments would use federal dollars (UDAGs) to leverage private dollars for projects and developments that the private sector was unwilling to finance on its own. Acting sometimes as a broker, sometimes as banker, sometimes as general partner, and sometimes as general contractor, elected officials, under the UDAG program, became the chief catalysts of downtown development, creating and implementing complex deals that brought together a combination of low-interest public loans, grants, union pension fund investment, and tax credits and shelters, in addition to private equity, which, for better or for worse, changed the face of downtown Buffalo. Beginning in the late 1970s and continuing into the 1990s, hotels, offices, and even restaurants and nightclubs were financed with UDAGs.

The first UDAG was a $4 million low-interest loan from the city to a San Francisco developer named Clement Chen. It was used in 1977 to build a new Hilton hotel near the waterfront in downtown Buffalo. The Hilton project had been a landmark, one of the first UDAGs in the country. It was risky, untried business, but the deal had worked. The hotel was built and the payments on the loan were made and recycled by the Griffin administration to begin the construction of new, owner-occupied homes in the Pratt-Willert section of the city's East Side. The mayor was pleased and described the role that the city was willing to play in the redevelopment process in entrepreneurial terms. "As long as it is not a free lunch we'll gamble some of our money if they gamble some of theirs."[31] Under the UDAG program, according to which most all of the risk was assumed by the city, not the private developers, there was no incentive not to build. Led by politicians eager for a groundbreaking photo-op and businessmen and developers eager to participate in a program that promised much reward at little risk, the city continued to build excess capacity by leveraging the creation of an ever-growing supply of commercial, office, and retail space at a time, everybody knew, of rapidly diminishing demand. Fund it and build it, even operate it and subsidize it, if necessary; but don't worry, they said, the supply will somehow create the demand, and eventually "they will come."

With the city's role as equal partner in a development project legitimized, Mayor Griffin now turned his attention to the two-block area on Main St. between Genesee and Chippewa, where he and his development team sought to use the powers of urban renewal to create a new "financial district" for downtown Buffalo. It was a vast, multifaceted project, consisting of a new headquarters for Buffalo Savings Bank (recently renamed "Goldome," in honor of its turn-of-the-century, sparkling gold-leaf dome), a new headquarters for the Liberty Bank, and another new hotel nearby. Costing in excess of $120 million, this elaborate and expensive project would be funded largely by the government, using the incentive of the UDAGs.

The package crafted by Griffin's team was complex; it was a fine example of just how multifaceted the urban renewal process had become. Because his plans for the new banks on Main Street would stimulate and help sustain the Main Street rapid transit line, Buffalo's congressional delegation was able to convince the federal Urban Mass Transit Authority (UMTA) to provide $3 million toward the land acquisition, tenant relocation, and demolition. Again, "the wreckers" went to work; they tore down all of the structures on the block, with the lone exception being the magnificent Buffalo Savings Bank building. Among the demolished buildings was a breathtaking art moderne masterpiece, the W. T. Grant store. Added to the funds from UMTA were $16.5 million in the form of a low-interest UDAG. New York State signed on as well, granting the city $7.5 million to build a new parking ramp across from a hotel planned for the area.

Griffin and his team were daring in their use of public money, taking on highly speculative development projects, like one called "Theatre Place," a mixed-use residential, commercial, and office development that would be housed in two remodeled commercial buildings on Main Street next to Shea's Theater. The city, eager to move ahead on the project, allocated more than $3.5 million to the project in the spring of 1979. Although no owner, developer, or tenants for the facility had been identified, it was a risk Griffin was willing to take. When a developer, Seneca Development, was finally found for the project, the money that the city had committed to the project was converted into an incentive-laden forty-year, low interest mortgage, the kind that no bank would ever touch, but that the city, in its newly entrepreneurial role, was willing to hold.[32] The heart of Theatre Place was a nightclub called the Tralfamador, which since the early 1970s had been a small, funky jazz club, located farther up Main Street, not far from the old campus of the University of Buffalo. It was known as one of the best jazz clubs west of the Hudson. Many of the city's jazz fans, who loved the club's former and more simple feel, felt the club's new and fancy digs were more like an airport. The

"Tralf" struggled, and it soon became clear that it (and the Theatre Place complex in which it was housed) was losing money. In order to protect their investments, the city and Seneca Development looked across Main Street to a vacant group of turn-of-the-century commercial buildings next to the Market Arcade Building. They needed something spectacular, they felt, something that would generate excitement and, above all, people. The Theater District needed people, lots of them, to create the density—"the critical mass"—that is essential if city districts are to be vital and dynamic. Only a movie complex, the city and Seneca Development felt, would do the trick.

Cinema complexes built in the suburbs were islands set in vast concrete parking lots. To see movies in the suburbs is to walk hurriedly through parking lots filled with idling automobiles, dodging cars backing in and pulling out, and rushing to beat the traffic jams that always follow the shows. Even the best movies somehow never seem as good when seen in the suburban theaters as opposed to movie houses in the city. But by the end of the 1970s, the dozens of movie theaters in the city—the large downtown movie palaces as well as the small ones in neighborhoods throughout the city—had almost all closed. Even the one or two downtown theaters that showed sleaze, martial arts, and "blaxploitation" films were on their last legs.

But Seneca Development and their eager partners and lenders in the Griffin administration believed otherwise, convinced, they said, that a market existed in the city for first-run quality films. General Cinema Corporation, one of the largest and most successful developers of suburban movie complexes in the country, was willing, Seneca Development reported in 1987, to build a complex of eight screens on Main Street, depending, of course, on the incentives.[33] Again, Griffin's development team crafted an enticing package calculated to lure a movie company that had never before built in a city. With a $4.2 million construction loan that required no money down and a repayment schedule that was not guaranteed but rather contingent upon ticket sales, the deal was too good to pass up, and, in 1988, the eight-screen movie complex opened. The largest audience for movies in downtown were the residents who lived nearby and soon General Cinema abandoned its stated commitment to program the broadest range of first-run films, concentrating instead on films that appealed primarily to an African American audience, particularly teenagers, who could walk easily from their East Side neighborhoods to the theater on Main Street. The growing number of black teenagers in the area threatened the viability of the larger vision for the Theater District. The magnificent Market Arcade Building, on which the city had spent close to $10 million to remodel still had no tenants by the early 1990s. Only the most generous "sweetheart" deal—a $600,000 low-interest, long-term, non-recourse loan—could lure a Denver-based company to locate the Breckenridge

Brew Pub in the building. Subsidies were also used to lure office tenants to the Market Arcade Building, which inexplicably, since it was arguably one of the most beautiful and unusual buildings in the state, failed to lure market-rate tenants. Gradually, by the early 1990s, state offices, a few not-for-profits, and a few lawyers attracted by the low rents, began to fill the building. However, they, like the tenants of all of the subsidized buildings in downtown, were not new to downtown, but came because they were lured from privately owned buildings that could no longer compete in a market increasingly inundated with empty space.

Depending on one's perspective, this approach to urban renewal was either a new form of capitalism or statism at its best. Like the position it took on the Main-Genesee project, the Theater District development cast city government in a high-risk venture traditionally the domain of speculative venture capitalists. To the protagonists—Mayor Griffin and his successor, Anthony Masiello—this was a new and courageous form of urban renewal. Others wondered, however, about the sustainability of projects for which there was no demonstrable demand; they were concerned that the public might have to support those projects longer than their proponents cared to admit. Worse still, some thought, was a growing culture of dependence in which the public sector, acting as venture capitalists, assumed most of the risk while the private sector, unwilling to participate unless on terms of their own making, reaped most of the rewards.

Was there any other choice? Could the businesspeople and politicians who cared, and who were confronted with a steadily eroding and increasingly shabby downtown, afford to wait for the private sector? After all, most of the players in the private sector—the businesspeople who worked there, the store owners who sought customers there, and the landlords who owned property there—were leaving downtown in droves. Had not actual conditions in downtown become so bad by the end of the century that government had no choice but to step in—to stir the pot, so to speak, in the hope that something could be done to stimulate downtown's revival, if not its renaissance?

During this time, genuine and lasting renewal was being achieved not by the developers and politicians but by the increasing efforts of historic preservationists, who not only valued the area's unique built environment but knew, like a growing number of people in cities throughout the nation, that preservation worked. By the early 1980s, preservationists, who had witnessed the devastation caused by decades of urban renewal, banded together to protect the city's historic infrastructure. The efforts of the preservationists, which had begun in Allentown during the 1960s, now spread to downtown, where they fought to preserve the city's best-known structure, the Guaranty Building, which had been designed and built by Louis Sullivan in 1896 at the corner of Church and Pearl streets. By the early 1970s, this magnificent building, an internationally recognized masterpiece of modern architecture, had gone to seed. Following construction of new and publicly subsidized buildings like the M&T Bank headquarters and the Main Place and Marine Midland towers, the Guaranty Building, also known as the Prudential, lost most of its better tenants. The building, increasingly abandoned, became blighted.

By the mid-1970s, the Guaranty Building's owners had defaulted on their mortgage and their tax payments, and, following a nearly disastrous fire in 1977, the building's primary creditor (a bank in Oklahoma), eager to rid itself of the problem, prepared to demolish it. Now, however, a group of preservationists, led and inspired by an architect named John Randall, who had moved to Buffalo in 1973 specifically to save the Guaranty, sought the support of New York's senator, Patrick Moynihan. Working together to assemble a creative financing package that involved a combination of a federal grant, tax-free loans, and other incentives, the building was sold to a new group of investors who, recognizing the value in its history, carefully restored it. Randall and the preservationists were thrilled. At a dedication ceremony in December 1983, Senator Moynihan recognized that historic preservation in Buffalo had become a force to be reckoned with. Referring to Sullivan's Guaranty Building, he said, "This is what America gave to the world and Buffalo chose to preserve it."[34] The preservation of the Genesee Building on Main Street and its adaptive reuse as the Hyatt Hotel in 1984 further inspired the hopes of the preservationists who, during the early 1980s, were enjoying the fruits of their labor. In 1981, a group of citizens formed the Preservation Coalition of Erie County and, inspired by the efforts in Allentown and appalled by the demolition in the late 1970s of such landmarks as the W. T. Grant store and "Jew" Murphy's Omega Café, they worked for and finally succeeded in creating, in 1983, the Joseph Ellicott Historic District. The designation of this nineteen-block area in downtown as a historic district, which contained such grand structures as the Guaranty Building, the Ellicott Square Building, the old Post Office, and both the city and the county hall, guaranteed that in some form at least the historic infrastructure of Buffalo's downtown would be preserved and protected.[35] Earlier that year, the Preservation Coalition, in an effort to call attention to the city's large and impressive stock of art deco architecture, sponsored what they called an "Art Deco Jazz Party," held at an old deco landmark, a restaurant on Exchange Street called "Dan Montgomery's." (This building, rich in history as well as in architectural detail, was demolished in 1987, replaced, like so many other buildings, with a parking lot.) Later that summer, Margaret Wooster, a local preservationist and editor of a short-lived journal called the *Buffalo Arts Review*, paddled her canoe up the Buffalo River to look for the grain elevators on what she called "The Buffalo River Museum." In 1986, Reyner Banham, one of the world's leading architectural historians (then working on the faculty at UB's School of Architecture and Environmental Design), wrote a book about those same grain elevators. Called *The Concrete Atlantis*, Banham told the rest of the world what preservationists in Buffalo already knew about the worth and value of their city's canyon of grain elevators. As people became more concerned about, interested in, and aware of Buffalo's heritage, still more books on the subject were published. In 1981, a citizen-led effort resulted in the publication of *Buffalo Architecture: A Guide* (MIT Press, 1981). In 1983, SUNY Press published a book by this author on Buffalo's history titled *High Hopes: The Rise and Decline of Buffalo, New York*, and, in 1989, MIT Press published Jack Quinan's *Larkin Building: Myth and Reality*.

The early 1980s were busy years for Buffalo's fledgling preservation movement. In 1982, a group called the Friends of Olmsted Park was formed. The Parkland Alliance, "composed of groups and individuals advocating the preservation …appreciation and enhancement of parks and open space in Buffalo," was formed in 1984. In 1986, the Parkside Community Association, so successful in achieving racial balance during the 1960s, secured the designation of their neighborhood as a "historic district" under the protection of the National Register of Historic Places. Despite the successes, and despite the increasing role that history and the awareness of the past was beginning to play in the thinking of the times, people remained concerned. In the summer of 1986, Susan McCartney, one of the founders of the Preservation Coalition, wrote: "As the city slowly but surely destroys the downtown that was, turning it into an area of growing parking lots, soulless banks, vacant lots and imaginary 'fountain plazas,' will there be anything of substance left downtown to make it worthwhile?"[36]

By the mid-1980s, the flow of business to the suburbs that had been building steadily since the 1920s reached flood-like proportions. Downtown, with the exception of law firms and bank headquarters, had been stripped of all but the most marginal of stores. The suburbs in general and Amherst in particular had become the preferred place to live and work within the metropolitan area. The impact on downtown was relentless, and not even the millions of dollars of public money that had, since the 1950s, been spent on urban renewal could stem the tide. In 1981, the gargantuan McKinley Mall opened in Hamburg, and in 1987, an even bigger mall, the Walden Galleria, opened in Cheektowaga. While having been a devastating blow to the city, the decision to locate UB in Amherst (and the subsequent economic spin-offs resulting from that decision) had made Amherst, with close to one hundred twenty thousand residents by the end of the 1900s, the fastest-growing town in New York State. Prompted by easy access to the "brains" of the community, UB fueled a seemingly endless cycle of growth in Amherst. It was, as one Amherst official said in 1987, "only natural that development should occur here. Companies tell us they need to be near the university, creating jobs for the twenty-first century."[37] What made the growth of Amherst so disturbing was that much of it was being aided by quasi-public organizations like the Amherst Industrial Development Agency. While it was perhaps understandable that downtown, desperately struggling to stay alive, would use public power and public funds to leverage private development, people wondered why a booming community like Amherst should be allowed to do the same. Nevertheless, throughout the 1980s, as Buffalo struggled against all odds, the Town of Amherst, like its neighbors in Cheektowaga, Hamburg, and other suburban locales, continued to dangle incentives designed to lure business away from the city.

Thus, despite hundreds of millions of dollars of public money, despite extensive new construction and rehabilitation, despite years of imaginative and Herculean political and financial legerdemain, the city's ambitious hopes to create a new Main Street remained unrealized. While the construction of new buildings, the rehabilitation of some old ones, and the opening of the rapid transit line added a degree of vitality to Main Street, there remained at the end of the 1980s a palpable sense of uncertainty about the future. Downtown's problems, while clearly rooted in powerful economic and demographic trends, were compounded by serious mistakes in conception and design. By focusing almost exclusively on trying to "bring back" the big-spending suburbanites, the politicians and developers who plotted downtown's revival completely neglected the patterns of the daily life of the people who lived nearby. By basing their plans on what they thought downtown should look like as opposed to how it actually worked, they were doomed to fail. The gritty yet lively urban places that made downtown vital were replaced by ones that, while clearly more sanitized and suburbanized, were far less appealing. While the Convention Center and the Marine Midland Tower are the most glaring examples of this process, many of the efforts to revitalize downtown put image ahead of function. The problems that the Tralfamador (the publicly leveraged nightclub) had were caused not by demographics or economics but, rather, by design. Forsaking the smoky, cramped, "city" feel of the old Tralf, designers of the new one opted for the cavernous and cold look of the shopping mall for the new facility. When, despite these extremely expensive efforts, the Tralf continued to fail, it remained easier and somehow more comforting to blame "historical forces"—the flight to the suburbs, the decline of the economy—than to rethink concept and design.

Artificiality of concept and design and an emphasis on image hampered other efforts to revitalize Main Street. Most of Main Street's most expensive and highly praised projects were made possible by the destruction of the city's retail core: Kobackers and J. N. Adams in the 1960s; W. T. Grant's, Grossman's, and Hens & Kelly in the 1970s; and Hengerer's in the 1980s. The reason, therefore, that so much of retail in downtown Buffalo died, is because so much of it was killed by urban renewal. These stores, eliminated as "blight" during the late 1970s and early

1980s, were what brought generations of shoppers—Poles, Italians, and African Americans from the East and West Sides, as well as the more genteel shoppers from the Delaware District—to the downtown area. On the new Main Street, now lined with banks, a hotel, and shiny buildings with "class A" office space, there is no place for these people to shop. As misguided politicians and developers concocted ever more complex and generous financial packages in a desperate effort to lure high-priced retailers like Brooks Brothers and Ann Taylor downtown, the area's natural constituency, the people who lived in the city and who craved the exciting and nurturing human environment that they knew was possible, remained frustrated and disappointed.

By the end of the 1980s, Buffalo needed to be renewed, not rebuilt; it needed to be healed, not reconstructed. But the money, the glory, and the photo ops are found in rebuilding and reconstructing, and politicians and business leaders, ever eager for headlines and the quick fix, did not pay much attention to healing. Besides, it's more difficult to repair human relations and more challenging to restore faith than it is to hire consultants who, with their elaborate plans, make it all seem so simple and exciting. Politicians in deeply distressed smaller cities like Buffalo are easily beguiled by the flattery of well-dressed and well-paid architects and consultants. For far too many years, these itinerant hired guns, peddling variations of the same boilerplate solutions, have been eagerly received by a local leadership contingent that should have known better. But they were blinded by the "sizzle" and misled by the grandiose visions of planners, architects, politicians, and developers. As they sat in the glow of these new and always better plans, the city rotted.

Almost daily, it seemed, throughout the 1970s and '80s, the people of Buffalo were assaulted by the horrors of living in a community caught in what appeared to be a relentless and irreversible cycle of decline. Hopes were dashed and illusions shattered, sometimes by what was happening in the city's plants and factories, sometimes by what was happening in the city's streets and neighborhoods. Few events hurt more than the death in February 1987 of Father Joseph Bissonette, a pillar of the community since the early 1960s, who had been one of Buffalo's great crusaders for social justice and interracial harmony. In the early 1980s, Father Bissonette worked at St. Bartholomew's Church on Grider Street, where, with barely a hundred parishioners left in the rapidly changing Fillmore-Leroy neighborhood, he passionately tried to build an interracial ministry.

Bissonette lived in the church rectory for years. Extraordinarily charismatic and a brilliant speaker, he was extremely popular throughout the community, drawing hundreds of people when he was invited to say mass and to speak at churches throughout the diocese. His brother Ray had urged him to move on, to accept an assignment at a larger, more prestigious parish where he would be better situated to reach community decision makers, and where he could encourage them to create the political and social changes necessary for ensuring the well-being of his parish. But Bissonette refused to leave St. Bartholomew's; he stayed on, continuing to minister to his dwindling congregation. He would say mass before a handful of old people who huddled in their coats in the underheated church and who often dozed off before he even got to the sermon. Bissonette rarely left the community (except, Ray remembered with a smile, to fly throughout the country to perform marriage ceremonies for friends who were former priests), and he never accepted his friend Father Jack Weimer's standing invitation to take a vacation in Florida. It wouldn't be appropriate, he politely said, to take a vacation that his parishioners could not afford.[38] Bissonette's concerns extended beyond the boundaries of his parish. In 1979, while working as an intern in Washington, DC, for John LaFalce, a Buffalo-area congressman (and another Canisius alumnus), Bissonette told an interviewer that he'd "never stayed within the narrow concept of church and religion." He said he'd always been interested in the "larger issues." In the early 1980s, Bissonette became increasingly distressed by US intervention in Central America. As president of the board at the Center for Justice in Buffalo, he soon became outspoken in his criticism of American foreign policy in El Salvador. Using the resources at hand, he turned his church into a haven for illegal immigrants and political refugees from El Salvador, Nicaragua, and Honduras who came to the United States and Canada seeking sanctuary.

On a late February night in 1987, Bissonette opened his rectory door to two young men from the neighborhood. Bissonette knew one of them, Ted Simmons, a nineteen-year-old kid who had been to see him several times to talk about the trouble he'd been having at school and at home. Simmons's mother had thrown him out of the house, he said, and he wondered if he and his friend, Milton Jones, a seventeen-year-old from down the street, could come in. Bissonette let them in and showed them to a table in the kitchen. They sat down and waited while he made them sandwiches. Suddenly, one of the boys produced a long hunting knife, cornered the priest, and demanded that he lead them to the rectory's safe. Pocketing barely $200, Simmons and Jones led Bissonette back into the kitchen, bound him to a chair, and gagged him with a pair of his own socks. Grabbing a large can from the kitchen cabinet, Jones smashed Bissonette on the head, knocking him unconscious. Simmons and Jones then passed the hunting knife back and forth between them, stabbing the priest repeatedly in the chest and heart. With Bissonette lying dead on the floor, the two teenagers fled the scene.[39]

The murder of Father Bissonette was announced in bold headlines in the *Buffalo News* the following morning. A well-known and extremely popular priest, Bissonette's death was greeted with shock and horror. Bill Stanton, his old friend and close colleague since their days at Bishop Turner High School, told the press that

Bissonette "was about the best we had." He was, said another, "a priest's priest." To Jack Weimer he was "the most courageous priest I know on any issue." Jim Mang, who had left the priesthood to become director of the Western New York Peace Center, said, "We've lost the most consistently principled priest on peace and justice issues in the diocese of Buffalo."

The police were baffled by the murder and unable to produce a suspect. Two illegal immigrants from Central America who had been staying in Bissonette's church were released after being briefly detained. Then, ten days later, Simmons and Jones knocked on the rectory door at St. Matthew's Church on Wyoming, just a few blocks away from St. Bartholomew's. Monsignor David Herlihy came to the door. Simmons knew Herlihy, too, and told the semiretired priest that his mother had thrown him out of the house. He was wondering, he asked, if he and his friend from the neighborhood could come in. Shortly after, Herlihy was found by another priest, lying dead on the rectory floor, stabbed seventeen times in the chest and heart. Early the next morning, Jones and Simmons were stopped while trying to cross the Peace Bridge to Canada. They were returned to Buffalo, and in 1988 they were tried for murder. Both received sentences of fifty years to life.

Many hoped that the murders of Father Bissonette and Monsignor Herlihy would be the low point for Buffalo, that things would get better because they couldn't get any worse. It was hoped that there might emerge from the sadness that followed in the wake of these horrific murders a new sense of healing, the deep and lasting renewal that so many people in Buffalo desperately longed for. So much had been lost during the 1970s and '80s—the jobs, the neighborhoods, the infrastructure that had for so long provided meaning and support to daily life in the city—and now, when so much was needed, the city's leadership could, as people would soon find out, provide so little.

NOTES

1. "Suburban Enrollment Rises in Buffalo Schools," *Buffalo Evening News*, September 9, 1980.

2. The details on Phase IIIx of *Arthur v. Nyquist* were kept in vertical files, which were stored in Judge Curtin's chambers and filed under "The Remedy Phase." When Curtin finally and formally declared the case concluded in the mid 1990s, these files were removed from Curtin's chambers. While dockets of the case are available from the federal district clerk's office, the materials that made up the daily business of the trial are no longer available.

3. These letters were never introduced in the case and therefore do not appear on the docket. They were kept by Judge Curtin and his clerks in a separate file under the heading "Letters."

4. "Kelly Urges Delay," *Courier Express*, February 11, 1981, p. 12.

5. "Griffin Assails School Pairings," *Courier Express*, February 21, 1981, p. 13.

6. Mozella Richardson, personal communication with the author, June 1989.

7. Curtin's clerk, Michael Brady, took notes at these community meetings. These notes are in the files pertaining to *Arthur v. Nyquist*, which are stored in Curtin's chambers.

8. "Cooperation the Watchword as Bussing Commences," *Courier Express*, September 9, 1981, p. l; "Parents, Students on Board with Bussing," *Buffalo Evening News*, September 8, 1981, p. A1.

9. "Diocese Reports Continued Decline in School Enrollments," *Buffalo Evening News*, September 11, 1981, p. B1.

10. "Further Desegregation Remedies Urged," *Buffalo Evening News*, March 12, 1982.

11. "Education Expert Touts Buffalo Plan," *Buffalo Evening News*, January 14, 1982.

12. See Sondra Astor Stave, *Achieving Racial Balance: Case Studies of Contemporary School Desegregation* (Greenwood, CT: Greenwood, 1995).

13. "Curtin Satisfied with Desegregation Pace," *Buffalo Evening News*, June 16, 1983, p. 1A.

14. Michael Winerip, "School Integration in Buffalo," *New York Times*, May 13, 1985.

15. "John T. Curtin," *Buffalo News Magazine*, January 26, 1988, p. 4.

16. Ibid.

17. "Williams Stresses Problems at Bethlehem," *Buffalo Evening News*, May 22, 1982.

18. "Strength of Buffalo Steel Industry Melting Away," *Buffalo Evening News*, June 14, 1982, p. Al.

19. "Bethlehem to Cease Steelmaking in Lackawanna," *Buffalo News*, December 27, 1982, p. A1.

20. Frank Palumbero, personal communication with the author, November 1988.

21. Alan Marquardt, personal communication with the author, April 1988.

22. United Steel Workers, Brochure, 1964.

23. "Lay-offs at Harrison Take Toll," *Courier Express*, July 17, 1982, p. 12.

24. Ray Hill, "A Year to Forget…" *Buffalo News*, December 1, 1982.

25. M. Beebe, "U.S. Plants Leave the Good-life Behind," *Buffalo News*, March 8, 1987, p. A1.

26. Norman Harper, personal communication with the author, October 1989.

27. International Union of Electrical Workers, *Union Messenger*, April 1986. Copies of this publication were provided to the author by Frank Perry in November 1988.

28. "Workers Fly Flag Upside Down to Signal Distress at Bethlehem, *Buffalo News*, August 17, 1983, p. B1.

29. "Once Mighty Bethlehem Being Reduced to Rubble," *Buffalo Evening News*, March 22, 1988, p. B9.

30. House Committee on Banking, Finance, and Urban Affairs, Hearings on the Housing and Community Development Act, 1977, 95th Cong., lst sess., February 24, 1977, p. 1.

31. Mayor James D. Griffin, personal communication with the author, August 1989.

32. Fred Fadel, former City of Buffalo commissioner for community development, personal communication with the author, February 1990.

33. Irving Korn, CEO, Seneca Development, personal communication with the author, April 1989.

34. For a detailed discussion of the effort to preserve the Guaranty, see Linda Levine and Maria Scrivani, *Beautiful Buffalo: Preserving a City* (Buffalo, NY: Canisius College Press, 2003), pp. 181ff.

35. *Preservation Report* 4, no. 6 (1983): 1–2. The *Preservation Report* can be found in the Grosvenor Collection at the BECPL.

36. *Preservation Report* 7, no. 5 (1986): 6.

37. Hubert Gerstman, former representative to the Amherst town board, personal communication with the author, November 1989.

38. Ray Bissonette, personal communication with the author, April 1989.

39. "Priest Found Slain in Rectory," *Buffalo News*, February 25, 1987, p. 1A.

chapter 13

STRANGE BEDFELLOWS

why Bad Things Happen to Good Cities

By the end of the twentieth century it had become increasingly apparent to community leaders that despite all the efforts that had been made over so many years, nothing, it seemed, could reverse what people saw and understood as the decline of their community. Increasingly frustrated, leaders in both the public and the private sector turned to ever-more desperate measures. In the process, they created new and strange bedfellows for the people of Western New York.

It started with hockey and the effort, beginning in 1990, to save Buffalo's beloved but beleaguered NHL franchise, the Buffalo Sabres. Founded in 1970 by two scions of Buffalo's leading family, Northrup and Seymour Knox III, the Sabres, despite a loyal fan base and a team that flirted perennially with the Stanley Cup, had never made any money. It had become an intolerable situation, even for the loyal Knox Brothers, who over the years had subsidized the team with massive infusions of their family's money. By the early 1990s, the Sabres, with lower than average ticket prices and mounting costs, announced that they were $18 million in the red. Saddled with a WPA-era municipally owned rink known as "the Aud," a place that lacked such state-of-the-art profit centers as luxury suites and box seats, the Knox brothers announced that without a new arena they would have to consider moving the team to another city. What they really wanted was what sports franchises in cities throughout the country were getting: a new arena with lots of room for concessions and as many big-ticket, high-profit luxury suites and seats as possible. Only with a new arena, the Knoxes argued, could the Sabres become profitable.[1]

The community heard the Knoxes loud and clear, and the effort to build a new arena for their team began. It was an effort that revealed a great deal about how money and power were used in Buffalo and Western New York at the end of the twentieth century. By early 1992, the outlines of the deal were crafted: the approximately $120 million required to build a new arena would be raised, as in other cities throughout the nation, by a creative mix of public- and private-sector dollars.

The city was first in line, despite the opposition of Mayor Griffin, who felt the city was "getting a pig in the poke." It promised, through the sale of bonds, to raise $3.5 million to purchase and clear the existing property and to lay the foundations for the new structure.[2] Erie County committed $20 million to the project. The funds would be raised, County Executive Dennis Gorski said (using the vague yet confident speech characteristic of so many politicians), "with some sort of service related tax." New York State followed Erie County when Governor Mario Cuomo said, at the end of 1992, that the state would provide a $25 million "loan" that "would only be repaid in an unlikely set of scenarios." The balance of the money needed for the project, $65 million, would, it was agreed, come from the Knoxes themselves.[3]

By the spring of 1993, however, Governor Cuomo's commitment seemed to be in danger of unraveling, and Seymour Knox, in what he said was a "last-ditch effort," personally went to Albany to lobby for the project. There, in language he would have been reluctant to use in his home town, he told the Western New York delegation in Albany that without the $25 million, "Buffalo will lose the Sabres. ...Come hell or high-water, we will move out of Buffalo.... There are," he said, "plenty of cities out there who want an NHL franchise."[4] Cuomo, shaking off his earlier hesitation, responded quickly. Undaunted by a lawsuit initiated by a statewide citizens group called the "All County Taxpayers' Association," which challenged the legality of using state funds for private enterprises, Cuomo flew to Buffalo and, with much fanfare, announced the state's contribution. The state, he said, "has found some money" for the arena: "It means thousands of jobs and the revitalization of a whole area of a city."[5] The Sabres, meanwhile, continued to bleed money. People began to fear that after sustaining so many years of such large losses, the team would go bankrupt. The prospect of a new arena with no tenant was frightening, and Knox, desperate to salvage his team as well as his dream of building a new arena, turned, according to the *Buffalo News*, to "a cable operator who is willing to pay twenty million dollars for part of the Sabres to keep the financially strapped hockey club afloat during construction of the arena." The timely infusion of funding came from John Rigas and his company, Adelphia Cable, which was quickly and quietly becoming one of the largest cable companies in the country and had been broadcasting Sabres games for almost a year. For Adelphia, like other cable companies that owned sports franchises, the team was the company's "soft ware," a loss leader that enabled Adelphia to sell advertising while at the same time marketing their own highly profitable products, like cell phones, pagers, and Internet access. This, far more than the team's potential for profit, was what captured Rigas's interest in the Sabres. The $20 million he invested in 1994, which represented the amount that the Sabres were projected to lose during the arena's construction, gave Rigas, now the team's largest single owner, a 40 percent stake.

Rigas, the son of Greek immigrants, grew up over his family's Texas Red Hots Restaurant in Wellsville, Pennsylvania. Following his discharge from the armed services, Rigas earned an engineering degree and opened a cable company in Coudersport, Pennsylvania, a small town on the border between New York and Pennsylvania. With more than 1.5 million customers, Adelphia had become, by 1990, the eighth-largest cable company in the nation.

He was happy, he said in 1994, to be able to invest in the Sabres. Sounding like a benign and generous savior, he said that he liked Buffalo: "It is one of the great cities of America." What impressed him most, he explained, was the city's "hardworking people with their great ethnic roots. I hope," he said, "that the people of Buffalo will come to the Rigas Family when they have a charitable cause."

Erland "Erkie" Kailbourne, CEO of Fleet Bank and one of the city's leading power brokers, was a friend of Rigas's from their childhood days in Wellsville. Kailbourne, who came to serve as Rigas's liaison to Buffalo's business establishment, vouched for his old friend. In an attempt to mollify those in Buffalo who were concerned about "Greeks bearing gifts," Kailbourne said that Rigas is "very community minded and he approaches business in the same way. He is," Kailbourne said, urging Buffalonians not to worry; he's "a family person and family values are very important to him. I think it is to Buffalo's benefit that he is becoming involved with the Sabres."[6]

For Seymour and Northrup Knox, however, it was a terrible blow. They recognized that they, unlike their father, who had succeeded in his mission to make his city a great mecca of modern art, had failed to realize their own dreams for Buffalo. By early 1994, it had become clear that the Knox brothers, who out of loyalty, sentiment, and love for their hometown had supported the Sabres for so many years, would soon lose ownership and control of the team they adored. Perhaps, some wondered, their father was right; perhaps there was indeed more to be realized by investing in the arts than in professional sports.

While Rigas was bailing out the hockey team in January 1994, another "angel," Jeremy M. Jacobs, came to the rescue of the foundering efforts to raise private funds for construction of the hockey arena. Jacobs, the richest if not the most powerful businessman in the city, was chairman of the board and CEO of Delaware North Companies, a massive concessionaire, which, valued at $1 billion, was far and away the largest privately owned business in Western New York. There were few deals made in Buffalo that did not in some way come across the desk of Jeremy Jacobs, and it was only a question of time before he became involved with the construction of the new arena. Jacobs was the rainmaker, the man who, far more than the politicians who went along for the usual ride, made the arena deal happen. Jacobs had the most to gain from the construction of the arena, and he knew that there was more than enough money in concessions to justify and guarantee his risk.

By 1994, Delaware North Companies had become a giant. As one of the largest privately owned corporations in the country, it had enormous reach and power. Known as "Sportsystems" until 1980 (when a decade of legal problems forced the company to change its name), Delaware North began in 1915 when three sons of Polish-Jewish immigrants moved to Buffalo and started peddling hot dogs, peanuts, and popcorn at local sporting events and in Delaware Park. Baseball games soon became their specialty. By 1919, they operated the concession stands at Buffalo Bisons games as well as at a ballpark occupied by the Baltimore team of the International League. Under the leadership of Louis Jacobs, the company was awarded its first major league concessions contract in 1927 at Navin Field, home of the Detroit Tigers. More major league deals followed as Jacobs, recognizing the profit in ballpark concessions, made inroads in the sport by lending money to struggling franchises in exchange for guaranteed concessions contracts. Extending the company's reach, Jacobs established a relationship with Bill Veeck who, as owner of several different teams, worked with Jacobs on franchise deals in Milwaukee, Cleveland, St. Louis, and Chicago.[7]

The company began to diversify in the 1930s and '40s, especially into professional hockey and pari-mutuel betting, first as food service providers, then later as the actual owners of the facilities. In 1939, the company received a long-term contract for concessions operations at Washington National Airport. By the early 1940s, the company had expanded its food service business to drive-in movies and racetracks in cities throughout the country. It was usually only a question of time before the food service contracts led to actual ownership. In 1954, for example, the company began running concessions at Magnolia Downs in Louisiana. When that operation came close to bankruptcy several years later, the Jacobses ended up controlling the facility. Bill Veeck later told reporters that "Louie Jacobs would not rise from his chair as a loser."[8]

The 1960s was a decade of dynamic growth for the Jacobses' company beginning with a contract to operate all of the food concessions at the 1960 Olympic Games in Rome. The following year, in an effort to keep the company's owner-ship of racetracks and sports arenas separate from the operation of Sportservice, its concessions wing, Jacobs created the Emprise Corporation. Meanwhile, in 1963, the Jacobs family acquired controlling interests in both the Cincinnati Royals of the NBA and their home court, the Cincinnati Gardens. Emprise's expansion went international as well. During the 1960s, Sportservice became the food concessionaire at England's Royal Ascot Race Track, the New York World's Fair, and the 1967 Montreal Expo. By the time of Louis Jacobs's death in 1968, the company had experienced enormous growth. It had over five hundred operating units and was, with more than $50 million in sales, easily the world's largest food service concessionaire.

Under the leadership of Louis's son Jeremy, Sportsystems grew even bigger. By lending large sums of money to struggling sports teams, the company acquired more concessions rights at a growing number of sports facilities throughout the country. A $2 million loan to the Montreal Expos, a similar deal with the Seattle Pilots, and a $12 million construction loan for the financing of Busch Stadium in St. Louis, resulted in each case in lucrative, multidecade deals for exclusive con-cessions rights.

By the early 1970s, these kinds of deals were coming under the scrutiny of the United States Department of Justice, which was concerned that the company's lending power gave it an unfair edge over other companies in the competition for sports concessions contracts. The Justice Department, besides investigating pos-sible antitrust violation, also began to look into the company's labor union con-tracts. In 1972, the House Committee on Crime began to hold hearings con-cerning Emprise's connection with organized crime figures. An in-depth report published in *Sports Illustrated* in 1972 outlined the case against Emprise. In a long, detailed article in which a photograph of Louis Jacobs was framed by a gallery of mob figures, the authors wrote, "In Washington a congressional committee is con-ducting hearings into the involvement of organized crime in sport. The name heard most is not that of a mobster but a company—Emprise—whose sports investments may exceed that of any company in the world."[9] The article stated that investigations revealed that Louis Jacobs had made interest-free loans in the 1950s to Anthony Zerilli and Jack Tocco, reputed members of the Detroit Mafia. In a related case, Emprise and six others, including Serilli and Michael Polizzi, were convicted of concealing their ownership of the Frontier Hotel and Casino in Las Vegas. In addition, they were found guilty on racketeering charges.

Emprise was forced to give up control of its betting facilities; its dog racing operations in Arizona were placed in trust; and the liquor control authorities in Missouri put the Emprise units operating concessions at Busch Stadium, the St.

Louis Arena, and the Kiel Auditorium into trusteeship. By the end of 1976, the company's fitness to retain its contracts had been challenged in eight of the twenty-eight states in which it held liquor licenses and in six of the nine states in which it had pari-mutuel operations. In 1977, Jeremy Jacobs's plea for a presidential pardon for his company was denied. As a result, a number of states refused to grant Emprise operating licenses in accordance with state laws that denied licenses to convicted felons. Despite this, the company prospered. In 1977, the year its request for a presidential pardon was denied, the company reported that its annual revenues had grown to $275 million. Of that, $125 million came from arena food service, $80 million from recently acquired subsidiaries in steel, smelting, and appliance distribution, and $70 million from eight horse tracks, eight dog tracks, and two jai alai frontons.

In 1980, the name of the parent company was changed from Sportsystems to Delaware North Companies Incorporated. Soon after, Sportservice, the company's concessions subsidiary, tapped into the south Florida leisure market when it acquired the concessions rights for the new Miami Metrozoo. By 1981, the company's revenue from food service alone was $174 million. By the late 1980s, Sportservice had expanded its convention center business, adding more than $50 million in annual revenues to company coffers.

Beginning in the 1990s, Delaware North expanded rapidly in Europe. While it had sold off most of its parking operations in the United States, the company maintained them in Australia and Hungary. Meanwhile, with the purchase of three Australian food companies and the purchase of concessions contracts at two racetracks in Budapest, overseas business flourished. Following the Gulf War in 1991, Delaware North won the contract to provide food and other concessions to firefighters and engineers working in the burned-out oil fields of Kuwait. One year later, Delaware North signed a forty-year contract to provide food and souvenir concessions for the Moscow Circus. Never before had their company motto—"From the earth to the stars and everything in between"—been more apt.[10]

It was only a question of time before Jacobs and Delaware North became involved in Buffalo's hockey arena deal. In January 1994, in a style patented by his father, Jacobs agreed to lend $35 million to the Sabres in return for the exclusive right to all the concessions in the new arena, including operations of a parking lot to be built by Erie County. His loan, along with $25 million promised by M&T Bank, would secure the construction of the arena. Six months later, however, M&T reconsidered its commitment and withdrew from the deal. The withdrawal of M&T was yet another opportunity for Jacobs. With little more than a phone call, he arranged for Fleet Bank, the primary financial backer of his privately owned Fleet Arena in Boston, to take M&T's place. Gail Edwards, Delaware North's treasurer, described the role of Jacobs's company: "We bring to the table introductions to banks and knowledge of how to structure the deals.... We are kind of a marriage broker."[11] By the summer of 1994, while Jacobs was in New York City negotiating to buy Madison Square Garden and with it the New York Knicks, the Rangers, and the Paramount Theatre, the outlines of the Buffalo arena deal were set in place. The new arena, with $10 million from the City of Buffalo, $20 million from Erie County, $25 million from the state, a small amount from HSBC Bank, and the rest from Jacobs and his Boston bankers, would finally be built.

While Rigas and the Knox brothers counted the days until the arena's September 1996 opening, the Sabres, even with the $20 million cash injection from the Rigas family, were desperately short of operating capital. Looking at a debt load they could not carry and a payroll they could barely meet, the Sabres again faced bankruptcy. In February 1996, Rigas came to the rescue, ponying up an additional $6.5 million.

Despite the sale of luxury seats and boxes and a winning team that sold out as much as any team in the NHL, the opening of the new arena, officially called the Marine Midland Arena, could not stem the team's losses. The Sabres had lost $32 million in their last three years at the Aud. After one year at their new arena, they had lost another $4 million (had it not been for the $7 million paid by Marine Midland Bank for naming rights, they would have lost $11 million). Burdened with construction debts in excess of $80 million, the Knox group, which still controlled the team, was choking, desperate, and looking for a way to get out. On January 2, 1998, Sabres president Northrup Knox (his brother Seymour had died of cancer in July 1996) resigned as chairman of the board. With $5 million in cash, $10.5 million more over the next few years, plus the assumption of all debts, John Rigas assumed complete ownership and control of the Buffalo Sabres.[12]

Most observers felt that the fall of the Knoxes was essential for the survival and long-term viability of the team. While some wondered if John Rigas and his sons would have the kind of commitment to Buffalo that had led the Knoxes to pump millions of dollars into their struggling hockey team, the Rigases were nonetheless greeted with a sense of relief and hope that finally the team would be able to realize financial security. "The Rigas Family and Adelphia," the *Buffalo News* said hopefully, "will bring a lot of financial stability to the team and to the entire city."[13] The Sabres, however, continued to lose money. Nothing seemed to have helped: not the $127 million arena with all those moneymaking suites; not the adoring fan base that despite a 17 percent increase in ticket prices still bought enough tickets to sell out two-thirds of all Sabres home games; and not the highly competitive team that made the playoffs three years in a row. Indeed, by season's end in the spring of 1998, the Sabres had lost more than $15 million. In addition, the arena, built as both a life preserver for the hockey team and a cornerstone for the city's waterfront development efforts, also lost money. The Rigases, crushed by the $80 million debt burden they had inherited from the Knoxes, ran more than three months behind on their arena rent. In the spring of 1999, they announced that they wanted a new arena lease, Rigas said, like the one the Bills had recently signed for the use of Ralph Wilson Stadium. Like savvy sports franchise owners nationwide, the Rigases wanted a lease where the public assumed all of the costs while the team enjoyed all of the revenues.[14]

Ralph C. Wilson Jr., the owner of the Buffalo Bills since the team's inception in 1960, and the only owner of an AFL franchise who had kept his team in its original city, had by the mid-1990s become restless. Though a multimillionaire from Detroit, Wilson was considered a "good" team owner and a man loyal to Buffalo. Under his ownership, the Bills had been among the more successful franchises in the league. During the mid-1970s and then again twenty years later, when the team went to an unprecedented four consecutive Super Bowls, the Bills almost yearly led the NFL in attendance figures and gate receipts. For the first twelve years of the franchise's history, the Bills, led by O. J. Simpson, had played at the War Memorial Stadium, a WPA-vintage all-purpose outdoor stadium endearingly called "The Rock Pile." By the early 1960s, the Rock Pile was doomed by both its age and its location at Jefferson and Best, in the heart of the African American East Side. To replace it, Wilson lobbied hard for the construction of a massive, state-of-the-art domed stadium in suburban Lancaster. (While some hoped the new stadium would be built on the city's waterfront, Lancaster was the first choice of the people who mattered.) The domed stadium project, riddled from the beginning with talk of scandal and projected construction costs of more than $60 million, was soon dropped and replaced with a far more modestly priced open-air stadium to be built in suburban Orchard Park. Built in 1972, Rich Stadium, named for the Rich family of Rich Products fame and paid for with $22 million from Erie County was, with more than eighty thousand seats, one of the largest in the NFL. It became the scene of the glory days of Buffalo Bills football, the home to die-hard fans who rarely failed to fill the massive stadium week in and week out during the long, cold months of Buffalo's football season.

Rich Stadium was owned and operated by Erie County, whose lease with the Bills was due to expire at the end of 1998. Wilson, everybody knew, was anxious not so much about his team but, rather, about the ability of Buffalo and Western New York to support it. In early 1997, as negotiations for a new lease with the county were about to begin, Wilson seemed ready to throw in the towel. No, he said, in an interview with the *Buffalo News*, he would not, as some had whispered, take the team to Toronto. But he hinted that Cleveland, which had just recently lost the Browns, was beckoning. In a long and rambling interview, Wilson groused about the local economy and expressed the proverbial complaints about taxes and the "high cost of doing business" in Western New York. Besides, he said, ticket sales for the 1997–1998 season were not going well. Wondering out loud in a rare interview, Wilson thought that perhaps the problem was not with the team, which had had so many winning seasons, but rather with Buffalo. "We've had no enthusiasm for ticket sales nor," he added, "anything else." "I don't know" he bemoaned, "what people here are focusing on." He did know, however, that they were "not focusing on the Bills."[15] After more than thirty years and four failed Super Bowl attempts, he seemed fed up. Why couldn't Buffalo be more like the rest of the country, Wilson pouted: "Everywhere I go things are growing, I can't believe the building that is going on in Denver, Florida, San Jose...." He was angry and upset: "We're at a big disadvantage in Buffalo. Who's going to come here and do any promotions with us?" Would Wilson, like Cleveland's notorious Art Modell, just pick up and leave? Would he, too, succumb to the temptation of what people said was a "relocation fee" of more than half a billion dollars? Or could he, somehow, be convinced to stay? Whether he was serious about Cleveland or simply bluffing in the hope of driving a hard bargain with New York State and Erie County, his comments and the suggestion that he might move the beloved Bills out of Buffalo led to the crafting of a new lease for the Bills. Worked out by Wilson, Governor George E. Pataki, and Erie County executive Dennis Gorksi, an outline of the new lease was announced to the public in July 1997.[16]

Like football owners throughout the country, Wilson wanted to tap the potential revenue of club suites and luxury seats. Unlike revenue from ticket sales, 40 percent of which had to be shared with the visiting team, proceeds from the sales of suites and boxes were considered "non-shared revenue," all of which went directly to the home team. While he wanted the proceeds from the sale of club suites and luxury seats, Wilson did not want the expense of building them. Predictably he turned to the state for help. This was the kind of deal Pataki, like Cuomo before him, loved. Besides, Pataki considered Wilson a friend. "Ralph," he said, "has proven that loyalty and commitment are not outdated ideals that are easily tossed aside." It was time, the governor said, for the state to reciprocate. In July 1997, Pataki said that New York State would contribute the $63 million needed to build the seventy-eight hundred club seats and seventy-six luxury boxes that Wilson wanted and said he needed.[17]

Erie County, under the leadership of Dennis Gorski, was next in line. Gorski promised that the county, using funds raised from a new "sin tax" on alcohol and tobacco, would cover all game-day expenses, including overtime pay for county police, for a total annual contribution of $3 million. The total package that had been created for Wilson consisted of more than $123 million in public funds over the five-year life of the lease. The deal was, according to a letter to the *Buffalo News*, "the stuff that business people fantasize about. Somebody else pays a lot of your expenses and you keep all of the profits."[18]

It wasn't over yet, however. Though thankful for the efforts of Pataki and Gorski, Wilson would not commit to the terms of the lease without a commitment from the people of Western New York first. It was a hard bargain. He insisted that he would not sign the contract unless not less than five years' worth of luxury suites and club seats—$11 million in tickets—were sold in advance. In the fall of 1997, he set a deadline for their sale: December 1, 1998.

It seemed at first that Wilson's goal was unrealistic, that perhaps he had been right about a local economy that simply did not have the corporate muscle to buy the suites and boxes that would make his already profitable team still more profitable. By midsummer of 1998, with Wilson's December deadline looming, the Bills were less than halfway toward their goal. Sensing that it now appeared more likely than not that Wilson would take his team and leave, "Erkie" Kailbourne summoned area business leaders and formed a group called "Business Backs the Bills." Often referred to in almost mythic language—alternatively described as "tireless," "dynamic," "heroic," and "magical"—Kailbourne organized and orchestrated a region-wide sales effort to save the Bills. Recalling the frantic yet successful effort in 1900 to bring the Pan-American Exposition to Buffalo, Erkie vowed, in increasingly Churchillian terms to bring "victory" to Buffalo ("As long as I have air in my lungs," he said in one speech, "I am going to fight to keep the Bills here").

The press, particularly the *Buffalo News*, fanned the flames, printing daily updates and countdowns in the paper. Under headlines that read "Touchdown Seat Sales Reach Goal," "Last Chance Running Out," and "White Knight Sought to Close Gap," the *News*, with the frenzy of a wartime bond drive, led the cheers. Everybody who was anybody in the business community signed on and became cheerleaders in an ever-more melodramatic effort to save the Bills and thereby save the city. To some, having a suite at Rich Stadium "was about networking." It was "like having every country club member in Buffalo and every business club in Buffalo in the same place. There is a tremendous networking opportunity there for ten days a year." To most people, however, the Bills were about more than networking. Indeed, the effort to keep the Bills had transcended concerns about sport and entertainment; maintaining the Bills as a Buffalo institution was essential, it seemed, to the well-being and stability of the communal psyche. The Bills were part of the culture of the community, and to many the Bills *were* Buffalo, a critical part of the landscape of people's daily lives, a balm for the easily hurt and long-disappointed hopes and aspirations of a sad and wounded community. Letters filled the *Buffalo News* during those months in late 1998 when the community rallied to help Ralph Wilson, thereby keeping the Bills in Buffalo. People wrote that the Bills "are what make us great" and that "they ... make us feel like a major-league town." "If the Bills moved," one fan said, "I think a lot of people would be lost." Unable to fathom life without the Bills, one *News* correspondent asked readers to "think about what it's like between seasons here." It was inconceivable, therefore, that the region, which had lost so much for so many years, would have allowed the Bills to leave no matter how one-sided the deal was.[19]

To seal the deal, and to make sure no stone was left unturned, Erkie Kailbourne prevailed on Stanford Lipsey, the president and publisher of the *Buffalo News*, to lure the paper's owner, Warren Buffett, to Buffalo. Buffett rarely came to Buffalo, and never on public missions. But when the Bills called in September 1998, Buffett listened. He was more aware than anybody of the close relationship between the success of the Bills and the profitability of his newspaper (newspaper sales more than doubled on the Mondays following a victory by the Bills). With profits at stake, Buffet decided to make the trip to Buffalo. While the four hundred people invited to hear him speak were far more interested in his views on the stock market, Buffett limited his comments to a pep talk about the Bills. "They are an under-priced asset to the citizens of Buffalo," he said. Urging reluctant corporations to join the drive to buy the boxes and save the team, Buffett exhorted: "You're getting a bargain. Don't pass it up."[20] While Buffett's visit helped, Kailbourne, with less than a week left on Wilson's deadline, was still $300,000 short. In heroic, almost superhuman terms, the *News* described him sweeping across Western New York from Rochester to Jamestown in a sleepless, last-ditch mission to close the deal. Finally, on December 2, 1998, one day past the deadline, Kailbourne announced "the miracle" that so many had doubted would ever happen. The premium seats had all been sold and the $11 million had been raised. State and county funds would be released, the stadium would be remodeled, and, most important of all, the Bills would stay in Buffalo.

While some complained that the deal was bad for Buffalo (in his run for governor in 1998, Tom Golisano said that Governor Pataki's proposed deal with the Bills "[was] a disgraceful example of corporate welfare... the super bowl of mismanagement"), most people, it seemed, were satisfied that as long as the Bills stayed, it was a good deal for Buffalo. Fans were happy that the Bills would be around for at least another five years, and nothing else seemed to really matter.[21] Few people paid much attention to the details of the deal and fewer still questioned it (certainly not the political and community leaders who had championed it). Indeed, unlike so many other public projects, which generated enormous public discussion and debate, there was none on the subject of the new Bills lease. The fact was that as far as these kinds of deals went, Buffalo's contribution was fairly modest. With the state assuming close to $100 million of the total $128 million package, the city got off relatively easily when compared to the price other communities paid to keep and attract NFL teams. Besides, it was said, Wilson didn't *have* to stay at all. Other owners, lured by relocation fees in excess of half a billion dollars, would likely have left without thinking twice. But

Ralph Wilson was lauded as a different kind of owner. Indeed, shortly after the lease was signed, Wilson, who chose not to sell the naming rights to the stadium, agreed with his friend Governor Pataki's suggestion to have the newly rehabbed stadium named after him.

Some, particularly some of the reporters who had been covering the Bills for years, saw through the mist of vanity that enshrouded the deal. "This is what you get," wrote the *News*'s, Jerry Sullivan on December 12, 1998,

> when you hold all the cards and play them to the hilt. The Buffalo Bills owner strong armed business and avid fans into forking over eleven million dollars for expensive club seats and luxury suites before agreeing to keep the team in town for the next five years. Plus he gets sixty three million in improvements for his football team's stadium and a three million dollar handout from the State each year. He alone gets all the revenue from the parking and concessions and lets Erie County pick up operating and game day expenses. The fact that it is only a five year reprieve got lost in the frenzied campaign to sell eleven million dollars a year in premium seating. Five years? It hurts to admit it, but that tells you how little faith Ralph Wilson has in this community and its rusty, broken down economy. That's how little clout the supplicants from county and state government had over him at the bargaining table.

"Wilson is," Sullivan concluded, "a nice enough man but we're at a time in sports when sheer economic forces can blow away the best human intentions. I'm glad he's obligated to stay at least five more years but this thing is far from over. Have the parade while the joy is still fresh because we'll be anguishing about it again before you know." In December 1998, David Robinson, another *News* reporter who had followed the story of the Bills and their new lease since the mid 1990s, also wondered about Wilson's motivations: "By driving a hard bargain Wilson goes from being the owner of a profitable team to being the owner of a fabulously profitable team."[22]

People loved their Bills, however, and despite the doubts, they accepted the deal. They knew it was corporate welfare; they knew that it meant less money for schools, the arts, and the long list of other underfunded programs and activities; but they didn't care. It didn't matter that the actual economic contribution of the Bills or of professional sports activity in general was insignificant in the life of the total regional economy. It didn't matter that based on an average manufacturing salary of around $40,000, the Bills generated no more economic impact than a manufacturing plant with four hundred ninety employees. None of it mattered. What did matter was that the Bills were staying. The people wanted it that way, and they got what they wanted. Perhaps sometime in the future it would be different, and a new generation of Buffalonians would make different choices and demand a different set of priorities. But those days, at the end of the twentieth century, were nowhere in sight.[23]

What was good enough for Ralph Wilson was good enough for John Rigas. During the summer of 1998, Rigas sought a new hockey arena deal that would give him Wilsonian perks and benefits. He was willing, he said, to give in order to get; in October 1998, the Rigases announced that they would join with Buffalo's Benderson Development Company and the Cordish Company of Baltimore to develop Buffalo's Inner Harbor (Mayor Anthony M. Masiello was fond of referring to Benderson, Cordish, and Adelphia as his "Dream Team"). It wasn't exactly clear what they were going to build—there was talk, as always, of a "family entertainment center," and the Cordish Company, who had brought Barnes and Noble and an ESPN "Sports Zone" to Baltimore's Inner Harbor, said that they could do the same for Buffalo. To Masiello, always desperate for downtown development, it was enough that they said they would do something. The Rigases, unlike their partners on the Dream Team, were more specific about their contribution. Their plan was to build a complex near the new arena, which would include 200,000 square feet of office space, 120,000 square feet of retail space, a 40,000-square-foot television studio, a fifty-bed hotel, and three practice hockey rinks. The Rigases promised in October 1998 to do all of this with their own money.[24] Masiello was ebullient, as if he had finally found the solution to all of his city's problems. When he officially announced the Dream Team in March 1999, the mayor urged the people of Buffalo to believe with him that the project would come to fruition: "It is in our collective best interests in the public sector," he said, "to do whatever we can to help them succeed because clearly they are presenting us with a great opportunity for real jobs and real economic growth."[25] The *Buffalo News* believed in the dream, too, and was quick to praise the Mayor's announcement despite its absence of details. "For now," a *News* editorial crowed, "it is enough to dream. But by putting those dreams in the right hands, local leaders have moved waterfront renovation one more welcome step closer to reality."[26] Despite the mayor's assurances about jobs, the Dream Team plan was still vague at best. Would Cordish build a Hard Rock Café or a Sports Zone? Would the Bendersons, who specialized in building strip malls and enormous gas stations, bring their questionable trademark to the city's waterfront, too? Of the various components of this pipe dream for the development of Buffalo's waterfront, only the Rigases' promise appeared to have substance. "It is not speculative," the mayor assured anybody who might have doubted, "because Adelphia is going to be the tenant."[27]

Meanwhile, Adelphia had gobbled up cable companies all over the country. In February 1999 alone, the company made two massive acquisitions; it bought both Frontier Vision Partners of Denver and Century, two of the largest cable companies in the country. By paying $550 million in cash for the former and $5.2 billion in cash for the latter, Adelphia, which now boasted 4.7 million cable subscribers, seemed invincible. As a result, the company, at least in the eyes of the city's business and political establishment, became the goose that would soon lay the golden egg in the city's Inner Harbor. John Rigas, already the savior of the Sabres and the go-to guy on waterfront development, was beyond reproach. In that February of frenzied buying, John Rigas took time out to receive St. Bonaventure University's prestigious Gaudette Medal, which honors business and community leaders "who exemplify the joyful spirit of St. Francis in their service to mankind."²⁸

Rigas's commitment, however, was expressly contingent on renegotiating the Sabres's arena lease. The arena, since the Hong-Kong Shanghai Banking Corporation's acquisition of Marine Midland Bank, was by then called HSBC Arena (according to a joke then circulating in Buffalo, the acronym really meant "Holy Shit the Bank's Chinese"). Insisting that the arena was costing the team more than $15 million a year, the Rigases demanded a quid pro quo that would provide them with the same kind of hold-harmless clauses that Wilson had negotiated for the Bills. By this time, however, all the key players in Western New York were on board. Everybody seemed to believe the mayor's ever-growing projections for the new jobs that the Adelphia project would create (the estimates had grown from twelve hundred to three thousand by the fall of 1999), and all the players —the business establishment, the banks, the Niagara Partnership (the recently changed named of the former Chamber of Commerce), the *Buffalo News*, the mayor, and a unanimous Common Council—were ready to work together to make the Adelphia deal happen. Meanwhile, the Dream Team's plans seemed to have become more concrete.

According to the cheerleading mayor, the plan consisted of a $160 million investment that would include a thirty-story office building to house Adelphia's corporate headquarters, dozens of apartments, a hotel, and a strip of shops, restaurants, and retail centers. For the hopeful mayor, the building would be a symbol, "a statement," he said, "that there will be a future in Buffalo."²⁹ In addition, the mayor promised that the old Aud would be converted into a six-level complex with still more retail, restaurants, and "a Cineplex" (this despite the reality that downtown's one movie theater could barely stay alive, and the handful of restaurants and retail operations, consisting of wig shops, sneaker stores, and a jewelry store called The King of Diamonds, were little better off). For Masiello, the crown jewel of the project was a planned "water wall," which would be two hundred feet wide and fifty feet tall. Referring to plans to project video images on the "water wall," Masiello said, "We feel that it is important to create a lot of sizzle here."³⁰

In April 2000, all the details of the deal had been set in place. The state, county, and city together committed more than $133 million in taxpayer funding for the project. The biggest sum came from the state, with Pataki promising a donation of $98 million in the form of a $50 million outright grant to build the new office building and another $48 million to pay off the existing loans that the Rigases had assumed from the Knoxes. In a deal similar to the one it struck with the Bills, the county promised the Sabres $1 million a year as an operating subsidy. In addition, the county relinquished its claims to an arena seat tax that had generated close to $300,000 a year in income. There was more: the county would build, at a cost of $12 million, a new parking lot for the project. The city, meanwhile, had its own role to play, and promised to forgo $500,000 of ground rent the Sabres owed. In addition, at an estimated cost of $15 million, the city would deliver to Adelphia an "environmentally clean shovel ready site" for their new office building.[31]

Within a year of Governor Pataki's April 2001 announcement of the deal's consummation, Adelphia's communications empire seemed to be crumbling. Rigas reported in April 2001 that the company had lost more than $600 million in 2000 and that losses would continue well into 2001. Seemingly alone among public officials, James Pitts, the president of Buffalo's Common Council, was concerned. "I am very worried about Adelphia's financials," he told the *Buffalo News* that same month. "When you look at their losses you have to be concerned."[32] Masiello, oblivious to any reality that could tarnish his increasingly desperate hope for the revival of his city, seemed not to notice. By this time, he, like Governor Pataki, had directed his attention toward efforts to bring to Buffalo the strangest and potentially the most corrupt bedfellows that the city had ever slept with: the Seneca Nation of Indians.

From their first contact with French missionaries to their utter defeat at the hands of the new Americans, the natives of the Seneca Nation had been beaten in war and, in peace, stripped of their dignity and their land. Caught off guard by history, the Senecas were punished terribly for having chosen the wrong side in the American Revolution. In 1799, General Washington, whose name in the Seneca language was "Town Destroyer," had ordered the notorious General Sullivan to "cut a swatch of terror" west of the Niagara Frontier. Sullivan did his job well. By the end of the American Revolution there was little left of the ancestral Seneca homeland in the Genesee River Valley. A few people struggled to survive on the ruins of their old lands, but most were dispersed. Some crowded into the undamaged settlements; many more, seeking food and protection, camped in flimsy cabins on the banks of the Niagara River, near the British-controlled Fort Niagara on Lake Ontario. By 1800, the Seneca Nation's villages had been destroyed and its population had diminished to fewer than three thousand. They reeled from the tidal wave of change: their bodies had been poisoned by alcohol; they had been misled by drunk, unreliable, and easily bribed leaders; and they had been deceived by state legislators in cahoots with voracious, land-grabbing speculators. Weakened and demoralized past the point of resistance, the Seneca acquiesced to forced relocation to ten reservations west of the Genesee River.

The War of 1812 and the opening of the Erie Canal dealt a further blow to any hopes the Senecas had for the survival of their ancestral ways in Western New York. Following yet another disastrous treaty, this one in 1848, the Seneca's territory in New York State was reduced yet again, this time to three small reservations on the Niagara Frontier: Cattaraugus, Allegheny, and a settlement surrounding a small body of water called Cuba Lake. By 1850, the Buffalo Creek Reservation, located at the fringes of the growing city of Buffalo, was abandoned and cleared for development; it soon became a part of Buffalo. That the Senecas had once been major actors in the city's history was mostly forgotten by the time the Senecas returned to the scene a hundred fifty years later with the advent of casino gaming in Western New York.

By the end of the 1990s, a handful of businessmen from the impoverished Seneca Nation had figured out a way to profit from the addictions of white people who trekked by the thousands to the Cattaraugus Reservation, just thirty-five miles south of Buffalo. Because it was a sovereign nation, no sales taxes were collected at reservation business establishments. This state of affairs encouraged area whites to shop on the reservations. Every year, Western New Yorkers bought millions of dollars worth of cheap gasoline and cigarettes from Seneca retailers at the expense of off-reservation, tax-paying businesses. Both Governor Cuomo and Governor Pataki made periodic but weak attempts to collect sales tax revenue from the Senecas. However, citing their claim to Indian sovereignty, the Senecas refused to pay the state sales tax. Instead, they threatened to use violence and, perhaps more significantly, they threatened to withdraw the funding they supplied to campaigning politicians. In this way, they convinced both governors to back down.

However, in 1997, under pressure from both the owners of gas stations and convenience stores (who bitterly resented the unfair competition) and state legislators (who were eager to capture the nearly $50 million in annual sales tax revenue that Seneca sales would generate), Pataki started to talk tough, insisting that the Indians pay taxes on any sales made to non-Indians. Scott Snyder, a Seneca firebrand, whose father Barry was one of the nation's most successful tobacco and gasoline merchants, warned that "Pataki is dangerously close to his first Indian war."[33] When Indian demonstrations threatened to spin out of control, Pataki, who had seemed so resolute, backed down. In May 1997, in a speech delivered before the Buffalo and Erie County Historical Society, Pataki announced that he had changed his mind. Instead of collecting state sales taxes from the Senecas, he instead planned to propose the repeal of all state regulations that mandated the collection of taxes on sales by Indians to non-Indians. The governor, who as recently as April of that year had dispatched state police to stop the entrance of delivery trucks with no tax certificates to the reservation, said, "Let me make my message to all Indian nations clear...it is your land. We respect your sovereignty. ...You will have the right to sell tax free gas and cigarettes free from interference from New York State." It was, wrote *News* correspondent Agnes Palazetti, who had been covering Indian affairs for the paper for years, "an utter, complete and abrupt about-face."[34] Wrapping himself in the blanket of Indian sovereignty, Pataki surrendered to the Indians without a fight, seduced not by wampum and alcohol, like the Senecas of old, but by the far more seductive drug of casino gambling.

The temptations of casino gambling in the Buffalo area became increasingly difficult to resist. News from reservations all over the country showed that casino gambling was beginning to pay big dividends. The first indications came from Foxwoods, a casino that the Pequot Indians opened on their reservation in central Connecticut in 1992. In 1994, Foxwoods, with its $400 million in annual profit on approximately $800 million in gross sales, was judged by industry analysts as the "most profitable casino in the world." On the July Fourth weekend of that year, 164,000 people came to Foxwoods and left behind more than $40 million. By the mid-1990s, more than fifteen thousand gamblers per day went to Foxwoods, which, with its forty-five hundred employees and an annual payroll of $100 million, had become Connecticut's leading tourist destination and the largest casino in the world. In New York State, Turning Stone, a casino on the Oneida reservation near Syracuse, had more than two thousand people on its payroll, and had become the largest employer in Central New York. And while Turning Stone shared none of its profits with New York State, it was responsible for more than $30 million per year in contracts with area vendors. Under the leadership of Ray Halbritter, a Harvard-educated Oneida who by the mid-1990s had assumed almost mythical status among Indian tribes throughout the country, the Oneida seemed to be on the verge of an unprecedented economic boom. By 1998, the Oneida had bought back more than seven thousand acres of what was considered their aboriginal land. They had also acquired a growing empire of tourist attractions that included hotels, golf courses, a convention center, numerous gas stations and convenience stores, and a pyrotechnic factory that manufactured flame-retardant suits for the motor sports industry. In 1998, Hulbritter diversified his holdings still more with the purchase of one of the oldest Indian newspapers in the country, *Indian Country Today*, which was published in South Dakota. In speaking engagements with tribes all over the country, Halbritter boasted that all Oneidas had health insurance and one hundred twenty had enrolled at four-year colleges. In 1998, Halbritter began to spread the wealth. Announcing that the Oneida no longer needed their annual $2.6 million tribal allocation from the federal government, he gave it to other tribes: $640,000 to the Mohawks, $450,000 for the creation in upstate New York of an Urban Indian Service Center, $800,000 to be divided among the nations of the Southwest, and, for his fellow Iroquois, the Seneca of the Niagara Frontier, $640,000.[35]

Who could resist the lure of casino gambling? Not Pataki, who knew just how generous the Indians were at campaign time; not the state's large and extremely influential gambling lobby; not the business leaders among the Seneca who never saw a tax-free business deal they did not like; and certainly not Anthony Masiello, the mayor of Buffalo. On June 21, 2001, all of these forces came together when Pataki, in a last-minute visit to Niagara Falls, New York, that surprised not only the press but the mayors of both Niagara Falls and Buffalo, announced against the majestic backdrop of the falls that he had signed a "memorandum of understanding" with the Seneca Nation of Indians that would bring casinos to both Buffalo and Niagara Falls. In the *Buffalo News*'s coverage of the event (much more a "photo op" than a press conference), reporters Tom Precious and Andrew Galarneau stated that the governor had announced that three Seneca-owned casinos would be built in Western New York: one in Niagara Falls, one on the Cattaraugus Reservation, and the third in downtown Buffalo. They reported that the plan the governor presented offered "few details." Indeed, Pataki left much unsaid. Yes, he said, he knew that any formal compact with the Senecas had to be approved not only by the Senecas themselves but also by the state legislature. He also knew that Indian gaming could not go forward without the approval of the Department of Interior. But these insignificant obstacles, he suggested in an offhand manner, would be easy to overcome. He made no effort to provide the details of the agreement nor did he shed any light on how, if at all, revenue from the casino would be shared with the host cities. And while he did say that the casino in Niagara Falls would be housed temporarily in the city's convention center, he offered no idea as to where in Buffalo the Seneca casino would be located.[36] While the devil may well have been in the details, the mayors of the two cities affected by the compact—Buffalo's Anthony Masiello and Niagara Falls' Irene Elia—were too elated to care. For Masiello, who had been addicted to casino gambling as an economic development strategy for years, and for Elia, whose impoverished city according to the *New York Times* made Buffalo "look like Paris," the deal was too good to be true. It was, said Mayor Elia, "a day that the Lord hath made. Let us rejoice and be glad."[37]

It quickly became apparent that there was far more to Pataki's gambling initiative than the mere construction of the three casinos. Thanks to hefty lobbying efforts of race track owners, the bill permitted the tracks to install ersatz slot machines called "video lottery terminals" (VLTS). In addition, the bill made it legal for New York State residents to participate in a multimillion-dollar, multistate lottery called Power Ball. Despite the magnitude and complexity of the legislation and the fact that some lawmakers were "upset that the Pataki Administration was dropping on their desks such a major issue with so few details," Pataki's gambling bill, with no debate or discussion, passed the Senate just one day after Pataki's Niagara Falls press conference.

In early September of that year, Pataki buried his complex gambling proposal in the fine print of a quickly constructed post-9/11 budget bill. So disguised, it easily passed the Assembly with little comment or examination. Several months later, Tom Precious, the *Buffalo News*'s Albany correspondent, who had been following the tortuous legislative history of gambling for years, revealed how such a controversial bill, one so fraught with significance for the state of New York and the City of Buffalo, had passed so easily. In an article written in February 2002 titled "Lobbying at Epic Level to Glorify Gambling,"[38] Precious called attention to the intense and generously funded lobbying effort that had led to the passage of the gambling bill. The Senecas had taken no chances, and following the advice of their Buffalo-based *consigliere*, former chairman of the Erie County Democratic Party, Joseph Crangle, they retained Aiken-Gump, one of Washington, DC's most politically connected law firms and lobbying companies, to handle their interests in Albany. Aiken-Gump, a firm that, according to its Web site, saw "litigation as strategy," represented, in addition to the Senecas, some of the largest and most powerful corporations in the nation. Under the leadership of one of its partners, L. William Paxon, a former Republican congressman from Buffalo and a close friend of Pataki, Aiken-Gump had raised hundreds of thousands of dollars for George W. Bush's presidential campaign in 2000. Now, working with Crangle, Paxon became Aiken-Gump's point man for Pataki's omnibus gambling bill. Joining Paxon on the case was another Aiken-Gump partner named Barry Brandon, an Oklahoma Creek, who, prior to coming to Aiken-Gump, had been the chief of staff of the Indian Gaming Commission, the federal agency that regulated Indian gambling operations. Crangle, however, sought still more muscle to help secure passage of the bill and, in the summer of 2001, he urged the Senecas to retain the expert lobbying services of Patricia Lynch, who, following her years of service as the top aide to Assembly Speaker Sheldon Silver (in the revolving-door fashion so commonplace in state and local politics), had opened an Albany-based lobbying firm of her own. Because there were few people who knew better how to grease the wheels in Albany, Lynch's company, whose roster of clients also included the Off Track Betting Corporation, grew to become the most lucrative lobbying firm in Albany. In 2002, she was retained by the Buffalo Niagara Partnership to be its Albany lobbyist at an annual cost of $50,000 plus expenses.[39]

By the end of the 1990s, Governor Pataki, increasingly blinded by the promise of casino gambling, recognized that by linking casino gambling to economic development he could trump the charge that he cared little about Western New York's economy. He also realized that his bill would raise cash for his reelection campaign. Few issues attracted more big spenders, both pro and con, than casino gambling. Nobody had spent more than the Connecticut Pequots, who, in 1994, gave more than $315,000 to the National Democratic Party, a contribution that earned the CEO of the tribe, a man named "Skip" Harper, the right to sleep in the Clintons' White House Lincoln Bedroom. Albany politicos, too, benefited from the largesse of casino interests. An article titled "Casino Interests Pour Money into Albany," written by the muckraking Precious in August 1998, documented some of the action in Albany. One company, known as G-Tech, ran the lottery for Rhode Island and stood to lose out if a casino opened in New York. In 1998, G-Tech gave Republican Senate Majority Leader Joseph Bruno, a long-standing opponent of casino gambling, and Assembly Speaker Sheldon Silver, a supporter, each a gift of $10,000. Another particularly generous lobbyist in 1998 was G. Michael "Mickey" Brown, the one-time CEO of Foxwoods who owned his own gambling company called Manhattan Cruises and was soon to be designated the chief point man for the Senecas at their casinos in Western New York. Manhattan Cruises operated a 32,000-ton cruise ship anchored at Sheepshead Bay in Brooklyn; it was a floating casino, which, according to Brown, "provided an overnight cruise experience with casino gambling in international waters." Brown, who did business with big casino operators all over the world, needed to protect his options in New York. He, too, gave Senator Bruno $10,000 in 1998.[40]

Because Native Americans, as members of a sovereign nation, are exempt from lobbying restrictions, the Senecas were able to spend lavishly. In their effort to secure the passage of Pataki's gambling bill, they made payments of more than $448,000 to Albany politicians in 2001, more than any other group or individual. Others were almost as generous. In their successful effort to ensure that they would not be left out of the Seneca casinos, the Hotel Employees and Restaurant Employees Union spent more than $170,000. Another big spender was Park Place Entertainment, the world's largest casino company. Eager to expand into new territory, Park Place spent $381,000 on lobbying and $36,000 in direct contributions to state officeholders. Meanwhile, Delaware North, the huge entertainment company owned by the Jacobs family of Buffalo, spent a total of $223,000 on lobbying and on direct contributions in 2001. Despite their size and ambition, Jacobs and Delaware North continued to worry about their smaller holdings. They were concerned that Finger Lakes, their racetrack in upstate New York, was losing money, and they hoped for the passage of Pataki's gambling bill, which would allow track owners to install video slot machines. With this in mind, Delaware North spent close to $300,000 on lobbying in 2001, with $25,000 going directly to Pataki. The New York Racing Association got in on the act, too, spending $444,000 in lobbying and direct donations. In 2001 alone, in their efforts to keep him "honest," companies, organizations, and individuals with an interest in legalized gambling gave $355,000 directly to Pataki. With outrage and dismay, Precious wrote that "the money came from blue-blood families of the thoroughbred racing industry, makers of lottery equipment, lawyers for the Senecas, Las Vegas casino interests, unions hoping to be in on future gambling halls and a host of Western New York firms and individuals with eyes on betting ventures."[41]

Before Pataki's dream of Indian-owned casinos in Niagara Falls and Buffalo could be realized, however, the Senecas themselves and, ultimately, the United States Department of the Interior would have to be convinced. Relying on his powerful allies on the reservation and his close connections with the Bush administration, Pataki worried about neither. For many years, the Seneca Nation of approximately sixty-five hundred people had been evenly split on the subject of casino gambling: it was opposed by a group calling themselves "Traditionalists" and supported by a group known as "the Businessmen." During the 1990s, control of the Nation seesawed between these two factions. As the casino referendum approached, the businessmen had established tentative control. None of these men was more successful than Barry Snyder. Snyder, who began his operations in the early 1980s with a lone hot dog stand on the Cattaraugus Reservation, had, ten years later, parlayed this into a full-service restaurant, a construction company, an industrial equipment rental company, and several gas stations and convenience stores. The various entities all operated under the name Seneca Hawk. From the beginning, Snyder tried the patience of the state. In 1987, he set up thirty video gambling devices in his restaurant and stores. When his businesses were raided and his gambling devices confiscated, Snyder hired Buffalo's leading criminal defense lawyer, Paul Cambria, to represent him. Five years later, as Albany prepared another attempt to crack down on the tax-free tobacco and gasoline businesses on the reservation, Snyder, who announced that "the word 'tax' is not in our Seneca language because it is detrimental to our survival as a sovereign nation," hired Joe Crangle, the former chairman of the Erie County Democratic Party. Snyder hoped that Crangle's influence in Albany would guarantee that no Indian sales tax bill would ever be passed.[42]

Another leader of the businessmen's faction that favored casino gambling was Cyrus Schindler. Like many Senecas his age, Schindler was a retired ironworker. And like Snyder, his friend and business associate, Schindler was the successful owner of a restaurant, smoke shop, and gas station on the Cattaraugus Reservation called the Smoke Signal Café. When state tax officials attempted to collect sales tax on the Cattaraugus Reservation in 1997, Schindler's resistance led to his arrest. When Schindler was elected president of the Seneca Nation in 2000, he installed in his office an "Indian" version of Mt. Rushmore that showed the heads of Chief Joseph, Sitting Bull, Crazy Horse, and Geronimo in place of Washington, Jefferson, Lincoln, and Roosevelt.

There is nothing merely titular about being president of the Seneca Nation, and Schindler used his power persuasively. With approximately sixty-five hundred members and an annual budget of $12 million, the government itself, with seven hundred employees, was the Seneca Nation's largest employer. Following his election in 2000, Schindler, like Snyder, a persuasive and powerful advocate of casino gambling, chose his friends and supporters to fill all of the government jobs.

While many on the reservation opposed casino gambling on the grounds that it was alien to Seneca traditions, at least as many were opposed to it because they did not trust the businessmen who ran the tribe. Despite the millions of dollars a year in bingo money that had been flowing to the nation, and despite the more than $60 million that they had received in 1990 from the federal government for an old land claim, the Senecas had nothing to show for it. In 2000, the Seneca Nation was as deeply mired in poverty as ever. More than 20 percent of its people survived on public assistance and more than half of them were out of work. Meanwhile, spousal, child, drug, and particularly alcohol abuse ran rampant on the three area reservations. Between 1970 and 2000, there were 474 "premature and preventable deaths" of Senecas due to drinking, a number that represented 8 percent of the population.[43] Life on the reservations was rough and often dangerous; shootouts among rival gangs within the tribe were common. In 1995, the Erie County sheriff said, "Everybody is armed. Every pick-up truck going down the road has a rifle in the front seat."[44] Many wondered if any of this would change with the arrival of casino gambling. Could they trust Schindler, Snyder, and their questionable cohorts with the nation's money? They held grave doubts. Like their neighbors in Buffalo, the Senecas wondered about their future and the direction their leaders were taking them.

The casino referendum among the Senecas was scheduled for May 14, 2002. Like all of their elections, bribery was acceptable and therefore rampant. (Because the Seneca Nation is sovereign, their elections are not within the jurisdiction of state or federal election laws.) When the referendum votes were counted, the pro-casino forces, who benefited from a less than 50 percent turnout, narrowly declared victory by 101 votes. On the reservation, as in Albany, it was the money—the promise of it as well as the bribes and "donations"—that carried the day.[45]

Despite the success of the casino referendum, there remained many obstacles to Pataki's vision of Western New York as one of the nation's great gambling destinations. While the state legislature had authorized the governor to enter into a compact with the Senecas (albeit after the agreement had already been reached), no compact had yet been officially agreed to. If and when one was signed, it would require the approval not only of the legislature but, more significantly, of the United States Department of the Interior, whose ruling on matters pertaining to Indian tribes was final. However, following a June 2002 ruling by United States

District Court Judge Joseph Arcara in a case regarding Seneca claims to Grand Island, federal approval of Indian gaming in Western New York seemed increasingly unlikely.

According to a law called the Indian Gaming Regulatory Act, the federal legislation that was passed in 1988 to monitor and control Indian gambling, casinos were legal only on or immediately adjacent to Indian reservations. If, however, it could be demonstrated that the land in question was what was considered "ancestral," casinos were permitted. It was this question of what constituted "ancestral land" that confronted Judge Arcara as he pondered the Seneca's claims to Grand Island.

Arguing that Grand Island, one of the area's most popular suburbs, was "ancestral land," lawyers for the Senecas insisted that it was theirs by history and by right, and demanded that the nation be paid a generous settlement to compensate for its loss. According to Joe Crangle, common sense indicated that most if not all of Western New York was ancestral Seneca land. Just look, he said, as he pointed out of the window of his office in downtown Buffalo at the street names below. "Why do you think that they have such names as 'Seneca,' 'Mohawk,' 'Huron,' 'Pawnee,' 'Shoshone,' 'Tuscarora,' and 'Scajaquada.' It's obvious, isn't it?"[46]

Others felt differently. Indeed, lawyers for New York State, which had hundreds of millions of dollars at stake in the ruling, argued that Seneca claims to Grand Island as ancestral land were illegitimate and specious and should therefore be denied. "The Senecas were not," lawyers for Pataki argued, "early inhabitants of the Niagara Frontier." Federal District Judge Joseph Arcara agreed with the defendants. In a decision that encouraged the opponents of Indian-operated casino gambling, he ruled that there was no archeological or historical evidence for the Seneca Nation's claims on Grand Island. "This is not a case," he said, "involving an Indian tribe's ancestral homelands. At the time of first European contact the villages of the Seneca were all east of the Genesee River. The Seneca Nation's ancestral homelands were located in the Genesee Valley not in the Niagara Region and certainly not in the Niagara Islands."[47] For the Senecas, whose hopes for casinos in Niagara Falls and Buffalo were based on convincing the Department of the Interior that these cities, like the rest of the Niagara Frontier, were "ancestral," Arcara's sweeping denial of all Seneca claims in the area was a setback. If they were unable to convince Arcara of the legitimacy of their ancestral claims to Grand Island, how, some wondered, would they ever prevail in Niagara Falls and Buffalo?

Proponents of the proposed compact, particularly Pataki, were not dissuaded. Seemingly unfazed about the contradiction in his position in the Grand Island case and his rationale for casinos in downtown Niagara Falls and Buffalo, Pataki continued his aggressive efforts to bring casino gambling to the area.

Indeed, in an action that typified the "shoot-from-the hip" gambling mentality that characterized this sad story, Pataki, Senate Majority Leader Bruno, and Assembly Speaker Silver—before the Seneca referendum, before the compact was signed, before it had been approved by the state legislature or the Department of Interior—counted as receipts in their 2003 state budget $600 million in revenue anticipated, they said, from gambling.

Many people in both Niagara Falls and Buffalo had also started counting their money. There were few in Niagara Falls who did not covet a casino. In that depressed and downtrodden city, there was nothing left to lose. An attraction for visitors from around the world since the 1850s, Niagara Falls was, a hundred years later, more than just the "Honeymoon Capital of the World." Indeed, by the late nineteenth century, the City of Niagara Falls had capitalized on one of the world's greatest sources of electricity to become an industrial giant. It was home to some of the largest chemical companies in the world. It was also home, as the world found out, to more than one hundred twenty contaminated sites, including Love Canal, which by the mid-1970s was one of the most polluted places in the United States.

Like other cities of the American rust belt, Niagara Falls went into steep decline in the last half of the twentieth century. By the early 1990s, with few honeymooners and tourists choosing to visit the US side of Niagara Falls (the Canadian side offered better attractions and better views), with even fewer factories still in operation, with its entire downtown demolished by urban renewal, and with its people betrayed by a seemingly endless line of corrupt politicians and developers, Niagara Falls had become one of the most desperate and downtrodden cities in the United States. To make matters worse, a brand-new casino, owned and operated by the Ontario provincial government, had opened to booming business in the fall of 1996 just across the Niagara River in Niagara Falls, Ontario. With gap-toothed streetscapes filled with vacant lots, abandoned office buildings and half-empty hotels, and a gigantic water slide whose owners declared bankruptcy soon after it opened, the American side of Niagara Falls, like the Love Canal that had made it notorious twenty years earlier, was more like a festering open wound. Desperate for hope, the people of Niagara Falls embraced the possibility that the city would finally be delivered.

Buffalo, however, presented a different situation. Despite the enthusiastic endorsement of Mayor Masiello, a *Buffalo News* poll conducted in the fall of 2002 showed that most Buffalonians were opposed to having a casino in their city. The third-term mayor, whose legacy was littered with unrealized large-scale development schemes, remained an exuberant supporter despite the evidence that he was at odds with his constituents. Desperate to latch onto anything that promised even the slightest economic benefit and eager to do to the bidding of Pataki, upon whose largesse he had come to depend to keep his city out of bankruptcy, Masiello strongly supported casino gambling. Many people wondered who he was speaking for when, in the spring of 2002, he proclaimed, "Without equivocation we welcome and support an Indian gaming casino in the core of our downtown business district."[48] While he knew he wanted casino gambling ("gaming," he euphemistically called it, as if by doing so he could erase the ugliness and pathology attached to the activity most people knew as "gambling"), he never successfully articulated his reasoning. Sometimes he said it was "about the money."[49] At other times, with the vapidity that characterized his style, he said it was "about jobs." Yes, he knew there were problems associated with gambling. He admitted to concerns about gambling addiction, the impact of increased credit card debt, and the strain the casino would place on his already poor community. But rubbing the thumb and forefinger of his right hand together, as he often did when talking about "gaming," he repeatedly stressed that it was "about the money." In a city where half the households earned less than $25,000 a year, casino jobs that started at $28,000 looked pretty good. And for a mayor more concerned with ribbon cutting ceremonies and photo-ops—a politician whose years in office were filled with promises made and never fulfilled—the proposed casino for his city was an opportunity that he simply could not refuse.

While the majority of people in Buffalo opposed casino gambling, the usual downtown suspects—the development hustlers, parking lot owners, and "players"—supported the mayor. Exhibiting a disturbing lack of concern about the frightening implications of their actions, this powerful minority bowed before the Senecas and scraped to Pataki, hoping that they could convince them to convert large chunks of their downtown into a sovereign Indian reservation dedicated to casino gambling.

The mayor's preferred site was the Statler, which until the mid-1960s had been the city's premier hotel. Like hotels in troubled downtowns throughout the nation, the Statler had slowly gone out of business. Even the construction of a convention center in the early 1970s and the hospitality spin-off that development promised could not save it; by 1980, the Statler had been converted into an office building. By the mid-1990s, the once grand building had declined still further. Neglected by its owner, Gerald Bucheit, who had purchased the building in 1992 for less than five dollars per square foot, the Statler, by the end of the century, was three-quarters empty. With malfunctioning elevators, dark and dank corridors, month-to-month tenants, and a giant discount jewelry store called the King of Gold in the lobby, the Statler had become a commercial tenement building. Had Bucheit spent half as much money fixing his hotel as he did on lobbying the governor, he might have had a profitable building, but the lure of gambling for him, like the bankrupt politicians he worked with, was too great. In the summer of 2002, Bucheit, with

Masiello as his chief pitchman, endorsed the advantages of the Statler as a permanent site of the Seneca casino in downtown Buffalo.

Meanwhile, despite both the absence of a signed compact and the questions raised by Arcara's ruling in the Grand Island case, work began on the casino in Niagara Falls. Indeed, said Mickey Brown, the man hired by the Senecas to build and operate their casino, they even had an opening date: New Year's Eve, December 31, 2002.

There were few men in the gambling business with the credentials of Mickey Brown. By the mid-1990s, he had become a one-stop shop for casino gambling, the go-to guy who could build, finance, and then operate the largest casinos in the world. Brown did it all. He negotiated compacts, arranged for financing, hired builders and architects, supervised construction, ordered dice, cards, chips, and slot machines, and then, when the casino was built, he oversaw its day-to-day operations. He had done it all at Foxwoods, and he promised to do it all in Niagara Falls and Buffalo, too.

Before Foxwoods, Brown had been a freelance casino consultant, an entrepreneur in the high-stakes world of international casino gambling. He had brokered the creation and construction of casinos in the Bahamas, Australia, South Africa, and Malaysia; as a result of his travels, he had befriended one of the wealthiest families in the world. Based in Malayasia, a Muslim country where religious laws forbade both gambling and alcohol, the Lim family, founded in the mid-1960s by Tan Sri Lim Goh Tong, had become one of the world's largest casino operators. Their company, called the Genting Group, employed fifteen thousand people and owned everything from palm plantations to paper mills to power plants. While it was best known for its expertise in tourism and recreation (it owned two of the world's largest cruise lines, Norwegian Cruises and Star Cruises), the real jewel in the company's crown was an enormous casino resort in Malaysia called Genting Highlands, "a vast casino and entertainment complex," according to its Web site, "shrouded in the mist of the mountains of Malaysia." Eventually, the Lims, like most everybody in the world of gambling, became involved with Brown. It was Brown who brokered the deal with Lim Kok Thay that created Foxwoods.[50] Brown liked the Lims. "They've got the Chinese business ethic," he told the *Buffalo News* on the eve of the opening of Seneca Niagara. "There's no night. There's no Sunday's. When it's time to work, you work because you have to."[51] And the Lims liked Brown, who, as CEO of Foxwoods, earned the Lim family more than $100 million a year on their $130 million dollar investment. They were natural partners for the new Seneca casinos in Niagara Falls and Buffalo. Brown was bullish on Niagara Falls as a casino location; soon after his arrival in the spring of 2002, he invited Lim Kok Thay to visit him there. "We believe," he told the *News* in September 2002, "that there is an enormous unsatisfied demand for gambling in New York, Ohio and Pennsylvania. This is what we're going to cater to." By October 2002, they had announced their deal. The Lims, who the *Buffalo News* referred to sometimes as Malaysian, sometimes as Asian, and sometimes as Chinese—but always as billionaires—would lend the Senecas upward of $80 million. The five-year term of the loan was steep and the interest rate, at 30 percent, was high. But Brown was confident. "This is as close to a sure thing as you're going to get in this industry," he said in describing the deal. "There is no doubt in my mind that we're just going to knock the cover off the ball."[52]

But there still was no deal. In the summer of 2002, negotiations between Pataki and the Seneca Nation had stalled over the former's insistence on the right of organized labor to have "access" to casino employees (the hotel workers union had contributed generously and regularly to Pataki's reelection campaigns). Adding to the uncertainty were rumblings within the Seneca Nation that led people to question whether any Seneca casino would ever be built. There wouldn't be a casino if it were up to him, said Arnold Cooper, the treasurer of the Seneca Nation, who announced in July that if elected president of the nation in the November 2002 election he would not authorize the use of tribal funds to purchase land for the construction of casinos. Cooper represented a growing number of Senecas who were deeply critical of Snyder, Schindler, and the other cigarette and gas merchants who were leading the casino efforts and who, in Cooper's words "[had] recklessly spent our money in pursuit of casino gambling."[53] Support for casino gambling had always been tenuous among the Senecas, and Cooper's strong challenge threatened to derail the plans of Schindler, Governor Pataki, Mayors Elia and Masiello, Mickey Brown, and the Lim family of billionaires. If the deal was not set in stone prior to the November elections and Cooper managed to unseat Schindler, then plans for Seneca-run casinos in Niagara Falls and Buffalo would have to be scrapped.

In August 2002, however, when the Senecas agreed to Mickey Brown's choice of a union-friendly contractor, a company called C. R. Klewin (the same contractor that Brown had used at Foxwoods), all obstacles to the compact were removed; on August 19, 2002, the parties signed the agreement. "This has been," Pataki said, "a long and difficult haul, but it is worth it. In still more of his tiring election-year rhetoric, he promised, "We're going to be getting the hotels, the restaurants, the jobs, the taxes, the benefits and the jobs, the jobs, the jobs."[54] Though there was still no word from the Department of the Interior, Brown was unconcerned. He pushed his crews hard in order to be ready for New Year's Eve. "The men," Brown told the *News*, "are working twenty hours a day, six days a week," to convert the old convention center into a casino, a temporary one but a big one, which would, he promised, accommodate three thousand five hundred to four thousand gamblers at a time until a newer, bigger, and much better one could be built. He had to hurry, he said: "The deadline for our slot machine order has to be by September 15 to start delivery on December l. Then we will install one hundred machines a day for twenty six days."[55]

Pataki was confident that the last obstacle to casino gambling in Western New York, namely approval by the Department of the Interior, would fall much like the others. And in November 2002, Arnold Cooper's campaign for the presidency of the Seneca Nation failed, putting an end to the last-ditch efforts by tribal members to prevent casino gambling. Many in the Department of the Interior, the career people, the nonpolitical professionals who worked at the Bureau of Indian Affairs (BIA), had serious reservations about the compact, believing that it violated the generally accepted principles that governed these kinds of deals. Given their mandate to protect, defend, and strengthen the legal, economic, and political conditions of Native Americans, the BIA professionals were concerned that the compact's provision that the Senecas share 25 percent of casino profits with Pataki was overly generous. It was this concern that had led them earlier in the year to reject a casino compact between Louisiana and the Choctaws. In that deal, Louisiana's 15.5 percent share of profits was considered too high. The BIA also worried that, whereas most compacts granted Native Americans the exclusive right to control gambling in the target region, Pataki's gambling bill, by allowing the use of video "slot machines" at area racetracks, did not.

Others were troubled by the provisions in Pataki's compact with the Senecas that clearly violated Judge Arcara's ruling in the recent Grand Island land claim case. Wasn't the placement of casinos on clearly nonancestral land such as downtown Buffalo and Niagara Falls inconsistent with Arcara's judgment in that case? Pataki, however, was unconcerned; he knew that Secretary of the Interior Gale Norton would approve his compact. He had confidence in his close relationship with the Bush administration. He had already briefed Vice President Cheney about the importance of the casinos and knew that Cheney would help him overcome any doubts that Norton may have had about the integrity of his compact with the Senecas.

The casino proponents were right not to worry. In October 2002, Secretary Norton allowed the backdoor approval of Pataki's compact with the Senecas. To do this, she relied on a loophole in the Indian Gaming Regulatory Act that provided that failure to respond to a request to approve a compact within forty-five days resulted in its automatic approval. By allowing the forty-five-day period to elapse without taking action, she effectively eased open the last gate that had stood between the Senecas and their casinos. "The Secretary will neither approve nor disapprove the gambling compact between the Seneca Nation of Indians and New York State. As a result," Secretary Norton said, "the compact will be considered to have been approved as of October 25, 2002."[56] Shortly thereafter, Norton revealed that she had found a way around Arcara's Grand Island ruling. Since the city is only fourteen miles from the Seneca's original reservation on Buffalo Creek, the site, she said, was "within or near proximity to former reservation lands" and therefore did not need to be ancestral land. John LaFalce, a long-time Democratic congressman from the area and a casino opponent, was furious. He expressed the feelings of many when he said: "I suppose that this has been wired by Governor Pataki and President Bush." He was concerned about "the deeply flawed process" and was convinced that Norton, under pressure from the White House, approved the deal "as a favor to . . . Pataki." He demanded an investigation of what he called Secretary Norton's "non-approval" of the compact.[57]

The people of Niagara Falls celebrated. They counted the days until New Year's Eve, when the opening of the Seneca Niagara Casino would, they believed, finally bring relief from years of bad breaks and bumbling leadership. Many people in Buffalo, however, were nervous. They feared that the same questionable process and shady dealing that had brought a Seneca casino to Niagara Falls would trump their efforts to develop a far more positive, enlightened, and creative effort to heal, revitalize, and renew the city that they loved. They were angry that their mayor and their governor, with the blessing of the Department of the Interior, had endorsed a plan that would allow the Senecas to buy property in downtown Buffalo, declare it part of their sovereign trust lands, and proceed to build a casino upon it. People were hurt, saddened, and insulted by what they regarded as a breach of the cardinal rule of democratic government, namely, consent of the governed. In Buffalo, citizen participation went beyond civics textbook cliché. In Buffalo, citizen participation was integrated into community life. Whether working to improve their schools and their parks, forcing the city and the state to desist from the construction of grade-level highways, or preventing the closure of branch libraries and the venerable Children's Hospital, Buffalonians had developed a tradition of organizing and fighting hard for their civic values. Unlike their leaders, the people of Buffalo were not desperate. The people had great faith in the nature and quality of life in the city. They loved their neighborhoods. They rejoiced in the wonderful architecture that graced street after street. They relished their park system and were proud of the strength of local community life. Increasingly, they were becoming angry that their city, which in fact had so much to offer, was about to become irredeemably known as just another depressed city with an Indian casino.

What motivated the opponents of casino gambling to fight was not that the plan was illegal but rather that casino gambling offended their notion of the good city and insulted their intelligence. For people who recognized the role of intelligence and creativity as the driving forces of city life, the idea that city leaders could embrace casino gambling, legal or illegal, as a panacea for what ailed it, was an offense. To those people who valued what was unique about Buffalo, casino gambling was anathema. For the Senecas, however, the placement of Seneca-owned casinos at key locations in Western New York represented an opportunity for them to finally have it their way.

Bolder leadership, in Buffalo at least, would have demanded a referendum, would have insisted that the people have an opportunity to express themselves on what many felt was the most controversial development scheme in the history of their city. While it is likely that Indian sovereignty would have been able to legally trump the outcome of any referendum, the mayor's zealous endorsement of Pataki's pact with the Senecas denied the people of Buffalo any opportunity to express themselves. They deserved better. Betrayed by leadership they believed was spineless and desperate, the city's citizens demanded more, and many in Buffalo vowed revenge. Afraid of the increasingly strange bedfellows that their leaders had chosen as partners, the good people of Buffalo watched, waited, and wondered what was going on.

NOTES

1. J. Heaney, "Knox Wants Deal," *Buffalo News*, June 21, 1992, p. A1.

2. K. Collison, "Council Restores Funds," *Buffalo News*, July 8, 1992, p. B1.

3. J. Heaney, "Sabres Outline Crossroads Plan," *Buffalo News*, November 1, 1992, p. A1.

4. J. Sorenson, "State Favors Unspecific Arena Funding Plan," *Buffalo News*, June 8, 1993, p. B1.

5. R. J. McCarthy, "Cuomo Signs Arena Bill," *Buffalo News*, July 13, 1993, p. A1.

6. K. Collison, "Cable TV Chief Tied to Offer," *Buffalo News*, January 11, 1994, p. A1.

7. David Robinson, "Why Delaware North?" *Buffalo News*, July 17, 1994, p. B13.

8. There is little written about the Jacobses and the growth and development of their company. The best generally available work is J. Underwood and M. Sharnik, "Look What Louie Wrought," *Sports Illustrated*, May 29, 1972, pp. 40ff. For general background information on the company, see Paula Koops, ed., *The International Directory of Company Histories*, vol. 7 (Chicago: St. James Press, 1993), pp. 133ff.

9. Underwood and Sharnik, "Look What Louie Wrought."

10. See Delaware North's Web site, http://www.delawarenorth.com/.

11. Underwood and Sharnik, "Look What Louie Wrought."

12. K. Collison, "Jacobs' Firm to Aid in Funding of Arena," *Buffalo News*, July 13, 1994, p. B1.

13. J. Kelley, "Rigas to Take Control of Sabres," *Buffalo News*, December 31, 1997, p. C1.

14. Ibid.

15. D. Esmonde, "Wilson Should Use His Business Sense, Not Blame Economy," *Buffalo News*, May 29, 1997, p. B1.

16. "Bills Lease: Who Benefits?" *Buffalo News*, December 27, 1997, p. B3.

17. T. Precious, "Funding Aimed at Keeping Bills in Buffalo," *Buffalo News*, July 30, 1997, A1.

18. D. Robinson, "Here Are Three of the Area's Sweetest Sweetheart Deals," *Buffalo News*, August 3, 1997, p. C1.

19. Throughout the summer and fall of 1997, the Letters to the Editor section of the *Buffalo News* was filled with letters, sometimes angry, always passionate, both pro and con, concerning the issue of the Bills lease.

20. G. Warner, "Buffett Brings Clout to Buffalo," *Buffalo News*, September 9, 1998, p. A1.

21. R. McCarthy, "Golisano Denounces Stadium Deal," *Buffalo News*, October 21, 1998, p. B1.

22. D. Robinson, "Ties That Bind Won't Seem So Snug," *Buffalo News*, December 9, 1998, p. C1.

23. Rod Watson, "City Would Be Better Place If Efforts to Boost the East Side Matched Those to Save the Bills," *Buffalo News*, December 3, 1998, p. B2. Ralph Wilson was not the only sports team owner who benefited handsomely from the eagerness of local politicians to lavish taxpayer money on professional sports during the 1990s. The city's minor league baseball franchise, the Buffalo Bisons, showed annual profits in excess of $10 million throughout the 1990s. The City of Buffalo, meanwhile, which along with the state and county had built the $61 million stadium in which the team played, was, as a result of its deal with Rich, paying over $500,000 annually to the state to cover the stadium's operational deficits. For information on Rich and the Bisons, see J. Bonfatti, et al., "Bottom Line Sports," *Buffalo News*, March 14, 1999, p. A1.

24. K. Collison, "Rigas Deal Closer," *Buffalo News*, October 31, 1998, p. A1.

25. K. Collison, "Inner Harbor Dream Team," *Buffalo News*, March 24, 1999, p. A1.

26. "Dream Team Offers Hope," *Buffalo News*, March 25, 1999.

27. K. Collison, "The Transformer Developer David Cordish," *Buffalo News*, May 30, 1999, p. A1

28. "Main Street," *Buffalo News*, February 22, 1999, p. B4.

29. K. Collison, "Ambitious Plan by Adelphia," *Buffalo News*, September 16, 1999, p. A1.

30. T. Precious, "$75 Million for Adelphia Project," *Buffalo News*, April 5, 2000, p. A1.

31. B. Meyer, "Adelphia Deal Ok'd," *Buffalo News*, April 7, 2001, p. A1.

32. F. O. Williams, "Adelphia Communications Stock Continues to Fall," *Buffalo News*, May 5, 2002, p. C4.

33. A. Palazzetti, "Seneca Businessman Warns Against Tax Plans," *Buffalo News*, April 8, 1997, p. B1.

34. A. Palazzetti, "Indians Win Sales Tax Battle," *Buffalo News*, May 23, 1997, p. A1.

35. A. Palazzetti, "Oneida Indian Leader," *Buffalo News*, April 4, 1993, p. A1.

36. T. Precious and A. Galarneau, "Casino Promised City," *Buffalo News*, June 21, 2001, p. A1.

37. Leslie Eaton, "Viva Niagara Falls," *New York Times*, December 12, 2002, p. B1.

38. T. Precious, "Lobbying at Epic Levels to Glorify Gambling," *Buffalo News*, Feb-

ruary 11, 2002, p. A1. See also J. Zremski, M. Beebe, and D. Herbeck, "Senecas Becoming Big-Spending Players on the Political Scene," *Buffalo News*, May 20, 2004, p. A1. According to these reporters, the goals of the Senecas' spending were not limited to merely ensuring the passage of the casino compact. They had also spent heavily in both Albany and Washington—upward of $400,000—to protect such valued Seneca interests as the tribe's collection of online smoke shops, the nation's largest.

39. T. Precious, "Senecas Recruit Lobbyist with Ties to State Gov't," *Buffalo News*, June 29, 2002, p. C12.

40. Four years earlier, Jeremy Jacobs had retained Brown to help him craft a proposal that would bring two casinos to Western New York. Tom Precious, "Casino Interests Pour Money into Albany," *Buffalo News*, August 20, 1998, p. A1.

41. Ibid.

42. A. Palazzetti, "Indian Group Hires Crangle," *Buffalo News*, May 10, 1989, p. B1.

43. A. Palazzetti, "Seneca Teens in Trouble," *Buffalo News*, May 22, 1989, p. B1.

44. A. Palazzetti, "Three Killed in Gunbattle," *Buffalo News*, March 26, 1995, p. B1.

45. A. Palazzetti, "Senecas Vote Yes," *Buffalo News*, May 15, 2002, p. A1.

46. Joe Crangle, personal communication with the author, February 2003.

47. D. Chen, "Federal Judge Denies Claim of Senecas," *New York Times*, June 22, 2002, p. B5.

48. Lou Michel, "City, Business Leaders Welcome Senecas," *Buffalo News*, May 19, 2002, p. A1.

49. Mayor Anthony M. Masiello, personal communication with the author, April 2003.

50. J. Zremski and A. Galarneau, "Seneca's Point Man," *Buffalo News*, October 12, 2002, p. A1.

51. Ibid.

52. Ibid.

53. K. Robinson, "Gambling Opponents See Fight," *Buffalo News*, April 21, 2002, p. A1.

54. A. Galarneau, "Senecas Aim for Falls Facility," *Buffalo News*, August 21, 2002, p. A1.

55. A. Galarneau, "Working on 'Wow,'" *Buffalo News*, December 6, 2002, p. A1.

56. Jerry Zremski, "Senecas Get to Buy Casino Land; Interior Secretary Ruling Removes Last Federal Obstacle," *Buffalo News*, November 13, 2002, p. A1J. See also Zremski, "Washington Approves Land Transfer," *Buffalo News*, November 30, 2002, p. A1.

57. Ibid.

chapter 14

WHAT'S GOING ON?

Buffalo at the Turn of the Twenty-First Century

t the turn of the twenty-first century, it seemed little was going right in Buffalo. The city's population had dropped precipitously, its economy continued to unravel, and its downtown was littered with the detritus of hundreds of millions of dollars of public spending—money wasted on a rapid transit system that perennially hovered on bankruptcy, half-empty office buildings, and an array of other failed projects, including restaurants, nightclubs, and movie theaters. The 1990s had been a difficult decade for the city, and by 2000, the situation had gotten worse. For the first time since the end of the nineteenth century, Buffalo's population had fallen below three hundred thousand (the 2000 census counted fewer than 297,000 residents). Driving the loss was the flight of one-quarter of the city's white population—53,149 people—which was equivalent to the entire population of Niagara Falls. Most of the people who left were young.

The loss of population was of great concern to business and political leaders. One of the most powerful of them was Robert G. Wilmers, president of M&T Bank. In his annual report to the bank's stockholders in the spring of 2006, he continued what had become annual jeremiads about the state of the city and the region. "Make no mistake: this is not business as usual," Wilmers said. "The magnitude and duration of population loss among the young is unprecedented in our history. There has never been a previous 10-year period in the history of the upstate region when there has been any decline in this most vital portion of our population."[1] Offset somewhat by the modest increase in the number of African Americans and Hispanics, Buffalo's net loss was more than thirty-five thousand people.[2]

The population loss mounted as the decade wore on, doubling from twenty-one hundred per year between 1990 and 1994 to forty-five hundred per year from 1995 to 1999. The trend, it seemed, was permanent, and people wondered when, or if, the cycle of decline would ever end. "The thing that surprised me is the rate of decline actually sped up from the previous decade," said David J. DiSalvo, the city's manager of planning analysis. "Ten years ago, we said the population was going to bottom out and stabilize at a number of around 300,000."[3]

Meanwhile, the city's economy continued to stagnate. The manufacturing sector suffered the most; employment in manufacturing dropped from approximately ninety-three thousand people in 1990 to seventy-two thousand in 2002. In a trend far worse than that affecting the national economy, the Buffalo area lost close to thirteen thousand jobs between 1999 and 2000, more than three thousand of them in manufacturing. The *Buffalo News* reminded its readers that "17 percent of the region's manufacturing jobs have disappeared in three years."[4] The decline in manufacturing had a significant impact on real personal income, which, between 1991 and 2001 grew (in what was now being called the "Buffalo Niagara Region") by a total of just 11.1 percent, or about 1.1 percent per year. As growth in the area slowed, so, too, did the area's per capita income, which at $27,852 was $2,560 less than the United States average.

In an attempt to stem the city's decline, in 1999, a few of the area's largest companies formed an organization dedicated to the creation of new jobs on the Niagara Frontier. Called the Buffalo Niagara Enterprise (BNE), its goal was to "re-brand the area as an attractive place to live and do business." The BNE stated that it would create ten thousand jobs per year by 2004. Operating on an annual budget of $7 million provided in part by Erie County and in part by the Buffalo Niagara Partnership, the BNE, which spent more than $2 million per year on advertising and promotions, was one of the best-funded privately led booster organizations in the country. Although its goals were lofty, realizing them was not out of the question, since to do so required an expanding labor market of just 1.5 percent a year (the labor market in New York State as a whole, it was pointed out, grew at approximately 2 percent per year). But poor leadership compounded by a recession from 2001 to 2002 proved too much to handle. Between 2000 and 2002, the local economy lost more than five thousand jobs, a drop of 8 percent a month. By the end of 2002, unemployment stood at 7 percent, the highest in many years. The BNE, a mere two years after its much-heralded initial job creation announcement, renounced its previous goals. The head of the organization admitted that they had been "unrealistic."

The private sector of the economy continued to decline throughout the last quarter of the century. By 2006, the area top ten employers were no longer great industrial giants; instead (they were in the following order): New York State with 16,655 employees; the United States government with 10,000; Tops Markets with 6,000; Erie County with 7,269; Kaleida Health with 6,866; the State University of New York at Buffalo with 6,488; the Buffalo public schools with 5,319; HSBC Bank with 5,100; the Catholic Health System with 4,702; and M&T Bank with 4,153. Of the 72,553 people who worked for them, close to 46,000—63 percent— were public employees.[5] The public sector bureaucracy was particularly bloated in Buffalo. In fact, Buffalo had, on a per capita basis, the most public workers of any city in the nation.[6] The big government payroll, however, did not translate into good governance. Indeed, in 2000, the Maxwell School of Citizenship and Public Affairs at Syracuse University, in what they said was the most comprehensive survey ever done, ranked Buffalo and New Orleans as the two worst run cities in the nation.[7]

That something was wrong with city government was immediately apparent upon entering city hall. Even in the best of times, most people agreed, it was frustrating and extremely difficult to get anything done in Buffalo. Led for twelve years by a mayor unable or unwilling to take on the Byzantine bureaucracy, the sleepy, old-boy culture of city hall had become encrusted with mediocrity and hidebound by rules and regulations that tried the patience of anybody who had to deal with it. While the city hall building itself was a marvel of art deco design filled with fantastical murals, sculptures, and other magical design motifs, the upkeep left something to be desired. The red limestone exterior was tarnished and dirty while the lobby and elevators were dark and dingy. The elevators that did work were staffed by men, often unshaven and wearing old Buffalo Bills sweatshirts, who seemed not to know and certainly not to care about why their passengers were there. Everything in city hall—the corridors, offices, and public rooms—bore the aura of decay. Nothing that looked this way could possibly function effectively. Even the telephones, the main lines of communication between the people and their government, barely worked; callers waited rarely fewer than twenty rings before the overworked operator finally picked up.

Perhaps none of this would have mattered had the place functioned properly, but it didn't. Indeed, at the beginning of the new century, there was no more common complaint in Buffalo than just how difficult it was to deal with city hall. The smallest improvement, something such as a request of a café owner to place two tables in front of his business, could involve hours of time and months of negotiations with as many as six different entities on almost as many floors in the building. While the city's leadership would point their fingers at the larger forces of change that had led to the decline of Buffalo, there were a growing number of people in Buffalo who had, as a result of their bitter and frustrating experiences, come to believe that the truth was closer to home—that in fact there was no greater obstacle to the energy, imagination, and creativity necessary for change than the arcane, lackadaisical, and often punitive culture of city government itself. Given the quality and culture of public leadership in turn-of-the-century Buffalo, it was no wonder that no strategies existed, that nobody, after twenty-five years of population loss and economic decline, had a plan, and that nobody, it seemed, had a clue about what to do. The mayor, who always seemed surprised when something went wrong, was essentially asleep at the wheel. In December 2002, for example, when Trico, the locally owned windshield wiper company that in 1985 had shocked the community when it moved more than two thousand employees to its new maquiladora plant on the Texas-Mexico border, announced that it would shut down the last of its Buffalo operations, Masiello (who six months before the Trico closing had hired a Canadian consulting firm at a cost of $100,000 to help draw up an economic development plan for Buffalo) said in response, "We're going to have to try to prevent companies from closing or leaving."[8]

While most of the regional economy sputtered, however, some companies, particularly M&T Bank, were phenomenally successful. At the time it was acquired by Robert Wilmers in 1982, M&T Bank had barely $2 billion in assets. By 2006, as a result of several key acquisitions, the bank had assets of more than $55 billion.[9] With more than thirteen thousand five hundred employees (fifty-five hundred in Western New York) and a stock that outperformed most bank stocks in the country, M&T had, by the turn of the new century, become the city's most influential institution. Wilmers himself, despite his quiet demeanor, had become "the Man," a person whose words, like those of Alan Greenspan or Warren Buffett, were greatly anticipated and highly respected. (Buffett, by the way, was not only a personal friend but the owner of 6 percent of the stock in the bank. By 2005, the $40 million dollar investment he had made in the bank in 1987 was worth $728 million.) Wilmers was an intriguing man; generous and charitable toward his adopted community, he was the subject of much speculation. How, people wondered, was it possible for M&T to be so successful despite two decades of relentless regional decline? What did Wilmers know that others didn't? If he could make it, why couldn't the rest?[10]

Questions like these took on particular urgency downtown, where there were few businesses that worked. Even the local McDonald's and Burger King couldn't make it. Located across the street from each other on the corner of Main and Mohawk, these two franchises, opened with the aid of public funds in the late

1970s, hung on for a while, supported by an increasingly obese population. In Buffalo, 124 people out of every one hundred thousand died of heart disease every year, one of the highest rates in the country. By the mid-1990s, even these fast food chains had had enough; both closed, leaving their signs and lights dangling from the building facades. By then, all of the property in downtown Buffalo had lost value. In 1996, an entire block of Main Street, from the Main Place Tower at one end to the Liberty Bank Building on the other, including the Main Place Mall in the middle (projects that had been lynchpins of the trumpeted Main Street urban renewal plan of 1965), sold for a total of $19 million, $10 million less than their assessed valuation.[11]

Other areas fared just as badly. In 1995 alone, the assessed value of the thirty-eight-story Marine Midland Center dropped by $2.7 million, while the former Goldome Bank, now owned by M&T, dropped to $21 million, slightly less than what it had cost to build thirteen years earlier. Publicly leveraged buildings suffered the most. In 1985, two suburban developers bought the Sibley's building (formerly Hengerer's Department Store) and renovated it with $2.8 million in UDAG money in a conversion that replaced the department store with offices. In 1995, with a vacancy rate of 60 percent, the building's owners succumbed to foreclosure. That same year, another generously subsidized office building, a place on Pearl Street called Olympic Towers, saw its $11 million mortgage sold for less than $3 million. Ten years after it had opened in 1985, the chairman of the Niagara Frontier Transportation Authority admitted that the metro line "was not the boon for downtown people were hoping it would be."[12] With more than twenty-five thousand daily riders, it was one of the most used systems per mile in the country. However, the good ridership numbers failed to generate the expected ripple effect on Main Street. Despite special zoning that had been created to stimulate development around the system's dozen stations, they remained barren, littered wastelands, disconnected from the surrounding streetscape in a way never imagined by their designers. The bottom was falling out of Main Street, as it had been for more than fifty years, and nothing that anybody did, let alone said, could stop it. "The whole area," *Buffalo News* art critic Richard Huntington wrote in 1994, "is devoid of people. It is one big stretched out mood piece, a stage set for dancing bears and organ grinders."[13]

By the end of the century, despite hundreds of millions of dollars of public money, despite massive demolition and reconstruction, despite years of clever, imaginative, and Herculean political and financial legerdemain, Buffalo's ambitious hopes to create a new Main Street were far from realized. Main Street in particular and downtown in general had yet to prove that they had regained their place as a destination of choice for the metropolitan area. Fighting a relentless uphill battle against a suburban area that continued to add extensive commercial, retail, and entertainment functions to its traditional residential ones, downtown Buffalo, despite all the money and gimmicks, all the festivals and hoopla, had failed to demonstrate that there was a constituency out there that cared enough to support it.

Perhaps most serious of all, the city, unable to bring stability to its weakening finances, lost most of its autonomy when, in the summer of 2003, it was placed under the authority of a fiscal control board. For years, Buffalo's weakening fiscal condition had been annually papered over when, at crunch time, the state invariably came through with emergency funds that would, for yet another year, bail out the city. Buffalo's reliance on state aid ballooned from $58 million to more than $100 million between 1995 and 2001, an increase of over 70 percent. Unable or unwilling to initiate or implement local spending reforms, the mayor concentrated most of his energies on passing his hat in Albany. However, in the wake of the dramatic fiscal crisis that followed the 9/11 catastrophe, state funds dried up. The city, according to Donn Esmonde, a popular columnist for the *Buffalo News*, had "maxed out its State credit card." "The structure of City government," Esmonde wrote in November 2001, "can't support its weight. The load of salaries and benefits is too heavy for taxes and fees. It should have collapsed years ago except Albany propped us up with millions of dollars. That crutch," Esmonde concluded starkly, "collapsed with the World Trade Center. Rome is burning. It is time to stop fiddling around."[14] Finally confronted with a crisis of unprecedented proportions, the mayor announced in the spring of 2002 that the city faced a $14 million deficit for the year and a $60 million gap for the year ahead. In a rare burst of candor from a man eager to "sugarcoat" the harsh realities of life in Buffalo, Masiello said: "I'm telling you things have never been this bad."[15] The mayor's projections, compounded with growing reports of missing funds and budgetary legerdemain, fueled the speculation that drastic change was in the air. According to the *Buffalo News*, "Buffalo's economic condition borders on the desperate. The city survives on the money the mayor receives from Albany each year at the annual begging ritual. These funds have run out and now the city faces bankruptcy."[16] As the crisis grew throughout the year, voices calling for creation of a financial control board became louder and clearer. It came as no surprise, therefore, when New York State Comptroller Alan Hevesi, in May 2003, recommended that the governor and the state legislature create what he called an "oversight and recovery board for Buffalo." The problems—a budget deficit more than twice that promised by the mayor, plus a $30 million dollar gap for the Board of Education—were such that Hevesi had no choice. While reluctant to cast blame, choosing instead to cite the deeply structural and long-term weaknesses of the area's economy as the cause of the problem, Hevesi made it clear that other factors—poor accounting practices, obstinate political leaders, intransigent public unions—were equally if not more responsible for Buffalo's fiscal and budgetary nightmare.

Under Hevesi's plan, a seven-member board advised by six additional non-voting members would have approval authority over a four-year recovery plan to be proposed by the mayor. Future budgets would have to be consistent with the plan, and revenue projections would be subject to board approval. Future pay raises could be put on hold, giving the board leverage to encourage the city and its unions to renegotiate damaging contracts. In addition, in a blow that was symbolic as much as it was real, the city could not spend more than $50,000 without the express permission of the board.[17]

Two years later, in the summer of 2005, Comptroller Hevesi appointed another control board, this one for Erie County. He said, "Erie County is facing a fiscal crisis, a cash crisis and a crisis of confidence. The ongoing strategy of cutting taxes without cutting spending and using gimmicks to cover up the deficits set the stage for this fiscal crisis years ago. I am recommending that the Governor and Legislature establish a control board to force Erie County to solve its financial problems. The people of Erie County deserve no less." In this stunning and deeply damning report of fiscal mismanagement and neglect, the comptroller explained that

> Erie County has suffered through many years of structurally imbalanced budgets, underestimated expenses and overestimated revenues; the chronic use of one-shot funding sources; the use of the entire fund balance leaving no reserve or contingency; and the use of debt to pay for operating expenses. In sum, Erie County has been systematically violating the fundamental rules of responsible financial management. That has left the County with limited options for fixing its fiscal mess. At this point, the problem is so big and it is so late in the year, that it will require every possible measure to deal with the problem this year and to close the huge future gaps. That means more budget cuts, tax increases such as the County Executive has already proposed, and deficit financing. Deficit financing and other assistance will require State action. And it is clear that it would be irresponsible to give the current Erie County government more resources unless there is a control board to ensure that those resources are used properly.[18]

With the finances of both the city and the county now under the jurisdiction of control boards, people also wondered about the sorry condition of the State of New York and the impact poor state governance might have on the city. The numbers gathered in *Governing* magazine's State & Local Source Book for 2005 and reported in the *Buffalo News* in the spring of 2006 told much of the story. Total state tax revenue, *Governing* reported, at $4,645 per person, was the nation's highest. Property tax revenue was fifth-highest among all states, at $1,402. Total spending was second-highest, at $10,376. Per capita state and local debt was second-highest, at $10,306. Welfare spending was highest, at $1,699, even though the number of recipients per ten thousand residents was only sixteenth-highest. Kindergarten through grade 12 education spending (state and local) was second-highest, at $2,001, even though school enrollment as a share of total population was the fourth-lowest. Spending per pupil was the highest, at $12,059. The average pay of state and local employees was second highest, at $52,450. The consequences of such numbers, the *News* reported, were both pernicious and predictable. People were leaving. According to the United States Census, New York's share of the national population had steadily eroded, from 9.8 percent at midcentury to 6.5 percent in 2004.[19]

The fiscal stringency of the times did not prevent the political leaders of Western New York from following wasteful and potentially illegal administrative procedures. According to a *Buffalo News* investigation in 2004, city hall, under the combined leadership of Mayors Griffin and Masiello, had squandered much of the half-billion dollars in federal aid the city had received over the past thirty years for revitalization of its downtown and neighborhoods. While Buffalo received more in federal aid from Community Development Block Grants per resident than all but one city in the country, most of it, the *News* found, was frittered away as a result of "parochial politics and bureaucratic ineptitude."[20]

The management of these massive funds by both the Griffin and Masiello administrations was careless and possibly corrupt—HUD for years had cited the administration of Buffalo's block grant program for faulty planning, poor management of projects, and deficient accounting systems. However, little was done to change it. According to Steven T. Banko, field office director of the Buffalo HUD office and Masiello's former chief of staff, the city suffered from a "lack of management expertise." The process itself was fundamentally broken. "The whole thing was in shambles," he said.

The mounting problems at city hall did not prevent the Masiello administration, prodded as always by Governor Pataki, from pursuing public policies that seemed disconnected from the reality of daily life in the area. Nothing was more emblematic than their obsession with laying out public funds and other incentives to lure Bass Pro, a giant sports retailer headquartered in St. Louis, to the city's inner harbor development area. Despite the city's fiscal and economic hardships, and despite the presence of city and county control boards, money always seemed to be available when it came to providing "incentives" for what critics had begun to call "silver bullet" projects (so long as these projects were proposed by people with the right connections). There had been talk about Bass Pro for several years. Its founder and president, Johnny Morris, was good friends with Bob and Mindy Rich, the billionaire owners of Rich Products. Founded in Buffalo during the 1930s by Bob Rich's father, the company, which specialized in frozen dairy products, had become, with sales in excess of $2 billion, one of the country's largest privately held companies. The Riches and Morris were neighbors in Florida, where the Riches lived just long enough each year to avoid New York State income tax levies. Once the Riches spread the word that their friend was interested in Buffalo, politicians and economic development czars from Albany to Buffalo were soon touting the advantages of a waterfront location for what the *Buffalo News* called "a mammoth sporting goods complex."

Once an arrangement was cobbled together, Governor Pataki flew to Buffalo in November 2004 to announce the Bass Pro deal. The agreement, Pataki proudly announced, would be sweetened by an $80 million package of incentives, which would transform the mothballed Memorial Auditorium into a retail/entertainment complex. Also attached to the deal were parking and related transportation projects that contained generous public subsidies. The grand plans would be implemented using $21 million from New York State (commonly referred to as the "Adelphia Money," which referred to the state's allocation for that now-defunct project), $12 million from "unspecified" state sources, $30 million in federal transportation dollars, and $17 million from Erie County and Buffalo. The local funds would come from borrowings against future sales tax revenues. Masiello argued that the local handouts were necessary "to provide seed funds for the retailer."[21] The ecstatic governor crowed that "when Bass Pro comes to town they don't just open a store . . . they change that town." Erie County Executive Joel Giambra said, "This is the hook that the Waterfront needs." The mayor added his increasingly hollow cheerleader's cry that "Bass Pro brings people, they bring sales tax dollars and they bring hope." Thomas Kucharski, the president of Buffalo Niagara Enterprise, was even more thrilled. "This," he said, "is a head-turner. When someone asks me what's new in Buffalo and I say, 'Well, we're getting the third largest Bass Pro in the country,' it makes a very, very positive impression."

The *Buffalo News* was as guilty of spinning the Bass Pro deal as were the politicians who saw it as yet another source of hope for the city's salvation. The *News*'s business reporter, whose writings on business developments contained far more cheerleading than reportage, extolled the project. Under headlines like "Hope Soars with Bass Pro" and "Bass Pro Key to Revitalizing Waterfront," the *News* conveyed the impression that this deal was not only "done," but, once completed, would do what over fifty years of efforts to revitalize Buffalo's waterfront had failed to do.

The *Buffalo News* also played an active role in recruiting GEICO, one of the largest automobile insurers in the nation, to locate significant operations in the Buffalo area. The company, which specializes in selling car insurance through telemarketing, announced in 2004 that it would open a call center in Amherst. GEICO, like the *Buffalo News*, a wholly owned subsidiary of Warren Buffett's Berkshire-

Hathaway, enjoyed the enthusiastic support of the newspaper. The paper's president and publisher, Stanford Lipsey, aggressively brokered the deal. Lipsey informed the public that GEICO would spend $36.9 million of its own money on the call center if the Buffett company could count on public subsidies to make the deal work. It quickly received them: $100 million in tax breaks from the state, a $14 million reduction in utility rates from the New York State Power Authority, and a $4 million state grant. An article in Buffett's *Buffalo News* explained that the subsidies would be used "to defer costs of equipping and furnishing the facility."[22]

While the *News*'s efforts paid off for GEICO, in late 2005 there was still no ink on the Bass Pro deal. In an effort to expedite this inexplicably bogged down project, Governor Pataki created a group of power brokers who would, he said, "shepherd" it through. Pataki described the group's members as people "who all have their heads and hearts in Western New York." One member was Mindy Rich. Another was Larry Quinn, president of the Buffalo Sabres, whose team stood to benefit as much as anyone by the location of Bass Pro at a waterfront location just a couple blocks away. Joining them was Jack Quinn, a recently retired Republican congressman, who had passed through the revolving door into a lucrative $500,000-a-year job as president of a large Washington lobbying firm. The chairman of the group, Anthony Gioia, was a wealthy and influential Pataki supporter, a local businessman, and the recently retired United States ambassador to Malta. The citizens of Western New York were assured that the group would bring the Bass Pro project to fruition. If, when, and how it would remain as unclear as ever.

So much public money had been extended to so many projects, but there was remarkably little to show for it. Fifty-six million of the public's dollars had been used to build the HSBC Arena for the Knox's Buffalo Sabres. And $42 million in public funds had been allocated to build Dunn Tire Park for Bob and Mindy Rich's minor league baseball team, the Buffalo Bisons. By 2004, even more—close to $60 million, most all of it under a federal loan program known as "108 money"—had been spent on the Theater District on Main Street. Desperately eager to leverage development, the city had loaned millions of dollars to almost anybody with an idea. Theater operators, night club owners, and restaurateurs had all been able to borrow under this program. By the turn of the new century, the default rate on 108 loans in Buffalo—22 percent—was twice the national average.[23] Among the defaulters were such high-profile downtown ventures as the Journey's End Hotel, TGI Friday's, General Cinema, Theatre Place, the Tralfamadore, the Breckenridge Brew Pub, and others. Compounding the high default rate was the fact that the city had to guarantee these loans out of current community development block grant funds. As a result, close to $1 million a year of those already sparse funds were being used to fund the defaulted 108 debts.[24] In addition to the 108 loans, the Masiello administration spent a fortune on consultants: $665,000 on fifty-six outside consultants, many of whom were former city employees who, upon retiring, had opened consulting firms. Allegedly, the mayor knew nothing about this and, when told, he promised, as usual, to "get to the bottom of this."

Meanwhile, nearly twenty-five years after Love Canal, another local neighborhood faced a major environmental disaster. This time it was the Hickory Woods development in South Buffalo. Hickory Woods was developed in the early 1990s when first Mayor Griffin and then Mayor Masiello initiated a scheme for the construction of new homes on land that had been occupied by Republic Steel for more than fifty years. Eager to foster new land use in his home base of South Buffalo, Griffin sent a letter to the LTV Corporation, Republic's parent company, in 1991. The letter expressed the city's interest in buying some of LTV's land for the creation of a residential community. Griffin was aware that there was a hazardous landfill just a few hundred yards from the proposed Hickory Woods project, so he made direct inquiries with LTV as to whether there was any history of land filling or environmental problems at the specific Hickory Woods site. The company wrote back that while there were no known environmental problems, there had never been any soil or groundwater tests conducted. One year later, Griffin ordered an environmental review of his own, which concluded that the site was in fact "free of environmental problems." The report, signed by the city's assistant environmental assessment coordinator, said that "the site is not located near any known industrial waste-disposal sites." One year after the review ordered by Griffin, Masiello, upon taking office, retained a consultant to conduct another soil test. This second test affirmed the conclusions of the first. State health officials disputed these findings and sent a letter to the mayor urging caution. "The report," they said, "does not have sufficient information to comment on the potential health concerns associated with the development of this parcel into residential property." According to the state official who wrote the letter, the city never responded.[25]

Eager to push the development, Masiello lent his full support to Hickory Woods, a new neighborhood that would include more than two hundred homes. Subsidies for purchase of homes in the Hickory Woods neighborhood would be provided by the city. Construction proceeded apace; homes were built and families moved in with no apparent problems or concerns until mid-1998, when a city inspector, noticing dry, black, gravelly material in the soil of a lot on Abby Street, ordered the project shut down. Construction came to a grinding halt. Facing mounting criticism for having promoted and subsidized the creation of a new neighborhood on clearly contaminated ground, the mayor said, "This is the first that I have heard about this. No one has brought this information to my attention." Finally recognizing that there was a problem at Hickory Woods, the city asked the United States Environmental Protection Agency to intervene. The city attorney said that the Masiello administration had done "an exemplary job" of identifying and responding to the problem. The mayor, too, seemed pleased with himself. "When Tony Masiello first knew there was a problem," he said, "the city acted expeditiously."[26]

Soon, the people of Hickory Woods began to abandon their homes altogether. "People have left because they are tired of waiting for compensation and tired of the constant stress that comes with living in a neighborhood contaminated with lead, arsenic and polycyclic hydrocarbons."[27] Angry at the inaction of city hall and frightened by the prospect of another Love Canal in their new South Buffalo neighborhood, the people of Hickory Woods wondered what the city government knew and when it knew it. They wondered, like so many others, what was going on.

In suburban Amherst, other kinds of environmental problems arose. Beginning in the late 1960s, as Amherst grew as quickly as any suburban area in the state, federal soil scientists warned politicians and developers of the dangers of building new homes in Amherst. According to the scientists, Amherst was on a flood plain and the soil they were building on was unsuitable for homes. In their zeal for expansion, town officials and real estate developers nevertheless encouraged housing developments in Amherst's federally regulated wetlands and floodplains. By the end of the 1990s, it became clear that their zeal had been foolhardy. Residents reported more than five hundred homes with foundation problems in the early 1990s. The *Buffalo News*, in a March 2003 article titled "Amherst Officials Ignored Data in Unstable Soil," reported that "today these warnings have come true... houses are sinking. Foundations are cracking. Walls are collapsing. Gas lines are snapping and hundreds of homeowners watch as their savings are drained and their futures are mortgaged on a house that may not be worth the money some are investing in them."

Amherst, particularly the 14051 zip code (including parts of East Amherst and Clarence), was one of the wealthiest areas in the state. According to *Money*, it was one of the wealthiest areas in the entire nation. Growth had been extraordinary. Endless cul-de-sacs and ever-larger and more expensive homes and golf courses had devoured the once-pristine landscape far removed from the gritty reality of life in the city. In opulent and ostentatious development oases like Spaulding Lake, multimillion-dollar "McMansions" were purchased as quickly as they were built. Advertisements, replete with large color photos that hawked the lifestyle as much as the homes, filled the Saturday Home Finder section of the *Buffalo News* with tantalizing descriptions: "Exquisite all brick Spaulding Lake mansion with three levels of lavish architectural detail." "Magnificent plaster moldings embellish the interiors of this 5 bedroom, 7 bath beauty.... Awesome gourmet kitchen, 2 staircases, 4 fireplaces, media room and wine cellar." One ad, describing a home with a "4.5 car garage," said that the sixty-eight-hundred-square-foot home would "[m]ake your dreams come true. $1,150,000."[28]

How was such growth possible? Where did the new residents who bought these opulent homes come from? What did they do? And how, given what everybody knew about the local economy, could they possibly afford it? The oddest disconnect was that the pace of new construction in East Amherst and Clarence outpaced the number of new households by a ratio of nearly four to one. Indeed, according to the Brookings Institute, the disparity between new construction and new households was greater in the Buffalo metropolitan area than anywhere else in the country. The continued trend of sprawl without population growth was, Brookings warned, "fraught with disaster that will lead sooner rather than later to continuing, inescapable population loss and real estate abandonment."[29]

David Rusk, a national expert on sprawl, agreed. In most cases, Rusk said, sprawl is a by-product of rapid and uncontrolled population growth, a response, however dangerous, to demographic trends and market forces. Rusk warned that this was not true of suburban sprawl in the Buffalo area. While sprawl is common in other metro areas, he said, it is usually driven by population growth. Between 1950 and 1990, Rusk said, the population of Erie County grew by only 7 percent. Its urbanized land area, however, grew by 133 percent, an alarming nineteen-to-one ratio, compared to an average three-to-one ratio nationally. When it came to sprawl in the absence of growth, Rusk said, "Buffalo is about the worst."[30]

The problem was ignored not only by the local developers who were somehow able to coax enough of the area's super rich to move, most of them from Williamsville to East Amherst and Clarence, but also by the public officials who touted the signs of growth, however inauspicious, as positive outcomes of their leadership. Most public officials, particularly the development officers in the Amherst Industrial Development Agency (AIDA), encouraged sprawl by dangling juicy tax incentives to companies willing to locate there. By 2003, the AIDA and two real estate development companies—Uniland Development and the Ciminelli Company—had been found guilty of violating an antipirating law by giving corporate tenants illegal tax abatements in an effort to lure them to Amherst.[31]

Meanwhile, the outlying suburbs, particularly East Amherst, Clarence, and Lancaster, with their strip plazas, traffic jams, McMansions, and seemingly endless lines of cars waiting at fast-food drive-throughs and cookie-cutter coffee "shops," continued to grow. By the middle of the first decade of the new century, these auto-friendly residential and shopping districts had become the destinations of choice in the Buffalo metropolitan area.

Meanwhile, in the city, all of the development deals for which the local leadership had energetically stumped seemed to be coming apart. The greatest collapse was "the Adelphia deal." Observers far more thoughtful than the governor and the mayor had long raised questions about Rigas's company. They wondered how Adelphia, with its high debt burden, could possibly succeed with its grand construction plans in downtown. Nevertheless, Pataki and Masiello, fully aware that Adelphia was carrying in excess of $14 million in reported debt in 2002, were not deterred from including the Rigases in their "dream team," which, as they never tired of promising, would renew Buffalo's waterfront. However, when the Rigases announced in the spring of 2002 that in addition to the massive debt that Adelphia actually reported there was another $3 billion of unrecorded debt, even the governor and the mayor became concerned. As news about the debt leaked, Adelphia stock fell precipitously from $31 per share in January to only eight cents per share by March. As people in Buffalo began to panic, wondering particularly about the fate of the Buffalo Sabres, the Rigases, closeted in their Coudersport, Pennsylvania, headquarters, were oddly silent. In June 2002, Adelphia declared bankruptcy. Shortly thereafter, John Rigas, his two sons, and two corporate executives, were arrested and indicted on conspiracy and fraud charges. The federal prosecution called it "one of the most elaborate and extensive corporate frauds in US history." The collapse of the Rigases also meant the collapse of the mayor's dream team and the end of his own dreams of waterfront revitalization. However, all hope was not lost. Masiello redoubled his dedication to landing a downtown casino, which would be owned and operated by the Seneca Nation of Indians.

While some people—Assemblyman Sam Hoyt and a citizens group called Citizens Against Casino Gambling—had railed against the Seneca Indian casino for years—most people were uncertain and confused. Though they sensed that there was something clearly wrong about the proposal, many hoped that the development of the casino downtown would play out just as Pataki and Masiello had promised. For politicians and downtown developers, there were just too many promises to ignore (and too many dollars to pass up). By 2006, the Seneca Gaming Corporation, with casinos in Niagara Falls and nearby Salamanca, and with annual revenues in excess of $300 million and more than three thousand employees, had become one of the largest companies in Western New York.[32] The Senecas were on a roll. In 2004, the tribe completed a bond sale of more than $300 million, the largest in the history of Indian gambling. Using their money and power, they had intimidated Masiello as well as the new mayor, Byron Brown. As site acquisition and demolition proceeded in the spring and summer of 2006, doubts about the casino grew. More than ever, a growing number of people began to ask the difficult questions that only a few had raised before. What, they wondered, would be Buffalo's actual share of casino proceeds? How would claims of Indian sovereignty affect the ability of federal, state, and local officials to enforce laws on the grounds of the casino? Finally, people began to ask questions about the Seneca Nation, and particularly their questionable leadership under Barry Snyder and the Seneca Party. Given the deeply troubled past of Snyder and his cohorts, could the people of Buffalo expect an honest accounting from the Senecas?[33] Besides, what would be the impact of the casino on existing downtown entertainment venues, most of which were already struggling to survive? What about the social costs—the increases in addictive behavior, credit card debt, and bankruptcy, all long known to be insidious side effects of casino gambling? What about the demolition of the historic H-O Oats grain elevator to make way for the new casino development? And perhaps most importantly, what about the impact of casino gambling on the spirit of the city?

Hope appeared in the form of a 2005 lawsuit filed in federal court by a group called Citizens for a Better Buffalo. Their petition argued that Pataki's compact with the Seneca Nation was illegal and should therefore be declared null and void. While a growing number of people in the community began to realize that the casino deal was "all snake-eyes and boxcars," as vocal casino critic Bruce Jackson put it, it was too little and too late. The die of casino gambling had already been cast; the deal was done.[34]

Linked to these "silver bullet" projects was the ongoing search for what were now called "shovel-ready sites," which the mayor, urged on by the big developers who made big political contributions, said were the essential ingredients for development. Shovel-ready sites referred to the creation, particularly downtown, of an inventory of fully cleared and fully cleaned-up sites that would be ever ready and instantly available for development. "Shovel-ready sites," they insisted, would jump-start development and, in the process, renew downtown. What little was still left of the traditional structure of a downtown already littered with parking lots and suburban-style buildings was threatened still further when in the early years of the new century everything became a target, including such noteworthy buildings as the landmark AM&A's store and the row of twentieth-century industrial buildings in the Washington Street Electric District. Many justifiably felt that city leadership had descended to a desperate and panicked grasping at straws.

Given his inclination to make deals, it was no surprise that after twelve years as mayor, Masiello took a job in December 2005 with a lobbying firm called Government Action Professionals (GAP). In addition to Masiello, the firm's only Democrat, GAP principals consisted of three of the best-connected Republicans in Western New York: two former deputies to the county executive, and Victor Farley, the former chairman of the Erie County Republican Party, who, according to the *Buffalo News*, "lobbied for the county and the city for years." Masiello, whether he realized it or not, had been preparing for this job for years. He joined a long list of local public officials who, after completion of their terms of public service, joined the mercenary culture of lobbyists. Among them were two former Republican congressmen. One was Bill Paxon, who, as a million-dollar-a-year man at Aiken-Gump, had been the Seneca's point man with Pataki. Another was Jack Quinn, who, upon leaving Congress in 2004, joined Paxon in Washington as a lobbyist for Cassidy and Associates, which, with more than $14 million in annual revenues and a client list that included Ford, USAir, and Wal-Mart, was one of the nation's largest lobbying firms. In addition, Eva Hassett, who was one of Masiello's closest advisors during his years as mayor and was the daughter of a well-connected Republican developer and lobbyist, went to work as a lobbyist for Savarino Construction, one of the area's largest and most aggressive real estate developers, at the end of Masiello's tenure.

According to *Buffalo News* reporter Tom Precious, Masiello, like the other politicians turned lobbyists, was "on familiar terrain." For more than thirty years he had worked in local and state politics. He had nurtured old relationships and cultivated new ones, and these relationships had taken him from councilman to state senator and eventually to mayor. Well liked, Masiello was seen as "nice," if not intelligent or competent. He had coasted for years on his likeability as he made slow progress up the ladder of local politics. He'd never known anything other than the back-slapping, old-boy network of Buffalo politics, the "hey, how ya' doin'" ways of people who'd been working, eating, playing, and doing business with each other since childhood. Everybody in Buffalo knew "Tony," first as "Big Red," a basketball standout at Canisius College, then as a friendly, big bear of a man on the Common Council, where he blandly represented his old West Side neighborhood for many years. With few ideas and little initiative, he was elected state senator in 1971, a post he dutifully filled until he was finally elected mayor of Buffalo in 1993. No matter how angry or frustrated people became with him, Masiello always remained "Tony," never "the mayor." Treated not as the leader of a great but challenged city, but instead as a good old boy from the neighborhood, people would often say, "Hey, don't worry. I'll take care of it. I'll talk to Tony about that." How, some wondered, could you expect higher and better standards of leadership when the boss was simply "Tony"? Convinced that he was hired as a lobbyist for *what* not *who* he knew, Masiello, forgetting the sorry record of his years in office, said upon accepting the job, "I think I bring a lot of expertise to help the city in Albany on many fronts. On the financial side, nobody knows their finances better than I do. I have an in-depth understanding of their government and what works and isn't working." A few eyebrows were raised when it became known that one of the firm's clients, Malcolm Pirnie, an environmental consulting firm, had done business for years with the mayor. Masiello addressed the question when he said he wouldn't lobby for Pirnie—"I can't do that and I won't do that"—

and most people in Buffalo were satisfied. "Hey," many seemed to say, "don't worry about Tony. Tony's a nice guy."[35]

Even the best of mayors would have been challenged by the problems in the city's public schools. With a rapidly dropping population (there were 37,000 students in 2006 as compared to 72,863 in 1975), the public schools of Buffalo, like those in cities throughout the country, were considered a failure by virtually everybody who lived there. No matter how hard the school system tried, no matter how many kids passed the standardized tests, and no matter how many feel-good stories the press told, the reality was that by the beginning of the new century the public schools had lost their most critical battle: the battle for the hearts and minds of the people who lived in Buffalo. With a student population plagued by a district-wide poverty rate of close to 80 percent, powerful professional and blue collar unions that impeded progress, a top-heavy bureaucracy that placed far too many people in offices and far too few in classrooms, the highest dropout rate in the state, and too many students prone to violence, the city's public schools were perceived as failures and were all but written off by the city's middle class. No longer able to blame the problem on lack of funding (at the end of 2005, the amount of money spent annually on each pupil in the Buffalo schools exceeded $16,000), people were baffled. The Buffalo school system increasingly served the poor, the blacks, and the Hispanics. Between 1999 and 2005, the percentage of low-income students eligible for free lunches jumped from 54 percent to 78 percent. In 1967, minorities represented 41.5 percent of the district's enrollment. By the end of the 2006 school year, they represented close to 80 percent.[36]

Suburban schools were different, of course, particularly in the rich districts where abundant property tax revenues were used to fund them. A *Buffalo News* article on rich and poor school districts described Clarence High School:

Enter past the arching picture windows, where a garden of greenery leads into an art gallery with recessed lighting, and you'll see what money can buy. Student announcements are read from television monitors on the walls. The state-of-the-art, eight-lane swimming pool area has skylights and second-story gallery seating. Labs have the newest equipment, with students recording experiments on computers. The Clarence library-media center—known among other educators as "Barnes & Noble"—is the most elaborate around, with cushy chairs, brick pillars and second-floor atrium. And then there's the rich tapestry of courses and extracurricular activities for students to choose from and enjoy. Sixteen Advanced Placement classes. Three photography courses. Fourth-year Latin. Engineering Design. A science/leadership course in which students go whitewater rafting and canoeing in the Adirondacks. A 175-member choir whose repertoire includes Bach's Sanctus in D Minor.[37]

In financially strapped Buffalo, meanwhile, where teachers, like police and fire-fighters, struggled under a pay freeze imposed by the control board, the most basic improvements were hard to come by. The gross discrepancies between schools in Buffalo and those in the suburbs led Phil Rumore, the president of the Buffalo Teachers Federation, to insist that unless New York State ended its reliance on property taxes to fund public education, "the poor will stay poor and the rich will stay rich."[38]

By the middle of the new century's first decade, the only students left in the city's public schools were either those few children who had the privilege of attending Buffalo's academic high schools (City Honors and Hutchinson Tech-nical) and special schools, such as Performing Arts and the Montessori School (located across from each other on Clinton Street), or thousands of others who were trapped without a choice. The charter school movement, which counted more than five thousand students in 2006, though seen by many as an effort by middle-class parents, mostly whites, to create safe havens in an unsettling public school environment, gave others hope that it was still possible to live in the city and obtain a decent education for their children.

Integrally tied to questions about the public schools were questions about race. Indeed, during the early years of the new century, nothing dominated the public and private agenda in Buffalo quite like race issues. In 2005, when African Americans accounted for close to 50 percent of the city's total population of 297,000, for the first time in the city's history, an African American politician was overwhelmingly elected mayor of Buffalo. It seemed that African Americans would finally exert significant control over the political life of the city. City gov-ernment was filled with, if not dominated by, African Americans. Many of Mayor Brown's closest advisors were African American, as were both the police commis-sioner and the fire commissioner. Blacks had significant representation on the Common Council, the Board of Education, and all other boards and bodies whose decisions influenced daily life in the city. In addition, African Americans held highly visible public jobs. The school superintendent, James A. Williams, was black, as was the president of Buffalo State College, Muriel A. Howard. At the University at Buffalo, African Americans were prominent, particularly in sports, where, alone among Division I schools, the director of athletics as well as the coaches of both the football and basketball teams were black. Because the City of Buffalo was represented by proud, accomplished, and dedicated African Ameri-cans, the public face of the city had, to a real extent, become black.

Unfortunately, the public picture of African Americans in Buffalo was char-acterized even more powerfully by what appeared, at least to many, as the growing influence of an African American underclass. With close to 50 percent of all African American households headed by single mothers (as compared to 16 percent for whites) and with 34 percent of all blacks in Buffalo living at or below the poverty line (as compared to 18 percent for whites), the problems of poverty clearly undermined the structure of Buffalo's African American community. Some of this had to do with the decline of industry, the impact of which was even more devastating in African American communities than it was in white ones. For years, Buffalo's African American community, like that in other cities throughout the "Rust Belt," consisted of thousands of blue collar workers. These workers had been protected by a union (most often the UAW); they had made good money, received great benefits, and earned a solid standing within the powerful world of the industrial economy. Because most of these well-paid individuals lived in the city (even in 2006, only 12 percent of the area's total suburban population was African American), they nurtured and sustained the neighborhoods in which they lived. These "Blue Collar Aristocrats" were the neighborhoods' most stable citizens: they owned their own homes, were active in the local churches and schools, and served as important role models to the children in the neighborhoods. The collateral damage to these neighborhoods, as much as the jobs and the dollars lost, was a blow from which Buffalo's African American community has yet to recover.

The black underclass emerged in the vacuum left by the shrinking African American blue collar middle class. In downtown and in the neighborhoods, on Connecticut and Vermont streets on the West Side, and on the side streets of Black Rock, Riverside, and North Buffalo, people worried about the growing presence of the African American underclass: the threatening sounds of rap and hip hop booming out of passing cars; young men hanging out on corners, sporting the apparel of "gangsta rap"; young black males, swaggering matador-like down the middle of the streets, challenging motorists, it seemed, to hit them. They worried about inner city kids at venerable high schools like Lafayette who attacked their schoolmates, abused their teachers, and degraded a learning environment that educators had taken so long to build. People thought twice about riding the metro, where the Niagara Frontier Transportation Authority piped classical music into stations in an effort to pacify the throngs of rowdy kids who crowded in on their way to and from school. People also worried about the high rates of homicide in the African American community and the dreaded gang wars and drive-by shootings that left so many people—most of them young, most of them black—dead or wounded. It was hard enough to live in Buffalo, and many people responded to these threats to peace of mind by leaving. Among them were a growing number of African Americans who, far more than whites, understood the challenges of life in the inner city. In a movement that would continue to grow, upwardly mobile African Americans began to join their white counterparts in an interracial march to the suburbs.

While the numbers were still insignificant (somewhere around 15 percent of the more than six hundred thousand people living in Buffalo's suburbs were African

American), more and more blacks—public school teachers and principals, government employees, and anyone with the means—moved to the suburbs, the less affluent to inner-ring suburbs like Cheektowaga and West Seneca, the more affluent to Amherst and North Tonawanda. Between 1990 and 2000, the African American population of Amherst grew by 30 percent to 4,544. During that same period, it tripled in Cheektowaga to 2,754. Indeed, in 2005, the first African American church in Buffalo, the Zion Dominion Church of God in Christ, moved from its inner city location on Genesee Street to the overwhelmingly white suburb of Amherst.[39]

Most African Americans, however (approximately one hundred thousand), continued to live in the city. The poorest were concentrated on the old East Side, on Broadway, Genesee, Sycamore, and William. In more recent years, a growing number of the city's poorest blacks moved from the East Side to the West Side, particularly into the area bounded by Grant and Niagara streets and by Massachusetts and Forest avenues. The tightly knit communities that once defined the area were gone, and nobody, neither landlord nor tenant, seemed to care about properties that were surrounded by poverty and decay.

Meanwhile, much of the East Side became an abandoned wasteland. Hundreds of homes on dozens of streets, built when the city was twice its current size, sat empty. In 2000, 18 percent of the available housing units in the city, most of them on the East Side, were vacant. The houses were both eyesores and hazards. In the absence of any demand for these houses, demolition was the only viable strategy, it seemed, despite the cries of hardcore preservationists. In 2000, more than 2,649 homes were demolished; more than a century of history was plowed into the ground. Compounding the public's ambivalent response to these demolitions was the fact that the city had no plan for reuse of the growing tracts of empty land that now characterized much of the East Side. Indeed, given the continued decline of the population, there was no plan, other than talk of creating an urban forest, which made any sense. As a result, block after block of the city's East Side became empty fields. No wonder so many people in Buffalo were willing to give a large chunk of their city "back to the Indians."

While some middle-class African American neighborhoods in Buffalo remained stable, such as the area around Humboldt Park—on Brunswick and Hamlin Park, and on Hedley, Blaine, and the other small side streets behind Canisius College—these neighborhoods were in jeopardy. While their inhabitants tried to preserve communal strength and stability, they fought battles, particularly against the rise in gang-related violence, against overwhelming odds.

For reasons that are difficult to identify and understand, very little mixing of the races occurred in Buffalo. Indeed, there were few public places in Buffalo where whites and blacks met in any significant numbers. While there was some racial overlap in Delaware Park, particularly on its golf course, virtually none occurred at the theaters, at the philharmonic, on the lawn at the Pine Grill Reunion, or at the Farmer's Market on Bidwell Parkway. Despite the growing size of the African American middle class, African Americans could be found at few of the better restaurants in the city. With the exception of the Anchor Bar, a well-known restaurant that sits astride the city's ancient racial divide at Main and North streets (indeed, it is no wonder that its location at a cultural crossroads led to the Anchor Bar's creation of "Buffalo Wings," a blend of Italian and African American culinary traditions), no restaurant, since the closing in 2001 of the Calumet Arts Café on Chippewa Street, could boast a racially mixed clientele.

Unlike African Americans, Buffalo's mostly Puerto Rican Hispanics, despite their growing numbers (over twenty-five thousand in the metropolitan area in 2006), remained largely invisible. It was not easy being Puerto Rican in Buffalo. There was nothing tropical about Buffalo; the culture, sounds, and colors of the Caribbean fell on fallow ground. With median family income at $18,500 (as compared to $28,000 for Buffalo's whites and $19,000 for African Americans), 45 percent of Buffalo's Hispanics lived below the poverty line. They were the poorest people in the city. Low incomes produced low rates of home ownership and, therefore, higher housing costs. In a city where home ownership was dwindling (only 50 percent of the city's whites owned their own homes, compared to 36 percent for blacks), the Hispanic rate of 25 percent meant that they were spending far more for housing than any other group in the city.[40]

It was even worse for Hispanic children in Buffalo, which had the highest poverty rate in the nation among Hispanic children. Jay Rey, the first *Buffalo News* reporter to pay significant attention to the city's Hispanic community, reported in 2003 that nearly 57 percent of Hispanic children in Buffalo were growing up poor. In a community where almost 40 percent of all children were growing up in poverty (the sixth-highest in the nation), the poverty rate for Hispanics was nonetheless shocking. Indeed, the rates of poverty among Hispanic children were only marginally lower in nearby Syracuse and Rochester.[41]

Buffalo's Puerto Ricans were isolated on the city's Lower West Side, an urban nook that was unknown to the community at large, particularly the more than six hundred thousand people who lived in the city's suburbs. There was no compelling reason for outsiders to visit, for the barrio on Buffalo's West Side bore little resemblance to those well-known centers of Hispanic vitality like Spanish Harlem in New York or Calle Ocho in Miami. Outsiders—"Americans" or "white people," the Puerto Ricans called them—sometimes barreled down Niagara Street on their way downtown or sped across town on Virginia Street (the proposed route of the long-forgotten Lower West Side Arterial) en route to the Thruway entrance at Niagara Street, but few of them comprehended the overwhelming challenge Hispanics faced in trying to establish a vibrant community in Buffalo.

Not much progress had been made in the thirty-odd years since Frankie Perez organized and led his people in the early 1970s against the construction of a highway arterial that would have obliterated the neighborhood that he tried so tirelessly to build. If anything, conditions in Buffalo's Lower West Side barrio, like the African American ghetto on the East Side, had worsened. Without decent job opportunities for unskilled workers, Hispanic migrants and their families found themselves caught up in an intergenerational cycle of poverty.

The decline of the Hispanics' economic condition was mirrored by their virtually nonexistent political voice. As a minority trapped within the Ellicott District, which was dominated by African Americans, Puerto Ricans had no direct access to the corridors of power. Indeed, although they comprised at least 10 percent of the city's total population, Ralph Hernandez, a member of the Buffalo School Board, was the only Puerto Rican who held an elected position. In a city where tribal ties, whether Irish, Italian, or African American, were what determined access, the Puerto Ricans were shut out, relying exclusively on the good graces of a local state assemblyman, Sam Hoyt, who almost alone among area politicians embraced Buffalo's Puerto Ricans. While there were power brokers in the community, "go-to guys" like Andres "Andy" Garcia, who cultivated relationships with the city's black and white political establishment, and who could, with a phone call, receive money for a heritage event, the sad truth was that whatever money Buffalo's Puerto Ricans received came as a gift, not as a result of power and influence. In the absence of meaningful access to political and economic opportunities in the wider community, young Puerto Ricans often turned to crime as a means of acquiring money and power within the neighborhood. In 2004, for example, violence spiked in the Puerto Rican Lower West Side. During the spring and summer, at least nine people were shot, three fatally, as local gangs named for streets—the "Tenth Street Gang" and the "Seventh Street Gang"—fought for control of the neighborhood's lucrative cocaine and heroin trade.

Despite its prevalence on the Lower West Side and on the East Side, poverty in Buffalo cut across the lines of color and race. In a city where the median household income hovered at just under $30,000 (as compared to $46,000 for Erie County and $49,000 for the nation), it was even lower in the decaying, still predominantly white neighborhoods of Black Rock and Riverside, or Lovejoy and Seneca-Babcock, places where the poverty level reached close to 30 percent.[42] Gone from these places was the vitality of once lively commercial streets like Ontario and Tonawanda, Amherst and Grant, Lovejoy and Seneca. They had been replaced by an abandoned and bedraggled landscape of postindustrial urban America. "Welcome," wrote *Buffalo News* columnist Rod Watson, "to the world of the working poor, where people with the least end up paying the most to make it from day to day. In this world, rent to own franchises are more prevalent than department stores, check cashers and predatory lenders replace banks that fled to richer communities and high-priced corner stores rush in where supermarkets fear to tread."[43]

At the turn of the century, Buffalo did not need to be rebuilt; it needed to be healed. Its people needed comfort and reassurance that somehow something would be done to restore the root systems of their daily lives, which had been so badly weakened by the effects of the past fifty years. The people of Buffalo needed to know that their personal landscapes would someday be improved and that their heroic efforts to strengthen and improve the quality of their lives would be rewarded, not betrayed. They needed to know that the faith they had in themselves and their community could undo the negative impacts of history. Certainly, history had been rough on Buffalo, and so much had been lost: neighborhoods, downtown, people, jobs, schools, elm trees, sidewalks, front porches, and all of those comforting qualities that are associated with the city as it was in the days before cars, suburbs, television, street crime, broken schools, and broken promises. The wounds of history could be seen everywhere in a landscape out of time, filled with old cars, old houses, old people, and old buildings. But despite all its problems, many people still believed in the promise of Buffalo, believed that somehow they could build new gates for an old and battered city. Beneath it all, under the layers of history's dust, there lay a city with color, character, commitment, energy, passion, intelligence, and creativity. If all of this could someday be harnessed, the potential of Buffalo and its people would be limitless.

NOTES

1. S. Roberts, "Flight of Young Adults Is Causing Worries," *New York Times,* June 13, 2006.

2. J. Rey, "City Falls Below 300,000," *Buffalo News,* March 16, 2001, p. A1.

3. Ibid.

4. D. Robinson, "Job Losses Increase in Buffalo Region," *Buffalo News,* June 20, 2003, p. C10.

5. Business First, *Book of Lists, 2006* (Charlotte, NC: American City Business Journals, 2005), p. 120.

6. B. Meyer, "Bureaucracy: Big and Bloated," *Buffalo News,* May 29, 2000, p. A1.

7. T. Dolan, "Researchers Soften Blow," *Buffalo News,* February 1, 2000, p. A1.

8. M. Glynn, "Trico Workers Hoped Against Hope," *Buffalo News,* December 4, 2002, p. B1.

9. Business First, *Book of Lists,* p. 8.

10. J. Epstein, "The Man Who Made M&T," *Buffalo News,* August 14, 2005, p. A1.

11. D. Robinson, "Can Downtown Property Values End Downward Spiral," *Buffalo*

News, December 15, 1996, p. C11.

12. K. Collison, "Ten Years Down the Line, Metro Rail Brings Satisfied Riders but Few Spin-offs for Buffalo," *Buffalo News*, May 21, 1995, B1.

13. R. Huntington, "Downtown Moodpiece," *Buffalo News*, April 3, 1994, p. B6.

14. D. Esmonde, "It's Time to Stop," *Buffalo News*, November 12, 2001, p. B1.

15. B. Meyer, "Conditions Worsen," *Buffalo News*, November 4, 2002, p. A1.

16. "Albany's Life Line to Buffalo," *Buffalo News*, May 10, 2001, B4.

17. T. Precious and B. Meyer, "State Plan Would Give City Control Board," *Buffalo News*, February 22, 2003, p. A1.

18. Office of the New York State Comptroller, Budget Review, Erie County, June, 2006, p. 11.

19. K. Walker, "The Numbers Tell the Story, *Buffalo News*, April 30, 2006, p. A1.

20. J. Heaney, "The Half-Billion Dollar Bust," *Buffalo News*, November 14, 2004, p. A1.

21. S. Lindsted, "Hopes Soar with Bass Pro," *Buffalo News*, November 20, 2004, p. A1.

22. P. Lakamp, "The High Price of Subsidies," *Buffalo News*, December 6, 2004, p. A1.

23. J. Heaney, "Failed Loans, Modest Job Gains Mark City Lending," *Buffalo News*, November 15, 2004, p. A1.

24. J. Heaney, "Artistic Success, Fiscal Failures," *Buffalo News*, November 16, 2004, p. A1.

25. Phil Fairbanks, "Toxin Neglect: City Had Early Warnings," *Buffalo News*, February 11, 2001, p. A1.

26. A. Cardinale, "Hickory Woods Alerted," *Buffalo News*, December 15, 2000, p. A1.

27. Phil Fairbanks, "Fleeing Their Dreams," *Buffalo News*, August 11, 2003, p. A1.

28. *Buffalo News Home Finder*, April 22, 2006, p. 12.

29. J. Rey, "Key Study Says Sprawl Has Hurt City," *Buffalo News*, May 30, 2004, p. A1.

30. J. Rey and N. Cervantes, "Shrinking Outward," *Buffalo News*, April 1, 2001, p. A1.

31. S. Schulman, "Court Rules Amherst Is Guilty of 'Pirating,'" *Buffalo News*, June 11, 2003, p. A1.

32. Business First, *Book of Lists*, p. 120.

33. In early 2003, members of Seneca Nation president Barry Snyder's family were implicated in a bizarre $10 million cigarette smuggling caper, which among other things was linked to aid for Hezbollah terrorists. See Michael Beebe, "Seneca Aide Faces Charges in Smuggling of Cigarettes," *Buffalo News*, February 22, 2003, p. B1.

34. Bruce Jackson, "Proposed Casino in Downtown Is a Bad Deal, Not a Done Deal," January 4, 2006, http://www.Buffaloreport.com/2006/060104Jackson.note.html.

35. For details on Masiello's job with Government Action Professionals, see Tom Precious, "As Lobbyist, Masiello Is on Familiar Terrain," *Buffalo News*, February 13, 2006, p. B1.

36. For demographic data on the children in the Buffalo public schools, see Buffalo Board of Education, "Compilation of Demographic and Other Pertinent Information," March 2006.

37. S. Schulman and N. Cervantes, "Halls of Injustice," *Buffalo News*, April 29, 2002, p. A1.

38. P. Simon, "Rumore Calls Aid Disparity a 'Disgrace,'" *Buffalo News*, February 1, 2006, p. B1.

39. V. Thomas, "For Zion Dominions Church, Move from Downtown to Amherst Is Historic," *Buffalo News*, June 13, 2005, p. B3.

40. J. Rey, "City Leads in Poverty of Hispanic Children," *Buffalo News*, May 24, 2003, p. A1.

41. Ibid.

42. R. Watson and J. D. Epstein, "The High Cost of Being Poor," *Buffalo News*, June 18, 2006, p. A1.

43. Ibid.

chapter 15

NOW IS THE TIME

Restoring a sense of Place

Community exists in the space where history and hope meet, where an awareness of the past and a belief in the future inspire people to identify with a place and to dedicate themselves to its improvement. In Buffalo there are many people living in such places—where the atmosphere is haunting, where the confluence of old and powerful architecture, of soaring trees and verdant gardens, of howling winds and soft breezes embrace the space and, in the process, call the people to a deeper commitment to community.

An intense sense of place exists in Buffalo. Most of the three hundred thousand people who still call Buffalo home really care about the city. We argue about it and worry about it, but we believe in our community, ourselves, and our ability as citizen activists to improve it. Tied deeply to the uniqueness of place is the strength and vitality of the countless citizens' groups whose energy and activities fill the streets and neighborhoods of the city. Combining education, community organization, astute lobbying, and sophisticated communication and public relations skills, we represent democracy at its best as we strive to guarantee that the future will be bright in Buffalo. There are so many groups of citizens, too many to list, and participation in them demands the time, energy, and commitment of thousands of people throughout the city. Citizen engagement and participation is, indeed, the mother's milk of this community. Despite a past filled with the hurts of history and the disappointments of poor leadership, our passion and our energy imbue every corner of the community with hope for the future.

Much of what motivates us is a deep appreciation of our history and our heritage. While history in Buffalo has always been challenging and occasionally cruel, we cherish our past and recognize its importance to the future. For years, few people valued our rich legacy, the breathtaking beauty of our natural environment, and the magnificence of our physical infrastructure. Indeed, frightened by a future that seemed to be leaving us behind, we acted as if our city's survival depended on obliterating our past, or at least forgetting it. But experience has taught us otherwise. We have come to understand and act on the belief that our best guides to the future are the gifts we have received from the past. By reclaiming our past and reinforcing our heritage, we have come to realize that we can create a more meaningful present and a still more promising future.

In the game of "place making," nothing is more important than the past. In Buffalo, as in cities everywhere, place making is at the root of the efforts that citizens have made to improve the quality and character of life in their communities. By engaging in stewardship of specific places that are simultaneously rooted in the past and reaching into the future, citizen activists preserve our history and maintain our communal memory. At the same time, such efforts become a driving force in our collective understanding of how best to heal, renew, and strengthen our city.

This holds true on Richmond Avenue, a street rich in history and breathtaking architecture. From Colonial Circle near its northern end to Symphony Circle at its southern terminus, Richmond retains the beauty and majesty that Fredrick Law Olmsted envisioned when he laid out the avenue as part of his master park plan for Buffalo. For the people who live on or near Richmond, knowledge of its history, appreciation of its architecture, and commitment to the ongoing evolution of the community rooted there has inspired many of them to join in stewardship efforts. In recent years, two different community groups—the Kleinhans Community Association and the Richmond Avenue Association—have been working on projects that have led to a rediscovery of the neighborhood's past and a strengthened commitment to its future. For many years, Richmond was marked for widening. Indeed, throughout the 1920s and '30s, as planners and politicians wrestled with the impact of the automobile, serious consideration was given to proposals for extending the street directly into downtown by cutting it through the neighborhood that has since become known as "Allentown." Fortunately, these plans were abandoned. Nonetheless, efforts to accommodate traffic were made during the late 1930s when two of the fountains of light that Fredrick Law Olmsted had designed—one at Symphony Circle and one at Ferry Street—

were removed. Hard times followed. Richmond, a street where the cathedral of elm trees was most glorious, suffered terribly during the 1950s and '60s as the blight of Dutch Elm disease coursed through the city. According to long-time city forester Ed Drabek, of the one hundred twenty-five thousand elms in Buffalo in 1950, close to 10 percent of them grew on Richmond. By 1970, only thirty-five thousand remained in the entire city, with only several hundred on Richmond. Stripped of its arboreal protection, Richmond sat exposed and vulnerable. Throughout the next twenty-five years, Richmond's decline continued, with the front lawns of the many glorious Victorian homes pockmarked with "For Sale" signs. However, by building on history and the invaluable legacy of Olmsted, a group of residents on Richmond began to plan for the future.

The process of community healing and renewal is a gradual, sometimes serendipitous unfolding; it often occurs as the result of the convergence of seemingly unrelated events. Such was the case on Richmond Avenue. First came the commitment of a handful of dedicated citizens to restore Kleinhans Music Hall, the world-renowned masterpiece designed by Eliel and Eero Saarinen. Ten years and $12 million later, the restoration of the music hall was complete. Today, it sits like a jewel nestled in Olmsted's wooded landscape. When a gentle summer breeze stirs the trees, its magnificent curved façade is a series of ripples on the surface of the restored semicircular reflecting pool that had for many years sat empty, collecting piles of dead leaves and litter. At the same time, both the Richmond Avenue Association and the Kleinhans Community Association planned to re-create not only the original circles that Olmsted had designed at Symphony Circle and at Richmond and Ferry, but to also re-create the tall, sculptured light standards that had for years identified these spaces. In November 2002, using a combination of public and private funds, and working closely with the Olmsted Conservancy, members of these two inspired community associations presided over the restoration of the old, knowing that in the process they strengthened the new. For the people on Richmond, the past and present have converged. The result has been the creation of a special sense of place: a place where passionate people have embraced the past and in the process have built a beacon for the future.

Located just around the corner, south of the First Presbyterian Church, which towers over the intersection of Wadsworth and Symphony Circle, the Allentown neighborhood blends a rich and kinetic tradition of both the genteel and the bohemian. In Allentown, healing and renewal began in the 1960s, as community activists banded together to defend the neighborhood's urban fabric from the threat of the wrecking ball; today there is no more interesting or stimulating place in the city. From Franklin on the east, Days Park in the west, Virginia Street in the south, and North Street in the north, Allentown represents everything that is hoped for in the neighborhoods of our city: the Victorian residential side streets of Park, Irving, and Mariner; the quiet glory of Arlington Park and Days Park; the funky mix of locally owned shops, bars, performance spaces, restaurants, and coffeeshops that combine to create an exciting and diverse mix of people and activities that make those who live there smile. Because it is vibrant, cheap, and welcoming, Allentown is the home to a growing number of immigrants from Africa, mostly refugees from Angola, Somalia, Liberia, and the Congo. They can be seen everywhere in Allentown: waiting with their children for the school bus at Hudson and Wadsworth, walking to and from the Adult Learning Center at Elmwood and Virginia, and attending church services at Holy Cross on Niagara. The men are tall and proud, and the women, wrapped in the multicolored dresses of their homelands, have a dignified bearing, which the insidious street culture of the ghetto cannot strip away. Foreigners, like native Buffalonians, sense the power of place. And they, too, are drawn to Allentown.

The peculiarity of place that distinguishes Allentown is its diversity, which is particularly noticeable at the Towne Restaurant. For more than twenty-five years, the Towne has been the focal point of Allentown. What was true then remains true today. Family owned and operated, the Towne is open twenty-four hours a day and serves the entire rainbow of people who make up the city. It thrives on diversity: dusty, paint-splattered contractors on break; business people meeting over a meal; neighborhood street people, gays, and musicians; local artists and shopkeepers, and well-dressed couples on their way to a Philharmonic concert at Kleinhans all seem comfortable in the no-questions-asked, come-as-you-are ambience of this local institution. At Towne, the food is good, the portions are large, the service is excellent, and the price is right.

The crowded community bulletin board in the vestibule of the restaurant proclaims that the Towne belongs to everyone. It is crowded with ads, posters, and announcements. Black letters on orange poster board announce "Nightmare on Allen Street," a Halloween rock 'n' roll jam to be held at Nietzsche's, the best live music bar in Buffalo, which is located just down the street. A beautiful silk-screened poster invites the public to a lecture sponsored by the Preservation Coalition of Erie County on "The English Country House" at St. John's Grace Episcopal Church. Under a richly detailed pen drawing, another sign says that there is a one-bedroom apartment available in the historic Tifft Row Houses, a group of early Victorian brick homes across the street from the Towne. Still another sign announces that two films are showing at the Polish Community Center; one is called *Polonia Lives: A Look at the Efforts of Polish and Black Residents Resisting Plans to Destroy Their Neighborhood to Make Way for an Auto Plant in Detroit.* In the polyglot community that is the Towne, everyone *is* a neighbor.

Allentown's history as a bohemian enclave open to outsiders has led to the creation of the Infringement Festival, Allentown's indigenous festival of the avant-garde. Originally organized by a handful of Allentown artists on a meager budget, the Infringement Festival has no stages or dedicated performance space of its own. Instead, it weaves its way through the fabric of the neighborhood. There are puppet shows in the tiny theater at the rear of Rust Belt Books and poetry readings at the Allen Street Hardware Café. Meanwhile, in an empty storefront on Allen, the Subversive Theatre Company performs Brecht while other actors perform Shakespeare in the parking lot next to Ali's Farm Store. As the artists who created the Infringement Festival know, the streets of Allentown are fertile ground for creative expression. The festival is an annual expression of the fun and excitement they experience on a daily basis just living there.

There are few finer, more identifiable places in Buffalo than Days Park, at the west end of Allen Street. Days Park was born in the 1850s when a brick manufacturer named Thomas Day bequeathed it to the city as a park. Its current design is Olmsted's, whose plans for it included the planting of dozens of trees and the central placement of a fountain surrounded by a wrought iron fence. By the end of the 1960s, there was no trace of any of the Olmsted design elements. The trees were gone, killed by the scourge of Dutch Elm disease, and the fountain, perhaps in anticipation of the extension of Richmond Avenue through Days Park, had been removed in 1923. Today, however, both the trees and the fountain are back, and the uniqueness of place in Days Park has been restored. Dozens of linden trees planted in the early 1970s by citizen activists now shelter and define the park. And a new fountain installed by the Days Park Block Club graces its center. In the process of researching the history of the park and restoring its lost glory, the block club, like its counterparts in the Kleinhans and Richmond neighborhoods, has reinforced the special sense of place that characterizes Days Park.

Not far from the Days Park neighborhood, the Lower West Side, whose boundaries are hard to precisely define, is bounded roughly by the Niagara River on the west, Porter Avenue in the north, city hall to the south, and a grouping of streets that converge around Virginia and Elmwood on the east. What Joanne Wypijewski wrote in 1994 about the area, in an introductory essay to *Triptychs*, Milton Rogovin's book of Lower West Side photographs, is as apt today as it was then:

> Almost nine thousand people live on the Lower West Side. Once called the Italian neighborhood...the area now has a decidedly Larin cast. Yet one would not say the Lower West Side is "the Spanish neighborhood" and leave it at that. On street corners and project drive ways, in the back and forth of social intercourse, the faces reflect layers of in-migration: Puerto Rican, Italian, black (from the city's East Side), American Indian, Arab, Vietnamese. More interracial exchange occurs here than in any other part of Buffalo. Pinwheels of children, of every color, whirl

about the side-walks. Among their elders one finds every shade of tolerance, every tint of good and bad, every addition and process of reform.[1]

While the racial and ethnic landscape is mixed and there are indeed a growing number of people from countries all over Africa, the dominant flavor of the Lower West Side remains the sabor de Puerto Rico. You can see it in the tropical scenes painted on murals throughout the neighborhood; at the tables of the Niagara Café, in the tiny botanica on Niagara Street; in the santero ceremonies held secretly in ancient wooden homes on Busti and Seventh Street; in the aisles of Tops Super Market; in the CD- and DVD-packed aisles of Willie and Maria Ruiz's record shop on Niagara, where Spanish is the loving tongue; on the streets and sidewalks on the first Saturday of September when, since 2003, the community has held a Puerto Rican Day Parade; on the pages of *Panorama Hispano*, a neighborhood Spanish-language weekly; in the passion of the bilingual teachers at the Herman Badillo School on Elmwood and Johnson Park; in the meetings of the Latin American Small Business Association at Lou Santiago's Niagara Street offices; in the bomba and plena performances of Frankie and Liliangina Quinones on the dance floor of La Luna, Buffalo's only Latin nightclub; in the productions of RAICES, Rolando Gomez's Puerto Rican theater company; in the eyes of the players on Los Leones de La Luna, the Puerto Rican softball team, proudly wearing their orange and black pin-striped uniform, who swept the competition in the Buffalo bar league in the summer of 2003; in the faces of the fishermen at the foot of Ferry Street; and in the parandas of Christmas and the Three Kings parade at Epiphany, when the winery streets of the Lower West Side are filled with the parading Boriquas of Buffalo. On the Lower West Side, the landscape and the streetscape are fluid—front yards, sidewalks, and commercial streets run together seamlessly, and there is little differentiation between private and public spaces. Color, character, vitality, and diversity define the Lower West Side, creating a sense of place that is utterly unique.

The uniqueness of place that characterizes the Lower West Side has been strengthened in recent years by a growing number of new immigrants, mostly from Africa. Recently, they have been arriving in Buffalo at a rate of about one thousand per year. On the historic side streets of the Lower West Side, they have begun to carve out new homes for themselves. Four not-for-profit agencies affiliated with international refugee relief organizations carry out the mission of resettling the new immigrants in Buffalo. Journey's End, located on Barton Street in the old studios of WNED, Buffalo's NPR affiliate, is one of these. The director of Journey's End, Robert Roggie, in referring to the growing number of African residents in the West Side, said in the spring of 2006 that "things are changing. I can feel it in the air." Roggie, who grew up in rural Marilla before moving to the Lower West Side to study

Spanish in the early 1980s, is convinced that when and if the city adopts a strategy for the acceptance and integration of new immigrants, the difficult obstacles that they face will be overcome. "There are 30,000 African refugees and immigrants in St. Paul, for goodness sake. We can get them here if we really wanted to."[2]

Even in the absence of a public policy that would welcome and aid in the integration of new immigrants, still they come: from Cuba, Burma, Somalia, Sudan, Angola, Chad, Liberia, Ethiopia, Ukraine, and Belorussia. The influx has brought new life to the streets and neighborhoods of the Lower West Side and beyond, to places like Connecticut and Grant Street, Massachusetts and Vermont, streets that for so long have been down, if not out. The foreign-born newcomers can be seen every day walking from the Lower West Side to the offices of the Immigrant and Refugee Association on Franklin Street, which is run by Catholic Charities. Both individuals and entire families—some from Bosnia and Albania, some from the Ukraine and Moldavia, and some, wearing traditional clothing of Sudan and Somalia—make their way on the narrow sidewalk of Edward Street. They dodge the speeding suburbanites for whom Edward Street is an access route to downtown, and hope that somehow, in some way, they will be able to find a new home for themselves and their families in Buffalo.

Despite the many difficulties, the new refugees and immigrants are finding their way in Buffalo, persisting in their struggles against the obstacles of history, language, climate, and attitude. Many have found success. Their children fill the halls of School 45 and Grover Cleveland High School, where more than six hundred of the nine hundred enrolled children speak a language other than English. The children's parents fill the classrooms of the Adult Learning Center, the International Institute, and the Western New York Literacy Volunteers. Working where and when they can, and buying homes when they are able, these newcomers are struggling to improve their lives and, in the process, the life of their neighborhoods and city as well.

People on the East Side, also increasingly aware of their community's history, have fostered a new sense of pride in the present and hope for the future. They have affirmed an awareness of place, and their commitment has strengthened the quality of daily life on the Lower East Side. A group of African Americans led by George Arthur, Kevin Cottrell, and Jesse Nash Jr., have been working since the early 1990s to make real the promises of an organization known as the Michigan Avenue Preservation Corporation. Since the early years of the nineteenth century, the neighborhood was at the center of the dynamic history of Buffalo's African American community. In 1845, on Michigan Avenue between William and Broadway, in a building that still stands, a group of free blacks living in Buffalo formed the Michigan Avenue Baptist Church. Several years later, in the same church, Frederick Douglass came to speak to a convention of African American abolitionists. The church's basement served as a station on the Underground Railroad; runaway slaves were hidden there as they awaited their final journey across the Niagara River to Canada and freedom. The church was also the site, in the early years of the twentieth century, where Mary Talbert, W. E. B. Du Bois, and others met to form the Niagara Movement, which soon after became the NAACP. It was from this church as well that Reverend Jesse Nash, a transcendent leader to his community, presided from the early 1920s until his death more than fifty years later. Finally, it was there, in 1993, that a young African American named Kenneth Cottrell formed the Underground Railroad Committee of the Niagara Frontier, which was dedicated to the commemoration of the church as one of the nation's major locales of African American heritage. By building on the rich foundation of this neighborhood's past, citizen activists continue to tie people to place, thereby ensuring a better future.

There's more in the East Side than the Michigan Avenue Baptist Church. Indeed, right across the street, looking out over Broadway, is the Colored Musicians Club, the last of its kind still standing in the United States. Founded in 1918, the Colored Musicians Local #533 was moved in 1935 to the building at 145 Broadway, which it still occupies today. On any night of the week, the small bandstand is packed with musicians—members of the Carol McLaughlin and the George Scott big bands—some white, some black, rehearsing in the historic hall. From the mid-1930s through the mid-1990s, it was a ritual for visiting black jazz artists like Duke Ellington, Billie Holiday, Dizzy Gillespie, Louis Armstrong, and others to pay a visit to "The Club," sit in, and make it a home away from home. Today, the restoration and renovation of the Colored Musicians Club is an integral part of the larger efforts to make heritage, history, and culture the building blocks of community renewal in the Michigan Avenue historical corridor.

History and heritage also converge at the Merriweather branch of the Buffalo and Erie County Public Library, where long-time Buffalo architect Robert T. Coles has created a special place that will anchor this neighborhood for generations. The branch was named in honor of Frank Merriweather, the founder of the city's oldest African American newspaper, the *Criterion*. Coles's design meshes six open circular rooms on the perimeter—symbolic of village huts—which nest against a stunning central circle topped by a towering, light-filled sky dome. The central area, symbolic of the village center, houses the circulation desk. The jewel of the library is the African American Resource Center, which houses the largest collection of African American history and research material outside of New York City. In the special place that is the Merriweather Library, history and heritage are the building blocks of community.

Similar happenings are going on in nearby Hamlin Park. Located just off of Humboldt Parkway, the neighborhood was planned and developed at the turn of the century on land that was owned by the Hamlin family. It was bisected and destroyed in the early 1960s when the Kensington Expressway cut through the neighborhood. Despite that devastation, the neighbors, now mostly African American, stayed on. After years of research, a committee of Hamlin Park residents presented a report to the Common Council in 1998 that led to the creation of the Hamlin Park Historic District. By strengthening their ties to the neighborhood's past, the people of Hamlin Park have resurrected their faith in the future.

South Buffalo, a geographically separate and ethnically distinct district, has always possessed a strong sense of place. There, too, the call of history is proving to be an effective tool for community renewal. While the neighborhood church is no longer used to store guns stockpiled for an invasion of Canada, and Fenians no longer congregate on neighborhood streets, Irish pride still runs deep in both the First Ward and in South Buffalo. St. Patrick's Day is momentous, marked by a seamless celebration that begins on a Friday and ends, reluctantly, after the Sunday parade. The annual Shamrock Run, where thousands of people, Irish and otherwise, descend on the area to compete in a five-mile road race through the streets of the neighborhood, is also cause for celebration. The Old First Ward Community Association, one of the race's sponsors, awards special prizes to runners in Irish costume. There is also an Irish Center, founded in 1970 and located on Abbott Road in South Buffalo, which, while serving as a meeting hall, a pub, and a recreation center, has also been a home to more than a dozen nonprofit Irish American organizations. The Buffalo Irish Center has become one of the most culturally and ethnically rich centers in Western New York, the place where South Buffalo's children, grandchildren, and great-grandchildren experience the wealth of Irish-American heritage the Buffalo area has to offer.

The uniqueness of place so strongly felt in South Buffalo is cemented by a long tradition of political leadership that goes back to the late-nineteenth-century days of First Ward leaders like "Blue-Eyed" Billy Sheehan and Tom "Fingy" Connors. The political tradition remains just as strong today. On the federal, state, and local levels, the delegations that have roots planted deep in the heritage-rich soil of South Buffalo are the envy of neighborhoods throughout Western New York.

Delaware Park represents another area in the city that is steeped in history. Conceived by Olmsted, eviscerated by the highway-building boom of the 1950s and '60s, revived by the citizen activists who, in the 1970s, constituted the Delaware Park Steering Committee, and renewed in our own day by the Olmsted Conservancy, Delaware Park is the city's greatest sanctuary and, more significantly, the embodiment of the transformative power of a loving understanding of the gifts of the past and their role for the future. There are few places more evocative to Buffalonians than Delaware Park. In winter, the meadow, blanketed in snow and framed by large, leafless trees, is still and meditative. In spring, summer, and fall, the meadow fills with people and activity: walkers, joggers, bicyclists, and rollerbladers on the Ring Road, golfers on the course's eighteen holes, baseball and softball teams on the diamonds, and on the soccer fields, hundreds of children, dressed in the green and white uniforms of the Delaware Soccer League, play all day. Everybody comes to bask in the beauty that was Olmsted's gift to future generations. The power of the park is transcendent in the life of the city. It is no wonder that the city's oldest tree, an oak, which, according to former city forester Ed Drabek, is more than three hundred years old, is located on the fairway of the seventeenth hole. It is no wonder, either, that for more than thirty years, "Shakespeare in Delaware Park" has flourished. Started in 1976 by Saul Elkin, a professor of theatre at UB, Shakespeare in Delaware Park is the oldest free Shakespeare festival in the country. The performances are mounted on a multitiered wooden stage built at the bottom of a small hill overlooking Hoyt Lake. On snowy winter days, the hill, filled with children and their families, is the best place to sled in Buffalo. On warm summer nights, the hill is filled with hundreds of people, some picnicking on blankets, others sitting on folding chairs, who come to watch yet another production of Elkin's public theater company. The theater company, which is supported completely by private donations, raises a third of its $300,000 annual budget during intermissions, when all of the actors in the company make their way through the crowds, Shakespearian hats in hand, raising money from the ever-growing number of people who enjoy what is one of the city's best attractions in one of the peoples' favorite places.

On the northeast side of Delaware Park lies Parkside, which, because of its brilliant Olmsted design and the uniqueness of its domestic architecture, was added to the National Register of Historic Places in 1987. Parkside is steeped in its history and architectural legacy. There is no prettier or more interesting residential neighborhood in the city than Parkside, which is defined by Olmsted's gently curvilinear street patterns and highlighted by large, mostly wood Victorian homes, many of them with large wraparound porches. Dotted with a few magnificent churches, replete with some of the best Victorian homes in New York State, and crowned with Frank Lloyd Wright's world-famous Darwin Martin House, Parkside celebrates its past while always looking to its future. When the Parkside Community Association formed in 1963, dedicated to the creation and perpetuation of a well-preserved and well-maintained neighborhood that was also racially mixed, few would have guessed that more than forty years later, their mission has been realized.

Like the other places that work in Buffalo, Elmwood Avenue remains rooted in its nineteenth- and early twentieth-century history as a middle-class neighborhood of homes, shops, schools, libraries, and churches. In recent years, as a result of efforts by hundreds of people who live and work there, a community has emerged that embodies the neighborhood's strong sense of place. Known as "Elmwood Village," or "Elmwood," as it is commonly referred to, the area has become a state of mind as well as the city's most vibrant and successful neighborhood. Elmwood is a place where the stores are locally owned and everything is within walking distance. Galvanized by a dedicated citizenry who know what they want and, more importantly, know how to get it, Elmwood has become as urban and sophisticated a neighborhood as it gets in Rust Belt America. Elmwood is a village, as a local bumper sticker says, where the ties that bind are strengthened by a common outlook and a highly developed public culture that encourages good contact, good communication, and good citizenship. Whether it's watching the World Cup at Caffe Aroma, using a computer at the Crane Branch Library, having a meal at any of the many good restaurants, following neighborhood gossip on Buffalo Rising, an increasingly popular electronic journal with roots on the avenue, Elmwood (a place that Walt Whitman would have loved and Bob Creeley did) contains the essential ingredients of the democratic city.

All of these great place-making elements come together on Bidwell Parkway, an Olmsted-designed, lushly treed parkway that connects Colonial and Soldier's circles. By the early years of the twenty-first century, Bidwell Parkway, like the agora in ancient Athens, had become the spatial conscience of the community, a beautiful, embracing place that served as the central stage in the theater that Elmwood had become. It was here that a weekend farmers' market set up its tents and stalls; here that the "Women in Black" stood, week in and week out, silently protesting the war in Iraq; here that the Buffalo Philharmonic Orchestra offered idyllic summertime concerts; and here, under a big white tent, that Tim Tielman, Buffalo's most passionate urbanist, convened his "Architectural Revival Meetings," an annual talk-fest that presents the best and most interesting contemporary ideas in architecture and urban affairs. Taking root on Bidwell Parkway, these ideas spread out onto Elmwood and into the rest of the city.

The strong commitment to place in Buffalo is reinforced by the way the city's various neighborhoods celebrate themselves. The Elmwood Festival of the Arts, for example, much like the Allentown Arts Festival and the Infringement Festival, is integrally tied to the neighborhood and the streets that make it up. The Italian Festival is tied inextricably to Hertel Avenue, for two decades now a solid Italian American neighborhood. Similarly, the Pine Grill Reunion, an annual outdoor jazz festival organized by the African American Cultural Center, is associated with Martin Luther King Park, in the heart of the East Side. Also linked to that park is Juneteenth, the largest festival in the African American community, when thousands of people are lured by the late afternoon and early evening smells of barbeque filling the air. Vendors, selling the brightly colored clothes of Africa, speckle the land-scape. At night, the park is filled with people, some sitting on lawn chairs listening, others dancing to the sounds of Pappy Martin's Love Supreme Jazz Ensemble or the Jimmy Gomes Quartet, featuring Doug "Trigger" Gaston on piano.

The growth of charter schools has also heightened the sense of place throughout the city. While legitimate questions and concerns about charter schools remain, their powerful impact on peoples' feelings about place is undeniable. For years, the sense of locale was reinforced by the city's public and parochial schools, which were located within walking distance of pupils and parents. In those days, parents knew the teachers because the teachers lived in the neighborhood too. Like the parish church and the local saloon, neighborhood schools strengthened the root systems of community. All of that ended, of course, in the years following Judge Curtin's 1976 desegregation order. As children began to be bused to schools in different parts of the city, their parents, particularly the white ones, left for newer, nicer, and far "whiter" schools in the suburbs. For a while, at least, court-mandated desegregation promoted a new kind of community school, but by contributing to the exodus of so many white families from the city, the desegregation program had the sadly ironic effect of contributing to the creation of a public school system that, by 2006, was almost 80 percent African American. While Judge Curtin, Eugene Reville, and the other actors in that intense drama struggled valiantly to create an interracial public school system, their efforts, sadly, were defeated by historical and cultural forces much stronger than the intentions of these eminently good men.

The public school system had fallen on hard times. Overwhelmed by the challenge of dealing with so many poor children, throttled by obsolete labor rules and contracts, and strangled by an antiquated, administration-heavy bureaucracy, the city's public schools, with the exception of the handful of highly regarded ones, such as the Montessori School, Hutch Tech, Performing Arts, and City Honors (which was chosen by *Newsweek* magazine in the spring of 2006 as the fourth-best school in the nation) had lost their credibility in the community. Angered by the decline of their public schools and fully aware of the importance of local schools in defining and strengthening local attachments, parents throughout the city leaped at the opportunity offered by the passage in 1998 of the New York State Charter School Act. Created, organized, and managed by citizens, charter schools, though public, functioned independently of the Board of Education. For passionate, well-organized, and neighborhood-oriented Buffalonians, charter schools were a godsend. For many, the charter school movement represented grassroots democracy at its best. "It takes us," said Steven Polowitz, one of the organizers of the Tapestry Charter School, "back to the roots."[3] By

2006, more than five thousand children in Buffalo, close to 14 percent of the total in the public school system, attended charter schools. While the educational promises of the charter school movement have yet to be realized, charter schools, as much as any other development in the city, have empowered parents of the children involved by connecting them to the fabric of everyday life in the city.

Perhaps nothing, however, creates, nurtures, and sustains a sense of place more powerfully or effectively than trees and gardens. The planting of trees and the creation of gardens are acts of faith; they are imbued with the belief that hard work now will reap enormous rewards later. These activities, powerful and significant for individuals, become still more so when they are pursued by groups of people. People who plant trees and nurture gardens believe in themselves and their community. Their work heals the city and intensifies the already strong sense of place. Much of their work has been inspired by the rich legacy bequeathed to the city by the work of Fredrick Law Olmsted, a legacy that is protected and sustained by the Olmsted Conservancy. Founded as the Friends of Olmsted Parks in 1978, the Olmsted Conservancy has emerged as one of the most dynamic, influential, and successful community advocacy groups in the area. After years as a volunteer-based community organization, the conservancy's efforts were rewarded when, in 2004, it entered into a groundbreaking partnership with the City of Buffalo, Erie County, and the community, which made the conservancy the official stewards of the Buffalo Olmsted Park System. The conservancy became the first not-for-profit organization in the nation to manage a park system. In a city of volunteers, no organization counts more than the Olmsted Conservancy—more than a thousand of them are involved in the ongoing campaign to return Buffalo's far-flung system of interconnecting green spaces to its pristine nineteenth-century beauty. According to Corinne Rice, chairwoman of the board, "People are starting to believe. They are willing to accept responsibility."[4] The Olmsted volunteers can be seen everywhere: on hands and knees tending to landscaping in the Olmsted circles; cutting grass in Delaware Park; and planting flowers in the Delaware Park Rose Garden. As Buffalonians honk and wave to the Olmsted volunteers as they drive by, they appreciate that these thousand-plus people bring to the community not only spirit and energy but savings as well. In Buffalo, according to the conservancy, the per capita cost to the taxpayers for park maintenance is $10 per year as compared to more than $100 per year in some other cities.[5]

Olmsted's influences are deeply felt in Riverside and in South Buffalo as well. The efforts to restore Olmsted's legacy in those neighborhoods led to the formation of neighborhood groups dedicated to the preservation of his work and vision. Much of his work in South Buffalo is virtually untouched. The rich landscaping of Cazenovia Park and the crashing falls of Cazenovia Creek provide a sense of serenity, while the parkways and circles that he designed—McClellan Circle and McKinley Circle—thanks to the work of a group of South Buffalo volunteers known as "South Buffalo Alive," are clean and well maintained.

Since the days of Frank Karpick, Buffalo has been blessed by both professionals and volunteers who believed deeply in the healing and restorative power of trees in the life of the city. Karpick, who labored against the scourge of Dutch Elm disease, was memorialized in 1972 when the Karpick Maple tree was named in his honor. Despite his efforts, Dutch Elm disease ravaged the city during the late 1960s. More than ninety-five thousand out of a total of one hundred thirty-five thousand elms had been lost, and the city, fighting its perennial fiscal problems, was unable to help. Into this vacuum stepped the Junior League. In 1973, a few of their members formed the Buffalo Green Fund. By creating a not-for-profit organization, the Green Fund was able to accept contributions from citizens eager for trees in the neighborhood. The Green Fund bought them, the city planted them, and the citizens got their trees and their tax deductions. For more than thirty years, the Green Fund has been working with community groups all over the city. Today, while there are fewer trees in the city than during the peak years before the onset of Dutch Elm disease, one would think, looking at the lush foliage, that the urban forest had been there forever.

Gardens, because they require sustained and concerted effort, reaffirm and sustain a sense of place. In recent years, there have been few events on the city's cultural calendar more powerful and more effective as a place maker than the annual Garden Walk, which in July 2006 celebrated its twelfth year. Founded by Marvin Lunenfeld, an inveterate gardener who, with his wife, Gail McCarthy, turned the backyard of his large Victorian home on Norwood Avenue into a wondrous garden, the Garden Walk, which attracts hundreds of thousands of people each year, winds its way through the back alleys and side streets of neighborhoods all over the West Side. There is no better showcase of the beauty of Buffalo's West Side neighborhoods than the Garden Walk. One can see the story-book streets of Irving, Mariner, and Arlington Park in Allentown; the piazza-like remnant of the old Rumsey Estate at Johnson Park; the passionately maintained parkway at Days Park; the compact and tightly knit streets—Orton, St. John's, and Hudson—that sit in the shadows of Kleinhans Music Hall; the dream-like "Cottage District" at Little Summer, Ketchum, and Union Place; and the list goes on. The Garden Walk reveals fantastical streets and neighborhoods, places with indescribable homes, where the scale is small, the pace is slow, and the goodwill, energy, and spirit are radiant. The thousands of Buffalonians who live out their daily lives in these neighborhoods understand the present. During the Garden Walk, they see the future and they know that it will work.

While the Garden Walk is a sort of retrospective of the highlights of well-established neighborhoods, even more inspiring are the enormous efforts to create community gardens, an activity whose primary goal is community renewal in struggling neighborhoods. One of the finest gardens, chosen annually as "Buffalo's Best Community Garden," is located on the Lower West Side, at the northwest corner of Jersey and West. The garden was started in 2000 by Gail Graham, a neighborhood activist and citywide leader in the community gardens movement. It is a five-stage perennial garden, maintained by neighborhood residents of all ages. When he is not working at the post office, Graham spends his days at different locations around the city where he coaches, coaxes, and inspires community gardeners. Graham works closely with other "guerilla" gardeners, people like Anna Church, a Brazilian immigrant who has worked with volunteers in her neighborhood to bring fruit trees and flowers to the long-empty lot at Niagara and Jersey. No soldier in this particular war is more passionate or effective than Rosa Gibson, whose community garden at Wohlers and Northampton provides a different way of seeing and understanding the streets of Buffalo's East Side neighborhoods. Gibson's organization, the Community Action Information Center, along with a rotating core of volunteers, has commandeered more than fifteen abandoned lots to make vegetable and flower gardens, an evergreen orchard, and on what was until 2003 a junkyard at the southwest corner of Wohlers and Northampton, a fully flowering orchard filled with apple, peach, cherry, and apricot trees. "Being near Dodge Street where there's a lot of drug traffic, in a block where there's a lot of drug traffic and drug pushers, I know I'm in a bad area," Gibson said. "But I'm not going anywhere. I'm staying in this neighborhood until it gets good. After all, it all starts with the soil."[6]

On Massachusetts Street on the West Side, just around the corner from LaNova Pizza, lies a large community garden that is part of the Growing Green program, operated by the Massachusetts Avenue Project (MAP). In the early years of the new century, the landscape of the neighborhood was filled with vacant lots—more than two hundred and twenty of them. The mostly rundown homes that remained were occupied by an increasingly poor population, with almost half of the residents under the age of eighteen.[6] By involving the neighborhood's youth in a comprehensive program of community gardening, MAP's vision is to fill both empty land and empty lives. Today, MAP's "Growing Green" program operates a half-acre lot at the corner of Massachusetts and Shields, which, with beds filled with all kinds of greens and with kids working everywhere, has the look and feel of a pioneer kibbutz. The group is building a greenhouse using a sustainable building technique consisting of straw bales. Soon the children who spend several hours of every week working there will be able to not only grow but to sell the produce that will be grown in the greenhouse. Diane Picard, director of the program, has still more ambitious plans for her urban kibbutz. She advocates for the repeal of the law prohibiting the raising of livestock in the city. Once this is accomplished, she says, "we can have our own chickens and our kids can go into the egg business, too."

There are hundreds of people in Buffalo involved in the community garden movement, and it is their faith, patience, and hard work that, as much as anything in the life of the contemporary city, gives us reason to hope. There is nothing easy about creating and sustaining a community garden. Indeed, given the vagaries of weather and human behavior, the odds are that they will fail. And yet, despite the odds and the obstacles, people in neighborhoods all over Buffalo, in places that have been decimated and destroyed by years of private neglect and poorly conceived public policies, are coming together to build gardens. The wounds are beginning to heal. Faith is being restored and people, believing in themselves and in their communities, are creating a brighter future for the city they love.

All of this—the gardens, the flowers, and especially the trees—over one hundred thousand of them—was threatened when during the evening of Thursday, October 12, 2006, a lake-effect snowstorm that, like the Blizzard of 1977 will be talked about for generations, struck the Buffalo area with a vicious and deafening force. By dawn on Friday morning it was clear that the damage was horrific and unprecedented. Within just a few hours, nearly two feet of snow had fallen. Power lines were downed and almost three hundred thousand people—close to 90 percent of the homes and businesses in Buffalo and the surrounding area—were without power. Most shocking was the fate of the trees. Tens of thousands of them were smashed, shattered, and destroyed: countless broken limbs on an apocalyptic battlefield. Particularly ravaged were the over twelve thousand trees that filled the majestic parks of Fredrick Law Olmsted. "The jewels of his vision," wrote *Buffalo News* reporter Gene Warner, "the stately maples, oaks and ash trees that line Olmsted's parks and parkways have been clobbered and destroyed."[7] An early morning walk on Friday the thirteenth confirmed the cataclysmic vision. Everywhere—in South Park and Cazenovia Park, on Richmond Avenue and Bidwell Parkway, on Colonial Circle and Soldiers Place, in Riverside and Martin Luther King parks—the view was similar: branches, overwhelmed by the weight of snow-laden leaves, had cracked, broken, and fallen to the ground. Whole trees, many of them the grand and ancient ones that had towered for generations, now lay eerily corpselike on the streets and sidewalks in neighborhoods throughout the city. During the course of the next several days, thousands of people, most of them still without power, took to the streets on foot to survey the wreckage.

For days and weeks after the storm, a deep sense of sadness, loss, and even despair lingered in the air. October, usually the region's most magnificent month, had turned into a nightmare of freakish weather. In the face of the havoc and devastation the weather had wrought, people wondered if their long cared for and lovingly tended natural environment would ever again be healed, repaired, and restored. But even in the midst of what local weekly *Artvoice* called "Arborgeddon," already the people of Buffalo were bending their backs to the hard task of recovery. Local residents removed debris from their own properties and carefully trimmed their trees in an effort to save them. In a surprisingly nimble response from city government, an army of tree care experts was mobilized to save the trees that were salvageable and to remove the trees that were downed altogether or were denuded beyond repair. In the weeks following the storm, the Buffalo Olmsted Parks Conservancy enlisted volunteers to clean up the city's parks. It also set up a series of fundraisers and benefit concerts to raise money for a comprehensive replanting effort. In Buffalo, a city of no illusions, a city staggered by hard weather and even harder economic realities, the people, as always, could be counted on to pick themselves up, dust themselves off, and turn their attention to making their city better in the little ways that, taken together, count for so much.

History, forever lengthening, always ends with an open question. It ends at the present moment and in the present place, where the accumulation of past events and the open array of future possibilities converge in our own lives. What's next? Where do we go from here? In asking the question, we venture the answers that make the future's potential real. The story of Buffalo is necessarily a story without an ending. The people of Buffalo, in the here and now, have the power to write the next chapter. Though long plagued by poor, misguided leadership, global economic forces beyond their control, racial tensions that originated in other places and at other times, and the collective depression that might be expected of such long suffering, Buffalonians nonetheless have the opportunity in the present moment to discover and renew their dedication to making their city a better place. In striving to make the place they call home stronger, healthier, and more livable, they enrich their own lives as well as the lives of their children and their children's children. The person and the place, the past and the future, are inextricably knitted together at the needlepoint of now, and this is where each of us resides. It is hoped that this volume, which has told of the great and glorious victories and the sad and humbling defeats of the city and its citizens over the last century, will one day be counted among the little things that together made Buffalo better.

As for me, I find that the summer sunsets are beautiful in Buffalo, especially along the shores of the Niagara River, at Front Park, or at the foot of Ferry. It is here, where the waters of Lake Erie flow with gathering speed into the Niagara River, that the setting sun is its most luminous. When the wind is quiet and the water calm, there are only a few sounds—the glide of a skull, the singsong of a swooping bird, the distant honks of geese passing in formation high above. The air is sublime and the mood is haunting. On quiet evenings such as these, all seems well in this city, which I now happily call my home.

NOTES

1. Milton Rogovin, *Triptychs: Buffalo Lower West Side Revisited* (New York: Norton, 1994), p. 16.

2. Robert Roggie, personal communication with the author, March 2006.

3. Steve Polowitz, personal communication with the author, June 2006.

4. See http://www.buffaloolmstedparks.org/.

5. D. Williams, "Vandalism at Community Gardens," *Buffalo News*, May 8, 2006, p. A1.

6. Diane Picard, director, Massachusetts Avenue Project, personal communication with the author, June 2006.

7. Gene Warner, "Parks' Treasures Badly Battered," *Buffalo News*, October 15, 2006.

NOTES ON SOURCES

PLACES TO LEARN ABOUT BUFFALO HISTORY

The Grosvenor Collection at the Buffalo and Erie County Public Library is staffed by a group of wonderful librarians—there is no better, more enjoyable place to do research on Buffalo history. The Grosvenor Collection contains every possible kind of material: from books, newspapers, and city directories to maps, personal journals, and photographs. In conducting research for *City on the Edge*, the numerous scrapbooks housed in the Grosvenor Collection have been essential.

The collection, which covers over four hundred square feet of wall space in the Grosvenor Room, was started in 1900 by Sara Palmer Sheldon, the director of the library's Newspaper Room. Following her retirement in 1932, the job of scouring through the local press to locate, clip, and sort articles into a variety of different topical scrapbooks fell to other staff members. The collection is a treasure trove of information for anybody interested in just about any aspect of Buffalo history.

The following is a partial list of the scrapbooks in this collection: four volumes on McKinley's visit to Buffalo and all that happened in the wake of his assassination; two volumes on Buffalo's

Foreign Population; twelve volumes on the Schools of Buffalo; five volumes on Art; three volumes on Theaters and Concert Halls; two volumes on City Planning; three volumes on Streets; two volumes on Buildings; eleven volumes on Industry; twelve volumes on Churches; two volumes on Trees; eleven volumes on Industry in Buffalo; and one volume on Weather. In addition, there are over thirty volumes of scrapbooks available on microfilm, which deal with the Pan-American Exposition. Go to the Grosvenor Room. Ask for Cynthia Van Ness, Pat Monahan, Amy Pickard, and Robert Alessi. Learn and have fun. And while there, have lunch at Fables, a great café in the library's lobby.

Linked to the scrapbook collection is the miraculous Local History Card Catalog. Arranged alphabetically, beginning with the "AAO Art Gallery" and ending with the obituary of a man named Edmund Zynda, this collection contains over one hundred drawers and thousands of cards, which reference just about any imaginable topic of local history. Also very helpful is the Grosvenor's vertical file collection, which contains random material with a wide and diverse range of topics.

The Grosvenor is also a very good place to start if you are researching the history of the arts in Buffalo. For those particularly interested in the history of the local music scene, Raya Then has created and cataloged a vast amount of material covering the history of music in Buffalo from the early village days through to the present. The collection is humbling both in its breadth and in the degree of dedication required of its creator.

There was a wonderful journal published in Buffalo for a few years during the 1920s called the *Buffalo Arts Journal*. It is an incredibly good source for information on the life of the arts in this community during those years. It also contains an annual roster of local artists, including short bios and photographs. Another great journal is *Buffalo Saturday Night*, which was published for several years in the early 1920s. Both of these sources are available at the Grosvenor Room.

The library at the Buffalo and Erie County Historical Society is another excellent source of material dealing with all aspects of the arts as well as just about every other aspect of Buffalo history. Helpful and knowledgeable librarians like Pat Virgil will lead you through their mountains of material. Most interesting is their incredible collection of manuscripts, which contains an unbelievable array of primary materials dealing with all aspects of Buffalo history from aboriginal days to the early years of the twentieth century.

The library at the Albright-Knox Art Gallery is thorough and complete. It contains all of the catalogs of all of the shows held there since the founding of the Buffalo Fine Arts Academy in 1862. In addition, there are countless vertical files filled with fascinating information. If you wish to visit, be sure to ask for Susanna Tejada.

The university archives at the State University of New York at Buffalo are housed on the fourth floor of Capen Hall, which is located on the north campus in Amherst, NY. The archives are a part of the university's "Special Collections." The archives are an indescribably rich source for all kinds of information dealing with any and all activities that have ever occurred in the life and the mind of this most fertile university. They contain university records, manuscript collections, faculty papers, student papers, theses and dissertations, blueprints and other campus architectural material, and all kinds of iconography, artifacts, and memorabilia... you name it, and it's there, for years lovingly cared for by Shonnie Finnegan, archivist emeritus, and now tended by archivists John Edsen and Bill Offhaus.

Sharing the warm and cozy space on the fourth floor of Capen Hall is the Poetry Collection. Founded by Thomas Lockwood and Charles Abbott in the early 1930s, the Poetry Collection is devoted to twentieth-century poetry in English and English translation. The Poetry Collection, which contains over a hundred thousand volumes, possesses manuscripts by nearly every major poet and many minor poets writing in English. Sound recordings of poets reading from their own works, poets' notebooks, letters and manuscripts, and a wide variety of literary magazines are also included in this collection. Approximately five thousand small-circulation magazines, twelve hundred current subscriptions, and a number of portraits, sculptures, and photographs round out the collection. For years headed by Robert Bertholf, the Poetry Collection is now under the direction of Mike Basinksi.

The Music Library at the State University of New York at Buffalo is another remarkably rich source of information. Although started only in 1967, the Music Library has a collection of uncommonly rich materials and resources that cover the whole history of world music. In addition, there is a large collection of materials dealing with "Buffalo Musicians" (those individuals who have been paid by the university for their various services to the music department; that is, faculty, visiting faculty, members of the Center for the Creative and Performing Arts, and music librarians). The earliest component of the list, UB Lecturers in Music, dates back to 1918. John Bewley, ever knowledgeable and helpful, is your guy there.

The archives at the Buffalo State College library contain a great deal of information invaluable for the study of local history, including the Butler Family Papers, the Tom Fontana Collection, the Dr. Francis E. Fronczak Collection, the Charles Rand Penney Collection, the Paul G. Reilly Indian Collection (Seneca Nation of Indians land claims), and the Monroe Fordham Regional History Center. Here, too, are the archives of the *Courier Express* as well as the *Buffalo Jewish Review*. For help negotiating Buffalo State College's wonderful local history resources, see Al Riese.

For an astounding collection of materials and photographs, including the complete Hare and Hare Brothers photo archives, visit the Lower Lakes Marine

Historical Society at 66 Erie Street in downtown Buffalo (or online at http://www.llmhs.org).

WEB SITES WITH INFORMATION ABOUT THE HISTORY OF BUFFALO

The electronic archive of the *Buffalo News* (http:buffalonews.com/newslibrary/) is the best source of daily news and information beginning in 1989. The articles can be searched chronologically by topic or by-line.

For Buffalo history, see the following Web sites:

- Buffalo Architecture and History, http://www.ah.bfn.org/. There is no better introduction to Buffalo history and architecture than this wonderful Web site, which is lovingly "created and maintained by Chuck LaChiusa as a community service." Filled with photos, maps, great history, and dozens of links, this Web site is the best place to begin your research on Buffalo.
- BuffaloResearch.com, http://www.buffaloresearch.com/. This site is passionately maintained by Cynthia Van Ness. She has created a staggering series of links that connect the user to maps, photos, books, written texts, and just about any other kind of material pertaining to the history of Buffalo. Cynthia's Web site and her many links (for example, to Western New York Heritage Press, at http://www.wnyheritagepress.org/ and to the Buffalonian, at http://www.buffalonian.com/) made the use of illustrations in this book unnecessary. See Cynthia's link "Offbeat Buffalo: Off the Beaten Cyberpath" for other Buffalo Web sites.

THANKS AND ACKNOWLEDGMENTS

To the keepers of our communal memory:

At the Buffalo and Erie County Historical Society, William Siener, director and Pat Virgil, director of the library;

at the Buffalo and Erie County Public Library's Grosvenor Collection, Raya Then, Herb Tinney, Cynthia Van Ness, Amy Pickard, Robert Alessi, and Pat Monahan;

at the University at Buffalo Archives, Shonnie Finnegan, archivist emeritus and archivists John Edsen and Bill Offhaus;

at the UB Poetry Collection, Bob Bertholf, Mike Basinski, and Luca Crispi;

at Kleinhans Music Hall, Carol Ann Strahl;

at the Albright-Knox Art Gallery Library, Susana Tejada;

at the Baird Music Library, University at Buffalo, John Bewley;

at the Buffalo Philharmonic, Ed Yadzinski, archivist and historian;

at the Burchfield-Penny Collection, Nancy Weekly and Gerald Mead;

at the library archives at Buffalo State College, Al Riese;

at the Archives of the Heart, Margaret P. Gordon.

To those in government:

Anthony J. Caldiero, Office of Strategic Planning;
Anthony M. Masiello, former mayor;
James D. Griffin, former mayor;
David Sengbusch, formerly of the Office of Strategic Planning;
Bill Grillo, director of zoning;
Frank Manuele, former director of city planning;
James Pitts, former president of the Common Council;
Nick Bonifacio, council member, Niagara District;
Brian Davis, council member, Ellicott District;
Jim Pavel, director of special services;
Carolyn Showers, Board of Education;
Federal District Judge John T. Curtin;
Joseph Murray, former associate superintendent, Buffalo Public Schools;
Eugene Reville, former superintendent, Buffalo Public Schools.

To those in the community:

Ansie Baird, daughter of Oscar Silverman and daughter-in-law of Cameron Baird;
Jan Williams, one of the first creative associates;
Harold Cohen, former dean of the School of Architecture and Planning at the
    University at Buffalo;
Ted Lownie, architect in charge of the renovation of Kleinhans Music Hall;
Wayne Wisbaum, chairman of Kleinhans Music Hall;
Wes Olmsted, Allentown artist;
Joe Crangle, former chairman of the Erie County Democratic Party;
Steve Halpern, activist lawyer and academic;
Aaron Bartley, community activist and founder of PUSH;
Dennis Moloney, founder of White Pine Press;
Stan Lipsey, Mike Beebe, and David Robinson at the *Buffalo News*;
Gail Graham, founder of the Jersey-West Community Garden;
Rosa Gibson, founder of the Wohlers Community Garden;
Ed Drabeck, former City of Buffalo forester;
Bette Blum, of the Buffalo Tree Fund;
Mitch Cummings and Robert Roggie, from Journey's End;
M. Francis Holmes, district director of US Citizenship and Immigration Services;
Steve Polowitz, attorney;
Frank Perez, activist and community leader;
Mark Schroeder, South Buffalo community leader and New York State assemblyman;

Celia White, grass-roots poetry organizer;
Irene Sipos, grass-roots editor;
Susan McCartney and Tim Tielman, urban guerrilla warriors;
Marge Ryan, South Buffalo community leader;
Anna Church, Prospect Avenue Block Club;
Diane Picard, Massachusetts Avenue Project;
William Schoellkopf, law clerk to Judge John T. Curtin;
Patrick Martin, attorney for the Buffalo and Erie County Public Library;
Jimmie Gilliam, poet;
Gabrielle Boulaine, organizer of the Nickel City Poetry Slam;
Kevin Cunningham, Elmwood Avenue Johnny Appleseed;
Greg Halpern, photographer from Buffalo and author of *Harvard Works Because We Do* (all photographs in this volume are courtesy of Greg Halpern, www.halpernphotography.com.);
Rachel Kane, editor;
Joan Fedeszyn, publicist;
Brian McMahon, editor extraordinaire at Prometheus Books;
and the countless others whose knowledge and experience have been invaluable to me during the course of this project.

INDEX